THE AMA HANDBOOK OF PROJECT MANAGEMENT

FOURTH EDITION

Edited By

PAUL C. DINSMORE, PMP

JEANNETTE CABANIS-BREWIN

AMACOM American Management Association

New York | Atlanta | Brussels | Chicago | Mexico City
San Francisco | Shanghai | Tokyo | Toronto | Washington, D.C.

Bulk discounts available. For details visit:
www.amacombooks.org/go/specialsales
Or contact special sales:
Phone: 800-250-5308
Email: specialsls@amanet.org
View all the AMACOM titles at: www.amacombooks.org
American Management Association: www.amanet.org

This publication is designed to provide accurate and authoritative information in regard to the subject matter covered. It is sold with the understanding that the publisher is not engaged in rendering legal, accounting, or other professional service. If legal advice or other expert assistance is required, the services of a competent professional person should be sought.

Library of Congress Cataloging-in-Publication Data

The AMA handbook of project management / edited by Paul C. Dinsmore, PMP. Jeannette Cabanis-Brewin. — Fourth edition.
    pages cm
    Includes bibliographical references and index.
    ISBN 978-0-8144-3339-3 — ISBN 0-8144-3332-4   1. Project management—Handbooks, manuals, etc. I. Dinsmore, Paul C. II. Cabanis-Brewin, Jeannette.
    HD69.P75A46 2014
    658.4'04—dc23   2013041497

Trademark information about PMI, the Project Management Institute, Inc., is to be found on Page x.

About AMA
American Management Association (www.amanet.org) is a world leader in talent development, advancing the skills of individuals to drive business success. Our mission is to support the goals of individuals and organizations through a complete range of products and services, including classroom and virtual seminars, webcasts, webinars, podcasts, conferences, corporate and government solutions, business books and research. AMA's approach to improving performance combines experiential learning—learning through doing—with opportunities for ongoing professional growth at every step of one's career journey.

Printing number

10 9 8 7 6 5 4 3 2 1

CONTENTS

SECTION ONE

The Project Management Body of Knowledge: Comprehension and Practice

American Management Association • www.amanet.org

SECTION TWO
The Profession of Project Management

SECTION THREE
Organizational Issues in Project Management

American Management Association • www.amanet.org

SECTION FOUR
Issues, Ideas, and Methods in Project Management Practice

SECTION FIVE
Industry Applications of Project Management Practice

PMI (the Project Management Institute)

"PMI" and the PMI logo are service and trademarks of the Project Management Institute, Inc., which are registered in the United States of America and other nations; "PMP" and the PMP logo are certification marks of the Project Management Institute, Inc., which are registered in the United States of America and other nations; "PMBOK," *"PM Network,"* and *"PMI Today"* are trademarks of the Project Management Institute, Inc., which are registered in the United States of America and other nations; ". . . building professionalism in project management . . ." is a trade and service mark of the Project Management Institute, Inc., which is registered in the United States of America and other nations; and the *Project Management Journal* logo is a trademark of the Project Management Institute, Inc.

PMI did not participate in the development of this publication and has not reviewed the content for accuracy. PMI does not endorse or otherwise sponsor this publication and makes no warranty, guarantees, or representation—expressed or implied—as to its accuracy or content. PMI does not have any financial interest in this publication and has not contributed any financial resources.

FOREWORD

Although it might be considered difficult to improve on a book that has already won the highest honor in its field—the Project Management Institute's 2007 literature award—the fourth edition of this classic handbook provides an updated set of principles and processes for those managers and professionals who want to expand their understanding of the theory and practice of project management.

There is a deluge of books being published about project management. Unfortunately, all too many of these books have taken information from existing books and cast them in a slightly different light, resulting in minor contributions to the growing book literature. This handbook by Paul Dinsmore and Jeannette Cabanis-Brewin is a refreshing change that presents the best state-of-the-art literature in the theory and process of project management.

The material in the book comes from authors who are notable contributors in the project management community, ranging from academics and practitioners who contend with teaching and managing stakeholders in the project management field.

This handbook should be readily available to anyone who works in the management of projects and deals with tactical and strategic change in contemporary organizations.

—**David I. Cleland, Ph.D., FPMI**
Professor Emeritus
Department of Industrial Engineering
School of Engineering
University of Pittsburgh

American Management Association • www.amanet.org

When the lunar module Eagle landed in the Sea of Tranquility at 13 hours, 19 minutes, 39.9 seconds Eastern Standard Time on July 20, 1969, the event was hailed as one of history's major milestones. It was also one of the most fascinating and significant spin-offs of the U.S. space program and was the development of flexible yet precise organizational structures, forms, and tools that allowed people to work together to reach challenging goals. Out of that grew the modern concept of project management.

Since the Apollo days, project management, applicable both to individual endeavors and to a series of projects called programs, has been applied to many new fields of activity. With the trend toward accelerated change, the scope of project management has expanded from construction projects and aerospace to encompass organizational change, research and development (R&D) projects, high-tech product development, banking and finance, nonprofit services, environmental remediation— in fact, just about every field of human endeavor.

When it first appeared in 1993, this handbook was a major contribution to the field, pulling together expert practitioners to share their advice on topics such as designing adequate organizational structures, generating and maintaining teamwork, and managing the project life cycle. The second edition, released in 2005, was designed to complement and supplement the Project Management Institute's *Guide to the Project Management Body of Knowledge (PMBOK® Guide),* third edition, and to provide supporting materials for those preparing to take the certification exam or working to maintain their certification. We have retained this feature, though the last two editions, updating the chapters in Section One to the new standard, the *PMBOK® Guide,* fifth edition, in this book.

As in previous editions, we have retained many of the original authors, keeping those chapters that stand as classics in the field. However, with the pace of change, we have also eliminated a few chapters that had become dated in order to include new developments in the discipline. As a brief overview, the fourth edition changes comprise the following:

- One hundred percent of the chapters have had editorial revisions.
- All of the chapters that repeat in this edition have been updated, either by the author or by another expert in the field.
- Four chapters have been deleted, either because they were no longer relevant or because we chose to replace them to improve coverage of the topic.
- Four chapters are by new authors, replacing chapters on the same topics with updated content and a fresh voice.

- Eleven chapters are on new topics by new authors, covering stakeholder management to sustainability, agile project management to project management in healthcare, closing processes, and everything in between.
- And, of course, it is all, to the best of our knowledge, in line with the fifth edition of the *PMBOK® Guide*.

HOW TO USE THIS BOOK

Students who are taking introductory courses in project management as part of a degree in another field (for example, engineering, information technology, business administration, manufacturing or production management, construction management, and so on), or who are studying for degrees in the field of project management, will find the book invaluable. As a complementary and supplementary text, the handbook does not contain materials already published in the *PMBOK® Guide*, but it is designed to help those studying project management understand and integrate the materials contained in that standard, as well as project management concepts and issues that currently are not included in the *PMBOK® Guide*.

The book targets a broad audience, including not only the traditional project management faithfuls, but also professionals involved in organizational development, research, and other associated fields. The book provides a ready reference for anyone involved in project tasks, including upper management executives, project sponsors, project managers, functional managers, and team members. It addresses those working in any of the major program- and project-oriented industries, such as defense, construction, architecture, engineering, product development, systems development, R&D, education, and community development. Whether you are preparing for advancement in the project management field through certification or by completing university courses in the field, this handbook will be a valuable reference. For those using the book in a classroom setting, discussion questions provided at the end of each chapter help students and peers initiate fruitful discussions about concepts, problems, and ideas in their chosen field.

Organization of the Handbook

Section One: The Project Management Body of Knowledge: Comprehension and Practice

This section is designed specifically to aid the reader in learning the basics of project management and in preparing for taking the Project Management Professional (PMP) certification exam. Chapters 3 through 17, in fact, correspond to chapters of the *PMBOK® Guide*, fifth edition, that are tested on the PMP exam. This section includes the fundamental knowledge areas and describes the processes required to ensure that projects are brought to successful completion.

The organization of the book is specifically designed to raise interest and to lead readers to further analysis of the project management field. Those preparing for certification are generally studying the field of project management for the first time. Thus, Section One introduces the student to the basic accepted practices and principles of project management, as practiced within the project. Note that the *PMBOK®*

American Management Association • www.amanet.org

Guide does not deal with, and the PMP certification process does not test, concepts of project management that extend beyond the bounds of the individual project. Yet the project manager must survive and thrive within highly competitive business organizations, interacting with other organizations both within their employer's organization and from other organizations that have an interest or stake in the project. It is anticipated that as students work through the materials in the first section, they will be generating questions concerning these other aspects of project management that clearly fall outside the individual project (for example, the individual's career potential, the expected contributions of projects to the organization, the requirements to manage multiple projects simultaneously, leadership concepts that cut across organizational lines, management of the power structures and conflicts that typically surround projects, and the interaction of the projects with other major departments of the organization, such as accounting, finance, and other groups being affected by the results of the project). These broader issues are explored in Sections Two through Five of the handbook.

Section Two: The Profession of Project Management

Section Two covers the field of project management as a rapidly growing profession that is being supported and developed by a number of professional organizations, particularly in the United States, Europe, and Australia. This section documents the growth and creation of the profession, identifies the major professional organizations contributing to its development, discusses the status of this new profession with a global perspective, and reviews the impact of this professionalizing process on the practitioner of project management and on the supporting organizations. Ethics, professionalism, and career development are the primary topics covered in this section.

Section Three: Organizational Issues in Project Management

Even a certified professional cannot escape the realities of organizational life, and increasingly, the role of the project manager catapults the individual out of the single-project milieu and into organizational issues: multiple projects, programs, performance measurement, portfolio selection and management, enterprise systems, organizational culture and structure, and alignment with strategy. These areas have become crucial issues in project management. Top professionals and academics with specific expertise in these areas have been sought out to provide tutorials on these topics in Section Three.

Section Four: Issues, Ideas, and Methods in Project Management Practice

Politics, new methodologies and organizational structures, globally diverse teams, breakthrough technologies, Agile, and sustainability—Section Four brings together writers on some of the leading-edge topics in project management. One thing that is certain about project management: it is not going to remain static for another ten years or even ten months. The chapters in this section provide a glimpse of where the discipline and the organizations in which it is practiced may be heading.

Section Five: Industry Applications of Project Management

With the growth of project management in all industry sectors, this section of the book could be one hundred chapters long; it was difficult to limit it to a handful of industries. As professionals, the students will need to understand how the basic accepted concepts of project management must be adapted to the environments found in different industries and professions. Section Five identifies a number of specific industries, technologies, and specialty areas in which project management is widely used and recognized, and examines the differing priorities of the project manager in each of these different venues. The overall thrust of this section is to demonstrate that the basic concepts of project management apply universally across these venues, even though the specific concepts and ideas may have different priorities and influences on project management practices in each venue. New to this section in the fourth edition are chapters on project management in healthcare, marketing, financial services, and infrastructure development.

About the Contributors

Finally, biographical information on all the contributing authors can be found at the end of the handbook. Some of the authors have provided email addresses or website URLs to encourage the interested student to ask questions, learn more, and engage in the kind of dialogue that spurs this fascinating discipline to growth and change.

ACKNOWLEDGMENTS

In completing this project, we drew upon the knowledge, comprehension, patience, and diligence of many people. In particular, we would like to thank our AMACOM editor, Robert Nirkind, for his encouragement and patience.

Thanks are also due to our own companies, DinsmoreCompass and PM Solutions, for making it possible for us to work on this book, and the families and friends who put up with our schedules over the course of the past year.

Most of all, we want to thank the authors who contributed so much of their time and talent to this project, as well as the contributors to previous editions, who laid the groundwork for this updated version. A special word of thanks is due to Paul Lombard, PMP, of the PM College who assisted in updating two chapters in addition to his own.

Finally, we would be remiss if we did not express our appreciation of the Project Management Institute for its work in developing and maintaining the project management standards that form the basis of our profession.

—PAUL C. DINSMORE, PMP,
RIO DE JANEIRO, BRAZIL

—JEANNETTE CABANIS-BREWIN,
CULLOWHEE, NORTH CAROLINA

PAUL C. DINSMORE

Paul C. Dinsmore, PMP, is an international speaker and seminar leader on project management. He has authored or coauthored twenty books including *Winning in Business with Enterprise Project Management* and *Enterprise Project Governance*, and has written more than one hundred professional papers and articles. Mr. Dinsmore is president of DinsmoreCompass, a training and consulting group focused on project management and team building. Prior to establishing his consulting practice in 1985, he worked for twenty years as a project manager and executive in the construction and engineering industry for Daniel International, Morrison Knudsen International, and Engevix Engineering.

Mr. Dinsmore has performed consulting and training services for major companies including IBM, ENI-Italy, Petrobras, General Electric, Mercedes Benz, Shell, Morrison Knudsen, the World Trade Institute, Westinghouse, Ford, Caterpillar, and Alcoa. His speaking and consulting practice has taken him to Europe, South America, South Africa, Japan, China, and Australia. The range of projects where Mr. Dinsmore has provided consulting services includes company reorganization, project start-up, development and implementation of project management systems, and training programs, as well as special advisory functions for the presidents of several organizations. Mr. Dinsmore participates actively in the Project Management Institute, which awarded him its Distinguished Contributions Award as well as the prestigious title of Fellow of the Institute. He also has served on the board of directors of the PMI Educational Institute.

Mr. Dinsmore graduated from Texas Tech University and completed the Advanced Management Program at Harvard Business School. He can be reached at paul.dinsmore@dinsmorecompass.com.br.

JEANNETTE CABANIS-BREWIN

Jeannette Cabanis-Brewin, principal of The WordSource, LLC, has written about the human and organizational aspects of project management for more than eighteen years, and has contributed, as editor or author, to more than twenty project-management books. She is editor in chief of the research arm (formerly the Center for Business Practices) of the project management consulting firm PM Solutions, Inc. A former staff writer and editor for the Project Management Institute's publishing division, she has researched and written hundreds of articles for print and online publications and has edited three award-winning project management books, including *The Strategic Project Office* by J. Kent Crawford, winner of PMI's 2002

David I. Cleland Literature Award. She is also the coauthor, with J. Kent Crawford, of *Optimizing Human Capital with a Strategic Project Office, Seven Steps to Strategy Execution,* and *An Inside Look at High-Performing PMOs.* Her new book, *Create a Healthy Workplace, Build a Healthy Bottom Line,* is forthcoming in 2014 from Maven House Press.

Jeannette Cabanis-Brewin has a BA in English, professional writing concentration (summa cum laude) from Western Carolina University and has done graduate work in organizational development (Western Carolina University) and nonprofit management (Duke University). In 2007, the Project Management Institute honored her with a Distinguished Contributions Award.

CHAPTER 1

What Is Project Management?
Project Management Concepts and Methodologies

JOAN KNUTSON, PMP, PM GURU UNLIMITED

**FRANCIS M. WEBSTER, JR., PHD,
WESTERN CAROLINA UNIVERSITY, RETIRED**

What do Wall Street and Main Street have in common? Both measure success relative to speed, quality, and teamwork. Growing behemoths and smaller emerging concerns tout project management as a vehicle to success. They use project management to plan and manage enterprise initiatives that generate revenue or contain costs. Those who compete to sell products or services use project management to differentiate themselves by creating a product of higher quality than that of their competitors and getting it to market sooner.

Project management is recognized as a necessary discipline within corporations and governmental agencies. The planning, organizing, and tracking of projects are recognized as core competencies by for-profit and nonprofit organizations of any size.

Projects are mini-enterprises, and each project is a crucial microcosm of any business or organization. You may not be an entrepreneur, but as a project manager you are an "intrapreneur." Think about it: projects consume money and create benefits. Consider the percentage of your organization's dollars that are invested in projects, and the amount of your organization's bottom line generated through projects.

PROJECTS: THE WORK

Pharmaceuticals, aerospace, construction, and information technology are industries that operate on a project basis, and all are notable for developments that have changed the way we live and work. But not all projects are of such magnitude. A community fund-raising or political campaign, the development of a new product, creating an advertising program, and training the sales and support staff to service a

1

product effectively are also projects. Indeed, it is probable that most executives spend more of their time planning and monitoring changes in their organizations—that is, projects—than they do in maintaining the status quo.

All of these descriptions focus on a few key notions. Projects involve change—the creation of something new or different—and they have a beginning and an ending. Indeed, these are the characteristics of a project that are embodied in the definition of *project* as found in *A Guide to the Project Body of Knowledge* (*PMBOK® Guide*, Fifth Edition) published by the Project Management Institute (PMI): *A temporary endeavor undertaken to create a unique product, service, or result.*[1] This definition, although useful to project managers, may not be sufficient to distinguish projects from other undertakings. Understanding some of the characteristics of projects and comparing projects to other types of undertakings may give a clearer perspective.

Some Characteristics of Projects

▶ *Projects are unique undertakings* that result in a single unit of output. The installation of an entertainment center by a homeowner, with the help of a few friends, is a project. The objective is to complete the installation and enjoy the product of the effort. It is a unique undertaking because the homeowner is not likely to repeat this process frequently.

▶ *Projects are composed of interdependent activities.* Projects are made up of activities. Consistent with the definition of a project, an activity has a beginning and an end. Activities are interrelated in one of three possible ways. In some situations, one activity must be completed before another can begin. Generally, these *mandatory* relationships are difficult to violate, or to do so just does not make sense. The relationship of other activities is not as obvious or as restrictive. These more *discretionary* interdependencies are based on the preferences of the people developing the plan. Some activities are dependent on some *external* event, such as receiving the materials from the vendor. In any of these three instances, mandatory, discretionary, or external, activities have a relationship one to another.

▶ *Projects create a quality deliverable.* Each project creates its own deliverable(s), which must meet standards of performance criteria. That is, each deliverable from every project must be quality controlled. If the deliverable does not meet its quantifiable quality criteria, that project cannot be considered complete.

▶ *Projects involve multiple resources,* both human and nonhuman, which require close coordination. Generally there are a variety of resources, each with its own unique technologies, skills, and traits. This aspect, in human resources, leads to an inherent characteristic of projects: conflict. There is conflict among resources as to their concepts, approaches, theories, techniques, and so on. In addition, there is conflict for resources as to quantity, timing, and specific assignments. Thus, a project manager must be skilled in managing both such conflicts.

▶ *Projects are not synonymous with the products of the project.* For some people, the word *project* refers to the planning and controlling of the effort. For others, project means the unique activities required to create the product of the project. This is not a trivial distinction, as both entities have characteristics specific to themselves.

The names of some of these characteristics apply to both. For example, the life cycle cost of a product includes the cost of creating it (a project), the cost of operating it (not a project), the cost of major repairs or refurbishing (typically done as projects), and the cost of dismantling it (often a project, if done at all). The project cost of creating the product is generally a relatively small proportion of the life cycle cost of the product.

▶ *Projects are driven by competing constraints.* These competing constraints represent the balance of scope, quality, schedule, budget, resources, and risks, among other factors. One of these constraints is the driving or gating factor of each project. Different projects may be driven by a different constraint, depending on the emphasis established by management. Being first in the market often determines long-term market position, thus creating time pressure as the major driver. Most projects require the investment of considerable money and labor the benefits of the resulting product can be enjoyed. Thus, containing resource expenditures may be the driving factor. A need exists for the resulting product of the project to be of the highest quality, as, for example, with a new system within the healthcare industry.

In summary, projects consist of activities, which have interrelationships among one another, produce quality-approved deliverables, and involve multiple resources. Projects are not synonymous with products. During the life cycle of any product, the concept of project management is used, whereas, at other times, product or operations management is appropriate. Finally, how projects are managed is determined by which of the competing project constraints is the driving factor.

Development Life Cycles

As one of the characteristics above stated, the work to create the product and the work to manage the project that creates the product are different. However, a development life cycle often integrates work efforts to accomplish both. A development life cycle defines the activities to create the product and designates other activities to plan and control work being performed to create the product. The work efforts related to creating the product might be *Design It, Build It, Quality Assure It,* and *Ship It,* whereas the processes to manage the project might be *Initiating, Planning, Executing, Monitoring and Controlling,* and *Closing.*

The activities to create the product are specific to the industry and to the product being created. In other words, the pharmaceutical product life cycle is very different from the software development life cycle. Yet the same project management life cycle could be used to organize and monitor either the pharmaceutical or the software product creation.

Traditional. The design and the use of the integrated product and project life cycles have changed. Traditionally, the product life cycle is decomposed into phases or stages, such as the example above. Each phase is performed, completed, and approved during a Phase Review effort, and then the next phase begins. This technique is called the waterfall development life cycle. The project management life cycle works in sync with the product life cycle. Each phase of the product life cycle (for example, the design phase) would be planned, executed, controlled, and possibly closed-out before the build phase begins. In other words, the work efforts to produce the product would be performed serially and only once. The efforts to project manage the effort would be repeated for each sequential phase of the product life cycle

Iterative. It is recognized that a phase of the product process might be revisited— for example, if something was discovered during the design phase that necessitated going back and revising the specifications created in the requirements phase. The traditional waterfall can be modified slightly. The modification of the waterfall is called a spiral, or an iterative, approach.

Relative to the project management efforts, the upcoming phase is planned and managed at a very detailed level, whereas the later phases are planned at a lesser level of detail until more information is gained, which justifies a detailed planning effort. This type of project management effort is referred to as the rolling wave, or the phased approach to project management.

Evolving. With time-to-market or time-to-money becoming more important, the above sequential techniques are ineffective. New approaches, such as incremental builds and prototyping, have emerged. A prototype (a working model) is produced. The customers play with it, modifying/adding/deleting specifications, until the product is the way that they want it. Only then is the product officially released to be used by the entire customer community. Incremental build suggests creating a minimally functional product and releasing it. Even before it is in the customer's hands, more features and functions are being added for the next release.

Still not fast enough? Deliverable-driven and time-boxed efforts, called "agile," become the basic premises for these faster (cheaper) and better development life cycles. Using the same theory as incremental and interactive, a new version of the product must be completed in a specified, but very short, period of time (often called a sprint). Typical project management schedule charts become extinct or at least modified to accommodate this agile development approach. Short-interval scheduling that produces quality-controlled deliverables becomes the mode of the day. Teams become closer and more energetic. Customers start seeing output quicker. Paperwork becomes less important and flexible decision making becomes a necessity. Risks, mistakes, and some wasted time are acceptable. Yet the product is produced faster, thus generating revenue or containing costs occurs sooner.

In summary, each of the above variations to product/project development life cycles has its place. The trend toward speed will increase. The desire for highest quality products created with minimal cost will influence these techniques as time goes on.

PROJECT MANAGEMENT PROCESS: THE DISCIPLINE

Project Management is a disciple that requires discipline.

The word *discipline* has the following two definitions: (1) the rules used to maintain control; and (2) a branch of learning supported by mental, moral, or physical training. Project management, therefore, is a discipline (definition 2) that requires discipline (definition 1). It is a branch of learning that deals with the planning, monitoring, and controlling of one-time endeavors. In other words, project management is *the application of knowledge, skills, tools, and techniques to project activities to meet project requirements.*

Some Characteristics of Project Management

▶ *Project management is a unique career and profession.* Its origins can be traced back to efforts such as U.S. Department of Defense major weapons systems development, NASA space missions, and major construction and maintenance efforts. The magnitude and complexity of these efforts were the driving force in the search for tools that could aid management in the planning, decision making, and control of the multitude of activities involved in the project, especially those occurring simultaneously.

▶ *Project management is not just scheduling software.* There is a misconception that project management is no more than scheduling using PERT (Program Evaluation and Review Technique) or CPM (Critical Path Method). A more realistic view is that scheduling software is a small part of project management. Software has permitted time scheduling, resource allocation, and cost management to be done much more efficiently and, therefore, in less time and in more detail. Thus, a project can be planned and executed more precisely, leaving more time to perform the other aspects of project management. Constantly improving software also has made it easier to manage the schedules, resources, and costs associated with multiple co-occurring projects.

▶ *Project management is different from operations and technical management.* Operations management can be characterized as managing the steady state; thus it is recurring and repetitive. As soon as the operation is established, the concern becomes maintaining the operation in a production mode for as long as possible. Technical management tends to focus on the theory, technology, and practice in a technical field concerning itself with questions of policy on strength of materials, safety factors in design, and checking procedures.

However, executives tend to be concerned about setting up a new operation (via a project) to implement organizational strategy. Project management, then, is the interface among general management, operations management, and technical management; it integrates all aspects of the project and causes the project to happen.

▶ *A focus on integration.* If there is a single word that characterizes project management, it is *integration*—the integration of this discipline with other driving factors within the organization.

Factors That Influence the Practice of Project Management

Below is a sampling of those driving factors that influence project management and, equally as important, which project management the discipline influences.

Strategic Planning: The Directive. Decisions from the strategic planning process become the directive from which projects are initiated. Project practitioners need to see the alignment between the strategic plan and the project. Strategic planning converted into an ongoing strategic management process continues to review strategic objectives and filter down any changes, so that project managers can redirect their efforts appropriately.

Resource Allocation: The Critical Success Factor. Resources used by projects are defined as *skilled human resources (specific disciplines either individually or in crews or teams), equipment, services, supplies, commodities, material, budgets, or funds.* The project manager must ensure that the allocation of specific resources is adequate but not overcommitted, and that the right resources are assigned to the right tasks. This is not a simple procedure because of the number of activities that can be in process simultaneously. Fortunately, project management software provides assistance by identifying overloading or underloading of any one resource or pool of resources. Having identified any problems, human judgment is still required to evaluate and make the final decisions. This essential process both determines the cost of the project (budget) and provides oversight.

Change Management: The Differentiator. *Modifications to documents, deliverables, or baselines associated with the project are identified, documented, approved, or rejected.* This is the definition of change management in the context of project management. However, every project creates significant changes in the culture of the business. Additional attention needs to be paid to planning and managing cultural and organizational change generated by projects.

Quality: Win/Win or Lose/Lose. A quality initiative is *the degree to which a set of inherent characteristics fulfills requirements;* it begins at the same time as the project management discipline. Quality management in the form of Six Sigma and other approaches combines project management techniques with the quality improvement techniques to ensure verifiable success.

Mentorship: Transfer from One Generation to the Next. Staff members who leave a company/agency or a division/department take with them a history and knowledge of past projects. Cultures survive by passing knowledge from the elders to the young. To keep the information needed to perpetuate the project management culture in house, proactive mentorship programs (as well as knowledge-based systems) are established to orchestrate the passing of the culture onto new project practitioners.

Metrics and Close-Out: Inspect What You Expect. Originally, metrics were the data collected after a project was completed to be used to plan for the next project(s). As project management has evolved, we have learned that we cannot wait until the end of a project to set thresholds and collect the data. Management wants measurement metrics throughout the project that can be managed using executive scorecards or dashboards. Control procedures need to be in place before the project proceeds so that the records can be complete from the beginning. If not, valuable effort can be consumed in retracing the records after the fact, and control can be lost before the project really gets started. Furthermore, legal tests of prudence are better dealt with when accurate and complete records of the project are available.

Productivity: Doing More with Less. The drive to do more with less money and fewer resources, to do it faster, and to produce the highest quality deliverable will never go away. To accomplish this mandate, the biggest bang for the buck comes from increasing productivity. Project practitioners use new and creative techniques (automated and nonautomated) to facilitate greater productivity.

Maturity Tracking: Managing the Evolution of the Project Management Discipline. With increased visibility, project management is being asked to account for what it has contributed lately and, more importantly, for what it plans to contribute tomorrow. To answer these questions, a reasonable maturity growth plan specifically designed for the project management discipline is constructed, which evaluates the growth of today's environment to ensure planned, rather than chaotic, growth.

Teams: Even More Distant. Remote or distant teams face the challenge of geography and diversity. Project management needs to address variables such as multifunctional, multicultural, multigenerational, multigender, and multipersonality project environment.

Risk: The Defeating Factor. Risks are the holes in the dike. Too much vulnerability in the dike can make it crumble. If risks are isolated and the potential holes they present are plugged up, the dike will remain sound and solid. The subdiscipline of risk management is a major area of focus. One emerging approach is to use these techniques for controlling negative risks (threats) as well as for harvesting positive risks (opportunities).

Competencies: Today and Tomorrow. Initially, project practitioners focus on their subject matter expertise, such as financial analysis, telecommunications design, and marketing creativity. Those who became involved in projects transition to project management competencies, such as scheduling, status reporting, and risk management. The next movement is to add general business awareness skills/competencies, such as financial knowledge, facilitation, leadership, problem solving/decision making, and creativity/innovation. Each of you must ask what's next in your world.

Behind these integrations exists a superstructure in the form of processes, procedures, and methodologies.

Project Management Process: The Superstructure

The definition of a project is a *temporary endeavor undertaken to create a unique product, service, or result.* This work is accomplished by instituting a project management process. As with any other discipline, a process or a methodology is created so that consistent rules and standards are employed. Consistent processes provide a common lexicon of terms, a regimented business system, and a frame of reference from which everyone can work. Below are the nine key knowledge areas[1] within a project management discipline.

▶ *Integration management* has been described earlier in this chapter.

▶ *Scope management* ensures *that the project includes all the work required, and only the work required, to complete the project successfully.*[1] The project scope management plan is *a component of the project or program management plan that describes how the scope will be defined, developed, monitored, controlled, and verified.*[1] Project scope includes the features and functions that characterize the product, service, or result, and includes the work that must be done to deliver it with its specified features and functions. Scoping a project is putting boundaries around the work to be done as well as the specifications of the product to be produced. When defining the scope, it is wise to articulate not only what is included but also what is excluded.

▶ *Time management* is *the processes required to manage the timely completion of the project.*[1] The management of time is crucial to the successful completion of a project. The function of time management is divided into six processes: *define the activities, sequence the activities, estimate the activity resources, estimate the activity durations, develop the schedule, and control the schedule.*[1] Definition and sequencing include depicting what work is intended to be done and in what order or sequence.

Estimating is the determination of the duration required to perform each activity, considering the availability and capacity of the resources to carry out the activity. *Scheduling* portrays the duration on a calendar, recognizing both time and resource constraints. The final deliverable from the scheduling process is the estimated time target to complete the entire project. Schedule control includes a recognition of what has happened and taking action to ensure that the project will be completed on time and within budget.

▶ **Cost management** processes maintain financial control of projects and *includes the processes involved in planning, estimating, budgeting, financing, funding, managing, and controlling costs so that the project can be completed within the approved budget.*[1] Cost estimating is the process of assembling and predicting costs of a project. The cost budgeting process involves rolling up those estimates in order to establish budgets, standards, and a monitoring system by which the cost of the project can be measured and managed. Cost control entails gathering, accumulating, analyzing, monitoring, reporting, and managing the costs on an ongoing basis.

▶ **Quality management** includes *the processes and activities of the performing organization that determine quality policies, objectives, and responsibilities so that the project will satisfy the needs for which it was undertaken.*[1] Quality management makes use of quality planning, quality assurance, quality control, and quality improvement techniques and tools. If the requirements for the product of the project are consistent with the real, or perceived, needs of the customers, then the customers are likely to be satisfied with the product of the project. The product either conforms to these requirements or it does not. If the product going to the customers has no defects, they can perform their task in the most efficient manner—and do the right thing right the first time.

▶ **Human resource management** comprises all the *processes that organize, manage, and lead the project team.*[1] It is all about making the most effective use of people, from sponsors, customers, and partners, to individual contributors. Human resource planning and the formation, development, and management of the project team are all part of human resources management. The project manager is responsible for developing the project team and building it into a cohesive group to complete the project. Two major types of tasks are recognized: behavioral and administrative. The behavioral aspects deal with the project team members, their interaction as a team, and their contacts with individuals outside the project itself. Included in these aspects are communicating, motivating, team building, and conflict management. Administrative tasks include employee relations, compensation, government regulations, and evaluation. Much of the administrative activity of the project manager is directed by organizations and agencies outside the project.

▶ **Communications management** includes *the processes required to ensure timely and appropriate planning, collection, creation, distribution, storage, retrieval, management control, and ultimate disposition of project information.*[1] These include communications planning and management, information distribution, and performance reporting. Successful project managers are constantly building consensus or confidence at critical junctures in a project by practicing active communications skills. The project manager must communicate to upper management, to the project team, and to other stakeholders. The communications process is not always easy because the project manager may find that barriers exist to communication, such as lack of clear communication channels and problems in a global team environment. The project manager has the responsibility of knowing what kind of messages to send, knowing when and to whom to send the messages, using the correct mode/medium, and translating the messages into a language that all recipients can understand.

▶ **Risk management** includes *the processes concerned with conducting risk management planning, identification, analysis, responses, and monitoring and controlling on a project.* Risk management is the formal process whereby risk factors are systematically identified, assessed, and provided for. The term *risk management* tends to be misleading because it implies control of events. Risk management must be seen as preparation for possible events in advance, rather than simply reacting to them as they happen.

▶ **Procurement management** includes *the processes to purchase or acquire the products, services, or results needed from outside the project team.* Planning for purchases or acquisitions, contracting, requesting seller responses, source selection, and contract administration (including closure) are all part of procurement management. Inherent in the process of managing a project is the procurement of a wide variety of resources. In most instances, this requires the negotiation of a formal, written contract. In a global business environment, it is essential to understand varying social, political, legal, and financial implications in this process.

▶ **Stakeholder management** includes *the processes required to identify the people, groups, or organizations that could impact or be impacted by the project.* The newest knowledge area in the standards, its addition reflects the growing realization that project management relies on people—not just the project manager and team, but also the executives, managers, clients or customers, vendors, partners, end-users, and communities that have a stake in the project's outcome. Identifying and analyzing the needs and roles of stakeholders is a critical basis for planning, risk management, and requirements gathering. A telling detail in the language about stakeholders in the fifth edition of the *PMBOK® Guide* is the change from "managing stakeholder expectations" to "managing stakeholder engagement."

In summary, the superstructure that supports the project management discipline relies on professional and practical scope, time, cost, quality, human resources, communications, risk, and procurement management—all coordinated through the practice of integration management. Each of these processes and their subordinated processes create the methodology by which projects are performed in a logical and consistent manner. The level of detail and the amount of rigor is defined by the culture as well as by the magnitude and complexity of the project itself.

CONCLUSION

Projects are ubiquitous. They are everywhere, and everybody does them. Projects are the driving force for many organizations in most industries. Projects can be looked upon as the change efforts of society, and the pace of change has been increasing.

Therefore, effectively and efficiently managing change efforts is the only way organizations can survive and grow in this modern world. It is the mode in which corporate strategy is implemented, business change is addressed, productive teams and their necessary competencies are dealt with, the quality of the deliverables is determined, preestablished metrics for management's decision making are tracked, the project is closed out, and the lessons learned are determined.

This discipline changes over time, but the basic business premise never changes: Accomplish the right thing right the first time within justifiable time, resources, and budget. Projects are the means for responding to, if not proactively anticipating, the environment and opportunities of the future.

DISCUSSION QUESTIONS

❶ Regarding the eleven driving factors discussed in the paragraph entitled A Focus on Integration, what is the maturity level of your organization: high, medium, or low? If the maturity level is low, is that acceptable within your evolution of project management or should something be done to change that?

❷ Regarding the six descriptors of projects found in the section entitled Some Characteristics of Projects, what is the awareness level of the key players within your organization's project management community: high, medium, or low? If the awareness is low, what will you do to move that score up to medium or even high?

❸ Regarding the key knowledge areas found in the section entitled Project Management Process: The Superstructure, to what degree are these processes being employed: high, medium, or low? If low, what action needs to be taken to increase competency and adherence to that process?

Though unscientific, this analysis should suggest to readers which of the chapters in this handbook might offer information about the challenges presently facing them.

REFERENCE

[1] This definition, and all others in this chapter, are derived from the Project Management Institute's *A Guide to the Project Management Body of Knowledge,* 5th edition (Newtown Square, PA: PMI).

The Project Management Body of Knowledge: Comprehension and Practice

Introduction

FOUNDATIONAL PROJECT MANAGEMENT KNOWLEDGE

Serious students and practitioners of project management are already familiar with the *PMBOK® Guide*—the professional standard published by the Project Management Institute (PMI). This document provides the foundation for the study and practice of our discipline. Like most standards, it is both very detailed and very high level. That is to say, each knowledge area and process group in the *PMBOK® Guide* is described in as much detail as possible when creating a document that, by definition, must apply to all projects in all fields of endeavor. For the new project manager or the project manager faced with a specific problem in need of a specific solution, such standards often seem frustratingly academic and far removed from the daily grind of getting the work done.

But the *Guide,* while of tremendous value in describing the parameters of the field, was never intended as a step-by-step manual for running a project. Instead, it functions more as an ideal, or pure, vision of project management. Meanwhile, between the vision and the reality, as the poet T.S. Eliot wrote, falls the Shadow.

Chapters 2 to 17 are designed to help you take the fundamentals of project management one step further into the sunlight. Respected expert practitioners discuss the processes and knowledge areas that, rather than reiterating what you can read in the *PMBOK® Guide*, will help you to apply the standards and principles of the profession.

Chapter 1 offered an overview of project management, its history and working parts. Chapter 2 provides an overview of the bodies of knowledge about project management that have been amassed by various professional societies worldwide. Chapters 3 to 7 discuss the processes that make up project management; in particular, initiating, planning, monitoring and controlling, and closing each receive a full chapter of coverage. Chapters 8 to 17 cover the ten knowledge areas accepted as the basis of project management.

Chapters that in previous editions appeared in this section as supplemental readings have been moved to the relevant sections later in the book or, in some cases, deleted.

Finally, all chapters in this section have been reviewed either by the author or by another knowledgeable party for compliance with the newest version of the PMI standard, *A Guide to the Project Management Body of Knowledge,* Fifth Edition.

American Management Association • www.amanet.org

Bodies of Knowledge and Competency Standards in Project Management

ALAN M. STRETTON, UNIVERSITY
OF MANAGEMENT AND TECHNOLOGY

LYNN H. CRAWFORD, HUMAN SYSTEMS
INTERNATIONAL LTD., INSTITUTE FOR THE
STUDY OF COHERENCE AND EMERGENCE (ISCE),
AND BOND UNIVERSITY

The original version of this chapter, published in the first edition of this handbook, was written when the only knowledge standard for project management was the 1987 *Project Management Body of Knowledge (PMBOK®)*[1] developed by the Project Management Institute (PMI), headquartered in the United States. After publication of the first edition, the *PMBOK®* was completely rewritten and renamed *A Guide to the Project Management Body of Knowledge (PMBOK® Guide)* in 1996,[2] with revised editions published in 2000, 2004, and 2008[3] and again in 2013,[4] with the basic 1996 structure largely unchanged. In the meantime, other bodies of knowledge of project management have been developed around the world, notably in the United Kingdom, other countries in Europe, and Japan. These are all markedly different from the *PMBOK® Guide,* but are the de facto project management knowledge guides in their respective geographic domains. All of these bodies of knowledge are often also referred to as project management standards, and although ISO 21500:2012[5] provides an international standard for guidance on project management, there is still no single universally accepted body of knowledge for project management.

Concurrent with these developments, some countries and some professional associations have adopted performance-based competency standards, rather than knowledge standards, as a basis for assessing and credentialing.

Proliferation of bodies of knowledge and standards, and, more significantly, associated qualifications, are problematic for practitioners who may be forced to pursue numerous qualifications to maintain employment in the field. Attempts to develop a global body of project management knowledge have led to acceptance that

13

different models with different underpinning philosophies will continue to coexist. Meanwhile, processes for transferability and mutual recognition of qualifications, based on comparison of bodies of knowledge and competency standards would address the practitioner's dilemma.

This challenge is being addressed by the Global Alliance for Project Performance Standards (GAPPS), which has developed the framework entitled Global Performance Based Standards for Project Management Personnel. This global initiative is discussed further below, but first we examine the origins and natures of key bodies of knowledge and competency standards for project management.

WHY A BODY OF KNOWLEDGE FOR PROJECT MANAGEMENT?

Knowledge standards or guides, which typically take the form of bodies of knowledge, focus primarily on what project management practitioners need to know to perform effectively.

The most compelling argument for having a body of knowledge for project management is to help overcome the "reinventing-the-wheel" problem. A good body of knowledge should help practitioners do their jobs better, by both direct referencing and by use in more formal educational processes.

Koontz and O'Donnell express the need as follows: "[U]nless practitioners are to learn by trial and error (and it has been said that managers' errors are their subordinates' trials), there is no other place they can turn for meaningful guidance than the accumulated knowledge underlying their practice. . . ."[6]

Accumulated and relevant knowledge in disciplines such as engineering, architecture, accounting, and medicine is introduced to practitioners through academic degree programs that are essential prerequisites to enable them legally to practice their profession. Project management is interdisciplinary. There are no mandatory certifications limiting those who can practice project management, and the majority of practitioners hold qualifications in other disciplines, most commonly in engineering. Defining the knowledge that is specific to project management practice therefore has been an important aspect of aspiring professional formation.

Beginning in 1981, PMI took formal steps to accumulate and codify relevant knowledge by initiating the development of what became their *Project Management Body of Knowledge (PMBOK®)*. The perceived need to do so arose from PMI's long-term commitment to the professionalization of project management.

The initial overambitious goal of trying to codify an entire body of knowledge—surely a dynamic and changeable thing—was tempered in 1996 by the change in title to *A Guide to . . .* and the statement that the *PMBOK® Guide* was in fact, "a subset of the . . . Body of Knowledge that is generally accepted as good practice."[2] That is to say, the *PMBOK® Guide* is designed to define a recommended subset rather than to describe the entire field.

In summary, PMI sees its subset of the body of knowledge, as set forth in the *PMBOK® Guide*, as a basis for the professionalization of project management. A further purpose is provision of a guide to practitioners and a basis for assessment and certification of project management practitioners. These purposes are shared by European and Japanese professional associations in developing their own bodies of knowledge.

Initial interest in project management focused on individual projects and their managers. Since 2000, there has been increasing interest in programs and portfolios of projects and the knowledge and competencies required for their management that are different from or extend beyond the individual project. This has led to a broadening of the scope of project management standards and in some cases to the development of specific and separate standards for the management of programs and portfolios. As stated in the sixth edition of the Association of Project Management (United Kingdom), ". . . the term 'project management body of knowledge' no longer does justice to the broader reaches of the profession" and the use of the term *P3 management* has become popular in referring to management of projects, programs, and portfolios.[7]

We now look at some of the principal bodies of knowledge of project management, encompassing management of projects, programs, and portfolios, in more detail.

PMI's *PMBOK® Guide*

PMI has produced the oldest and most widely used body of knowledge of project management, which has been modified substantially over the years. In the words of an editor of the *Project Management Journal:* "It was never intended that the body of knowledge could remain static. Indeed, if we have a dynamic and growing profession, then we must also have a dynamic and growing body of knowledge."[8] For this reason, bodies of knowledge and standards are subject to regular review.

The precursor of the *PMBOK®* was PMI's ESA (Ethics, Standards, and Accreditation) report of 1983,[9] which nominated six primary components, namely the management of scope, cost, time, quality, human resources, and communications.

The 1987 *PMBOK®*[1] was an entirely new document, and the first separately published body of knowledge of project management. It added contract/procurement management and risk management to the previous six primary components. The 1996 *PMBOK® Guide*[2] was a completely rewritten document, which added project integration management to the existing eight primary components. The nine components were then renamed project management knowledge areas, with a separate chapter for each. Each knowledge area has a number of component processes, each discussed in terms of inputs, tools and techniques, and outputs. These component processes are also categorized into five project management process groups: initiating, planning, executing, monitoring and controlling, and closing. The knowledge areas and their component processes are listed in Table 2-1.

The forty-two component processes identified in the fourth edition of the Guide were increased to forty-seven in the fifth edition. The most noticeable change was the separation of stakeholder management processes from communications management to create a new, tenth knowledge area, project stakeholder management, taking the number of knowledge areas from nine to ten.

The ten chapters in the fifth edition of the *PMBOK® Guide* that address the knowledge areas and component processes are preceded by one chapter dealing with the organizational context of projects and their life cycles and phases, and another chapter primarily concerned with the project management process groups. The relationship of project management with program, portfolio, and organizational project management is addressed in an introductory chapter, making it clear that these are

Knowledge Area/ Subject Groups	PMBOK® Guide, Fifth Edition		ISO 21500:2012	
Integration	4.1	Develop project charter	4.3.2	Develop project charter
	4.2	Develop project management plan	4.3.3	Develop project plans
	4.3	Direct and manage project work	4.3.4	Direct project work
	4.4	Monitor and control project work	4.3.5	Control project work
	4.5	Perform integrated change control	4.3.6	Control project changes
	4.6	Close project or phase	4.3.7	Close project phase or project
			4.3.8	Collect lessons learned
Scope	5.1	Plan scope management	4.3.11	Define scope
	5.2	Collect requirements	4.3.12	Create work breakdown structure
	5.3	Define scope	4.3.13	Define activities
	5.4	Create WBS	4.3.14	Control scope
	5.5	Validate scope		
	5.6	Control scope		
Time	6.1	Plan schedule management	4.3.21	Sequence activities
	6.2	Define activities	4.3.22	Estimate activity durations
	6.3	Sequence activities	4.3.23	Develop schedule
	6.4	Estimate activity resources	4.3.24	Control schedule
	6.5	Estimate activity durations		
	6.6	Develop schedule		
	6.7	Control schedule		
Cost	7.1	Plan cost management	4.3.25	Estimate costs
	7.2	Estimate costs	4.3.26	Develop budget
	7.3	Determine budget	4.3.27	Control costs
	7.4	Control costs		
Quality	8.1	Plan quality management	4.3.32	Plan quality
	8.2	Perform quality assurance	4.3.33	Perform quality assurance
	8.3	Control quality	4.3.34	Perform quality control
Human Resources	9.1	Plan human resource management	4.3.15	Establish project team
	9.2	Acquire project team	4.3.16	Estimate resources
	9.3	Develop project team	4.3.17	Define project organization
	9.4	Manage project team	4.3.18	Develop project team
			4.3.19	Control resources
			4.3.20	Manage project team
Communications	10.1	Plan communications management	4.3.38	Plan communications
	10.2	Manage communications	4.3.39	Distribute information
	10.3	Control communications	4.3.40	Manage communications

TABLE 2-1. **COMPARISON OF KNOWLEDGE AREAS/SUBJECT GROUPS IN FIFTH EDITION OF THE** *PMBOK® GUIDE* **AND ISO 21500:2012**

Knowledge Area/ Subject Groups	PMBOK® Guide, Fifth Edition	ISO 21500:2012
Risk	11.1 Plan risk management 11.2 Identify risks 11.3 Perform qualitative risk analysis 11.4 Perform quantitative risk analysis 11.5 Plan risk responses 11.6 Control risks	4.3.28 Identify risks 4.3.29 Assess risks 4.3.30 Treat risks 4.3.31 Control risks
Procurement	12.1 Plan procurement management 12.2 Conduct procurements 12.3 Control procurements 12.4 Close procurements	4.3.35 Plan procurements 4.3.36 Select suppliers 4.3.37 Administer procurements
Stakeholder	13.1 Identify stakeholders 13.2 Plan stakeholder management 13.3 Manage stakeholder engagement 13.4 Control stakeholder engagement	4.3.9 Identify stakeholders 4.3.10 Manage stakeholders

WBS, work breakdown structure.

Source: This table is based on information found in the fifth edition of the *PMBOK® Guide,* PMI, 2013.

TABLE 2-1. CONTINUED

outside the scope of the *PMBOK® Guide* and the subject of specific, separate PMI standards.

In 1998, PMI was accredited as a standards developer by the American National Standards Institute (ANSI) and from the second edition of the *PMBOK® Guide* onward only the section of the guide dealing with project management processes has been identified as the standard. In the fifth edition this was clarified by including the standard for project management of a project as an annex to the *Guide*.

The aim of the *PMBOK® Guide* is to identify and describe "that subset of the Project Management Body of Knowledge that is *generally recognized as good practice*" [author's italics], and they go on to explain that "'generally recognized' means the knowledge and practices . . . applicable to most projects most of the time" and

> "good practice" means there is general agreement that the application of these skills, tools, and techniques can enhance the chances of success over many projects. "Good practice" does not mean that the knowledge described should always be applied uniformly on all projects; the organization and/or project management team is responsible for determining what is appropriate for any given project.[10]

In summary, the *PMBOK® Guide* has focused on (project) management knowledge and processes that are generally recognized as good practice in the context of individual projects and has not included knowledge areas and component processes that may be relevant only on some projects or only on some occasions.

PMI has produced separate documents that it refers to as standards rather than knowledge guides, which specifically address the management of programs and portfolios. These are the standard for program management and the standard for portfolio management, both initially released in 2006. Their third editions were published in 2013.

The Association of Project Management Body of Knowledge (*APMBOK®*)

Morris notes that when the United Kingdom's Association of Project Management (APM) launched its certification program in the early 1990s, it was because the APM felt that PMI's *PMBOK®* did not adequately reflect the knowledge base that project management professionals need. It therefore developed its own body of knowledge, which differs markedly from PMI's.[11]

The fifth edition (2006) of *APMBOK®*[12] was organized into seven main sections, with a total of fifty-three component items. In the document there are brief discussions of all headings and topics, and references given for each topic. Morris discusses the reasons why APM did not use the *PMBOK®* model. In essence, he says that the different models reflect different views of the project management discipline. He notes that while the PMI model is focused on the generic processes required to accomplish a project "on time, in budget, and to scope," APM's reflects a wider view of the discipline, "addressing both the context of project management and the technological, commercial, and general management issues, which it believes are important to successfully accomplishing projects."[11]

Morris goes on to say

> . . . all the research evidence . . . shows that in order to deliver successful projects, managing scope, time, cost, resources, quality, risk, procurement, and so forth . . . alone are not enough. Just as important—sometimes more important—are issues of technology and design management, environment and external issues, people matters, business and commercial issues, and so on. Further, the research shows that defining the project is absolutely central to achieving project success. The job of managing the project begins early in the project, at the time the project definition is beginning to be explored and developed, not just after the scope, schedule, budget, and other factors have been defined. . . . APM looked for a structure that gave more recognition to these matters.[11]

One of the key differences between the PMI and APM approaches is that the *PMBOK® Guide's* knowledge areas have focused on project management skills that are generally recognized as good practice, whereas contextual issues and the like are discussed separately in its Framework section. On the other hand, the *APMBOK®* includes knowledge and practices that may apply to *some* projects or *part* of the time, which is a much more inclusive approach. This is exampled by the fact that the *PMBOK® Guide* specifically excludes safety, while the *APMBOK®* specifically includes safety.

The sixth edition of the *APMBOK®*, released in 2012,[7] retained the inclusive philosophy of previous versions but changed significantly in terms of structure and delivery. The structure was reduced from seven sections with fifty-three components, to four main sections covering context, people, delivery and interfaces, fifteen subsections, and fifty-three components. The section on delivery equates most directly to the *PMBOK® Guide*, but the approach and content are noticeably different. The *PMBOK® Guide* knowledge areas are presented in considerable detail, more or less in the form that might be expected in a textbook, and, as noted previously, relate only to projects. The *APMBOK®* is much broader in scope, covering projects, programs, and portfolios, in the form of an overview, providing references for further reading. In part because the scope is broader, topic coverage is more expansive, including benefits management, which is not mentioned in the *PMBOK® Guide*. In terms of delivery modes, although it is still available in traditional book form, both hardcover and paperback, the *APMBOK®* is also provided online in interactive format. This enables users to search it, to access material that is either generic or specific to management at the level of project, programs or portfolios, and to provide real-time feedback and suggestions for review. Table 2-2 displays the structure of the *APMBOK®*, Sixth Edition.

International Project Management Association Competency Baseline (ICB)

Following the publication and translation of the first editions of the *APMBOK®* in 1992 and 1994, several European countries, including Austria, France, Germany, Switzerland, and the Netherlands, developed their own bodies of knowledge.

Drawing on these bodies of knowledge, the International Project Management Association (IPMA), a federation of national project management associations, mainly European, developed an IPMA Competence Baseline (ICB) in the late 1990s. This was reviewed and updated in 1999 (Version 2) and again in 2006 (Version 3.0). The primary purpose of the ICB is to provide a reference basis for its member associations to develop their own national competence baselines (NCBs). Another purpose of the ICB was to "harmonize" the then-existing European bodies of knowledge, particularly those of the United Kingdom, France, Germany, and Switzerland. The majority of members have since developed their own baselines, which may include additional elements to reflect any cultural differences and provide a basis for certification of their project managers.[13]

In spite of its name, the majority of the content of the ICB Version 3.0 can be seen primarily as a knowledge guide, although it is explicitly intended as a basis for assessment and certification at four levels—IPMA A, B, C, and D. Competence in the ICB is defined as a "collection of knowledge, personal attitudes, skills and relevant experience needed to be successful in a certain function."

The ICB comprises some forty-six competence elements of which twenty are classified as technical, fifteen as behavioral, and eleven as contextual. The forty-six competence elements are required to be included in each member's national competence baseline (NCB). Like the *APMBOK®*, the ICB is inclusive in that it considers not only the project, but also the program and portfolio.

Japan's *P2M*

In mid-1999, Japan's Engineering Advancement Association (ENAA) received a commission from the Ministry of Economy, Trade, and Industry to establish a new Japanese-type project management knowledge system and a qualification system. ENAA established a committee for the introduction, development, and research on

Section	Subsection	Components
1. Context	1.1 Governance	1.1.1 Project management
		1.1.2 Program management
		1.1.3 Portfolio management
		1.1.4 Infrastructure
		1.1.5 Knowledge management
		1.1.6 Life cycle
		1.1.7 Success factors and maturity
		1.1.8 Sponsorship
	1.2 Setting	1.2.1 Environment
		1.2.2 Operations management
		1.2.3 Strategic management
2. People	2.1 Interpersonal skills	2.1.1 Communication
		2.1.2 Conflict management
		2.1.3 Delegation
		2.1.4 Influencing
		2.1.5 Leadership
		2.1.6 Negotiation
		2.1.7 Teamwork
	2.2 Professionalism	2.2.1 Communities of practice
		2.2.2 Competence
		2.2.3 Ethics frameworks
		2.2.4 Learning and development
3. Delivery	3.1 Integrative management	3.1.1 Business case
		3.1.2 Control
		3.1.3 Information management
		3.1.4 Organization
		3.1.5 Planning
		3.1.6 Stakeholder management
	3.2 Scope management	3.2.1 Benefits management
		3.2.2 Change control
		3.2.3 Configuration management
		3.2.4 Change management
		3.2.5 Requirements management
		3.2.6 Solutions development
	3.3 Schedule management	3.3.1 Resource scheduling
		3.3.2 Time scheduling
	3.4 Financial and cost management	3.4.1 Budgeting and cost control
		3.4.2 Funding
		3.4.3 Investment appraisal
	3.5 Risk management	3.5.1 Resource scheduling
		3.5.2 Time scheduling
	3.6 Quality management	3.6.1 P3 assurance
		3.6.2 Reviews
	3.7 Resource management	3.7.1 Contract
		3.7.2 Mobilization
		3.7.3 Procurement
		3.7.4 Provider selection and management

TABLE 2-2. **CONTENT AND STRUCTURE OF *APM BODY OF KNOWLEDGE* (SIXTH EDITION)**

Section	Subsection	Components
4. Interfaces	4.1 Accounting 4.2 Health and safety 4.3 Human resource management 4.4 Law 4.5 Security 4.6 Sustainability	No components

TABLE 2-2. CONTINUED

project management, which produced *A Guidebook of Project and Program Management for Enterprise Innovation* (officially abbreviated as *P2M*) in 2001, with English revisions in 2002, 2004, and 2008.[14] The Japanese approach was from the start both broad and inclusive.

The task of issuing, maintaining, and upgrading *P2M* was undertaken by the Project Management Professionals Certification Center (PMCC) of Japan (formed in 2002), which also implemented a certification system for project professionals in Japan, based on *P2M*. The PMCC consolidated its organization with that of the Japan Project Management Forum [(JPMF), which was originally inaugurated in 1998] in November 2005, to make a fresh start as the Project Management Association of Japan (PMAJ), which is the publisher of the 2008 edition of *P2M*.

The rationale for developing *P2M* and the certification system was a perceived need for Japanese enterprises to institute more innovative approaches to developing their businesses, particularly in the context of the increasingly competitive global business environment, and also a perceived need to provide improved public services. The key concept in addressing this need is "value creation." The recommended means of achieving value creation is through developing an enterprise mission, then strategies to accomplish this mission, followed by planned programs to implement these strategies, and then specific projects to achieve each of the programs. The focus of *P2M* is on how to facilitate the effective planning, management, and implementation of such programs and projects.

The original Japanese document comprises 420 pages, so it is a large and very detailed document. The *P2M* not only covers the management of single projects, but also has a major section specifically on program management. It has chapters on the following topics, under the overall heading of Domain Management, applicable to projects and programs:

1. Project Strategy Management
2. Project Finance Management
3. Project Systems Management
4. Project Organization Management
5. Project Objectives Management
6. Project Resources Management
7. Risk Management
8. Program and Project Information Management
9. Project Relationships Management

10. Project Value Management
11. Project Communications Management

TOWARD A GLOBAL BODY OF KNOWLEDGE

No single, globally accepted, body of knowledge of project management currently exists. Each major professional association has a vested interest in maintaining its own body of knowledge, as each case has entailed a considerable investment in, and commitment to, subsequent certification processes. It is, therefore, difficult to envisage any situation that might prompt professional associations to voluntarily cooperate to develop a global body of knowledge to which they would commit themselves. Representatives of thirty-one countries and a wide range of project management professional associations were brought together by the International Organization for Standardization (ISO) to develop ISO 21500:2012 Guidance on Project Management, but it is not intended as a body of knowledge or basis for education and certification. It may influence the content of the various bodies of knowledge, but there is no indication that it is likely to replace them.

Nonetheless, since the mid-1990s, discussions at global forums, often in association with major project management conferences, indicated that there is a wide recognition that a globally recognized body of knowledge would be highly desirable.

One particular initiative was the coming together of a small group of internationally recognized experts to initiate workshops, beginning in 1998, to develop a global body of project management knowledge. This group, known as the OLCI (Operational Level Coordination Initiative) recognized that one single document cannot realistically capture the entire body of project management knowledge, particularly emerging practices, such as in managing "soft" projects (e.g., organizational change projects), cutting-edge research work, unpublished materials, and implicit as well as explicit knowledge and practice. Rather, there has emerged a shared recognition that the various guides and standards represent different and enriching views of selected aspects of the same overall body of knowledge.[15]

COMPETENCY STANDARDS

Competency has been defined as "the ability to perform the activities within an occupation or function to the standard expected in employment."[16] There are two primary approaches to inferring competency: attribute based and performance based.

The *attribute-based* approach involves definition of a series of personal attributes (e.g., a set of skills, knowledge, and attitudes) that are believed to underlie competence, and then testing whether those attributes are present at an appropriate level in the individual.

The performance-based approach is to observe the performance of individuals in the actual workplace, from which underlying competence can be inferred. This has been the approach adopted by the Australian Institute of Project Management (AIPM) as a basis for its certification/registration program.

Several factors combined to lead AIPM to adopt the competency standards approach. First, there was recognition that the possession of knowledge about a subject does not necessarily mean competence in applying that knowledge in practice. More significantly, however, in the early 1990s when the AIPM was developing its certification program for project managers, the Australian government, through its Department of Employment, Education, and Training (DEET) and National Office of Overseas Skills Recognition (NOOSR), was very actively promoting the development of national competency standards for the professions.

With support of the Australian government the AIPM led the development of the first Australian National Competency Standards for Project Management (NCSPM), which were released in 1996 in the context of the Australian Qualifications Framework. A conscious decision was made to align the NCSPM units of competency with the nine knowledge areas of the *PMBOK® Guide,* which was released in the same year. For well over a decade the Australian national standards provided the basis for AIPM's professional registration program.[17]

The format of Australian Competency Standards, which is similar to frameworks developed by the United Kingdom, New Zealand, and South African governments, emphasizes performance-oriented recognition of competence in the workplace, and includes the following main components:

- *Units of competency*: the significant major functions of the profession
- *Elements of competency*: the building blocks of each unit of competency
- *Performance criteria*: the type of performance in the workplace that would constitute adequate evidence of personal competence
- *Range indicators*: the precise circumstances in which the performance criteria would be applied

The elements of competency are expressed in action words, such as *determine, guide, conduct, implement, assess outcomes,* and the like. There are generally three elements of competency for each unit, but occasionally more. There are typically two to four performance criteria for each element of competency.

In 2008 the AIPM released its own Professional Competency Standards for Project Management, so that its registration program was no longer directly aligned with the Australian Qualifications Framework. In keeping with the competency standards approach, standards are written for specific roles. The AIPM has standards for roles of project practitioner, project manager and project director for which the units of competence remain closely aligned to the knowledge areas of the *PMBOK® Guide.* More recently released standards for the role of project portfolio executive have a different focus that reflects the broadening context of project management.

The units of the 2013 version of the government-endorsed Australian National Competency Standards for Project Management remain focused on the project and continue to reflect the knowledge areas of the *PMBOK® Guide.* They are presented in the form of qualifications that are generally applicable to roles of project team members, project managers, and project directors.[18]

Other Competency Standards

Both the United Kingdom and South Africa have performance-based competency standards for project management that form part of the national qualifications frameworks. The Occupational Standards Council for Engineering first produced standards for project controls (1996) and for project management (1997). These are maintained and reviewed by the Engineering Construction Industry Training Board (ECITB). These United Kingdom and South African standards are formally recognized and provide the basis for award of qualifications within their respective national qualifications frameworks.[19]

PMI has produced a Project Manager Competency Development Framework that is not considered a standard but is intended as a resource for practitioner development.[20] In the United Kingdom, the Association for Project Management published the APM Competence Framework in 2008. This is linked to the *APMBOK®* (Fifth Edition) and the ICB-IPMA Competence Baseline Version 3.0.[21]

Toward Global Performance-Based Competency Standards

A global effort for the development of a framework of Global Performance-Based Standards for Project Management Personnel (now known as the Global Alliance for Project Performance Standards [GAPPS]) was initiated in 2003, with preparatory work going back to the late 1990s. The work of an international group, with representatives from major international project management associations, industry, and academia, the intent of this endeavor is to provide a basis for comparison of standards and mutual recognition of qualifications.[22]

The GAPPS has two main streams of activity: the development of performance based standards for project management in its broadest sense, and the mapping or comparison of project management standards and qualifications. The primary purpose of the development of standards is to provide a neutral core against which the content of other standards can be mapped, but in some cases, notably the role of project sponsor, standards are developed in response to demand where no other standards currently exist. The process for development of performance-based standards has been well developed since the late 1980s by governments in the United Kingdom, Australia, New Zealand, and South Africa. The GAPPS draws upon this depth of experience, following established standards development practices and drawing upon existing standards, the input of practitioners, and relevant research.

The GAPPS Project Manager Standard was first released in 2006. A table for evaluating the management complexity of project roles, the Crawford-Ishikura Factor Table for Evaluating Roles (CIFTER), was developed and has been adopted by a number of global organizations as a basis for categorization of projects and determining the level of competence required to manage them. Based on this categorization, two levels of project manager standards, global level 1 and global level 2, are identified. The GAPPS project manager standard focuses on the project but does not adopt the knowledge or functional area structure followed by the majority of other project management standards taking a more integrated and practice-based approach. There are only five units of competence required at global level 1 and six units at global level 2, as illustrated in Figure 2-1.[23]

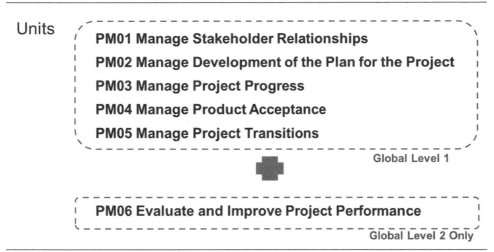

Units

PM01 Manage Stakeholder Relationships

PM02 Manage Development of the Plan for the Project

PM03 Manage Project Progress

PM04 Manage Product Acceptance

PM05 Manage Project Transitions

Global Level 1

PM06 Evaluate and Improve Project Performance

Global Level 2 Only

FIGURE 2-1. **UNITS OF COMPETENCY—GAPPS PROJECT MANAGER STANDARD**

In 2011 a Program Manager Standard was released. This standard has five core units of competence, applicable to all program managers and three additional units applicable only in some contexts (see Figure 2-2).[24]

Combinations of these core and additional units produce six different categories of program manager role. A tool for assessing program management complexity, the Aitken-Carnegie-Duncan Complexity (ACDC) Table, is provided as a basis for differentiating levels of program manager role.

In addition to providing a basis for mapping and comparison of content, these GAPPS standards are being used and adapted by organizations often in association with the knowledge-based standards of the various professional associations as a basis for determining competence, based on evidence of workplace application.

All work of the GAPPS is undertaken by volunteers, and the output is made freely available via the GAPPS website (www.globalpmstandards.org), which offers

1. Provide Leadership for the Program
2. Facilitate Stakeholder Engagement
3. Craft the Program
4. Orchestrate the Attainment of Benefits
5. Sustain Program Progress

Core Units

6. Manage Organizational Change
7. Direct the Management of Contracts
8. Engage in Collaborative Alliances

Additional Units

FIGURE 2-2. **UNITS OF COMPETENCY—GAPPS PROGRAM MANAGER STANDARD**

Chapter 2 • Bodies of Knowledge and Competency Standards in Project Management **25**

a valuable and continually updated resource providing guidance on the comparability of project management bodies of knowledge, standards, and assessment processes.

DISCUSSION QUESTIONS

❶ In your own career, what aspects of general management are equally important to project management skills and knowledge? Should project management perhaps be considered a "general management" skill?

❷ There are many competing bodies of knowledge and competency standards for project management. Do you consider this an advantage or disadvantage for practice and for the development of a profession of project management?

❸ Discuss the difference between attribute-based and performance-based competency models. If your competency were required to be measured, which would you prefer to be gauged by?

REFERENCES

[1] Project Management Institute, *Project Management Body of Knowledge* (Drexel Hill, PA: PMI, 1987).

[2] Project Management Institute, *A Guide to the Project Management Body of Knowledge,* (*PMBOK® Guide*) (Newtown Square, PA: PMI, 1996).

[3] *A Guide to the Project Management Body of Knowledge* (*PMBOK® Guide*), 4th edition (Newtown Square, PA: PMI, 2008), p. 4.

[4] Project Management Institute, *A Guide to the Project Management Body of Knowledge* (*PMBOK® Guide*), 5th edition (Newtown Square, PA: PMI, 2013).

[5] International Organization for Standardization, *ISO 21500:2012 Guidance on Project Management* (Geneva, Switzerland: ISO, 2012).

[6] H. Koontz and C. O'Donnell, *Essentials of Management* (New Delhi, India: Tata McGraw-Hill, 1978).

[7] Association for Project Management, *APM Body of Knowledge,* 6th edition (Princes Risborough, UK: APM, 2012).

[8] Project Management Institute, "Project management body of knowledge: special summer issue," *Project Management Journal* 17, No. 3 (1986), p. 15.

[9] Project Management Institute, "Ethics, standards, accreditation: special report," *Project Management Quarterly.* PMI: Newtown Square, PA. August, 1983.

[10] PMI, 2008, p. 4.

[11] Peter W.G. Morris, "Updating the project management bodies of knowledge," *Project Management Journal* 32 (2001), p. 22.

[12] Association for Project Management, *APM Body of Knowledge,* 5th edition (High Wycombe: UK, 2006).

[13] International Project Management Association, *ICB: IPMA Competence Baseline Version 3.0.* (Nijkerk, The Netherlands: IPMA, 2006).

[14] Project Management Association of Japan, *P2M: Project and Program Management for Enterprise Innovation: Guidebook* (Tokyo, Japan: PMAJ, 2008).

[15] Lynn Crawford, "Global body of project management knowledge and standards," in P.W.G. Morris and J.K. Pinto (editors), *The Wiley Guide to Managing Projects*, Chapter 46. (Hoboken, NJ: John Wiley & Sons, 2004).

[16] L. Heywood, A. Gonczi, and P. Hager, *A Guide to Development of Competency Standards for Professions: Research Paper 7*, (Australia: Australian Government Publishing Service, 1992).

[17] Australian Institute of Project Management (Sponsor), *National Competency Standards for Project Management*. (Sydney, Australia: AIPM, 1996). Standard can be viewed at www.aipm.com.au.

[18] Innovation and Business Skills Australia *BSB07—Business Services Training Package: Release 8.1.* (East Melbourne, Australia: Commonwealth of Australia, 2013).

[19] Engineering Construction Industry Training Board, *National Occupation Standards for Project Management* (Kings Langley, UK: ECITB, 2002).

[20] Project Management Institute, *Project Manager Competency Development Framework* (Newtown Square, PA: PMI, 2007).

[21] Association for Project Management, *APM Competence Framework* (Princes Risborough, UK: APM, 2008).

[22] Lynn Crawford and J.B. Pollack, "Developing a basis for global reciprocity: negotiating between the many standards for project management," *International Journal of IT Standards and Standardization Research* 6 (2008), pp. 70 84.

[23] Global Alliance for Project Performance Standards, *A Framework for Performance Based Competency Standards for Global Level 1 and 2 Project Managers* (Johannesburg, South Africa: GAPPS, 2006, with technical revision, 2007).

[24] Global Alliance for Project Performance Standards, *A Framework for Performance Based Competency Standards for Program Managers* (Sydney, Australia: GAPPS, 2011). Accessible online at www.globalpm standards.org.

CHAPTER 3

Project Management Process Groups
Project Management Knowledge in Action

GEREE STREUN, PMP, CSQE, PMI-ACP, CSSGB, CSM,
GV SOFTWARE SOLUTIONS, INC.

The project management profession's standard, *A Guide to the Project Management Body of Knowledge (PMBOK® Guide),* is described as consisting of ten knowledge areas. What is left out of this description is the equally important segment of the standard that describes the processes used by the project manager to apply that knowledge appropriately.

The ten knowledge areas can be effectively arranged in logical groups for ease of consistent application. These process groups are initiating, planning, executing, monitoring and controlling, and closing. They describe how a project manager integrates activities across the various knowledge areas as a project moves through its life cycle. So, while the knowledge areas within the standard describe what a project manager needs to know, the process groups describe what steps the project managers must take and the approximate order of those steps.[1] Historically, the definition of the processes that make up the project management body of knowledge was a tremendous milestone in the evolution of project management as a profession. Understanding the processes as described in the *PMBOK® Guide* is a first step in mastering project management.

However, as the practice of this profession matures, our understanding of its processes will also mature and evolve. This is reflected in the additions and changes made in successive editions of the standard over the years.

In 2000 edition of the *PMBOK® Guide,* processes were divided into two classifications that were essentially virtual groupings of the project management knowledge areas: core processes and facilitating processes.[2] This classification provided a focus to guide project managers through the application of the knowledge areas and to help in implementing the appropriate ones for their projects. However, a clear differentiation between the core processes and facilitating processes was not provided. Project managers also needed information about when and how to use the processes in those classifications. Subsequently, many inexperienced project managers used the differen-

29

tiation to focus only on the core processes; they addressed the facilitating processes only if time permitted. After all, the latter processes were merely "facilitating" processes.

Therefore, a key change was made in 2004 in the third edition of the *PMBOK® Guide* that was maintained throughout subsequent editions. The artificial focus classifications of core processes and facilitating processes were removed, and since then all of the processes within the knowledge areas are treated equally in the *PMBOK® Guide*.[3] In order to understand this, it is important to know that a process is a set of activities performed to achieve defined objectives. All project management processes are equally important for every project; there are no unimportant processes. A project manager uses knowledge and skills to evaluate every process and to tailor each one as needed for each project. This tailoring is required because there has never been a "one size fits all" project management approach; this is especially important when integrating Agile techniques into a project management process. Every company and organization faces different constraints and requirements on each project. Therefore, tailoring must be performed to ensure that the competing demands of scope, time and cost, and quality are addressed to fulfill those constraints and requirements. Some processes can require a stronger focus on quality and time while also minimizing cost, which is an interesting project management challenge.

The odds of a project being successful are much higher if a defined approach is used when planning and executing it. The project manager chooses an approach for the project's specific constraints after the tailoring effort is completed. This approach must cover all processes needed to adapt, capture, and analyze customer interests, plan and manage any technology evolution, define product specifications, produce a plan, and manage all the activities planned to develop the required product.

PROJECT MANAGEMENT PROCESS GROUPS

Project management process groups are a logical way to categorize and implement the knowledge areas. The fifth edition of the *PMBOK® Guide* recommends addressing every process group for every project. However, the tailoring and rigor applied to implementing each process group are based on the complexity of, and risk for, the specific project.[4] The project manager uses the process groups to address the interactions and required trade-offs among specified product requirements to achieve the project's final product objective. These process groups may appear to be defined as a strict linear model. However, a skilled project manager knows that a project is iterative in nature. Furthermore, artifacts like the business case statement, preliminary plan, and scope statements are rarely complete in their first drafts. Therefore, in most projects, the project manager must iterate through the various processes as many times as needed to define the requirements and then to refine the project management plan that is used to produce a product that meets its requirements. This iteration activity can be done as a series of sprints or iterations to drive to the final deliverable.

Project managers iteratively perform the activities within the process groups on their projects as shown in Figure 3-1, which illustrates how the output of one process group provides one or more inputs for another process group, or even how an output may be the key deliverable for the overall project.

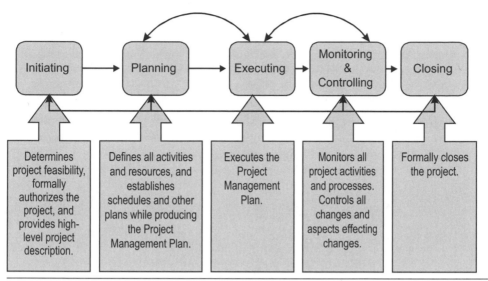

FIGURE 3-1. **PROJECT MANAGEMENT PROCESS GROUPS' INTERACTIONS**

These process groups are tightly coupled since they are linked by their inputs and outputs. This coupling makes it clear that the project manager must ensure that each process is aligned with the other processes for a successful project. When managing a successful project, the process groups and their interactions provide a specific outcome from the application of the project management knowledge areas. A project manager skilled in applying these knowledge areas never confuses the process group interactions with the phases in a product life cycle and is able to apply the interactions in the process groups to drive a project life cycle to its successful completion.

Many project managers have been involved with a project that was started without appropriate analysis and preparation and then ended up costing the company a significant amount over its budget. A case in point: a high-level manager at a customer site might mention an idea to someone in a development company and that idea hits a spark. The company takes the idea and launches into production. When the finished product is completed, there is surprise all around. The customer does not remember any request for this product and the production company cannot sell it to anyone else. The following issues are apparent in this scenario:

- It is not clear whether the idea expressed a valid need.
- It is not clear whether there were real or imagined requirements.
- It is not clear if there was an analysis of a return on investment.
- It is not clear whether there was a delivery date.
- It is not clear whether needed resources were pulled from other projects or if there was impact on other schedules.
- It is not clear that a market need was established prior to development.

The initiating process group is required to answer these types of questions and to formally begin project activities.[5] The project manager uses the initiating processes to start the project by gathering and analyzing customer interests and then addressing any issues or risks and project specifics. The project manager must iterate through the needed initiation activities to identify the service or product requiring the project's effort. The organization must take a critical look at the feasibility and technical capability of creating the product or service as the requirements become more refined. After the appropriate analysis, a project charter is produced that addresses at a minimum the following issues:

- It provides formal authorization for the project.
- It provides a high-level description of the product or service that will be created.
- It defines the initial project requirements, constraints, and assumptions. The constraints and assumptions typically provide the initial set of negotiating points for the project plan.
- It designates the project manager and defines the project manager's authority level.
- It specifies any hard delivery dates if those dates are required by the contract.
- It provides an initial view of stakeholder expectations.
- It provides an indication of the project budget.

The project manager works with the customer to capture the customer's interests and analyze them to develop the initial scope statement. Typically, content detail varies depending on the product's complexity or the application area. This document provides a high-level project definition and should define the project boundaries and project success criteria. It should also address project characteristics, constraints, and assumptions.

The documents developed during this series of processes are provided as input to the planning effort. A plan is a tool that can be used like a map. Unfortunately, some project managers learn a hard lesson about the importance of a defined project plan. A plan is not just a way to focus on tasks; it is a tool to focus efforts and accomplish what is required by the due date. The plan is used to keep the project on track so that the project manager and the team know where the project is in relation to the plan, and they can work together to determine the next steps, especially if discovery is needed. Attempting to run a project without a plan would be like trying to travel to a destination via an unknown route, not knowing one's current location and having no indication of which direction to take. In such a situation, even a map would be useless.

Additional confusion is introduced when some project managers confuse the Gantt chart, which is defined by commercial tools as a "project plan," with an actual project management plan as defined in the fifth edition of the *PMBOK® Guide*.[6] A real project management plan provides needed information about the following:

- Which knowledge area processes are needed, how each is tailored for this particular project, and especially how rigorously each of those processes will be implemented in the project
- How the project team will be built from the resources across the organization or will be brought in through contract, hiring of full-time employees, or outsourcing
- Which quality standards will be applied to the project, and the degree of quality control that will be needed for the project to be successful
- How risks will be identified and mitigated

- Which method will be used for communicating with all of the stakeholders to facilitate the timing of their participation to facilitate addressing open issues and pending decisions
- Which configuration management requirements will be implemented and how they will be performed on this project
- A list of scheduled activities, including major deliverables and their associated milestone dates
- The budget for the project based on the projected costs
- How the project management plan will be executed to accomplish the project objectives, including the required project phases, any reviews, and the documented results from those phases or reviews

Planning is the central activity the project manager continues performing throughout the project. The plan is iteratively revisited at multiple points in the project. Every aspect of the project is impacted by the project management plan or, conversely, impacts the plan. The plan provides input to the executing processes, to the monitoring and controlling processes, and to the closing processes. If a problem occurs, the planning activities can even provide input back to the initiating activities, which can cause a project to be re-scoped and to have a new delivery date authorized. The project manager integrates and iterates the executing processes until the work planned in the project management plan has produced the required deliverables. The project manager uses the project management plan and manages the project resources to perform the work to produce the project deliverables. During execution, the project manager also facilitates the quality assurance activities. The project manager also ensures that approved change requests are implemented by the project team. This effort ensures that the product and project artifacts are modified only per the approved changes. The project manager communicates status information so that the stakeholders will know the project status, which activities have been started or are finished, and which activities are late. Key outputs from executing the project management plan are the deliverables for the next phase and the final deliverables to the customer.

The project manager uses monitoring and controlling processes to observe all aspects of the project. These processes help the project manager proactively know whether or not there are potential problems so corrective action can be started before a crisis results. Monitoring project execution is important, because a majority of the project's resources are expended during this phase. Monitoring includes collecting data, assessing the data, measuring performance, and assessing measurements. This information is used to show trends and is communicated to show performance against the project management plan.

Configuration management is an essential aspect of establishing project control. Therefore, configuration management is required across the entire organization, including procedures that ensure that versions of the project are controlled and that only approved changes are implemented. The project implements aspects of change control necessary to continuously manage changes to project deliverables. Some organizations implement a change control board to formally address change approval issues to ensure the project baseline is maintained by only allowing approved changes into the documentation or product.

Project managers must integrate their monitoring and controlling activities to provide feedback to the executing process. Some of this information feeds back to the planning process. However, if there is a high-impact change to the project scope or overall plan, then there will also be input to the initiating processes.

The closing processes require the project manager to develop any procedures required to formally close a project or a phase.[7] This group of processes covers the transfer of the completed product to the final customer and project information to the appropriate organization within the company. The procedure also covers the closure and transfer of an aborted project and any reasons the project was terminated prior to completion.

The process groups described above represent the standard processes defined by the fifth edition of the *PMBOK® Guide* and required for every project.[8] These processes indicate when and where to integrate the many knowledge areas to produce a useful project management plan. Those processes, when executed, produce the result defined by the project's scope.

DISCUSSION QUESTIONS

❶ During which project management process are risk and stakeholders' ability to influence outcomes the highest at the beginning of the process?

❷ You are a project manager for a major copier company. You are heading up a project to develop a new line of copiers. You are ready to write the scope statement. What should it contain?

❸ You are a project manager working on gathering requirements and establishing estimates for the projects. Which process group are you in? How does knowing this clarify the steps you need to take to perform your assigned tasks?

REFERENCES

[1] Project Management Institute, *A Guide to the Project Management Body of Knowledge (PMBOK® Guide)*, 3rd edition (Newtown Square, PA: PMI, 2004), p. 30.

[2] Project Management Institute, *A Guide to the Project Management Body of Knowledge, (PMBOK® Guide)*, 2000 edition (Newtown Square, PA: PMI, 2000), p. 29.

[3] Project Management Institute, *A Guide to the Project Management Body of Knowledge (PMBOK® Guide)*, 5th edition (Newtown Square, PA: PMI, 2013), p. 49.

[4] *Ibid.*, p. 46.

[5] *Ibid.*, p. 54.

[6] *Ibid.*, p. 55.

[7] *Ibid.*, p. 56.

[8] *Ibid.*, p. 52.

CHAPTER 4

Project Initiation
Managing the Front End

PETER W.G. MORRIS AND ANDREW EDKINS,
UNIVERSITY COLLEGE LONDON

We have been asked to update a chapter on the initiation of projects originally written 20 years ago for the first edition of this handbook. First, what do we mean by *initiation*? With respect to projects, to what does it refer? It might be the beginning of a substage of the project; it could be mobilization on site. More critically, it could refer to the initiation of the whole project.

The 1993 chapter, and its update of 2006, discussed initiation in the second of these two perspectives—as the front end of a project. It focused particularly on major projects. In doing so it used the framework of, and much of the data and evidence from, the research published in 1987 as the book *The Anatomy of Major Projects.*[1] Much of this handbook, however, reflects a different framework: that of *A Guide to the Project Management Body of Knowledge (PMBOK® Guide).* There is nothing necessarily wrong in choosing one framework over another, so long as they are both valid, but the effect of doing so needs to be acknowledged; otherwise, what one person thinks is meant by initiation will be different from what another person thinks. The *PMBOK® Guide* takes initiation as the first of five process stages that can occur several times as the project is developed and implemented.[2] In this chapter, on the other hand, we shall be focusing on initiation more as a part of the work associated with establishing the project's "front end." Doing this provides much more opportunity to influence the project outcome for the better, as we shall see.

THE *PMBOK® GUIDE*

The well-known *Guide* process (initiate → plan → execute → monitor and control → close) is laid out across ten knowledge areas: scope, time, cost, quality, human resources, communications, risk, contract/procurement, integration, and stakeholder management. The recursive character of this progression does not in our view reflect the dominating importance of the project development life cycle—the one feature of

35

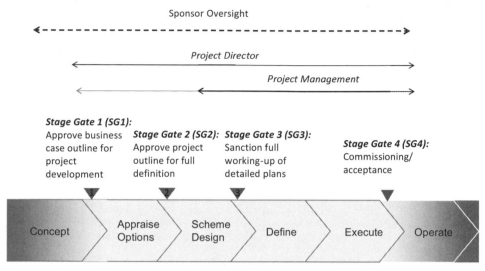

The front end is defined either as the stage SG1 to SG2, or SG1 to SG3; or the stage where the project's requirements are defined.

FIGURE 4-1. **THE PROJECT DEVELOPMENT LIFE CYCLE**

projects that distinguishes them from nonprojects (Figure 4-1). This in turn leads to the following:

- An underappreciation of the characteristics of the project's full life cycle and its stages, and the impact of these on the management of projects.
- Insufficient weight being given to managing the early phase of the project, which we call the front-end stages of the project—that is, the project's initiation stage(s)—where the project's scope, cost, schedule, and other targets and risk profiles are first established.

Project management, as seen in the *PMBOK® Guide,* is essentially focused on the execution phases of projects. The ethos is one of controlling—planning and then monitoring—once the requirements have been defined. But many of the factors that have been shown to be important to the effective management of projects, including many that occur in the front end (governance, strategy, contextualization, technology selection, and even people factors) are either missing from the *Guide* or are substantially underplayed.

MANAGEMENT OF PROJECTS

An alternative model, originally proposed largely by Morris in the late 1980s and early 1990s and refined thereafter, is the management of projects (MoP).[3] This is the framework used to discuss initiation in the previous editions of this handbook. In the MoP framework, the unit of analysis is the project. Projects are defined by their development life cycle. The MoP is as concerned with managing the front end as with downstream execution. ("Front end" is defined as either the period prior to definition of the project's or program's requirements, or the period prior to the execution being sanctioned.) The MoP stresses the need for the project's strategy to flow from, and support, the project sponsor's business drivers. Its ethos is not just controlling against the plan but creating value for the sponsor. It includes proactive stakeholder management. It recognizes the challenges frequently found in technology, and the benefit and challenges of innovation. It includes selecting and managing an appropriate commercial platform. It also acknowledges that people are central to projects and programs. "Projects are built by people, for people, through people."[4]

We now turn the topic of managing initiation.

INITIATION

The *PMBOK® Guide* says initiation is about obtaining authorization to spend and to commit resources. Stakeholders are identified. A project charter is approved. "A key purpose . . . is to align stakeholders' expectation with the project's purpose, giving them visibility about the scope and objectives, and how their participation in the project and its associated phases can ensure that their expectations are achieved."[5] But there is more to it than that!

For many project management personnel, initiation entails contract bidding, followed, when successful, by mobilization for execution. We argue that the richer, more useful issue is that of the project development cycle. Here initiation refers to the project's front end, which, in this second, broader view, begins with the authorization by management of the expenditure of effort, time, and most probably money to develop the potential project's definition, and ends either with acceptance by the sponsor/board of the project definition documentation, or with the acceptance of the project requirements, or with either the project's termination or its shelving. The important point is that work is done (sometimes a substantial amount) on developing the project definition before and in the process of leading up to the submission of the project proposal, that is, the formal request to sanction full implementation of the project.[6] Figure 4-2 shows the addition of this layer of context compared with the traditional concept of initiation. While traditional project management focuses on "on time, in budget, to scope" execution and delivery, the MoP also focuses on the project in its context, particularly on early definition of the conditions for stakcholder success. Within this framework, project, program, and even aspects of portfolio management are encompassed.

GOVERNANCE, SPONSORS, AND STRATEGY

There have been some substantial changes in thinking since the earlier editions of this handbook. For example, we have come to pay more attention now to how the project is influenced by its context, be that the parent body's institutional practices or the characteristics of the project and the environment in which it is to be realized.[7]

One group that potentially has a huge influence on the conduct of the project, yet crucially is external to the project, is the project sponsor. The sponsor is "the holder of the business case"[8]—the person responsible for the project and accountable for the satisfactory realization of the project proposal. The nexus between owner/sponsor and project director/manager is critical in the early initiation stages of the project.

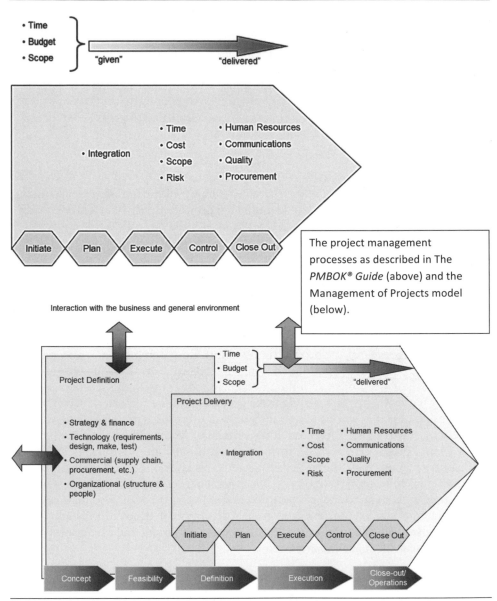

FIGURE 4-2. **MANAGEMENT OF PROJECTS (MOP) COMPARED WITH THE *PMBOK® GUIDE***

The project team should support the project sponsor actively. To shape the project effectively, the team must understand the sponsor's objectives and business strategy and ensure that the project strategy is aligned with them.[9]

Many project professionals view the project execution plan (PEP) as the project strategy document, but this is not its purpose; it addresses only the project implementation strategy, that is, the plan for the work to be performed after formal authorization and capital expenditure on the project have been sanctioned. Some more mature project organizations, however, also have a separate development strategy plan that sets the strategy for the project or program pre-sanction. Others roll the two together into one continuous strategy document.[10]

The project strategy establishes the why, what, how, who, how much, and when of the project development—all that is needed to be done to meet the project objectives and goals: what the project has to achieve and how its success is to be evaluated. As Morris and Jamieson found, the project strategy should cover, at a minimum:

- A definition of overall objectives and goals
- Statements on how these should be achieved (and verified)
- Technical descriptions of the product (requirements, specifications, etc.) and the proposed development strategy
- Project organization (and the policy and strategy for the procurement of resources)
- Key roles of players within and without the project team
- Estimates of the time required, phasing, and implementation strategy
- Budget and related financial strategy issues (cash, insurances, bonds, penalties, etc.)
- Risks and opportunities faced and strategies for managing them
- Configuration and change management policies and plans
- Quality policy and plans
- Safety, health, and environmental policies and plans
- Reporting requirements
- Communications policy and document (information) management
- Expected behaviors

There may be several levels within the enterprise at which the project's objectives, goals, and strategies are stated, and they may be "emergent" as well as be formulated in a "deliberate" manner[11]—emergent in that implementing strategy does not always go as planned, and deliberate in that projects are the mechanisms through which most organizational strategy is realized. Events arise that change the strategic landscape. Sponsors and their project and program teams should be sensitive to these emergent changes and address their implications.

This discussion underscores the active, shaping nature of managing strategy. Mintzberg, for example, stresses the personal side to crafting strategy to fit the organization's context and the conditions unfolding around its realization.[12] "Ploy," "perspective," and "pattern" all require insight and judgment and are as important, Mintzberg contends, as "position" and "plan." This is a view echoed by Artto et al, who concluded, after an exhaustive study, that project strategy "is a direction in a project that contributes to success of the project in its environment."[13] Strategy shapes, and gives momentum to, the project's course: the project and its strategy are dynamic.

Governance determines the principles on which management is to operate. The United Kingdom's Association for Project Management (APM) has elaborated what this means to the discipline of managing projects:

- The board has overall responsibility for governance of project management.
- The roles, responsibilities, and performance criteria for the governance of project management are clearly defined.

- Disciplined governance arrangements, supported by appropriate methods and controls, are applied throughout the project life cycle.
- A coherent and supportive relationship is demonstrated between the overall business strategy and the project portfolio.
- All projects have an approved plan containing authorization points at which the business case is reviewed and approved. Decisions made at authorization points are recorded and communicated.
- Members of delegated authorization bodies have sufficient representation, competence, authority, and resources to enable them to make appropriate decisions.
- The project business case is supported by relevant and realistic information that provides a reliable basis for making authorization decisions.
- The board or its delegated agents decide when independent scrutiny of projects and project management systems is required, and implement such scrutiny accordingly.
- There are clearly defined criteria for reporting project status and for the escalation of risks and issues to the levels required by the organization.
- The organization fosters a culture of improvement and of frank internal disclosure of project information.[14]

The project management-governance relationship is central to achieving good project initiation and to getting effective strategy formulation and good practice applied. The lead responsibility for this is surely not wholly the job of the sponsor, but must lie to a large extent with the project team. As professionals with specialist knowledge in the world of projects, the project manager and his team should have the knowledge and the sense of duty to make this relationship work as effectively as possible. To do this requires a proactive style of management.

TECHNICAL DEFINITION

Historically, many of the cost and schedule overruns experienced by projects were caused by poor management of new technology or of design.[15] Evidence suggests that on average we have done better in this area in recent years,[16] although in some sectors, such as defense and intelligence, gaining a technical edge coupled with urgency (threat) means that unproven technology often still has to be incorporated into the project, with obvious risk to the desired outcome.[17] In any case, the landscape with regard to managing the technical base of the project is now more mature compared with that discussed in earlier editions of this handbook.

The real challenge in the front end remains, however, as it has for years—that of eliciting requirements. Does this happen quasi-automatically or does it have to be actively managed, and if the latter, who manages it—the systems engineer or the project manager? We would argue that of course it must be managed, and since the results of doing so may profoundly affect the fortunes of the project, the manager of the project needs to be involved in this critical activity. To put it another way, anyone responsible for overall project success ought to ensure that the requirements are elicited properly.

How ambitious should the user requirements be? The answer must depend on how they relate to the project or program strategy, on the views about what level and types of risk are deemed acceptable, and on the risk management system employed. Unwarranted, undermanaged technical risk is foolish; technical risk that the project is prepared for might be a different thing. Innovation (sometimes ground-breaking) may be central to what the project or program is trying to achieve.

COMMERCIAL PLATFORM

At some point within the front end, the contracting and procurement strategy need to be determined. It is certainly needed for deployment as part of execution, post-sanction, but there may well have been benefit in involving members of the supply chain earlier. One of the basic decisions that needs to be made is who will be responsible for individual work packages? Should there be a single integrating supplier, or should work packages be allocated to separate organizational units with some form of project management function integrating them?

The degree of active control that the owner/sponsor wishes to exert over the evolving work package affects the way this integration is organized. The integration is essential if the work packages are to come together to produce the value and benefits expected of the project for the sponsor. It is the appreciation of this inter-connectedness that has led to renewed interest in systems thinking and systemic and holistic solutions. This is becoming increasingly important as clients seek out solutions that encompass whole-life performance risk management. From buildings to aircraft jet engines, there is evidence of the risk related to the design, build, operate, and maintain steps being handled in an integrated and aligned way.

Pricing also influences risk. The spectrum varies from fixed price to cost reimbursable. The former transfers financial responsibility largely, though not necessarily wholly, onto the supplier; the latter transfers it more onto the owner/client. Agreeing on a fixed price bid too early in the development cycle (before the design is sufficiently developed and before change can be effectively controlled) increases the risk significantly, and hence the need for contingency allowances. It is naive to expect that risk can be transferred to suppliers or subcontractors regardless of their ability to properly bear that risk. In the event of failure, collapse may ensue and the transferring party will end up suffering even if it seeks redress from the defaulting parties. This commercial positioning strongly links to the subsequent culture of the project, with options ranging from the highly adversarial to positively collaborative.

CONTROL

The essence of project management is control—delivering securely—but the nature of that control is different in the front end than in later execution. Work in the front end often involves the interplay of uncertainty and innovation. As a result, the form of organization is more "organic."[18] In execution, control is about planning, monitoring, and correcting to make sure the project is completed on time, within budget, and to scope. As a result, the organization is more "mechanistic."

The effective management of projects entails effective estimating. The estimating competency deployed in a project directly influences the chances of project management success in that it establishes the data that many will use to decide if the project was completed successfully—at its most obvious, on time, within budget, and to scope.

There may be a tendency for at best enthusiasm and at worst contrived positioning to lead to undue estimating optimism—"optimism bias." Feedback and lessons learned logically ought to be (but too often in practice are not) inputs to the estimator's knowledge base. It is important that the assumptions underlying the makeup of the estimate be documented, and that an audit trail be available so that any downstream changes can be understood and set within the appropriate context.

Risks should be identified and assessed, and effective risk management must be built into the project management strategy to address them. Risks should be distinguished from uncertainties. Risks are simply understood to be possible negative events for which there is sufficient information to ascribe a probability of occurrence. Uncertainties, on the other hand, are the result of a lack of reliable information. Uncertainty generally should decrease as the project definition improves, but risks may not, as the development within the front end could reveal many new downstream risks.

PEOPLE AND ORGANIZATION

If leadership is about vision and establishing goals and values, then leadership is central to the front end. Managers can be leaders; we should not assume that leadership is the preserve of just a few very senior people. There is much leadership activity that is required in addition to creating and communicating a vision of the project outcome.

It has long been known that organizations need to fit their environment and technology, but we are now recognizing that managers may be able to influence context, to some extent at least. For some project managers, the early engagement with stakeholders, increasingly including the media, can make significant differences to the wider understanding of the project. This is especially the case where the project will have impact on the physical or social environments.

Project management professionals may need to influence politicians, legislators, regulators, community representatives, potential partners, financiers, suppliers, and others. This may seem unusual to readers who see the role of project managers as preeminently execution managers, which is not a role of subtlety or diplomacy. But if one takes the professional responsibility of project management to include the shaping of the project in the front-end definition phases, then project managers need to be diplomats!

Indeed, acquiring the knowledge and skill sets—the competencies—required to manage the project, both in initiation and for future execution, is a major task of front-end work. Doing this is not easy since the competency sets required are a function not just of the characteristics of the project—its complexity, urgency, risk, significance, size, and so on—but also of its context. And these characteristics may not be clear at the front-end stage.

CONCLUSION

We have defined initiation in a broader sense as the front end of the project development process. The front end is crucial to the project's character and eventual success (or failure). It is challenging to work in unstructured, aspirational, organic, and dynamic settings. Working in the initiation phase of a project calls for maturity and diplomacy. It is in many ways far from traditional project managers' usual comfort zones. The discussion questions below provide a checklist for exploring new projects in the front end.

DISCUSSION QUESTIONS

❶ What is the reason for the project and where did it come from?

❷ Who set the delivery date, budget, specification, and scope? How and on what basis? What are the measures of success? Can they be improved on?

❸ Who are the sponsors and what will they need to do to create a successful project? What should project management be doing to support them?

❹ What and who is driving the technical base? How can we innovate better?

❺ Have we got the people with the appropriate knowledge, skills, and behaviors?

❻ Is there a plan to build a cohesive team that can carry knowledge of the project forward?

REFERENCES

[1] Peter W.G. Morris and G.H. Hough, *The Anatomy of Major Projects* (Chichester, UK: John Wiley and Sons, 1987).

[2] Project Management Institute, *A Guide to the Project Management Body of Knowledge* (*PMBOK® Guide*), 5th edition (Newtown Square, PA: PMI, 2013).

[3] Peter W.G. Morris, *The Management of Projects* (London: Thomas Telford, 1994); see also Peter W.G. Morris and J.K. Pinto, *The Wiley Guide to Managing Projects* (Hoboken, NJ: John Wiley & Sons, 2004).

[4] Peter W.G. Morris, *Reconstructing Project Management* (Chichester, UK: Wiley-Blackwell, 2013), p. 235.

[5] PMI, 2013: p. 54.

[6] K. Samset and G.H. Volden, "The Proposal," in T. Williams and K. Samset (editors), *Project Governance: Getting Investments Right* (Basingstoke, UK: Palgrave Macmillan, 2012), pp. 46–80.

[7] Peter W.G. Morris and J. Geraldi, "Managing the institutional context for projects," *Project Management Journal* 42, No. 6 (2011): pp. 20–32.

[8] Association for Project Management, *Body of Knowledge*, 6th edition (Princes Risborough, UK: APM, 2013).

[9] K. Artto, J. Kujala, P. Dietrich, and M. Martinsuo, "What is project strategy?" *International Journal of Project Management* 26, No. 1 (2008), pp. 4–12.

[10] A. Edkins and A. Smith, "Designing the Project," in T. Williams and K. Samset (editors) *Project Governance: Getting Investments Right* (Basingstoke, UK: Palgrave Macmillan, 2012), pp. 135–175.

[11] H. Mintzberg and J.B. Quinn, *The Strategy Process: Concepts, Contexts, Cases* (Upper Saddle River, NJ: Prentice Hall, 1996).

[12] H. Mintzberg, "Crafting strategy," *Harvard Business Review*, July–August (1987), pp. 66–75.

[13] K. Artto, J.M. Lehtonen, and J. Saranen, "Managing projects front-end: incorporating a strategic early view to project management with simulation," *International Journal of Project Management* 5 (2001), pp. 255–264.

[14] Association for Project Management, *Directing Change: A Guide to Governance of Project Management* (High Wycombe, UK: APM, 2004), p. 6.

[15] Morris and Hough, 1987; Morris, 1994.

[16] L. Crawford, J. Pollack, and D. England, "Uncovering the trends in project management: journal emphases over the last 10 years," *International Journal of Project Management* 24 (2006), pp. 175–184.

[17] S.R. Meier, "Best project management and systems engineering practices in pre-acquisition practices in the federal intelligence and defense agencies," *Project Management Journal*, 39, No. 1 (2008), pp. 59–71.

[18] T. Burns and G.M. Stalker, *The Management of Innovation* (London: Tavistock, 1961).

CHAPTER 5

Comprehensive Planning for Complex Projects

DAVID L. PELLS, PM WORLD SERVICES

Preparing a project management (PM) plan is a straightforward effort that promotes and ensures comprehensive project planning. The PM plan is a combination of two plans that are often prepared separately: the traditional management plan, which describes operational management systems and approaches, and the project plan, which includes the work breakdown structure (WBS), logic, schedules, and cost estimates. Thus, it is more comprehensive than either management plans or project plans and reflects an awareness that the team members, the system, and the detailed planning are all critical to project success.

ELEMENTS OF A PROJECT MANAGEMENT PLAN

The project management plan should cover seventeen topics:

1. Introduction/overview
2. Mission and objectives
3. Work scope
4. Planning basis
5. Work breakdown structure
6. Organization development plan
7. Resource plan
8. Procurement and logistics plan
9. Logic and schedules
10. Cost estimates, budgets, and financial management
11. Risk analysis and contingency plan
12. Quality and productivity plan
13. Environmental, safety, and health protection plan
14. Security plan
15. Project planning, control, and administration plan

16. Documentation and configuration management plan
17. Appendix

Introduction/Overview

This is an introduction both to the specific project and to the PM plan document itself. Some background information should be included to provide perspective on the information that follows, such as how the project was initiated, who the customer or sponsor is, how the project is funded, and other contextual factors that may be important to those who read the plan. External factors, such as economic trends, constraints, or opportunities; political or governmental conditions; demographics; or internal organizational factors, can be discussed, but since the introduction should be short, allowing the reader to move into the PM plan quickly, additional external or historical information can be included in the appendix.

Mission and Objectives

The purpose or mission of the project is stated in one or two paragraphs, followed by a set of concrete objectives. The mission statement is all-encompassing, establishing why the project exists (and referencing the business case). Mission statements should reference the customer if the project is being performed under contract or for a third party.

Project objectives are outlined as specific goals to be accomplished and to which status can be applied. For instance, objectives for a small construction project might include a good location; a modern energy-efficient economic design; a fully furnished facility; a complete set of project documents; compliance with all laws, codes, and requirements; a standard profit margin; and a completion date.

Planning becomes straightforward when objectives are defined for key areas. Objectives can be established for every aspect of the project, including the following:

- Technical objectives
- Schedule objectives
- Cost objectives
- Organizational/personnel-related objectives
- Quality objectives
- Environmental safety and health objectives
- Contracting/procurement objectives
- Management system objectives

Well-defined objectives enhance the reliability of subsequent planning. Once objectives are stated in concise terms, they allow for the development of the project scope of work and the work breakdown structure. Mission and objectives should always be agreed to by the customer or project sponsor, and must be understood and supported by the project implementation team.

Work Scope

The work scope section of the PM plan demonstrates how well the project is understood. It includes narrative descriptions of all elements of the project's scope of work. It clearly identifies the products or services to be provided to the customer. The statement of work should contain enough information to allow development of the WBS, schedules, and cost estimates, as well as assignment of responsibilities.

This section can address the project phases and include special plans associated with those phases, such as the research and development (R&D) plan, engineering/design plans, construction plan, manufacturing plan, facility start-up plan, and transition plan. It may also describe the systems management activities, including systems engineering and integration, to ensure project life cycle perspective. To simplify preparation, the work scope can be prepared in outline form, which can then be used to develop the WBS. Often the WBS and work scope are prepared in parallel, with the resultant narrative description of the work called a WBS dictionary.

Planning Basis

The planning basis section provides for the documentation of key assumptions, requirements, and other factors considered during preparation of the PM plan. Below are some items covered in this section of the PM plan.

Project Deliverables/End Products: A list of all products, documents, and services to be delivered to the customer over the life of the project is required.

Requirements: Requirements may include technical requirements, facilities requirements, data requirements, management requirements, or special instructions. Technical requirements may include codes, standards, laws, engineering or design specifications, models, or examples of the mandatory or recommended compliance of the project. When there are mandatory requirements, such as laws, these must be identified and listed, or the project staff runs the risk of noncompliance and legal prosecution.

Facilities requirements include an initial assessment of types, amount, and quality of facilities needed for the project, along with related utilities, furniture, and equipment. This provides initial bases for estimating quantities and costs associated with those resources. Overlooking facilities issues during project planning leads to schedule slippages, cost overruns, unhappy project participants, and untold headaches for the project managers. For small projects, facility requirements may not be a big issue; for larger projects, they can be critical.

Functional and operational requirements (F&ORs) spell out what the system, facility, or product being produced is intended to do. Where F&ORs exist, listing or identifying them greatly simplifies and facilitates the design process. Mandatory data requirements, management directives, or special instructions are also identified and documented during the planning process. Requirements are often defined or captured in other documents, which are then referenced in the PM plan.

Constraints: Constraints may include known technical limitations, financial ceilings, or schedule "drop-dead" dates. Technical constraints may be related to state-of-the-art capabilities, interface requirements with other systems, or user-related issues (e.g., software that must run on certain types of personal computers). Financial and schedule constraints can be introduced by the customer, and include the lead time associated with procured hardware or funding/budgetary limits.

Approaches/Strategies: The approach or strategies to be utilized can have a major impact on planning. For instance, if all project work is to be performed within the parent (host) organization with minimal subcontract support, that approach impacts planning of resources and organizational issues. If work is to be "fast tracked" by overlapping design and construction activities, or by performing more work in parallel, then that approach can be described. Communication of strategies to project participants begins with devoting several paragraphs to that topic in this section of the PM plan.

Key Assumptions: Every project is planned under some degree of uncertainty. Therefore, assumptions are required to estimate work scope, schedule durations, resource requirements, and cost estimates. Assumptions are also required when defining the management strategies, systems, and procedures to be utilized.

Major assumptions have a significant impact on planning and estimating. The major reason for documenting key assumptions is to provide the project manager with a basis for revising plans when the assumptions are changed (i.e., when a customer changes his or her mind). Key assumptions should be revisited and up-dated over the life of the project—a major reason why the PM plan should be a living document.

Specifically Excluded Scope: This subject limits the scope of work. It highlights specific issues, such as documentation, training, or follow-on support, which cus-tomers often assume but which cost money and have not been included in the project plan. Clarification of these scoping questions saves headaches later, in some cases even avoiding litigation.

Work Breakdown Structure

The WBS, a mandatory component of the PM plan, is a product-oriented hierarchy of the scope of work embodied in a numbered structure that provides a system for organizing the scope in a logical manner. The WBS is prepared in conjunction with the scope of work, and it should be developed to the level of detail where responsi-bility for work performance is assigned. Responsibility for each element of a WBS is then established.

The most popular presentation of a project WBS is in graphic form, similar to an organization chart. This WBS chart displays project elements and tasks in levels and boxes, representing smaller parts of the project. (For more about the WBS, see Chapter 9, Project Scope Management in Practice.)

Organization Development Plan

This section of the PM plan addresses organization structure, responsibilities, authorities, interfaces, and personnel development, and therefore serves as a frame-work for planning stakeholder management. For every project, how the people involved are organized, assigned responsibilities, and directed needs to be defined and communicated to the participants. In addition, interfaces among participants both inside and outside the project team require planning. Equally important, training and team-building plans need to be established to promote the quality and productivity of the project work. It is crucial to identify all stakeholders, whether in management, functional areas, project teams, vendors, partners, and clients, customers, or end-users. Understanding the influence, authority, and responsibility of these stakeholders forms the basis for planning.

Organizational Structure: Although not all participants may be involved during early project planning, key positions and participating organizations are identifiable fairly early. A preliminary organization structure in graphic form can be prepared and included in the PM plan. Where possible, names, titles, and phone numbers are included to promote understanding and communication. Organization charts are dated but not finalized until resource allocation plans are prepared, based on detailed work planning and cost estimates. Sample organization charts for three common types of project organization structures can be found in Figures 5-1, 5-2, and 5-3. The functional structure shown in Figure 5-1 is a widespread organizational form. It is characterized by a hierarchical, "chain-of-command" power structure and specialization into functional "silos."

Authorities: Much has been written about the "authority versus responsibility" issues in project management, especially in matrix organizations (Figure 5-2). The matrix structure seeks to combine the advantages of the functional and the projectized organization, while avoiding their disadvantages. Project and functional components are administratively independent, but interdependent in the execution of projects. Project managers or other project participants are often responsible for project accomplishment without having authority over the resources being employed. For all projects, it is helpful to recognize these issues and to document procedures for resolving conflicts as necessary. Where multiple companies or organizations are integrated into a project organization, contract relationships are referenced or defined, as appropriate. Procedures for resolving problems related to work direction may also need to be established.

Responsibilities: Specific responsibilities of individual project participants should be defined to promote communication and teamwork and to avoid confusion. For large projects, responsibilities of positions or participating organizations are defined. One of the advantages of the projectized organization is the clarity of responsibility for project deliverables and outcomes (Figure 5-3). The fully projectized structure makes projects independent from the rest of the organization, gives the project manager full authority over resources, and facilitates the development of multidisciplinary technical terms.

Interfaces: On projects involving technical activity, it is common for personnel from the customer's organization to talk directly with technical staff in the project organization. However, when multiple project participants are interfacing with outside entities—customer representatives, the general public, the press, or others—it is easy for conflicting information to be transmitted. These interfaces can generally be identified and controlled via established protocols. Clearly defining the interfaces highlights where communication is needed and which areas may cause potential communication problems.

Personnel Development: This section of the PM plan outlines the types of training and team-building activities planned for the project. Establishing a plan demonstrates that the project leaders are aware of these issues and plan to improve communication, teamwork, and productivity on the project. Additional training may be necessary if the project utilizes new technologies, equipment, systems, or approaches.

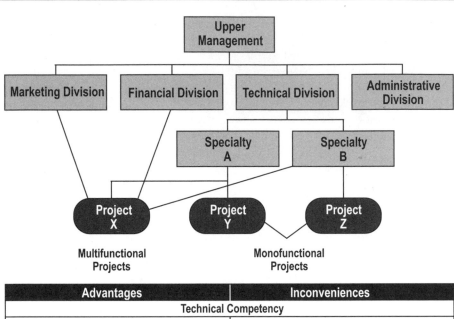

Advantages	Inconveniences
Technical Competency	
• Development and maintenance of technical competency in specialized fields • Synergy among specialists	• Filtered perception; lack of an overall view • Difficulty in integrating several specialties: possible conflicts among specialists • Difficulty in creating motivation for the project • Lack of openness to the environment • Risk of neglecting the aspects not related to the specialty
Objectives	
• Concentration on the objectives of the function • Pursuing long-term development objectives • Easy reconciliation of internal objectives	• Conflict of priorities with other functional activities • Difficulty in making effective compromises between the variables quality-time-cost • Nobody is exclusively responsible for project objectives • Subordination of the managerial to the technical
Permanence and Stability	
• Horizontal relations are clear • Clear definitions of roles and responsibilities • Efficiency improved by standardization • Stability in interpersonal relations • Well-defined career paths • The possibility for organizational learning	• Difficulty in adapting; resistance to change • Difficulties in the internal circulation of information • Slow decision making
Control	
• Easier control of quality and performance • Flexibility and economy in the use of labor	• The time variable is less well controlled • Limited liaisons with the outside • Lack of visibility for the client • Limited development of management capabilities among the personnel

FIGURE 5-1. **CHARACTERISTICS OF THE FUNCTIONAL STRUCTURE**

Adapted from Brain Hobbs and Pierre Menard, "Organizational Choices for Project Management," in *AMA Handbook of Project Management,* 1st edition. AMACOM: 1993, pp. 85 and 88.

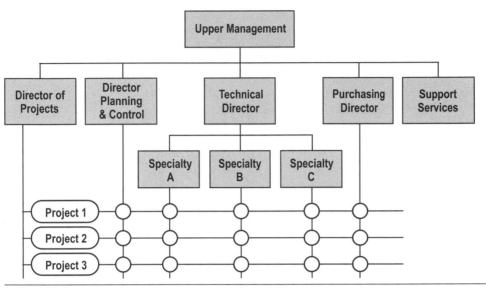

FIGURE 5-2. **THE MATRIX STRUCTURE**

Adapted from Brain Hobbs and Pierre Menard, "Organizational Choices for Project Management," in *AMA Handbook of Project Management,* 1st edition. AMACOM: 1993, p. 91.

ADVANTAGES	INCONVENIENCES
Clear identification of overall project responsibility	Duplication of effort and resources
Good systems integration	Limited development and accumulation of know-how
More direct contact among different disciplines	Employment instability
Clear communications channels with client and other outside stakeholders	
Clear priorities	
Effective trade-offs among cost, schedule, and quality	May tend to sacrifice technical quality for the more visible variables of schedule and cost
Client-oriented	
Results-oriented	

FIGURE 5-3. **CHARACTERISTICS OF THE FULLY PROJECTIZED STRUCTURE**

Adapted from Brain Hobbs and Pierre Menard, "Organizational Choices for Project Management," in *AMA Handbook of Project Management,* 1st edition. AMACOM: 1993, p. 90.

Resource Plan

The resources needed to accomplish the project—personnel, supplies, materials, facilities, utilities, and information/expertise—are identified here. Resource availability also needs to be determined, including expertise that is not available within the organization, which can be supplied via hiring, contract, or partnership. Material resources may be available only on the other side of the world, requiring additional planning, time, and expense to secure.

The primary resource planning issues are identification and qualification of the resources required; availability of those resources; quantification, or amount, of the resources required; and timing, or "allocation," of the resources. Identification and availability of resources are addressed in this section of the PM plan. Quantities and timing of those resources are established during the cost-estimating process and finalized after schedules have been determined. Pricing of resources is how cost estimates are established and becomes the basis for project budgets. Resource allocation is also normally included in the cost estimate section of the PM plan, in the form of a time-phased cost estimate.

Procurement and Logistics Plan

Logistics issues related to major equipment, supplies, or materials need to be planned in advance to ensure manufacturing, transportation, and storage by cost-efficient, safe, and timely means. These issues have become even more critical in the global economy where supply chains are international.

Subcontracting Plans: Subcontracting activity has a direct effect on project costs, schedules, and success, so it normally receives attention early in the planning process. A primary contracting organization may have overall project management and planning responsibilities, but one or more other subcontractors will perform portions of the project, so if subcontracting arrangements are not planned early, project work can be delayed.

This section of the PM plan includes identification of subcontracting laws, regulations, and requirements to be complied with; identification and description of the major subcontracts anticipated for the project; timing of those subcontracts; potential problems or issues associated with the contracts; and approaches and expertise to be employed during the contracting process.

Procurement Plans: The procurement of equipment, materials, and supplies requires planning to reduce the risk of impacting project schedules and to ensure efficient and cost-effective acquisition. On large projects or projects involving R&D or manufacturing of new systems, key equipment or parts may themselves need to be developed and specially manufactured. In cases involving long lead-time items, procurement planning occurs long before the items are needed on the project, in order to initiate the design and procurement processes for those items.

Logistics Plans: The timing, transportation, delivery, storage, and usage of project materials, supplies, parts, or equipment must be planned, coordinated, and managed for the project to be successful. Unavailability or damage during shipment, storage, or handling causes major problems at the job site. Large organizations may have well-established systems and procedures, or organizations responsible for logistics; those organizations and procedures should be identified in the PM plan.

This section of the PM plan includes plans related to the physical aspects of procurement: when items will be delivered by vendors; transportation and handling during shipment; warehousing, storage, kiting, and handling at the job site, including inspection, testing, and acceptance procedures; and distribution to project participants as needed for completion of project tasks. Systems and expertise needed to track, manage, and report status on procured items are identified, along with the schedule and approach for establishing those systems and functions. Responsibilities and procedures are identified and defined.

Logic and Schedules

All project work must be scheduled. Schedules include milestone lists, summary schedules, and detailed schedules. This section of the PM plan includes those schedules and the logic and network plans necessary to develop them.

Networks and Logic: Network planning, not to be confused with the computer networking application of the term, is the practice of identifying activity relationships so that they can be factored into the schedule. In their simplest form, network plans are simple flow diagrams displaying the order in which activities are to be performed, which activities cannot be started or completed before other activities are started or completed, and what activities must be completed before the overall project is complete. The PM plan, however, should describe the logic applied and establish networks as the basis for the schedules.

Summary Schedules: The summary schedule corresponds to the upper levels of the WBS and identifies key milestones. Additional levels of schedules are developed as required and are compatible with one another, the management summary schedule, and the WBS.

Milestone schedules are simple lists of top-level events (i.e., the completion of the key tasks or activities) with planned dates. These same lists are used for reporting schedule progress by adding a column for completion date information. Milestone schedules, networks, bar charts, and activity listings can be included in the PM plan. Detailed schedules may be provided in the appendix.

Cost Estimates, Budgets, and Financial Management

Every PM plan includes a cost estimate, a budget, or both. The cost estimate is normally in table format and includes a summary of costs for each major task or element of the project. Financial management includes systems and procedures for establishing budgets, reporting financial information, controlling costs, and managing cash flow.

Cost Estimates: The most straightforward method of estimating costs is to assign a cost to each element of the WBS or each activity in the schedule or network. Costs are estimated by identifying the resources needed for each activity, in what quantities, and at what price. The pricing of the resources depends on the timing, so normally a cost estimate is not finalized until project activities have been scheduled.

Budgets: Budgets are cost estimates that have been approved by management and formally established for cost control. Actual costs are compared to budgets as the project is completed, to identify variances and potential problems, and to provide information on what the costs will eventually be (at completion). The budgeting process often includes extensive reviews and revisions of cost estimates to arrive at the final budget.

Financial Management: The requirements, systems, procedures, and responsibilities for project financial planning, management, and control are addressed in this section. Financial control includes cash flow management as well as conventional cost control (standard cost accounting, cost performance reporting, and cost productivity assessment).

Cash flow management involves traditional income and expenditure reporting and analysis. On most projects, funding and funds management are critical, representing the timing at which resources can be scheduled and work accomplished. Cash flow planning and reporting procedures and responsibilities are established in the PM plan. Where corporate or enterprise financial information systems will be used for financial management, those systems and procedures should be identified.

Risk and Opportunity Plan

Project activities associated with new research, technical developments, or other tasks that have never been done before must be assessed for potential risk events. Opportunities should also be considered. Risks and opportunities may be associated with the external environment—economic or political conditions, weather, geography, public opinion, or labor-related factors. Stakeholders are an important source of increased uncertainty, so they should be carefully assessed. This section of the PM plan provides an opportunity to consider project risks, opportunities, and contingency plans. Topics suggested for this section are risk and opportunity identification, analysis, and mitigation, as well as contingency plans and reserves.

Risk and Opportunity Identification: The stakeholder management plan and the WBS can be used to identify risks and opportunities associated with specific elements of the project. Each WBS element should be assessed. Risk is higher when new or unproven technologies are required, but these may also yield opportunities. Greater uncertainty is expected when all aspects of a task or project element are not yet planned in detail. Finally, risks, both positive and negative, are generally higher during the early stages of a project.

Risk Analysis: Risk analysis includes a detailed discussion of the risk or opportunity, including both internal and external factors. An impact table is prepared with factors assigned based on technology status, planning status, and design/project status. Finally, the potential cost and schedule impact is assessed. The impact table includes a worst-case (or best-case) cost estimate for each of the project elements included.

Risk Mitigation Plans: Once risks have been identified and assessed, strategies are needed to mitigate them: technology development, modeling, demonstrations, peer reviews, replanning, changes in project logic, reorganization of project participants, contractual changes, and so on. The idea is to adapt a proactive, planning-based approach to risk assessment and to minimize project risks through specific actions. A similar approach can be taken to maximize benefits from potential opportunities.

Contingency Plans and Reserves: Changes to technical requirements or schedules require a reevaluation of contingency reserves. Risk analysis can be performed in conjunction with cost estimating when estimates of contingency reserves are calculated. Cost estimates may be inaccurate for various reasons, such as engineering errors or oversights, schedule changes, cost or rate changes, external factors, construction or implementation problems, or estimating errors. The amount of reserves depends on the funds available, overall riskiness of the project, the management approach, and other factors.

Quality and Productivity Plan

Project management planning itself is a productivity improvement process. This section of the PM plan is where total quality management planning, quality management systems planning, quality assurance/quality control planning, technical performance measurement, and productivity improvement are discussed.

Quality Management Systems Planning: Although quality may be defined in terms of technical performance of end products, value to the customer is also a key measure. Technical quality and customer satisfaction are increased by establishing systems and procedures for ensuring high performance. That means well-defined project requirements or specifications, systems for comparing progress to specifications, and effective feedback mechanisms. This part of the PM plan contains or refers to quality management systems or procedures to be utilized on the project.

Quality Assurance/Quality Control: Quality assurance (QA) is a process of establishing performance standards, measuring and evaluating performance to those standards, reporting performance, and taking action when performance deviates from standards. Quality control (QC) includes those aspects of QA related to monitoring, inspecting, testing, or gathering performance information, as well as actions needed to ensure that standards are met. QA and QC both require discipline and systematic approaches to defining and measuring technical performance. For large projects, formal systems and procedures are necessary, and these can be described or listed in this section of the PM plan.

Technical Performance Measurement: Technical performance measurement is the evaluation of performance against standards, criteria, or requirements established for a project. A procedure is established to evaluate each element of the WBS for technical performance status and for taking corrective action. Evaluation can be by a design committee, chief engineer, QA organization, or group of technical experts.

Productivity Improvement: Productivity improvement, or reductions in the time and costs to accomplish project objectives, calls for planning and monitoring. Plans, schedules, and cost estimates can be evaluated for process and performance improvements. Cost-saving methodologies, such as value engineering, can be applied to designs and technical plans. Cost estimates can be subjected to "sensitivity analysis," which identifies areas of the project where the most probable savings can occur. Company procedures, systems, or processes can be reassessed for improvements regarding paperwork, staffing, or time. New products, methodologies, or technologies might increase productivity. Employees also may be encouraged to identify productivity improvements, cost savings, or time-saving processes. This section of the PM plan identifies which of those strategies will be used.

Environmental, Safety, and Health (ES&H) Protection Plan

This section identifies the environmental compliance laws, regulations, and requirements that must be satisfied on the project, and how they will be complied with. It describes steps to be taken by the project team to protect the environment, the public, and project participants.

Safety and Health Protection Plan: In the project safety plan, each element of the WBS is assessed for safety issues, including potential hazards, opportunities for accidents, and government regulatory requirements. The systems, procedures, and steps to be employed to ensure a safe workplace are described. Organizational procedures can be referenced as needed, but must be identified for each project.

ES&H Management/Information Systems: The systems and procedures to be used for managing and reporting information related to environmental, safety, and health (ES&H) activities on the project are identified and described. Responsibilities and interfaces with outside organizations, often key to compliance with ES&H regulations, are also documented. A matrix chart is used for projects where multiple regulations, systems, and organizations are involved.

Emergency Preparedness Plan: Emergency preparedness addresses such issues as fires, storms, floods, power outages, sabotage, terrorism, and the loss of key personnel. Preliminary planning identifies the people who will take charge in each type of emergency. Public services such as fire stations, ambulances, hospitals, police, and evacuation routes can be identified.

Security Plan

Every project involves security issues that need to be dealt with.

Physical Security: Plans for providing physical security (gates and fences, guards, electronic access systems or surveillance devices, badges, or contracted security services)—including requirements, responsibilities, tasks and activities, timetables, and procedures—are described or referenced in the PM plan.

Property Protection: Property protection against loss, theft, or damage is needed whenever a project involves the acquisition or use of materials or equipment, including hardware, software, vehicles, tools, and other assets. Property protection may also require detailed property management information systems, procurement tracking systems, training, and experienced personnel.

Information Security: For some projects, information security may be the most important security issue facing the project manager. As a project proceeds, key information is generated, including technical information (e.g., design specifications, vendor data, engineering data), cost and schedule information, contract-related information, correspondence, plans, and progress information. Loss of such information could be devastating to a project or, indeed, to the entire organization. This section of the PM plan contains the plans for insuring against loss or damage of key project information. An information security manager for the project may be needed to control access to information; to coordinate passwords, codes, and file names; to ensure backup systems and databases; and to ensure proper usage of procedures and protocols.

Project Planning, Control, and Administration Plan

The PM plan is the major plan for the project, yet it may be just one of many plans prepared, especially if the project is large, complex, and involves many different organizations. If more than one management plan is prepared for the project, they are identified and described here. On large projects a hierarchy of management plans is common, with each participating organization preparing a management plan for its portion of the project. A table should be developed identifying all the plans to be prepared and their relationship to one other.

Detailed Work Package Plans: Work packages are the lowest level of project work assigned to individuals. Project activity at the lowest levels of the WBS is planned in work packages, which describe in detail the work scope, schedules, and costs associated with the work. Work package plans are summarized and consolidated to support the information contained in the PM plan. The work package planning process to be used, the assignment of responsibilities, the formats to be used, and the planning procedure can be described in this section of the PM plan.

Project Control: Project control involves procedures, processes, and methods used to determine project status, assess performance, report progress, and implement changes. In addition, on large projects there may also be the need for a formal work authorization process, which documents task agreements prior to the start of work.

Work Authorization: Work authorizations are documents that describe work to be performed, have cost estimates (or budgets) and scheduled performance dates identified, and are negotiated and agreed to by a "requesting" organization and a "performing" organization. Work authorizations are common in large companies doing business with the United States government. The work authorization forms and procedures to be used on a project are described in this section of the PM plan.

Cost and Schedule Performance Measurement: The methods and procedures to be used to assess schedule status and how much work has been accomplished over the life of the project are described in this section of the PM plan. For instance, the process and responsibilities for assessing the completion status of each activity in the project schedule are outlined here, as well as any methods to be used for measuring quantities of work completed. Systems and procedures for cost collection, accounting, and reporting are outlined in this section as well. The procedures, systems, and responsibilities for administering and controlling changes to a project's work scope, schedule, and budgets (or cost estimates) are also described in this section of the PM plan. Formal change control systems are required to ensure that plans, baselines, design, and documentation are not revised without appropriate reviews and approvals.

Project Administration: This section of the PM plan describes the reports, meetings, and record-keeping processes. Formats, procedures, and responsibilities are outlined and defined for major reports. A list of reports to be prepared, with distribution and responsibilities identified, can be included in this section or in the appendix. Major management meetings to be conducted are identified, including review meetings with customers or management, status meetings, change control meetings, and special meetings to transmit key information. The system, procedures, and responsibilities for administrative records management on the project may be addressed in the document control section of the PM plan, or included here.

This section may also contain an overview of procedures and responsibilities associated with administering key contracts. Performance measurement and reporting by contractors is described, contract requirements identified, and subcontract management activities identified, including site visits, meetings, and technical reviews.

Documentation and Configuration Management Plan

This section of the PM plan identifies the documents to be prepared on a project and establishes the administrative approach, systems, and procedures to be used to manage that documentation.

Documents include plans, administrative documents and records, technical data, engineering and construction documents, procedures and systems-related documents, reports, and correspondence.

For each major element of the WBS, a list of documents for each participating functional organization is developed. That list includes documents related to management and administration; technical specifications and requirements; R&D, design, and engineering; manufacturing; construction; start-up; operation or production; and contracts, compliance documents, and documents prepared by entities external to the project.

Responsibilities are identified, from initial preparation of the documents through changes, reviews, and approvals, and a distribution list. In addition, document storage and control is addressed. A document responsibility matrix is a simple method for communicating the plan for document control. The responsibility matrix lists the documents, and then identifies responsibilities for document preparation, revisions, approvals, distribution, and storage.

Document storage is a huge issue for large projects, no less now than when it entailed buildings full of file cabinets. Document storage issues include document identification, version control, data security, and so on.

A document numbering system can be based on the WBS, the project organizational structure, the date, or any other logical order. The numbering system is then used to organize and store project documents and to find the documents over the life of the project.

Security against fire, damage, or theft is also addressed and described in the PM plan, as are backup files for automated data storage systems. Access requirements and plans are also described, including a list of those who will need access, what kind of access (e.g., online, complete, extracts, etc.), the frequency of access, and how that access will be monitored.

Configuration Management. Configuration management can be defined as the process of identifying and documenting the functional and physical characteristics of products, facilities, or systems; of controlling changes to those items and associated documents; and of reporting status of the items or changes to those who need to know. [Note: The term *configuration management* has had other precise connotations on information technology (IT) projects. When communicating between project management and IT personnel, be careful in your use of terms to avoid misunderstanding.] The objective is to keep project technical documentation consistent with the project systems, products, hardware, or facilities involved. Where a comprehensive document control system has been implemented, configuration management can be an expansion of the processes for the technical documents and systems.

On projects for government agencies, configuration management requirements may include compliance with detailed laws, regulations, or contract clauses. This is especially true in such industries as nuclear power, military/weapons systems and procurement, space-related contracting, transportation, and other areas potentially involving environmental, health, or safety issues concerning the general public.

The technical systems, components, facilities, and products that comprise the project and associated technical documents are identified in the PM plan. Technical baseline documents consist of the documents associated with research, design, engineering, fabrication, installation, construction, start up, and operation of each of the technical systems/components of the technical baseline.

Configuration control involves the procedures for administering and controlling changes to the technical baseline and associated documents. Configuration control parallels the more general document control process but places more emphasis on controlling changes to the design and technical configuration of the systems themselves. The configuration control section identifies how changes to the technical baseline are made and fixes the associated responsibilities and procedures for keeping technical documents current. Procedures and responsibilities are identified in a matrix format along with necessary narrative explanations.

A method is established for communicating configuration changes and status information to those who need that information. In general, a procedure with distribution lists for specific documents or system will suffice, provided that responsibilities are assigned for distribution of technical information and documentation.

Appendix

The appendix provides a place to include or identify supporting information, allowing the body of the PM plan to be kept concise. In some cases, where a section of the PM plan is prepared as a separate document (for instance, when required by law), it can be included in the appendix and referenced in the PM plan.

DISCUSSION QUESTIONS

❶ The project management plan combines two plans sometimes prepared separately. What are the advantages of joining those plans?

❷ What are the drawbacks of joining the two types of plans?

❸ What differences are there in the logic of the project management plan as compared to that discussed in the Project Management Institute's *Guide to the Project Management Body of Knowledge* (*PMBOK® Guide*)? Why do you think the plan outline differs?

CHAPTER 6

Monitoring and Control of Projects

WILLIAM P. ATHAYDE, JD, PMP, PM COLLEGE

Project control promotes the achievement of project goals by analyzing project information, monitoring the variation from the plan, and responding to variations as appropriate. Project managers should commence their monitoring and control by ascertaining the quality of the existing project management plan and its myriad parts.

Today, a large percentage of projects approach planning and controlling in ways very different from traditional project management. Many organizations are trying to apply project management tools and techniques that were developed for projects with clear specifications and detailed scope statements to situations where neither exists. Worse yet, some senior managers don't seem to understand why those tools fail to provide the quality of insights and predictability in non-construction projects that can be achieved in construction projects, and they blame project managers and their teams when the results don't match management's expectations.

One of the most common examples of this problem is seen in projects that largely entail the creative activities of thinking, problem solving, and design. Innovation and new product development projects do not always start with a complete set of specifications or a clear understanding of the final result. They often have goals of finding a major breakthrough in a material, design, or process with strategic goals of being faster to market, manufacturing more efficiently, and utilizing less expensive raw materials. Estimating with any precision how long it will take to develop an idea or approach is often extremely difficult if not impossible, and the activities leading to completion of certain deliverables or milestones are not easily measured.

How projects are monitored and controlled depends on the type of project, the project management approach being employed, and the level of experience with both the project methodology and the project subject matter. The ability to monitor and control (i.e., "manage") the project depends on the foundation laid at the beginning of the project, and on all the subsequent actions, decisions, and outcomes that are built on that foundation. The documentation of those activities and outcomes is our window on what has occurred. Critical to understanding the foundation is the transparency of the time and cost estimating and the risk management systems in use. If project managers have a clear understanding of the basis-of-estimate and well-informed insights into the risk profile for each activity, they can assess the value of that information, develop appropriate options, and use the information to make reasonable decisions or to provide good information and advice to the other decision makers.

Part of the problem with the project foundation is that project managers are often tasked to "execute" projects that have not had any formal project initiation or planning activities. Those projects arrive "ready" for the execution phase based on what someone promised to a customer or to senior management without a project team ever being asked for any inputs. The schedule and budgets for such projects are often arbitrary numbers, and the scope is often vague or incomplete. In such situations, project managers joining those projects frequently have to go back and fill in the project foundation by conducting activities that should have happened in the initiation and planning phases. So before they can effectively monitor and control the project, they have to start over or rework part of the project, resulting in at least an unplanned delay and frequently resulting in discovery of increased project scope and the need for increased budget and schedule duration.

To do proper monitoring and controlling requires good project management, which, in turn, requires the participation of proper resources from the start. Shortcuts in the initiation and planning phases can condemn even the best project manager's chances of success. This issue is raised to emphasize how pervasive it is and how strongly it undermines the project manager's ability to control the project.

Monitoring and controlling activities in a project should be an "umbrella-like" function covering the entire project from start to finish; it should start as soon as the project does. We immediately are comparing the actual situation with the desired future state. For instance, if you inherit a project and discover that nothing has been done, although the "late start" date was a month ago, you immediately see a warning signal. Even when taking on a project at its inception, we often see a disconnect between the desired completion date and what our experience tells us about how long it usually takes to complete a similar project. From the outset, project managers need to assess how realistic the schedule and budget are based on all available information and on their experience.

Clearly, some underlying principles guide the thought and action processes when we approach the tasks of monitoring and control a project. First, that the system employed must include an ongoing process that will apply throughout the project (standardization). Second, the system should be the minimum necessary to achieve the desired results (efficiency). Third, we have to focus on measuring the right things in the right way (focus, efficiency, intensity, and process). Fourth, the system must be understood by all staff members who have to interface with it (simplicity and logic). Fifth, in order to convert the raw outputs from any system of measurement to meaningful information, one must apply experience and judgment. As a way to further conceptualize and unify the entire project control process, many authors have cited Shewhart's Plan–Do–Check–Act model (made popular by Deming) as a way to illustrate the overall methodology that must apply, thereby placing emphasis on the iterative nature of the entire project control process (Figure 6-1). With these ideas in mind, let's consider more of the details of the realities of project monitoring and control.

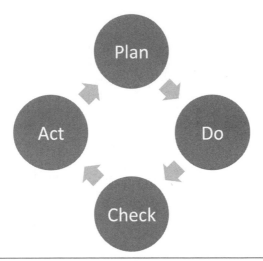

FIGURE 6-1. **THE SHEWHART CYCLE**

Adapted from multiple sources; for examples, see http://www.citelighter.com/business/management/knowledgecards/pdca-plan-do-check-adjust.

Critical to any tracking effort is this basic question: How accurate and realistic are your estimates? Clearly, if estimates were "pulled from the air" instead of based on data and experience, they are suspect, and relying on them may set us up for failure. Another problem is when "padding" (also called "contingency") has been included in the estimates and not disclosed.

The accuracy and realism of the estimates are functions of the quality of the data, the tools used to collect and analyze the data, the team's experience with those tools, and whether the team had adequate time to properly conduct the process. Good estimates are like good cooking—they require good ingredients (data), the right tools, the ability to use those tools, and the time to do the work correctly. Often, one or more of those elements are missing from an estimate's life history!

PROJECT TYPE: A STARTING POINT

Because the construction industry typically has established engineering principles, centuries of experience, clear standards, physical control of the raw materials and final product, known effort, and predictable costs, its projects tend to be easier to monitor and control than projects in many other industries. In addition, construction projects normally have clear requirements, detailed plans, and standard processes for estimating and conducting the work, so their high success rate is understandable. Much of that industry's world revolves around "go–no go" standards. The projects typically have a complete and detailed work breakdown structure, accurate estimates, and reporting systems that minimize the ability to "spin" or shade the data. In contrast, intellectual activity is much harder to estimate. Asking a scientist how long it will take to develop a new medical device, employing yet-to-be-developed technology, is not likely to elicit a precise answer.

New product development or innovation projects seem to be almost polar opposites of construction projects in aspects such as having clear requirements and having well-tested, detailed processes for completing the specific product. Many software development projects, while designing the desired functionality within the boundaries of an existing IT system, are plagued by an extraordinary number of scope change requests, which can require reworking and sometimes redesigning the underlying system. When not well controlled, such changes have inadvertently caused projects to grow to three or four times their original size, requiring a total redesign of the product and resulting in massive budget and schedule overruns.

Some of these scope change problems can be attributed to changes in technology or in the customer environment, but a large percentage are the result of key stakeholders not participating fully in the requirements gathering processes, and the failure of the project manager or the organization to have firm cut-off dates for changes to the project. Thus, project managers must exercise available control in this area, and even if they lack the ability to exercise control over late changes being forced upon the project, they must communicate to upper management the impacts on schedule, budget, quality, and customer satisfaction of each proposed change. Upper management must then decide whether or not to agree to those changes. Should management approve the changes, but not approve the extra time or resources to accomplish the added work, then management is responsible for the overrun(s).

While the manner in which the estimates were "nurtured" may be a critical consideration, we need to revisit the project's "nature." For projects that have new discoveries or innovations as their goal, it is very difficult to estimate or even to develop detailed work breakdown structures during the initiation phase. Many of the project leaders and subject matter experts are hesitant to get locked into a schedule for things they cannot predict. These projects often require a "rolling-wave" approach to planning and estimating because unexpected failures and new discoveries create an ever-changing landscape for the project. Thus, such projects must be planned a phase at a time based on what has been learned in the project.

Interestingly, one major manufacturer of medical devices looked at this issue several years ago, and after analyzing many past projects concluded that there was a pattern in its projects that could assist in estimating even those projects that had traditionally only been estimated one phase at a time. While their scientists and engineers were unwilling (and maybe unable) to commit to estimates for completion of an entire research and development (R&D) or new product development project, they were able to accurately estimate the duration of the first phase of the project—the feasibility study. And, surprisingly, the manufacturer discovered that there was a very high correlation between the length of the feasibility study phase and the overall length of the project. The manufacturer found that multiplying the time estimate for the feasibility study by a factor of four usually arrived at an accurate estimate of the overall duration of the project (within 10 to 15 percent)! Not a perfect solution, but a reasonably effective one for estimating even those new product development projects.

THE MONITORING AND CONTROL PROCESS: AN OVERVIEW

The ability to control a project starts with stakeholder identification—the ability to understand who the stakeholders are and specifically what they need (in both project outcomes and communications during the project). The "voice of the customer" provides the requirements that are communicated in the scope statement and achieved through the work detailed in work breakdown structure (WBS). The WBS must be decomposed to the appropriate level to create accurate estimates and for the appropriate level of monitoring. The work packages become the activities and are sequenced to start the schedule development. Available resources will then be applied to determine the schedule. The schedule, along with the scope and cost, will create the "baseline" against which the project's performance will be compared.

Sadly, many organizations do not adequately decompose the project work, which reduces the ability to make an accurate estimate and to track and control the work. Some new product and innovation organizations create product breakdown structures (PBS) and assign the work using that approach. Their process usually delegates the creation of the WBS and the estimate to the functional areas responsible for the PBS deliverable(s), without the project manager having any details or responsibility to track progress except at the highest levels. Such approaches distance the project manager from understanding the basis of estimates, and usually prevent close tracking of any elements so delegated.

Prior to, or simultaneous with, the WBS development, the project control system needs to be established. The system sets up procedures and criteria for collecting data, establishing and tracking milestones, and determining what metrics will be applied. As the project progresses, cost and performance data will be collected and evaluated in comparison to the baseline. Corrective action may or not be taken depending on the extent of deviation from the plan.

One of the big questions in many projects is how progress will be tracked. Part of the work to be scheduled is the creation of the system/structure for monitoring and control. That system needs to be easily understood by all of the people involved in it. Questions that need to be answered include the following:

- Is the information to be gathered worth the effort?
- Does it tell us what we need to know?
- What metrics will be used, and are they clear and concise?
- Can we get the information on a timely basis so that we can effectively react to it?
- When and how and by whom is the data collected?
- What is the quality of the data (or observations) to be gathered? Is it objective or subjective?

Factors Affecting Monitoring and Controlling

Throughout the process of monitoring and control, the project manager should keep in mind and be on the lookout for the top five causes of troubled projects:

1. Lack of sponsor or customer involvement
2. Failure to follow a project management methodology
3. Poorly defined or incomplete requirements
4. Not establishing or not following a change management process
5. Not establishing or not following a risk management process[1]

Resource Availability and Ability

Are we using dedicated resources? Multitasking, which is promoted by many organizations, undermines focus and productivity, and is a root cause of many project delays. We all know that by focusing on one activity we can get it done more efficiently. There are also much more extreme examples of the dangers of multitasking, such as the higher automobile accident rate for drivers who are texting while driving. By addressing multitasking, many organizations not only reduce delay in projects, but also, even more importantly, have been able to cut project cycle times by 20 to 50 percent by using critical chain project management. The critical chain approach, which uses the theory of constraints, promotes worker focus by eliminating multitasking and clearly prioritizing work. It also uses 50 percent probability estimates, and controls schedule contingency (buffer) at the project level. While the use of critical chain requires a corporate cultural change, when correctly implemented the results are remarkable. Its approach is applicable across a much wider range of projects and industries than is commonly understood.[2]

In addition to multitasking, there are other important resource considerations when monitoring and controlling projects:

- Are we relying on "superstars" to do some of the work on the project? Our most capable resources are frequently stretched thin and are often pulled away to assist troubled projects. The more skilled the resource, the more likely that it will be lost to higher priority work.
- Planning task durations based on high skill level is risky. Best practice dictates that estimates should be based on average skill levels, unless you know that you have new or lesser skilled workers who made take longer and may also need coaching or mentoring from more experienced or outsourced resources. Those situations would require longer than average durations and longer estimates of how much time the coaches or mentors would be involved.

Availability and Accuracy of Information

Many readers will be surprised to learn that another issue to be decided is whether or not timesheets will be kept. Many organizations, especially those doing R&D, product development, and innovation projects, don't track resource hours expended. They recognize that creative activity is not easy to measure in minutes and hours. Much of that work requires collaborative activity that is not tied to a clock. Other organizations direct employees not to report more than the nominal workday on their time records! But if timesheets are inputs to your control process, then it is important that they be kept accurately. Recording time once a week for resources that are not 100 percent dedicated to a single project is an invitation for problems. Can you recall in adequate detail all of the projects and issues that you dealt with last week? Most of us cannot! So, for resources that are not 100 percent dedicated to a single project, daily time recording is necessary, and unpaid overtime hours need to be part of that record! If all hours are not recorded, you really don't know what the project is costing in time and budget, and you lack accurate information to use in future estimating.

A major organizational culture issue that must be considered is whether your project information system promotes inaccurate reporting or delayed information sharing. If reporting a negative or less-than-expected status results in negative consequences, the reporting parties will usually find a way to report in a most favorable light or may withhold some of the bad news in hopes of turning the situation around before the next reporting interval. Sometimes the sources of the inaccurate reporting are intermediate managers who block, change, or reinterpret some of the reports in order to serve their own goals. A historical example of this problem is the overruling of subordinates regarding O-ring risks before the Space Shuttle Challenger disaster.[3,4]

Analysis of many situations where management was "surprised" by the project dashboard suddenly going to "red" has verified that many project stakeholders engage in inaccurate status reporting. The best defense against this is a culture of open and honest communication where the priorities focus on determining how we can remedy the current problem and achieve our responsibilities to the project, and are not focused on affixing blame. Control requires accurate information on the status of work, and it is surprising how often the very systems developed to obtain and report that information encourages either reporting misinformation or withholding information.

Keeping all of the above issues and considerations in mind, we now discuss a tool for monitoring the progress of the project. Whether you are using a Gantt chart or a system such as Earned Value Management (EVM; see Chapter 33), most systems develop their outputs by using a "percentage complete" analysis and compare that information to what the project plan predicted at a given point in time. Points must be established throughout the project where the value of the work is a given in our project plan. While we noted that tracking the percentage of work completed in a construction project seems relatively easy, it is much harder in other fields. The most common approach is to establish milestones throughout the project and set values for those milestones.

The metrics report the project history, but that's only half of the story! We could predict the future of a project based only on the progress to a specific point in time, but that is not a complete view of the path ahead. In addition to metrics of past activities, we also need the benefit of team members' observations and intuition. Their experience and insights regarding the meaning of the data as well as those regarding upcoming activities need to be considered by the project manager. Team members usually have the best insight into the risk picture that awaits the project. It is crucial for the monitoring and controlling processes to take that information into account. How do you promote this information flow while not making it overwhelming for those reporting and receiving the information? One approach is to institute a standard reporting format that is simple to use, that communicates essential information, and that serves as a basis for determining the lessons learned. By requiring reports of completions, successes, and problems that briefly answer the following five questions within 24 hours of an event, the project manager not only promotes information flow, but also has the feedback for the lessons learned process:

1. What happened?
2. What did our plan say to do about it?

3. What did we really do about it?
4. How did it work?
5. What are the recommendations for the next time the problem occurs?

These answers can be archived, and, where appropriate, applied to the lessons learned process, which should be part of each phase of the project. These lessons can be learned even if the team members have moved on to other projects.

Communication of project status is a critical element of any successful project control process. The receipt and reporting of timely and accurate information are essential. Any reporting system must meet these criteria. The project team should consider the value of graphical representations in enhancing communications. Gantt charts are easily understood and quickly communicate a lot of information upon completion of the work. Communicating the project's status based on work progress and actual costs as compared to the project plan is a particular benefit of the charts used in EVM.

Monitoring and control starts at the beginning of the project and extends until it is done. We have discussed some of the issues to consider, but only the project team can fully assess the many factors in each project situation.

DISCUSSION QUESTIONS

❶ What questions need to be answered regarding how progress will be tracked in a project?

❷ What actions should a project manager take to determine the validity of cost and schedule estimates when taking over an ongoing project?

❸ What five questions should form the basis of your lessons learned documentation approach?

❹ How do monitoring and control activities differ between new product development projects and construction projects?

REFERENCES

[1] James S. Pennypacker, *Troubled Projects: Project Failure or Project Recovery* (Glen Mills, PA: Center for Business Practices, 2006).

[2] Numerous examples can be found at websites for ProChain Solutions (http://www.prochain.com/clients/results.html), and the Goldratt Institute (http://www.goldratt.com/resultsoverview.shtml) or in the third edition of this handbook, Chapter 29.

[3] Malcolm McConnell, *Challenger: A Major Malfunction, A True Story of Politics, Greed, and the Wrong Stuff* (Garden City, New York: Doubleday, 1987).

[4] Joseph Trento, *Prescription for Disaster* (New York: Crown, 1987).

CHAPTER 7

Closing Processes
The End, and a Foundation for New Beginnings

LYNN H. CRAWFORD, HUMAN SYSTEMS
INTERNATIONAL LTD., INSTITUTE FOR THE
STUDY OF COHERENCE AND EMERGENCE (ISCE),
AND BOND UNIVERSITY

Closing processes are possibly the most important and least well executed of the activities associated with projects. They are important because they are associated with effective handover from one project phase to another, and with termination or finalization, which is one of the key distinguishing characteristics of projects. Project closeout is also the point at which the project is handed over to clients and end users and judgments are made, either formally or informally, objectively or subjectively, about its success. Furthermore, research indicates that the more involved project managers are in management of project finalization, the more likely they are to be perceived as a top performer by clients and employers.[1] Yet despite the importance of closing processes, they are often neglected. Consequences of this neglect are clearly expressed in the well-known project management proverb: "Projects progress quickly until they become 90 percent complete; then they remain at 90 percent complete forever!"[2] Major reasons for this phenomenon are that the initiating and planning processes of projects are more interesting and exciting, and the executing, monitoring, and controlling processes are more demanding and action-oriented, than are the closing processes. Energy and enthusiasm are often exhausted by the time the project team begins to focus on closing a project or project phase. The team members are often keen to move onto the next phase of the project, and toward the end of a project they are thinking about where they will move next. Either by natural attrition or by design, closing processes are poorly resourced or given low priority. The most effective way to reverse this trend is to give closing processes the priority they warrant, and the best way to improve their execution is to plan for the closing processes at the start of the project.

CLOSING PROCESSES IN PROJECT MANAGEMENT STANDARDS

Closing processes bring together all aspects of a project, so it is not surprising that they are generally treated as integrative activities in project management standards. In the Project Management Institute's *Guide to the Project Management Body of Knowledge (PMBOK® Guide)*, closing processes are identified with project integration and procurement knowledge areas.[3] The International Organization for Standardization's *Guidance on Project Management* (ISO 21500:2012) also treats closing processes as integrative, primarily concerned with formal project closure and capture and use of lessons learned.[4] The Association for Project Management's *Body of Knowledge (APMBOK)* considers closing processes as part of the project or program life cycle, which also provides a structure for governance of project work.[5] There is no specific section devoted to project closure. In the International Project Management Association's *IPMA Competence Baseline* (ICB),[6] a discussion of various competence elements refers to such closing processes as the capturing of lessons learned, contract completion, and archiving of documents. There is also a specific competence element, titled "Close-Out," that addresses formal closure, evaluation, and documentation, checking that objectives and customer expectations have been met for each phase of the project. In the Global Alliance for Project Performance Standards (GAPPS) *Project Manager Standard,*[7] closing processes are integrated throughout, with references to securing stakeholder agreement to criteria for success and completion when developing the plan for the project; in the context of product acceptance, project transitions and an entire unit are devoted to project evaluation and improvement.

Closing processes are generally considered to apply both to phases throughout the project and to final project closeout. This is made most explicit in the *PMBOK® Guide* and ISO 21500:2012, in which closing processes are expected to be carried out in each phase of a project alongside initiating, planning, executing, monitoring, and controlling processes. In this sense, closing involves all the processes associated with finalization and handover, from one project phase to the next, or at the closeout of the entire project. Final closure of the project may be as planned or contracted, or it may be the result of early termination or cancellation.

Each standard places slightly different emphasis on particular aspects of phase or project closure, treating it at different levels of detail.

Closing Processes in Practice

Planning for Closure

Closing processes are most often associated with the end of the phase or project, but to be effective they have to be considered and planned for at the start of the project. The second of Covey's *Seven Habits of Highly Effective People* is to "begin with the end in mind,"[8] and this is the first principle of effective project closure. Planning for closure at the start of the project helps to counteract the challenges of reduced enthusiasm and resources toward the end.

When determining the project objectives, criteria should be developed for judging whether, at the end of the project, the objectives have been met. When developing the scope baseline, consideration should be given to how the delivery of scope will be assessed so that at closure of a phase or the entire project, there is confidence that all planned scope has been delivered. Associated with this should be clear criteria for completion.

How will the success or failure of the project be assessed? If measurable criteria for success are determined at the start of the project and agreed to by the client, the customer, and other relevant stakeholders, then the project team has a clear understanding of what it needs to achieve, and, as the saying goes, what gets measured is what gets done.

Engagement of the client, customer, end users, and other relevant stakeholders in determining and agreeing on the objectives, the scope to be delivered, and the criteria for completion and success is a vital part of the process. If they have not been involved in the process and have not signed off on it, then they may have changed their minds or forgotten what was agreed to by the time it comes to close the project. Getting stakeholders to sign off on anything is always a challenge but doing this in the early stages provides a sound basis for closure. It makes sense to keep checking back with stakeholders throughout the project to ensure that their expectations are managed and to minimize surprises.

Each of the subprocesses discussed below should be considered at start up and planned into each phase and project.

Product Acceptance

Gaining acceptance of the product or output of the phase or project from the customer or sponsor is a key closing process. It is made much easier if key stakeholders have agreed to measurable criteria for acceptance in the early stages of the phase or project. Delivery may be progressive, throughout the project, and good records of acceptance of each deliverable are necessary at closing to avoid potential disputes.

Good quality management practices suggest that customers and end users should be involved in determining, at the start of the project and at closure, what is to be delivered and at what quality. The quality of the product is a factor in gaining acceptance. For some product types, acceptance testing is required. Such testing processes need to be planned at the start so that the time required is factored in, the resources are available for testing, and the acceptance criteria are agreed upon.

Opportunities for customer feedback should be considered and planned into the overall project process. It should not be an afterthought. Seeking feedback progressively throughout the project is good practice because it enables corrective action to be taken while it still has the potential to favorably affect the customer experience.

At closing, the product of the project or phase, in addition to being accepted "by the sponsor on behalf of the users,"[9] needs to be handed over and transitioned into operation.

Commissioning and Handover

Commissioning is a term often associated only with large engineering projects where it entails all the processes involved in checking, inspecting, testing, and generally ensuring that everything has been delivered in accordance with specification and is functioning as intended. In settings such as hospitals, data centers, and power plants, commissioning may be treated as a separate project conducted by a specialized team. Here the project team will hand over to the commissioning team.

Commissioning does not apply only to large and complex engineering projects. All projects need to be commissioned, although this means different things for different projects. Even if all that is being handed over at the end of a project is a report, thought should be given to how the report will be used, and work should be planned into the project to address this issue. Where the deliverable is a report, ensuring that it is both usable and used when handed over may involve planning a presentation to senior management and other specific stakeholder engagements. Where new information systems or organizational change are the intended result of a project, good change management processes entail the preparation of users to embed change and ensure that new systems can and will be used. Many projects, on completion, are handed over to the business to support it in its operations and to deliver specific benefits. Research suggests that facilitating the integration of the product of the project into the business is a critical success factor for all projects.[10] Commissioning the project to ensure it is operational, whatever that may mean for the particular project type, is therefore an important aspect of successful transfer and handover.

Commissioning and handover also require attention to warranty conditions that may need to be updated or agreed to, and there may be follow-on work involved in transitioning to the next phase or to production or operations. Such work might include setting up maintenance agreements, product support, training, or providing "as built" documentation. Processes should have been established early in the project to deal with any outstanding issues.

Much of the work involved in commissioning and handover may be specified in contracts, and wise clients will be sure that everything they want is specified in a contract.

Contractual Closure

Contractual closure involves finalizing all agreements with contractors and other suppliers, completing all financial transactions, and closing the project accounts. To do this it is necessary to ensure that all contracted work is completed. Often it is only the work that is specified in the contract that is completed at the end of a project because of the legal and financial ramifications associated with failing to meet the terms of the contract. As contracts are set up at the start of a project or phase, this underlines the importance of planning upfront with closure in mind. Closing processes associated with contract finalization are normally spelled out in the contract. All contracts entered into, therefore, need to be carefully read to ensure that all obligations are met.

If for any reason a project is terminated prior to completion, the contractual implications need to be carefully considered, as this may results in claims and disputes.

Administrative Closure

Contractual closure is generally given priority over administrative closure because there are usually penalties associated with contractual nonperformance. Administrative closure, which involves finalizing and archiving all project records, is often seen as something that is less urgent and can be done in due course. It is particularly affected by the dispersal of the project team to new projects.

Good quality management systems and ISO certification can be useful in ensuring that project records are signed off and systematically archived. It is important to understand any legal and other compliance issues relating to storage of documents, such as confidentiality and security.

There are many benefits of paying attention to administrative closure, although they are not necessarily obvious at the time it needs to be done. First, it is important to be sure that all records are in order, in case any disputes arise after the project is closed. This can happen, for instance, as a result of faults discovered some time after the product of the project has gone into operation or where unexpected safety issues arise. Where there is any form of post-project investigation, well-organized and archived documentation will be of benefit to all concerned. There are often legal requirements that documentation be maintained and available. A repeat project may be initiated requiring the reuse of project documentation. Similarly, a client may request follow-on work. Good documentation makes this much easier to do.

Particularly important is the maintenance of historical data that can be used to provide comparative performance information on projects within an organization. This is fundamental to an organization's ability to benchmark and improve the performance of projects over time.

Review and Learning

Capturing of performance data and the conduct of various types of end-of-phase and end-of-project review contribute to project and corporate knowledge management and organizational learning. The GAPPS Project Manager Standard has a unit that deals with evaluation and improvement of performance. This unit has the following three elements:

6.1 Develop a plan for project evaluation.
6.2 Evaluate the project in accordance with the plan.
6.3 Capture and apply learning.[11]

Sadly, the practices in this unit are used significantly less than those in the other five units in the standard, supporting the widespread experience that there is considerable room for improvement in review and learning within and between projects. Closing processes, including administrative closure (capture of project data), and reviews, provide an opportunity to support learning.

Various types of review and audit are recommended and may at times be required. The *APMBOK* defines a review as a "critical evaluation of a deliverable, business case or P3 [project, program, and portfolio] management process"[12] and identifies three specific types of review:

- Gate review: conducted at the end of a phase to confirm ongoing viability
- Post-project review: conducted after handover of project deliverables but before formal closure of the project or program to document lessons learned for future use

- Benefit review: to measure the achievement of benefits against the business case.[13]

In 2001, the United Kingdom government initiated a formal gateway review process that has been widely adopted with only minor modifications by other governments and by public and private sector organizations worldwide.[14] The primary intention of these gateway reviews is to evaluate the readiness of a project or program to progress to the next phase. The original U.K. government process identified six key stages or gates in the life of the project, as shown in Table 7-1.[15]

Many private sector organizations now have similar gateway review processes that form part of their project and corporate governance processes. The gates are designed to suit the specific needs of each organization but primarily occur at the end of each project life cycle phase.

While primarily intended to assess readiness to progress to the next phase, these gateway reviews can also be used to stimulate the progressive review and gathering of lessons learned. Gathering and disseminating learning from projects in flight is far more effective than waiting to do so at the completion of the project. It provides opportunities for immediate implementation of learning for the benefit of the cur-

Gate 0	Strategic assessment	Investigates the direction and planned outcomes of the project or program and can be repeated at key decision points throughout the life of the project
Gate 1	Business justification	Follows preparation of the business case and focuses on the project's business justification prior to the key decision on approval for development proposal
Gate 2	Delivery strategy	Reviews the business case and delivery strategy before any formal approaches are made to prospective suppliers and delivery partners
Gate 3	Investment decision	Focuses on the full business case to confirm that the project is still required, affordable, and achievable
Gate 4	Readiness for service	Focuses on the readiness of the organization to transition from project delivery to operations
Gate 5	Operations review and benefits evaluation	Confirms that the desired benefits of the project are being achieved, and business changes are operating smoothly

Sources: The State of Queensland (Queensland Treasury and Trade), *Gateway Review Guidebook for Project Owners and Review Teams* (Queensland Government, Department of Instrastructure and Planning, 2013);

State of Queensland Office of Government Commerce (OGC), Successful delivery toolkit. [On-line]. Accessed September 13, 2013 at http://www.best-management-practice.com/?DI=571293;

State of Queensland Department of Finance and Deregulation, *Gateway Review Process.* [On-line]. http://www.treasury.qld.gov.au/office/services/financial/gateway-review-process.shtml

State of Victoria Department of Treasury and Finance, *What Is the Gateway Review Process?* [On-line]. Accessed September 13, 2013 at http://www.dtf.vic.gov.au/Investment-Planning-and-Evaluation/Understanding-investment-planning-and-review/What-is-the-Gateway-review-process

TABLE 7-1. GATEWAY REVIEWS IN THE UNITED KINGDOM GOVERNMENT'S GATEWAY PROCESS AND DERIVATIVES USED BY OTHER GOVERNMENT ORGANIZATIONS

- Evaluating effectiveness of project management
- Comparing what was actually delivered against the original requirements
- Identifying lessons learned
- Assessing performance
- Capturing stakeholder's opinion of how the project was delivered
- Disseminating findings

Source: *APMBOK*,[5] p. 197.

TABLE 7-2. **OBJECTIVES OF A POST-PROJECT REVIEW**

rent project and, if effectively disseminated, to other concurrent projects. It is a far more timely and immediate approach especially where projects take place over several years. Many of the objectives of post-project reviews can be beneficially incorporated into reviews conducted periodically throughout the project, thereby enhancing the opportunities to capture learning and learn from experience (Table 7-2).

It is important to note that the *APMBOK* recommends that post-project reviews be conducted after the handover of project deliverables but before formal project closure. Adopting this approach and ensuring that reviews are planned at the start of the project will increase the likelihood that this aspect of closing is done well. Further assurance is provided where such review processes form part of the required governance of the project or projects within an organization.

Releasing Resources

Different types and numbers of resources may be required at various phases of the project so human resources and other assets should be reviewed and refreshed, released or redeployed at each phase and finally at the end of the project. Project managers must also obtain release from their project management role at the end of the project, handing over responsibility to the project owner. The organization established to carry out the project must be disbanded or in some cases may be partially transitioned to take on a new project.

In addition to review of the project, the performance of all team members should be assessed and feedback given, and, as with reviews, it is most beneficial if feedback is provided progressively throughout the project, offering opportunities for improvement. This can also be an important factor in maintaining motivation of team members, ensuring that they have opportunities for individual development. Processes for assessment of performance of individuals may be done entirely within the context of the project or it may be done in consultation with the organizational human resources function in which case specific processes may be required. However it is done, it is good practice to ensure that the processes for performance assessment are clearly outlined and equitable with associated appeal processes. As with all other closing processes, assessment of individual team member performance should be planned at the start, ideally in consultation with those that will be affected.

Performance of the project team can also be assessed. NASA has found that assessment of team performance at various points throughout a project is one of the key contributors to improved project performance.[16]

One of the most important but often overlooked aspects of project closure is attending to the emotional aspects affecting all stakeholders. Effective emotional closure can positively impact stakeholder perceptions of project success, paving the way for repeat business and providing motivation and encouragement for good teams and team members to work together again in the future. If you handle the emotional aspects of project closure well, you will build a stock of great team members who will want to work with you in future.

People often become passionate about their projects. They may have to work long hours, so their projects become an important part of their lives. Project closure represents a big change and even perhaps a sense of letdown that may be mitigated by the excitement of moving on to a new project but may be exacerbated by some anxiety about what comes next. It is therefore important to plan some form of celebration, not only at completion but also at important milestones throughout the project, such as when key resources change. Some industries have their own celebratory traditions. Examples are the ceremonies held for naming and launching of ships and the "topping out" of a completed building by placing a tree on the structure to symbolize growth and to bring luck. Everyone involved in the project is invited to the ceremonies, which may be treated as a media event for public relations purposes. Recognition of the performance and contribution of individuals, teams, and even suppliers and contractors may form part of a completion event.

One organization has a small team of people who are responsible for capturing on video footage projects in progress and upon completion, including interviews with stakeholders. At the end of the project the video team produces a CD/DVD of the "successful" project, copies of which are given to the client, project team members, and other stakeholders. This is a very clever way of taking control of the lasting image and memories the project manager would like all stakeholders to have of their performance on the project.

Not every project is big enough or of long enough duration to warrant such an investment or a major celebratory event, but budget provision should be made in the planning of the project to enable the project team, at a minimum, to get together to celebrate a successful completion. This recognition may be fairly low key but should be genuine and should not be overlooked.

CONCLUSION

Clients and employers value seamless and effective handover and closure of their projects, so doing it well contributes positively to the project manager's career and reputation.

The impression that is left with the project owner and users at the end of the project, and the way they talk about it, significantly affect the reputation of the project, the performing organization, and the project manager and teams involved.

REFERENCES

[1] Lynn Crawford, "Senior managment perceptions of project management competence," _International Journal of Project Management_ 23 (2005), pp. 7–16.

[2] I first encountered this "proverb" in the 1990s when it was in a list of project management proverbs on the NASA APPEL website. When writing this chapter I could no longer find it on the NASA site. An internet search provided numerous hits but no original source.

[3] Project Management Institute, *A Guide to the Project Management Body of Knowledge* (*PMBOK® Guide*), 5th edition (Newtown Square, PA: PMI, 2013).

[4] International Organization for Standardization, *ISO 21500:2012 Guidance on Project Management* (Geneva, Switzerland: ISO, 2012).

[5] Association for Project Management, *APM Body of Knowledge,* 6th edition (Princes Risborough: Association for Project Management, 2012).

[6] International Project Management Association, *ICB: IPMA Competence Baseline Version 3.0.* (Nijkerk, The Netherlands: International Project Management Association, 2006).

[7] GAPPS, *A Framework for Performance Based Competency Standards for Global Level 1 and 2 Project Managers.* (Johannesburg: Global Alliance for Project Performance Standards, 2006, with technical revision, 2007), p. 29.

[8] Steven Covey, *The Seven Habits of Highly Effective People* (New York: Fireside–Simon and Schuster, 1990).

[9] Association for Project Management, 2012, p. 28.

[10] Lynn Crawford, A. Aitken, and A. Hassner-Nahmias, *Project Management and Organizational Change* (Newtown Square, PA: Project Management Institute, 2013).

[11] GAPPS, 2007, p. 29.

[12] Association for Project Management, 2012, p. 196.

[13] Association for Project Management, 2012, p. 26.

[14] The State of Queensland (Queensland Treasury and Trade), *Gateway Review Guidebook for Project Owners and Review Teams* (Queensland, Australia: Queensland Government, Department of Instrastructure and Planning, 2013).

[15] Office of Government Commerce (OGC) (2008). Successful delivery toolkit [online] originally at http://www.ogc.gov.uk/resource_toolkit.asp, and then moved to http://webarchive.nationalarchives.gov .uk/20100503135839/http://www.ogc.gov.uk/what_is_ogc_gateway_review.asp. Also, Department of Finance and Deregulation (2013). Gateway review process [online] at http://www.finance.gov.au/gateway/ review-process.html; and Department of Treasury and Finance (2013). What is the gateway review process? [online] at http://www.dtf.vic.gov.au/Investment-Planning-and-Evaluation/Understanding -investment-planning-and-review/What-is-the-Gateway-review-process.

[16] C. J. Pellerin, *How NASA Builds Teams: Mission Critical Soft Skills for Scientists, Engineers, and Project Teams* (Hoboken, NJ: John Wiley & Sons, 2009).

CHAPTER 8

Project Management Integration in Practice

GEREE STREUN, PMP, CSQE, PMI-ACP, CSSGB, CSM, GV SOFTWARE SOLUTIONS, INC.

Integration was added to the project management body of knowledge as a ninth knowledge area in the 2000 edition of the Project Management Institute's *Guide to the Project Management Body of Knowledge* (*PMBOK® Guide*). This addition validated the experiences many project managers have had throughout their careers. It underscored the important project management role of coordinating and creating linkages among the various aspects of knowledge, activities, and processes with the integration of all project processes to effectively manage a project to meet its objective.

THE EVOLUTION OF THE INTEGRATION KNOWLEDGE AREA

The 2000 edition of the *PMBOK® Guide* defined the project management processes necessary to integrate the project management activities needed on a project. The three processes described in that document were (1) developing a plan, (2) executing the project activities in the plan, and (3) coordinating changes across the project.[1] In describing integration as a knowledge area, the Project Management Institute (PMI) provided a foundation to ensure that project management activities are properly integrated and coordinated. However, the description of integration fell short of what a project manager actually needs to do to effectively manage a project. For example, no mention was made of initiating project management processes, monitoring tasks in the published plan, and integrating the closing activities across all project phases.

In 2004, the third edition of the *PMBOK® Guide* was expanded to provide more detail on the planning, executing, and controlling processes, and to emphasize two areas that had not been adequately addressed in any previous editions: project initiation and project closure.[2] Because a project has a very small chance of succeeding when either initiating or closing is done incorrectly, additional information about these two areas was provided in subsequent updates.[3] The project manager now has specific processes to provide guidance for the initial activities needed to develop both the project charter and a preliminary project scope statement. The project manager can also find guidance for performing the integrative processes needed to produce a comprehensive project management plan, rather than nine individual documents that were implied in the 2000 edition of the *PMBOK® Guide*. A clear emphasis is also placed on what must be done during project execution. While monitoring and controlling now have a desired emphasis for projects of any size, the integration activities needed to effectively close a project are also defined.

Project managers have learned through trial and error that project management is really an integrated series of processes and activities. These processes are iteratively applied by skilled project managers to effectively lead a project to its completion. While planning and managing a project, the project manager must make decisions about needed resources, as well as anticipate problems and plan their resolutions. Trade-offs made between conflicting objectives and the needed alternatives are also detailed within those groups. If the project processes have been properly integrated, the project manager will be attuned to all aspects of the project effort and can effectively communicate that information to the stakeholders.

The need for integration among the project processes is evident wherever interfaces must be established for the processes to interact,[4] such as the situation where a project is assigned a specific delivery date without any regard for the overall product scope. The project manager must identify any risks resulting from this approach and communicate that information to the stakeholders. The stakeholders and the project manager use that information to negotiate a decision on whether the schedule should be extended or to reduce the overall product scope to meet the original schedule. The project manager usually performs many activities concurrently during initiation, including the following:

- Assigning members of the project team to perform activities to analyze the scope and to understand the requirements, as well as any assumptions, constraints, and potential risks.
- Working with appropriate stakeholders to establish an initial schedule.
- Setting initial customer expectations. If done effectively, subsequent efforts are facilitated when a consensus among the stakeholders must be negotiated on a difficult request. A fine-grained application of this is communicating risk mitigations, including any risks that cannot be avoided or resolved.

Companies typically perform a feasibility study after becoming aware of a perceived opportunity. The company uses various methods to make a decision to start a project and to establish a value returned against the projected costs. The company may consider a project for various reasons:

- The high cost of fuel requires a more efficient and clean energy source. Analysis would determine if a real market demand exists before the project is considered.
- A company does a business process analysis on its billing and receiving system and finds several areas that are costing the company a great deal of money. Therefore, a new project is established to improve that system.

- A company wants to enter the worldwide market and finds it is required to adhere to a new, more restrictive standard to even enter the market in Europe or Asia.
- A start-up wants to build a new, ultra-small, implantable medical device to aid patient mobility. A project can be started to research this idea and the impact of adding a high-tech manufacturing facility needed to produce microcomponents.

The analysis process must also support picking alternative ways of executing the project to meet defined constraints, such as doing the project offshore or purchasing a turn-key system. The result is a project charter document that answers at a minimum the following questions:

- What is the relationship between what is being created and the stimuli that cause the need?
- What are the projected budget limits that will ensure a profit?
- Who is the project manager, and what is the authority level given for this project?
- What is the initial milestone schedule and will it impact the cost?
- What are the first-cut assumptions and constraints identified for the project?[5]

During the upfront effort, the project manager begins gathering data for a preliminary scope document that defines the project and its expected result. This document should address the project's characteristics and boundaries and its resulting products. Document content will vary depending on the application area and project complexity; for instance, is the project to erect a terminal extension at an international airport, or is it building an online billing system for a pet supply company? The differences in product complexity and the required coordination efforts are very clear to see in these two examples. Skilled project managers can identify the nuances in the scope of their projects and respond appropriately to meet the project objectives; the product requirements; any acceptance criteria; assumptions, constraints, and risks; and any contract specifics, such as a nonnegotiable delivery date.

The key tool a project manager uses is the project management plan. However, the manager must first perform all activities required to define, prepare, and integrate the activities in the project management plan. An integrated and cohesive plan defines all information about how the project will be executed, controlled, and closed. The required contents for a project management plan are fairly standard. It should essentially define what, who, the process, and when (with cost):

- *The what:* the project objective and deliverables
- *The who:* the personnel and resources required on the project
- *The process:* the project life cycle that will be incorporated into the plan. A diagram can be included to indicate needed process interactions.
- *The when/cost:* the scheduled due date for each deliverable, including all major milestones
- The project's *production and delivery locations*
- The *communication requirements*: what is needed to build the stakeholders' support and keep them involved[6]

The project application area directly affects project execution more than any other project process. Deliverables are produced through the project team's effort as directed by the project manager. In addition, during execution, the team is acquired and trained if necessary. Goods and tools may also be obtained so that they can be used during project execution. The project manager leads the team, as the approved changes to the product are received and implemented. While managing all of this, the project manager also supervises any technical and organizational interfaces required between the project and the rest of the organization. Documents produced during the project effort are also updated.

Monitoring the project requires the project manager to collect, measure, and analyze information, and to assess measurements to determine trends. Those trends are analyzed, and project performance may be modified as a result. The project manager compares status data to the project management plan to determine whether the project will meet its planned objectives on the specified dates. The project manager also keeps detailed information on any identified risks to ensure the mitigation plans are implemented quickly enough to minimize negative impact to the project.

Change control is a fundamental integration concept, as it touches all project processes. Changes to the project documents and other deliverables are controlled by continually assessing any factors that cause changes and by controlling attempts at any ad hoc changes. The project manager controls project changes by identifying and approving only those changes that are necessary. The project manager does that by ensuring that any changes are completely documented and approved prior to allowing a baseline update.

An automated configuration management system supporting version control is an effective and efficient way to manage changes to project artifacts. An automated system typically supports a high level of security and controls baseline changes. A change control board is typically implemented in many companies to support and enforce integrated change control at the highest level. A corporate configuration policy defines the change control board's responsibilities and the needed interaction with all projects.

How does the project manager know when to start closing a project? A skilled project manager knows that every project process must be properly performed, since each process is needed to successfully lead to project completion. The project manager uses the closing processes to establish the integrated procedures to close and transfer a project's deliverables. Administrative and contractual activities must be defined and completed to officially close out a project or a project phase. When the project is closed, documentation and project data must be transferred to the corporate knowledge base for future reference. The finished product must also be formally accepted by the customer as one of the last closing activities.

These closing procedures also establish the activities required if the project has to be canceled before it successfully achieves its objectives. If a project is canceled, there may be penalties or legal ramifications for the company, so project records and data are transferred to the appropriate authorities in the company to resolve those issues.

American Management Association • www.amanet.org

CONCLUSION

In practice, there is no clear definition of how to integrate project processes, activities, and knowledge. The project manager's role is made both challenging and rewarding by the skill gained while managing the project to facilitate and monitor efforts for success. In fact, a case can be made that integration is the capstone skill for excellent project managers—the skill that, more than any other, reflects the project management role.

It is also clear that the various tasks that the project manager performs are not individual one-time events. Rather, they are overlapping, integrated activities that occur at varying levels throughout the project. The project manager must be proficient in the project management knowledge areas; experienced managers can skillfully integrate those knowledge areas to effectively deliver the project's desired result.

DISCUSSION QUESTIONS

❶ Effective project integration requires emphasis on what issues?

❷ When is historical information useful during the project?

❸ What does integration mean in project management?

REFERENCES

[1] Project Management Institute, *A Guide to the Project Management Body of Knowledge* (*PMBOK® Guide*), 2nd edition (Newtown Square, PA: PMI, 2000), p. 41.

[2] Project Management Institute, *A Guide to the Project Management Body of Knowledge* (*PMBOK® Guide*), 3rd edition (Newtown Square, PA: PMI, 2004), p. 77.

[3] Project Management Institute, *A Guide to the Project Management Body of Knowledge,* 4th edition (Newtown Square, PA: PMI, 2008), p. 33; and Project Management Institute, *A Guide to the Project Management Body of Knowledge,* 5th edition, (Newtown Square, PA: PMI, 2013), p. 62.

[4] Institute of Electrical and Electronics Engineers, Inc., *IEEE Standard for Developing Software Life Cycle Processes,* Std. 1074-1991 (New York: ANSI/IEEE, 1992).

[5] PMI, 2013, p. 69.

[6] Institute of Electrical and Electronics Engineers, Inc., IEEE Standard for Developing Software Project Management Plans, Std. 1058.1-1987 (New York: ANSI/IEEE, 1988 [reaff. 1993]).

CHAPTER 9

Project Scope Management in Practice

RUTH H. ELSWICK, PMP, PM COLLEGE

For many project managers, as well as other stakeholders, managing scope is truly a mystery. We could even give it a name: "The Case of the Creeping Scope." Project managers must get into the "crime prevention" mode rather than the solution mode to effectively define and manage scope!

The first step in the scope creep prevention process is to understand exactly what is meant by scope. The Project Management Institute (PMI) breaks scope down into product scope and project scope. Product scope is defined as the "features and functions that characterize a product, service, or result." Project scope, on the other hand, includes all the work that needs to be done to deliver the product, service, or result as defined in the product scope. Figure 9-1 shows how most projects are structured. At the top we have the project level. On the left are the project management activities that focus on the processes needed to carry out the project. On the right is the product or technical side, which contains the deliverables to produce the product, service, or result for which the project was undertaken. Product scope is only the right side of the equation, while project scope is the top level and includes both sides of the equation.

Most project managers focus on the product side and, during estimating, often forget the time and money that it takes to produce and monitor the project management activities. Resources, as well, focus on the product side and forget that they need to participate in the project management activities such as developing the team charter, work breakdown structure (WBS), schedule, and so on. The bottom line is that there is a real need to understand the two types of scope.

Also key to effectively managing scope is to know exactly what is required. PMI describes this process as follows:

- Plan the approach you will take.
- Collect all the requirements.
- Define what you want the scope to be.
- Create the WBS.
- Verify that all the deliverables have been accepted.
- Monitor and control the scope.[1]

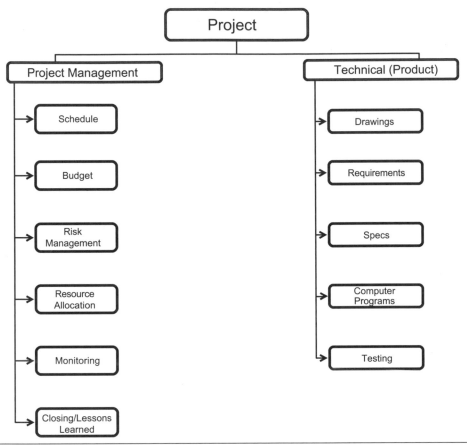

FIGURE 9-1. **PRODUCT SCOPE VS. PROJECT SCOPE**

PLANNING THE APPROACH

Planning the approach to the scope is a new concept for many project managers. The plan that is put into place gives all stakeholders an idea of how the scope, both product and project, will be managed throughout the project. Notice that it is managed throughout the project—not just in planning. Often the approach to scope planning, if it is done at all, is to put a WBS together, wipe the sweat off the forehead, and say, "Wow, I'm glad that's done!" Scope planning, and replanning, admittedly has heavy emphasis during the planning process, but it is also essential during the monitoring and controlling process, where a comparison can be made between what was thought to be a good approach and how the plan actually measures up. The project manager should tap into the experiences and knowledge of the team members as well as other stakeholders to gather lessons learned and suggestions on how to best approach the scope. This input from the various sources not only results in a better, more manageable plan, but also (1) generates commitment from the stakeholders to the plan, (2) gives more credibility and reality to the plan, and (3) ensures that everything has been covered.

COLLECTING *ALL* THE REQUIREMENTS

Once the scope management and requirements plan is in place, the real fun begins, as it is time to collect all of the requirements— "all," not just some. The key to successfully gathering requirements is to use different methods of information gathering. Focus groups and facilitated workshops work well in an environment where everyone can attend the meetings. In a virtual environment, the Delphi technique or questionnaires and surveys may better fit the bill. Interviews can be used in either environment. The environment should dictate your techniques. The challenge is that there may be conflicts in what the requirements should be as well as what the priorities are. The good news is that the project manager realizes early on that there is a difference in priority perceptions. Once those differences are recognized, they can be addressed early in the project rather than trying to address them further into the project where more is at stake. Group decision making techniques such as the pairwise comparison can be very helpful in determining priorities.

The output of collecting requirements should be a traceability matrix, which traditionally has been used in software development, but now has found its way into the project management environment to ensure that each requirement relates to the business and project objectives. Table 9-1 is a suggested template, but there is no set standard for the traceability matrix and it should be adapted to the individual projects.

DEFINE THE SCOPE

Scope definition is primarily accomplished through the use of a project scope statement; Table 9-2 is a suggested template.

This statement can be considered a "handshake document." After the sponsor or other executive, often with the assistance of the project manager, has issued the charter, the team then develops the project scope statement, which is a high-level document ensuring that all stakeholders have a common understanding of the project's deliverables and the work that will be required to create those deliverables. The statement takes the project deliverable that is described in the project charter and details it for one level in the WBS. Figure 9-2 is a graphic depiction of the relationship between the charter and the project scope statement for an project involving the development of a training course.

Although there may be some variance in the content, typically the project scope statement includes the following:

- Product scope description of the product, service, or result.
- Acceptance criteria: what will determine if the deliverables have been met.
- Deliverables: the tangible product, result, or capability that the project delivers.
- Project exclusions: what will not be included in the project. Often the comment is made that if it isn't included in the deliverables, it is excluded. The problem with this theory is that people have different perceptions of what the deliverable entails. For example, included in the construction of a new house may be a three-car garage. Some people picture a three-car garage as having wiring, sheetrock, and a finished floor. Other perceptions may be that is just the building

(*text continues on page 90*)

Traceability Matrix

Project Name:

Project Number:

Project Manager:

Requirement Number	Business Need/Project Objective (Rationale for Inclusion)	Requirement Description	WBS Deliverable	Priority of the Requirement	Current Status (Active, Cancelled, Deferred, etc.)	Responsibility	Comments

TABLE 9-1. TRACEABILITY MATRIX TEMPLATE

Project Title   **Date Prepared:**

Purpose: The project scope statement is used to define, develop, and constrain the project and product scope. The scope statement should directly include, or include by reference, the items described below.

Product Scope Description:

Product scope is progressively elaborated from the project description and the product requirements in the project charter.

Deliverables:

Project deliverables are progressively elaborated from the project description, the product characteristics, and the product requirements in the project charter.

Acceptance Criteria:

The acceptance criteria that will need to be met in order for a stakeholder to accept a deliverable. Acceptance criteria can be developed for the entire project or for each component of the project.

Project Exclusions:

Project exclusions clearly define what is considered out of scope for the project.

Project Constraints:

Constraints that may be imposed on the project may include a fixed budget, hard deliverable dates, and specific technology.

Project Assumptions:

Assumptions about deliverables, resources, estimates, and any other aspect of the project that the team holds to be true, real, or correct but have not been validated.

Approvals:

_____   _____
Project Manager Signature   Sponsor or Originator Signature

_____   _____
Project Manager Name   Sponsor or Originator Name

_____   _____
Date   Date

TABLE 9-2. **EXAMPLE OF A PROJECT SCOPE STATEMENT TEMPLATE**

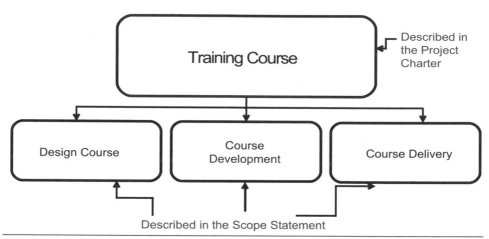

FIGURE 9-2. **THE RELATIONSHIP BETWEEN THE PROJECT CHARTER AND SCOPE STATEMENT**

with just sheetrock or just wiring. It is far better to preclude any differences in perception and simply specify the exclusions.

- Constraints: the items that limit the team's options. A number, whether it is budgetary amount, a date, or number of resources, is typically a constraint. "The project will start on July 20," or "The project must complete by December 10," or "The project budget cannot exceed $100,000," or even "The project will not exceed three resources"—these are all constraints that contain numbers. It is important to note, however, that a constraint could be something other than a number, such as "The project will only use internal resources."
- Assumptions: anything that is considered to be true, real, or certain and often allows you to move forward. The key learning point here is that assumptions must be validated as you move through the project.

CREATE THE WORK BREAKDOWN STRUCTURE

Once there is stakeholder agreement on the project scope statement, the team then creates the WBS. Just as the scope statement is based on the project charter, the WBS is based on the scope statement. The WBS helps the project manager and the team members organize the work so that all project deliverables are identified, estimated, and scheduled. The WBS defines the what, who, how much, and how long. This is accomplished by deconstructing each of the major deliverables, identified in the scope statement, down to its lowest level, termed a work package. It is at the work package level (the "what") that resources are assigned (the "who"), the time or effort to complete it is estimated (the "how long"), and what it will cost to produce that work package (the "how much") is determined. It is important that the team actively contributes to the development of the WBS. The project manager may choose to further define the elements of the WBS, including the work package elements, in a document that provides such things as detailed deliverables, a list of associated activities, milestones, start and end dates, resources required, cost estimates, technical references, and quality requirements. This document is referred to as a WBS dictionary.

Since developing a WBS from scratch can be difficult and contentious, it is strongly recommended that a WBS from a previous, similar project be used as a template for the WBS development, or the project manager can develop a "straw man" to get the team moving in the right direction. Another way that a project manager can efficiently facilitate the WBS construction is to assign core team members to each of the major deliverables identified in the scope statement. These core team members will manage getting input from resources who will be working on those deliverables, and then all the core team members, along with the project manager, will meet to blend the deliverable areas.

The WBS becomes a key tool in tracking project progress. The prudent project manager will consider how tracking and reporting WBS deliverables will be accomplished to better track progress on the project.

It is important to note that the scope statement, in combination with the WBS and the WBS dictionary, makes up the scope baseline for the project.

The WBS facilitates the following:

- Understanding the work involved
- Planning the work
- Identifying end products and deliverables
- Defining the work in successively greater detail
- Relating end items to objectives
- Assigning responsibility for all the work
- Estimating costs and schedules
- Planning and allocating resources
- Integrating scope, schedule, and cost
- Monitoring cost, schedule, and technical performance
- Summarizing information for management and reporting
- Providing traceability to lower levels of detail
- Controlling changes

The WBS provides a common, ordered framework for summarizing information and for quantitative and narrative reporting to customers and management.[2]

VALIDATE THAT ALL DELIVERABLES HAVE BEEN ACCEPTED

Scope validation is accomplished when all the stakeholders formally agree on what the project deliverables are; each deliverable is objectively validated.

The basic idea of scope validation is to take the deliverables, which have been objectively validated using the quality control process to ensure that they meet the customer's expectations, and then present them to the customer for formal acceptance. These could be classified as *interim* deliverables, with the final deliverables formally accepted as part of the closing process. Although scope validation is certainly closely aligned with the quality control process, they have a major difference in objectives. Scope validation is concerned with the acceptance of the deliverables while quality control is concerned with how correct the deliverables are. The tools used to accomplish scope validation vary from organization to organization and project to project. Usually the tools consist of work performance information that indicates the status of the deliverables, change requests to track changes to the deliverables, and updated documents such as WBS.

MONITORING AND CONTROLLING SCOPE

Information from the following documents contributes to controlling scope:

- The scope baseline compares actual results to determine if any changes or preventive action is necessary.
- The scope management plan describes how the project scope will be monitored and controlled.
- The change management plan defines how change management will be managed on the project.
- The configuration management plan addresses change to the technical side of the project.
- The requirements management is a part of the change management plan but addresses only changes to requirements on the project.[3]

Monitoring these items aids the project manager in determining the causes and degree of difference between the scope baseline and actual performance. Getting to the root cause of variance is key in determining whether or not corrective, or even preventive, action is necessary.

The output of controlling scope is a true picture of work performance information, what changes are required, and what documentation needs to be updated.

DISCUSSION QUESTIONS

❶ What are some examples of project scope in your organization? What are some examples of product scope in your organization? Who would manage each type of scope?

❷ What is the primary difference between a scope description and acceptance criteria as elements of a scope statement? Give some general examples of each.

❸ What are some items that would be included in the WBS dictionary? Under what circumstances would you use the WBS dictionary?

REFERENCES

[1] Project Management Institute, *A Guide to the Project Management Body of Knowledge* (*PMBOK® Guide*), 5th edition (Newtown Square, PA: PMI, 2013).

[2] David Pells, "Comprehensive Planning for Complex Projects," in Paul C. Dinsmore and J. Cabanis-Brewin (editors), *The AMA Handbook of Project Management,* 3rd edition (New York: AMACOM, 2010), p. 51.

[3] PMI, 2013, p. 138.

CHAPTER 10

Time Management in Practice

VALIS HOUSTON, PMP, ACACIA PM CONSULTING

"Plan the work, work the plan." This simple phrase can be your guide through many difficult times in a project management career. The project time management knowledge area should be applied with the support of a project scheduling tool, although it can be done with 3 × 5 cards to gather information, and then organized in a spreadsheet. However, the spreadsheet only communicates the proposed plan. Once the project starts and the dynamics of a project ensue—dates slip, unplanned scope is added, resources are suddenly unavailable—managing from the spreadsheet will probably become quite frustrating. The plan will no longer be a tool to provide project tracking and oversight. At that point, you will have lost control of your project.

Let's look at how the scheduling processes outlined in Chapter 6 of the Project Management Institute's *Guide to the Project Management Body of Knowledge (PMBOK® Guide),* Fifth Edition, work in practice.[1]

PLAN SCHEDULE MANAGEMENT

In this step, the project manager and team decide how much rigor they want to apply to the project based on their understanding of the size and complexity of the effort. Large projects require a great amount of rigor, while, conversely, smaller projects require very little. Thus, when planning any aspect of a project, the effort in that area should be scaled to the expected dynamics of that project. When identifying key components of its time management plan, the team should consider the other elements of the plan already in place, the tasking in the project charter, and the potential impact of any applicable environmental factors or the requirements of organizational time and planning guidelines. Once the schedule management plan is in place, the team can then begin the harder work of time and schedule management, the detailed planning beginning with the definition of activities.

DEFINE ACTIVITIES

For the process of defining activities described in the Project Management Institute (PMI) standard, the goal is to identify, completely and correctly, those activities that enable you to accomplish the project objectives. Usually, the work breakdown structure (WBS) is the tool used by project teams to accomplish this objective. Although later it will be necessary to come back and look at how the "realistic" plan fits into the needs of the business, at this stage it is important to determine what the team believes are the necessary tasks required for project completion.

Such activity definition can be done relatively easily in a project scheduling tool such as MS Project. Using this tool makes it easier to accomplish the remaining tasks of project time management. However, this task can also be done with sticky notes or 3 × 5 cards. Give a descriptive title to the task and a brief definition, along with notes gleaned from the team. Detailed notes are helpful, as you will come back to these notes throughout the project. There is a "notes" section for each task within MS Project to capture this information, or use the back of the 3 × 5 card.

At this point, it is not imperative to have the entire team available, as the focus is not on creating dependencies. The leads for each area (in an information technology project these might be the requirements lead, development lead, test lead, lead architect, etc.) can provide enough input to develop the activities. Essentially, this initial meeting answers this question: What specific actions need to happen to deliver the product defined in the scope statement?

Keep milestones in mind, both external milestones to clients or upper management and internal milestones for the team.

Be cautious about identifying tasks that are too broad in scope, for example, "develop Web site" or "create design document." Dig into the details; push to understand what must be done and how it ties into other activities. If you know something needs to happen, but neither you nor your team lead can put your finger on it, create "placeholders." Keep these "to be determined" placeholders in the plan until you have fleshed them out fully. As you continue to refine the plan (and even after the plan is finished), you may expect to come across activities that were "forgotten" or "unknown" at this early stage of the project. *Expect the plan to change.*

SEQUENCE ACTIVITIES

After developing an understanding of what needs to be done to make your project a success, the next step is to identify and document the dependencies between the activities. There are many different tools and models that can be used here, though one of the most popular is the network diagram (which can be created in a scheduling tool such as MS Project) to visually display how the work in a project comes together. Your project's network diagram helps to flesh out relationships between tasks, within a team and between teams. As you focus on the workflow, look for areas where work can be done in parallel. If you do not have a project scheduling tool or are uncomfortable using it at this point, the 3 × 5 cards or sticky notes that you used to define the activities can be placed on a wall or white board to facilitate team discussion. This technique of sequencing manually using sticky notes is widely known as "walking the wall."

Focus first on those tasks within a particular team of the project, such as the developers or testers. This process is made effective by frequently asking questions such as, "What happens after task X?" and "What do you need to get started with task Y?" Push for a healthy discussion on what is needed for each of the activities to get started. Are tasks X and Y needed for task Z to start? Are there dependencies from outside this immediate team or even from outside the project that are required? For example, do the testers require access to test data that are created by another part of the company? Balance the push for details with the risk of documenting too much detail. One helpful guideline is to base the amount of detail on the complexity and length of the project.

High complexity with a large variety of unknowns often requires gathering more detail. On a small project of a few months' duration, you can capture tasks of as little as half-day duration if they are critical ones, but going into greater detail than that is not recommended. Remember that this will become your plan, and the tracking and oversight of the project will be your responsibility and become administrative overhead for your project team to report out on. Do not make the plan overly burdensome to yourself and your project team.

Ask if tasks can start sooner, as opposed to a "finish-to-start" relationship, although this can be a tricky area. Performing tasks in parallel could potentially result in over-allocation of resources and cause more reworking than necessary if a problem occurs with the first task. Beware of overlapping dependencies—tasks that have a start-to-start or finish-to-finish dependency. These can prove to be a choke point in the timeline if resources are waiting for work to be completed; they can also be a cause for communication breakdown among team members. You probably will not be able to avoid such activities, as they are inherent to all projects, but be sure to add a note that it can be a risk area and needs to be watched carefully.

To determine the sequence of events, bring in a few experts/leads from each subteam to discuss the dependencies, paying special attention to what is being completed when. Again, as this will become your plan, do not be ashamed if everyone else in the room seems to understand and you do not. Keep asking until the sequence of events is clear. Start tying together activities that come out of these discussions. As you did within teams, push to understand if one team's activities can be started before another team's activity is complete. Is it possible, for example, to overlap development and integration testing? Can completed modules be delivered to the integration test environment so that integration testing can get started? Or is there something that precludes this from happening? Again, ask the subteam leads "What happens next?" and "What do you need to get started?"

If there is disagreement among the subteam leads, document any dissenting opinions. If the majority of the team can agree and any additional risks are documented, that should suffice. If not, as the project manager, the decision is yours to make. Investigate the issue further, but do not let issues during planning linger. Again, if necessary create placeholders in the plan for these unknowns and continue to push forward. Remember, the plan will change, so strive for the 80 percent solution.

ESTIMATE ACTIVITY RESOURCES

You cannot create a plan without taking into consideration the most important aspect: the people. In this process the project team is trying to estimate the type and quantities of material, human resources, equipment, or supplies required to perform each activity.

For each defined activity, the project manager will need to examine each element of the project to understand the type(s) and quantity of each skill set required. For example, if your project is producing a film, how many of a certain type of camera will be needed? Will these cameras be available only during the mornings because another film will use those same cameras in the afternoon? Along the same line of thinking, you need to know if you will be able to fill all the necessary activities with a name from your project team. If your team lead needs more time to ascertain resource availability, assign a generic, yet descriptive, resource to the task: "Sr. Java Developer" or "Jr. Tester" should suffice until the team lead can provide an exact name. Be sure to highlight this activity, as you will need to come back to it to assign a specific resource. If after reviewing the team's capacity the resource to fill that slot is not available, this is a red flag that you may have more on your hands than the project team can handle. Raise this issue early and try to obtain the necessary skill set from within your organization or, if feasible, from outside the company.

At times, it becomes necessary to assign a resource without fully knowing the details behind an activity. Do not let this be a reason to *not* assign a resource. Someone must be responsible for every activity. Push accountability down to the lowest level possible; ensure that these decisions are not done in a vacuum, but—at a minimum—with the support of the team lead for those resources.

Be sure to document any resource constraints that will impact the effort, such as a shared resource who has only 60 percent of his or her time available for your project or a resource who is assigned 100 percent on your project but does not work on Fridays. Be sure to also capture holidays, vacations, and administrative time during the course of the project. (This can be done in MS Project under the "Change Working Time" dialogue box.) Individual resource constraints can be applied as well as modifying the base calendar from an 8-hour day to a 7-hour day. (If you are not using a scheduling tool, this exercise can also be captured in a spreadsheet.)

Three pieces of information are needed to develop a schedule: the actual activities, resource estimating (knowing who will be working on those activities), and the duration of the activities. Do not take lightly the task of estimating activity resources, as not digging in and understanding the constraints and availability of your resources can have serious repercussions on the timeline that may not become known until it is too late.

ESTIMATE ACTIVITY DURATIONS

At this point, it begins to become apparent how all this planning results in a timeline. For each activity, the project manager needs to understand how much effort is required. Be careful to separate "duration" from "effort." For example, an activity with an effort of 10 days will take 12.5 days (duration) if the assigned resource can only give 80 percent of his time to your project. On the other hand, if the same 10-day activity has two full-time resources assigned, it is possible for it to be completed faster, with a duration of 5 days. This is why the process of estimating activity resources is so important.

Estimating activity durations is not a one-time task but a process executed at the start of the project and again with each approved change to the project plan. It is the process of estimating the number of work periods needed to complete individual activities with the estimated resources. Plan to perform this exercise iteratively, at key points in the project—what the *PMBOK® Guide* refers to as "progressive elaboration." This simply means that as we learn more about "what" we are building (requirements) and "how" we are building it (design), we are able to refine these estimates and further define a timeline that is more accurate and more attainable.

Early on, the project manager will be asked to let upper management know when the project will deliver results. Progressive elaboration enables you to provide a more precise date of when the project will actually be delivered, but not until the project is sufficiently well along. This is the dilemma that faces many projects: committing to a date without having enough information about scope and resources. Although you will likely be told that these dates are just for planning purposes and the team will not be held to them, this is seldom the case. What can help is to instead provide a range of dates, and commit to providing better estimates as further information makes itself available.

There are quite a few estimating tools and techniques available, ranging from parametric estimating and wide-band Delphi to three-point estimating (most likely, optimistic, and pessimistic). (For more detail on these methods, see Chapter 11.)

Bottom-up estimating, paired with one of the techniques mentioned above or commonly used at your company, is the recommended approach, as it focuses on the low-level details that can only come from your project team. The project time management chapter of the *PMBOK® Guide* states: "When a schedule activity cannot be estimated with a reasonable degree of confidence, the work within the schedule activity is decomposed into more detail." Stress to the project team that these tasks will be worked by them and they will be held accountable for these estimates. Push for as much information as is appropriate at that particular phase of the project. If you have finished design reviews and the development lead is not able to provide estimates for a number of activities, then you need to go back to design.

MS Project allows for the creation of columns in Gantt view in which you can assign "duration" and "effort." If using a spreadsheet, you can also update it similarly.

Be sure to keep all the documentation used in this process. As you progress through the project and refine the estimates, this documentation will help remind the team why it made certain decisions. This helps to further refine your estimates with the new knowledge that has been gained. It also helps to build your company's historical database.

DEVELOP THE SCHEDULE

You have defined all the activities and documented all the predecessors and successors, a resource calendar is in hand, and you have allocated the proper duration for each activity. Now you are ready to develop the schedule. In this step you analyze the needs of stakeholders; analyze the sequence of the work; consider durations, resource requirements, and schedule constraints to ultimately select a schedule model to document; and track and control the project time.

Remember that the schedule is meant to be updated and refined throughout the project. This first iteration becomes the baseline. Unless something major in the project causes you to re-scope and change the baseline, this baseline becomes the "square and level" by which progress is tracked.

When creating the schedule, start with external and internal milestones. All activities should support these milestones.

It is also a good idea to group milestones together and at the top of the schedule. This will provide easy access when you have to give an executive overview of your plan.

Now comes the step in which you apply the time constraints you documented during the sequence activities step. "Start no earlier than" or "Start as soon as possible" will help to create a dynamic plan that will change as a reflection of tasks completing earlier or later than scheduled. This is where the spreadsheet loses its appeal and project management software becomes a necessity. Remember to apply any lead and lag times that you discovered during activity sequencing.

A number of scheduling techniques are available. Critical Path is probably the most widely used and is the underlying technique behind MS Project. Also gaining in prominence has been Goldratt's critical chain method (see Chapter 35 for a more detailed discussion of critical chain). Be sure that the technique you choose is supported by your project management software.

Do not forget to apply the resource calendar with its holidays, vacations, shifts, and so on. It is possible for key resources to become over-allocated, for example, assigning Joe Developer to four 8-hour activities on the same day, resulting in a 32-hour day. Resource leveling is moving these activities to provide a "best fit" to keep resources from being over-allocated or to execute activities when key resources are only available at certain times. Be aware that resource leveling, although necessary, could result in extending the schedule.

What about replanning? Often you will be asked to expedite the schedule, while keeping the scope intact. Crashing (trade-offs between cost and schedule to determine how to obtain the greatest amount of compression for the least incremental cost) and fast tracking (normally sequential tasks done in parallel) are high-risk techniques that, in an effort to deliver faster, can increase cost, increase the probability of rework, and increase the threat of missing the earlier date. When these requests come in, try to work on them with as little interruption to the project team as possible. It always seems that these requests come at the worst time, when taking team members off current work to look at a potential replan of the schedule will assuredly result in missing deadlines on the current work. Instead, pull as few team leads as possible to look at replanning. If you are comfortable and have enough knowledge of the project, you can perform this exercise yourself. Have a seasoned project manager review the result to catch any errors in the replan. Try to encapsulate the project team away from these interruptions and keep them working towards the baseline schedule until it is ultimately decided that a replan is necessary.

Congratulations: You now have a project schedule. Review it once more with the team to get buy-in on the schedule baseline, as this is foundation for project tracking and oversight. Once you see the actual schedule laid out, it will be obvious why scheduling by this method is sometimes called "waterfall," as each activity flows into the next one in an ordered sequence.

CONTROL SCHEDULE

Even though you have a baseline schedule in hand, you are far from finished. This process includes those steps you take to monitor the status of project activities to update project progress and manage changes to the schedule baseline to achieve the plan and project objectives. In other words, you will have to keep it current in order to track progress, to facilitate the inevitable change requests, and to assist in providing project status. In the hands of a mature organization with proper structures in place, earned value (see Chapter 33) is a valuable asset. Even if your organization does not utilize earned value, take the time to understand its concepts and try to apply them, even if in a piecemeal fashion.

Probably the hardest aspect of controlling the schedule is gathering actual progress from the team. Gathering progress is not the problem; rather, it is the subjective sense that "we are at 90 percent" for over half the duration of the task that can be frustrating, not only to management leaders who hear each week that "we are still at 90 percent," but also to the developer struggling to complete the task. Be wary of this trap. This is a sign that further deconstruction of the task might be necessary to gain better insight into what has been completed and what work still remains.

Receive the progress reporting template from management or create one that is judged satisfactory to management and make sure your team is aware of the activities that are being reported to management. At a minimum, key deliverables and critical path items should be represented on your status report. Be sure to include start and finish dates and whether that task is ahead of or behind schedule.

If using MS Project, the tracking Gantt view is recommended. It shows the baseline versus current task start/finish dates. It also provides percentage completes for both the activity and the summary task level. This view can quickly show which areas of the project are falling behind and by how much. Continue to ask questions to get a better feel for how much of the activity has been completed and how much is left. Along with asking about the percentage complete, also ask if the activity will be completed by the baseline end date.

Schedule controlling is one of the most important roles in the project. While controlling, continue to be alert for areas in the plan that require refinement. Be on the lookout for schedule slips and take immediate corrective action. Track against the baseline and be prepared for change requests.

... AND THEN THERE'S AGILE

No chapter on scheduling today would be complete without mentioning that there is another way, one that adds flexibility to the processes described above. For its devotees (including this author), Agile has almost crowded traditional schedule management off the page; however, for the majority of project managers it is a relatively new concept. Here are a few techniques for introducing a new team to Agile, which can also be used on waterfall projects. These techniques help to improve communication and transparency, expedite the team's work load, identify bottlenecks, and keep your client abreast of the current state of the project, which usually veers from the original plan on day two. These powerful tools can be used alongside the project time management processes outlined above. [Note: Agile methods bring a whole new language to projects. For definitions of terms unfamiliar to you in this chapter, please consult Chapter 44.]

TECHNIQUES DURING A SPRINT

During a Sprint, I use a Kanban or task board to facilitate the Scrum stand-up meeting (Figure 10-1). The task board is a visual tool that immediately shows what is on the backlog, what the team is working on, and more importantly, gives the viewer insight into the flow of work.[2] The board encompasses the current Sprint. Each column identifies a key hand-off or milestone for tasks as the work makes its way from concept/user story to working product accepted by the business. As with everything Agile, modify to fit your team and adjust as necessary.

Use rows for user stories and note cards to represent the tasks needed to complete each user story. All the note cards start in the backlog column. The team members responsible for the work associated with each note card move their note card down the row into each new column as work progresses. Though most Agile software tools come with a Kanban feature, there is nothing like a physical Kanban board. The ability to touch and move tasks and allow team members to brief the team on what they are doing facilitates information sharing within the team. It is wonderful to see team members move one task card an inch to the right, but still within the bounds of the column to signify they have done something productive. It instills a sense of progress and ownership in your team. Think of it as your team's living game board. Note that it is the *team's* board, not yours to manage or own.

Incorporating a Kanban board into the daily Scrum stand-up meeting allows the team to quickly identify, due to the visual nature of Kanban, what the rest of the

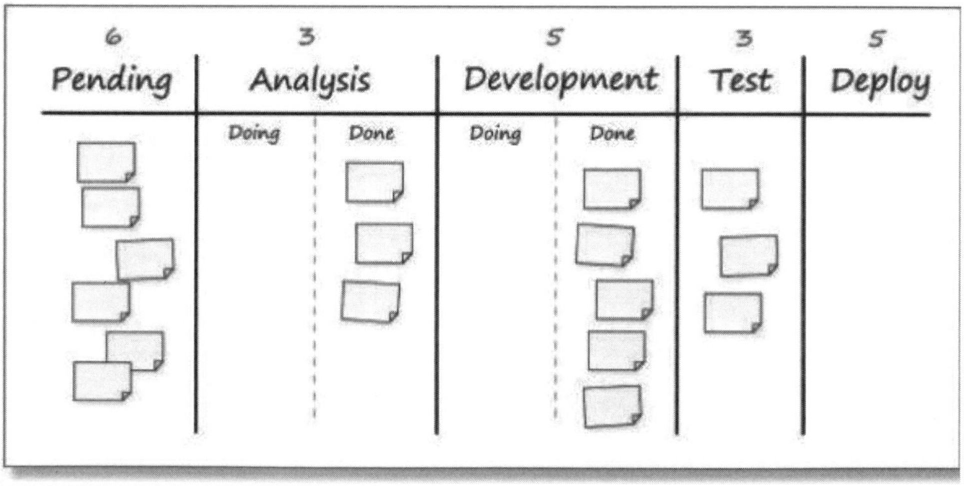

FIGURE 10-1. **EXAMPLE OF A SIMPLE KANBAN BOARD**

Source: Roni C. Thomas, Introduction to Kanban (slideshow), at http://www.slideshare.net/Intelligrape/ introduction-to-kanban-21088273. This work is licensed under the Creative Commons Attribution-Noncommercial-ShareAlike 3.0 License.

team is working on. This allows for immediate feedback on potential issues; for example, if two developers are working in the same area of the code, they can discuss how to work with each other without stepping on each other's updates. Also, what is appreciated by the next team members in the flow is the ability to gauge when code will be coming their way. This allows them to prioritize their work so that they can be ready to accept the deliverable. The team members adjust and balance their work in order to expedite the expected hand-off of work. Facilitate communication during the stand-ups to ensure awareness of progress throughout the team. Your team will quickly see the usefulness of a Kanban board, but the Scrum master/project manager will need to highlight important hand-offs.

With a Kanban board, when one team member starts to become a bottleneck, with items queued up behind her, this is visibly apparent to the entire team. At that point, those team members being underutilized have an opportunity to step up and assist, which allows them the chance to learn new skills. These individuals derive satisfaction knowing that they are building a new skill set and being a contributor beyond their basic role. The team becomes more than just self-managing; it is self-correcting, with individuals stretching their skills further than they had previously imagined.

A key problem arises when a team member starts a number of tasks, but has not moved any into the next column. The team member has done quite a bit of work— 80 percent complete on a number of tasks—but since none of the tasks are 100 percent, he has not delivered any value. Because the next step in the chain is not able to proceed, this has slowed down the flow of work. Push to have no more than two tasks active at any one time with the same team member. This ensures that work is flowing through the team and minimizes the amount of work in progress (WIP).

HOW THE KANBAN HELPS WITH ESTIMATING

Mike Cohn, in *Agile Estimation and Planning,* says, "A key tenet of agile estimating and planning is that we estimate size but derive duration."[3] A bit controversial, but I shy away from assigning hours to tasks. After the team has spent time understanding what is required to deliver a user story and we have conducted a roundtable discussion on the "size" of the user story and everyone has been given an opportunity to explain their position, just assign a story point and be done with the estimation. The next step is to break out tasks, but not spend more of the team's time to assign hours to each task. Everyone will be able to see early on if work is not getting accomplished. The team will have a fairly steady velocity, so focus on committing to the story points trend that the team has established. The estimated hour burn-down is a nice chart for management, but it does not focus on delivered value, which should be the only real measure of progress.

LESSONS LEARNED, CONTINUOUSLY

Since lessons-learned sessions are invaluable, why conduct them only at the end of the project? When dealing with waterfall/traditional teams, try not to overwhelm the team with new terms that you have learned from your recent certified Scrum master course. Start with one idea. Conducting lessons learned (or retrospectives) throughout the project is a great introductory experiment. Lessons-learned sessions allow the team members to consider how they are operating and whether or not their current processes need to change. On a waterfall project, conduct the lessons learned every few weeks. The format I prefer is the "start, stop, continue" method. It, along with many other retrospective techniques, is detailed on the Agile Retrospective Resource Wiki.[4] We begin in the start quadrant, where the team members get to elaborate on a something that they want to see the team start doing in the next Sprint. Then, as a team, we identify how we will make this happen. We then move to the stop quadrant, repeating the process for items that we want to stop doing in the next Sprint. Then we highlight key areas that occurred during this Sprint that we want to continue doing in the continue quadrant. I modify the method by dropping the "more of, less of" and adding the "shout out." At the shout-out quadrant, any team member can give a shout out or compliment to another team member. This ends the retrospective on a positive note.

TECHNIQUES FOR RELEASE PLANNING

The best way to keep the business (product owner and stakeholders) involved is continually to groom and update the release plan. If you conduct two-week Sprints, a few days before the end of the Sprint you have an idea of the team's progress/velocity and if the commitments made during the Sprint planning session will be achieved. At this time, collaboratively with the product owner and development lead, you can update the release plan. Review the release backlog and determine if there are any user stories that can be removed, or if there are any new user stories to be added. Then, always (always!) reprioritize the backlog.

As you gain an understanding of the team's velocity, make adjusts to the original release plan. Are you going slower than planned and not completing as many user stories? Are user stories are not making it to "done done" within a Sprint? If so, modify the original release plan accordingly and update future Sprints with the new priority. Adjust each Sprint's capacity based on new velocity.

By keeping your product owner involved, she will begin to understand the team's velocity, even if she does not really know what story points are. Your product owner will understand why, four Sprints later, the current release plan does not look like the original release plan. Also, because you have kept the product owner aware on how the release is evolving, there will be no surprises.

Next, brief the other stakeholders on the new release plan. This allows all stakeholders to be aware of changes. They become accustomed to seeing an evolution of the release plan along with the evolution of the product. Again, the goal is to ensure that at the end of the release there are no surprises, and that everyone understands how and why we ended up with a product that is different from the original release. And honestly, how often has your original day-one plan never been adjusted?

Ken Schwaber's *Agile Project Management with Scrum*[5] gives an excellent overview of the roles and rules of using Scrum along with practical examples. Be mindful that there is more to being Agile than just Scrum. And not every rule needs to apply to your project, nor should you keep a rule that the team believes is no longer value added.

Continue to research and try out the various techniques and tools described here. You are not limited to only one, and only one might not be the best fit for your project. And lastly, remember that you must diligently "plan the work," as this will become the measure of your success and then, just as aggressively, "work the plan" to ensure the project's success. Whether your team is Agile or waterfall, remember that the goal is to create a quality product that makes money for your company. If your team is spending time on activities that do not support that goal, you are not only wasting time and money, but your team's morale will suffer for it.

There are many tools that you should have in your tool kit; choose those that push the team to communicate, foster transparency, and break down artificial barriers between team members. This leads to a team that is more harmonious, which leads to a highly efficient team.

DISCUSSION QUESTIONS

❶ When have you experienced the impact of a poor estimate of activity resources on project outcomes? Discuss how the problems might have been prevented using the technique described in this chapter.

❷ Practice identifying activities using a project you are involved in or familiar with. What issues impact your ability to define the activities in a project?

❸ How would you handle a persistent request from executives for a specific deployment date for your project before having requirements completed?

❹ Thinking back to a recent project that was challenged by schedule over-runs, "rerun" it mentally using Agile techniques. Would a more flexible process have been helpful?

ACKNOWLEDGMENT

I gratefully acknowledge Paul Lombard, PMP, for providing updates to the standard scheduling processes in this chapter for the fourth edition.

REFERENCES

[1] Project Management Institute, *A Guide to the Project Management Body of Knowledge* (*PMBOK® Guide*), 5th edition (Newtown Square, PA: PMI, 2013).

[2] Alan Shalloway, Guy Beaver, and James Trott, *Lean-Agile Software Development* (Boston: Addison-Wesley, 2010).

[3] Mike Cohn, *Agile Estimating and Planning* (Upper Saddle River, NJ: Prentice Hall, 2006).

[4] Retrospective Plans. At http://retrospectivewiki.org/index.php?title=Retrospective_Plans.

[5] Ken Schwaber, *Agile Project Management with Scrum* (Redmond, WA: Microsoft Press, 2004).

CHAPTER 11

Project Cost Management in Practice

PAUL LOMBARD, PMP, CQM, PM COLLEGE

Project cost management is so easy and yet so hard. It affects many aspects of project work and is affected by factors within and outside the project. How do we overcome this problem? An important first step is to have an effective cost management system on your project. As you might expect, no single cost management system is correct in all cases, so it is more effective to speak in terms of the general attributes, or key elements, of an *effective cost management system*. The foundation of that system must be the guidance and procedures defined and promoted by your organization's leaders. This guidance must also be coupled with the cost management needs of all the project's key stakeholders. In defining the necessary elements of this system, you should remember that you may need to interact with elements outside of your project domain, so it is usually best to use generally accepted or recognized standards. The cost management knowledge area in the Project Management Institute's *Guide to the Project Management Body of Knowledge* (*PMBOK® Guide*) suggests a four-process cost management system: plan cost management, estimate costs, determine budget, and control costs.[2] These four processes, either formally or informally, should be considered for all projects, and they can be performed as discrete activities or combined as the needs of the project dictate.

PLAN COST MANAGEMENT

The first step in establishing your cost system is the plan cost management process. This planning process consists of actions taken by the project manager, usually with the project team, to define what the cost management system will look like on your project. To determine this, the team needs to think about the amount of rigor, or the degree of formality, it will want to implement. This means identifying the right mix of procedures, processes, reporting mechanisms, governance, documentation, and other methods deemed appropriate to ensure that all the elements of project cost (planning, managing, expensing, and controlling) are included and attended to. This requires the team to prepare by reviewing existing information in the organization such as current plans, existing standards and guidelines, the project charter, and the current operating environment. In essence, the team is discovering what exists already in terms of guidance and what is going on internally and externally that must be planned for. This discovery process cannot be limited to narrowly defined costs only. For example, a common dilemma today arises when companies buy expensive portfolio management software systems. The goal of a portfolio system is to provide automation that enables the leadership team to manage key investments. However, when that same organization does not have a consistent practice of program and project management, it becomes very hard to gather the data needed to support the portfolio system because there is no consistent process in place for producing the data. For this reason, some companies fail in their initial portfolio management efforts.

So, in defining the cost management system, project leaders should review appropriate inputs, use the right tools, make use of expert judgment, analyze all relevant data, and, during a good kickoff meeting, establish an effective cost management plan that is the right size for the project. Armed with this guidance the team is ready to perform the next step: cost estimation.

COST ESTIMATION

The objective of estimating cost is to "approximate the monetary resources needed to complete project activities."[3] For many years as a project manager, I thought the most common approach to estimating was PIDOOMA, an acronym for *Pulled It Directly Out of Mid-Air.* In other words, we guessed. Guesses are seldom based on reality, and clearly this approach is fraught with problems, because the game often becomes guess and guess again. Without clarity, the target result keeps shifting. How can projects be effectively managed if the target is constantly shifting? They can't. A more disciplined approach is required. As a first step, review existing project and cost plans, especially the scope and schedule baselines, depending on the size of the project, and other plans and documents should be reviewed as well (e.g., the human resource staffing plan, the risk register, etc.). In addition, the team should review and consider any external factors that could impact the project, such as market segment information, economic trend information, and so on. After reviewing the relevant documentation, the team can begin to build the estimate. The goal is to achieve a project cost "baseline." The baseline is the approved version of a work product (e.g., the project plan) that can be changed only through formal change control procedures and serves as a basis for comparison.[4] It is an excellent tool for comparison, because when it is complete it functions as an "area of order" for the project against which the project manager can assess variation and deviation from the plan. Without it, there is no context, and variation does not appear to exist. To create this baseline, the team must first develop a cost estimate. Although many estimating tools and techniques are available, the collection of common activities performed fall into two general categories: estimate development methods and estimate verification methods.

Estimate Development Methods

Methods employed to build and sustain the cost estimate include the following:

▶ *Expert Judgment.* In this method, one or more "experts" are solicited to analyze characteristics of part of a project or the whole project and to provide an estimate of the costs based on their knowledge or experience. This technique is often used when no prior data exists.

▶ *Analogous.* This approach uses actual costs or data from prior projects to develop an estimate for the current project. The estimate is usually adjusted to compensate for complexity or other factors, such as time or the time value of money. Rightly or wrongly, this technique is often used to develop a quick estimate of costs. However, this can be dangerous if the previous project is not exactly the same and critical special complexities are overlooked.

▶ *Parametric:* This method builds on the statistical relationship between historical data and other variables to calculate an estimate for a given activity. For example, a construction company knows it costs 100,000 euros for each mile of straight road. That cost is then multiplied by the number of miles to be built and then adjusted for other considerations. Usually, parametric estimating is best when used in conjunction with other methods, such as expert judgment or bottom up.

▶ *Bottom Up:* Also known as the "definitive method," this approach requires a more detailed view of the project. Normally, all or many of the component work packages or activities have been identified, and each is estimated (cost, time, resources, etc.). These individual estimates are then rolled up or summed up at the next higher level. The bottom-up estimate is considered to be the most accurate estimate. (Some sources quote the level of accuracy of the bottom-up estimate to be between –5% to +10%,[5] because of the level of detail, but it does take time and knowledge to develop.) The bottom-up estimate is believed to provide the team with the ability to closely track and control a project because of the level of detail. The good thing about this estimate is that it tells you how much your project will really cost; the bad thing is . . . it tells you how much your project will really cost![6]

▶ *Three-Point Estimates:* In some cases, there is uncertainty about the task to be performed or disagreement about some aspect of it (e.g., cost, duration, risk, etc.). The three-point estimating approach arrives at an estimate that considers these uncertainties. This approach triangulates three estimates to compensate for risk or uncertainty:

- Most likely (ML): often provided by the resource owner or performer, this is the assessment of the real effort required to accomplish the work.
- Optimistic (O): assumes that those performing this task will have perfect or near-perfect results. Implicit in this estimate is that the ideal circumstances exist (e.g., perfect requirements, right tools available, best worker, excellent design, etc.).

- Pessimistic (P): assumes "worst case scenario" performance of the task. For example, requirements are poor, equipment is not available, workers are unskilled, and so on.

There are two common methods for calculating the three-point estimates; triangulation and beta distribution. The formula for each approach is as follows:

$$\text{Triangular Distribution} = cE = (cO + cML + cP) / 3$$

$$\text{Beta Distribution} = cE = (cO + 4cML + cP) / 6$$

Note that E = estimate and c = cost. Each formula has its benefits and drawbacks. The common expected distribution of events is represented by the triangular distribution formula, while a distribution of events with *high degrees of uncertainty* is represented in the beta distribution formula (also known as the program evaluation and review technique [PERT] formula). The use of triangular or PERT estimating is sometimes a required activity when developing a project schedule, and PERT is especially useful when there is uncertainty about cost or work durations. PERT functionality is a common feature in most popular project scheduling tools.

Estimate Verification Methods

The following are additional methods to verify the completeness or assess the accuracy of the cost estimate:

▶ *Reserve Analysis:* A contingency reserve or allowance is added to the developed estimate to account for risk or uncertainty; these items are often referred to as the "unknown unknowns." It is usually a set amount (e.g., 10 or 20 percent) based on organizational guidance or the best estimate of the project team.

▶ *Cost of Quality:* The four traditional "costs of quality" are prevention costs, appraisal costs, internal failure costs, and external failure costs. The measure for a given organization can be gathered over time, and historical data can be used to verify and, if necessary, adjust the estimate. Cost of quality performance from prior projects can be very helpful in strategizing your cost estimate and managing your current project.

▶ *Vendor Bid Analysis:* An assessment of vendor bids can be compared with the estimate developed by the project team. The result can be used to verify and adjust the cost, if necessary. Once the cost has been an agreed upon by both parties, the resulting cost estimate becomes a baseline against which vendor work can be tracked and controlled.

After the cost estimating is complete, the project team will have tools to help them and management understand how the estimate was derived (basis of estimate [BOE]) and to track and control the project (activity cost estimates).

American Management Association • www.amanet.org

Determine Budget

Budgeting, ideally, is the act of "aggregating the estimated costs of individual activities or work packages to establish an authorized cost baseline."[7] In other words, the budget is the money *allocated* to accomplish the project. In preparing to establish the budget, the project team should review and validate all relevant information (e.g., cost management plan, BOE, key project plan elements (e.g., scope documentation, schedule, resource calendars, risk registers, activity cost estimates, etc.) as well as any agreements, contracts, and organizational process assets.

Once this has been accomplished, the team should begin to define the budget. If done properly, budget development initially involves assembling or bringing together in a structured format the estimating data already derived. The team should ensure the estimate includes not only work items but also other key factors, such as risk, profit, overheads, and so on, before it is presented to stakeholders for agreement or approval. In many cases, contingency costs have been added at the work package level in anticipation of known risk; this is known as planning for known unknowns. However, at this stage of budget development, the project team typically adds some contingency for the unknown unknowns, as we discussed earlier. Another important activity the team should consider is seeking expert opinion to ensure that the budget is "sufficient and complete" to accomplish the project objectives. The team may also consider comparing their initial budget against similar projects, or historical information, to determine if any area varies excessively. If there is a large variance, it should be analyzed to ensure it is appropriate. Each project is unique and some large variance is correct. Using prior project experience can be very helpful in ensuring that all key factors have been considered and that you have not overlooked key details or are too optimistic in your estimates. Once the above steps have been accomplished, the last step should be to ensure that your budget is consistent with the amount allocated for it. This reconciliation ensures your project will be properly funded.

The goal of the "determine budget" activities is to efficiently arrive at a budget that is realistic, executable, and amenable to your organization's monitoring and control activities. Project budgets are of no value if they are not tracked and controlled. Two important considerations for budget developers warrant mention here: market viability and game playing. The budget serves as a baseline for tracking and controlling costs. Unfortunately, many budgets are based on faulty historical, or no historical, information. The historical information that does exist in many organizations is based on performance of processes that are not efficient. Such data are of limited use and will cause your budget to be either uncompetitive, as it is on the high side, or unrealistic, as it is on the low side. It is unfortunate to lose a work project because of an inflated budget, but it is worse to win a work project that cannot be delivered within the budget assigned. It not only hurts relationships with customers, it can also adversely affect the motivation of the performers of the work. Also, the project manager should be alert for "game playing"[8] in the budget. Game playing is the addition of added cost elements based on faulty assumptions, fears, or power. These items can inflate your budget and reduce your marketability.

Control Costs

"The importance of project control and its impact on business performance has long been recognized. Effective control helps run the project according to plan, often in spite of changes, contingencies and work-related contingencies."[9] Any organization concerned with its business performance in these uncertain times must implement effective cost control as one of its key control mechanisms when managing projects. Cost control "is the process of monitoring the status of the project to update the project costs and managing changes to the cost baseline."[10]

Not developing an estimate and establishing a budget is essentially the same as not knowing where you want to go. There is no mechanism for controlling cost, because data have no meaning without context. In project management terms, the baseline serves as the context, and one critical element of that project baseline should be cost. Without it, any expenditure is OK! Controlling project costs requires a baseline that includes cost.

An even more confusing practice is to create an initial cost baseline but not update it when changes are approved or project performance requires it. Remember, a baseline is the approved version of a work product that can be changed *only* through formal change control procedures and *is used as a basis for comparison.*[4] Controlling cost should be thought of as an iterative process, repeated many times through the life of the project. It is comprised of gathering, organizing, analyzing, and deciding (GOAD) project information to enable achievement of the project result in a manner that enables effective project management. The first three steps of the GOAD model, G, O, and A, are most applicable to the monitoring activities; the last part, D, is the control function that we will discuss later in this chapter. In project terms, these steps are as follows:

▶ *Gather:* This set of activities is associated with collecting actual project performance information. However, before undertaking the data collection process, a cost control system should be established to provide guidance on how data will be collected on your project. In establishing the cost control system, all relevant project documentation should be reviewed, including the existing project management plan, project funding information, work performance data, as well as organizational process assets. As part of this review process, special attention should be given to key tools (e.g., project software, financial and accounting procedures, etc.) and templates that may help streamline the data gathering process. Once the system is established, gathering is the process of collecting the defined data in accordance with the system.

▶ *Organize:* In this step, the team assembles and prepares the data for analysis according to organizational guidelines and personal preferences in assembling project performance data in a way that enables effective analysis. The key considerations are who will be reviewing and analyzing the data, and what format lends itself to effective analysis. Organizations often use the "dashboard" features available on most popular software programs to help organize data. A dashboard is a display similar to those you might see in a cockpit or an automobile that has key information relating to cost (or time or resources) structured in an easy-to-read graphical format.

▶ *Analyze:* Once the data have been organized, they need to be effectively analyzed to understand current status and implications for the future. As a suggested rule, look at data for one cycle back and three cycles forward. You should not become too fascinated with past data for the same reason you cannot drive a car forward looking through the rearview mirror. Data analysis may be carried out by the project team, the project management office, or the leadership oversight team. In all cases data should be analyzed against the project: the baseline to assess how much the project has varied, what that means in future terms, and, if necessary, what the causes are of problematic variance.

▶ *Decide:* Analysis of data reveals information that may require action. The goal at this point, in accordance with organizational guidance and effective project practice, is to take appropriate action(s) to keep the project on track. The two big failures of project teams are to act when they shouldn't and to not act when they should. This usually happens when the fundamentals are not in place. As a result, team members do not know the real status of the project and, thus, do not act appropriately.

COMMON TOOLS FOR MONITORING AND CONTROLLING PROJECT COSTS

Deliverable and Milestone Tracking

In this approach a cost is determined and assigned to each milestone or deliverable. As costs are incurred, they are attached to a deliverable for management and control. Many organizations like this approach because it is simple, less bureaucratic, easy to define, and fits well with most work breakdown structures. However, the long time between deliverables can obscure problems in the system, so getting each party to agree on the attributes of a complete and correct deliverable or milestone result can frequently be a challenge that causes disagreement, delay, and added cost.

Measurement by Work Percentages

Many organizations use this approach. They associate cost with work on the basis of reported percentages of work complete. For example, if the team has accomplished one day's work on a five-day task, the organization might assign a figure of 20 percent complete to that task. This does enable easy financial reporting, because 20 percent of a 1,000-euro task is easy to calculate. It is also popular because most stakeholders understand (or believe they do) what 40 percent complete means, and that makes project reporting simpler. However, this approach has several problems. The first and probably the most important is the challenge of defining exactly what 40 percent complete means. Percentage data are easily misunderstood, confused, or misrepresented. In addition, some projects and tasks can reach 80 percent very quickly and might therefore be considered to be in great shape, but the most challenging piece might be the last 20 percent. In some cases, that last 20 percent never gets finished![11]

Customer Satisfaction Measures

Occasionally an organization selects customer satisfaction as the key measure to control projects because it often speaks directly to a specific area that organizational leaders track quite closely, and it forms a common basis between the customer and the providing organization. However, using customer satisfaction as the primary measure usually leads to more problems. For example, customers can be delighted when they receive every change they requested at minimal or no cost. However, the profitability of the providing organization is sinking. Also, customer measures are too subjective to function as a stand-alone cost management tool. These measures can be used effectively when coupled with other project data, but they are normally not effective when used alone.

Earned Value Management

Organizations use this technique because it combines the best of the measurement approaches discussed above and extends them to a greater precision. The strength of earned value management (EVM) lies in its approach to representing the data. It combines the concepts of budget, cost, work performance planned, and work performance completed to arrive at a representation of current performance. This means that EVM can be applied to all projects in all industries and can be accomplished at any level of the project domain. It also provides the capability to forecast results derived from current performance. Sometimes organizations resist its use because it requires learning a new approach. Further, it might not be used because it relies on up-to-date project information. Gathering these data leads to added work on the project, and the data are not easily understood by the leaders to whom the data will be presented. However, its use is growing and, in some cases, is mandated because of the insights provided by its use.[12] EVM is covered in more detail in Chapter 33.

CONCLUSION

There are several effective techniques for project cost management, most of which are used by numerous organizations around the world. The technique selected to control costs on the project should be based on careful consideration of project factors, such as size, complexity, corporate procedures and guidelines, and client or customer needs. The goal of any system should be to enable effective management without creating an unnecessary burden.

Once the tools for controlling costs are selected, project leadership is responsible for defining at what intervals performance reviews will be conducted. The content of the review depends on the goals of the reviewer. For example, a high-level leadership team may review project cost performance as compared with the contract, project charter, or project plan. Project managers may be concerned about other factors in addition to core cost and status. For example, they may also compare documents, such as the actual spending plan against the original planned spending rate, staffing costs, and so on. Other entities may review other financial aspects of the project. The key is that if your documentation is in order, the project will be easier to manage and costs easier to control, no matter who reviews the project.

DISCUSSION QUESTIONS

❶ Who should define the cost data that will be reviewed at end of phases in the project? Why is it necessary to define the elements in advance? What are the attributes of effective data?

❷ What is the formula for a PERT estimate and under what circumstances in cost management could it be used?

❸ What are the four key processes that should exist formally or informally on every project?

REFERENCES

[1] "Lessons learned, again, and again," *ASK Magazine*, NASA, issue 12 (June 2003).

[2] Project Management Institute, *A Guide to the Project Management Body of Knowledge,* 5th edition (Newtown Square, PA: PMI, 2013).

[3] Ibid.

[4] Ibid.

[5] James C. Taylor, *Project Scheduling and Cost Control* (Plantation, FL: J. Ross Publishing, 1997).

[6] Lionel Galway, "Quantitative Risk Analysis for Project Management: A Critical Review," RAND Corporation Report WR-112-RC, February, 2004.

[7] PMI, 2013, p. 208.

[8] Integrated Master Schedule Directive, Office of the Under Secretary of Defense, DI-MGMT-81650, 2005.

[9] Eliyahu Goldratt, *Critical Chain* (North River Press, 1997).

[10] PMI, 2013, p. 193.

[11] J. K. Pinto and J. W. Trailer, *Essentials of Project Control* (Newton Square, PA: PMI Publications, 1999).

[12] *Flight School, An Accelerated Project Management Learning Experience,* PM College Training Course, www.PMCollege.com.

CHAPTER 12

Project Quality Management in Practice

GEREE STREUN, PMP, CSQE, PMI-ACP, CSSGB, CSM
GV SOFTWARE SOLUTIONS, INC.

What do we mean by "quality management" on projects? Often, discussions of quality become confused when it is not clear whether we are referring to the quality of the process, or the quality of the finished product. The project quality management processes described in the Project Management Institute's *Guide to the Project Management Body of Knowledge (PMBOK® Guide),* fifth edition, address that confusion by including all the activities that determine quality standards, objectives, and responsibilities so that the project will satisfy the quality requirements and result in a product that meets quality standards. .

The quality management approach described in the *PMBOK® Guide* is compatible with other quality approaches.[1] Quality processes should be used on all types of projects. The quality approach when building a house is different from that used when developing software for an embedded medical device. In either case, the failure to meet quality requirements can have a negative impact on both the customer and the company building the product. For instance, building a house without the proper architectural diagrams or building inspections can necessitate costly reworking after the customer takes possession of the dwelling, which could leave the developer liable for damages. In the case of an embedded medical device, a patient may be harmed, thus leaving the developing company open for prosecution by the Food and Drug Administration and the legal system.

Quality has many different perspectives, as meanings have evolved from different industries, organizations, and application areas. The International Organization for Standardization's (ISO) definition of quality is "the totality of characteristics of an entity that bear on its ability to satisfy stated and implied needs."[2] Additionally, quality can refer to the following:

- Relative quality—the quality of the product or service as compared with other products or services

- Fitness for use—the product or service is usable
- Fitness for purpose—the product or service meets its intended purpose
- Meets requirements—the product or service in relation to the customer's requirements
- Quality is inherent—quality cannot be tested in; the process must support designing in quality, not attempting to test it in at the end of the process

Quality management processes, when properly implemented on a project, drive the project to advance a company's market position:

▶ A high-performing quality organization has process improvement initiatives that result in the following:

- Improving all processes in an organization
- Lowering correction costs
- Stopping recall costs
- Recognizing the impact of implementing quality improvement objectives
- Building a historical repository of lessons learned for future improvement

▶ Use the quality process to build quality into the product throughout the development process. This costs less than trying to test quality into the product during the verification phase, and costs much less than a product recall after a failure in the field. Long-term costs can even include the loss of current and future customers.

▶ Know your customer's expectations. What do they really want or need to satisfy their requirements? Keep in mind that sometimes customers provide information that is more appropriately a proposed solution; an effective quality effort strive to elicit their real need.

QUALITY'S TIE TO PROJECT MANAGEMENT

The focus for providing quality services or products has evolved over the years from something that is nice to have, to a hard demand by customers for quality products. Customers are becoming more educated in their rights and are holding producers to a higher standard. Global competition has also resulted in a stronger emphasis on quality. A company's position in the global market improves when a company increases quality by meeting customer requirements worldwide. The return on investment comes to the company when the quality equation is appropriately applied and the value of the outcome is greater than the sum of the inputs, thereby reducing overall costs. Quality efforts typically increase overall profitability by making sure the quality costs are less than the cost of delivering a substandard product.

A project is defined as a series of processes by the project management process groups, and it is important to continually improve project processes as the project management plan is executed.[3] A skilled project manager recognizes that for projects to be successful, they must involve a continual improvement effort as part of the project tasks. The project manager develops the project management plan, anticipating problems and developing solutions to achieve the required outcome. This guarantees that activities documented in the project management plan are executed to meet the organization and customer's quality requirements. When planning a project and meeting the project's quality requirements, the project manager must be skilled enough to consider multiple quality aspects:

- The interactions among all project processes provide a focus on quality. The project manager must ensure the upfront analysis is thorough enough to identify any bottlenecks that will negatively impact process interactions during the project effort.
- The degrees of influence result from the conflicting project demands. For instance, will the resources needed on the project be overloaded and not readily available?
- The communication needs to maintain a project's appropriate quality focus. The project manager should define what communication media will be used and the communication frequency required to track quality issues to resolution.

Shortcuts taken during initial project processes lead to negative impact in both project and product quality and drive up the overall cost to the producing organization; for instance, the project initiation activities could be waived, or the project manager is assigned late in the project, or the project manager is never granted the proper authority to do the job.

Cost of quality is a concept that is often overlooked when planning the quality effort in a project. The term *cost of quality* reflects the total price of all efforts to achieve quality in a product or service. The calculations must also take into account the impact from delivering a bad product and any retrofit that may result. Key project decisions that impact the cost of quality come from either striving for zero defects, which entails determining how much it will cost the project to achieve this high level of quality, or striving for "good enough" quality, which may entail costly product recall or warranty claims. A project is temporary; however, the product may have a life of twenty years or more, which means investments in defect prevention should be compared with the life of the product to determine the possibility of an appropriate return on the quality investment. If the customer is dissatisfied as a result of an injury or a financial loss, the risk to future business is immense, and total quality cost is potentially beyond measure for a company with unrealized future sales and negative market growth.

Quality planning requires that the project manager anticipate situations and plan activities that resolve those situations. Including planned quality activities in the project management plan is critical, because any project activity that is not planned typically will not be done. Therefore, it is essential to anticipate quality activities to achieve the defined quality criteria and build them into the plan very early in the process.

The quality management plan is a subset of the overall project management plan, and it addresses quality assurance and quality control as components of the continual process improvement effort within any project.[4] It also includes activities to facilitate improving the overall process by planning activities for analyzing the processes to identify all non–value-added activities and then removing them or modifying them to add value.

Quality assurance is a series of umbrella activities for continual process improvement. Project quality assurance activities are an essential aspect of building in quality rather than trying to test in quality at the end of the development life cycle. Quality assurance continually improves the process of reducing waste, while allowing processes to operate at increased levels of efficiency.

Quality audits of project activities ensure that the project complies with quality policies, processes, and procedures. Correcting the noted deficiencies results in reduced quality costs and increases the likelihood of the customer accepting the product. Quality audits also confirm that implemented change requests, corrective actions, defect repairs, and preventative actions are correct. Process assessment is very similar to quality audits, but identifies inefficiencies in the process. Root-cause analysis is a follow-on activity to both audits and assessments, which analyzes the identified problem, then determines one or more underlying causes, and lastly addresses that problem at an organizational level to prevent future occurrences.

The project manager must have some knowledge of quality control techniques and tools, such as the following[5]:

- *A cause-and-effect diagram* (Ishikawa diagrams or fishbone diagram) is a tool used to show how various factors are linked to identified problems or adverse effects. Figure 12-1 is an example of a cause-and-effect diagram.
- *Control charts* are used to show if a process is stable or has performance that can be predicted. Effectively used control charts illustrate how a process behaves over time. By monitoring and graphing a process's output over time, the chart shows if a process is within acceptable limits over that timeframe. Control charts can be used to monitor plan variances or other outputs to determine if the project management process is in control. Any process found to be outside the defined limits should be targeted for adjustment. Figure 12-2 is an example of such a control chart.
- *Pareto charts* are histograms representing a distribution that is ordered by occurrence frequency. Pareto diagrams are based on Pareto's law, often called the 80/20 principle, which means a low number of causes or issues (approximately 20 percent) produce the majority of the problems.

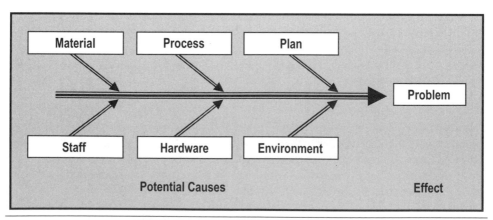

FIGURE 12-1. **A CAUSE-AND-EFFECT DIAGRAM**

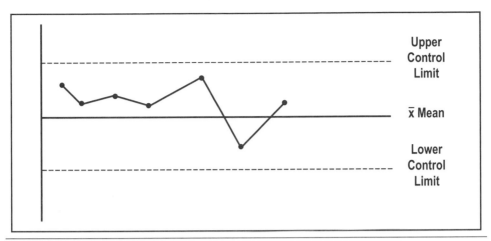

FIGURE 12-2. **A CONTROL CHART OF PROCESS PERFORMANCE**

- *Statistical sampling* entails selecting a limited (e.g., 80 percent) part of the population to test. Appropriate application statistical sampling often reduces the customer's chance of receiving defective parts or output variation.
- *Inspections* examine a project's artifacts to determine conformance to standards and validate defect repairs. The results of an inspection include measurements and can be generated at any level in the process. Inspections are also used to ensure that processes are being followed as documented.

Quality improvement recommendations and audit findings are used to evolve the project process, the project management plan, and other project deliverables. The quality measurements are fed back to the project management processes to reevaluate and analyze project processes. Planned quality activities ensure a high degree of project and product success, which ensures a high return on investment for the effort made by the production organization.

DISCUSSION QUESTIONS

❶ What is the purpose of a quality audit?

❷ Discuss how schedule variances can impact the overall schedule, giving examples from projects you are familiar with.

❸ Can you think of examples where Pareto diagrams and the Pareto theory would be useful in improving the quality of a product? In improving the quality of a process?

REFERENCES

[1] Project Management Institute, *A Guide to the Project Management Body of Knowledge* (*PMBOK*® *Guide*), 5th edition (Newtown Square, PA: PMI, 2013), p. 226.

[2] International Organization for Standardization, *ISO 9000 Quality Management, Standards Compendium,* 5th edition, ISO 8402:1994, Quality management and quality assurance vocabulary.

[3] PMI, 2013, p. 52.

[4] Ibid., p. 228.

[5] G. Gordon Schulmeyer and James I. McManus, Handbook of Software Quality Assurance, 2nd edition (London: International Thomson Computer Press, 1996).

CHAPTER 13

Human Resource Management
The People Side of Projects

HANS J. THAMHAIN, PHD, PMP, BENTLEY UNIVERSITY

Virtually every organization recognizes the importance of people—their attitudes, skills, personal efforts and collaboration. In project environments, where time and resource effectiveness are critical components of performance, this is especially obvious.[1-8] Yet managing people effectively is very difficult. It is especially challenging in today's complex business environment, with many operations distributed across the globe. This requires working with people from different support organizations, vendors, partners, customers, and government agencies; it requires effective networking and cooperation among organizations with different cultures, values and languages.[9-15] Thus, managers today must be capable of dealing effectively with economic, political, social, and regulatory issues, and the associated uncertainties and risks.[16-18]

Many of the issues involved in managing people overlap between functional and project management since the project organization is generally an overlay to the functional organization, which project managers depend on for many of their needed resources. (Note: Although organizational charts are one of the aspects of human resource management covered in the chapter on human resource management in the Project Management Institute's *Guide to the Project Management Body of Knowledge* (*PMBOK® Guide*), we will not discuss types of organization here, as these charts were covered in Chapter 5.)

WHAT DRIVES PROJECT-BASED PERFORMANCE?

Project managers often describe their organizational environments as "unorthodox," with ambiguous authority and responsibility relations. The multidisciplinary settings common to projects create a unique organizational culture with its own norms, values, and work ethics, requiring broader management skill sets and more sophisticated leadership than do traditional business situations. These cultures are more

Activity	Individual or Resource			
	Project Manager	Team Member 1	Team Member 2	Sponsor(s)
Create project management plan	R, A	C	C	C, I
Gather requirements	C, I	R	C	C, I
Approve budget	C	I	I	R
Create marketing plan	C, I	C	R	I

Source: Adapted from Project Management Institute, *A Guide to the Project Management Body of Knowledge (PMBOK® Guide),* 5th edition (Newtown Square, PA: PMI, 2013), p. 262.

TABLE 13-1. **EXAMPLE RACI MATRIX TEMPLATE**

team-oriented regarding decision making, work flow, performance evaluation, and work group management. Authority must often be earned and emerges within the work group as a result of credibility, trust, and respect, rather than organizational status and position. Rewards come to a considerable degree from satisfaction with the work and its surroundings, with recognition of accomplishments as important motivational factors for stimulating enthusiasm, cooperation, and innovation. Tools such as the RACI matrix (Responsible, Accountable, Consult, Inform) help project managers to understand the complex interplay among stakeholders (Table 13-1). Understanding who is responsible and/or accountable for various project tasks, as well as who it is important to consult or inform about project progress, is an important first step for leading project teams and dealing with sponsors and customers.

While overall project performance is determined by a complex array of variables, the importance of teamwork and team management cannot be overstated. This is why the Project Management Institute's (PMI) standard chapter on human resource management describes the major process areas as follows:

- Plan human resources management: identify project roles and responsibilities, as well as the skills needed and the reporting relationships. Tools such as resource calendars, skills database, and competency assessments assist the project manager in this planning.
- Acquire project team: confirm the availability of appropriately skilled individuals, and obtain their commitment. This may involve negotiation skills or interface with procurement processes when outsourced talent is required.
- Develop project team: address competency, interpersonal skills, and building an environment conducive to achievement.
- Manage project team: track team member performance, provide feedback, resolve conflicts, facilitate meetings, and support team members in achieving personal, team, and project success.[19]

Such a "team-centered" management style is based on the thorough understanding of the motivational forces and their interaction with the enterprise environment.

(Note: Team building, conflict resolution, and other related skills are covered in detail in Chapter 39.)

HOW TO MOTIVATE AND INSPIRE

Leaders who succeed in project environments must work with cross-functional groups and gain services from personnel not reporting directly to them. They have to deal with line departments, staff groups, team members, clients, and senior management, each having different cultures, interests, expectations, and charters. Transforming these multidisciplinary groups into cohesive teams is difficult. To get results, these project leaders must relate socially as well as technically, and understand the culture and value system of the organization in which they work. It is no longer possible for managers to get by with only technical expertise or pure administrative skills.

What works best? Observations of best-in-class practices show consistently and measurably three important characteristics of high-performing project teams: (1) team members enjoy work and are excited about the contributions they make to their company and society; (2) they feel confident about their assignment regarding the overall probability of success, their perception of the risks involved, their lack of personal embarrassment and anxiety, and their mutual trust and respect; and (3) they have their professional and personal needs fulfilled.

MOTIVATION AS A FUNCTION OF RISKS AND CHALLENGES

Motivational strength is a function of the probability and desire to achieve the goal. Understanding this fundamental model of human behavior is critical to motivating people on project assignments that are often challenging or less desirable for many reasons. Personal motivation toward reaching a goal changes with the probability of success (perception of doability) and challenge.[20] Figure 13-1 expresses the relationship graphically. A person's motivation is very low if the probability of achieving the goal is very low or zero. As the probability of reaching the goal increases, so does

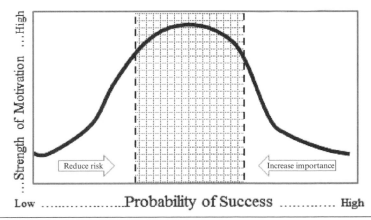

FIGURE 13-1. **RELATIONSHIP BETWEEN PROBABILITY OF SUCCESS AND STRENGTH OF MOTIVATION**

motivational strength. However, this increase continues only up to a level where the goal is still seen as desirable and challenging. When success is more or less assured, motivation often decreases. This is an area where work is often perceived as routine, uninteresting, and holding little potential for professional growth. The challenge is for team leaders to build an image of low risk and high professional interest by showing the team, for example, that the project is well planned, resourced, and supported, and emphasizing the importance of the outcome to the enterprise and society, and the excitement of working on this project and its mission.

HIGH-PERFORMANCE TEAM LEADERSHIP

As organizations have become flatter, leaner, more agile, and self-directed, they share responsibilities, resources, and power to a greater extent. Today's project organizations rely extensively on cross-functional teamwork, including multi-company alliances and complex forms of work integration with member-generated performance norms and work processes. Self-directed team concepts are gradually replacing the traditional, more hierarchically structured organization,[21,22] requiring a radical departure from traditional management practices of top-down, centralized command, control, and communications. To be effective, project managers have to direct their personnel and obtain cross-functional support without much organizationally derived power. They must develop, or "earn," their own bases of influence and build their own power spectrum, which derives from personal knowledge, expertise, and the image of a sound decision maker. The basic concept of *power and authority* has been known for a long time. Four decades ago, French and Raven[23] presented a typology that included five bases of interpersonal power: authority, reward, punishment, expertise, and referent power (i.e., friendship, charisma, empathy), which are summarized in Figure 13-2. To this day, these are still the most commonly recognized influences of managerial power. For some time, the first three bases—authority, reward, and

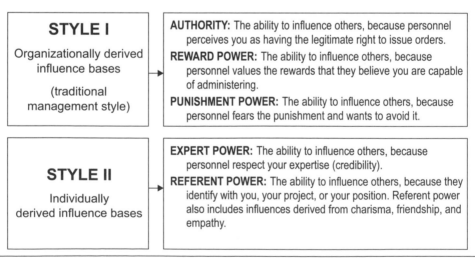

FIGURE 13-2. **COMMON BASES OF MANAGERIAL INFLUENCE**

punishment—were perceived as being derived entirely from the organization. However, more recent studies provide measurable evidence that all bases of power can be individually developed, at least to some degree. (For a fuller discussion of power and politics in project organizations, see Chapter 34.)

Today's organizations grant power to their leaders in many forms. Some of it is still derived from the organizational construct and vested in the leader via organizational position, status, and other traditional components of legitimacy, including the power to mete out rewards and discipline. However, contemporary project managers must *earn* most of their authority and influence bases for managing their multifunctional teams. Since earned authority depends largely on the image of trust, respect, credibility, and competence, it is strongly influenced by the manager's ability to foster a work environment in which the team feels comfortable, accomplishes results, and receives recognition, and the team members have their professional and personal needs met.[24] This includes images of managerial expertise, friendship, work challenge, promotional opportunities, fund allocations, charisma, personal favors, project goal identification, recognition, and visibility of the work and its importance.

Rewards are very important bases of managerial power. They must be used judiciously, consistent with the employee's output, efforts, and contributions, and fair and equitable across the organization. Effectively, employee communication, such as explaining the rationale for any financial award, which is supported with well-earned recognition of the accomplishments, is a good starting point for optimizing the motivational benefits of financial and other types of rewards.

Motivation, and the project manager's ability to influence it, is not necessarily fixed or stable, but changes with the work environment and team dynamics. This situational dependency is graphically shown in Figure 13-3. It shows that intrinsic motivation increases with the manager's emphasis on work challenge, expertise, and ability to provide professional growth opportunities. On the other hand, emphasis on

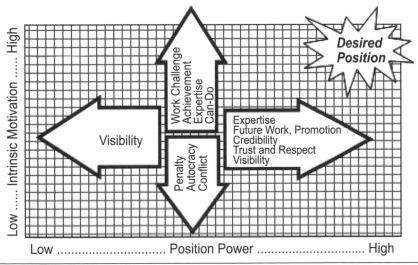

FIGURE 13-3. **HOW ENVIRONMENTAL FACTORS INFLUENCE MOTIVATION**

penalties and authority, and the inability to manage conflict, lowers team members' motivation. Project managers who can foster a climate of high motivation not only obtain greater support from their personnel, but also achieve high overall performance ratings from their superiors.

RECOMMENDATIONS FOR WORKING EFFECTIVELY WITH PEOPLE ON PROJECTS

The following suggestions are valid for any project situation. However, projects of higher complexity require an even stronger focus on the human side of management and more sophisticated leadership. This is particularly true in high-tech environments, where the work culture favors expert power, individual autonomy, and creativity.

1. *Clear task assignment:* At the outset of any new assignment, managers and project leaders should discuss with their staff/team members the overall task and its scope, timing, resources, deliverables, and objectives.

2. *Early project/mission involvement and ownership:* A thorough understanding of the task requirements comes usually with intense personal involvement, which can be stimulated through participation in project planning, requirements analysis, interface definition, or feasibility studies. Involvement of the team members during the early phases of the assignment, such as bid proposals and project planning, can produce great benefits toward plan acceptance, realism, buy-in, personnel matching, and unification of the task team.

3. *Priority image:* Management should clearly articulate the importance of the assignment and its impact on the company and its mission. Senior management can help develop such a "priority image" by their involvement and by effectively communicating key mission parameters. The relationship and contribution of individual work to overall business plans, as well as of individual project objectives and their importance to the organizational mission, must be clear to all personnel.

4. *Team image:* Building a favorable image for an ongoing project and its team, in terms of high priority, interesting work, importance to the organization, high visibility, and potential for professional rewards is crucial for attracting and holding high-quality people. Senior management can help develop a priority image and communicate clear top-down objectives, building an image of high visibility, importance, priority, and interesting work.

5. *Effective project planning and team structure:* Formal planning, using proven tools and techniques, early in the life cycle of a project is critical to any project success. These plans and their methods don't have to be far out, but should be effective in defining the basic team structure and cross-functional linkages for effective project execution. This requires the participation of the entire multidisciplinary team, including support departments, subcontractors, and management.

6. *Professionally stimulating work*: Whenever possible, managers should try to accommodate the professional interests and desires of their personnel. Interesting and challenging work is a perception that can be enhanced by the visibility of the work, management attention and support, priority image, and the overlap of personnel values and perceived benefits with organizational objectives. Making work more interesting leads to increased involvement, better communication, lower conflict, higher commitment, stronger work effort, and higher levels of creativity.

7. *Senior management engagement:* It is critically important that senior management provide the proper environment for a technology team to function effectively. Early in the project life cycle the project manager should negotiate the needed resources with the sponsor organization, and obtain commitment from management that these resources will be available. An effective working relationship among resource managers, project leaders, and senior management critically affects the credibility, visibility, and priority image perceived by the project team.

8. *Clear communication:* Poor communication is a major barrier to teamwork and effective performance. In addition to technology tools, such as voice mail, email, electronic bulletin boards, and conferencing, management can facilitate the free flow of information, both horizontally and vertically, by work space design, regular meetings, reviews, and information sessions. Further, well-defined interfaces, task responsibilities, reporting relations, communication channels, and work transfer protocols can greatly enhance communications within the work team and its interfaces, especially in complex organizational settings.

9. *Leadership positions:* Leadership positions should be carefully defined and staffed for all projects and support functions. Especially critical is the credibility of project leaders among team members, with senior management and with the program sponsor, for the leader's ability to manage multidisciplinary activities effectively across functional lines.

10. *Reward system:* Personnel evaluation and reward systems should be designed to reflect the desired behavior and focus of the people on the team. Rewards should encompass the whole spectrum of intrinsic and extrinsic motivators, and reward both individual and team performance.

11. *Problem resolution:* Project managers should focus their efforts on problem identification and early problem solving. That is, managers and team leaders, through experience, should recognize potential problems and conflicts at their onset, and deal with them before they become big and their resolutions consume a large amount of time and effort.

12. *Personal drive and leadership:* Managers can influence the work environment by their own actions. Concern for the team members, the ability to integrate personal needs of their staff with the goals of the organization, and the ability to create personal enthusiasm for a particular project can foster a climate of high motivation, work involvement, open communication, and ultimately high team performance.

CONCLUSION

Managerial leadership has significant impact on the work environment, affecting project personnel and performance. Other important influences include effective communications among team members and support units across organizational lines, good team spirit, mutual trust and respect, low interpersonal conflict, and opportunities for career development and job security. These conditions serve as a bridging mechanism between personal and organizational goals, helpful in building a unified project team capable of producing integrated results in support of the organization's mission.

Taking a bird's-eye look at the people side of project management, the following three recommendations stand out as particularly important to effective role performance:

1. *Understand motivational needs.* Project managers need to understand the interaction of organizational and behavioral elements in order to build an environment conducive to their personnel's motivational needs. Two conditions seem to be especially critical to high performance: professional interest and work support. However, identifying and satisfying these needs across a complex diversified work group is challenging and requires special techniques and skills. Conventional tools, such as focus groups, action teams, suggestion systems, open-door policies, and management-by-wandering-around, complemented with computer-aided tools, such as PeopleSoft and online surveys, can provide a useful framework for identifying and profiling the needs of various segments of the project team.

2. *Accommodate professional interests, and build enthusiasm and excitement.* Project managers should try to accommodate the professional interests and desires of their personnel when negotiating tasks and during the execution. This leads to employee ownership and commitment, resulting in increased involvement, better communication, lower conflict, stronger work effort, and higher levels of creativity. Equally important, factors that satisfy professional interests and needs strongly effect team unification and overall project performance. While the scope of the work group may be fixed, the manager has the flexibility of allocating task assignments among various members. Well-established practices, such as front-end involvement of team members during the project planning or proposal phase and one-on-one discussions are effective tools for matching team member interests and project needs.

3. *Adapt leadership to the situation.* Because their environment is temporary and often untested, project managers should develop a leadership style that allows them to adapt to the dynamics of their organizations, support departments, customers, and senior management. They must learn to "test" the expectations of others by observation and experimentation. Leading a technology team can rarely be done "top down," but requires a great deal of interactive team management skills and senior management support. Although difficult, managers must be able to alter their leadership style as demanded by the specific work situation and its people. This is particularly important in the increasingly prevalent use of virtual teams, where the ability of the manager to communicate is not facilitated by collocation at a work site. Not only the virtual team member but also the project manager must adjust his or her methods of setting clear expectations, giving feedback, resolving conflict, and sharing information.

DISCUSSION QUESTIONS

❶ How can managers and team leaders "earn" their authority, especially when crossing functional lines and dealing with organizations over which they have no formal authority?

❷ Discuss the characteristics of effective project teams. How could you measure team effectiveness? How can you develop these qualities?

❸ Thinking of the issues involved in working virtually, what are some of the ways the project manager can support and include virtual team members?

REFERENCES

[1] D. Anconda and H. Bresman, *X-Teams: How to Build Teams That Lead, Innovate and Succeed* (Boston, MA: Harvard Business School Publishing Company, 2007).

[2] "The five dysfunctions of a team: A leadership fable," *Academy of Management Perspectives*, 20 (2006), pp. 122–125.

[3] I. Kruglianskas and H. Thamhain, "Managing technology-based projects in multinational environments," *IEEE Transactions on Engineering Management*, 47, No. 1 (2000), pp. 55–64.

[4] A. Nurick and H. Thamhain, "Team Leadership in Global Project Environments," in David I. Cleland (editor), *Global Project Management Handbook* (New York: McGraw-Hill, 2002).

[5] B. Schmid and J. Adams, "Motivation in project management: a project manager's perspective," *Project Management Journal* 39, No. 2 (2008), pp. 60–71.

[6] A. Shenhar, "What great projects have in common," *MIT Sloan Management Review* 52, No. 3 (2008), pp. 19–21.

[7] S. Sidle, "Building a committed workforce: does what employers want depend on culture?" *Academy of Management Perspectives* 23, No. 1 (2009), pp. 79–80.

[8] H. Thamhain, "Critical success factors for managing technology-intensive teams the global enterprise." *Engineering Management Journal* 23, No. 3 (2011), pp. 30–36.

[9] D. Armstrong, "Building teams across borders," *Executive Excellence* 17, No. 3 (2000), pp. 10–11.

[10] H. Barkema, J. Baum, and E. Mannix, "Management challenges in a new time," *Academy of Management Journal* 45, No. 5 (2002), pp. 916–930.

[11] R. Barner, "The new millennium workplace," *Engineering Management Review (IEEE)* 25, No. 3 (1997), pp. 114–119.

[12] A. Bhatnager, "Great teams," *Academy of Management Executive* 13, No. 3 (1999), pp. 50–63.

[13] C. Gray and E. Larson, *Project Management* (New York: Irwin McGraw-Hill, 2000).

[14] A. Shenhar, "What great projects have in common," *MIT Sloan Management Review* 52, No. 3 (2011), pp. 19–21.

[15] H. Thamhain, "Criteria for Effective Leadership in Technology-Oriented Project Teams," in Slevin, Cleland, and Pinto, *The Frontiers of Project Management Research* (Newton Square, PA: Project Management Institute, 2002), pp. 259–270.

[16] R. Keller, "Cross-functional project groups in research and new product development," *Academy of Management Journal* 44, No. 3 (2001), pp. 547–556.

[17] S. Manning, S. Massini, and A. Lewin, "A dynamic perspective on next-generation offshoring: the global sourcing of science and engineering talents," *Academy of Management Perspectives* 22, No. 3 (2008), pp. 35–54.

[18] H. Thamhain, "Managing globally dispersed R&D teams." *International Journal of Information Technology and Management (IJITM)* 8, No. 1 (2009), pp. 107–126.

[19] Project Management Institute, *A Guide to the Project Management Body of Knowledge (PMBOK® Guide),* 5th edition (Newtown Square, PA: PMI, 2013).

[20] M. Hoegl and K. Parboteeah, "Team goal commitment in innovative projects," *International Journal of Innovation Management* 10, No. 3 (2006), pp. 299–324.

[21] D. Cleland and L. Ireland, *Project Management: Strategic Design and Implementation* (New York: McGraw-Hill, 2007).

[22] J. Polzer, C. Crisp, S. Jarvenpaa, and J. Kim, "Extending the fault line model to geographically dispersed teams," *Academy of Management Journal* 49, No. 4 (2006), pp. 679–692.

[23] J. French and B. Raven, "The basis of social power," in D. Cartwright (editor), *Studies in Social Power* (Ann Arbor: Research Center for Group Dynamics, 1959), pp. 150–165.

[24] H. Thamhain, "Team leadership effectiveness in technology-based project environments," *IEEE Engineering Management Review* 36, No. 1 (2008), pp. 165–180.

CHAPTER 14

Project Communication Management

RUTH H. ELSWICK, PMP, PM COLLEGE

Recently an engineer who had successfully managed a very large aerospace project—a multimillion dollar, technically complex project that had expanded to five years and involved hundreds of resources and thousands of activities—told me that the hardest part of managing that project, "far and above anything else" was trying to manage the communication. He said, "I felt like a traffic cop in the middle of all the stakeholders trying to direct the flow of all the information."

This project manager's experience sums up what most project managers feel as they try to manage communications on a project. Often there is pressure to shortcut the planning process and jump right into the project. In reality, the time spent in planning how communication will be handled can be invaluable in helping the project manager better manage and control the entire project environment. Communication has been identified as one of the biggest reasons for success or failure on a project. To ensure communications success, project managers should do the following:

- Establish (and maintain) the support of those involved, including project sponsors, team members, and those who will use the project deliverables.
- Educate decision makers on the "whats" and "whys" of the project.
- Inform the ultimate beneficiaries and others who will be affected by the project, and prepare them for what to expect.

In addition to the effect on those closest to the project, other impacts include the following:

- Any phase of project implementation (testing, for example) may involve some change or even disruption in regular services to some or all users. These impacts need to be communicated in advance.
- Implementation also may involve changes in local procedures, new training for users, and other effects. All possible impacts need to be communicated in a timely manner.

It is important to understand that like any other part of project management, effective communication is a process. Like any process, it is impossible to extract those items that are convenient and forget those parts of the process that are inconvenient. The Project Management Institute (PMI) defines three processes of communications management:

- *Plan communications management* based on the results of the stakeholder analysis. Particular attention here is placed on the key stakeholders as they are the ones that need to be managed closely and have the most frequent interactions.
- *Manage communications* by executing all of the elements of the communications plan.
- *Control communications* by monitoring the communications plan and its effectiveness in meeting stakeholder needs.[1]

To effectively plan for communication, it is necessary to have several elements already in place. The primary tool to be used is the stakeholder register, which, at a minimum, identifies every stakeholder along with their role in the project, their expectations, their potential influence on the project, and their interest in the project. It is helpful, as well, to include some the strategies for managing the stakeholders. All of this helps the project manager to better determine what is the best method, or methods, of communicating with the individual stakeholders. This information is included as part of the communications requirements matrix or communication plan (Table 14-1).

It is important, at a minimum, to include the following elements as part of the communication plan:

- *Audience:* Who is the audience for each communication? Check the project charter, scope statement, work breakdown structure (WBS), and other project documents to determine audiences.
- *Message:* What message should go out to the audience? Elements include the following: What does the project need to communicate to its audiences? Who is authoring or sponsoring the message? How will it take place and in what steps or increments? What does the recipient need to do and by what date?
- *Intent:* Why is this communication taking place? What is the intended effect? What do we hope to achieve? What are the benefits?
- *Media:* How to communicate depends on the phase of the project, the audience, and other factors. It generally takes face-to-face communication to achieve buy-in, gain support, and motivate someone to action. At other times, you can use hardcopy print and electronic media, or combinations of media.
- *When:* Consider the scope statement, the evolving project plan, and the advice of project leaders and key stakeholders to determine a communication approach and timing.
- *Frequency:* How often does the communication need to occur?
- *Responsibilities:* For each message in the communication plan, ask the following questions: Who will prepare the message, develop the media, and coordinate the delivery? Who will author or sign the communications? Who is sending the message?

PROJECT COMMUNICATIONS PLAN TEMPLATE

Attachments to each communication should include:

■ List of recipients
■ Message text

■ Media requirements
■ Delivery schedule and who delivers

AUDIENCE	MESSAGE (WHAT)	INTENT (WHY)	MEDIA (HOW)	WHEN	RESPONSIBILITIES

TABLE 14-1. **EXAMPLE OF A COMMUNICATIONS PLAN TEMPLATE**

In this day of virtual teams, communication can be particularly challenging. There are several considerations when developing the communication plan:

- Urgency of the information (will it cause us to fail?): If we are relying on technology, how reliable is it? Time zones can make a difference here; if the information is urgent, will there be a delay in the recipient receiving the information?
- Availability of technology (access?): Countries vary in their technological compatibility, different availability of media, and accessibility. Do you have backup if one method fails?
- Expected project staffing (training necessary?): Project stakeholders, including team members, have different skill levels in various software programs. If training is required, it could have an impact on the cost of the project as well as potentially delaying the schedule.
- Duration of project (how long is the project?): Communication for a project that lasts one week will be different from one that lasts seven years.

Other issues to think through might be the project environment itself—is it virtual or face to face? Confidentiality of information could have a huge impact on the media that will be used for communications.

One important aspect of communication is to determine the best method to use. These methods are defined by PMI as follows:

Interactive communication is the most efficient and preferred method. It ensures that the receiver is providing feedback to the sender. We typically think of interactive communication as one-on-one meetings, phone calls, instant messages, and so on.

Push communication is where information is sent to the receiver with no pressing need to receive feedback. Typically push communication is reports, emails, voice mails, and even blogs.

Pull communication is used for large amounts of information where feedback is not required. Receivers access the information, usually from a database or project workbook, as they need it. We typically think of pull communication as a data site such as Sharepoint or other Internet or Intranet sites.[2]

No discussion of communication planning would be complete without a description of a communication model. There are as many models available as there are people thinking them up. The most common, and simplest, model is found in Figure 14-1. As shown in the figure:

- The sender is the originator of the message.
- Encoding is the act that begins the communication process.
- The receiver is the one who receives the message.
- Decoding is the process of understanding the message.
- Noise is interference with the decoding of messages, and it can be literal noise, distractions, cultural factors that cause misunderstanding, or aspects of the receiver's immediate environment that make listening difficult.
- The medium can be email, telephone, written documents, or even face-to-face communication.

Feedback is crucial, as it closes the communication loop by ensuring that the message sent was interpreted correctly by the receiver. We must never forget that,

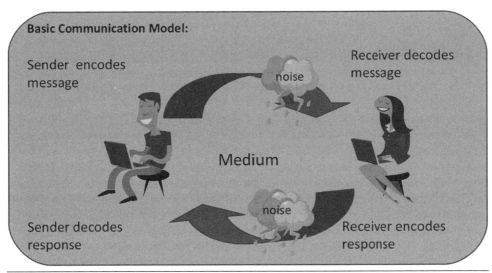

FIGURE 14-1. **A BASIC COMMUNICATION MODEL**

unless our messages have been received and understood, we cannot really be said to have communicated.[3]

The advantage of having knowledge of the communication model is that it describes how communication takes place between stakeholders. Distortions, ambiguities, and inconsistencies all increase uncertainty and dissatisfaction. An awareness of the circular nature of potential distortion that could occur within a team may well prevent miscommunication, particularly where team members are from different parts of the world. Differences in language may cause noise that may impact the medium that is used, which, in turn, could have an impact on who the sender should be.

An important aspect to consider when discussing written communication is the use of email. The effective project manager will discuss email etiquette at the beginning of the project, typically as part of the team charter. Suggested topics of discussion could include the following:

Include a subject and get to the point: Try to state your point within the first sentence or two. Be sure to denote within the first few sentences whether action is needed. Not many people enjoy playing the game "What's your secret?" when it comes to email topics.

Be careful of your "tone": It is very difficult to describe tone in writing, but it is easily interpreted in the negative. It is important that the sender come across as approachable and professional, yet friendly. Avoid using all capitals, exclamation points, or other punctuation that could be interpreted negatively. Also avoid abbreviations and, as tempting as it may be, don't use those little smiley face emoticons!

Take advantage of the Spell Check: Poor grammar or misspellings are a turn-off and give the impression that you don't care. That said, never completely rely on the Spell Check to find your mistakes; many a "project manger his loved" to regret this!

Don't send the email prematurely: Wait to complete the "Send To" and "Copy To" fields. This is particularly true if you are concerned about your tone or professionalism in the email. Sometimes even the writing of the email allows you to more objectively think about what you are saying.

Send it as "urgent" only if it really is: Have your team determine what will be considered an "urgent" message.

The discussion so far has dealt with the two primary types of communication: written and verbal. But it is also important to note a third type of communication: body language. Body language is technically known as kinesics, and it is a significant aspect of modern communications and relationships. It is safe to say that body language represents a very significant proportion of meaning that is conveyed and interpreted between people. Many experts in kinesiology agree that between 50 and 80 percent of all human communications are nonverbal. So while body language statistics vary according to situation, it is generally accepted that nonverbal communications are very important in how we understand each other (or fail to), especially in face-to-face and one-on-one communications, and most definitely when the communications involve an emotional or attitudinal element.

Body language is a crucial factor when meeting someone for the first time. It takes only a few seconds for a person to form an opinion based on a first meeting. This initial instinctual assessment is based far more on what we see and feel about the other person than on the words he or she speaks. On many occasions we form a strong view about a new person before we hear a single word. This is also true in reverse—others form their opinion of us based on body language.

Although the interpretation of body language certainly can't be a part of a communication plan, the effective project manager needs to be aware of body language when communicating with key stakeholders, including the project team. Here are some general rules for interpreting body language:

▶ When translating body language, keep in mind that one signal does not necessarily indicate a meaning. It is often said that if people cross their arms during a discussion, it means that they are shutting you out. However, it is just the opposite for some people, who cross their arms when they are intently listening. Crossing of the arms combined with looking down and sitting back in the chair is more of an indication that a person is no longer listening to you.

▶ Cultural differences influence body language signals and their interpretation. The general interpretation of guidelines is usually based on Western or North European behaviors. What may be the norm in one culture can mean something entirely different in another culture. As an example, I was teaching a course in Japan a few years ago. In the middle of an intense explanation, two of the class participants sat back in their chairs, crossed their arms, and closed their eyes. I thought that I had gotten a little boring, so I stepped up my intensity. More participants sat back, crossed their arms, and closed their eyes. At the next break I told my host that I was boring them to death. He burst out laughing. "No," he said, "in our culture when they close their eyes they are listening carefully!"

▶ In a multicultural environment, refrain from using colloquial hand gestures. Hand gestures mean different things in different cultures, so to avoid an embarrassing situation, use restraint when gesturing. Also be careful of slouching, resting your foot on your leg, and other casual postures, as these, too, can be misinterpreted. (More tips on cross-cultural communication on projects can be found in Chapter 39.)

It is important to remember that perfect communication is impossible. But taking the time to plan up front will go a long way in improving communication. The communication process, as defined by PMI, represents an effective way of giving and receiving information within the project environment. Choosing the correct communication, being knowledgeable of different ways to communicate, being an effective sender, and providing effective feedback as a receiver makes for more effective communication.

DISCUSSION QUESTIONS

❶ What are the three types of communication, and when would each be used?

❷ What type of meeting would be used to exchange and analyze information about project performance and progress? What should you *not* do in this meeting?

❸ What is the purpose of providing feedback, and why is it crucial in communications?

REFERENCES

[1] Project Management Institute, *A Guide to the Project Management Body of Knowledge* (*PMBOK® Guide*), 5th edition (Newtown Square, PA: PMI, 2013).

[2] PMI, 2013, pp. 294–295.

[3] Patrick J. Montana and Bruce H. Charnov, *Management—Classical Management Theory, Organizational Structure, Human Resource Management, Work Group Dynamics,* 4th edition (Hauppauge, NY: Barron's Educational Series, 2008), pp. 325 and 333.

CHAPTER 15

Project Risk Management in Practice

DAVID HILLSON, PHD, PMP, PMI FELLOW, HONFAPM, FIRM, FRSA, RISK DOCTOR & PARTNERS

The word *risk* is a widely used part of our daily vocabulary, relating to personal circumstances (such as health, pensions, insurance, and investments), society (such as terrorism, economic performance, and food safety), and business (such as corporate governance, strategy, and business continuity). One area where risk management has found particular prominence is in the management of projects, perhaps because of the risky nature of projects themselves.[1] All projects, in varying degrees, are characterized by the following:

- Uniqueness
- Complexity
- Change
- Assumptions
- Constraints
- Dependencies
- . . . and People

Each of these factors introduces significant risk into every project, requiring a structured and proactive approach to the management of risk if the project is to succeed.

Many see risk management as a key contributor to the success of projects and businesses. This arises from the clear link between risk and objectives, embodied in the definition of the word. For example, the Project Management Institute's *Guide to the Project Management Body of Knowledge* (*PMBOK® Guide*), Fifth Edition states, "Project risk is an uncertain event or condition that, if it occurs, has a positive or negative effect on one or more project objectives."[2] Other international standards and guidelines[3–10] use similar definitions, always linking risk with objectives, particularly the International Organization for Standardization's ISO 31000:2009, where the definition of risk is "effect of uncertainty on objectives."[5]

This is why risk management is so important and not just another project management technique. Risk management aims to identify those uncertainties that have the potential to harm the project, assess them so that they are understood, and develop and implement actions to stop them from occurring or minimize their impact on achievement of objectives. Risk management also has the goal of identifying, assessing, and responding to uncertainties that could help achieve objectives. Because it focuses attention on the uncertainties that matter, either negatively or positively, risk management is a critical factor for project (and business) success. Where risk management is ineffective, a project can only succeed if the project team is lucky. Effective risk management optimizes the chances of success, even in the face of bad luck.

Fortunately, risk management is not difficult. The process, tools and techniques outlined in the *PMBOK® Guide* and similar guides offer a straightforward way of implementing an effective approach to managing risk on projects.

DEFINITION OF RISK

Before describing the risk management process, it is important to understand what we are trying to manage. The PMI definition of risk quoted above 2 includes one distinct type of uncertainty—that which, if it occurs, will have a negative effect on a project objective. But the standard also acknowledges that there are risks that create the possibility of a positive outcome. In other words, *risk includes both threat and opportunity*. At first this causes some hesitation for people new to the concept. They might say, "Surely everyone knows that risk is bad! Risk is the same as threat, but isn't opportunity something different?"

In adopting an inclusive mindset about risk, the Project Management Institute (PMI) is not unusual, and it is completely consistent with the current trend in international best-practice risk management. Many other leading standards and guidelines from project management organizations worldwide take a similar position,[3–10] including ISO 31000:2009, which comments that "deviation from objectives can be positive and/or negative."[5]

Taking this position has significant implications for all aspects of risk management, including thinking, language, and process.[11] That is why, as the body of knowledge documents have evolved, they have come to include a wider definition of risk. For example, in the *PMBOK® Guide,* Fifth Edition, both threat and opportunity are treated equitably, and the objectives of risk management are stated as "to increase the likelihood and impact of positive events, and decrease the likelihood and impact of negative events in the project."[12] The aim is to use the same risk process to handle both threats and opportunities alongside each other, giving double benefits from a single investment.

There has been one other important development in the way risk is defined for projects: the recognition that there are two distinct levels of risk in every project. This is best illustrated by asking the question "How risky is this project?" The risk register lists all identified risks, prioritized for attention and action, with responses and owners allocated to each risk. But a list of risks cannot answer the "How risky" question. A different concept is needed to describe the overall risk exposure of a project, which is different from the individual risks that need to be managed.

PMI has addressed this in the Practice Standard for Project Risk Management, which has two distinct definitions of risk.[8] The first is individual risk, which is defined as "an uncertain event or condition that, if it occurs, has a positive or negative effect on a project's objectives." The second is overall project risk, which is defined as "the effect of uncertainty on the project as a whole." The United Kingdom's Association for Project Management (APM) also has two similar definitions of risk in its *Body of Knowledge*.[13]

This dual concept of risk is important and useful when considering how to manage risk in projects. At one level the project manager is responsible for identifying, assessing, and managing the individual risks that are recorded in the risk register. At another higher level, the project manager is also required to account to the project sponsor, the project owner, and other stakeholders for the overall risk of the project. These two levels might be distinguished as the risks in the project and the risk of the project.

Managing risk requires action at both of these levels. But the typical project risk management process addresses only the lower level of individual risks within the project, which are recorded in the risk register. It is far less common to consider the overall risk exposure of the project as a whole, or to have any structured approach to managing risk at that higher level.

So how can overall project risk be identified, assessed, and managed? The first place to address overall project risk is during the pre-project or concept phase, when the scope and objectives of the project are being clarified and agreed upon. Here the project sponsor or owner defines the benefits that the project is expected to deliver, together with the degree of risk that can be tolerated within the overall project. Each decision about the risk–reward balance involves an assessment of overall project risk, representing the inherent risk associated with a particular project scope and its expected benefits. At this level, overall project risk is managed implicitly through the decisions made about the scope, structure, content, and context of the project.

Once these decisions have been made and the project is initiated, then the traditional project risk management process can be used to address explicitly the individual risks that lie within the project. At key points within the project it will be necessary to revisit the assessment of overall project risk to ensure that the defined risk thresholds have not been breached, before returning to the ongoing task of managing individual risks within the project.

So two levels of risk management are important for projects:

- Implicit risk management, which addresses overall project risk through decisions made about the scope, structure, context, and content of the project
- Explicit risk management, which deals with individual project risks through the standard risk management process to identify, analyze, respond to, and control risks

Both types of risk need to be understood and managed in order to answer the question "How risky is this project?"

PROCESS SUMMARY

Risk management is not rocket science, and the risk process simply represents structured common sense. The steps in the process follow a natural way of thinking about the uncertain future, by asking and attempting to answer the following questions:

- What are we trying to achieve? (Planning)
- What uncertainties could affect us, for better or worse? (Identification)
- Which are the most important uncertainties to address? (Analysis)
- What could we do to tackle these uncertainties, and what will we do? (Response planning)
- Let's do it—and how do things change as a result? (Monitoring and control)

These questions are reflected in the typical risk management process embodied in the various risk standards and guideline. For example, the risk management process outlined in both the PMI *PMBOK® Guide*[2] and the PMI Practice Standard for Project Risk Management[8] includes the following six processes, which clearly map to the questions above:

- Plan risk management—deciding how to conduct risk management activities for a project
- Identify risks—determining which risks might affect the project
- Perform qualitative risk analysis—prioritizing risks for subsequent further analysis or action
- Perform quantitative risk analysis—numerically analyzing the effect on overall project objectives of identified risks
- Plan risk responses—developing options and actions to enhance opportunities and to reduce threats to project objectives
- Control risks—tracking identified risks, monitoring residual risks, identifying new risks, executing risk response plans, and evaluating effectiveness

Various tools and techniques can be used to assist with each step, and they can be implemented at differing levels of detail on different projects. Successful risk management, however, requires only structured thinking and action, following a commonsense process in the face of uncertainty.

Plan Risk Management

The first step of the risk management process is *not* risk identification. Because risk is defined in terms of objectives, it is necessary first to define those objectives that are at risk, that is, the scope of the risk process. The *PMBOK® Guide*[2] describes this as "the process of deciding how to conduct the risk management activities for a project."

This statement indicates that risk management is not "one-size-fits-all." It is necessary to scale the risk process to meet the risk challenge of each particular project. Projects that are risky or strategically important require a more robust approach to risk management than do those that are simple or routine. Scalable aspects include methodology, tools and techniques, organization and staffing, reporting requirements, and the update and review cycle.

A number of other factors need to be decided before embarking on the risk management process:

- Setting the thresholds of how much risk is acceptable for the project by identifying the risk tolerances of key stakeholders, resolving any differences, and communicating the conclusions to the project team.
- Defining terms for qualitative analysis of probability and impact on the project, related to specific project objectives. Where terms such as *high, medium,* and *low* are used, their meanings must be agreed on to provide a consistent framework for assessment of identified risks.
- Defining potential sources of risk to the project. This may be presented as a hierarchical risk breakdown structure (RBS), perhaps drawing on an industry standard or an organization template. An example RBS is given in Figure 15-1.

The decisions made during this step of the process are documented in a risk management plan, which forms an integral part of the project management plan. The risk management plan should be reviewed during the project and updated where necessary if the risk process is modified.

Identify Risks

Because it is not possible to manage a risk that has not first been identified, some view this initial step as the most important in the risk process. Many good techniques are available for risk identification, the most common of which include the following:

- Use of brainstorming in a workshop setting, perhaps structured into a SWOT analysis to identify organizational strengths/weaknesses and project opportunities/threats
- Checklists or prompt lists to capture learning from previous risk assessments
- Detailed analysis of project assumptions and constraints to expose those that are most risky
- Interviews with key project stakeholders to gain their perspective on possible risks facing the project
- Review of completed similar projects to identify common risks and effective responses

For each of these techniques, it is important to involve the right people with the necessary perspective and experience to identify risks facing the project. In addition, use a combination of risk identification techniques rather than relying on just one approach—for example, using a creative group technique, such as brainstorming, together with a checklist based on past similar projects. The project manager should select appropriate techniques based on the risk challenge faced by the project, as defined in the risk management plan.

It is also important to consider risks arising from a broad range of potential sources, and the RBS provides a useful framework to ensure that no key areas are overlooked.

Another good idea is to consider immediate "candidate" responses during the risk identification phase. Sometimes an appropriate response becomes clear as soon as the risk is identified, and in such cases it might be advisable to tackle the

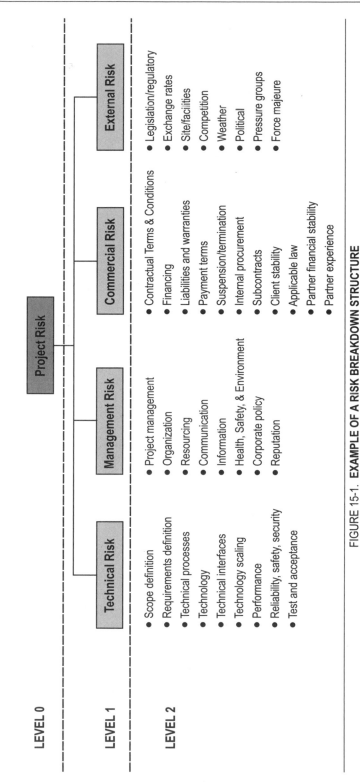

FIGURE 15-1. **EXAMPLE OF A RISK BREAKDOWN STRUCTURE**

risk immediately if possible, as long as the proposed response is cost effective and feasible.

Whichever technique is used, it is important to remember that the aim of risk identification is to identify risks. While this may sound self-evident, in fact this step in the risk management process often exposes things that are not risks, including problems, issues, or constraints. The most common mistake is to identify causes of risks or the effects of risks, and to confuse these with risks.[14]

▶ *Causes* are definite events or sets of circumstances that exist in the project or its environment, and that give rise to uncertainty. Examples include the requirement to implement the project in a developing country, the need to use an unproven new technology, the lack of skilled personnel, or the fact that the organization has never done a similar project before. Causes themselves are not uncertain because they are facts or requirements, so they are not the main focus of the risk management process. However, tackling a cause can avoid or mitigate a threat or allow an opportunity to be exploited.

▶ *Risks* are uncertainties that, if they occur, would affect the project objectives either negatively (threats) or positively (opportunities). Examples include the possibilities that planned productivity targets might not be met, that interest or exchange rates might fluctuate significantly, that client expectations may be misunderstood, or that a contractor might deliver earlier than planned. These uncertainties should be managed proactively through the risk management process.

▶ *Effects* are unplanned variations from project objectives, either positive or negative, which would arise as a result of risks occurring. Examples include being early for a milestone, exceeding the authorized budget, or failing to meet contractually agreed performance targets. Effects are contingent events, unplanned potential future variations that will not occur unless risks happen. As effects do not yet exist, and indeed they may never exist, they cannot be managed directly through the risk management process.

Including causes or effects in the list of identified risks can obscure genuine risks, which may not then receive the appropriate degree of attention they warrant. One way to clearly separate risks from their causes and effects is to use *risk meta-language* (a formal description with required elements) to provide a three-part structured risk statement, as follows: "As a result of [*definite cause*], [*uncertain event*] may occur, which would lead to [*effect on objective(s)*]." Examples include the following:

- "*As a result of using novel hardware* [a definite requirement], *unexpected system integration errors may occur* [an uncertain risk] *that would lead to overspend on the project* [an effect on the budget objective]."
- "*Because our organization has never done a project like this before* [fact = cause], *we might misunderstand the customer's requirement* [uncertainty = risk], *and our solution would not meet the performance criteria* [contingent possibility = effect on objective]."
- "*We have to outsource production* [cause]; *we may be able to learn new practices from our selected partner* [risk], *leading to increased productivity and profitability* [effect]."

The use of risk meta-language should ensure that risk identification actually identifies risks, distinct from causes or effects. Without this discipline, risk identification can produce a mixed list containing risks and non-risks, leading to confusion and distraction later in the risk process.

Finally, the risk identification step of the risk process is where the risk register is launched, to document identified risks and their characteristics. Where software tools are used to support the risk process, these usually offer a risk register format, though some organizations develop their own. The risk register is updated following each of the subsequent steps in the risk process, to capture and communicate risk information and allow appropriate analysis and action to be undertaken.

Perform Qualitative Risk Analysis

Risk identification usually produces a long list of risks, perhaps categorized in various ways. However, all risks cannot be addressed with the same degree of attention because of limitations of time and resources. And not all risks warrant the same level of attention. Therefore, risks should be prioritized for further attention to identify the worst threats and best opportunities, which is the purpose of the qualitative risk analysis phase.

Risk, as we are defining it, two dimensions: uncertainty and its potential effect on objectives. The word *probability* is usually used to describe the uncertainty dimension (although we might use *likelihood* or *frequency*), and *impact* (or *consequence* or *effect*) is used to describe the effect on objectives. For qualitative analysis, these two dimensions are assessed as being high, medium, or low, as defined in the risk management plan. The probability of each risk occurring is assessed, as well as its potential impact if it were to occur. Impact is assessed against each project objective, usually including time and cost, and possibly other factors such as performance, quality, and regulatory compliance. For threats, impacts are negative (such as lost time and extra cost), but opportunities have positive impacts (such as saved time and reduced cost).

The two-dimensional assessment is used to plot each risk onto a probability-impact matrix, with high, medium, and low priority zones. It is common to use a double mirror matrix, to allow threats and opportunities to be prioritized separately, and creating a central zone of focus (Figure 15-2). This zone contains the worst threats (with high probability so they are likely to happen unless managed, and high impact so they would be very bad for the project) and the best opportunities (where high probability makes them easy to capture, and high impact means it is very good).

Another important output from qualitative analysis is the pattern of risk on the project, and it is important to understand whether there are common causes of risk or hotspots of exposure. This can be assessed by mapping risks into the RBS to determine whether any particular causes give rise to large numbers of risks, and by mapping risks into the work breakdown structure (WBS) to identify areas of the project potentially affected by many risks.

Perform Quantitative Risk Analysis

On most projects, risks do not happen one at a time or independently of each other. Instead, they interact in groups, with some risks causing others to be more likely and

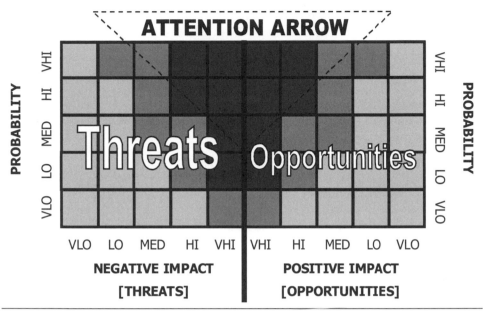

FIGURE 15-2. **MIRROR PROBABILITY-IMPACT MATRIX FOR THREATS AND OPPORTUNITIES**

some risks making others impossible. Qualitative risk analysis considers risks individually and allows development of a good understanding of each one. It is, however, sometimes necessary to analyze the combined effect of risks on project outcomes, particularly in terms of how they might affect overall time and cost. This requires a quantitative model, and various techniques are available, including sensitivity analysis, decision trees, and Monte Carlo simulation.

Monte Carlo is the most popular quantitative risk analysis technique because it uses simple statistics, takes project plans as its starting point, and is supported by many good software tools. However, decision trees can also be useful for analyzing key strategic decisions or major option points.

One often overlooked key aspect of quantitative risk analysis models is the need to include both threats and opportunities. If only threats are considered, then the analysis is only modeling the potential downside, and the result will always be pessimistic. Because the risk process aims to tackle threats and opportunities, both must be included in any analysis of the effect of risk on the project. Indeed, some vital elements of the risk model, such as three-point estimates, cannot be properly determined without considering both the upside (to produce the minimum/optimistic/best-case estimate) as well as the downside (to produce the maximum/pessimistic/worst-case estimate).

When developing Monte Carlo risk models, it is often too easy to use available software tools to create simple and simplistic models that do not reflect the complexities of the risks facing the project. In particular, simply taking single values of duration or cost in a project plan or cost estimate and replacing them with three-point estimates is not sufficient to model risk quantitatively. Other modeling techniques should be used to reflect reality, including the following:

- Different input data distributions, not just the typical three-point estimate (for example, the modified triangular, uniform, spike/discrete, or various curves)
- Use of stochastic branches to model alternative logic (these can also be used to model key risks)
- Correlation (also called dependency) between various elements of the model, to reduce statistical variability

It is important to recognize that additional investment is required to implement quantitative risk analysis, including software tools, associated training, and the time and effort required to generate input data, run the model, and interpret the outputs. As a result, in many cases the use of quantitative techniques may not always be justified. Often, information can be obtained from qualitative analysis to allow effective management of risks, and quantitative analysis techniques can be seen as optional. Quantitative analysis is most useful when projects are particularly complex or risky, or when quantitative decisions must be made, for example, concerning bid price, contingency, milestones, and delivery dates.

Three potential shortfalls should be mentioned when considering quantitative risk analysis techniques. First, the data should be of sufficient quality to avoid the GIGO (garbage in–garbage out) situation, ensuring good quality inputs to the model. Second, outputs from risk models always need to be interpreted, and quantitative analysis will not tell the project manager what decision to make. Third, be prepared to use the results of risk modeling and to make decisions based on the analysis. We should beware of "analysis paralysis," because quantitative risk analysis is merely a means to an end and must lead to action.

Plan Risk Responses

Having identified and analyzed risks, it is essential that something be done in response. As a result, many believe that the risk response planning phase is the most important in the risk process, since this is where the project team has an opportunity to make a difference to the risk exposure facing the project.

When introducing tools and techniques for risk response planning, the *PMBOK®Guide* uses an important word, stating the following: "Several risk response *strategies* are available" [italics mine]. It is important to adopt a *strategic* approach to developing risk responses to focus attention on what is being attempted. Too often, project teams resort to a scattershot approach, trying a wide range of different responses to a given risk, some of which may be counterproductive. It is better first to select an appropriate strategy for a particular risk, and then to design actions to implement that strategy, producing a more focused "rifle shot" aimed at managing the risk effectively.

The double-sided nature of risk means that it is vital to have strategies for addressing opportunities along with threat-focused strategies. The opportunity strategies match the common threat strategies, creating three pairs of proactive response strategies, and a final last-resort strategy:

- *Avoid/Exploit:* For threats, the aim of avoidance is to eliminate the uncertainty, making the threat impossible or irrelevant. To exploit an opportunity means to make it definitely happen, ensuring that the project gains the additional benefits.
- *Transfer/Share:* These strategies require involving another person or party in managing the risk. For threats, the pain is transferred, together with the responsibility for managing the potential downside. In a similar way the potential gain from an upside risk can be shared, in return for the other party taking responsibility for managing the opportunity.
- *Mitigate/Enhance:* Mitigation of a threat aims to reduce its probability or impact, while enhancing an opportunity seeks to increase it.
- *Accept:* For residual threats and opportunities where proactive action is not possible or not cost-effective, acceptance is the last resort, taking the risk either without special action or with contingency.

Having chosen a strategy, the project team should then develop specific actions to put the strategy into practice. This is the point at which most risk management processes fail. Whichever response strategy is selected, it is vital to go from options to actions; otherwise nothing changes. Many project teams, however, identify and analyze risks, develop response plans, write a risk report, and then "file and forget." Actions are not implemented, and the risk exposure remains the same.

The key to making sure risk responses are implemented is not to allow risk responses to be seen as "extra work" to be done when project tasks are complete. Risk responses are genuine project tasks, that is, work to be done for the project to succeed. Therefore, they should be treated like any other project task. Each risk response should be fully defined, with a duration, budget, resource requirement, owner, and completion criteria. A new task should then be added to the project plan for each agreed risk response, and these should be completed, reviewed, and reported on like all other project tasks.

Control Risks

The purpose of this final phase of the risk process is to ensure that the planned responses are achieving what was expected and to develop new responses where necessary. It is also important to determine whether new risks have arisen on the project and to assess the overall effectiveness of the risk management process. These aims are best achieved through a risk review meeting, although it is possible on smaller projects to review risk as part of a regular project progress meeting.

This step also involves producing risk reports at various levels and for different stakeholders. It is important to communicate the results of the risk process, since the aim is to actively manage the risks, and this is likely to require action by stakeholders outside the immediate project team. Risk reports should form a basis for action and include clear conclusions ("What we have found") and recommendations ("What should be done").

Risk management is a cyclic iterative process and should never be done just once on a project. Risk exposure changes daily, as a result of external events, as well as from the actions (and inactions) of the project team and others elsewhere in the organization. To optimize the chances of meeting the project's objectives, it is essential that the project team have a current view of the risks facing the project, including both threats and opportunities. For risk management, standing still is going backward.

OTHER ISSUES

The risk process outlined in standards and guidelines such as the *PMBOK® Guide*[2–10] forms a good basis on which to build effective management of project risk. However, the following issues also must be considered if risk management is to be fully effective. First, all risk management is done by people. This introduces the human factor into the picture, requiring proactive management like any other aspect of the risk process. The risk attitudes of both individuals and groups exercise a major influence over the risk process, which must be recognized and managed. The situation is complicated by the action of subconscious perceptual factors, biases, and heuristics that affect the risk attitudes adopted by people, operating at both individual and group levels.[15–16]

Second, organizational culture has a significant influence over the effectiveness of the risk management process. Where senior management does not recognize the existence of risk, or sees risk identification as a sign of weakness, or views resources allocated to contingency or risk responses as wasted, risk management will be an uphill struggle. Conversely, the organization that knows how to take risk intelligently will reap the benefits from minimizing threats and capturing opportunities.

Third, there is a need for internal sponsorship of the risk process. A risk champion within an organization can promote buy-in for its use at all levels, encouraging project teams and senior management to recognize risk and manage it proactively, sharing best practice and developing corporate experience. This is one of the accepted success factors for risk management and should not be neglected.

Fourth, the need for an efficient infrastructure to support the risk process must also be recognized. Software tools, training, templates, and specialized resources all have a part to play in making risk management effective. The organization must be prepared to invest in risk infrastructure, and ensure that it is well integrated with project management and other parts of the business.

By considering the above factors in addition to the risk process, the team and the organization develop risk maturity. This represents a position where all the necessary pieces are in place to allow risk to be managed proactively and effectively, with a supportive culture, efficient processes, experienced people, and consistent application. When these elements are present, together with the tools and techniques described above, risk need not be feared on any project. Instead, it should be welcomed as an opportunity to address the uncertainties inherent in all projects, optimizing the chances of achieving project objectives and delivering successful projects.

Not only is risk management essential, it is also not difficult. A simple structured process exists to identify, analyze, and respond to risks, and this can be applied to any project whether it is simple or complex, innovative or routine. The benefits of adopting a structured approach to managing risk are obvious: more successful projects, fewer surprises, less waste, improved team motivation, enhanced professionalism and reputation, increased efficiency and effectiveness, and so on. With these benefits available from adopting such a simple process, risk management deserves its place as one of the most important elements of project management.

American Management Association • www.amanet.org

DISCUSSION QUESTIONS

❶ Define project risk, and explain the relationship among uncertainty, risk, threat, and opportunity.

❷ What are the differences between a cause, a risk, and an effect? Use risk meta-language to describe a situation on a project you are familiar with. Does this help you distinguish between them?

❸ Name the basic risk response strategies for threats and opportunities, and give an example of each.

REFERENCES

[1] David A. Hillson, *Managing Risk in Projects* (Farnham, UK: Gower, 2009).

[2] Project Management Institute, *A Guide to the Project Management Body of Knowledge,* 5th edition (Newtown Square, PA: Project Management Institute, 2013), pp. 310 and 558.

[3] Association for Project Management, *Project Risk Analysis & Management (PRAM) Guide,* 2nd edition (High Wycombe, Bucks UK: APM Publishing, 2004).

[4] British Standards Institute, British Standard BS 31100:2011 "Risk Management—Code of Practice and Guidance for the Implementation of BS ISO 31000" (London, UK: British Standards Institute, 2009).

[5] International Organization for Standardization ISO 31000:2009. "Risk Management—Principles and Guidelines" (Geneva, Switzerland: International Organization for Standardization, 2009).

[6] International Organization for Standardization Guide 73:2009. *Risk Management—Vocabulary* (Geneva, Switzerland: International Organization for Standardization, 2009).

[7] International Organization for Standardization ISO IEC 31010:2009. *Risk Management—Risk Assessment Techniques* (Geneva, Switzerland: International Organization for Standardization, 2009).

[8] Project Management Institute. *Practice Standard for Project Risk Management* (Newtown Square, PA: Project Management Institute, 2009).

[9] Canadian Standards Association, CAN/CSA-Q850-97 "Risk Management: Guideline for Decision-Makers" (Ontario, Canada: Canadian Standards Association, 1997; reaffirmed 2002).

[10] United Kingdom Office of Government Commerce, "Management of Risk: Guidance for Practitioners," 3rd edition (London, UK: Office of Government Commerce, 2010).

[11] David A. Hillson, *Effective opportunity Management for Projects: Exploiting Positive Risk* (New York: Marcel Dekker, 2003).

[12] PMI, 2013, p. 309.

[13] Association for Project Management, *APM Body of Knowledge,* 6th edition" (Princes Risborough, UK: APM, 2012).

[14] David A. Hillson, "Project Risks—Identifying Causes, Risks and Effects." *PM Network*, 14 (2000), pp. 48–51.

[15] David A. Hillson and R. Murray-Webster, *Understanding and Managing Risk Attitude,* 2nd edition (Aldershot, UK: Gower, 2007).

[16] Ruth Murray-Webster and Hillson D. A. *Managing Group Risk Attitude* (Aldershot, UK: Gower, 2008).

FURTHER READING

C.B. Chapman and S.C. Ward, *Managing Project Risk and Uncertainty* (Chichester, UK: John Wiley, 2002).

C.B. Chapman and S.C. Ward, *How to Manage Project Opportunity and Risk*, updated 3rd edition of Project Risk Management (Chichester, UK: John Wiley, 2012).

R.J. Chapman, *Simple Tools and Techniques for Enterprise Risk Management,* 2nd edition (Chichester, UK: John Wiley, 2011).

Dale Cooper, P. Bosnich, S. Grey, G. Purdy, G. Raymond, P. Walker, and M Wood. *Project Risk Management Guidelines: Managing Risk with ISO 31000 and IEC 62198* (Chichester, UK: Wiley, 2014).

D.A. Hillson, *Exploiting Future Uncertainty: Creating Value from Risk* (Farnham, UK: Gower, 2010).

D.A. Hillson and P.W. Simon, *Practical Project Risk Management: The ATOM Methodology,* 2nd edition (Vienna, VA: Management Concepts, 2012).

D.T. Hulett, *Integrated Cost-Schedule Risk Analysis* (Farnham, UK: Gower, 2011).

N.N. Taleb, The Black Swan: The Impact of the Highly Improbable (London: Allen Lane/Penguin, 2007).

D. Vose. *Risk Analysis—A Quantitative Guide,* third edition (Chichester, UK: Wiley, 2008).

CHAPTER 16

Project Procurement Management in Practice

JUDITH A. EDWARDS, PHD, PMP, IEEE (SM), CONSULTANT

Procurement practice is one of those things that organizations and teams acknowledge is important up to a point—the point of actually *performing* the practice. The management rationale for not implementing the procurement practice is that it (1) costs too much or (2) takes too long. In fact, the standard practices for procurements are reasonably scalable. Many failed outcomes have root cause in avoiding key elements in the process. The risk of not performing the process is seldom assessed. Alternately, many organizations owe their successful outcomes to project procurement management best practice. Nonprofits are not immune from procurement difficulties and could benefit from the process.

PROCUREMENT PROCESS AND PROJECTS

Procurements should be a "project" and managed as such, even for small efforts. Successful procurements adhere to standard processes and implement a project management approach. A variety of process standards and guides are available to organizations, including the Institute of Electrical and Electronics Engineering (IEEE) standard 1062 from the software standards collection,[1] as well as from the Software Engineering Institute (SEI)[2] and other sources.[3,4] Those sources' processes are very similar to that found in the Project Management Institute's *Guide to the Project Management Body of Knowledge (PMBOK® Guide)*, Fifth Edition.[5] Although the first two references describe software procurement standards, those process descriptions are essentially tailored for a general procurement. Each process step evolved to solve many problems and issues with procurements in meeting the desired business objectives. Standard procurement processes were developed to do the following:

- Overcome or reduce instances of contract fraud abuses.
- Reduce risk.
- Describe the needed goods and services.

153

- Monitor and control costs and performance.
- Determine criteria for selection and acceptance.

Keeping these objectives in mind, the procurement chapter in the *PMBOK®
Guide,* Fifth Edition, describes four basic streamlined processes to obtain inputs to
a project:

1. Plan procurement management
2. Conduct procurements
3. Control procurements
4. Close procurements

The guide reflects an efficient supply chain by adapting technological advancements
with little bureaucracy. It recognizes economies gained by partnering arrangements,
including items on "teaming agreements" in planning and conducting procurement.
For small operation levels, tasks may have simple agreements, invoices, or requisition
forms.

Procurement efforts satisfy the definition of "project" with specific required outcomes, varying complexity, and time frames. A procurement effort could be embedded in a larger project effort. Such efforts should have a project manager role to ensure
the processes are completed and the team functions toward the desired objectives.
This should be the case regardless of scaling for the following scope efforts: short
duration for simple tasks, mobile environments, commodity purchases, long-term
significant outsourcing, and new product development. Oversight for multiple efforts
may be assigned a specific manager or agent.

Figure 16-1 shows typical timelines for a moderate scoped procurement effort
where the time scale represents periods after initiating the effort from the strategic
planning. After the make-or-buy decision point, other strategic milestone reviews

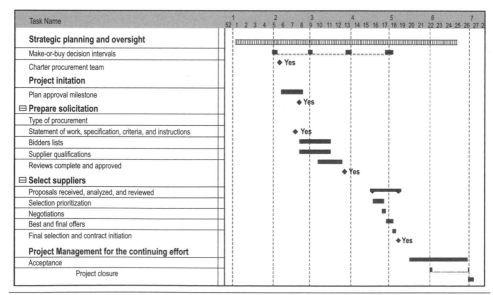

FIGURE 16-1. **PROCUREMENT PROJECT MANAGEMENT ACTIVITIES AND DURATION**

may indicate "go" or "no go," based on the information obtained during the various project phases or processes.

In scheduling a procurement effort, the project actually starts with initiation and planning to cover the preparation of solicitation documents, qualifying sellers (if necessary), and performing the selection. The execution of the project includes the monitoring and control of the seller while the seller executes the project. Procurement could involve co-developments with others and with the buyer organization. Acceptance of deliverables may occur at varying points depending on the contract agreements. The project completion includes the closure of the effort as well as the contract. The project effort depends on a variety of knowledge worker experiences, as discussed in the next section.

ROLES/RESPONSIBILITIES

Typically, no one person has the entire set of skills for completing the entire set of tasks in the areas of legal requirements, technical skills, business, purchasing, and project management. Therefore, forming a team with members from various disciplines is beneficial in providing checks and balances in the procurement tasks. Another justification for the procurement process becoming a project lies in this variety of teaming relationships, the set of stakeholders, and the unique business needs situations. Coordination of the procurement should come from an assigned project manager who understands the business and technical needs.

Table 16-1, the responsibility assignment matrix (RAM), shows the complexity of activities and roles in a typical medium-sized organization. Note that in the RAM, the following situations may occur for the project:

- One person may hold more than one role.
- Some roles may be outsourced.
- Role tasks may be delegated.
- Other stakeholders will be involved as procurement situations and issues arise during the executing or monitoring and control phases.

The project RAM should be updated as changes occur during project phase transitions. Some phases require more experienced knowledge workers who are tasked to integrate and deploy the procured items.

Contention in roles and responsibilities will be reduced when organizational processes and procedures address how the team is formed, the functional requirements for the roles, the processes to be performed, and approvals of the top-level project plans. The plan should be derived from organization standard practices addressing the following:

- Obtaining inputs for planning for solicitations
- Managing the acceptable sellers
- Qualifying new, potential sellers
- Defining the selection process
- Deriving the criteria based on type of purchase
- Controlling scope changes
- Reporting for oversight, defined for the project, approvals, and processes

Phase	Initiating	Solicitation	Selection	Management/ Executing	Monitoring & Controlling	Closing
Role	Typical responsibility per phase					
Project manager	Receives the charter; integrates directions into project planning; reviews past lessons learned	Procurement planning; prepares statement of work; approves specifications; submits solicitation documents	Co-lead: technical selection tasks	Project interface to stakeholders	Monitors project; communicates status	Completes archival for the project; creates lessons learned
Buyer*	Review planning	Reviewer	Co-lead: business tasks	Business and finance interface	Monitors seller performance and payment milestones	Completes procurement records and files
Legal	Participates	Creates contract terms & conditions; defines end-item data rights	Reviews; handles negotiations	Reviews	Issues reviews; change management	Contract closure
Technical specialist or lead	Review planning	Prepares technical specifications	Supports technical issues and reviews	Reviews and supports acceptance	Technical status of the effort	Supports archival efforts
Business unit manager	Strategic plan	Make-or-buy decisions	Reviews and approvals	Receives performance status	May require scope changes	Business deployment
Steering committee	Oversight	Oversight	Oversight	Oversight	Oversight	Oversight

*Notes:
- Typically the buyer role is from the procurement or purchasing organization.
- Outsourcing roles adds risk to be managed in addition to procurement risks.
- Other oversight may be needed to assure accountability of all participants to guard against fraud or mismanagement.

TABLE 16-1. **RESPONSIBILITY ASSIGNMENT MATRIX (RAM)**

SELECTION OF THE PROCUREMENT PROJECT MANAGEMENT TEAM

As you initiate the project, thought must be given to the makeup and training of the team members. The following factors should be considered in the selection:

- Members who interface with the seller should be "peers" who can gain the seller's confidence and establish a working relationship.
- Task leads need project management and negotiating skills.
- Responsibility and methods for accepting the product or services need to be clearly defined in, for example, a joint RAM for the seller and the buying organization.

American Management Association • www.amanet.org

- The size of the team depends on the business and technology factors, as well as on the complexity and risk entailed in the procurement process.
- Stakeholders involvement needs to be identified in the project planning.

Other stakeholders' considerations may be needed for the procurement project. They may include the project management office, line management, managers who are dependent on the procurement outcome, the quality-control organization, business units, other services, manufacturing, and clients/customers. The next section provides some experiences, lessons learned, and best practices from a variety of procurements.

SOME NEW CONSIDERATIONS IN PROCUREMENT

The fifth edition of the *PMBOK® Guide* updates the procurement practices to cover issues commonly faced in today's marketplace. For example, the tools and techniques section of the chapter stresses the importance of market research, including examination of specific vendor capabilities. At the same time, procurement managers are cautioned not to rely on market research alone, but to collaborate with potential bidders and strive to develop a mutually beneficial approach or product. This is in keeping with the current practice of including vendors as stakeholders in the project success.

In addition, the chapter discusses the Procurement Statement of Work document, which provides suppliers with a clearly stated set of goals, requirements, and outcomes from which they can provide a quantifiable response. The statements of work may include, but are not limited to, the following:

- Specifications
- Quantity desired
- Quality levels
- Performance data
- Period of performance
- Work location

Also new in the fifth edition of the standard is that procurement managers are urged to use care in defining each need in such a way that vendors can bring value through their offerings, and to examine past performance information from former projects and contracts to identify areas of risk (for example, a vendor that has previously created issues for a product due to failure to meet a deadline or a specification). "To ensure that the need can be and is met, analytical techniques can help organizations identify the readiness of a vendor to provide the desired end state, determine the cost expected to support budgeting, and avoid cost overruns due to changes."[6]

Similarly, project managers are advised to track work performance to better identify current or potential problems to support later claims or new procurements. "By reporting on the performance of a vendor, the organization increases knowledge of the performance of the procurement, which supports improved forecasting, risk management, and decision making. Performance reports also assist in the event there is a dispute with the vendor."[7] While such tracking includes traditional areas of concern, such as reporting compliance of contracts, it also advises the use of procurement agreements—sometimes termed a memorandum of understanding, a subcontract, or a purchase order—that include terms and conditions and may incorporate other items that the buyer specifies regarding what the seller is to perform or provide.

CONTRACTS AND OTHER DOCUMENTATION

Updated information in the new standard stresses the importance of creating and archiving procurement documentation, which may include the procurement contract with all supporting schedules, requested unapproved contract changes, and approved change requests. Procurement documentation also includes any seller-developed technical documentation and other work performance information, such as deliverables, seller performance reports and warranties, financial documents including invoices and payment records, and the results of contract-related inspections.

In addition to the discussion of different types of contracts traditionally found in the standard, the fifth edition spells out the major components, which will vary, but may include the following:

- Statement of work or deliverables
- Schedule baseline
- Performance reporting
- Period of performance
- Roles and responsibilities
- Seller's place of performance
- Pricing
- Payment terms
- Place of delivery
- Inspection and acceptance criteria
- Warranty
- Product support
- Limitation of liability
- Fees and retainer
- Penalties
- Incentives
- Insurance and performance bonds
- Subordinate subcontractor approvals
- Change request handling
- Termination clause and alternative dispute resolution (ADR) mechanisms (the ADR method can be decided in advance as a part of the procurement award)[8]

PROCUREMENT LESSONS LEARNED AND BEST PRACTICES

Drawing from experience in a variety of procurement projects, including those of long duration, and expensive efforts as well as relatively simple commodity purchases for both defense and commercial projects, Table 16-2 organizes lessons learned and best practices by knowledge area or project management phase. These suggestions,

Project Management Area or Phase	Lesson Learned or Best Practices
Process	• Risks increase by avoiding steps in the process. The standard process evolved to avoid risks or correct a failure or issue. • Incomplete steps in procurement may add costs and time later. • For a trained knowledge worker, the effort to follow the process is not excessive. • Organizational tools and standard templates aid the preparation of the solicitation documents and reinforce training on procurement processes.
Contract types	• Large organizations with supply chain management require interface processes based on purchase type, seller category, qualifications, and information automation access. • Cost control begins with the specifications and seller qualification processes. • Ownership rights for end-deliverables must be clearly specified. • Commercial-off-the-shelf purchases are often called COTS. If these are inappropriate or not planned, then the purchase might better be called COSTS.
Seller selection	• Time spent in qualifying sellers often means better working relationships and less risk. • It is not practical to expect the seller's systems to duplicate those of the buying organization. Where common processes or infrastructure is important, then define the needed capability in the work statements. • The low-cost bidder may be the highest risk. • Reference checking is a good way to learn of others' experiences in dealing with candidate sellers.
Planning	• Procurement needs to be managed to ensure that the products meet the specifications and work statements. • Plans need to address risk management.
Risk management	• Payment milestones ensure that the buyer is getting specified deliverables while reducing risks. The payment criteria should be defined in the work statements. • Risks must be managed regardless of the seller size and experience.
Training	• Often procurement processes are so rarely exercised that refresher training is necessary to ensure compliance with the organization practices.
Project management	• Detailed specifications and work statements reduce the potential future claims for scope changes. • Outsourcing should be a project supported by a project manager and a plan. • Recurring commodity purchases may still need technical acceptance and change management. • Interfaces to the seller must be controlled by the buyer and project manager to prevent unauthorized scope changes.

TABLE 16-2. **LESSONS LEARNED AND BEST PRACTICES, ORGANIZED BY PROJECT MANAGEMENT KNOWLEDGE AREA OR PHASE**

(continued)

Project Management Area or Phase	Lesson Learned or Best Practices
	• Project manager for the procurement project should be a peer of the seller's team so as to effectively manage the effort. • Problems occur if the seller becomes the primary project management interface to the end customer.
Business management strategy	• "Buy" objectives may have little to do with buyer core capability. The technical team needs to understand the roles and relationships and strategy. • "Should cost" needs to be determined for the life cycle and total cost of ownership, not just the cost of the delivered items or services. • Outsourcing does not necessarily save staff, time, or costs. The organization objective should support strategic business needs. • Outsourcing should not be a "me too" decision because it appears cheaper than in country; some end strategy must be considered. • It is unlikely that a procurement will succeed without a project team.
Roles and responsibilities	• Technical team needs to perform the acceptance and validation of the delivered items that are defined in the planning. • Often companies assume that the purchasing organization is responsible for the entire process. The development organization then fails to understand their role in the upfront planning. This results in key elements of the process being missed.
Change management	• If the specification needs to be changed to eliminate unneeded features or tasks or to assure success of project, then is must be done. Obtaining the wrong system will be most likely lead to sunk costs or major rework.

TABLE 16-2. CONTINUED

based on experience in the field, do not repeat but amplify recommendations or practices described in the *PMBOK® Guide*. They emphasize the need to follow or adapt procurement processes and not to neglect the steps for seeming short term gain.

Some table items were adopted from significant support software procurement for a defense project.[9] The software project procurement practices are no different from procurement process in general. Because of the invisible nature of both software development and other services, these efforts often incur more risk without the planning, coordination, and oversight.

INCREASING OPPORTUNITIES FOR SUCCESS

Procurements of all types involve risks.[10,11] Some techniques have been shown to improve the opportunity for project success. Starting with an attitude for "getting it right the first time," here are some suggestions:

▶ Hold early "bidders" conferences to obtain feedback on the statement of work and specifications. These can be held by teleconference or mobile communications techniques. It is essential that all potential sellers hear the same message. Seller comments need to be managed for nondisclosure of competition sensitive information. From the feedback, hold a follow-up conference to show the updated documents. This also helps the sellers to determine their response strategy.

▶ Obtain bidders list from social media connections and check bidder's social media presence, which should be used to form interview questions for capability and experience.[12]

▶ Obtain a "should cost" during the make-or-buy decision period to gauge the seller responses more accurately. Underbids by significant amounts require reasonable justifications for how the effort can be managed at that low cost without defaulting.

▶ Do not rush through the procurement process steps only to find that the best opportunities were missed or the specifications are incomplete or inaccurate.

▶ If changes are made to the solicitation documents, the process and procedures should require an update, and new bids should be obtained.

▶ Competitive bidding is considered a risk reduction method that avoids locked-in solutions or favoritism. If the procurement process is performed well, then the procurement effort should yield the best outcome for the buyer.

▶ Determine how to impose on the seller reasonable quality standards for the end product or service. The end result cannot be better than the weakest quality component.

▶ Form integrated product development teams as part of the project team and stakeholders.

▶ Ensure that the team is adequately trained on procurement processes. Provide refresher training for those with immediate need.

▶ Update organization practices with lessons learned and best practices.

▶ Define the responsibility and accountability for the team. Retain visibility into the project procurement practices and results. Audit the project for adherence to the practice and the project work statement and specifications.

▶ Reduce risks by using the two-person (or more) rule to ensure oversight and ensure that evaluations are fair.

▶ Require justifications for sole-source purchases to avoid buying in haste and repenting later. Cost/benefit analysis should be part of each decision process step.

▶ Exercise strict change control on both sides of the buyer/seller relationship.

▶ Define and know what acceptance means and the associated payment terms.

Thoroughly understanding the procurement process and practicing project management tenets aid efficiencies for the organization in getting products and services to market. Next, let's examine some considerations in applying lessons learned to several different sizes, or classes, of procurements.

SCENARIOS BASED ON "SCALE" OR "CLASS" OF PROCUREMENT

Five scenarios show the tailoring of the process and summarize procurement considerations based on scale, scope, size, or class of procurement. The "class" is a category of procurements that address embedded, secure, highly reliable, or special requirements. Organizations may define processes and procedures according to the scale. Guidance is given to increase the probability of successful outcomes, avoid defaults, and reduce sunk costs.

Scenario 1: Existing Items from Catalogs or Commercial-Off-the-Shelf (COTS)

In buying existing items, some requirement specifications or criteria need to be defined for their selection. Often much time and money is wasted when the purchased item becomes "shelfware" because the desired capability was never defined. The definition needs to be more than just that someone saw a demonstration or that the competition uses it. The goal is to satisfy a business need.

The purchased items should be evaluated against the requirements. When deficiencies are found, an estimate is needed to determine the total cost to integrate the items into the end product. Often a slightly more expensive item would save integration and troubleshooting efforts. Therefore, conduct product evaluations to find the minimum cost impact for including the item in the final product.

Experience or training is also needed to assess purchased items' quality. Volume purchase requires higher levels of specification for reducing rework or recalls. The selection of an existing item is dependent on the degree of risk the organization wants to assume. The result may end up with throwaway items and unnecessary costs for efforts. Key to the approach is investing in upfront feasibility or prototyping.

Scenario 2: Simple Contracting for Services or Support

Simple contractor or service efforts can be as disappointing and difficult as the large efforts. Obtaining mobile applications capabilities fit in this scenario. It is also important to have in writing what is expected, how completion is determined, and when the milestones will be finished. Payment should be in agreement with milestones met with mutual satisfaction. Warranties may be granted. Planned services should be structured as much as possible for direction of the effort and for follow-up of outstanding issues.

Scenario 3: Minimum Modifications to Existing Seller Items

An existing item may not completely meet the business needs unless it is modified. Ensure that you have the right to perform changes and to include the upgrade in your products or services. The procurement strategy may be to hire a seller to update an existing product to meet the specification. The solicitation documents need to clearly describe the responsibilities of the buyer and seller for the integrated solution and its support. If both organizations work on the item, then the responsibility is not clear, nor can it easily be determined how to maintain the item. Defined separation of responsibility and efforts is a good management approach. It is also important to focus domain knowledge on areas of expertise. The seller may be an expert in its technology but not in the business application where its products will be deployed. The buyer can provide the needed interface for the domain.

Strict management of product development interfaces aids in isolating difficulties and solutions. Decomposition allows better estimating of costs and integration efforts. Managing to clearly defined interfaces simplifies the tasks. It is difficult to have total knowledge of complex systems. By partitioning the effort along defined decomposition and interfaces, the buyer/seller teams need to know only their functionality and the interface requirements.

Scenario 4: Major New Development

This scenario considers allocating the entire component to the seller for development, as the buyer is procuring totally new technology or unique solutions. The size of the effort may be small, but it may be critical for some autonomous or embedded systems. The buying organization may be dealing with what Moore called "crossing the chasm"[10] to plan and manage the delivered items from feasibility or research developments through integration to a stable environment. Specification practices may need to go through a variety of stages for preliminary to final versions. For risk reduction, a "go/no go" decision can be made based on performance at each stage. At some point, the buyer can even require a proposal for the subsequent stage. If performance is poor or the objective is not met, then the effort can be re-competed.

In this scenario, the procurement goal is typically to transform a unique feature or capability into a stable product. A high degree of new technology or special implementations incurs more risk. The procurement strategy should involve a phased approach to prove various incremental deliveries. In a phased approach, stage the effort of development from minimum required functionality in pre-production to several increased capability solutions. Key parts of the procurement project involve planning, risk management, monitoring and control, integrated change management, quality control acceptance, and communications.

Scenario 5: Offshoring or Outsourcing

Companies are tempted to outsource by sending major development offshore without enough risk analysis or management support planning. Core competencies are lost and difficult to recover.[7] Unsuccessful procurements projects are numerous and have immense impact on productivity. What looks like a cost advantage is soon sacrificed because of lack of project management. A "me too" is not enough motivation for sending development out of the country. The rationale for more successful outcomes includes the amount of business the offshore will support in country. It is easy to lose branding and commonality if the entire development is sent offshore. The outsourcing may provide significant applied research advantages to the supplier, to the detriment of the buyer's core capability. Also, the cost advantage may be fleeting, with the changes in the economy, the environment, and organizations.

Following are some considerations to include in the plan:

- The management approach
- Communications and travel
- Standards, which should be established
- Product acceptance and quality controls
- Additional procurements may be required
- Tracking and metrics established
- Cost reporting and containment
- Customer satisfaction

It would be advisable for all parties to see the project plan and create their own plan with approval. Before the project is initiated, significant organizational portfolio analysis and a core competency review for strategic advantages and disadvantages should be completed. Near-term gains will not sustain long-term losses. Eliminating process steps without safeguards will increase the risk in obtaining successful outcomes.

CONCLUSION

At several checkpoints, the decision can be made to go forward with the procurement to the next phase. The project procurement process steps are as follows:

1. Plan the purchase and acquisition.
2. Plan the contracting.
3. Request seller responses.
4. Select sellers.
5. Perform contract administration.
6. Perform contract closure.

Supporting project processes include the overall project planning, monitoring and control, stakeholder communications, and integrated change management.

The effort should be established as a two-phase project to cover (1) the activities through seller selection and (2) managing the sellers through project and contract closure.

Important aspects of this knowledge area's processes include the following:

- Documentation, including plans, work statements, specifications, and acceptance criteria
- Project management performed by both the buyer and seller
- Skills training covering procurement processes, negotiations, assessment of capabilities, and performance
- Defined roles and responsibilities throughout the procurement project

"Classes" or "scenarios" of procurement may range from commodities, to COTS, to minor modifications to existing products, to special services, to unique/customized developments. Managing old and new technologies is always a challenge. Different controls and risk management are needed for each class, scenario, and scope.

DISCUSSION QUESTIONS

❶ You are planning to buy new technology for a product or service. Use reference materials and the Internet to determine a beginning supplier list to answer the following:

- What sections do you need in your project plan to facilitate your plan for procurement of goods or services?
- What should go into the make-or-buy analysis?
- What are your seller selection criteria?
- Using cost-benefit analysis, what are the pros and cons of sole source procurement versus competitive selection?

❷ In performing due diligence at the candidate sellers, what are the questions that you would want to ask before entering into a business relationship? What project methods would be used to monitor and control the seller's effort?

❸ Under what circumstances and for what functions would it be reasonable to outsource or to send offshore?

❹ How might you use social media to automate procurements in the five scenarios outlined in this chapter?

REFERENCES

[1] IEEE Standard 1062, *Recommended Practice for Software Acquisition* (New York: Institute of Electrical and Electronics Engineering).

[2] M.B. Chrissis, M. Konrad, and S. Shrum. *CMMI Guidelines for process Integration and Product Improvement* (Boston: Addison Wesley, 2003).

[3] F.A. Mitulski, *Managing Your Vendor* (Englewood Cliffs, NJ: Prentice-Hall ECS Professional, 1993).

[4] Q.W. Fleming, Project Procurement Management (Turstin, CA: FMC Press, 2003).

[5] Project Management Institute, *A Guide to the Project Management Body of Knowledge* (*PMBOK*® *Guide*), 5th edition (Newtown Square, PA: PMI, 2013).

[6] PMI, 2013, p. 365.

[7] PMI, 2013, p. 383.

[8] PMI, 2013, p. 378.

[9] J.A. Edwards and B.L. Mowday. "How to buy a compiler," in *WADAS: Washington Ada Symposium 1984 (March 1984)–1994 (July 1994)* (New York: Association for Computing Machinery).

[10] G.A. Moore, *Crossing the Chasm* (New York: Harper Business; Revised edition, 2002).

[11] M.C. Lacity and R. Hirschheim, *Outsourcing* (New York: John Wiley & Sons, 1993).

[12] Lon Safko, *The Social Media Bible: Tactics, Tools, and Strategies for Business Success* (New York: Wiley Desktop Editions, 2012).

CHAPTER 17

Stakeholder Management for Project Success

RANDALL L. ENGLUND, EXECUTIVE CONSULTANT

In recent years, it has become increasingly evident that projects struggle when project leaders fail to pay attention to the needs of all project stakeholders as well as the needs of the project itself. To ensure or increase the probability of successful project outcomes, it is important to work with the people who will make it happen. Thus, in 2013, the Project Management Institute added project stakeholder management to the standard as the tenth knowledge area.[1] For those who have long recommended more focus on people and less on tools in the project management arena, this is a welcome and long overdue addition.

WHO ARE OUR STAKEHOLDERS?

A stakeholder is anyone who has a "stake in the ground" and cares about the effort—sponsoring the change, supplying, or executing it. Stakeholder management is about identifying, establishing, and maintaining relationships and adapting to changes. A stakeholder management plan consists of identifying key participants, understanding their expectations and motivations, defining what project success looks like, managing conflicts that arise, and engaging, aligning, and influencing stakeholders throughout the project life cycle.

STAKEHOLDER ANALYSIS

Identifying stakeholders early on leads to better stakeholder management through-out the project. Use diagnostic tools and identified traits of key powerful people to analyze stakeholders. Ask, "Who could stop this effort?" Table 17-1 is an example of a stakeholder register or stakeholder analysis template.)

To be thorough, visualize all stakeholders as points on a compass. To the north is the management chain; direct reports are to the south. To the west are customers and end users; other functional areas are to the east. In between are other entities,

Stakeholder Name	Support or Opposition (+5 to −5)	Why? Own Interests?	Relative Power	Management / Communication

TABLE 17-1. **EXAMPLE OF A STAKEHOLDER REGISTER TEMPLATE**

vendors, or regulatory agencies. Identify all players. Write down names and get to know people in each area. What motivates them, how are they measured, and what are their concerns?

Use a stakeholder engagement assessment matrix (Table 17-2) to record starting and ending points for stakeholders within a stakeholder management plan.

Approach a stakeholder analysis using these steps:

1. Who are the stakeholders?

   - Brainstorm to identify all possible stakeholders.
   - Identify where each stakeholder is located.
   - Identify the relationship the project team has with each stakeholder in terms of power and influence during the project life cycle.

2. What are stakeholder expectations?

   - Identify primary high-level project expectations for each stakeholder.

3. How does the project or products affect stakeholders?

   - Analyze how the products and deliverables affect each stakeholder.
   - Determine what actions the stakeholder could take that would affect the success or failure of the project.
   - Prioritize the stakeholders, based on who has the most positive or negative effect on project success or failure.
   - Incorporate information from previous steps into a risk analysis plan to develop mitigation procedures for stakeholders who might negatively impact the project.

Stakeholder	Unaware	Resistant	Neutral	Supportive	Leading
End User Group			C		D
Key VP		C	D	D	
External Client				C	D

C, current state of the stakeholder; D, a desired state.

TABLE 17-2. **EXAMPLE OF A STAKEHOLDER ENGAGEMENT ASSESSMENT MATRIX**

4. What information do stakeholders need?

- Identify from the information collected, what information needs to be furnished to each of them, when it should be provided, and how.

Prepare an action plan for using a stakeholder "map" to resolve potential issues. That plan might include actions such as the following:

- Face-to-face meetings with every middle level manager, explaining the project mission and objectives, and getting them to share their real needs and expectations.
- Sessions with all middle managers, using "mind-mapping" techniques to brainstorm ideas and get suggestions and real needs from various perspectives, leading up to a more aligned vision for the project.
- Identifying and avoiding barriers like organizational climate, perceptions, customer pressure, and too many communication links.

Approach stakeholders in each area starting from the position of strength. When, for instance, power is high but agreement about the project is low, start by reinforcing the effective working relationship that exists and how the person may contribute to and benefit from the project. Express desire that this bond will help work through any differences. Only after establishing agreement on these objectives is it then appropriate to address the problem area. People often jump right into the problem. This prompts defensive behavior from the other person. Taking time to reestablish rapport first can prove far more effective in reaching a mutually satisfying solution. It is then possible to discover misinformation or negotiate a change in outcome, cost, or schedule that lessens the levels of concern and increases people's support of the project.

To illustrate, a customer says to the project manager, "I'm okay with most of your status reports, but I have a big problem with progress on resolving the resourcing issue." Most people only hear the problem and immediately jump into defensive mode. Instead, start with, "I hear that you're satisfied with how we implemented your requests and can continue moving forward. Is that correct? Great! Okay, so now we only have this one issue to work through . . . ." The tenor of this approach is positive, the topics on the table for discussion are bounded, and rapport is present, setting the stage for a creative solution.

CONFLICT

Stakeholders' competing interests are inherently in conflict. Upper managers and customers want more features, lower cost, less time, and more changes. Accountants mainly care about lower costs. Team members typically want fewer features to work on, more money, more time, and fewer changes.

Conflict is natural and normal. Too little, however, and there is excessive cooperation—"Whatever the group wants." Too much, and there is excessive conviction—"My mind's made up." These represent the flight or fight extremes of human behavior. The ideal is to create constructive contention where the attitude is "Let's work together to figure this out." This middle ground happens when:

- A *common objective* is present to which all parties can relate.
- People understand how they make a *contribution.*

- The issue under discussion has *significance,* both to the parties involved and to the organization.
- People are *empowered* to act on the issue and do not have to seek resolution elsewhere.
- Everyone accepts *accountability* for the success of the project or organizational venture.

For example, a materials engineering manager was in a rage and called the task force project manager to complain about how the project was proceeding. The project manager asked the other manager to come talk with him in person. Rather than putting up a defensive shield to ward off an upcoming attack, the project manager started the meeting by reviewing the project objectives and eliciting agreement that developing a process with consistent expectations and common terminology was a good thing. He next asked the materials manager about his concerns. He found out that inserting cross-check steps early in the process would ensure that inventory overages would not happen when new products were designed with different parts. This represented a major contribution to the project. These individuals were empowered to make this change, which would have significant impact because all projects would be using the checklists generated by this project. Rather than creating a political battle, the two parties resolved the conflict through a simple process, the project achieved an improved outcome, and the two parties walked off arm in arm in the same direction.

Start any new initiative or change that affects stakeholders by thinking big but starting small. First implement a prototype and achieve a victory. Plan a strategy of small wins to develop credibility, feasibility, and to demonstrate value. Get increased support to expand based on this solid foundation.

DEFINE PROJECT SUCCESS

Make a listing of all success and failure factors from previous project experiences. Take a high-level view and identify what thread runs through all key factors identified. What they have in common is that they all are about people. People do matter.

Projects typically succeed or fail depending on how well people work together. When you lose sight of the importance of people issues, such as clarity of purpose, effective and efficient communications, and management support, then you are doomed to struggle. Engaged people find ways to work through all problems. The challenge of leaders is to create environments for people to do their best work.

The list usually brings out a bountiful harvest of definitions for project success as well as what causes them to fail. Meeting the constraints of scope, schedule, and resources is just a starting point. Sometimes you can be right on these constraints and still fail to be successful, perhaps because the market changed, or a competitor outdid you, or a client changed his mind. You could also miss on all constraints but still have a successful project when viewed over time. It is important to get all requirements specified as accurately as possible; it is also important to be flexible since needs and conditions change over time or even when more becomes known about the project as it progresses.

Here is a suggested overarching criterion for project success: check with key stakeholders and ask them for their definitions of success. Pin them down to one key area each. Some surprising replies may surface: "Don't embarrass me." "Keep me out of the newspaper." "Just get something finished." There may even be conflicting responses. The job is to integrate the replies and work to make them happen. Having this dialogue early in the project life cycle provides clear marching orders—and forewarning about what is important to key stakeholders. An objective of this discussion is to tailor success expectations to organizations and to specific stakeholder expectations.

Perceptions about project success are relative and real. One manager states, "About the perception that the project had been successful, this 'perception' was stronger than any other factor, such as work completed, cost, measureable return of investment, et cetera. It appeared as though the actual work performed and the end result were by-products of the opinions of stakeholders and end users."

Having identified that success or failure is all about people, the goal now is to learn how to be better leaders and managers of people, not just of projects. Embrace the tenets of becoming a *complete project manager*, developing skill sets adapted from multiple disciplines.[2]

AUTHENTIC LEADERSHIP IN ACTION

How do you create an environment that achieves results, trust, and learning instead of undermining them? To get stakeholders working collaboratively, consider ways for them to receive more value from this effort: the project provides means to meet organizational needs; they have more fun; the experience is stimulating; they get more help and assistance when needed; they get constructive feedback; they are excited by the vision; they learn more from this project; their professional needs are met; they travel and meet people; it's good for their careers; together they'll accomplish more than separately; this is neat. . . .

Ways to demonstrate authentic leadership in action:

- Say what you believe.
- Act on what you say.
- Believe and demonstrate that being trustworthy is a priority.
- Avoid "integrity crimes" where people feel violated by actions not consistent with words.
- Involve team members in designing strategic implementation plans.
- Align values, projects, and organizational goals by asking questions, listening, and using an explicit process to link all actions to strategic goals.
- Foster an environment in which project teams can succeed by learning together and operating in a trusting, open organization.
- Develop the skill of "organizational awareness"—the ability to read the currents of emotions and political realities in groups. This is a competence vital to the behind-the-scenes networking and coalition building that allows individuals to wield influence, no matter what their professional role. Tap the energy that comes from acting upon the courage of convictions—from doing the right thing—and from being prepared.

For example, a contractor came to the project manager's office, made demands about resources on the project, and left. This was out of character, for the two people had formed a close relationship. The project manager decided not to act on the critical demands that could have severe negative impact on project relations. Later he sought out the contractor and found him in a different mood. The contractor confessed he was told by his company to make those demands. By correctly reading the emotional state and assessing that something below the surface was going on in that transaction, the project manager was able to work with the other person, keep the issue from escalating, and find a solution.

Leaders who commit "integrity crimes" shift the burden away from a fundamental solution to their personal effectiveness. Trust cannot develop under these conditions. Leaders either get into problems or else tap the energy and loyalty of others to succeed.

In systems thinking terms, this is a classic example of a "shifting the burden" archetype, in which a short-term fix actually undermines a leader's ability to take action at a more fundamental level. When under pressure for results, many project managers resort to the "quick fix"—a command and control approach, which on a surface appears to lessen the pressure. This has an opposite effect on the people they want to influence or persuade. These people do not do their best work, so more pressure is felt to get results.

A more fundamental solution is to develop skills of persuasion. Help people come to believe in the vision and mission and aid them in figuring out why it is in their best interest to put their best work into the project. Use Table 17-1 to help analyze their interests and concerns. People usually respond positively to this approach and accomplish the work with less pressure.

Tools of persuasion include the following:

- *Reciprocity:* Give an unsolicited gift. People will feel the need to give something back. Perhaps a big contract, or maybe just another opportunity to continue building a strong relationship.
- *Consistency:* Draw people into public commitments, even very small ones, and enforce those commitments. This can be very effective in directing future action.
- *Social validation:* Let people know that this approach is considered "the standard" by others. People often determine what they should do by looking at what others are doing.
- *Liking:* Let people know that we like them and that we are likable too. People like to do business with people they like. Elements that build "liking" include physical attractiveness, similarity, compliments, and cooperation.
- *Authority:* Be professional and personable in dress and demeanor. Other factors are experience, expertise, and scientific credentials.
- *Scarcity:* Remember just how rare good project management practice is, not to mention people who can transform a very culture. This applies to the value both of commodities and information. Not everyone knows what it takes to make a program successful.

To summarize the science and practice of persuasion, it usually makes great sense to repay favors, behave consistently, follow the lead of similar others, favor the requests of those we like, heed legitimate authorities, and value scare resources.[3]

To assess effective practices and apply a simple tool for stakeholder analysis, consider these steps:

1. Identify basic leadership traits and their consequences.
2. Assess and compare leadership approaches in complex situations.
3. Apply a shifting-the-burden structure to create a positive culture.
4. Appreciate the value of authentic leadership and commit to act with integrity.

DOCUMENT A STAKEHOLDER MANAGEMENT PLAN

A stakeholder management strategy usually comprises these elements:

- A stakeholder register
- Stakeholder engagement assessment matrix
- A communications plan, including communications requirements (see Chapter 14)
- Change management and change control plans to assess and mitigate the impact of change to the stakeholders and project
- Training and development of stakeholders' skills when appropriate
- Stakeholder relationship management strategy

People are driven by different motivations. To keep stakeholders engaged and aligned, track, monitor, and document progress and challenges (issues), have procedures for following up on progress and completion of tasks, challenges, and issues resolved. Rather than looking at managing stakeholders as an irritation, be aware of and honor the sensitive nature of a stakeholder analysis. Recognize that everyone involved in the project has valid concerns and meaningful hopes for the work you undertake together.

ENVISION A SUCCESSFUL, COOPERATIVE ENVIRONMENT

A vision for project stakeholder management is for all persons to cooperate willingly and productively, applying standard project management techniques, and operating in project-based organizations. Achieving this state requires forming a dream of what it would be like: Project managers would be like current department managers. Upper managers would be an integral part of the project management process. The organizational building block would be the team. Therefore, upper managers would function as members of upper management teams. Project positions would be based on influence, which is based on trust and interdependence. Any one project would be part of a system of projects, not pitted against one another for resources but rather part of a coordinated plan to achieve organizational goals and strategies. This means project managers would themselves be a team. The upper manager's team would develop the organization structure and lead the project system, or project portfolio. Trust would be supported by open and explicit communication. Upper managers would oversee a project management information system to answer questions and provide information on all projects. There would be less emphasis on rules but a strong emphasis on organizational mission to guide action. There would be clear relationships between individual jobs and the mission. A process for taming project chaos would be based on linking projects to strategy, a focus on values and direction, the free flow of information, and organizing to support project teams.

CONCLUSION

Implement a stakeholder management strategy whose goal is to engage, align, and proactively influence all stakeholders. Clearly define project success, according to each key stakeholder. Identify and document stakeholder characteristics in a stakeholder register. Proactively manage conflicts that arise, knowing that those conflicts represent engaged participants. Develop persuasive skills. Be trustworthy, authentic, and act with integrity. With positive reinforcement, stakeholders will have a positive influence on the project and contribute to its success.

DISCUSSION QUESTIONS

❶ Starting with yourself, how would you assess your stakeholder characteristics? What strengths can you leverage and what areas need development?

❷ Is fulfilling the triple constraints sufficient to determine if a project is successful? What criteria might evaluate project success more accurately? How does your organization describe success?

❸ As a project leader, how do you want to be perceived? Describe your desired reputation, especially with regard to how stakeholders perceive you and to achieving project success.

REFERENCES

[1] Project Management Institute, *A Guide to the Project Management Body of Knowledge* (*PMBOK® Guide*), 5th edition (Newtown Square, PA: PMI, 2013).

[2] Randall Englund and Alfonso Bucero, *The Complete Project Manager: Integrating People, Organizational, and Technical Skills* (Vienna, VA: Management Concepts Press, 2012).

[3] R.B. Cialdini, *Influence: Science and Practice,* 4th edition (New York: Pearson Allyn & Bacon, 2000).

The Profession of Project Management

Introduction

THE GROWTH OF THE PROJECT MANAGEMENT PROFESSION

Project management has evolved from the "accidental profession" of years ago—when no one actually planned to become a project manager, but just happened into the position—to a profession based on formalized bodies of knowledge, such as the Project Management Institute's *Guide to the Project Management Body of Knowledge* (*PMBOK® Guide*) and those developed by other professional organizations—the International Project Management Association (Europe) and the Association of Project Managers (UK), among others.

Where once project management was merely an add-on to the role of a civil engineer or systems engineer, today it is more commonly identified as a career choice in and of itself. The rapid growth of the discipline's primary professional organization—the Project Management Institute (PMI)—from less than 15,000 members when the first edition of this handbook was published in 1993, to well over a half-million members and credential holders (and increasing), gives us a good indication of the rapid "mainstreaming" of the project manager role.

Since formal certification programs appeared in the 1990s, more emphasis has been given to seeing project management as a profession—something that has a defined body of knowledge based on specific principles and is subject to qualifications and knowledge testing based on a formal process. There is an evolving trend toward developing professional certification that is not only knowledge based but also competency based, thus taking into consideration experience records and other formal professional qualifications.

PMI increasingly has focused on certification as the primary benefit to its membership, offering additional targeted certifications, such as the Certified Associate in Project Management (CAPM), designed to be a stepping stone to Project Management Professional (PMP) certification or a terminal certification for project administration roles, the Program Management Professional (PgMP) for program managers on the more experienced end of the scale, and, most recently, a certification in Agile methods.

Many companies require certification for advancement or recognize certification as part of the advancement path in careers. In formal bidding processes for professional services related to projects, client organizations often call for certified project professionals.

Professionalism is a personal commitment, but it must be supported by institutions, including professional societies, educational institutions, and the organizations that employ project managers. It also requires a great deal from the individual. The more seriously an occupation is taken as it moves into the category of the professions, the more serious are the implications of unprofessional or unethical behavior on the part of the practitioner.

This section of the handbook focuses on the career of project management. First, what must one do to become a certified project management professional? In Chapter 18, Theodore R. Boccuzzi takes us step by step through the various stages of qualification. What competencies are required of the project manager, and how are these developed? What does the new project manager have to look forward to in the course of his or her career? In Chapter 19, J. Kent Crawford and Jeannette Cabanis-Brewin discuss project management competencies and career paths. What are the ethical issues facing project managers? In Chapter 20, Thomas Mengel, a visiting professor of management at a number of Canadian universities, explores this topic and provides thought-provoking ethical cases for your consideration. Is project management in fact a profession? If not, what must we do to ensure that it becomes one? In Chapter 21, Janice Thomas addresses these issues. In Chapter 22, Deborah Bigelow Crawford (herself a former Executive Director of PMI) provides a look at how project managers today can ramp up their careers by developing business acumen.

CHAPTER 18

Preparing for the Project Management Professional Certification Exam

THEODORE R. BOCCUZZI, PMP, TRB CONSULTING

The Project Management Institute (PMI) provides a comprehensive certification program for project management practitioners with varying levels of experience. The certification program is designed to support a career in the project management profession. There are currently six credentials available: Certified Associate in Project Management (CAPM®), PMI Scheduling Professional (PMI-SP®), PMI Risk Management Professional (PMI-RMP®), PMI Agile Certified Practitioner (PMI-ACP®), Project Management Professional (PMP®), and Program Management Professional (PgMP®). None of the credentials serves as a prerequisite for another. PMI's certification and credentials are transferable across industries and geographic borders, and are not tied to any single method, standard, or organization

The credential awarded under this program to those who lead and direct project teams is the Project Management Professional (PMP), which is accredited by the American National Standards Institute (ANSI) against the International Organization for Standardization (ISO) 17024 and is ISO 9001-certified in quality management systems. The PMP has become the credential of choice for many industries and corporations that provide project management services. Although it is not the only project management–related certification, the PMP is highly regarded throughout the world. Many organizations have begun to require it for individual advancement or for employment. Although the PMP is not a license or registration and does not provide legal authority to practice project management, as do certifications that are legally required and competency based (such as the Australian certification program), it does advance project management competency of the individual and of the organizations for which they perform projects.

The information in this chapter is the most up-to-date available, but the profession and the certification process will undergo many changes, and the specific details of the exam and other certification requirements are expected to change. Even the body of knowledge, as testified to by the fact that the Project Management Institute's *Guide to the Project Management Body of Knowledge* (*PMBOK® Guide*) is now in its fifth revised edition,[1] changes over time. Project management as a profession is relatively young. Like other professions, its standards and certifications are evolving in response to business and social pressures. The parallel can be drawn to the evolution of other professional certifications, such as the certified public accountant (CPA).

In the early days of that profession, accountants managed the financial records of businesses, but they did not always treat accounting events consistently. As the accounting profession recognized the inconsistencies of accounting techniques, its members worked to form a series of generally accepted practices. Changing economic times (notably the 1929 stock market crash) and increased criticism added impetus to the development of uniform standards and a certification program to enhance credibility and professionalism. Early versions of the CPA examination were not as comprehensive or as difficult as the versions given today; twenty years ago, it was not necessary to have a degree to be eligible to take the exam. Similarly, we can expect the PMP itself to evolve and go through a series of changes reflecting the changing standards and requirements of the project management profession. In the event that project management is truly recognized as a profession, with all the serious accountability issues that this designation raises (malpractice and licensing for example), those changes will become even more significant.[2]

To achieve the PMP credential, four sets of requirements must be met in level of education, project management experience, project management education, and ethical behavior. One must meet the educational and experiential requirements required, agree to follow the PMI Code of Ethics and Professional Conduct, and pass the PMP credential examination. Passing the exam is a mark of official and public recognition of an individual's ability to meet specified standards in field of project management.

To get complete details about the credential process and the most current information available about the credential exam, as well as any upcoming or possible changes, visit PMI's website to download the latest *Project Management Professional (PMP)[SM] Credential Handbook* from PMI.[3] Before submitting a PMP credential exam application, PMI requires that the applicant affirm that he or she has read and understood the entire handbook.

THE PROJECT MANAGEMENT PROFESSIONAL CREDENTIAL PROCESS: AN OVERVIEW

To be eligible for the PMP credential, candidates must agree to abide by PMI's Code of Ethics and Professional Conduct, complete a specified number of hours of formal project management training (thirty-five hours as of this writing), and meet the educational and experiential requirements that are described in detail in the *PMP Credential Handbook*. Preparing the application packet is a project in itself. The documentation required includes the examination application, experience verification forms, project management education forms, the application fee schedule, other demographic information, and the PMI Code of Ethics and Professional Conduct. Signing the application indicates that you accept the responsibilities outlined in the PMI Certification Application/Renewal Agreement, including abiding by the PMI Code of Ethics and Professional Conduct, which states that as a PMP you will always act with integrity and professionalism, contribute to the project management knowledge base, enhance individual competence, balance stakeholder interests, and respect personal, ethnic, and cultural differences.[4] The following qualifications must be documented:

▶ *Project management education.* Candidates must provide documentation for the required number of hours of formal project management training in any of the ten knowledge areas: scope, time, cost, quality, human resources, communications, risk, procurement, stakeholder, and integration management. To fulfill this requirement, candidates must have successfully completed courses offered through a university or college academic or continuing education program, or any course or program offered by training companies, consultants, PMI component organizations, distance-learning companies, employer-company sponsored programs, or PMI registered education providers (REPs). Note that PMI chapter meetings and self-study activities (e.g., reading books) cannot be included as part of this requirement. The courses must be complete at the time of application.

▶ *Level of education and project management experience.* The certification requirements acknowledge that not all project managers are formed in the classroom by offering options that allow credit for practical experience. Educational and experiential requirements are divided in two categories:

1. Candidates with a baccalaureate or global equivalent degree should be able to demonstrate a minimum of 4,500 hours of experience in leading and directing projects within the five process groups. The candidate must show a minimum of thirty-six nonoverlapping months of project management experience.

2. Candidates with a high school diploma, associate's degree, or global equivalent credential must demonstrate a minimum of 7,500 hours experience of leading and directing projects within the five process groups. The candidate must show a minimum of sixty nonoverlapping months of project management experience.

Regardless of the category, project management experience must be within a consecutive eight-year period prior to the application submission date.

Table 18-1 shows how to calculate hours of experience in the case of projects with overlapping months. This candidate has forty-three months of project management experience within a fifty-three-month time frame. However, within these forty-three months, two projects overlap a total of five months. The five overlapping months are subtracted from the forty-three months of total project experience demonstrated, allowing the candidate to indicate thirty-eight months of project management experience. Candidates are not required to subtract the overlapping hours; the total hours worked on all projects is counted.

The Project Management Experience Verification Form included in the application is used to summarize your role, the deliverables you managed, and the hours you spent on the project. Deliverables that you managed are reported by process groups. For example, you might report your activities on a project as follows (note that these deliverables are described in very general terms for the purpose of this example; on an actual application form, you would want to be more specific and detailed in your descriptions):

- Initiating process
  - Project charter development
  - Identify stakeholders

Project	Dates	Length (Months)	Hours
Project A	02/01/2000—09/31/2000	8	1,000
Project B	06/01/2001—10/31/2001	5	500
Project C	02/01/2002—08/31/2002	8	1,000
Project D	06/01/2002—11/31/2002	6	750
Project E	04/01/2003—09/31/2003	6	750
Project F	08/01/2003—05/31/2004	10	1,200
Total	02/01/2000—06/31/2004	**43**	**5,200**
Less Overlap 1 (D–C)	06/01/2002—08/31/2002	3	
Less Overlap 2 (F–E)	08/01/2003—09/31/2003	2	
Qualifying Months/Hours		**38**	**5,200**

TABLE 18-1. **CALCULATING HOURS OF PROJECT EXPERIENCE**

- Feasibility study
- Business case development
- Preliminary project scope statement development
- Planning process
  - Scope planning
  - Scope definition
  - Create work breakdown structure (WBS)
  - Schedule development
  - Make or buy decisions
  - Cost estimating
  - Risk identification.
- Executing process
  - Direct and manage project execution
  - Perform quality assurance
  - Information distribution
  - Create work packages
  - Conduct procurements
- Monitoring and controlling process
  - Monitor and control project work
  - Manage stakeholders
  - Performance reporting
  - Integrated change control
  - Scope control
  - Schedule control
  - Cost control

Project	Initiating Process	Planning Process	Executing Process	Monitoring & Controlling Process	Closing Process	Total Hours
Project A	0	525	300	150	25	1,000
Project B	0	300	150	50	0	500
Project C	100	400	300	150	50	1,000
Project D	0	425	200	100	25	750
Project E	0	475	175	50	50	750
Project F	200	450	300	150	100	1,200
Total	300	2,575	1,425	650	250	5,200

TABLE 18-2. **SORTING PROJECT EXPERIENCE INTO PROCESS GROUPS**

- Closing process
  - Close project
  - Contract closure

Candidates report only the hours that they actually worked on the project. The hours are listed by the amount of time spent in any one or more of the five process groups. Table 18-2 shows how to summarize qualifying hours into process groups.

You are not required to report a minimum number of hours in any of the five process groups for an individual project. However, candidates must show experience in all five process groups when the hours are totaled.

PMI certification department selects at random a percentage of applications for audit prior to granting eligibility. If selected, the candidates may be asked to submit verification of the projects documented on the Experience Verification Forms (for example, a signed letter from a supervisor or manager). Copies of degrees or transcripts may also be required.

Once you have passed the application hurdle, PMI will issue you a letter confirming your eligibility to take the exam. Now, the real work begins.

PREPARING FOR THE EXAM

The process of preparing to take the exam differs widely from individual to individual. It is important to have a good understanding of your own study habits, strengths, and weaknesses. Some candidates attend a specialized course, of which there are many available. Some prefer to study on their own, using some of the many materials on the market. Candidates can choose from books, sample exams, flash cards, online sites, and training courses. Many PMI chapters have study classes or networks where members meet to help one another study.

Differences in age, social relationships, family position, maturity, patience, and interests require different training approaches. People also have different learning speeds and styles based on their cognitive styles. The typical student's attention span for a standup lecture is seven to ten minutes. Thus, effective training delivery must vary among lecture, hands-on, textbook, video, CD, computer, and other media to keep your attention. Distance learning has a great potential application for teaching the theory behind project management and acquiring the basic concepts and language. One benefit of computer-based training via CD-ROM or the Internet is timely delivery, which may in fact be more important than depth of content. However, classroom training will never go away, because the classroom is where students get to apply concepts and get feedback on an immediate basis from teachers and from fellow students, so that performance and understanding are validated.

Regardless of how you choose to prepare, the first step is to understand the nature of the examination itself.

What's on the Test?

The PMP certification examination tests the applicant's knowledge and understanding of project management skills, tools, and techniques with a battery of multiple-choice questions (two hundred questions as of this writing) randomly selected from a large database. The examination questions are derived from the *Project Management Professional Role Delineation Study,*[5] which describes, in statements, the specific tasks project managers perform during the planning and execution of a project, why each task is performed, and how each task should be completed. Identified with each task statement are the associated skills, tools, and techniques required to complete the task. Examination questions developed from these task statements assess the candidate's knowledge and ability to apply the proper project management skill, tool, or technique. The candidate must correctly answer at least 81 percent of the questions to pass. (Unanswered questions are scored as wrong answers.)

The questions are organized into five domains that contain the tasks, knowledge, and skills identified in the *Project Management Professional Role Delineation Study*. PMI determined the relative importance of each domain to the practice of project management and applied a weight to each domain; the domains weighted most heavily are covered by the highest percentages of questions on the exam. The domains (and the percentage of questions relating to them) are as follows, as of this writing:

1. *Initiating* (13%): Tests knowledge of how to determine project goals, deliverables, process outputs, and resource requirements; how to document the project constraints and assumptions; how to define the project strategy and budget; how to identify the project performance criteria; and how to produce formal documentation.
2. *Planning* (24%): Tests knowledge of how to refine the project strategy, how to create the WBS, how to develop the resource management plan, how to refine the time and cost estimates, how to establish project controls, how to develop the project plan, and how to obtain project plan approval.
3. *Executing* (30%): Tests knowledge of how to commit and implement project resources, how to manage and communicate project progress, and how to implement quality assurance procedures.
4. *Monitoring and controlling* (25%): Tests knowledge of how to measure project performance, how to refine project control limits, how to manage

American Management Association • www.amanet.org

project changes and take corrective action, how to evaluate the effectiveness of correction action, how to ensure project plan compliance, how to reassess project control plans, how to respond to risk event triggers, and how to monitor project activity.

5. *Closing* (8%): Tests knowledge of how to obtain acceptance of project deliverables, how to document lessons learned, how to facilitate project closure, how to preserve product records and tools, and how to release resources.

What's Not on the Exam

As comprehensive as the exam strives to be in testing the candidate's knowledge of project management processes and methods, much in the daily life of the project manager is not on the exam. For example, it does not test for leadership or interpersonal communication skills, which are critical to being a successful project manager. Being certified is a good thing, but it is by no means enough. Simply winning the PMP designation does not guarantee success. A good project manager has general management skills and industry knowledge in addition to project management knowledge. Just as with any certification or degree, you still must turn theory into practice. Any credential is only worth the paper it is written on if you cannot apply what you have learned.

Getting Started

To organize your study time, first perform a gap analysis of your existing project management knowledge.

The certification process starts with an assessment of the gaps in skills and knowledge. Having identified areas needing more attention, the candidate should undertake a study of the most current edition of the *PMBOK® Guide*. This is the foundation document used to both create and prepare for the exam, but it is not the sole reference. Candidates should read widely on the topic of project management. PMI maintains a list of suggested materials for PMP exam preparation on its bookstore website; many of them, like this handbook, are designed to help candidates deepen their knowledge of both the body of knowledge and its applications. Ideally, the background gained from studying the standards document will be deepened through a more detailed study of suggested readings and other methods, such as participation in professional symposia, training, online learning, and networking with fellow project managers to discuss professional problems and share best practices. (Note: older materials may reference earlier editions of the standard; check and compare release dates to be sure you are working with up-to-date materials.)

Preparing for the exam takes time and dedication. The amount of time you will need to study depends on your current knowledge base. Some "fast-track" courses claim to prepare you for the exam in five days or less. However, it is more reasonable to expect that it may take from one hundred to as many as four hundred hours to properly prepare for the exam. One expert suggests that, even if you plan to take a "fast-track" course, you spend hundreds of hours studying *before* taking the course.[6] Historically, approximately 70 percent of candidates pass the certification exam the first time; one of the main reasons candidates fail is the lack of proper preparation.

It is recommended that the candidate prepare for the exam before submitting an application. This enables you to take all the time you need to properly prepare without the stress of meeting the eligibility deadline.

Study Tips

Studying should begin by knowledge area. A step-by-step approach to preparation might include the following milestones:

- Perform gap analysis to determine the areas in which your knowledge is lacking.
- Learn the purpose of each knowledge area. (See Annex A-1 in the *PMBOK® Guide* for a useful summary.)
- Learn the definitions of key terms in each knowledge area, referencing the glossary in the *PMBOK® Guide*.
- Memorize the names of process groups.
- Learn the process steps within each knowledge area.
- Learn the inputs, tools and techniques, and outputs to each of the forty-seven process steps.
- Learn formulas, particularly earned value calculations.
- Learn which of the forty-seven process steps is required in each of the five process groups.
- Learn how to apply these processes to projects, as many of the questions on the certification exam are situational. This is where the individual's own professional experience on projects comes into play.[7]

To make the process easier on your personal time, keep your study materials handy wherever you go. If you are waiting in the airport or a doctor's office, spend the time studying. Take practice exams and analyze your results, comparing attempts to see where you have improved and where you still have work to do. Keep the scores as a motivator to do better.

Don't try to memorize definitions first. Concentrate your efforts first on the high-level ordered lists: the five process groups, the nine knowledge areas, and the forty-seven component processes.

Be on the lookout for how the processes flow, how the output of one process becomes the input of another. Make note of their exceptions, for example, where change requests are an input or where they are an output.[8]

Note the differences between the processes in each knowledge area. Know the tools and techniques, especially where they involve further analysis—for risk management in particular.[9]

Some candidates for the PMP are put off by the aspects of preparation that appear to be simply rote memorization. However, the value of the PMP is largely the result of the understanding that comes from sharing a common terminology, the importance of which cannot be overstressed. The experience of studying for the exam in itself is valuable because of this—even if you never take or pass the test.

This is one reason why "fast-track" programs have earned some criticism. As one project management writer notes:

They encourage cramming, not the development of long-term knowledge and comprehension. When we were in high school, our learning choices often reflected one of two avenues: learn the fundamentals of the principles being taught and, through a relatively deep understanding, be able to apply them to different situations and problems; or cram at the last minute, relying on short-term memory and triggers to recall the essentials, never to be recollected or used again. We face the same choice preparing for our PMP.[9]

Therefore, try to plan an exam preparation approach that prepares you not just for taking the exam but for your life as a project manager after the exam.

TAKING THE EXAM

The computer-based exam is administered at locations across the globe, on dates scheduled by PMI. Generally, candidates can schedule a time and place that are convenient to their schedule. Candidates are allotted four hours to complete the exam. Prior to starting the exam, the candidate should record any relevant reference information, including formulas, on scratch paper, because having only 240 minutes to answer two hundred questions means that time is of the essence. If you can quickly answer questions from the recorded information, it gives you extra time to spend on the more difficult questions.

As with any test, read each question thoroughly to be sure you understand what the question is asking. Carefully review each of the four multiple-choice options, eliminating options that are obviously incorrect, and select the answer. Avoid spending too much time on difficult questions; flag those questions for review afterward. One important strategy is to remember that the questions are based on the concepts presented in the *PMBOK® Guide*. If an answer to a question in the *PMBOK® Guide* conflicts with your professional experience, the answer from the *PMBOK® Guide* is the correct one in the context of the exam. If you are unable to answer, it is better to guess at an answer than leave the question unanswered.

Candidates learn whether they have passed or failed immediately after completing the exam, when their results are displayed on the screen. The exam administrator provides a report that will indicate how many questions were answered correctly within each process domain. Candidate can access their exam report from PMI on the online certification system ten business days after the examination date. These reports will be most useful to those who do not pass the exam, forming the basis for their study plan for the next attempt.

Those who pass the computer-based exam may begin using their PMP designation immediately. Candidates who do not pass the PMP certification exam may retake the exam, up to three attempts within one year.

PMI allows for paper-based testing under limited circumstances. Candidates who qualify to take a paper-based examination will receive their examination scheduling instructions from PMI twenty days before their scheduled appointment. This confirmation will contain all information required for sitting and taking the exam, including exam date, time, location, and contact person. Candidates who take the paper-based examination will not receive their exam report the day of the exam.

They will be able to access their exam report from PMI on the online certification system approximately six to eight weeks after the examination date.

KEEPING CERTIFICATION CURRENT

Project management is an ever-changing field, so certification is not forever. The PMP certification is granted for three years and must be maintained by fulfilling the continuing certification requirements (CCRs). All PMPs are required to achieve a minimum of sixty professional development units (PDUs) during a three-year CCR cycle. One PDU is earned for each hour the PMP participates in a classroom, workshop, or conference on a project management topic. A PDU may also be earned for activities that advance the profession of project management. There are six categories in which PDUs may be earned:

1. Completing formal academic training
2. Performing professional activities or completing self-directed learning activities, including credit for a published article, for example
3. Attending classes offered by PMI registered education providers
4. Attending classes offered by other education providers
5. Volunteering services to professional or community organizations
6. Working as a practitioner in project management

Project Management Professionals may report their PDUs or view their CCR transcript online. It is recommended that you keep all documentation of PDUs for at least eighteen months after the end of the three-year CCR cycle for which they were submitted, just in case you are randomly selected for a CCR audit. Those who earn greater than sixty PDUs during a three-year CCR cycle may transfer up to a maximum of twenty hours to their next three-year CCR cycle. Those who fail to submit their required sixty PDUs by the end of their three-year CCR cycle will have their certification suspended; if the required PDUs are not submitted within six months after the completion of their three-year CCR cycle, certification is revoked and the ex-PMP must begin the application process over and retake the exam.

Becoming a PMP places you in a prestigious group of project managers. It demonstrates to current and potential future employers that you possess the skills necessary to lead projects to successful completion. Having the PMP credential after your name gives you the confidence, respect, and recognition that you desire from your peers. It indicates that you know how to apply proven project management processes and methodologies that will bring projects to a successful completion, regardless of the industry. In addition, your pursuit of PMP certification makes your career choice and direction clear to a potential employer: it says that you are serious about project management. A certification provides proof of your commitment, willingness to learn, and desire to succeed—a proactive approach by someone willing to take charge.

DISCUSSION QUESTIONS

❶ Taking into account your work schedule, personal commitments, and learning styles, and using the information on the process and study tips in this chapter, make up a schedule for the project of earning your PMP.

❷ Considering your past experience and study, which areas of the test do you expect will prove most challenging to you? Use the results of your self-assessment to compile a set of study resources.

❸ How will your professional life change once you have earned your certification? In what ways will it be more rewarding? More challenging?

ACKNOWLEDGMENT

The author gratefully acknowledges the contribution of content for this chapter by Muhamed Abdomerovic, PMP.

REFERENCES

[1] Project Management Institute (PMI), *A Guide to the Project Management Body of Knowledge,* 5th edition (Newtown Square, PA: PMI, 2004).

[2] Mark E. Mullaly, "The 'P' in PMP: Are We Really a Profession?" On Gantthead.com, http://www.projectmanagement.com/contentPages/article.cfm?forcemobile=on&ID=220429&thisPageURL=/articles/220429/The-P-In-PMP--Are-We-Really-A-Profession-.

[3] Project Management Institute (PMI), *Project Management Professional (PMP)^{SM} Credential Handbook,* http://www.pmi.org. (On the PMI website, see also *Continuing Certification Requirements [CCR] Program Handbook.*)

[4] Project Management Institute (PMI), *PMI Code of Ethics and Professional Conduct,* http://www.pmi.org.

[5] *Project Management Professional Role Delineation Study* (PMI, 2011).

[6] Peter Nathan and Gerald Everett Jones, *PMP Certification For Dummies* (New York: John Wiley, 2003).

[7] Table 3-1 of the *PMBOK® Guide,* 5th edition, maps the forty-seven project management processes into the five project management process groups and the ten project management knowledge areas; p. 61.

[8] Nathan and Jones, op cit.

[9] Mark E. Mullaly, "Training for PM Certification: The Good the Bad and the Highly Questionable," www.gantthead.com, posted on October 16, 2002; now archived at http://bepmpcertified.blogspot.com/.

Competency and Careers in Project Management

J. KENT CRAWFORD, PMP, CEO, PM SOLUTIONS

JEANNETTE CABANIS-BREWIN, EDITOR IN CHIEF, PM SOLUTIONS RESEARCH

Research into the causes of project failures has identified a primary cause of troubled or unsuccessful projects: the lack of qualified project managers.[1] At one time, this lack was primarily due to the fact that qualified project managers were quite rare. Project management was "the accidental profession," not one chosen and studied for.

Today, with the proliferation of degree programs, training courses, and a growing professional body, this is less true. The problem facing projects now is an organizational one. In many organizations, employees have little incentive to assume the position of project manager, largely because organizations have historically assumed that technical capabilities of individuals could be translated into project management expertise. Because of this, professionals who have worked for years to earn the title of senior engineer or technical specialist have been unwilling to exchange their current jobs for the role of project manager. The role is added to their regular job description, instead of being viewed as a legitimate function to be valued by the organization, and which requires a special set of skills. Therefore, many organizations still have not connected the value of the project manager to the success of the organization. Additionally, when companies do perform project management training, they rarely if ever measure the impact of that training on business outcomes, so the value of the trained project manager is still subjective for many organizations.[2]

A second, related cause of troubled or unsuccessful projects is that poor role definition—for all the roles in a project, but especially for the project manager—places even qualified personnel in situations where they are doomed to failure by requiring them to do too much and be expert in everything.

Clearly it is time for organizations to become more systematic in the way they deal with the human resource challenges posed by the project environment. To explore a framework for the division of labor on projects that we think works both for the people and for the project outcomes, let's start by examining the historical role of the project manager.

WHAT DOES A PROJECT MANAGER DO?

The project manager's challenge is to combine two discrete areas of competence:

▶ *The art of project management:* effective communications, trust, values, integrity, honesty, sociability, leadership, staff development, flexibility, decision making, perspective, sound business judgment, negotiations, customer relations, problem solving, managing change, managing expectations, training, mentoring, and consulting

▶ *The science of project management:* plans, WBS, Gantt charts, standards, CPM/precedence diagrams, controls variance analysis, metrics, methods, earned value, s-curves, risk management, status reporting, resource estimating, and leveling

The military, utility, and construction industries were early adopters of project management, so the profession "grew up" in an environment with a strong cost accounting view and developed a focus on project planning and controls—an emphasis on the science. This is the kind of project management that we think of as being "traditional" or "classic" project management. However, it simply represents an early evolutionary stage in the life of the discipline.

Today, however, project management is being used in nearly all industries and across all functions within those industries. Organizations have flattened out, and new information technology has allowed people to communicate more effectively and reduce cycle times across all business processes. As a result, management began pushing more projects onto an increasingly complex organization. The role of project manager is now very demanding and requires an ever-expanding arsenal of skills, especially "soft" or interpersonal skills.

WHAT MAKES A GOOD PROJECT MANAGER?

The debate about project manager skills and competencies is well into its third decade. Thus, we have lists compiled by a dozen or so organizations, academics, and consultancies expressing views on "the good project manager." What project manager skills, competencies, and characteristics do these lists agree on?

Technical or Industry Expertise

A baseline of technical or industry knowledge is what gets a project manager candidate in the door. Commonly, a project manager has an undergraduate degree in some technical specialty, and while that can mean engineering or computer science, with the broadening of the project management field, it can also mean a degree in marketing or one of the helping professions (e.g., health care, social work, education, law). Industry knowledge gained from work in a particular field, such as construction, information technology, or health care, is added to that baseline. Into this category also fall the technical aspects of project management, such as facility with project management software tools.

Interpersonal and General Management Skills

The skills upon which the role seems to succeed or fail are those that are variously termed "organization and people competencies" (Association for Project Management, UK), "personal competencies" (Project Management Institute [PMI]), or "high-performance work practices" (*Academy of Management Journal*). PMI's list of project manager roles reads like a soft skills wish list: decision maker, coach, communication channel, encourager, facilitator, and behavior model.[3]

Thus, the "new project management" is characterized by a more holistic view of the project that goes beyond planning and controls to encompass business issues, human resource issues, organizational strategy portfolios, and marketing. The new project management places its focus on leadership and communication rather than a narrow set of technical tools, and advocates the use of the project management office in order to change corporate culture in a more project-oriented direction.

As a result, the role of the project manager has expanded in both directions: becoming more business- and leadership-oriented on one hand, while growing in technical complexity on the other. This puts both project managers and the organizations they serve in a bind. The solution to this overload is being worked out in many best-practice companies where the implementation of enterprise-level project management offices allows the development of specialized project roles and career paths. Our research studies on the state of the project management organization (PMO) have shown a steady rise in the number of enterprise PMOs and the number of employees supervised within them. The research has also demonstrated that mature PMOs with large staffs of project managers and supporting project roles displayed better organizational performance.[4] Best-practice companies define specific competencies for these roles, and provide "a fork in the road" that allows individuals who are gifted strongly either on the art side of the ledger—as program and project managers and mentors—to flourish, while allowing those whose skill lies in the science of project management to specialize in roles that provide efficiency in planning and controlling projects.

The Fork in the Road

Because the project leader has been found to be one of the most (if not the single most) critical factors to project success, much effort has been devoted to understanding what project managers can/should do to enhance the chances of project success. Leadership, communication, and networking skills top the list. In spite of the importance of leadership characteristics for project managers, researchers and practitioners have observed that project managers in many organizations are seen by senior management as implementers only.[5]

Confusion of roles and responsibilities would be averted if these two very different roles—leader and implementer—were not both referred to as "project managers." Organizations can avoid this problem by determining beforehand who has the best mix of traits and skills to be a superior project manager, or the potential to become one, and by creating career paths for both technically oriented project managers and leadership-oriented project managers. Technical project managers tend to focus more on process while business project managers are more concerned with business results. Ideally, a balance between the two is required.[6]

In addition, other roles can be broken out of the "monster" job description, further streamlining the leadership work of the project manager. Many tasks that have long been part of the project management landscape feature elements of administrative work, for example.

IDENTIFYING AND ASSESSING COMPETENCY

One of the first things an organization must do is inventory the skills required for effective project management at all levels. After a skills inventory is developed, the key attributes of those skills must be determined and a profile developed. This is also the first step in developing competency requirements. Christopher Sauer, in his study of successful project-based organizations, points out that organizational capability is built from the ground up: by making it possible for the people who do projects to do their best.[7] Focusing on building project manager competencies to the "best" level means first identifying what needs to be improved. To do this requires a competency assessment program.

Dimensions of Individual Competence

Competence may be described in different ways, but there are four dimensions that seem to be universally acknowledged:

▶ *Knowledge:* For project managers, the "body of knowledge" contains more than simply specific knowledge about how to plan and control projects—the knowledge outlined in the Project Management Institute's *Guide to the Project Management Body of Knowledge* (*PMBOK® Guide*). There is also knowledge in their chosen discipline (engineering, marketing, information systems, etc.); knowledge of other disciplines that come into play in the industry in which they work, such as regulatory law or technology advancements; and knowledge of the business side (finance, personnel, strategic planning).

▶ *Skills:* For a project manager, skills may fall into any of three areas: their area of subject matter expertise (engineering, marketing, information systems); project management skills related to planning and controlling; or human skills (influencing, negotiating, communicating, facilitating, mentoring, coaching). The technical skills become less and less important as the project manager's responsibility for the managerial skills grows; this is one reason why excellent technologists have often failed as project managers.

▶ *Personal characteristics:* On the intangible, but extremely important, side of the ledger, are things like energy and drive, enthusiasm, professional integrity, morale, determination, and commitment. In recent years, a number of project management writers have focused on these traits as being perhaps the most important for

American Management Association • www.amanet.org

project managers, outweighing technical knowledge and skills. To focus on a few of these:

- *Honesty:* Project managers are role models for the entire project team. They must conduct themselves ethically to instill a sense of confidence, pride, loyalty, and trust. An honest and trustworthy project organization leads to greater efficiency, fewer risks, decreased costs, and improved profitability. Dr. Frank Toney, in his book *The Superior Project Manager,* wrote that honesty trumps education, experience, and even intelligence as a desirable quality in project managers.[8]
- *Ambition:* Ambition is an important factor in business goal achievement. Achievement orientation, as defined in the work on motivation by David McClelland, comprises a focus on excellence, results orientation, innovation and initiative, and a bias toward action, and is very desirable in project managers.[9]
- *Confidence:* Leaders who are confident in their decisions are most likely to succeed. The most confident project managers believe that they have full control of their actions and decisions, versus the belief that outcomes are due to luck, fate, or chance. Superior project managers are confident in their decisions, proactive rather than reactive, and assume ownership for their actions and any consequences.

▶ *Experience:* When knowledge can be applied to practice, and skills polished, experience is gained. Experience also increases knowledge and skill. Experience can be gained in the workplace or as a result of volunteer activities.

COMPETENCY MODELS

The first step toward competency-based management is to understand the patterns that are repeated by the most effective employees in their knowledge, skills, and behaviors—in other words, competencies that enable them to be high performers. This "architecture" of effectiveness for a given position is a *competency model.*[10] A competency model comprises a list of differentiating competencies for a role or job family, the definition of each competency, and the descriptors or behavioral indicators describing how the competency is displayed by high performers.

Models for Project Management

The seminal research in this field was done by the Australian Institute of Project Management (AIPM), whose National Competency Standard for Project Management was adopted by the Australian government as part of that country's national qualification system. In England, the Association for Project Management (APM) created competency standards for project controls specialists and project managers. The publication of the United States–based PMI's competency standard in 2002,[11] after five years of developmental work, established another framework for thinking about the components of competence in a project management context. The existence of project manager competency models streamlines the adoption of competency-based management for project-oriented companies. Although all these assessment frameworks are quite different, they do have certain themes in common.

Once competencies are defined, it is time to conduct an assessment of the identified project management populations. The assessment process should be clearly focused on building strengths, not on eliminating staff; mitigating fear of assessments through open communication is critical.

Let's look at one model in detail: the Project Manager Competency Assessment Program (PMCAP) co-developed by PM College and Caliper International, a human resources assessment firm. Like other competency assessment systems, the PMCAP has three components: a multilevel knowledge test, a personality and cognitive assessment, and a multi-rater survey reviewing the current workplace performance of project managers. These three instruments address three aspects of competence: knowledge of project management concepts, terminology, and theories; behavior and performance in the workplace; and personal traits indicative of the individual's project manager potential.

▶ *Knowledge:* The Knowledge Assessment Tool tests the candidate's working knowledge of the language, concepts, and practices of the profession with questions based on the *PMBOK® Guide*. On an individual basis, candidates can see how they scored on each knowledge area, how they compared to the highest score, their percentile ranking, and how many areas they passed. For the organization, an aggregate table provides insight into the areas that need improvement for their entire population. This information is used to begin developing a targeted education and training program.

▶ *Behavioral assessment:* A second area of assessment is in behaviors exhibited in the workplace. This requires the use of a multi-rater tool (sometimes called a 360-degree tool), which allows the acquisition of feedback on the project manager's behavior from a variety of sources—typically peers, subordinates, supervisors, or clients, but always someone who has first-hand knowledge of the candidate's behavior in the workplace. Individuals rate themselves on their competency in several key performance areas. The independent assessors then rate the individuals on those same criteria. Ratings are compared. A multi-rater assessment serves as a gauge for determining which behaviors demonstrate areas for potential growth.

▶ *Potential:* The potential to perform the project manager role is evaluated through a series of questions that test the ability to solve problems, handle stress, be flexible, negotiate, deal with corporate politics, manage personal time, and manage conflict. The candidate's score is compared to high performers (project managers who show the highest level of competency). The results of this assessment indicate an individual's potential to survive and thrive in the role of a project manager.

Project Manager Competencies

According to research conducted by PM College in conjunction with Caliper, 70 percent of the competencies of a project manager overlap with the competencies of a typical mid-level functional manager. These competencies can be summarized as follows:

▶ *Leadership:* This is usually characterized by a sense of ownership and sense of mission, a long-term perspective, assertiveness, and a managerial orientation. Leaders focus on creatively challenging the system, and inspiring others to act.

▶ *Communication:* This includes written and oral communication, as well as listening skills, and competent use of all available communication tools. Skilled project managers know when to speak, when to listen, and how to resolve issues and conflicts in a calm and professional manner. A related skill, *negotiation,* is a daily feature of the project manager's life. Among the issues that must be negotiated with clients, executives, contractors, functional managers, and team members are scope, changes, contracts, assignments, resources, personnel issues, and conflict resolution.

▶ *Problem-solving skills:* These include proactive information gathering/strategic inquiry; project managers actively seek out information that might impact the project instead of waiting for it to surface, and apply that information in creative ways.

▶ *Self-assessment/mastery:* Best practice project managers are able to critically evaluate their own performance. This introspective ability enables the great project managers to adjust for mistakes, adapt for differences in team personalities, and remold their approaches to maximize team output.[12]

▶ *Influencing ability:* This is the ability to influence others' decisions and opinions through reason and persuasion, strategic and political awareness, the relationship development skills that are the basis for influence, and the ability to get things done in an organizational context.

Gap analysis is the next step after assessment of competency. The knowledge gaps are determined by examining the differences between the demonstrated level of knowledge and the level of knowledge that is required. The behavioral gaps are identified by examining the differences between the self-rating of the project manager candidate and the rater's score. The gaps in both knowledge and behavior, based on the size of the gap, are targeted as developmental opportunities. The results of this integrated assessment are used to create professional development plans for project manager candidates.

While an individual assessment is being conducted, the organization should be determining what roles it will need to ensure an improved level of project performance. Possible roles include team leaders, multiple levels of project managers, program managers, project portfolio managers, project executives, project office directors, and chief project officers. With each of these roles, the organization needs to create effective job/role descriptions that define performance/competency expectations, experiential requirements, and prerequisites of whatever technical skills are required.[13–15]

As project managers expand into new industries, additional areas of competency will emerge. The project manager's role is evolving away from technical, tool-based project management and toward a broader "art" of leadership. But that does not mean the science can be left behind. These equally important competencies many companies are successfully sorting into a new "starring role": the project planner.

THE EMERGENCE OF THE PROJECT PLANNER ROLE

A project planner supports the project manager by taking over critical, detail-oriented, time-intensive tasks, such as the ones discussed above. As a result, the project manager is free to focus on more strategic project goals and objectives. Earlier in this chapter, we discussed the core tasks of the *leader*. It is worthwhile noting that the core tasks of the *manager* have been identified as follows:

- Planning the work
- Organizing the work
- Implementing the plan
- Controlling results

These tasks align with the role of planner. Together, the project manager and planner/controller resolve the leader/manager dilemma by supplying both aspects of these roles in collaboration.

What Makes a Good Project Planner?

To efficiently handle the responsibilities outlined above, the successful project controller/planner must possess technical expertise in project management software and related spreadsheet or database (financial, resource) tools, as well as business process expertise in cost budgeting and estimating, risk analysis, critical path diagramming and analysis, resource forecasting, and change control. In contrast to the project manager candidate, the ideal project planner has the following personal and professional characteristics:

- Logical thinker and problem solver
- Organized and detail focused
- Numbers oriented
- Ability to interpret complicated and interconnected data
- Communication skills, especially as they apply to project information
- PM software expertise
- Application software expertise (accounting, procurement, etc.)

Just as with project managers of varying experience and skill, there is a hierarchy in the project planning and controls arena. A serious project controls person has a breadth of experience that encompasses many of what we have termed "specialty areas," such as change (configuration) control, risk management (from the perspective of quantifying risks with the tools), issues management, action item tracking, multi-project reporting, executive reporting, scheduling integration, organizational resource management, multi-project resource analysis, forecasting, leveling, multi-project what-if analysis, management of the organizational (enterprise) resource library, schedule estimating, cost estimating, and so on. And, just as with project managers, the organization will benefit from establishing a career path from the specialist team member level to a sophisticated divisional project controls position.

PROJECT TEAM MEMBERS: SPECIALTY ROLES IN PROJECT MANAGEMENT

The team member position is where the actual day-to-day work of the project planning, estimating, statusing, and analysis is done. Within this level, more definitive project management roles—depending on the organization—can include project controllers, project analysts, schedulers, business analysts, estimators, systems analysts, knowledge management coordinator, methodologist, resource manager, organizational development analyst, metrics analyst, and others.[16]

Competence-Building Activities

▶ *Case studies:* To approximate the real-world application of professional skills, create cases that highlight complex situations. Reading and studying such cases, the learner sees how to exercise judgment in applying any particular guideline or rule of thumb. As an organizational learning activity, project personnel can practice their problem-solving skills, either online or at lunch-hour learning sessions, by reviewing cases based on an actual organizational story or event.

▶ *Mentoring and coaching:* Mentoring is a perfect match for project management development. For project managers, mentoring—whether we called it that or not—has always played an important role in professional development. As members of the "accidental profession," project managers more often than not learned how to manage projects by managing projects and by observing other project managers in action. Beyond mentoring, professional coaching combines self-focused personal value measurements, personality-type testing, and style-preference identification with feedback on personal and professional behaviors from a broad group of people. The professional coach is most likely educated in a behavioral field, such as psychology, and combines education and training with years of experience working with other clients to provide extremely valuable insight. The coach's counsel will help leverage strengths and eliminate behaviors that might derail success.

▶ *Personal development plans:* Professional growth is also personal growth—a commitment to self-improvement. People who continuously seek feedback, work on their listening skills, polish communication skills, build relationships, and demonstrate control of their personal lives will rise above their peers. Yet many individuals passively accept (or grumble about) whatever growth programs are on offer by the organization. Instead, individuals should be encouraged to construct a personal development plan. The essence of this plan is to know yourself and the environment, build a road map to adapt and grow, and take personal ownership for change. Constructing a personal development plan requires openness to feedback, maturity to change behaviors, and willingness to practice new techniques. Reading is another critical resource for gaining new insights. Experiential education—conferences, seminars, and the like—is another important source for personal growth.[17]

Organizational Issues

Often in our discussion of competence, we focus narrowly on the personal traits and abilities of individuals. But even capable individuals cannot work miracles within dysfunctional organizations. That is why culture change, not merely individual competence assessments, is required. "Organizational pathology," says J. Davidson Frame, is behavior rooted in an organizational culture that works against the best interest of the organization and its members. Organizations that punish the bearers of bad news are an example.[18] To develop the organization's project management capability, says Christopher Sauer, it is desirable both to institutionalize the development of individual capabilities and to create learning that extends beyond the individual project manager's skills and experience. He recommends the PMO, as "a focal point in the organization," where an environment conducive to the development and practice of project management capabilities can flourish.[19]

PROJECT MANAGEMENT CAREER PATHS

One thing that companies can do to support competence is to ensure that project managers have a clear and desirable career path that includes training, promotion criteria, recognition of achievement, and the opportunity to progress to the highest possible levels in the organization. Developing a career structure is essential to the development of an organization's project management capability. The career path structure serves three purposes:

1. It allows the organization to match a project manager's level of competence/ experience to the difficulty and importance of a project.
2. It assures project managers that the investments they make in developing their professional skills will be rewarded.
3. It provides an incentive for people to stay with the company, because they can see a clear promotion path.

Tables 19-1 and 19-2 show examples of career path structures for project management, on both the leadership ("art") and technical sides ("science").

A career path includes at least three elements in order to be valuable: experiential requirements, education/training requirements (knowledge acquisition), and documentation and tracking mechanisms. The *experiential requirements* detail the types

Project Controller:
A project controller brings knowledge of and experience with implementing and using project controls to the team. Professionals in this category are hands-on experts in using project management software to plan and schedule tasks, manage interdependencies, roll-up and/or integrate plans and schedules, report status, and produce suggestions on how to make control process improvements.
Project Team Leader:
A professional, the project team leader has a proven track record in effectively applying the project management principles to project performance, attainment of the triple constraint, and high team performance/ motivation. The project team leader has led medium project initiatives (generally six months in duration) with up to ten core team members.

TABLE 19.1. **EXAMPLE OF A CAREER PATH FOR A PROJECT MANAGER**

Project Manager:

An experienced manager capable of successfully directing the planning, development, and implementation of medium-large projects according to cost, schedule, and scope requirements. The project manager participates in project initiation activities, including plan and budget preparation; leads the project management team in successfully executing the project as planned and budgeted throughout the project life cycle; and oversees the project closure activities including the collection of lessons learned.

Program Manager:

A recognized leader and manager well versed in the principles of project management, strategic and tactical planning, coordinating, and integrating multiple large and complex projects into a comprehensive program. The program manager is capable of working with the clients in defining their business drivers and defining how the program and project objectives meet the benefit triggers for business success.

Senior Project Manager:

A recognized leader and manager capable of successfully directing the planning, development, and implementation of large and complex projects according to cost, schedule, and scope requirements. The senior project manager participates in all phases of the project (from concept to closure) and often has worked in a global environment or setting.

Mentor:

A project management professional with extensive project and program experience capable of working with project managers and project teams to help them put the processes, skills, and support structure in place to effectively establish and manage projects. Typically, mentors provide consulting services to program managers, project managers, program/project teams, and corporate managers. The project management mentor is well versed in leading and managing program/project team members from diverse backgrounds, and within global and virtual settings. In program/project crisis the mentor can be called in to fill in for an extended period of time for the senior project manager or program manager.

PMO Director:

With years of experience in managing projects, programs, and project personnel, the PMO Director also displays a high degree of business acumen and is capable of not only organizing and managing project management improvement initiatives but also communicating the value of PM to the C-Level.

Portfolio Manager:

Portfolio management increasingly rests within the PMO, and sometimes the PMO Director may also take on this role. The portfolio manager, in an enterprise PMO, sits at the strategy table on the executive steering committee and has a voice in how projects are selected and prioritized, as well as in overseeing portfolio tracking.

VP for Strategic Projects and Programs or Chief Project Officer:

In large organizations, there may be multiple PMOs in the various business units—IT, R&D, Marketing, etc. Overseeing the enterprise's strategy for project management is a VP—or even C-level role responsible for optimizing the value that projects and programs deliver to the enterprise.

TABLE 19.1. CONTINUED

Chapter 19 • Competency and Careers in Project Management **199**

Level I	Level II	Level III
Project Coordinator	**Planner I**	**Planner II**
A professional educated and trained in project management principles and knowledge areas (scope, schedule, cost, quality, risk, human resources, communications, and procurement). Project coordinators have particular knowledge in the area's triple constraint: schedule, budget and scope/quality development, and monitoring. Project coordinators are also involved with reviewing project deliverables and technical documentation.	A professional educated and trained in project management principles and knowledge areas (scope, schedule, cost, quality, risk, human resources, communications, and procurement). Project planner I has a strong knowledge base in defining and tracking the project's triple constraint: schedule, budget and scope/quality development, and monitoring. Project planner I has often led small project initiatives (generally less than a month in duration with one to two people). Project planner I has often become involved with creating and reviewing project deliverables and technical documentation, and is capable of leading facilitation sessions for group reviews and project charter definitions.	A professional educated and trained in the project management principles and knowledge areas (scope, schedule, cost, quality, risk, human resources, communications, and procurement). Project planner II has a proven track record in effectively applying the project management principles both to the project's triple constraint—schedule, budget and scope/ quality development, and monitoring—and to managing risks, quality, communications, and resourcing. Project planner II has led small-medium project initiatives (generally one to three months in duration with three to six people). Project planner II often leads the creation of and facilitates the review of project deliverables and technical documentation.

TABLE 19.2. **PROJECT COORDINATOR AND PROJECT PLANNER ROLES AND RESPONSIBILITIES**

of on-the-job activities that have to be accomplished for each level in the career path. Experiential opportunities need to be coordinated with the appropriate resource manager and the human resource department in the organization. A broad range of experiences are required for future project managers. It is not possible to develop them by restricting their experiences to one function. Thus, rather than climbing the ladder up the functional silo, project managers benefit from being exposed to a number of functions, perhaps moving back to functions they have fulfilled before, but in a more senior role. One writer has labeled this "the spiral staircase" career path.[20]

The *education and training requirements* detail the types of knowledge that are required for each rung on the career ladder. At the lower levels, these tend to be basic courses designed to provide exposure and practice to the rudimentary skills required of that level. The upper-level positions require more advanced strategic or tactical types of educational experiences. These may include topics that go beyond the realm of project management into business strategy, financial, or leadership opportunities. The educational program should be targeted to the requirements identified in the career path, and be designed in a progressive nature. In other words, the training requirements of team members are prerequisites for project managers and so on.

Documentation mechanisms include the attainment of certificates, degrees, or other credentials that substantiate the acquisition of the desired set of skills.

The first important criterion for project manager success is the desire to be a manager in general and a project manager in particular. Many organizations force people into the position even if they are not adept at it and do not desire to become one. The step from technical specialist to project manager may be the assumed progression when there is no way to move up a technical ladder. It is better, however, if alternative upward paths exist—one through technical managership and one through project leadership. With such dual promotional ladders, technical managers can stay in their departments and become core team members responsible for the technical portions of projects. Dual ladders also allow progression through project management, but project managers must be able to motivate technical specialists to do their best work.

REFERENCES

[1] PM Solutions Research, *Strategies for Project Recovery* (Glen Mills, PA: PM Solutions Research, 2012).

[2] PM College, *Building Project Manager Competency Improves Business Outcomes* (Glen Mills, PA: PM Solutions Research, 2012).

[3] James S. Pennypacker and Jeannette Cabanis-Brewin (editors), *What Makes A Good Project Manager?* (Glen Mills, PA: PM Solutions Research [formerly the Center for Business Practices], 2003).

[4] PM Solutions Research, *The State of the PMO 2012* (Glen Mills, PA: PM Solutions Research, 2012).

[5] J.D. Frame, *The New Project Management: Corporate Reengineering and Other Business Realities* (San Francisco: Jossey-Bass, 1994).

[6] R. Graham and R. Englund, *Creating an Environment for Successful Projects,* 2nd edition (San Francisco: Jossey-Bass, 2003).

[7] Christopher Sauer, L.I. Liu, Kim Johnston, "Where project managers are kings," *PM Network* 32, No. 4 (2001), pp. 39–49.

[8] Frank Toney, *The Superior Project Manager* (New York: Marcel Dekker/Center for Business Practices, 2001).

[9] David McClelland, *The Achieving Society* (New York: Van Nostrand-Reinholdt, 1961).

[10] Howard Risher, *Aligning Pay and Results* (New York: AMACOM, 1999).

[11] Project Management Institute, *Project Manager Competency Development Framework* (Newtown Square, PA: PMI, 2002).

[12] Personal mastery is a concept discussed at length in the works of Stephen Covey, Peter Senge, and especially Daniel Goleman, *Emotional Intelligence* (New York: Bantam Books, 1995).

[13] Jimmie West and Deborah Bigelow, "Competency assessment programs," *Chief Learning Officer*, May 2003.

[14] J. Kent Crawford and Jeannette Cabanis-Brewin, *Optimizing Human Capital with a Strategic Project Office* (Auerbach, 2005).

[15] PM College Competency Resource Center, http://www.pmcollege.com/content/resource-center-project-manager-competency-0.

[16] J. Kent Crawford et al, *Project Management Roles and Responsibilities,* 2nd edition (Glen Mills, PA: PM Solutions Research, 2008).

[17] Mark Morgan, "Career-building strategies: are your skills helping you up the corporate ladder?" *Strategic Finance*, June 1, 2002.

[18] J. Davidson Frame, *Building Project Management Competence*, (San Francisco: Jossey-Bass, 1999).

[19] Sauer, 1999.

[20] J. Rodney Turner, Anne Keegan, and Lynn Crawford, "Learning by experience in the project-based organization," *Proceedings of PMI Research Conference,* PMI, 2000.

CHAPTER 20

Project Management Ethics
Responsibility, Values, and Ethics in Project Environments

THOMAS MENGEL, PHD, PMP, UNIVERSITY OF NEW BRUNSWICK

The construction of a new dam and power generator increases the service and viability of a regional supplier of electrical power, it decreases the emissions of greenhouse gas through a reduced need for power generated by fossil fuel, and it generates local employment and revenues not easily available otherwise. However, it also disrupts the scenic environment and changes the habitats for humans and other beings in a rural river valley and it will most likely be followed by other projects to come.

Good or bad? Right or wrong? In trying to meet requirements, project management includes decision making based on choices and criteria. Ethics are considered as one basis for the decisions to be made.

TERMS AND CONCEPTS OF ETHICS AND ETHICAL DECISION MAKING: VALUES, MORALS, AND ETHICS

Values are the major motif of our actions and endeavors (e.g., preserving our environment, making a profit). They provide us with orientation and serve as a basis for responsible decisions.[1]

To make daily choices about good or bad behavior easier, societies and groups tend to develop principles and rules that guide our conduct. These *morals* are codified convictions and expectations as to what is considered good behavior (e.g., shop locally).

Ethics are the systematic combination of values and morals to enable rational and values-based judgments and decisions about what ought to be done. Ethics include criteria and processes enabling us to arrive at or to assess personal decisions or behavior in terms of good or bad and right or wrong (e.g., religious ethics, corporate codes of conduct).

SYSTEMS OF ETHICAL DECISION MAKING

Ethical decision making tends to be easy in the case of one option serving one value. Facing several options serving one value or conflicting choices (e.g., the above-cited dam project), we need to enter a decision-making process based on ethical considerations helping us to sort out the ethical dilemma and arrive at an ethically sound decision.[2]

Results-based systems focus on the "good" end. They are interested in good results, ignoring how they came about. In a rather simplistic economic environment, for example, a cost-benefit analysis will lead to a decision in favor of the greatest gain. In more complex situations, however, it becomes difficult to weigh the level of gain of a majority against the level of pain for a minority. A more elaborate approach by Rawls[3] is built on the concepts of fairness and cooperation. Trying to eliminate personal preferences by pretending that the actors were under a "veil of ignorance" hiding their personal situation and status, Rawls argues that not knowing who exactly will benefit from any given decision will most likely produce just decisions.

Rules-based systems focus on "right" conduct. Behavior is considered "right" if based on "right" principles, independent of its results. Good will and universal applicability of the principles of actions provide the major criteria for evaluating decisions. However, this approach does not easily help us to decide in the case of conflicting principles.

ETHICAL CONSIDERATIONS IN PROJECT MANAGEMENT

Ethics deals with right actions and good results. Project management strives for meeting project requirements through project activities. Hence, every aspect of project management involves ethical considerations and may produce an ethical dilemma. However, "ethical hot spots"[4] in project management are areas of interest to the public and issues that touch on basic, generally accepted values (human rights, preservation of our environment, financial honesty, etc.).

Benefits of Managing Ethics in Project Environments

Enron, Arthur Andersen, WorldCom, and other companies have brought ethical questions to the forefront of business and project environments. Thus, managing ethics is expected to lessen the liability and maintain the professional integrity of executives and project managers. Furthermore, managing ethics has been proven to provide companies with financial advantages and an improved public image.[5] However, beyond tactical considerations, ethical reasoning per se and values-oriented leadership[6] become part of a comprehensive organizational and project strategy in trying to "maintain a moral course in turbulent times . . . [and to] support employee growth and meaning."[7]

Existing Approaches to Managing Ethics in Project Management

While many project teams implement codes of conduct for their projects, ethical reasoning begins to emerge in some particular project management areas. The Centre for Computing and Social Responsibility at De Montfort University in the United

Kingdom is striving to make implicit ethical considerations explicit for software project management.[8] Some dominant ethical principles (honor, honesty, bias, adequacy, due care, fairness, social cost, and action) are used within the project management process to produce a software development impact statement. First, stakeholders and ethical issues are identified (generic). Then, this process is applied to the work breakdown structure (specific), ensuring the consideration of ethical aspects in all project activities. Approaches like these may be the cornerstone of managing ethics comprehensively in project environments.

Ethical Standards in Business

International Standards of Business Ethics

In trying to increase awareness and appreciation of cultural differences, various standards of global business ethics have been published.[9] Kofi Annan, the former secretary-general of the United Nations, started the latest and most comprehensive initiative in January 1999. In challenging business and other leaders to support and implement core values within their corporate and public practices and policies, Annan initiated the United Nations Global Compact[10] and put forward nine principles regarding human rights, labor, and the environment. At its first leaders' summit on June 24, 2004, in New York, the principles were enhanced by a tenth principle against corruption, and the awareness of the need for global cooperation is growing continually. "This ever-increasing understanding is reflected in the growth of the Global Compact's rapid growth. With over 10,000 corporate participants and other stakeholders from over 130 countries, it is the largest voluntary corporate responsibility initiative in the world."[11]

Project Management Institute Standards of Ethics

The Project Management Institute (PMI), "one of the world's largest not-for-profit membership associations for project management,"[12] takes professional responsibility and ethical conduct of its members and certified project management professionals (PMPs) seriously. Thus, the institute has presented respective statements and codes at two levels.

While the 2000 edition of the Project Management Institute's *Guide to the Project Management Body of Knowledge* (*PMBOK® Guide*) only briefly touched on ethical norms that may "affect the way that people and organizations interact" and on "social-economic, environmental sustainability,"[13] the editions of 2004, 2008, and 2013 put greater emphasis on the professional responsibility the project management team has to its stakeholders and refers to the respective Code of Ethic and Professional Conduct[14] that PMI members, volunteers, and PMI-certified professionals need to adhere to. Furthermore, the later editions suggest considering the social, economic, political, and physical impact of projects beyond the existence of the project organization. Finally, they point out the need for project teams to consider and understand their environment, including ethical issues.

In particular, the PMI Code of Ethics and Professional Conduct "describes the expectations that we have of ourselves and our fellow practitioners in the global project management community. It articulates the ideals to which we aspire as well as the behaviors that are mandatory in our professional and volunteer roles. . . . We also believe that this Code will assist us in making wise decisions, particularly when faced with difficult situations where we may be asked to compromise our integrity or our values."[15] The Code affirms and in more detail describes the values of responsibility, respect, fairness, and honesty. Furthermore, for each value, it lays out aspirational and mandatory standards.

Finally, the Code describes the history of these standards and the open and collaborative process for their development; it concludes with a glossary of key terms including *conflict of interest* and *duty of loyalty.* The mandatory standards require professionals to adhere to all relevant regulations and legal requirements; to report unethical and illegal conduct; to negotiate and act in respect of others; to disclose and withdraw from conflict-of-interest situations; to refrain from favoritism, bribery, and discrimination; and to not engage in deceptive or other dishonest behavior. In its aspirational standards, the Code lays out the expectations for professional conduct such as serving the best of public interests, accountability, confidentiality, respectful and fair behavior, truthful communication, and good faith.

The fifth and latest edition (2013) of the *PMBOK® Guide* maintains and even strengthens that approach by adding *stakeholder management* as additional knowledge area and thus giving the management of relations with various stakeholders—implicitly including the perspective of ethics and social responsibility—more weight.[16]

MANAGING ETHICS IN PROJECT ENVIRONMENTS

Ethical Considerations for the Project Life Cycle and Organization

Phases in projects are supposed to reduce complexity, increase transparency, and allow for controlled transitions and reviewed handoffs.[17] *Reviews* are meant to detect problems and suggest solutions. Reviews may even be used to stop projects that no longer seem to be feasible within the given constraints. Project managers and team members are responsible for honestly and truthfully reporting any problems regarding phase deliverables and preparing a thorough review of the phase they are about to close. Although rushing could be tempting and may even be supported by time constraints put forward by stakeholders, giving in without clearly discussing the impact and associated risk is irresponsible and unprofessional conduct.

Communication with and management of project stakeholders is at the heart of successful project management. Furthermore, identifying stakeholders, determining their requirements, and managing their influence involve ethical considerations, including varying levels of responsibility. Project managers need to comprehensively determine the impact of any decision to be made. Expectations of funding or otherwise powerful authorities need to be balanced with conflicting requirements of other stakeholders. To comprehensively manage stakeholder expectations and conflicting issues, objectives and values need to be carefully addressed and openly discussed. The focus needs to be on customer satisfaction without disregarding others.

Furthermore, project needs have to be balanced with *organizational influences;* systems, cultures, and structures need to be considered. While team and project cultures may be innovative and leading the change, the possible difference to organizational culture and hierarchy has to be "managed" in loyalty to superiors and to the organization as a whole.[18]

Ethical "Hot Spots" in the Project Management Processes and Knowledge Areas

The project manager is responsible for tailoring project management processes according to the needs of the project and the organization. Since trade-offs are inevitable, the ethical implications of all decisions need to be assessed.

While defining the project during the *initiating processes,* the project team needs to understand the values, concerns, and expectations of stakeholders and analyze the possible impact of the project. That may help the project manager to create buy-in and evaluate the existence of a strong and broad-enough basis for the project to move forward.

The focus of ethical considerations in the *planning processes* is defining the detailed objectives and preparing the best course of action. Translating the general impact analysis of the project on various stakeholders into the detailed project activities and deliverables documented in the work breakdown structure is a helpful approach to base planning decisions on ethical reasoning. Furthermore, all planning processes need to be conducted and communicated honestly and thoroughly both internally and externally.

Executing, monitoring, and *controlling processes* implement the plans, with the ethical focus again being on communicating timely and truthfully with all stakeholders and on continuing to manage their expectations in balance with changes in and around the project environment. In spite of daily pressures and necessary control measures, not losing sight of stakeholders as human beings having values, objectives, and feelings, rather than as mere resources or obstacles of project improvement, becomes the major ethical challenge of execution and control. Customer satisfaction and team development are the main criteria for measuring project progress and success. Both depend on correct, comprehensive, and careful information and feedback in a timely manner.

Finally, the *closing processes* need to formalize acceptance, evaluate stakeholder satisfaction, and bring the project to an orderly end. Including evaluations of the impact analysis and stakeholder management processes in final lessons learned and post-implementation reviews will further improve the processes of ethical decision making and conduct.

Guidelines for Managing Ethics in Project Environments

Some ethical principles for project management have emerged in our earlier discussions. A clear vision—including values—needs to be part of project leadership and should be aligned with policy, practice, and communication to become effective. Project managers need to be "obsessed"[19] with basic values like fairness, honesty, due care, and integrity. They need to feel comfortable communicating intensely with a variety of internal and external stakeholders and taking their perspectives seriously. Ethical decision making requires commitment to solving problems collaboratively based on shared values. However, accountability calls for personal rather than collective responsibility in a professional context. The human, social, and environmental cost and impact of decisions and actions need to be analyzed, considered, and balanced with other project and stakeholder requirements in a local and global perspective. The initial results of that process and later changes need to be documented in a product- or service-oriented project deliverables impact statement (ProDIS) and a process-oriented project management impact statement (ProMIS).

Specific project management guidelines on ethical decision making can help implementing the ethical principles:

- Include ethical dimensions in all decision-making procedures.
- Use checklists and samples for the ProDIS and ProMIS.
- Make ethics decisions in groups and make them public (use of the "veil of ignorance" approach).
- Define a joint process and mutually agreeable criterion for ethical decision making.
- Apply both ethical principles and evaluation of the possible results and impact.
- Continually evaluate and improve the procedures of ethical decision making.

Finally, although corporate project management policies and procedures for man-aging ethics are not prerequisites for managing ethics in individual projects, they substantially help in doing so. However, top-down commitment is paramount. If senior executives do not live up to the core values of the corporation and fail to communicate both their shortcomings and their continual striving for ethical growth, all further efforts in ethical programs will be perceived as dummy activities merely aimed at deceiving the public. Thus, on top of the possible development of codes of ethics or conduct, ethics management needs to be implemented as a comprehensive and corporate-wide process using cross-functional teams.

Furthermore, ethics management needs to be integrated in other management practices to become effective. Ethicists and ethics committees may then be functions supporting the ethics management process by designing and implementing procedures to develop the impact statements (ProDIS and ProMIS) and to resolve ethical dilemmas based on vivid corporate values and principles. Both leaders and managers as well as staff members charged with special ethics functions need to hold and support regular challenging meetings confronting values statements with practical conduct and procedures, and thus updating and improving both. Everyone involved in that process needs to be educated and trained in ethics management and ethical reasoning and decision making.

Finally, leaders and managers need to install a corporate culture that values forgiveness and a continual effort for improvement. The survival of such a culture depends on the valued perception of ethical integrity and moral courage, even in the light of their occasional negative impact on the bottom line. Most probably this culture can best be implemented and nurtured by leaders serving both their various stakeholders and a joint mission based on shared values.[20]

SAMPLE EXERCISES

1. You are a passionate nonsmoker concerned about public health and a member of an antismoking organization. As a PMP, you are being offered an assignment as the responsible project manager for an external client in the tobacco industry. Your job would be to design and implement a sales initiative aimed at an increased market share of that client. How do you respond?

a. I accept. My boss has told me that increasing the market share of one company in a saturated market will most probably not increase smoking. In addition, if I don't accept, somebody else will.

b. I accept. My involvement with the antismoking organization is my business and not publicly known.

c. I decline and insist on my company's rejecting the assignment due to its general unethical background.

d. I decline and report my private involvement to my boss and state my concern that I cannot serve both the external client and my antismoking organization.

Answer: d. Your affiliation creates a conflict of interest that according to the PMI Code of Ethics and Professional Conduct needs to be reported to your superior.

2. As a project manager in a foreign country, you are in charge of contracting various suppliers. During the solicitation process one of the applicants for a contract offers your team free and preferred on-site housing. How do you respond?

a. I politely but firmly reject that offer. Accepting gifts from suppliers is perceived to be unethical by both global and professional standards.

b. I accept. In the culture of that particular country, this is not considered unethical but rather a common and friendly gesture among business partners.

c. I decline. Acceptance would create a dependency that will make objective negotiations regarding costs, time, and quality of the work performed more difficult.

d. I accept. That offer does not provide me with a personal advantage because I will be staying in a first-class hotel when I am on-site. Instead, it improves the situation of my team.

Answer: a. Accepting a gift from a supplier is explicitly mentioned as being unethical by professional standards and standards of global business ethics.

3. You are a project manager bidding for a project management contract. The contracting agency approaches you with the request to reduce the estimated costs by 30 percent based on the same deliverables and constraints. How do you respond?

a. I recalculate the bid by considering cheaper material and labor for items that have not explicitly been mentioned in the bid.

b. After seriously reconsidering, I truthfully present all the details and reaffirm that delivering the expected level of quality in the given time frame has its price.

c. Cost projections at this stage are rough estimates only. So, reducing the bid by 30 percent now to get the contract and recovering the missing amount "elsewhere" during the run of the project is a rather "normal" way of managing projects on a contract basis.

d. I know that competitors have underestimated the actual costs to get the contract. Thus I need to do the same in order not to disadvantage my company.

Answer: b. Professional codes of conduct require project managers to truthfully present all information to the best of their knowledge.

CONCLUSION

A comprehensive model of project management ethics and of managing ethics in a project environment needs an integrative approach, including an ethical analysis of the process as well as of the impact of project decisions. Existing approaches of business ethics and of project management–related codes of conduct and ethical guidelines serve as a first basis for ethical decision making in project environments based on professional responsibility and conduct. Managing ethics in project environments needs to inspire an appropriate project culture and include the mechanisms that ensure and improve ethical decision making, actions, and results.

Corporate leadership based on the model of servant- and values-oriented leadership will certainly support managing ethics in project environments. However, professionals in project management are challenged to implement project management ethics even in an unfavorable corporate or organizational environment. They may succeed if they passionately lead and manage projects by comprehensively serving both the project mission and requirements as well as the expectations of their stakeholders, and by orienting toward mutually acceptable values throughout the various project phases and processes.

DISCUSSION QUESTIONS

❶ How would you define "integrity"?

❷ What are the key elements of the PMI Code of Ethics and Professional Conduct? Do you feel they cover well the issues that may arise in practice? Why (not)?

REFERENCES

[1] Victor E. Frankl, *Man's Search for Meaning* (New York: Simon & Schuster, 1985); Thomas Mengel, *"High Potential" Can Be Deceiving—Utilizing the Reiss Motivational Profile® in HR and Leadership Development. FMI*IGF Journal* 23, No. 3 (2012), pp. 10–12; Thomas Mengel, "Motivation," in J. Gosling and A. Marturano (editors) *Key Concepts in Leadership Studies* (Milton Park, Oxfordshire, UK: Routledge, 2008), pp. 111–114.

[2] J.W. Weiss, *Business Ethics: A Stakeholder and Issues Management Approach with Cases,* 5th edition (Mason, OH: South-Western Cengage Learning, 2009); Laura P. Hartman (editor), *Perspectives in Business Ethics* (New York: McGraw-Hill, 2002), pp. 6–10; Peter Singer (editor), *A Companion to Ethics* (Malden: Blackwell Publishers, 1999), pp. 205–218, 230–248.

[3] John Rawls, *A Theory of Justice* (Cambridge, MA: Harvard University Press, 1971).

[4] Simon Rogerson and Donald Gotterbarn "The Ethics of Software Project Management," in G. Collste (editor), *Ethics and Information Technology*. (Delhi: New Academic Publishers, 1998), pp. 137–154.

[5] Lynn S. Paine, *Value Shift: Why Companies Must Merge Social and Financial Imperatives to Achieve Superior Performance.* (New York: McGraw-Hill, 2003); Rebecca Barnett, "How business ethics failed corporate America (and what we must do next)," *Project Magazine* 3, No. 7 (2002), http://www.project magazine.com/v3i7/ethicsv3i7.html.

[6] Thomas Mengel, K. Cowan-Sahadath, and F. Follert, "The value of project management to organizations in Canada and Germany, or do values add value? Five case studies, *Journal of Project Management* 40, No. 1 (2009), pp. 28–41; T. Mengel and K. Cowan-Sahadath, "The value of project management to Canadian government organizations, or do values add value?" *PMI Research Conference 2008 proceedings* (Warsaw, Poland: PMI, 2008); T. Mengel, "Leadership development for complex environments—helping create a meaningful future," *FMI Journal—Financial Management Institute of Canada* 19, No. 1 (2007), pp. 13–15.

[7] Carter McNamara, *Complete Guide to Ethics Management: An Ethics Toolkit for Managers,* 1999, http://www.managementhelp.org/ethics/ethxgde.htm.

[8] Rogerson and Gotterbarn, pp. 137–154.

[9] Hartman, pp. 730–746.

[10] *The Global Compact,* http://www.unglobalcompact.org.

[11] http://www.unglobalcompact.org/AboutTheGC/index.html.

[12] http://www.pmi.org/About-Us.aspx.

[13] Project Management Institute, *A Guide to the Project Management Body of Knowledge* (Newtown Square, PA: PMI, 2000), p. 27.

[14] Project Management Institute, *Code of Ethics and Professional Conduct* (Newtown Square, PA: PMI, 2007), http://www.pmi.org/~/media/PDF/Ethics/ap_pmicodeofethics.ashx. See also http://www.pmi.org/About-Us/Ethics/Code-of-Ethics.aspx and http://www.pmi.org/about-us/ethics.aspx.

[15] Ibid.

[16] Project Management Institute, *A Guide to the Project Management Body of Knowledge,* 5th edition (Newtown Square, PA: PMI, 2013).

[17] PMI 2008, pp. 18–21.

[18] Ibid., pp. 27–33.

[19] Carter McNamara, *Complete Guide to Ethics Management: An Ethics Toolkit for Managers,* 1999, http://www.managementhelp.org/ethics/ethxgde.htm.

[20] Robert K. Greenleaf, *Servant Leadership: A Journey into the Nature of Legitimate Power and Greatness* (Mahwah, NJ: Paulist Press, 1977).

CHAPTER 21

Professionalization of Project Management
What Does It Mean for Practice?

JANICE THOMAS, PHD, CENTER FOR INNOVATIVE
MANAGEMENT, ATHABASCA UNIVERSITY

As work has become more knowledge oriented, information workers in various occupations have recognized the similarity of their work to the traditional professions of the twentieth century. Many of these occupations, led by teaching, nursing, and social work, and including financial planners, surveyors, and many others, have embarked on professionalization initiatives seeking the recognition and privileges traditionally associated with medicine, law, accounting, engineering, and very few other occupations.

In the last decade of the twentieth century, project managers launched a similar professionalization mission. The Project Management Institute (PMI) stated that its mission was "to further the professionalization of project management" with the explicit intent of developing a new profession. Today, many project managers view project management as a profession. By 1999, more than 65 percent of PMI's membership explicitly recognized project management as a profession.[1]

There is no question that these individuals conduct themselves in a professional manner when carrying out their paid responsibilities. Yet there is equally no doubt that project management has not today attained the status of a traditional profession as defined in sociological terms, in which a profession is recognized as a special kind of occupation with a particular set of characteristics that carry with them a set of privileges and responsibilities. Formally, law in the Western world recognizes professions, and there are very few accepted in most Western jurisdictions.[2]

DEFINITION OF A PROFESSION

Professions have been studied for more than seventy-five years, starting when it was first recognized that there existed a class of occupations typically accorded a higher degree of privilege and rewards than other occupations. Original studies of the professions focused on identifying the unique characteristics that distinguished

213

Exclusive control—esoteric and systematic BOK	Members have a monopoly on understanding and applying the BOK
Autonomy of practice	Members control the standards of society
Norm of altruism	Members act in best interest of client
Authority over clients	Professionals control the client/practitioner relationship
Distinctive occupational culture	Occupation is set apart by a distinctive set of norms, values, and symbols
Recognition	Usually legal requirement for specific training and preparation prior to practice

FIGURE 21-1. **TRAITS OF A PROFESSION**

professions from nonprofessions. This "trait approach" to professionalization typically identified the set of characteristics outlined in Figure 21-1 as fundamental to a profession.[3,4]

These studies also identified the need to drive out malpractice, and thus protect the public, as a driving force in the legal recognition of the profession. The occupations of law, medicine, and, lately, engineering and accounting typically formed the basis of study for research on the traditional professions.

According to trait theory, nursing, teaching, and social work (among others) are classified as "semiprofessions," as they possess only some of the traits or have only partially developed some of the traits required by an occupation to be considered fully professional. Project management clearly fits into the "semiprofession" category,[5] as explained below.

Professionalization, or the path to professional status, requires consideration of both what a profession looks like (the traits) and the process by which these characteristics are attained. Figure 21-2 identifies the key activities usually associated with professionalization.

Abbott[6] suggested that professions begin with the recognition by people that they are doing something that is not covered by other professions and so they form a professional association. Forming a professional association defines a "competence territory" that members claim as their exclusive area of competent practice. The professionalization activity and its claims to professional status must be placed in historical, economic, political, and social context, and must be seen as being fundamentally shaped by these conditions, rather than assuming that claims to professional status are objective, inevitable, and timeless. Claims to professional status (for example, "autonomy" or "esoteric knowledge") are perceived as strategies in exerting occupational control and autonomy vis-à-vis other groups, including bureaucratic managers.[7]

Understanding professionalization as a struggle between occupations to exert control and gain autonomy can provide superior insights into the historical struggle

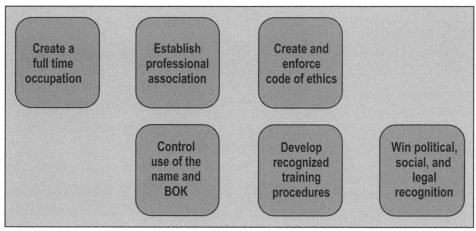

FIGURE 21-2. **THE PROCESS OF PROFESSIONALIZATION**

of occupations such as nursing, teaching, social work, and project management to achieve professional status. Indeed, some have pointed out that even the firmly established professions (such as medicine and law) are increasingly subject to broad social change questioning their traditional status, especially in the age of cutbacks.[8,9] Thus, we turn to an examination of the status of project management in attaining the characteristics of a profession and then the requirements of professionalization through the processes and exercise of power with particular emphasis on what project management can learn from the struggles of other "semiprofessions" and the actions of the various professional associations worldwide to advance this initiative.

STATUS OF PROJECT MANAGEMENT

Figure 21-3 summarizes project management's status in terms of developing the characteristics of a profession. Clearly, project management has not yet achieved most of the characteristics of a traditional profession. Next we will look at the activities various project management bodies and practitioners have embarked on to achieve these characteristics.

THE PATH TO PROFESSIONALIZATION

The path to professionalization is composed of several lines of activity, as introduced in Figure 21-3. Each of these activities is introduced below, with reference to the actions of other emerging professions and to the implications for project management in accomplishing this goal.

Full-Time Occupation

Being recognized as a full-time occupation rather than a skill or technical tool required of a variety of occupations can be seen as the first step toward formal

Exclusive control-esoteric and systematic BOK	No—BOKs are beginning to be recognized but still highly contested
Autonomy of practice	No—members *contribute* to the standards of practice
Norm of altruism	Not usually—societal impact of failed projects not recognized
Authority over clients	Not usually—project managers tend to work within corporations
Distinctive occupational culture	Possibly—certain aspects exist
Recognition	Not yet—PM not legally recognized as a profession in any jurisdiction

FIGURE 21-3. **THE STATUS OF PROJECT MANAGEMENT**

recognition of the worth of an occupation as separate from the other potential occupations within which this skill is practiced. An occupation has truly arrived in most Western jurisdictions when governments begin to collect occupational statistics. Until recently, the only statistics available on the number of project managers worldwide came as estimates provided by PMI; no occupational statistics were available. Without being a recognized occupation, project management could never attain professional status and would always be seen as an attribute perhaps of some other profession (like architecture). About five years ago, we are told, the United States government recognized project management as an occupation and would collect occupational statistics (though this has not been confirmed at press time). Thus, it appears that project management has been recognized as an occupation.

Monopoly Over Use of the Name

While the occupation has been recognized, there is still no clear definition of what a project manager is. To reach profession status, the term *project manager* must be captured and controlled. As long as anyone can use that designation without regard to training or certification, it will be impossible to create an occupation that can lay claim to professional status. To date, it appears that anyone can claim to be a member of the project management occupation without reference to qualifications.

All analyses of professionalization processes include this criterion, but it should not be viewed in absolute terms. All claims to professionalization include a negotiated statement regarding what the practitioners include in their claims and what they leave out. Doctors don't claim control or competency over everything in the domain of health work. Teachers don't claim the exclusive right to practice in all learning situations. Gaining control over the name will require defining which project management activities are to be the sole jurisdiction of professional project managers. What projects will professional project managers assume as theirs, and what will be left to anyone else who wants them? Where does the casual practitioner fit into the world of projects and where does the professional project manager enter? Not all projects are equal and not all projects require a professional. Currently, some of this activity is happening in individual organizations, as they create career ladders for project managers and define what qualifications are required for the use of the term *project manager* within their organizational activities, and within some national jurisdictions in terms of competency rankings.

The protection of that designation or name will be ongoing, a continuing part of the struggle among occupations, and between occupations and employers, to achieve control over the work. Through this ongoing process, the limits of the practice will be negotiated over time. Nurses do a number of things today that they did not do twenty years ago, as witnessed by the arrival of the nurse practitioner. This process will require lobbying activities to win the right to that name and continuing efforts to police the use of the name. Conducted in a piecemeal fashion within various organizations and professional associations, this is likely to be a messy process.

Control Over the Body of Knowledge

The claim to professional status ultimately rests on the ability of the practitioners to lay claim to more or less exclusive command of an esoteric body of knowledge that they declare to be essential to good practice. The inability to make this claim convincingly is, perhaps, the primary factor responsible for the failure of teachers and social workers to achieve full recognition as professionals. Nurses, on the other hand, suffer not from the lack of a hard scientific body of knowledge, but rather from the fact that another group of professionals, physicians and surgeons, has laid claim to controlling that body of knowledge. Project management fits somewhere between these extremes.

The emergence of project management bodies of knowledge (BOKs) is a significant step in the right direction, but the development of a full-blown BOK for project management will require a great deal of elaboration. In particular, professional bodies will have to be able to argue convincingly that the methods, ideas, and tools embedded in the project management BOKs and mastered by the professional project managers improve their ability to deliver projects and add value to clients. This is not a claim that can be substantiated yet by solid research evidence, despite ongoing and serious efforts to address this gap in understanding.[10]

Indeed, while the creation and maintenance of project management BOKs is a step in the right direction, so far there is no exclusive BOK that holds the position of generally accepted accounting principles or recognized medical diagnostic tests in the world of project management doctrines. Project management guidelines are promulgated by several project management professional associations worldwide as well as those crafted by individual gurus and large companies. Without agreement on what this BOK is and who is in charge of developing and maintaining it, professionalization will be difficult to achieve.

A further threat to our ability to develop and recognize a common BOK is the resistance that existing BOKs, such as that produced by the United Kingdom's Association of Project Management (APMBOK) and PMI's *Guide to the Project Management Body of Knowledge (PMBOK® Guide)*, have shown to change or incorporation of research findings into the documented "best practices." Comparing the original BOKs with the current editions illustrates this conundrum. Content remains much the same over the last twenty years since the publication of the first BOKs and largely ignores research findings from the same period.[11]

Education

Upgrading knowledge and developing recognized and ever more comprehensive educational programs has been a key aspect of professionalization in every case of a modern occupation striving to upgrade to professional status. The major established professions and the three semiprofessions of particular interest to project management—teaching, social work, and nursing—all lay claim to their own faculty/ college within the university higher education system. Accounting is the only profession that resides in someone else's home (business or management faculty/colleges); the others all have their own deans. To date, project management has no clear home within the university setting. It is found in one of several places, including business, engineering, or planning, and many universities provide no academic project management education, focusing only on providing project management training and professional certification preparation. Most training in project management still resides within corporate training, consulting, and professional organizations—entirely outside higher education. Development of a recognized academic discipline is crucial to the professionalization project. While there will always be a demand for a wide array of educational offerings, the emergence of the academic discipline will entail negotiations between professional associations and academics.

Role of the Professional Associations

Professional associations in traditional professions are the center of control for practitioners; they represent the interests of the practitioners to the outside world and enforce standards within the profession. A strong association mediates between public and private authorities on behalf of practitioners and directly influences the power and influence that accrues to that profession.

Today, a variety of local and global professional associations are alternately vying for recognition and authority in the project management world and cooperating to improve project management's chances of becoming a twenty-first-century profession.[12,13] These and other important association initiatives are introduced below.

International Project Management Association (IPMA)

The IPMA began as a community of practice for managers of international projects in 1965 but has evolved into a federation of approximately forty national project management associations representing 50,000 members around the world (see the IPMA Web site). The IPMA has developed its own standards and certification program, which is composed of a central framework and quality assurance process plus national programs developed by association members. This association competes on a global basis with the programs of PMI. However, recently the two organizations have been trying to find common ground for working together.

Project Management Institute

PMI began as the national project management association for the United States in 1969. Until the 1990s, this was a relatively small professional association. However, the 1990s witnessed exponential membership growth. By the late 1990s, PMI recognized that its membership of more than 100,000 was becoming international in nature. While PMI's headquarters continues to be in Philadelphia and the organization continues to be subject to the laws of that state, in 2003 the first of three planned regional service centers was opened in Europe. PMI's large membership and global mandate suggests that it is the "leading nonprofit professional association in the area of project management." However, it is still largely American in membership, nature, and approach.[13]

In recognition of the need for academic support in building a profession, PMI has increased its efforts to influence academic institutions over the last decade. In addition to certification and registered education programs, PMI has instituted university accreditation programs. To date all of these programs are voluntary in nature. PMI has also initiated government lobbying both in North America and in emerging markets like China in recent years.

Up until 2004, PMI's tag line was "building the profession." After thoroughly investigating the professionalization process through a commissioned research project,[14] the board of PMI agreed to change the tagline to "making project management indispensable for organizations." This seemed to have been the end of the professionalization journey for this organization. In 2012, PMI took direct opposition to a United Kingdom effort to achieve professional status for the occupation in that jurisdiction.

Regional Project Management Associations

There are almost three hundred regional PMI chapters, national members of IPMA, or other national associations in the world today. A few are notable because of their size or activity in developing bodies of knowledge, standards, or certification programs.

The Association for Project Management (APM) of the United Kingdom has a membership of over 19,000 individuals and five hundred corporations, and has been actively involved in defining the project management BOK over the years. In 2007, this group took steps to begin the path to professionalization for project management by marshaling resources to apply for a royal charter for the occupation. The application was submitted in 2008. PMI took steps to thwart this application, asking its membership in the United Kingdom to contest this effort. To date the application remains before the Privy Council for decision.

The Australian Institute of Project Management (AIPM) began in 1976 and operates independently of both PMI and IPMA. It has been a leader in encouraging the development of national project management associations in the Asia Pacific region. The AIPM has also worked closely with the Australian government to develop national competency standards, in effect furthering the recognition of the worth and nature of project manager as a recognized occupation.

American Management Association • www.amanet.org

Project Management South Africa is another independent professional association that has worked closely with the government to define performance-based competency standards.

The Japan Project Management Forum is based on corporate rather than individual membership and has been actively involved in capability enhancement, the promotion of project management, and the development of a Japanese project management BOK.

The Project Management Research Committee of China has also been active in publishing the China National Competence Baseline.

Global Efforts

In addition, there have been efforts underway for the last decade to define a global approach to project management integrating the efforts of the independent associations and perhaps setting the foundations for a future global profession. These are discussed in more detail in Chapter 2 of this handbook.

Certification/Licensing and Control

To attain professional status, professional associations must be given legal responsibility for designating who is qualified to practice. This may be very complicated, with a number of certification and licensing alternatives, such as those found in medicine, or much simpler, as in the more generic licensing of teachers. If there is no effective certification or licensing scheme, then it will be impossible for practitioners to lay claim to any sort of special status or privileges. Certification is the key to control of the name and to control of admission to practice. In project management today, there are a number of largely voluntary certification approaches in project management ranging from knowledge-based assessment to competency standards based on practice.

In North America (and increasingly globally), PMI has a largely knowledge-based approach that entails acquiring five years of project experience and then passing a test assessing knowledge of the concepts and terms included in their body of knowledge. Aggressive global growth over the last decade has given the Project Management Professional (PMP) designation widespread recognition, and many organizations are using it as an entrance requirement when hiring project managers. In this way, the PMP certification is beginning to control entry into the practice of project management in many jurisdictions.

Other professional associations (for example, IPMA and AIPM) have more comprehensive certification processes that assess levels of project management knowledge and performance starting at the team member level and progressing up to project or program directors. All of these certification processes are largely voluntary, but in some countries (such as Africa or Australia) government involvement in certification has come close to providing legal recognition for certification. If the APM association achieves royal charter status for the occupation, the United Kingdom will be the first country to actively effect licensing status and control over the title.

AREAS OF CHALLENGE OR CONCERN

To date, no government has recognized the imperative to protect the public from the malpractice of individuals calling themselves project managers, even in the face of billion-dollar overruns on public projects. It is unlikely that governments will independently pursue actions to create a project management profession. In most jurisdictions, there is some question as to whether they even understand that there is a developed occupation of project management, despite the fact that individual organizations and associations establish standards and define programs for hiring and advancing project managers. It is also unlikely that private corporations will request or require the formation of a profession, as protecting their short-term interests is not likely to encompass creating this situation. Some may support the initiative, but many will resist in order to protect their autonomy and rights over the management of work.

For project management to become a profession, it requires the concerted effort of its practitioners and professional associations in pursuing this objective. Keys to achieving this status are as follows:

- Developing a defensible definition of project management that can be used to gain protection of the occupational name
- Developing a well-defined and complex BOK that can be claimed by the profession and unequivocally asserted to create value
- Elaborating significant independent academic educational programs with an associated set of research programs
- Creating and enforcing a code of ethics for all practitioners using the title *project manager*
- Winning political, social, and legal recognition of the value of regulating project management for the good of society

The most significant challenge facing the professionalization effort is gaining recognition and acceptance of the changes required of both professional associations and practitioners. Under a profession model, professional associations refocus from supporting the advancement and growth of practice in general to defining, regulating, and representing the collective "rights" of professional project managers. Practitioners at the same time need to decide whether they see project management as a profession that should be self-regulating and to which they are willing to submit their practice for judgment, or whether they would rather see it continue as an occupation subject to the whims of the market or even a tool kit of use in many occupations. These differences are significant in scope and have serious implications for development of either the occupation or profession.[14,15]

The battle between groups holding different perspectives on the costs and benefits of professionalization is being fought in the United Kingdom today. The results of this battle will have serious implications for us all.

IMPLICATIONS FOR PRACTITIONERS

Regardless of the potential for project management to achieve professional status, the promulgation of written standards, and the acceptance of these standards by important jurisdictions and organizations, has serious implications for the way a craft is practiced. Today, courts and other organizations can take these standards into account in defining negligent or competent practice. Some feel that it is only a matter of time before project managers are held legally accountable for the outcomes of projects. The auditor general's office of Canada and many other organizations are attempting to use the American National Standards Institute (ANSI) standard *PMBOK® Guide* as a measure of project manager competence.

Clearly the professionalization effort has already created some serious implications for practitioners. Several of these are discussed below.

Bureaucratization of Practice

Practice standards and official guidelines in professional practice require that either practitioners follow the guidelines appropriately or justify why the particular context of activity required some other approach. Members of traditional professions maintain copious case notes and journals to enable them to reconstruct their professional reasoning if necessary. Professionals must be able to show that they followed established practice guidelines or justify why they did not. Many project managers operating in fast-paced environments may see this as unnecessary and time-consuming when there is no clear evidence that the guidelines provide better results than other approaches.

In many ways, this bureaucratization of project management has led to complaints of increased overhead costs of project management at exactly the time practitioners are striving to streamline practice to increase the value added. Trade-offs between following guidelines and getting things done in a timely fashion are already replete in project management discussions. Further professionalization without clear identification of when and where these guidelines need to be applied and when they can be shortcutted will exacerbate these conflicts. Interesting paradoxes are sure to arise.

Value of Certification

The value of certification is a hotly contested issue in project management. Many argue that the knowledge-based certifications that exist today simply show that you have some background knowledge and can pass an examination, not that you can successfully manage projects.[16] Again, there is no clear evidence that certification increases the success of project managers on any clearly definable criteria.

In fact, certification and licensing are not designed to eliminate poor performance or to guarantee a very high standard in all cases. It has more to do with providing an adequate screening mechanism and controlling the entry of individuals into the profession. The value of licensing doctors came from eliminating thousands of quacks and incompetents and raising the general standard. But as a consumer or patient, it is still up to you to find a good physician. The potential values arising through certification/licensing (professionalization) of project management are as follows:

- Raising the general level of practice
- Increasing the status of the practitioners

- Increasing the rewards for practicing project managers
- Screening out most of the individuals who should not be claiming that they are competent to practice

However, most of these benefits come from setting the entrance criteria significantly high so that not anyone who takes a course and studies can pass the exam. Failure rates on these "bar exams" are usually kept to a significant level. As the value of holding the certification rises, individual practitioners can expect the educational bar to be raised on attaining certification.

Benefits and Costs of Professionalization

The benefits of professionalization accrue to the majority of practitioners in terms of providing guidelines of practice, increased status, and recognition, but superstars often fail to see any benefit. Michael Jordan doesn't need the players' union, but most NBA players benefit from it. All professional project managers would benefit from increased status, pay, and authority in the project environment. However, many of the most successful practitioners probably already enjoy these benefits and are likely to oppose any constraints imposed on them. Those practitioners for whom managing projects has become an intuitive process of doing what is necessary will chafe against the need to document their decision processes. Expert project managers will be required to certify and abide by the laws of the professional association if they intend to continue practicing.

Professionalization also creates legal liability. Costs of insurance and personal liability can be quite high, as evidenced by malpractice costs in medicine. The liability assumed by an uncertified, unlicensed worker is considerably less than that assumed by a registered, licensed member of a profession. The seal of the profession carries with it a personal liability associated with bad practice. In projects that go terribly wrong, these costs could be substantial.

Costs to projects and organizations also rise when requiring professional project management practice. These costs are usually seen in two particular areas. The first is in the cost of acquiring the services of a professional. The second is in the loss of control over organizational practices. Using a professional project manager requires recognizing the judgment of the project manager in many areas that were traditionally the responsibility of the organization's management alone. Internal project management standards can only be applied as long as they adhere to the standards promulgated by the profession. Where there is a discrepancy, a professional project manager must go with the professional standard. Both of these can increase the costs of projects.

Costs to individual practitioners include the necessity to maintain current understanding of the body of knowledge and to continually update and upgrade skills. It will no longer be enough to master a body of knowledge and apply it as well as possible. It will now be necessary to ensure that your practice lives up to the evolving standards set by an outside body. Maintaining professional status becomes a cost and necessity of carrying out your professional practice. Certification will no longer be voluntary, and membership costs will usually rise to cover the increased costs of policing and developing the profession. Some form of insurance against malpractice is also likely to become a necessity.

Professionalization is often seen as a noble goal for emerging knowledge occupations. The activities of many project management associations throughout the world reflect the growing efforts to attain this goal by achieving professional recognition. However, there remains much to be done to develop the characteristics and recognition of a traditional profession. Obtaining the status of a full profession will require significant effort from the members of an occupation to work together to achieve recognition. Gaining control over the characteristics of a profession requires both heavy initial investment and ongoing efforts directed at maintaining this status. Recognizing the benefits and costs of this type of initiative are a solid first step to developing the necessary commitment of practitioners to this lofty goal.

CONCLUSION

It is important that practitioners have the background to clearly understand the issues involved in professionalization. From this foundation it is possible for individual practitioners to make informed choices about the activities they undertake to ensure their practice fits within this model and the implications of doing so. The process of initiating project managers into these practices will make a difference in how project management is understood and practiced in organizations.

DISCUSSION QUESTIONS

❶ If project management were formally recognized as a profession, how would it make a difference to you in your practice of project management?

❷ What aspects of professionalization do you think would improve project management practice? Hamper it?

❸ How can you contribute to the development of a project management profession?

REFERENCES

[1] Project Management Institute, *Project Management Factbook* (Newtown Square, PA: PMI, 1999).

[2] Italy is a noted exception where many occupations, if not most, are recognized as professions with a legal mandate enforcing privileges and responsibilities of membership.

[3] Sharyn L. Roach Anleu, "The professionalisation of social work? A case study of three organizational settings," *Sociology* 26 (1992), pp. 23–43.

[4] Richard Hugman, "Organization and professionalism: the social work agenda in the 1990s," *British Journal of Social Work* 21 (1991), pp. 199–216.

[5] B. Zwerman and J. Thomas, "Potential barriers on the road to professionalization," *PM Network*, 15 (2001), pp. 50–62.

[6] Andrew Abbott, *The System of Professions* (Chicago: University of Chicago Press, 1988).

[7] Meryl Aldridge, "Dragged to market: being a profession in the postmodern world," *British Journal of Social Work* 26 (1996), pp. 177–194.

[8] Richard Hugman, "Professionalization in social work: the challenge of diversity," *International Social Work* 39 (1996), pp. 131–147.

[9] David F. Labaree, "Power, knowledge, and the rationalization of teaching: a genealogy of the movement to professionalize teaching," *Harvard Educational Review* 62 (1992), pp. 123–154.

[10] S. Cicmil, T. Williams, J. Thomas, and D. Hodgson, "Researching the actuality of projects," *International Journal of Project Management: Special Issue on Rethinking Project Management* 24 (2006), pp. 675–686.

[11] P.W.G. Morris, L. Crawford, D. Hodgson, M.M. Shepherd, and J. Thomas, "Exploring the role of formal bodies of knowledge in defining a profession: the case of project management," *International Journal of Project Management* 24, No. 8 (2006), pp. 710–721.

[12] L.H. Crawford, "Global Body of Project Management Knowledge and Standards," in P.W.G. Morris and J.K. Pinto (editors), *The Wiley Guide to Managing Projects,* Chapter 46 (Hoboken, NJ: John Wiley and Sons, 2004).

[13] L.H. Crawford, "Professional Associations and Global Initiatives," in P.W.G. Morris and J.K. Pinto (editors), *The Wiley Guide to Managing Projects,* Chapter 56 (Hoboken, NJ: John Wiley and Sons, 2004).

[14] B. Zwerman, J. Thomas, S. Haydt, and T. Williams, *Professionalization of Project Management: Exploring the Past to Map the Future* (Newtown Square, PA: Project Management Institute, 2004).

[15] D.Y. Hodgson and D.Muzio, "Prospects for Professionalism in Project Management," in *Oxford Handbook of Project Management* (Oxford: Oxford University Press, 2011).

[16] Crawford, "Global Body of Project Management Knowledge and Standards."

CHAPTER 22

Business Acumen for Today's Project Manager

DEBORAH BIGELOW CRAWFORD, PMP, PRESIDENT, PM COLLEGE

The "flat" organization, an idea first floated in the 1940s, has come into its own, as Gartner Vice President Mike Rollins has noted, because "the nature of work is fundamentally changing" as the marketplace demands companies to become more customer-relationship oriented.[1] Driving decision making down to frontline employees has meant, in most cases, removing levels of hierarchy. Nearly a decade ago, the National Bureau of Economic Research reported that "layers of intervening management are being eliminated and the CEO is coming into direct contact with more managers in the organization . . . while managerial responsibility is being extended downwards.[2]

Technology has played a role in this "delayering" of the organization as well. In particular, the development of enterprise project management and project portfolio management software has led to increased visibility for project and program managers and teams. As companies seek to align strategic initiatives with corporate business objectives, project management organizations (PMOs) have risen to the enterprise level. In the 2012 State of the PMO study, 66 percent of PMO leaders now report to an executive vice president or to the CEO.[3] The PMO leaders themselves more and more frequently have "VP" in their titles, as shown by trends in the PMO-of-the-year award applications.[4] The barrier that once existed between project managers and the business side has grown very thin, and the career ladder can now lead from projects up to the executive level.

This new visibility brings new challenges and new relationships within the organization, and requires a new kind of communication. While once a narrow, technical focus was expected of project managers, this new organizational climate demands a broader, more business-driven focus. The business reason for initiating a project is now paramount; project managers who focus too closely on schedule performance metrics are likely to overlook what matters most to their executives. This was underscored by findings in the State of the PMO study showing that, in response to the

227

question "What matters most to your executives?" 75 percent of PMO leaders in high-performing organizations responded that "alignment with business objectives" mattered most. Only 61 percent responded that "delivering projects on time" was a top management priority.[5]

The following story from the annals of project management illustrates why business outcomes are superseding traditional cost and schedule metrics. The Ford Taurus was introduced in 1986, and became one of the best-selling cars in Ford's history. It had a revolutionary design and exceeded quality expectations, creating a new standard in the industry. Customers loved it. In 2012, it is still rated number one in the affordable large car category for performance, design, safety, and reliability. Yet when the original project was completed, the project manager was demoted because the project was completed three months behind schedule.[6]

That was the old project management mindset. Today, benefits realization metrics would have told the organization that the schedule slip was an acceptable variance, given the successful business outcome of the initiative.

Today's organizations must prepare project managers and teams for roles that include working closely with stakeholders in marketing, finance, and the executive suite. The importance of the managing stakeholders and their expectations is exemplified by the Project Management Institute (PMI) incorporating stakeholder management as its tenth knowledge area in the newly revised standard.[7]

Project managers must now concentrate on the three areas where a business-focused leader must shift from the traditional thinking:

1. Communicating to drive results
2. Managing for business impact
3. Demonstrating project value to the C-suite

PROJECT COMMUNICATION THAT DRIVES BUSINESS RESULTS

A project manager is no longer "just a project manager." Project managers are consultants, trusted advisors, and change agents. Thus, their communication style must change with the needs of the audience and the role they play. The impact of tailored communications cannot be overstated.

In the "business consultant" role, the project manager must constantly reinforce the strategic reasons for the project and identify the business impact of any changes. Savvy project managers ask a lot of questions to understand the business purpose of the project. Here are some considerations for business value:

- *Cost reduction:* How will this project specifically cut or reduce costs out of the operating budget for the overall organization?
- *Business growth:* If this is a new product or service, or even an internal project, how will it help the business grow?
- *Maintaining operations:* Most of these types of projects are basically "to keep the lights on," but you still need to consider what the cost of NOT doing this project is? Lost profits? Loss of compliance?
- *Speed and efficiency:* A project that improves productivity, speed to market, or overall operational efficiencies will generally have impacts on the bottom line.

Business value can be identified in a number of ways, but inevitably it all comes down to improved outcomes for the organization in one way or another.

Aligning communication style with the audience includes using the appropriate business terminology to help others shift their mindset from traditional to business-focused project management. The role of project managers is to ensure that they keep their project sponsor, their project team, and those interfacing with this project in alignment with the *project* and *business* goals.

Traditionally, project managers talk about cost, schedule, scope, and quality. That has not changed. However, in shifting to a business mindset, the project manager needs to bridge the gap between project terms and business terms, as follows:

- Cost translates to financial impact.
- Schedule translates to time to market.
- Scope translates to parameters for success.
- Quality translates to service integrity.

In the consultant role, the project manager may need to make tough calls, sometimes be "intelligently disobedient," and deliver bad news immediately—even recommend killing a project.

Project leaders also need to earn the right to be a trusted advisor. They need to demonstrate that they care about both the project and the customer and about how the project impacts them and the overall organization. Project leaders who give advice effectively, honestly, and genuinely build trust with teams and stakeholders. By doing so, they develop more collaborative relationships, which foster better communications and more successful projects.

Because projects drive business innovation and change, project managers also act as a "change agents." They engage leaders to play an active leadership role in the change and help those involved with the project understand the project vision. They facilitate involvement of high-level stakeholders to manage resistance to change, and build plans to ensure that people are motivated and have the skills to meet the demands of the change.

When the 2012 PMO-of-the-year award winner, Verizon Wireless Marketing PMO, was asked what contributed most to its success, the answer was "our leader was a great change agent, who walked the halls making sure everyone knew where we were headed and why."[8]

One of the competencies of strong project managers is being detail oriented. But in an expanded role as project leaders, they need to shift from a natural tendency to give project detail to giving more of an "elevator pitch" about the project. An elevator pitch sums up the unique aspects of the project in a way that excites others. An elevator pitch helps you move away from speaking about the technical details and to focus on the overall value of a project—and of project management in general.

Then, the next area of focus for the business- and value-focused leader is to shift from "managing the project to be completed on time and on budget" to "managing the project to realize the desired business impact."

MANAGING PROJECT OUTCOMES FOR BUSINESS IMPACT

As noted, the project management business environment has changed. The project manager is becoming more of an *organizational* leader. It is not uncommon today for project managers to need to communicate directly with executives about strategic initiatives crucial to the enterprise. The layers of bureaucracy that buffered project managers from executives are largely gone. Therefore, the project manager must communicate in terms of the business drivers and outcomes that are meaningful to executives. Some of the business drivers in organizations today that project managers are focusing on are the following:

- Competitive advantage
- Time to market
- Increased profits
- Best utilization of resource management
- Business growth

To truly manage the outcome of a project for business impact, four steps are necessary, and each step is critically important in relaying how to make this shift as successful as possible:

Step 1 in getting to business focused project management is linking organization goals to project goals. Organizations must transform goals into company-wide programs that translate corporate goals into action. These programs are divided into projects and managed by project managers who look at corporate objectives and execute accordingly. A business-focused project manager learns to think more strategically and become more responsible for project business results and not just for closing out the project. Figure 22-1 illustrates how a project should link to the objectives and overall vision of the organization. The organization's strategic plans cascade down from corporate strategy to business unit strategy to portfolio, program, and project strategy. As strategy cascades down the organization, performance measures are established at each level to link up with the strategic performance expectations of the entire company.

Step 2 is getting clarity from the project sponsor. It is imperative that project managers understand why this project is more important than others and what the expectations are regarding project outcomes. What outcomes will satisfy the project sponsor so that the project will be deemed a success?

Not all of this is up to the project manager, of course. The organization has to support project managers in becoming "all they can be" as business allies. Business-focused project managers will thrive in organizations that:

- Are strategically driven.
- Are strong at prioritizing projects.
- Actively manage and monitor the project portfolio.
- Are good at ensuring project sponsors act as project owners.
- Are change ready.
- Hold stakeholders accountable.

Step 3 is using business-driven project language. Begin talking about projects in both project and business terms. There should also be a shift in how success criteria

FIGURE 22-1. **THE PATH FROM CORPORATE VISION TO PROJECT EXECUTION**

are viewed. "On time, within budget" is still important, but the business-focused project manager broadens the criteria to answer the following questions: Did it have the economic impact we were expecting? What was the return on investment? What were the customer impacts?[9]

Step 4 in getting to business-focused project management is building a business case. Building a business case helps the project manager to think strategically about the project and how it aligns with the organization's strategies. Every project may not need a business case. However, the concept provides a framework to think about and map out how the project aligns with organizational goals.

A good business case starts with a comprehensive and clear understanding of the customer's expectations. This is typically completed in conjunction with the project initiation document or project charter. However, projects that are handed down after the portfolio prioritization process should have already been determined to be critical to the business, so the project manager may want to use the project business case before the actual initiation to get clarity about the reasons for the project and how it ties into the overall strategy. This document will also help to build a better business-aligned project charter, project initiation document, scope statement, and so on, and it can be used at project closeout to help determine if the benefits and value were achieved.

One might ask, Doesn't a project charter accomplish the same goals as a business case? The project charter tends to be one-dimensional and much more focused on the triple constraint, whereas the project business case is multidimensional and places the project in the business world. It strategically aligns the project with the overall organizational goals.

Thus, in developing a business focus for projects, organizations must consider a wide range of issues and follow a process that enables the right projects to be chosen to support the company's strategy. Upper management needs to support project management and encourage a cross-functional interface with projects. Portfolio management must be in place and proactively managed. Project selection and prioritization are critical factors of success. If an organization does not create a process to link projects to strategies, projects will surface across the organization in an uncontrolled manner, resulting in confusion and a higher project failure rate.

DEMONSTRATING PROJECT VALUE TO THE C-SUITE

The bottom line is that it all comes back to value. As noted above, the business case can help to outline the project value. It should include the following:

- Identified and quantified benefits
- Identified risks to achieving benefits and the associated risk management plan
- Estimated cost to deliver benefits
- Anticipated time frame for delivery of benefits

It's important to remember that the project value may not align with the project completion dates. Full project value may not be realized until "X" happens or is realized. Some projects are not viewed as a success upon their completion, but become successful as benefits accrue.

Executives tend to focus on business goals, results, and outcomes of projects. Practitioners tend to focus on tactics, tools, techniques, and finish lines. They both need to understand that there is a difference between project success and business success. Research has shown that only 30 percent of the business benefits will actually be achieved from the implementation of the project; 70 percent will come from putting in place a process for making people accountable for the change and having a system in place for realizing the project benefits long after the project has been implemented. That is a difference between project success and business success.[10]

In your communications, recognize that executives have limited time to spend on a single issue and that their focus is always going to be on the value of the project to the organization. Project managers that are the most successful in getting the C-suite executive's support are those that frame their project communications around business results.

Table 22-1 below highlights the major differences between business-focused and traditional project management. The business world has already integrated into the project management environment. This is most evident in the new role of the project manager.

Today's project manager enjoys an expanded perspective of success and greater career opportunities, but to optimize these opportunities it is necessary to embrace the business perspective.

Traditional	Business-Focused
Tactical	Strategically driven
Management of a singular project	Integration, coordination, and control of multiple and prioritized projects
Project-wide and not necessarily cross-functional	Organization-wide and cross-functional
A discipline	An operating environment
A specialist function	A business philosophy integrated with project management

Source: Adapted from D. Comninos and E. Frigenti, "Business Focused Project Management," 2006, http://www.alusani.biz/web_files/bfpm.pdf.

TABLE 22-1. **ATTRIBUTES OF TRADITIONAL PROJECT MANAGEMENT AND BUSINESS-FOCUSED PROJECT MANAGEMENT**

DISCUSSION QUESTIONS

❶ Think about a project with which you are presently involved. Why was this project selected? What are the strategic goals it serves? How will success be measured by the executives?

❷ Write the "elevator pitch" about your project. If you had to express to your CEO in one minute how things are going and what outcome she can expect, what would you say?

REFERENCES

[1] M. Rollings, "Replacing Taylorism as our management doctrine," Gartner, Inc. blog entry, April 18, 2011, http://blogs.gartner.com/mike-rollings/2011/04/18/replacing-taylorism-as-our-management-doctrine.

[2] R. Rajan and J. Wulf, J. (2003) "The Flattening Firm: Evidence from Panel Data on the Changing Nature of Corporate Hierarchies," Working Paper 9633 (Cambridge, MA: National Bureau of Economic Research, 2003), p. 1. http://Www.Nber.Org/Papers/W9633.

[3] PM Solutions Research, *The State of the PMO 2012 Executive Summary* (Glen Mills, PA: PM Solutions, 2012), p. 4.

[4] J.K. Crawford and Jeannette Cabanis-Brewin, *An Inside Look at High-Performing PMOs* (Glen Mills, PA: PM Solutions, 2011).

[5] PM Solutions Research, *The State of the PMO 2012* (Glen Mills, PA: PM Solutions, 2012), p. 77.

[6] A.J. Shenhar, "Strategic Project Leadership: Toward a strategic approach to project management," *R&D Management* 34, No. 5 (2011), Blackwell Publishing, p. 570.

[7] Project Management Institute, *A Guide to the Project Management Body of Knowledge* (*PMBOK® Guide*), 5th edition (Newtown Square, PA: PMI, 2013).

[8] PM Solutions Research, 2012 PMO of the Year Award ebook, http://www.pmsolutions.com/resources/view/pmo-of-the-year-award-2012-ebook/.

[9] R. Cossland, "The fatal assumptions of executive communication," Projectimes.com, 2009, http://www.projecttimes.com/articles/the-fatal-assumptions-of-executive-communication.

[10] J. Berman, *Maximizing Project Value* (New York: AMACOM Books, 2007), p. 3.

Organizational Issues in Project Management

Introduction

Until the early 1990s, the organizational issues related to project management were largely centered on how a specific project should be organized: Should it be put into a task force mode or be handled from a matrix management standpoint? The concern was based on single-project logic.

Because of the booming number of projects in organizations and the time pressure and cost squeeze associated with them, the organizational concern has moved toward managing multiple projects in a short time frame, with limited resources. This brings focus on more holistic issues in terms of organization. The concerns become of a larger nature than single projects, and thus involve topics such as the following:

▶ *Strategic project management* (using project management to implement strategies and using a strategic approach in each of the projects underway), about which Kam Jugdev in Chapter 24 offers a contrarian view that asks the reader to consider whether, in fact, project management truly is a strategic resource. The flip side of the coin is offered by Jeannette Cabanis-Brewin and James S. Pennypacker in Chapter 23, who discuss research showing that top-performing companies are those that align project management and strategic execution.

▶ *Enterprise project management* (how to manage all projects across an enterprise), which is discussed by Chris Vandersluis in Chapter 25 from both a cultural and tools viewpoint.

▶ *Project portfolio management* (how to pick and manage the right projects), which is touched on in a number of the chapters in this section, but is described in detail by Gerald I. Kendall in Chapter 26.

▶ *Governance* of projects and portfolios, which is examined by Paul C. Dinsmore and Luiz Rocha in Chapter 27.

▶ *Measuring the capability and value of project management processes,* both within projects and across the enterprise, which is discussed by James S. Pennypacker and Deborah Bigelow Crawford in Chapter 28.

- ▶ *Organizational change management,* which means keeping in mind that any project management improvement initiative is a change initiative, is described by D. Allen Young in Chapter 29.

- ▶ *Multiple-project management,* which means that projects, programs, multiple projects, and portfolios all have organizational or enterprise implications. Lowell Dye in Chapter 30 clarifies the differences and describes accepted multi-project practices.

- ▶ *Program management*, as a discipline in its own right, is described by Ginger Levin in Chapter 31.

- ▶ *The PMO,* described by J. Kent Crawford in Chapter 32, has been updated by Jeannette Cabanis-Brewin with research information about the changing role of project management organizations.

American Management Association • www.amanet.org

CHAPTER 23

Projects
The Engine of Strategy Execution

JEANNETTE CABANIS-BREWIN,
PM SOLUTIONS RESEARCH

JAMES S. PENNYPACKER,
PENNYPACKER AND ASSOCIATES

Most of us have participated in strategic planning sessions and later wondered what became of all those great ideas. There has long been a disconnect between the vision of strategy and its implementation. *Fortune* magazine has reported that nine out of ten corporate strategies devised on the executive level never come to fruition.[1] One reason is found in a survey conducted by the Society for Human Resource Management and the Balanced Scorecard Collaborative: 73 percent of polled organizations said they had a clearly articulated strategic direction, but only 44 percent of them communicated that strategy well to the employees who must implement it. These companies "are like a body whose brain is unable to tell it what to do."[2] Another reason is because strategic planning becomes meaningless in the absence of a way to execute planned strategies. Organizations pursue their strategies through the creation of "strategic initiatives"—portfolios of programs and projects—which become the vehicles for executing the strategy.

To what extent does integrating corporate strategy with project portfolio management contribute to organizational success? To seek an answer to this question, which has significant importance for executives and project managers alike, the Center for Business Practices (formerly the research arm of Project Management Solutions, Inc.) conducted a survey in November 2005, targeting of a broad spectrum of organizations.[3] Representatives of eighty-seven leading companies responded. The results: companies using identified "best practices" for aligning strategy and project most consistently also had the highest rates of project and organizational success.[4]

Many studies have cited the lack of executive support as a key contributor to project failure. Project managers complain that their projects do not receive the resources they need. Projects completed "successfully" by project management standards (on time, on budget, to spec) have been considered failures because they did not address a business need. All these issues are alleviated in a company that ties strategic planning to portfolio selection and project execution.

STRATEGY AND PROJECTS: A RESEARCH STUDY

The *Strategy and Projects* report was the first of a three-part research project. Part One reviewed management literature to develop a list of practices for aligning projects and corporate strategy. We first identified those practices that lead to high performance by searching the literature on the integration of strategy execution, portfolio, program, project, and performance management. This research revealed a set of best practices that we organized into a framework adapted from the McKinsey 7S framework.[5] The elements include the following[6]:

1. Governance
2. Processes
3. Strategy management
4. Project portfolio management
5. Program/project management
6. Structure
7. Information technology (IT)
8. People
9. Culture

Best practices were defined under each process area based on the management research reviewed. These practices were used to develop the questions in the survey. The goal of the survey was to learn whether organizations that exhibit these practices are, indeed, high performing, to confirm whether the practices identified are really "best practices," and to identify those practices that are most critical to the success of the organization. Participants rated their organizations on the frequency of their use of the best practices against a seven-point scale, where 1 = "not at all" and 7 = "to a great extent."

The Survey

Members of the Center for Business Practices Research Network (senior practitioners with knowledge of their organizations' project management practices business results) were invited to participate in a Web-based survey. Of eighty-seven respondents, eighty-four completed the survey in its entirety. We compared high-performing organizations, low-performing organizations, and all organizations, focusing on whether high-performing organizations exhibited the identified best practices more than the average of all organizations and whether low-performing organizations were below average in exhibiting these practices.

How "Performance" Was Defined

Most of the measures we used to ascertain which organizations performed well are familiar to all project stakeholders. We asked not only about the success of project management by conformance to schedule, budget, requirements, and so forth, but also about the overall success of the organization. Practices related to the organizational value of project management, such as the rational allocation of project resources, the skillful selection and prioritization of projects, and the alignment of projects to business strategy, are being supported today by organizations' increasing use of portfolio management systems and processes. As project management becomes more and more essential to the achievement of strategic organizational goals, these practices will gain in importance for all project stakeholders. The performance measures included the following:

- The organization's strategies are executed according to plan.
- The organization's shareholders are satisfied.
- The organization is financially successful.
- Projects are completed on schedule and on budget.
- Project customers are satisfied.
- Project resources are allocated optimally.
- Projects are aligned to the organization's business strategy.
- The organization works on the right projects.

Participants rated their organizations on the frequency of their achievement of these measures against a seven-point scale, where 1 = "not at all" and 7 = "to a great extent." Organizations termed "high performing" in the results reported better-than-average performance in all areas measured. In particular, high-performing organizations are significantly better than average in allocating project resources optimally, followed by completing projects on schedule and on budget and executing strategy according to plan. Low-performing organizations are significantly poorer than average in allocating project resources optimally, followed by completing projects on schedule and on budget and satisfying the organization's shareholders.

Key Findings

The results confirmed the best practices proposed by the management literature and described in this report. This underscores the value of using *Strategy & Projects* best practices in executing an organization's strategy. High-performing organizations use *Strategy & Projects* best practices in all areas more than other organizations, consistently and significantly. Low-performing organizations consistently underutilize *Strategy & Projects* best practices in all areas. Figure 23-1 shows how widely high performers differed from low performers.

THE STRATEGY & PROJECTS FRAMEWORK

Governance

Governance is the policy framework within which an organization's leaders make strategic decisions. With an effective governance framework, all strategic decisions throughout the organization are made in the same manner. Each level within the organization must apply the same principles of setting objectives, providing and getting direction, and providing and evaluating performance measures. Using a common governance framework ensures that decisions are made the same way up and down the organization.

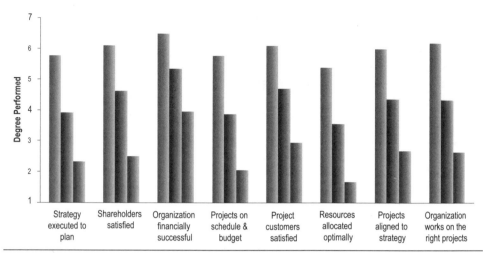

FIGURE 23-1. **PERFORMANCE INDICATORS**

Left bar indicates the frequency with which each measure was reported by the top-performing companies in the survey; right bar indicates frequency with which that measure was reported the low performers in the survey. Central bar expresses the mean of all companies.

The best practices identified for governance included:

- The organization has a well-defined strategy.
- A documented strategy execution plan guides strategy execution efforts.
- Strategy is communicated clearly to those developing portfolio and program/ project plans to ensure that those initiatives support the organization's strategy.
- Portfolio, program, and project managers feel a sense of ownership about the organization's strategy execution plans.
- Appropriate and effective processes are in place to monitor and manage risk.

The most often used governance practice by high-performing organizations is having a well-defined strategy. They also are significantly better than average at having project managers feel ownership of their strategy execution plans, followed by having appropriate and effective processes in place to monitor and manage risk.

The Seven Processes

Strategy Management

Strategy management moves the organization from its present position to a future strategic position in order to exploit new products and markets. Strategy management is accomplished through the application and integration of strategy management processes, such as mission-vision formulation, strategy formulation, planning, execution, and monitoring/control. Best practices identified for strategy management included the following:

- Strategy performance is measured, compared to objectives, and activities are redirected or objectives changed where necessary.

- There is an understanding of the impact of projects or project management activities on the creation and implementation of strategy.
- The organization's strategic plans cascade down from corporate strategy to business unit strategy to portfolio, program, and project strategy.
- Corporate and business units assemble a strategic portfolio of programs and projects, measure the strategic contribution of a program or project, and adopt or reject programs/projects based on this information.
- As strategy cascades down the organization, performance measures are established at each level (business unit, portfolio, program, project) to link up with the strategic performance expectations of the entire company.

The most often used practice by high-performing organizations is having strategic plans that cascade down from corporate strategy to business unit strategy to portfolio, program, and project strategy. High-performing organizations are significantly better than average at having performance measures established at each organizational level (business unit, portfolio, program, project) link up with the strategic performance expectations of the entire company. Figure 23-2 shows the rate of adoption of each of the best practices for strategy management; note that high performers are much more likely to use these practices.

Project Portfolio Management

One goal of portfolio management is to maximize the value of the portfolio by careful examination of candidate projects and programs for inclusion in the portfolio

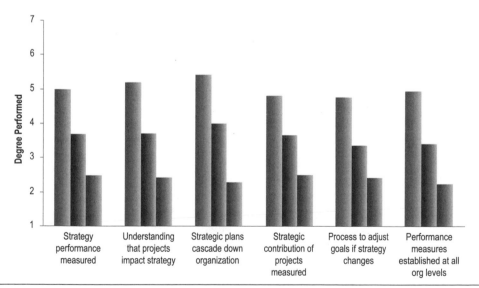

FIGURE 23-2. **STRATEGY MANAGEMENT AND PROJECTS**

The left bar in each set indicates the frequency with which that metric was reported by the top performers in the survey; right bar indicates the reported use of that best practice by low performers. The central bar expresses the mean. Note the dramatic difference between high and low performers on each measure.

and the timely exclusion of projects not meeting the portfolio's strategic objectives. Portfolio management is accomplished through the application and integration of portfolio management processes such as the following:

- Inventory: process for capturing project data and organizing for portfolio analysis
- Analysis: process for aligning projects to business strategy, examining business and project risks, and prioritizing projects in the portfolio
- Planning: process for approving and funding the project business plans; allocating resources and scheduling projects
- Execution: process for executing the portfolio of programs and projects by means of budgeted resource allocations; focus on getting the work done efficiently and effectively
- Monitoring/control: process for tracking a portfolio as programs/projects are executed, detecting problems or changes in underlying premises, and reporting to appropriate management levels
- Portfolio improvement: process for making necessary adjustments to portfolio

Best practices identified for PPM included the following:

- A list of current projects (active, proposed, on hold) is documented.
- Projects are prioritized using a scoring system that uses strategic alignment as a criterion to determine the priority of the project with respect to other projects.
- Metrics are captured to assess the performance of the project portfolio.
- Performance results of the project portfolio are communicated to stakeholders.
- Reviews of portfolio performance and changes in the business environment may cause decision makers to realign the portfolio (killing projects or putting them on hold, reallocating resources).
- Enough resources are in place to make the project portfolio achievable.

The most often used practice by high-performing organizations is having a documented list of the organization's current projects; they are also significantly better than average at having enough resources in place to make the project portfolio achievable.

Program/Project Management

Programs are collections of projects that unify and leverage the contributions of projects in the portfolio; a program of projects may be established to meet a key strategic objective. Program/project management is accomplished through the application and integration of program/project management processes familiar to us all: opportunity assessment, initiation, planning, execution, monitoring/control, and closing, including lessons learned. Best practices identified for program/project management were as follows:

- The organization's strategic objectives are an input to the project initiation process.
- The organization has a process for identifying project opportunities and determining if those opportunities are in line with the corporate strategic direction.

- Review of the program/project involves a re-verification of critical success factors, including resource availability and the continued validity of the business case.
- Project performance is monitored (schedule variance, budget variance, earned value).
- Program/project performance feedback is used for managing strategy execution.

The most often used practices by high-performing organizations are monitoring project performance and having a process for identifying project opportunities and determining if they are in line with the corporate strategic direction. They also are significantly better than average in using program/project performance feedback for managing strategy execution.

Structure

Corporate strategy affects the choice of organizational structures. Similarly, organizational structures are important to the execution of corporate strategy. To execute strategy effectively, managers must make sound decisions about structures and develop methods or processes to achieve the needed integration of structural units. Organizational structures take many forms, each affecting the speed at which change can be brought about. They include line and staff structures, functionalized structures, matrix structures, multidimensional matrix structures, strategic business units, laissez-faire structures, and virtual structures (listed here in order of their increasing ability to adapt to rapid changes in strategic direction demanded by changing market conditions). The best practices identified included the following:

- A strategic (enterprise) project office (sometimes called the Office of Strategy Management) plays a role in linking the organization's projects to its strategic plans.
- The company has an organizational structure (strategic project office, office of strategy management, strategic steering committee, etc.) responsible for managing strategy execution.
- Project management is clearly established and embedded within the organization's business management structure.
- Information about strategy and projects flows freely between business units facilitating strategy execution.

The most often used practice by high-performing organizations is having project management clearly established and embedded within the organization's business management structure, along with having project management clearly established and embedded within the organization's business management structure.

Information Technology

Organizations need appropriate information tools are in place to implement and automate the *Strategy & Projects* processes, as well as align the other elements of the framework.

Information technology is a supporting system that provides simple, actionable information to decision makers, thereby enabling the continuous planning and execution of strategy. Strategy execution involves participation and communication up and down the organization, as well as lateral flows of information and coordination across organizational units. Making strategy work also requires feedback about organizational and project performance and then using that information to fine tune strategy, objectives, and the execution process itself. Some of the best practices identified the following functions of information technology (IT) tools:

- Enabling appropriate communication of strategy and strategic performance throughout the strategic management chain, both top to bottom and bottom to top
- Providing real-time visibility into resources, budgets, costs, programs, and projects
- Developing alternative strategic and project portfolio scenarios
- Integrating strategy execution management, portfolio management, program/project management, and performance management functions
- Providing the capability to monitor and control risks, issues, and financials across portfolios
- Providing information on the availability of resources

The most often used practice by high-performing organizations is having IT tools that provide the capability to monitor and control risks, issues, and financials across portfolios. They also are significantly better than average at having IT tools that integrate strategy execution management, portfolio management, program/project management, and performance management functions.

People

The execution of strategy ultimately depends on individual organizational members, particularly key managers. So aligning strategy with training, managing, measuring, rewarding, and promoting people are key ingredients in effective strategy execution. Best practices identified for "people management" included the following:

- Project stakeholders understand how they can influence the successful execution of strategy and how their work is important to execution outcomes.
- Project stakeholders have clearly defined individual and team performance targets that are aligned with strategic objectives.
- Performance management reviews are structured to reward or correct individual performance based on the employee's contribution to strategic objectives.
- Project stakeholders clearly understand and buy into the organization's strategies.
- The project management staff is capable of creating, deploying, and maintaining enterprise, portfolio, program, and project strategies.

The most often used practice by high-performing organizations is having project stakeholders' buy-in to the organization's strategies. High-performing organizations are significantly better than average at having performance management reviews structured to reward or correct individual performance based on the employee's contribution to strategic objectives.

Culture

Corporate culture—the beliefs, behaviors, and assumptions shared by individuals within an organization—includes such things as procedures, values, and unspoken norms.

Culture can have a significant influence on how well strategy is executed in organizations. The importance of achieving strategic objectives, how performance is communicated, whether or not changes create competition or cooperation, who can access and use *Strategy & Projects* technology, whether or not decision making is done in command-and-control environments or by self-directed teams, how functional units work with each other—these are just a few of the issues of culture that need to be addressed in creating a structured approach to executing strategy. Best practices include the following:

- Project management is valued throughout the organization.
- A focus on strategy execution is an important part of the organization's culture.
- Risk planning is an important part of the organization's culture.
- Senior management is trusted, and consistently rewards successful project behaviors.
- There is a shared understanding and commitment about the organization's long-term objectives and its strategy for achieving them.

The most often used practice by high-performing organizations is having leadership that is trusted. High-performing organizations are significantly better than average at having senior management that consistently rewards successful project behaviors.

Top Ten Best Practices That Set High Performers Apart

The following best practices were used significantly more often by high-performing organizations than other organizations. Information technology best practices in particular set high performers apart. The practices are listed in order of their significance:

1. Information technology tools integrate strategy execution management, portfolio management, program/project management, and performance management functions.
2. Information technology tools are used to develop alternative strategic and project portfolio scenarios.
3. Project management is clearly established and embedded within the organization's business management structure.
4. Information technology tools provide information on the availability of resources.
5. Senior management consistently rewards successful project behaviors.

6. The enterprise project office allows the organization to manage its entire collection of projects as one or more interrelated portfolios.
7. Program/project performance feedback is used for managing strategy execution.
8. Information technology tools provide the capability to monitor and control risks, issues, and financials across portfolios.
9. Project management is valued throughout the organization.
10. The company has an organizational structure (strategic project office, office of strategy management, strategic steering committee, etc.) that is responsible for managing strategy execution.

Investigating the Link with Company Performance

A corollary of this research was an attempt to track financial performance of the companies responding to the survey to determine whether these practices can be shown also to lead to an improved bottom line. Most accounting measures of performance are based on the assumption that a business firm's efficiency of *operations* is the best way to assess goal attainment, so finding a measure that reflects wise investments in the project portfolio, based on strategy, proved to be a challenge. The group of companies participating in the study proved challenging to assess because they included publicly traded companies, nonprofits, government agencies, and state-owned foreign operations, as well as small privately held service firms. However, one striking, though admittedly anecdotal, correlation that came to light as we inquired further into the results was that nearly every organization in the top twenty performers is the recipient of at least one, and in some cases, many award(s) specific to their field of endeavor. We submit that this is no coincidence, but proof of the efficacy of aligning projects and strategy.

REFERENCES

[1] Jeannette Cabanis-Brewin, "Interview with Richard Russell of the Balanced Scorecard Collaborative," *Project Management Best Practices Report* 2, No. 9 (2000), p. 1.

[2] J. Mullich, "Human resources' goals work best when they're tied to company success," *Workforce Management* 82, No. 13 (2003), pp. 49–54.

[3] Results from this study were first published in the *Proceedings of the 2006 PMI Global Congress,* where we presented the study under the auspices of PM Solutions/Center for Business Practices.

[4] Center for Business Practices, *Strategy & Projects: A Benchmark of Current Best Practices* (Havertown, PA: CBP, 2006).

[5] BuldingBrands.com. (2006) The McKinsey 7S Model. http://www.mindtools.com/pages/article/newSTR_91.htm.

[6] This framework was later featured in our book, Seven Steps to Strategy Execution, written with J. Kent Crawford for PM Solutions, and published in 2007 under the Center for Business Practices mark. [Note: Center for Business Practices is now PM Solutions Research.]

CHAPTER 24

Competing Through Project Management

KAM JUGDEV, PHD, PMP, PROFESSOR, CENTER FOR INNOVATIVE MANAGEMENT, ATHABASCA UNIVERSITY

Strategy is about success.[1]

WHAT IS STRATEGY?

Increasingly, companies are turning to project management as part of their business strategy. In doing so, companies want to ensure that they are investing in the right resources that will allow them to be efficient and effective. Successful projects contribute to business performance, and this can translate into an improved chance of the company's surviving the cutthroat environment. However, research in project management using strategic management theories is just starting to emerge. We have yet to fully understand the dimensions of project management in terms of what aspects make it a source of competitive advantage. This is an important topic because it has the potential to help companies make decisions regarding which practices they plan to invest in and continue to support. This chapter discusses several strategic management frameworks that relate to project management.

In the strategic management field, the two broad approaches to strategy are the industry framework (outward focused) approach, which is often called the industry view, and the internally focused view, which is often called the resource-based view. The industry view was popularized by Michael Porter, and it examines an industry in terms of (1) strengths, weaknesses, opportunities, and threats (known as SWOT analysis), and (2) the five forces of competitive advantage (bargaining power of suppliers, bargaining power of customers, threats of new entrants, threats of product substitutes, and rivalry within the industry itself).[2] The internal framework of the firm focuses on a company's resources or assets. (We use the terms *strategic resource* and *asset* interchangeably in this chapter.) More often than not, these assets are knowledge based, as opposed to physical assets, such as property and technology, or financial resources. The resource-based view is the theory that subjectively assesses competitive advantage in terms of a company's internal assets.[3]

American Management Association • www.amanet.org

We begin with a brief overview of strategic management from a historical perspective.

A BRIEF HISTORICAL OVERVIEW OF STRATEGIC MANAGEMENT

Since the 1900s, strategic management has evolved from a focus on financial goals and strategic plans to aspects of corporate identity, where such models as the SWOT analysis emerged in the 1960s. This was followed by analytic tools and techniques such as scenario planning and experience curves. In the 1980s, due to some disillusionment with earlier strategic management practices that were limiting because industry factors could not fully explain profit differences between companies, the focus turned to what was happening within a company, the resource-based view. In the 1990s, with technology-driven disruptive innovations, the chief executive officer became a more important player at the executive level. Currently strategic management is often thought of as strategic renewal, spanning human capital, knowledge management, and organizational learning.

Mintzberg's classic book, *Strategy Safari: A Guided Tour Through the Wilds of Strategic Management,*[4] discusses the various schools of thought on strategy and describes the following types of schools of thought about strategy:

- Design school—strategy is a process of conception
- Planning school—strategy formation is a formal process
- Positioning school—strategy formation is an analytical process
- Entrepreneurial school—strategy formation is a visionary process
- Cognitive school—strategy formation is a mental process
- Learning school—strategy formation is an emergent process
- Power school—strategy formation is a process of negotiation
- Cultural school—strategy formation is a collective process
- Environmental school—strategy formation is a reactive process
- Configurational school—strategy formation is a process of transformation

Strategy is not just one of the above schools but rather a blend of them. Strategic management is comprehensive, aligned, and integrated; it pertains to all business disciplines; it is dynamic; it entails a constant search for competitive edge; it involves unique strategic capabilities; it requires spontaneous thinking and doing; and it involves frequent strategic change.[5]

Mintzberg also introduced us to the **five P's,** whereby strategy is a plan, a pattern, a position, a perspective, and a ploy. Whereas Mintzberg favors the concept of "crafting" strategy as an art, others support a more systematic and analytic approach, whereby strategy helps companies make decisions to remain competitive; it is a process for coordination and communication and it involves a target (vision).[6]

It is clear that strategy is a dynamic and multifaceted concept. Strategy is not about straightforward answers. Strategy is more about *understanding* what is happening in the dynamic internal and external environments to better grasp the issues and complexities that impact a company. These different perspectives on strategy will help readers refine their understanding of business strategy—the topic of *how* companies compete.

American Management Association • www.amanet.org

COMPETITIVE CONVERGENCE AND COMPETITIVE ADVANTAGE

Both formally and informally, companies conduct internal assessments (strengths and weaknesses) and external, environmental assessments (opportunities and threats) to plan their market positions and strategies using the SWOT analysis. Both shareholders and stakeholders have vested interests in companies. Shareholders are individuals who have a financial stake in a company because they own its stock. In contrast, stakeholders, which include shareholders, can either influence or impact a company positively or negatively or be impacted by a company.

Firms are primarily interested in improving financial returns and shareholder value to avoid situations of competitive convergence, which means that no one firm has a distinct advantage over its rivals for extended time periods (typically considered to be less than a few years). Competitive convergence occurs when companies try to do similar activities as their rivals with some variations. Some examples of similar activities include those that span operational effectiveness, such as quality improvement and outsourcing. These practices are necessary for a company's survival, but they do not lead to a sustained competitive advantage. The reason is that after a while, all the companies look and act the same and this leads to shrinking returns. In contrast, having a competitive advantage entails either doing different activities from one's rivals or doing similar activities differently. A competitive advantage involves being nimble, innovative, adaptive, and creative. A competitive advantage involves maintaining a long-term advantage (commonly interpreted as beyond five years).

Competitive Advantage Frameworks: Looking Within (Resource-Based View) and Looking Externally (Industry View)

A very important question in the strategy literature asks, "Why do firms differ and how does it matter?"[7] Examining the external environment to help explain company performance is the industry view of strategy. This approach helps firms look to the marketplace to determine the areas in which they want to compete. Analyzing the external environment involves an examination of the demographic, economic, political, environmental, social, and technological (yielding the acronym DEPEST) factors within the industry. The SWOT analysis and the five structural forces approach (consisting of threats of new entrants, bargaining power of suppliers, rivalry among existing competitors, bargaining power of buyers, and threats of substitute products or services) are useful techniques, but they are not strategy in and of themselves. The industry view provides a good description of market conditions and allows firms to identify some of the conditions for making a profit, but this approach does not provide complete information on how to make above normal profits. The industry view also downplays sources of competitive advantage that stem from resource variations between companies.

According to the resource-based view, a competitive advantage is sustained by developing key resources that are different from what rivals are doing. In contrast to the industry view, the resource-based view explains why firms exist (and others do not over time) on the basis of internal resources that are valuable, rare, and inimitable, and that have organizational support (acronym VRIO).[8] Resources that meet the VRIO criteria contribute to a firm's competitive advantage (Table 24-1).

Valuable?	Rare?	Difficult to Imitate?	Supported by Organization?	Competitive Implications	Performance
No	-	-		Competitive Disadvantage	Below Normal
Yes	No	-		Competitive Parity	Normal
Yes	Yes	No		Temporary Competitive Advantage	Above Normal
Yes	Yes	Yes		Sustained Competitive Advantage	Above Normal

Adapted from Barney, Jay B., *Gaining and Sustaining Competitive Advantage, Second Edition,* 2002. Reprinted by permission of Pearson Education, Inc., Upper Saddle River, NJ.

TABLE 24-1. **THE VRIO FRAMEWORK**

Currently, the project management literature emphasizes tangible (concrete and visible) practices. Another way to think about tangible resources is to think of these resources as ones that can be documented or experienced with the physical senses; that is, you can see it or touch it. To exemplify, in the 1970s and 1980s, the literature focused on various tools and techniques (i.e., software, work breakdown structures, program evaluation and review techniques, design-to-cost, life-cycle costing, risk management, cost and schedule control, and control systems). The approach whereby normative advice (meaning that this is how things should be done) on planning and managing projects from a systems approach contributed to the general understanding of project management as a tactical tool.[9]

As confirmed in the strategic management literature, although tangible resources enable a company to execute its business processes, it is the intangible ones (meaning those resources that are tacit and almost invisible) that are more likely to be sources of competitive advantage.[10]

Knowledge is created, acquired, captured, shared, and used. The common thread among knowledge, data, and information is that they all involve a personal dimension. This can be visualized using the iceberg analogy. The tip of the iceberg represents the explicit or visible body of knowledge, such as the knowledge developed and shared through the tangible project management practices discussed in this chapter (e.g., project management office and methodologies). Explicit knowledge is more formal, codified, and transmitted systematically. Explicit knowledge is the "know-what" that can be documented. However, the larger component of the iceberg is ignored, submerged, and tacit.

Tacit knowledge is personal, experiential, context-specific, and rooted in action. Nonaka and Konno divide tacit knowledge into technical and cognitive dimensions.[11] The technical dimension covers informal personal skills and crafts and could be called "know-how." The cognitive dimension involves beliefs, ideals, values, and mental models. Tacit knowledge involves the ability to innovate, which can be a source of competitive advantage.

Tacit knowledge has also been compared to the currency of the informal economy. Tacit knowledge is shared through socialization. Social capital is an intangible attribute of the relationships among members of a social unit.[12] Project teams share what they know through communities of practice. Communities of practice are based on social relationships as developed and sustained through trust and cooperation.

Most companies have many resources (both tangible and intangible), but few are strategic in nature. Examples of strategic assets include quality, reputation, brand recognition, patents, culture, technological capability, customer focus, and superior managerial skills. Notice how these strategic assets are valuable, difficult to copy, unique, and involve strong organizational support. Furthermore, such strengths are difficult to purchase. Most strategic assets also tend to be knowledge based, and knowledge-based resources are intangible. In essence, strategic assets are embedded in a company's unique internal resources, skills, and knowledge. Strategic assets contribute to a firm's ability to move from competitive convergence toward a competitive advantage.

The resource-based view is relevant to project management because project management is a knowledge-based discipline that emphasizes human and organizational assets based on explicit and tacit knowledge, skills, and know-how. Some other synonyms used in the strategy literature to describe complex resources that are sources of competitive advantage include dynamic capabilities, dynamic competences, and knowledge-based assets.

Research continues to unfold on both the industry view and resource-based view as we continue to make sense of how factors within the company and external to a company can improve company performance. To summarize, it is not a question of one approach being better at explaining company performance than the other, as much as it is a question of the context in which industry and firm-level effects may predominate.

BARNEY'S VRIO FRAMEWORK

Barney's four VRIO concepts, cited above, are defined as follows:

1. *Valuable:* To what extent do a company's resources and capabilities help it deal effectively with environmental threats or opportunities? The value of a resource is defined in economic terms, whereby the resource generates above-normal returns for the company. Valuable resources contribute to a firm's efficiency and effectiveness.

2. *Rare:* To what extent is the resource controlled by a small number of competitors? Generic resources are not sources of competitive advantage because they can be copied by rival companies. At best, select generic resources allow companies to survive. However, rare (unique) resources can offer a temporary competitive advantage and thus be sources of strength because few companies have them.

3. *Inimitable:* Are competitors without this resource at a cost disadvantage in trying to obtain or develop it? Inimitable resources are those that companies protect so that competitors cannot easily copy them or find substitutes for them. For example, Southwest Airlines use extensive selection processes to hire individuals with spirit and spunk to serve and entertain customers. These characteristics are rewarded

and encouraged by the company and are not easy for competitors to duplicate. To offer another example, the ability to be innovative is an intangible strategic resource for 3M, a diversified technology company known for ingenious and creative inventions, including the well-known Post-It Notes. 3M is widely known for its culture of innovation, an inimitable resource. With over 22,000 patents, 3M is able to protect its innovative products for many years. Similarly, Lululemon Athletica patents its materials and designs.

4. *Organizational support:* Are a company's policies and procedures organized to support and exploit (leverage) the valuable, rare, and costly-to-imitate resources? Organizational support refers to integrated and aligned managerial practices, routines, and processes. Organizational support also connotes managerial leadership and decisions that support key assets and how they are developed and sustained.

Within the VRIO framework, if a resource is only valuable, it leads to competitive parity, meaning that the company is no better than its rivals. Both value and rarity are required for a temporary competitive advantage, meaning that there is a short-term advantage. Value, rarity, and inimitability are required for a sustained competitive advantage. In addition to these three criteria, organizational support is necessary to both develop a competitive advantage and sustain it.

Analyzing Project Management Using the VRIO Framework

We can use the VRIO framework to examine key project management practices and assess if they contribute to a competitive advantage. Investments in physical, technological, and financial assets are valuable to a company. Project management involves the use of methodologies, bodies of knowledge, project management offices, and project management maturity models.

Tools and Techniques

Some tools and techniques are specific to planning (work breakdown structures) and scheduling (network techniques such as critical path methods, Gantt charts, and program evaluation and review techniques). Other tools and techniques are used to address project finances, project monitoring and control, project audits, project termination, and resource allocation. Throughout the project, technology (including hardware and software) is often used to help improve information and knowledge flow and assist in the decision-making process (e.g., project management information systems, knowledge management systems, and executive decision tools). The array of physical tools and techniques are readily available on the market so they are not rare. These assets are also readily imitable so they do not meet the VRIO criteria in full, even though they may reflect elements of organizational support whereby companies appreciate the merits of tools and techniques and invest in them.

Methodologies

An investment in project management methodologies helps companies understand the steps to be followed to achieve project success throughout the project lifecycle. Methodologies also provide guidelines and checklists to ensure that the practices are being followed properly and that the right outcomes are achieved before moving to the next step. Companies develop their own project management methodologies and many are based on the project management bodies of knowledge. Numerous companies, such as project management consulting firms and information technology firms, use project management practices to advertise and sell to clients. If such methodologies are readily available and imitable, do they meet the VRIO criteria? Are they sources of a sustained competitive advantage?

Bodies of Knowledge

Worldwide, there are a number of project management associations (see Chapter 2) that have bodies of knowledge to guide practitioners. The bodies of knowledge provide explicit standards on practice in the knowledge areas of time, cost, scope, quality, human resources, risk, communications, procurement, and integration. The guides represent codified knowledge and emphasize the rationalistic view of project management tools and techniques. The bodies of knowledge are important but not rare. Instead, they are readily imitable as evident by how similar the bodies of knowledge are between countries. An underlying assumption is that these bodies of knowledge are meaningful regardless of industry or firm-level context. However, knowledge is inseparable from context and involves a tacit and experiential dimension. As the bodies of knowledge do not meet the VRIO criteria, they are not sources of competitive advantage.

Project Management Offices (PMOs)

These days, more and more companies are establishing PMOs to coordinate the use of tools, techniques, and technology to support projects, ensure consistency of use, and provide training and guidance, particularly on troubled projects. The PMOs have taken on increasingly important role in some companies as a way to improve organizational performance.[13] For the most part, PMOs tend to provide methodologies and templates for teams to use, conduct project audits, and serve as a reporting channel. They may help reduce project costs, decrease time to market for new products, increase corporate profits, improve competences, and ensure quality and project success, but empirical findings on these factors are rare. (See Chapter 32 for a discussion of existing research.)

Since PMOs are lauded in the literature as offering tools and techniques, they are primarily vehicles for coordinating the use of tangible physical assets that help improve project management processes. Furthermore, the tools, techniques, and practices can be readily purchased and are easily transferred between companies, particularly as people move from one organization to another. According to the resource-based view logic, then, PMOs do not explain significant variation among companies.

Project Management Maturity Models

The emphasis on codified and tangible assets in project management is made clear with management maturity models, which were promoted in the literature as sources of competitive advantage.[14] Historically, the project management maturity models were based on the Carnegie-Mellon Software Engineering Institute's capability maturity model for software development. The models consisted of five linear stages reflecting software processes and practices that were increasingly more defined and repeatable. The models used a rational and mechanistic view of organizations, but did not address social and inter-relational aspects. The models addressed tangible assets but not intangible assets. Maturity models have limited value because it does not take long for rivals to mimic documented practices or institute similar practices and procedures. The codified knowledge is easily transferable between firms. Vendors used to indicate that their models were based on best-practices databases. Furthermore, the models did not initially emphasize *organizational* processes and practices and they lacked a clear connection between operations management and strategy. These models seem to have fallen out of favor in the literature, and the more recent literature emphasizes nonprocessed factors such as context, trust, and creativity.[15] A recent paper analyzed the project management maturity models to assess them against the VRIO framework and found that they did not meet the criteria.[16] Therefore, the arguments put forth for winning in the marketplace with such models are weak.

As companies invest in project management, they primarily invest in various tools and techniques, as discussed above. When these concrete practices are assessed with the VRIO framework, they do not meet all four criteria whereby the assets are valuable, rare, inimitable, and have organizational support. Some companies find themselves investing in project management practices that do not contribute to project or business improvements. Not only can this impact the bottom line, but it can also create negative impressions about project management.

Projects are conducted in complex, dynamic environments and involve a strong knowledge-based component. They cannot continue to be assessed as sources of competitive advantage if they are only thought of and evaluated on the basis of concrete, codified practices. In order to assess project management's potential as a strategic resource, it is prudent to examine the intangible dimensions of the discipline, such as knowledge-based assets, tacit knowledge, and social capital practices.

An extensive literature review found that a narrow stream of research using strategic management theories, including the resource-based view, dynamic capabilities, and absorptive capacity, is emerging. Without going into detail (which I would be pleased to provide upon request), the recent literature on assessing project management resources on the basis of use and complexity indicates that the intangible resources based on mentoring and communities of practice are two of the most complex resources that offer the most value. Another study used the resource-based view to show that while tangible resources are valuable and involve organizational support, intangible resources such as sharing know-how (otherwise known as tacit knowledge, as shared through mentoring, stories, brainstorming, and shadowing) are much more significant because they offer a company a temporary competitive advantage. The study found that sharing know-how significantly predicted the project management process as rare. Subsequently, the authors of this study identified other difficult-to-copy and embedded intangible project management resources such as social capital, tacit knowledge, communities of practice, and mentoring.

American Management Association • www.amanet.org

CONCLUSION

Companies that turn to project management for competitive advantage will place the discipline under increasing scrutiny to ensure that the investments are value-adding. These companies will also take with a grain of salt some of the publications that purport to offer competitive advantages through project management maturity models, program and portfolio management practices, and software and hardware, to name a few, especially if clear explanations of how these practices contribute to firm performance are lacking.

Project management practitioners should start thinking of project management as more than its tangible components. Companies need to view project management as a set of knowledge-based assets. The intangible elements of project management are very important and emerging as a small but viable stream of research in the literature. Viewing project management as a source of competitive advantage or as a strategic resource is new to many in the field. However, companies that assess their project management assets using the frameworks from strategy may be better positioned to understand which aspects of project management they should focus on (e.g., tacit knowledge-sharing practices such as through communities of practice, and social CapitaLand knowledge-based assets.) Over time, we hope to achieve an improved appreciation of how tangible and intangible assets in project management are complementary.

DISCUSSION QUESTIONS

❶ To what extent do you support the view that project management is a source of competitive advantage (versus competitive convergence) for your organization?

❷ What are some ways in which project management is a source of strategic advantage in your department or company?

REFERENCES

[1] Robert M. Grant and Judith Jordan, *Foundations of Strategy*. (San Francisco: John Wiley and Sons, 2012), p. 2.

[2] M.E. Porter, "What is strategy?" *Harvard Business Review* 74, No. 6 (1996), pp. 61–78.

[3] Jay Barney, "Firm resources and sustained competitive advantage," *Journal of Management* 17, No. 1 (1991), pp. 99–120.

[4] Henry Mintzberg, Bruce Ahlstrand, and Joseph Lampel. "And Over Here, Ladies and Gentlemen: The Strategic Mangement Beast," in *Strategy Safari: A Guided Tour through the Wilds of Strategic Management* (New York: The Free Press, 1998), pp. 1–21.

[5] Larry E. Greiner, Arvind Bhambri, and Thomas G. Cummings, "Searching for a strategy to teach strategy," *Academy of Management Learning and Education* 2, No. 4 (2003), pp. 402–420.

[6] Robert M. Grant, *Contemporary Strategy Analysis: Concepts, Techniques, Applications,* 8th edition (Chichester, West Sussex, UK: Wiley, 2013).

[7] Richard R. Nelson, "Why Do Firms Differ, and How Does It Matter?" in Nicolai Foss (editor), *Resources, Firms, and Strategies: A Reader in the Resource-Based Perspective* (Oxford, United Kingdom: Oxford University Press, 1991), pp. 257–267.

[8] Jay Barney, *Gaining and Sustaining Competitive Advantage* (New York: Prentice-Hall, 2010).

[9] Bruno Ulri and Didier Ulri, "Project management in north america: stability of the concepts," *Project Management Journal* 31, No. 3 (2000), pp. 33–43.

[10] Kathleen Eisenhardt and Filipe Santos, "Knowledge-Based View: A New Theory of Strategy?" in Andrew Pettigrew, Howard Thomas, and Richard Whittington (editors), *Handbook of Strategy and Management* (London: Sage Publications, 2000), pp. 139–162.

[11] Ikujiro Nonaka and Noboru Konno, "The concept of 'Ba': building a foundation for knowledge creation," *California Management Review* 40, No. 3 (1998), pp. 40–54.

[12] Janine Nahapiet and Sumantra Ghoshal, "Social Capital, Intellectual Capital, and the Organizational Advantage," in Eric L. Lesser (editor), *Knowledge and Social Capital: Foundations and Applications* (Boston: Butterworth & Heinemann, 1998), pp. 119–157.

[13] Monique Aubry and Brian Hobbs, "A fresh look at the contribution of project management to organizational performance," *Project Management Journal* 42, No. 1 (2011), pp. 3–16.

[14] C.W. Ibbs and Y.H.Kwak, "Assessing project management maturity," *Project Management Journal* 31, No. 1 (2000), pp. 32–43.

[15] Beverly Pasian, Spike Boydell, and Shankar Sankaran, "Project management maturity: a critical analysis of existing and emergent factors," *International Journal of Managing Projects in Business* 5, No. 1 (2011), p. 8.

[16] Kam Jugdev and Gita Mathur, "Classifying project management resources by complexity and leverage," *International Journal of Managing Projects in Business* 5, No. 1 (2012), pp. 105–124.

CHAPTER 25

Enterprise Project Management
Elements and Deployment Issues

CHRIS VANDERSLUIS, HMS SOFTWARE

Enterprise project management (EPM) is often thought of as the Holy Grail of project management: an environment where all project management information, reporting, and analysis is part of an all-encompassing system where virtually every activity, every hour of time, and every dollar planned and spent can be instantly identified.

Both senior management and the project management office (PMO)—or, in its absence, a centralized project management group of professional project schedulers and project managers—is highly interested in getting access to all levels of data regarding project management. The most common scenario we find in organizations today is ad hoc project management, where each project is managed in whatever way each individual project manager decides to do it. A PMO cannot function without project data, and if everyone is doing something different, the consistent collection of project management data gathered at the lowest level of detail is very attractive.

Enterprise project management can also be of great interest to individual team leaders who want to see the inter-project impact of different project groups, and who must resolve resource conflicts between teams. Even team members will find the prospect of less "management by emergency" a worthy path to bring order to chaos.

But before you embark on your own EPM deployment, it is important to know that EPM isn't for everyone.

WHAT IS ENTERPRISE PROJECT MANAGEMENT?

Enterprise project management is the integration of project and resource data, practices, and analysis into a single process. For organizations that manage more than one project at a time or that have projects so large they must be broken down into component subprojects, the management of two significant elements is critical. First is the interrelation between projects. If any project is dependent on the completion or delivery of elements from another, the impact of changes in one project can have dramatic effects on the second. For example, one project might be to install a new database on which new software deployments will depend. If the database project is delayed for any reason, all dependent projects will be delayed. Having a process that allows the downstream projects to see potential impact on their projects from other areas of the organization is a fundamental goal of EPM.

Second is the management of restricted resources. There is virtually no effective project management environment in the world where resources are in excess. It is more likely that workloads far exceed the availability of key resources to accomplish them. The prioritization of that work and the resolution of conflicts over those resources is a prevalent management concern in organizations around the world.

PROJECT MANAGEMENT MATURITY

A project management maturity (PMM) model can help identify whether migrating to an EPM model is right for your organization. There are several popular PMM models including the OPM[3] from the Project Management Institute (PMI), but the underlying concepts are the same.[1] All models show ad hoc project management, with the least mature way being that project managers manage the project in whatever way they decide to do it. The most mature would be a fully integrated enterprise with all project management being managed in a consistent, centrally managed structure.

It is an interesting concept, but the central premise—that the more integrated the project management environment of an organization is, the more mature it is—is not necessarily accurate. In some organizations, it is more effective to eschew the concepts of EPM altogether and to let individual project managers use whatever systems they wish.

The potential benefits to management of EPM seem obvious but they come with costs that are not all obvious. A centralized structure implicates several levels of management in project decisions. This may give management better visibility and serve to level the playing field, but it can hamper more experienced and connected project managers who know how to navigate their project through the corporate structure. Before accepting that the top level of the project management maturity model you are using is ideal for your organization, you must ask if that is the right level for you or if you would be better served being less centralized.

If EPM is right for you, then let's look at how you can create your own EPM environment.

ELEMENTS OF ENTERPRISE PROJECT MANAGEMENT

The following subsections describe the five basic elements of an EPM environment.

Storage of All Project Data in a Single Location

Any EPM deployment must start with gathering data into a single location and, as the first element, it is often highly contentious. Gathering data does not mean focusing only on software; in fact, it is certainly possible to create an EPM environment that is completely computerless. In such an environment, the basic requirement of getting all data together is still fundamental.

American Management Association • www.amanet.org

In today's modern organization, many managers equate control of data with power, and there are few managers who will willingly sacrifice what they consider power. Each aspect of project data may be jealously guarded by its incumbent owner. For make an enterprise system possible, all project data must be stored in the same place and managed consistently. This may require negotiating access and control of some of these data.

Once you have access to the project data, there is still work to be done. Let's start off with naming conventions. For example, if we talk about project resources, let's assume that one group refers to the CEO as "ME," short for Mike Edwards. Another group uses the letters "ME" to refer to the discipline of mechanical engineers. Yet another uses "ME" to mean maintenance engineers (i.e., janitors). If we don't first come to some understanding of how to name resources, when the data are brought together, we will find janitors, mechanical engineers, and the CEO all grouped together.

To bring these data together, standards must be agreed on to avoid this type of conflict. The same thing has to be done for project names, task names, department names, document names, change management issues, and so on. You also need to agree on the frequency of the data collection and the level of detail that makes sense for your projects.

The use of the word *standards* implies that someone will be the keeper and arbiter of those standards, and that almost certainly means that if you are committed to EPM, there will have to be some kind of central office to be responsible for elements of your EPM environment, such as naming conventions. Without some kind of PMO, there is little hope that the standards required for managing projects together will ever be agreed upon, and if they are, they'll never be enforced.

Along with naming conventions, you also must agree on the repository for the data. If you are implementing an EPM software package, then this part of your design may have been decided for you. The new system will have a set method of storing data, usually in a commercial database like Microsoft's SQL Server or Oracle. Then all you have to decide is where that data will reside. Different groups may argue that their project management needs are so unique that it is absolutely impossible for them to comply with a single repository for their data that is located somewhere else. These various interest groups must be dealt with one at a time. Your first mantra for deploying project management has to be "all project data, one location" until there is broad compliance.

Grouping Data by Different Criteria

The ability to group data by multiple criteria is an issue for reporting and analysis, so it is often spoken of last. However, the definition of the data structure makes all those reports and analyses possible, so it really needs to be dealt with early in your design. If there is no coding of data at all, bundling all the project data together essentially will just give you one enormously long list of tasks with no method of subdivision. That's not too useful. Once your data can be gathered in one place, project coding is your next challenge.

Coding comes in a variety of flavors. It is easy to think of grouping by project, by task, and by resource. The easiest way to think of what coding will be required is to think of the outputs of your EPM system either as reports or views of the data. If you need a report by department, you will need a department code. If you need a report by location, location will have to become a code.

You can further think of coding in two large categories: codes that apply to the entire project data structure to which everyone must comply, and codes that can be personalized project by project.

Here are some examples of coding:

- A project-level code that identifies the client of this project. This would allow projects to be grouped and sorted by client. This is key for client billing purposes.
- A resource-level code that identifies the department a particular resource belongs to. This would allow resources to be grouped by department as well as by project.
- A task-level code that identifies the project phase. This might enable us to create a report of tasks in different categories, such as design, documentation, and deployment.

Coding can be a simple list of values, such as a list of possible locations for a project, or it can be a hierarchical tree of values such as a work breakdown structure (WBS) or an "organigram" of resources often referred to as a resource breakdown structure (RBS).[2]

If you are wondering how to decide what coding is appropriate to your organization, here is a simple method of determining 90 percent of all coding requirements. First, put key personnel into a room with a large white board. At the far right of the board, start listing important business decisions that will be made using the resulting analysis or reports from the EPM system. An example might be the decision of selecting priorities for each project. Think of this business decision as the output from your EPM process. From each decision, work your way on the board from right to left. To the left of the decision, show the final report or reports that would berequired in order to make that decision. An example might be a resource conflict report and a project priority report. Draw an arrow from the report(s) to the decision. To the left of the report, show a box with the calculations or analysis that would have to be done by the system in order to create that report. An example of an analysis might be a resource leveling calculation of all projects. An arrow goes from the analysis or analyses to the report(s) that require it. To the left of the analysis you can now list the elements of data that the analysis requires. This list defines your key enterprise coding. Using this simple technique, you will quickly determine which data and coding requirements are critical to getting the business output required from the system.

Resolving Conflicts Such as Use of Resources

For many managers, an excessive amount of time is spent trying to figure out how to respond to resource capacity conflicts. These conflicts are exacerbated when there is no portfolio prioritization in place.

Resolving resource conflicts entails comparing resource availability with resource requirements. This may seem obvious, but remember that we are referring to *all* the resource availability and *all* the requirements. This means that all project and non-project loads, as well as all availability, must be defined in similar ways. There are several issues to deal with here. First, you need to decide on the level of detail of the data. In some organizations, one group wants to manage resources at a category level (e.g., engineers) and another wants to work at the individual level. There is no hard-and-fast rule that says which one is better, but you'll need to be consistent.

Next, you've got to define resource requirements in a common manner. Some project managers may, for example, attempt to overestimate their resource requirements in order to lock their project team together for an extended period. Other project managers might not do this, and the result may be an unfair allocation of key resources.

Should you allow staff members to be switched from a project they've already started work on? Analysis might show that resources are available between tasks on one project, and it might look attractive to put them on other work, but simple analysis usually does not allow for the impact of changing from one team to another. Just the time it takes to change gears from one project to another and to get the momentum required to do anything productive with that team can often take a lot longer than thirty minutes. There are exceptions, of course, but you'll have to decide whether this kind of change makes sense in your environment. Studies have shown that interruptions of any kind can take as long as twenty-five minutes to recover from.[3]

Finally, projects must be prioritized. This can often be a highly contentious issue for the most senior levels of management. Managers tend to request that their projects carry the highest priority so as not to lose access to resources. Prioritizing projects based on empirical analysis can help align key resources to those projects that are best for the organization. The rules for determining the level of priority of a project are much easier to get agreement on prior to deployment of your EPM environment than afterward.

Regardless of the process you create for resolving resource priorities, you need to set up some kind of referee to arbiter disagreements. This should be a person or committee that does not have a vested interest in the result and that can overcome personal bias.

Portfolio Management

For some, portfolio management is all about being able to group projects together for analysis and reporting. For others, it is mostly about a method of project approvals from the earliest concept to final completion, such as "stage-gating."[4]

Key aspects in portfolio management include the ability to code projects so that they can be grouped together for reporting or analysis. This is something you may have dealt with in your coding phase. The ability to organize the projects by priority from whatever perspectives are important to you is also key. Some examples include ranking projects by risk, by return on investment, by alignment to corporate strategy, by cost, by revenue, by manager, or by client.

One of the most interesting aspects of this kind of management is the ability to do forward-looking resource capacity planning. Given that all projects must now be stored in a central location, for the first time you may have the ability to see all resource loads simultaneously. This enables a "what-if?" analysis where the impact of a proposed project can be assessed instantly. The old practice where a client, department, or manager invents a delivery date based on a hoped-for schedule can be eliminated in favor of a promise based on actual capacity.

When you have this type of portfolio process, seeing the impact of a proposed project on all other work can usually be determined in seconds. The impact on management of such a process can be significant.

The Ability for Project Team Members to Interrelate

Collaboration

Collaboration has spawned an entire category of project management tools— "collaborative" project management. It is an interesting notion because collaboration is something that can only be *enabled* by technology, not *created* by it.

Enabling collaboration would seem to be a natural aspect of project management. Project managers never work in a vacuum; they communicate with team members, sponsors, clients, and others.

Collaboration can play a key role in an EPM environment. Collaboration functions include chatting with team members, notifying team members of events in the EPM system through their regular email, or using instant messaging or a mobile device. It may also include the ability to create elements such as mini-websites, online surveys, or online update forms. When we think of the work required for many team members to interact on documents or the necessity of being alerted to change management issues in a timely fashion or when they exceed established thresholds, collaboration takes on a whole new level of significance.

This kind of functionality isn't trivial. In the past ten years, the entire project management industry has focused more on having project team members communicate and work together than it has on the algorithmic nature of project scheduling. As interesting as it might be to create the ultimate theoretical schedule, actually managing a project has everything to do with communicating and only a little to do with calculations. We now see more new courses in "soft skills" than in critical path calculations and more new software functions that are communications oriented than in high-end analysis. The rapid expansion of smart phone use and of a ubiquitous Internet means that project managers, team members, clients, and sponsors have an unprecedented ability to communicate in near-real time. Need a picture? It now arrives instantly. Need to see a video of that new problem? It can be sent from your phone to a computer screen on the other side of the world in seconds.

One of the pitfalls in looking at EPM systems is the tendency for some to believe that if they purchase an EPM system with collaborative functionality, project team members will automatically collaborate. This may not be the case. If this is one of your goals in deploying EPM, it is worthwhile to ask why team members don't collaborate already.

Here are some questions that you can ask to determine if you've got more work to do on the cultural side of deployment than the technical side in order to enable a collaborative environment:

- If project managers share their data with the organization, will the executives use the data to punish them?

- Does it concern you that if you share your data with other project managers, they may use the data to take unfair advantage?
- If staff members detail all their work on a single integrated timesheet, will they be concerned that the data will be used to unfairly evaluate them?

If project team members are not collaborating now, the reasons are almost always cultural rather than technical. You'll need to do some work to evangelize the benefits of collaborating and even make changes in procedure to ensure you remove roadblocks to participation by team members.

ENTERPRISE PROJECT MANAGEMENT SYSTEMS

Given the interest in bringing all project data together, computer systems are ideally suited to showcase this kind of process, and numerous vendors are keen to show what they can do for you—too many to discuss here. Also, these systems are being updated constantly, with new functionality being released on what sometimes seems to be a daily basis. The trend in the EPM systems industry is in itself interesting. In the late 1970s and early 1980s, we saw the first multi-project systems available as commercial packages. Their orientation was very algorithmic, focused on the calculation of the schedule and the calculation of resource requirements. More recently, there has been a major trend away from the algorithmic perspective and toward a more collaborative approach. This makes sense; while the theoretical best schedule is useful information, most project managers spend most of their time working on human issues and on dynamic decision making to resolve issues that arise on the fly.

What functionality should you be looking for in an EPM system? The following subsections discuss some fundamentals.

Single Data Repository

The system should provide for storing data from all projects in a single repository. For large-scale deployments, you need to look at functionality for amalgamating data from several large repositories into a single repository for reporting and analysis. Depending on your organization, you may have to consider multinational access, access from slow communications connections, and other security and accessibility issues.

Portfolio Management

The system should have an ability to manage at a project level, allowing projects to be added or removed at will and to be grouped by multiple types of coding. A flexible coding structure should allow you to code the projects for use in a stage-gating approval and selection system. Also important is the ability to prioritize projects for resource management purposes.

On Premises or Online?

Many systems are now available online as a subscription service, accessible from anywhere you can access the Internet. For some, this will be very attractive, as the hardware and technical hurdles are managed by the vendor. For others this type of service is unattractive either because they must work in a highly secure environment and are prohibited from storing project data outside the office network or because they have users who will not be able to access the Internet. So ask if the system is available for installation on your premises or as a subscription service or both.

Enterprise Coding

When all data must come together, they need to be coded. In an enterprise project system, the first priority is a high degree of flexibility. No two organizations are the same and, therefore, no one can predict how you will need to group and analyze your project data. Ensure that the system you are looking at will be able to adapt to whatever coding you envision now and will have the capacity to extend to the grouping and coding you haven't even imagined yet. Also critical in this area is the ability to impose some coding as mandatory. Can the system ensure compliance with some critical code elements you have created? This is important when you are linking the EPM system to other corporate systems. For example, in a link with finance systems, you must ensure that work is only coded to accounts that exist and that 100 percent of the work is coded. Can the system impose this on all tasks?

Collaboration

Look for the basic building blocks of collaboration and communication. Does the system enable project management personnel to interact? Look for automatic notifications that can be integrated into your standard email or instant messaging systems. The ability to create communications areas such as project websites that are dynamically integrated with the project data can be of great benefit.

Document Control

Enterprise project management systems must also have the ability to integrate with or include functionality for document management, issue and change management, and other ancillary data that may not be schedule based.

Workflow

In larger organizations, the ability to define a sequence of procedures that must occur in a particular order can be of great benefit. Workflow need not be a complicated affair. Can you list a series of steps and then identify when a step has been completed? This type of functionality is important when looking at phased project approvals or when considering any kind of change management, such as a change in project scope.

SELECTING YOUR ENTERPRISE PROJECT MANAGEMENT SYSTEM

When looking at project software, the overwhelming number of products that purport to serve EPM requirements can be daunting. Start your analysis by looking around organizations you know already. When you look at vendors' websites, look at the client lists to see if you know any of them. Ask to speak to or even visit existing deployments where you can ask not only what has gone well but also what the most challenging aspects of the deployment were. With so many vendors on the market, references are often a critical tool in system selection.

A simple search of the Internet will reveal numerous vendors, but don't be fooled by claims or even independent analysis of who is best. There is really no such thing. Given that each organization has a different environment, a different maturity level, and different requirements, it is perhaps better to ask what the most appropriate tool for your particular situation would be.

Don't be too enthralled with or concerned about functionality that you haven't identified in your list of requirements. Virtually every system includes functionality that you can't take advantage of right away. Focus on your key challenges.

One of the best things you can do when evaluating EPM software is to think of yourself as a "solution buyer." If these systems are the solution, then you should put some time into thinking about what problem they are to solve for you.

Some organizations get caught up too quickly in making a list of functions to be responded to. This is the worst way to look for a new system. Start instead with the business challenges you wish to address, and then ask the vendors to respond with how they will enable you to address those challenges. The responses you get show you not only which vendors understand your problem but also which vendors are imaginative in addressing your situation.

DEPLOYING YOUR ENTERPRISE PROJECT MANAGEMENT SYSTEM

Deployment is where all of this theory moves into practice. There are many pitfalls in an EPM deployment, but you can avoid most of them by focusing on a few key factors.

By far, the most critical success factor is an appreciation by management of the nature of an EPM deployment. Too often senior management mistakenly believes that an EPM deployment is only a technology project. Thinking of deploying EPM as a change management project is the number one factor for success.

As with all change management projects, the next key element is ensuring you have sufficient management support for the duration of the project. This has to come from a senior-enough level to ensure compliance. There may be great interest in EPM from one level or another of the organization, but if it is not shared by an executive who can speak for everyone who would be affected, then the deployment is not going very far.

Whichever executive is sponsoring the project has to commit for the duration, and that is longer than the installation of some software. A typical deployment of EPM from the initial concept to final deployment can take anywhere from several months to a couple of years.

If you've overcome these challenges, the next is to pick a deployment methodology. A "phased approach" where the concepts and technology are rolled out to the organization over a period of time is almost always the most effective. Start your deployment with a small group that is committed to the success of the deployment. Plan to have these group members become part of a core group of users who will assist the deployment effort. They will be able to work on evangelizing the deployment, on training, and on fine-tuning your project management processes.

Finally, if you are deploying EPM, treat your EPM deployment as a project with all the controls and structure you would use with any change management project, and your chances of success increase dramatically.

DISCUSSION QUESTIONS

❶ While there is general expectation that scoring higher on a project management maturity model is better than scoring lower, a case could be made that some organizations might be most effective at other levels. Assuming a five-level model where level 1 is ad-hoc project management, level 2 is project tracking, level 3 is integrated project management, level 4 is consistent methodology, and level 5 is self-improving process, what might be the most effective level for your particular organization, and why?

❷ Portfolio management is a top-down approach to looking at groups of projects at one time. Budgeting is often done at the top level and then drilled down to the project level. Integrated project management is a bottom-up approach to looking at multiple projects at once. Both of these aspects are part of enterprise project management. How might you reconcile the two perspectives into one working process?

❸ Once a project is underway, the majority of a project manager's time turns from the analytic viewpoint to the business of managing people. With smartphones, tablets, and an always-on Internet, everyone on the project is enabled to talk to anyone else. How can you encourage effective communication and avoid the chaos of everyone "talking" at once to one another?

REFERENCES

[1] Suhail Iqbal, "Organizational Maturity: Managing Programs Better," in Ginger Levin (editor), *Program Management: A Life Cycle Approach* (Boca Raton, FL: CRC Press, 2012).

[2] For more about the resource breakdown structure, consult a project management glossary, such as http:www.maxwideman.com/pmglossary/PMG_R03.htm.

[3] Clive Thompson, "Meet the life hackers," *New York Times Magazine*, October 16, 2005, www.nytimes.com/2005/10/16/magazine/16guru.html?pagewanted=all&_r=0.

[4] Robert G. Cooper and Scott J. Edgett, "Best Practices in the Idea-to-Launch Process and Its Governance," www.stage-gate.com.

CHAPTER 26

Project Portfolio Management
Principles and Best Practices

GERALD I. KENDALL, PMP, TOC INTERNATIONAL

Project portfolio management (PPM) is a set of processes to analyze, recommend, authorize, activate, accelerate, and monitor projects to meet organization improvement goals (Figure 26-1). When performed successfully, PPM has yielded the following benefits:

- 20 to 30 percent improvement in time to market[1]
- 25 to 300 percent improvement in number of projects completed with the same resources[2]
- Average project duration cut by 25 to 50 percent[3]
- Over 90 percent project success rate, with double the profit margin[4]
- 50 percent improvement in research and development (R&D) productivity[5]

These achievements apply to government, not-for-profit, and for-profit entities.

The principles and best practices of PPM presented here are backed up by research, case studies, and many years of experience. To accomplish its primary objective of improved return on investment (ROI), PPM must ensure that all three of the following activities are performed expertly:

1. *Choosing the right project mix:* Choose those projects that will leverage the organization's precious resources to bring large, measurable value to the stakeholders.
2. *Ensuring the correct scope:* Align project content cross-functionally to ensure that the combined changes will result in the magnitude of improvement necessary to meet organization goals. Many of today's projects have technical scope relevant to a single, functional area, but lack the organization-wide policy, measurement, and content changes necessary to have a significant impact on organization goals.
3. *Executing quickly, in the correct sequence:* To accomplish this, people performing PPM must understand and convince the organization to adhere

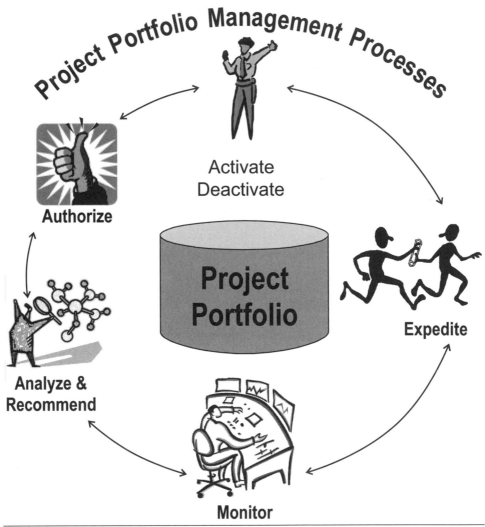

Project Portfolio Management Processes

Activate
Deactivate

Authorize

Project
Portfolio

Expedite

**Analyze &
Recommend**

Monitor

FIGURE 26-1. **PROJECT PORTFOLIO MANAGEMENT PROCESSES**

to the organization's project capacity. Any organization that is overloaded with too many projects sees a dramatic increase in resource multitasking, with a devastating slowdown in project flow. Project durations climb exponentially. Quick execution also demands that PPM effectively monitor project execution to ensure that out-of-control situations are speedily recognized and acted upon.

Executives without effective PPM experience suffer from cross-functional resource conflicts with continual top management refereeing, poor or anemic organizational performance, and projects that are habitually delivered late, over budget, or not within scope. Most executives are aware of the need for drastic changes in multi-project management practices, but many put the emphasis in the wrong place. Unfortunately, a great deal of such investment is misdirected into multiyear efforts to implement software tools and time sheets before dealing with the highest leverage points.

THREE ROLES: GOVERNANCE, MANAGEMENT, AND PROJECT PORTFOLIO MANAGEMENT

To have an effective project portfolio management system, an organization must formally define three distinct roles:

1. *Governance:* This executive role is one of decision making, usually conducted by top management teams. In the most effective implementations that I have evaluated, this role includes the "C"-level executives (CFO, CEO, COO, CIO) who meet monthly to make the following decisions:

- Which projects to approve/reject
- When to activate projects
- How many projects to activate and which projects to deactivate
- Due dates for projects
- Criteria for project proposals
- Priorities
- Resource allocation, including capital expenditure, people, and operating expense budget
- Project reviews, with approval for a project to proceed to the next stage or to kill the project, or approval/rejection of project improvement plans
- Investment in project management methodology and tools

2. *Management:* Relative to PPM, management's job is to ensure that the project management system is "in control." According to the late quality guru W. Edwards Deming, a system is in control when the goals of the system can be predictably met more than 95 percent of the time without management intervention. Every project has three distinct goals—to be delivered on time, on budget, and within scope, according to the original commitments (not the tenth revision to a due date). This role includes providing the project management processes for planning and execution to deliver projects according to their goals. Usually, this is done by a project management office or similar organization. Where such an office does not exist, this role is filled by the project portfolio management person.

3. *Project portfolio management:* The person undertaking this role provides information and recommendations to the governance group for improved ROI, and monitors execution of projects. Usually, there is a close relationship between the person responsible for strategic planning and the project portfolio manager. While strategic planners identify the ideas necessary to meet organization goals, the portfolio manager makes sure that there are corresponding programs and projects sufficient to accomplish those ideas. Furthermore, the portfolio manager maps and tracks the project execution against the strategies and raises the red flag when there is danger of missing a goal. Finally, the portfolio manager also lets strategic planning know when the strategy is not practical relative to project resources available.

CHOOSING THE RIGHT PROJECT MIX

There are three common problems with the way that projects are sanctioned in most organizations:

1. Goals set by the senior executive are *not measurably tied* to projects. Even when a functional VP insists that a project is essential to meet a goal, the *percentage* of the goal that the project will accomplish is often not identified or committed to. This is vital information for the portfolio manager to be able to assess the health of the portfolio.

2. The collection of active projects is *not formally tracked* to see if it is meeting the goals (on time and magnitude of improvement promised). My experience is that many projects, even in multibillion-dollar companies, lack formal, valid resource-based project plans. Furthermore, even when the plans exist, they are often sitting on a shelf rather than being used as the performance base to judge the project.

3. Organizations breed *many projects that are not sanctioned* by any executive. In a June 2004 research effort, this problem was reported by 70 percent of respondents.

A formal portfolio management and governance process, including multi-project software, helps to overcome these problems. This is a prerequisite foundation for analyzing and improving the project mix.

When considering an organization's project mix, two areas of analysis are very important. The first is whether the projects will provide high leverage on the organization's precious project resources—people and capital—to generate measurable, bottom-line improvements within the coming year. The second area is portfolio balance.

To leverage project resources, a portfolio manager must understand the overall "business" of the organization. Every organization has one major constraint—one area that, more than any other, limits the performance of the organization. In this sense, an organization is like a chain with one weakest link. Leverage is based on finding and improving the weakest link of the organization. The weakest link can be anywhere in the supply chain—with suppliers who cannot provide enough resource (materials or people), or internally, for example, in production or operations, engineering, information technology (IT), in the distribution channels, in retail, or in the market (end customer).

For most for-profit organizations (about 70 percent), their constraint is in the market. This means that the organization has enough internal capacity to handle more business. To have dramatically better results, what they need is more customers who will buy from them. Given this scenario, a healthy project portfolio should have an *imbalance*. The project mix should include a disproportionately larger number of projects to address the market constraint. Many organizations in this situation have a large number of sales campaign projects, but few real market R&D projects. They must understand the deeper needs of their markets enough to overcome their constraint.

Many project portfolios have significant IT components. To know that the IT projects in the portfolio are correct, the portfolio manager must be able to answer six questions about these projects.[6] One of the questions is, What current technological limitation does the organization or its customers have that the new technology will remove, and, if the limitation is removed, what impact will that have on the organization's bottom line? When this question is asked rigorously, it turns out, surprisingly, that few currently active IT projects make sense for the organization.

In a June 2004 survey, over 90 percent of organizations recognizing a constrained resource cited a technology resource. Since IT resources are often badly multitasked, working on far too many projects, the organization can achieve a much higher return on the IT investment by focusing these resources on those few areas that address the organization's constraint. In many organizations, the focus on deeper customer needs suggests a different answer in terms of IT projects. For example, many organizations have poor systems in their supply chain (relying on forecasts rather than pull systems, for example), inadequate customer resource management systems, and poor customer service systems.

If an organization does not have the correct balance of projects, with focus on meeting important customer needs, then the project portfolio often contains many projects focused on greater internal efficiencies. Without increased sales and profits, greater internal efficiencies often require layoffs to translate those efficiencies into bottom-line savings. The result, for project management, is that many people become less enthusiastic about working on projects.

Therefore, the second area of analysis of the project mix is vital. The portfolio manager must examine portfolio balance in the following areas:

- *Focus on market and customer needs vs. focus on internal improvements.* If the company has cash flow or other serious financial issues, then internal improvements might be the desired "imbalance." However, an organization cannot cost-cut itself to long-term health. It must be able to grow its business. The portfolio manager must assess and report an undesirable imbalance in terms of marketing projects.

- *Short term vs. long term.* Often, too many projects spend money this fiscal year without bringing benefits until the next fiscal year or far in the future. This is a huge red flag. Who knows what will happen one or two years from now? The portfolio manager should be asking the tough questions about project benefits and why they can't happen sooner.

- *Research vs. development.* To have a secure future, every organization must invest some of its project resources in research. Such projects need to focus on market research, experimentation with new methods, tools and processes, training and human development, motivation, and other areas.

- *Which organization assets are project dollars and human resources focused on?* Assets are not just bricks and mortar. They include those assets that are strategic to the company's future, such as the web site, customers, external sales agents, and distribution channels. The portfolio manager should look at the distribution of project investments to the organization's strategic assets, and determine whether or not the distribution makes sense, relative to the top five assets.

- *Sponsorship from IT vs. other functional areas.* I have noticed that in many organizations, over 70 percent of the projects in the portfolio are sponsored by IT. This is a red flag indicating a lack of balanced ownership of project initiatives. It signifies that functional heads are not holding ownership—and therefore ultimate responsibility—for bottom-line results.

ENSURING THE CORRECT PROJECT SCOPE

Two current common practices are at the heart of project scope problems. One is the dissection of organizations into silos (functional areas) combined with the initiation of projects that try to optimize within a silo.

The portfolio manager must actively seek to replace this common practice of project scope *within a silo* by looking at the organization *as a whole*. Projects must be connected, cross-functionally, to make sure that the bottom-line benefit to the entire organization is increased.

The second common practice that hurts scope is for technology solution providers (internal and external to an organization) to take responsibility solely for the delivery of the technology rather than partnering in responsibility for the business result that the technology is intended for. Technology providers argue that they have no control over the business results. This is correct in the current paradigm. In the future, they must become full collaborators with the functional heads.

For this current paradigm to change, one or both of the following two scenarios much occur:

1. Technology solution providers must develop a much better understanding of the business requirements to be willing to take a stake in the business results.
2. Business leaders must develop a much better understanding of the technology to better specify their needs.

In either case, the IT resource crisis that we find so common across most organizations could be resolved overnight, simply by significantly reducing the project rework and waste through a strong, collaboration model. Recent application of a methodology called "Agile" has brought IT organizations closer to achieving desired end-user results with reduced rework.

In general, to begin to overcome these two scope issues and create a much more successful project portfolio management outcome, organizations must initiate cross-functional business training to help their top functional leaders, including IT, better understand the cause-and-effect relationships and conflicts between functions. Further, the organization must be sure that their metrics for each functional area (and the scope for any associated projects) are holistic, not silo-oriented. Finally, IT internal resources and external vendors should be asked to identify the limitation that any new technology is intended to overcome, what rules (policies and procedures) the organization is currently using to cope with those limitations, and how the rules need to change when the new technology is put in place. Project portfolio management serves as a clearinghouse for these and other issues by defining business case criteria and taking a holistic view of the organization's investments.

EXECUTING QUICKLY: PROJECT FLOW

One of the two keys to managing a project portfolio to execute quickly is to have an anchor mechanism for strictly activating projects according to the organization's capacity. Many organizations make the mistake of trying to balance workload across all project resources. Managing project workload in this manner is far too complex to yield predictable results due to variability of both project task work and operational responsibilities. The result is an overload of critical project resources and lack of management attention when needed to respond quickly to project issues or questions.

There are two possible anchor mechanisms that work to ensure fast project flow. One is to stagger projects according to one strategic resource—that one resource pool, within each collection of projects, that determines how many projects the organization can handle without badly multitasking that resource; it is usually the resource that is the most heavily loaded, or the resource that project managers and sponsors fight over the most, or the resource that most delays projects. In many organizations, it is an IT resource, an engineering resource, or an integration group. In smaller organizations, it is often the availability of a project manager that governs how many projects the organization can accomplish.

A second possible anchor mechanism is to control the number of active projects allowed within a phase, such as integration or final testing. This mechanism allows a new project to start a phase only when an existing project completes that phase.

The governance process, with the portfolio manager's help, must accommodate the deactivation of projects if the strategic resource is overloaded. In organizations such as Alcan Aluminum and TESSCO Technologies,[7] this meant deactivating over 50 percent of the active projects. The portfolio manager must ensure that projects are staggered strictly according to the capacity of the strategic resource. Only then will project flow dramatically improve.

The second key to quick execution is to embed a relay runner work ethic for people working on the critical path tasks in projects. One current best practice embeds a process of daily task management, performed by expert coaches who ask two simple questions: (1) How many days are left to complete the task? (2) Is there any way to accelerate the task?

These two keys—staggering projects and relay runner work ethic—are part of a project management methodology called critical chain[8] (discussed in Chapter 35).

EIGHT MANDATORY STEPS FOR EFFECTIVE PROJECT PORTFOLIO MANAGEMENT

The following steps can be easily and quickly executed to launch an effective PPM process:

1. *Collect current project portfolio information.* If you are new to PPM, focus on basic information. Make a list of the formally recognized projects/programs that the functional heads see as essential to meet the organization's goals. If the list has more than fifty projects, this is a red flag that the organization is not focused on its key constraint. Collect any project plans associated with those projects, including resources allocated. Determine if there are financial and other justifications. Get a green, yellow, or red summary status on each active project (green: project is on target; yellow: project has some minor problems; red: project is seriously off-track). Document the sponsor.

2. *Collect goal, asset, and resource portfolio information.* Determine the official company goals (increasing revenues, market share, profit growth, etc.). Make a list of the top five organization assets, according to executive perception. For resources, do not go into individual detail. The resource portfolio should include a list of the twenty-five to thirty-five resource pools (skill sets) used by projects, how many resources exist within each pool, and the approximate percentage utilization of those resource pools.

3. *Measurably link project, goal, asset, and resource portfolios and assess.* In this step, the portfolio manager determines if all projects are connected to organization goals, and to what extent they will meet the goals if executed successfully. Projects are also linked to the asset portfolio to determine the extent of investment in the company's strategic assets. The link between the project and resource portfolios determines resource loads and to what extent the organization has the capacity to execute successfully and on time.

4. *Determine if the project portfolio is balanced or imbalanced correctly.* See the discussion above regarding balance.

5. *Determine the organization's project capacity.* Every collection of interdependent projects flows at a given rate (e.g., number of projects completed per quarter or total net present value generated per year). By reducing project work in process, and reassigning freed-up resources to remaining projects, the projects flow faster. Byconcentrating on task acceleration during execution rather than on estimates, organizations can increase their project capacity.

6. *Develop and gain consensus on prioritization criteria and perform initial prioritization.* There are dozens of criteria that you can use. However, almost every management team prefers simplicity. Some of the popular criteria that appear in opportunity template rating forms include relationship to organization goals, customer impact, competitive impact, risk, cash flow, level of difficulty to complete the project, and amount of strategic resource needed.

7. *Develop recommendations for the governance board, relative to improving the portfolio ROI.* Based on the information that you have gathered, make specific recommendations for executive decisions at the next governance board meeting.

8. *Prepare for and facilitate the governance meeting.* Part of the preparation involves gathering information about new project proposals and circulating recommendations among functional heads prior to the meeting.

MONITORING MULTI-PROJECT EXECUTION

When an organization has twenty or more large projects active simultaneously (and this is just a rule of thumb), it usually needs a software tool with real-time, online status to help monitor project execution. This is necessary so that all the project and resource managers have a real-time understanding of the impact on their projects and resources—enough to make good decisions on priorities and expediting. It is also necessary for the strategic resource manager to be able to do "what-if" analysis for new projects and stagger the projects correctly so as not to overload the strategic resource.

Executives cannot govern effectively with poor or nonexistent data. The data from execution of projects, based on performance against a resource-based project

American Management Association • www.amanet.org

plan, is essential to give executives a meaningful status of any project. Today's common practice is to provide summary reports to executives showing a green, yellow, or red status, as described above. However, the summary status often masks or does not have good enough data to really help executives understand the organization-wide resource issues or trend analysis to identify threats early enough to avoid disaster.

With poor data, executives often end up as referees, shifting resources to the major disaster areas. While this often solves one problem in one project, it also creates waves of effects on other projects. The underlying root cause of scheduling beyond the organization's project capacity is not solved permanently, because the anchor mechanism is never identified or accepted in principle. The data do not exist to convince executives of the problem.

Therefore, three essential components of enterprise-wide multi-project management are multi-project software that shows trend analysis for each project, the recognition and acceptance by top management of the anchor mechanism by which all projects are scheduled, and an indication of whether or not each project's work is completing quickly enough to finish on time.[7] With these pieces implemented, a governance committee has the tool to identify a negative trend within a project. From that identification, the portfolio manager should be able to state what task, right now, is causing the problem, what action the project manager is taking, and whether or not the portfolio manager believes that action is sufficient to overcome the problem. Then, the governance committee has a basis to take action or leave the project alone.

BEST MULTI-PROJECT PRACTICES

The following processes were cited as having the highest value for multi-project management by companies that claimed that 70 percent or more of their projects were completed on time and within scope:

- Visibility of the processes to senior management, with their involvement. This included regular and timely status reporting to senior management and program management, which was used to facilitate multiple business unit and product integration.
- Stage gate project reviews, especially those conducted by the governance board with staged funding. This brings "faster kills and better clarity on risks." It also helps to prioritize new projects early on.
- Prioritization of all projects, based on their value proposition with tangible ROI.
- Much better resource management and allocation.
- Consistency of applying best project management practices to all projects.[9]

EXEMPLARY ORGANIZATIONS

I posed the following question to several organizations that were achieving much higher-than-average success rates in delivering projects on time, on budget, and within scope: "What do you think is the major reason why your organization has better-than-average success in managing its collection of projects?" Here are a few responses:

Part of our success is attributable to the process surrounding the annual budget cycle by which we select our investments for the year. The process drives toward a set of outcomes: to prevent poorly conceived projects before they start, to select only projects aligned with our organizational goals, and to generate broad support for the resulting portfolio of investments. This helps avoid having a number of executive pet projects, projects to placate a squeaky wheel, or projects that serve only larger departments, with no priorities established among them. We put significant effort into constructing a decision-making framework that results in a balanced and prioritized investment portfolio that is grounded in our organization's values. The confidence in the selection process at the executive level and the project manager level gives the organization a vested interest in the success of the project. As an initiative encounters difficulty, there is a measure of corporate resolve to right the project and see it through to completion.

Once the best projects are put into the pipeline, the PMO [project management office] helps keep them flowing by increasing their visibility through regular, standardized status reporting back to the committee that authorized them in the first place. We have structured our status report to convey both milestones and budget in terms of planned (baseline), actual, and forecast, along with a statement of the status of risks and issues affecting the project. Status reporting by itself, however, is insufficient; the value of the status report lies in the ability of the executives to accurately interpret the information presented and from it make informed decisions.

As a further benefit, the visibility into the health of the project creates a powerful dynamic with both the project managers and the project sponsors. Both of these parties want their projects to show well before the executive committee. If project managers are aware of the visibility into their projects' performance, they will be more inclined to pursue their projects responsibly and raise red flags earlier than would be the case if their projects did not appear on the radar screen. This is a healthy and productive dynamic to have in place. However, for it to work effectively, it is essential to establish attainable performance standards.

There are many, many other factors to successful project portfolio management, but in Arlington we have found two pieces of the magic that the PMO can work: provide a relevant framework for analysis and decision making and lead the organization toward an ongoing dialogue about desired outcomes and the path to reach them.

—Denise Hart, Program Management Officer, Arlington County Government, Virginia

The BASC PMO credits its strong foundation to the development of a strategic partnership with all operational organizations. This strategic partnership and the continuing efforts in promoting project management with executive sponsorship are the key success factors in meeting customer expectations and overall project success.

The strategic partnership emphasizes a mutual goal of defining and implementing best practices. As part of this effort, the PMO meets regularly with the executive director to review the projects within the portfolio. The creation and management of the portfolio includes the PMO conducting interviews with the operational organizations, IT, and finance departments. Several scenarios are then built based on different priorities: ROI, risk, business need, and so on. These are then presented to the executive director and his team for review. The PMO is involved in all stages of managing the portfolio, thus creating value for the organization by assisting the operational entities with their resource allocations, requirements, and reemphasizing the value of project management methodology. This enables the organization to experience first hand the value of the PMO and assists the PMO in assigning the best-suited resource to a project, thereby increasing the probability of a successful project.

—Luke Foster, PMP, with BellSouth Affiliate Services

Tinker Federal Credit Union achieves success in managing its projects through its electronic services committee, made up primarily of senior managers from all of the organization's operational areas. The committee ranks projects in order of their strategic priority, and only allows one to be activated if adequate resources will be available for its successful completion. By selecting the projects most closely aligned with their strategic plans, the committee guarantees that completed projects will make the most significant impact possible on the organization's future growth and direction.

Tinker Federal Credit Union's project managers closely monitor each active project's progress and try to spot problems as early as possible so that corrective actions can be taken. Problems that cannot be resolved at the project team level are elevated to the appropriate senior managers on the electronic services committee. This high level of visibility and authority allows resolutions to occur quickly and with minimal disruption to the project's momentum.

—Ben Mannahan, Tinker Federal Credit Union Project Manager

CONCLUSION

Executive understanding, buy-in, and direct involvement at the beginning of any project portfolio management effort are key ingredients for success. While executive understanding can be fostered by education in the form of reading and presentations, do not expect the executives to buy in to a different approach without giving them some logical data and analysis. The data and analysis are needed to prove that there are too many active projects (well beyond the capacity of the organization to do its work without multitasking). Furthermore, the analysis of the collection of projects, when linked to the goals of the organization, must clearly identify the gaps. Otherwise, executives will perceive the portfolio management recommendations to be illogical and unfounded.

The portfolio managers' challenge is to perform their analysis and make recommendations in a way that gets top management to act. If the data presented to senior executives lack credibility, the portfolio manager will be asked to do more research and find more data, and thus will be continually caught in the web of analysis paralysis. Use the eight-step process recommended in this chapter to build a robust portfolio data warehouse that can be continually enhanced.

With the correct understanding of the executives, through the governance committee, project portfolio managers will be able to move their entire organization up in portfolio management and project execution maturity level. Communications and collaboration in cross-functional projects will improve dramatically. Most importantly, the organization will move closer to meeting or exceeding its goals, with ever greater predictability on positive project results.

DISCUSSION QUESTIONS

❶ If a project portfolio management process is meeting its objectives, what tangible outcomes would you expect to see in any organization?

❷ How would you bring a top management team to agreement on the choice of projects in a portfolio?

❸ Discuss how the knowledge of an organization's "strategic resource" is helpful in project selection.

REFERENCES

[1] Performance Measurement Group, "Better Project Management Practices Drop Time-to-Market 20–percent," in *Signals of Performance,* volume 2, number 1 (Waltham, MA: Performance Measurement Group, LLC).

[2] See case studies in Chapter 22 of Harold Kerzner, *Project Management, A Systems Approach,* 8th edition (New York: John Wiley & Sons, 2002).

[3] See case studies in Appendix B of Gerald Kendall and Kathleen Austin, *Advanced Multi-Project Management* (Plantation, FL: J. Ross Publishing, 2012).

[4] Performance Management Group, "Portfolio Best Practices Yield Higher Profits," in *Signals of Performance,* volume 3, number 1 (Waltham, MA: Performance Management Group, LLC).

[5] "How to boost R&D productivity by 50 percent," *Insight Magazine,* Summer/Fall 2001.

[6] For a full discussion of the IT implications of projects and the six questions, see Gerald I. Kendall, *Viable Vision* (Boca Raton, FL: J. Ross Publishing, 2004).

[7] Gerald I. Kendall, *Advanced Project Portfolio Management and the PMO* (Boca Raton, FL: J. Ross Publishing, 2003).

[8] Ibid., for a more detailed description and case studies.

[9] Results of research study conducted by the author in June 2004. Quotes from survey participants were also collected during the course of this research.

CHAPTER 27

Enterprise Project Governance
Directing and Structuring Organizational Project Decisions

PAUL C. DINSMORE, PMP, DINSMORECOMPASS

LUIZ ROCHA, PMP, FEDERAL UNIVERSITY OF RIO
DE JANEIRO

Projects and programs need alignment with strategic intent in order to enhance value creation and ultimately increase competitive advantage while, at the same time, mitigating risk. It is not only a matter of doing the projects right. It is not only a matter of doing the right projects. It is not only a matter of ensuring that the right combination of right projects is done right. It is also essential that the correct approach of oversight be applied to guarantee strategic differentiation and value creation through the right combination of right projects done right.

The evolution of project management, once relegated to tactical concerns, has reached the level of enterprise project governance (EPG)—the umbrella of policies and criteria that comprise the laws for the sundry components that make up an organization. Enterprise project governance takes the evolution a step further, encompassing an all-inclusive approach to projects across an enterprise, involving all players, including board members, the CEO and other C-level executives, portfolio managers, project management office (PMO) managers, and project managers.

Overall governance of projects includes the classic components of project management, such as portfolios, stakeholders, programs, and support structures. But EPG reaches beyond outstanding project performance and organizational pillars such as project management maturity and continuous improvement to embrace an enterprise-wide perspective, including the organizational risks, the essential issues, and the business opportunities.

HOW DOES ENTERPRISE PROJECT GOVERNANCE RELATE TO CORPORATE GOVERNANCE?

The increasing focus on corporate governance can be traced to the stock market collapse of the late 1980s, which precipitated numerous corporate failures through the early 1990s. The concept started becoming more visible in 1999 when the Organization for Economic Co-operation and Development (OECD) released its "Principles of Corporate Governance."[1] Since then, over thirty-five codes or statements of principles on corporate governance have been issued in OECD countries.

The evolution of corporate governance was prompted by cycles of scandals followed by reactive corporate reforms and government regulations intended to improve the practice. Investors, unions, government, and assorted pressure groups are increasingly likely to condemn businesses that fail to follow the rules of good practice.

Increasing governance oversight structures is not an easy task. James Wolfensohn, former president of World Bank, stated:

> A number of high profile failures in 2001–2002 have brought a renewed focus on corporate governance, bringing the topic to a broader audience. . . . The basic principles are the same everywhere: fairness, transparency, accountability, and responsibility. . . . However, applying these standards across a wide variety of legal, economic, and social systems is not easy. Capacity is often weak, vested interests prevail, and incentives are uncertain.[2]

The high visibility heaped on corporate governance sparked by the scandals at the beginning of the twenty-first century brought attention to the lack of governance policies in more specific disciplines. In the early 1990s, information technology (IT) executives perceived a crying need to put order into the then-chaotic industry. Various programs and standards were developed, such that IT governance has become a solid cornerstone of the profession. After the turn of the century, a similar need became evident in the burgeoning field of project management.

Thus, EPG is a natural evolution in organizations that wrestle with countless demands for new projects to be completed within tighter time frames, at less cost and with fewer resources.

The need for EPG becomes more apparent as the world becomes increasingly projectized. With more projects clamoring for attention, the demand to undertake, manage, and complete multiple projects creates a need to provide greater governance and structure to multiple decision layers. While corporate governance addresses the concerns of the ongoing organization, with its status quo activities and operational issues, EPG, under the corporate umbrella, focuses on the projectized parts of organizations.[3]

KEY COMPONENTS OF ENTERPRISE PROJECT GOVERNANCE

In fulfilling the EPG role, the key activities for project sponsors and steering committee members to address are strategic alignment, risk management, portfolio management, organization and stakeholder management, performance evaluation, and business transformation. Implementing project governance requires a framework based on these major components, as presented in Figure 27-1.

Strategic Alignment

The responsibility of EPG is to ensure that projects are consistent with company strategies and goals and that the projects are implemented productively and effec-

FIGURE 27-1. **COMPONENTS OF ENTERPRISE PROJECT GOVERNANCE**

tively. All investment activities are subject to the governance process in that they need to be resourced and financed adequately. For mandatory projects, the decision is not whether to undertake the project but how to manage it in order to meet the required standard with minimum risk. For discretionary projects, more focus is required on the go/no-go decision and whether the project supports the strategic objectives and the investment gives best value compared with other alternatives.

Risk Management

Risk management is a systematic process of identifying and assessing risks and taking actions to protect a company against them. Organizations need risk management to analyze possible risks in order to balance potential gains against potential losses and avoid expensive mistakes. Risk management is best used as a preventive measure rather than as a reactive consequence. Managing risk in an integrated way can mean everything from using financial instruments to managing specific financial exposures, from effectively responding to rapid changes in the organizational environment, to reacting to natural disasters and political instability.

Portfolio Management

The project portfolio provides a big-picture view. It enables managers to become aware of all of the individual projects in the portfolio and provides a deeper understanding of the collection as a whole. It facilitates sensible sorting, adding, and removing projects from the collection. A single project inventory can be constructed containing all of the organization's ongoing and proposed projects. Alternatively, multiple project inventories can be created representing project portfolios for different departments, programs, or businesses. Since project portfolio management can be conducted at any level, the choice of one portfolio versus many depends on the size of the organization, its structure, and the nature and interrelationships among the projects that are being conducted.

Organization

There are three main organizational components to EPG: executive leadership, the portfolio management team, and program and project managers. Effective EPG requires that the individuals who direct and oversee governance activities be organized, and their contributions should be modeled to ensure that authority and decision making have a clear source, that the oversight is efficient, and that the needs for direction and decisions are addressed. Much of EPG may be carried out by multiple committees working at different levels. The committees or work teams used depend on organizational structures and culture, so not all organizations employ these committees at the same time. Thus, EPG is a collaborative process requiring a healthy mix of corporate, business units, and technical support services.

Stakeholder Management

Everyone has expectations that determine their behavior. Expectations are visions of a future state, often not formally manifested, but which are critical to success. Expectation management is crucial in all settings where people must collaborate to achieve a shared result, and EPG is no exception.

Performance Evaluation

For EPG to be effective, overall performance has to be measured and monitored on a periodic basis to ensure that it contributes to the business objectives while at the same time remaining responsive to the changing environment. Performance is typically evaluated during execution of an implementation plan, yet due attention is required for ongoing monitoring as well.

Business Transformation

Vision and strategy require adaptation and refinement to adjust to changing economic influences. Business agility, or the ability to achieve business transformation, is a measure of both management and corporate success and, as such, essential in pursuing the implementation EPG. Establishing change capability enables clients to continue optimizing performance in response to changing service demands and new strategic drivers

The relationship between the EPG factors and other organizational components is shown in Figure 27-2.

FIGURE 27-2. **THE BIG PICTURE: HOW EPG RELATES TO OTHER ORGANIZATIONAL COMPONENTS**

THREE GOVERNANCE STRUCTURES

Board-Sponsored Enterprise Project Governance

In this scenario, corporate governance creates specific committees related to EPG, with names like *strategic planning and implementation, operations oversight, product development,* or *events and programs.* These committees can influence EPG policies as well as maintain oversight rights. As examples of organizations with corporate governance committees having scopes that relate to governance of projects, the Global Fund (a major organization aimed at fighting AIDS, tuberculosis, and malaria) has a portfolio and implementation committee, and L'Oreal, the French cosmetics conglomerate, has a strategy and implementation committee.

How might these board-level committees help shape EPG policies? Although overall executive responsibility for implementing projects resides with the CEO and management team, a board-level committee can exert influence on the selection and implementation of strategic projects—those that will ultimately affect the company's future. Here are actions appropriate for board-level committees that propose to focus on issues such as planning, strategy, and implementation:

- Require policies for selecting and prioritizing strategic projects.
- Require the organization to addresses issues of EPG, including project portfolio management.
- Set up a policy for oversight review of a few key initiatives (but avoiding micromanagement).
- Establish appropriate communication channels.
- Require periodic project management maturity assessments.

A CEO-Sponsored EPG

This governance structure is similar in concept to the first scenario except that the board delegates full responsibility to the CEO.

The common practice among many boards is to concentrate only on broad issues related to business ethics, risks, auditing, CEO succession, and internal board administration. All other responsibilities are handled by the permanent executive staff under the leadership of the CEO and executive team. Enterprise project governance takes place fully within the scope of the company's full-time professional leadership. Policies, structures, and procedures for EPG are therefore developed under the umbrella of the CEO and C-level colleagues, and delegated to appropriate levels within the organization.

Enterprise project governance, then, is just one of several responsibilities of the CEO, who is charged with making projects and everything else work effectively. The board's role regarding EPG is limited to hiring and firing the CEO, who, it is hoped, will be enlightened with respect to project governance policies. This limited EPG scope for board committees is prevalent in the corporate world and is adopted in organizations such as General Electric, Accenture, Roche, and Volkswagen. Enterprise project governance, then, is a matter to be organized and structured by the CEO and the executive team.

Where corporate governance has delegated full responsibility to the CEO to deal with all management and organizational matters, including strategies and projects, it falls on the CEO to provide for interface between the strategists (upper management and business planners) and the implementers (program and project managers). The following subsections discuss some of the ways the CEO can effectively deal with the project-related issues across the organization

The Chief Project Officer

In large organizations, the challenge of effectively coordinating hundreds of complex projects can be too much for a conventional hierarchical organization to handle. A solution to this is to designate a project-wise C-level executive to help coordinate the governance and oversight of multiple projects and major programs. This executive, called the chief project officer (CPO), shoulders the overall responsibility for EPG in the organization. Other titles, like VP for Special Projects or Head of Program Management, are also used to describe the same function. How a CPO operates depends on the maturity level of the organization with respect to project management (methodologies, past experience, and support), and the size and complexity of the projects. It also depends on the conviction of top management with regard to using an enterprise project approach to managing, and the nature of the organization— whether it is project-driven, like an engineering company, or functionally based, like a manufacturer of toothpaste that uses project management as a means to an end.

The CPO function makes particular sense in organizations that are global, multidisciplined, and require timely delivery of multiple, complex projects. A CPO's responsibility is to care for the organization's portfolio of projects—from the business case to final implementation, which includes the following tasks:

- Involvement in the business decisions that result in new projects
- Strategic project planning
- Setting priorities and negotiating resources for projects
- Oversight of strategic project implementation
- Oversight of an enterprise-wide project management system
- Development of project-management awareness and capability throughout the organization
- Periodic project review, including decision to discontinue projects
- Top-level stakeholder management, facilitation and mentoring

The Corporate Project Management Office

The corporate project management office (CPMO) is a small, strategic group, sometimes called the strategic project office. The CPMO is the link between the executive vision and the project-related work of the organization. Its functions include overseeing strategic items such as project management maturity, project culture, enterprise-wide systems integration, managing quality and resources across projects and portfolios, and project portfolio management. The CPMO is responsible for the project portfolio management process, and ensures that the organization's projects are linked to corporate strategies. The CPMO ensures that the organization's project portfolio continues to meet the needs of the business, even as these needs continue to change over time. It serves as the critical link between business strategy and execution of tactical plans.

The Program Management Office and Committees

The program management office (abbreviated PgMO to distinguish from the project management office, PMO), operates at a less strategic level than the CPMO and is designed to provide coordination and alignment for projects that are interrelated under the umbrella of a given program. An alternative approach for dealing with EPG issues involves the use of committees to provide the strategic guidance and oversight coverage for project management endeavors, for examples, the committee for strategic projects, the strategic steering committee, and the portfolio review committee. These committees have authority for prioritizing projects that cut across functional departments and are composed of executives from throughout the organization to ensure consensus and balance.

The CEO thus has multiple options for providing strategic guidance for managing projects across the enterprise. Which approach is the best fit and how the organization will be structured depend on the existing company culture, the developing needs within the organization, and the opinions of the principal decision makers.

Distributed Responsibility

In scenario 3, corporate governance provides no committee coverage for EPG, and the organization under the CEO establishes no formal structure such as a CPO or CPMO to deal with issues of portfolios, programs, and projects. Here, the challenge of dealing with multiple projects persists, yet the responsibility is scattered throughout the organization.

In this setting, a growing awareness exists at the middle management and professional levels regarding the need for a coherent enterprise-wide set of policies, competencies, and methodologies for managing projects of all natures and types. At this hands-on level, benefits for an EPG-type approach is evident to participating stakeholders, because this holistic view implies that the organization will be supported with appropriate systems, trained personnel, and an overall project culture.

The awareness, however, is not as evident to upper management. Proposals to top decision makers for an overarching program like EPG fall on deaf ears. This leaves the interested parties with two options. The first is to "go with the flow" and keep plugging away as best as possible and hope that something will sway opinions in the future. The other option is to take a proactive stance and embark on a policy of advocacy for the EPG cause. This implies using techniques of influence management to create interest and awareness. Here are some effective approaches:

- Target potential champions that might help carry the flag for the EPG cause.
- Distribute published literature, including magazines and Internet publications, that documents how competitors or other organizations take project management to a higher levels.
- Use indirect influencing by involving people who have access to the ears of the decision makers.
- Prepare a business case showing feasibility and proposing a step-by-step approach.

Such a bottom-up approach may be articulated by existing PMOs because they surely have awareness and interest in articulating such a movement.

IMPLEMENTING ENTERPRISE PROJECT GOVERNANCE

How to proceed depends on factors such as the actual need, the existing culture, the presence of a champion, and a feasible plan for making the implementation. Initiative for promoting the EPG concept may start at different levels, such as the board, CEO and executive team, middle management, or the "bottom-up" approach. Here are a few suggestions.

A Simplified Incremental Approach

Formal EPG is in reality an evolutionary approach. Like other project management improvement initiatives have done in the past, EPG can be introduced and upgraded incrementally. If there is minimal awareness in the organization about the impact project management has on organizational results, lack of a project management culture, insufficient sponsorship to champion the cause, or a lack of expertise in change management, partial initiatives may be appropriate. Here are some starting points:

- Intensify training programs in project management basics.
- Stimulate use of project management techniques across the enterprise in all types of projects, including engineering, IT, research and development (R&D), new product development, marketing, and human resources.
- Create awareness at the executive level through literature, benchmarking, and conferences.
- Identify potential sponsors for a broader program.
- Stimulate implementation and development of PMOs.

With these measures in place, an organization will be on its way to producing highly successful projects of all types across the enterprise. That said, a comprehensive EPG program offers the best way to guarantee optimal project performance and boost overall organization results.

Enterprise Project Governance Roadmap

The elaboration of an EPG plan may ultimately develop into a manual for maintaining the concept in place. Such a manual becomes a repository for definitions, approaches, processes, and lessons learned from execution, becoming an organizational asset. As time goes on, the document will be subject to adaptation, review, change, and improvement, creating an organizational learning cycle. There are nine factors to be considered in the EPG plan:

Stakeholder Size Up

The principal stakeholders fall into the organization´s main publics of interest. These publics of interest may be internal "champions" or the organization´s external publics. The champions have the power to initiate projects and shape their ultimate impact on the organization. In generic terms, the champions include board and project committee participants, project sponsors, and upper management overseers. On the other hand, there is a growing concern about the impacts that projects may have on certain communities and the power they may have to paralyze organizational projects. External publics include investors, clients, consumers, suppliers, and regulatory agencies.

Context and Culture

To understand the internal and external business context and current culture in which the organization operates, scenario and SWOT (strengths, weaknesses, opportunities, and threats) analysis from the corporate strategic plan must be translated into assumptions. Project competency gaps identified by human resources must be addressed. Organizational climate and attitudes toward projects and compliance and the characteristics of the culture that may impact the EPG framework must be analyzed.

Strategy Alignment

Enterprise project governance needs to clearly align organizational mission, vision, values, and strategic intentions as stated into the corporation's strategic plan to all the programs and projects in the organization. For mandatory projects, the decision is not whether to undertake the project but how to oversee them in order to guarantee all the compliances required. For successful program and project selection, attention is focused on alignment with strategic objectives and the "go/no-go" decision with respect to best value. All the projects must individually consider not only the deliverables but also the organizational benefits resulting from the deliverables' implementation.

Directing

Promote and motivate expected behaviors by organizing the policies, methodologies, standards, and guidelines applicable to EPG. In addition, all the systems related to project implementation must be clearly defined and an effort made to standardize them instead of having a software Tower of Babel. Finally, develop a glossary because standardizing project language is key to EPG.

Risk Management

Managing risk in an integrated way allows effective responses to rapid changes in the organizational environment, natural disasters, and political instability. For such, a link between EPG and the organizational risk management approach is required pinpointing the critical organizational risks, and outlining how the approach to portfolio, programs, and projects are integrated with the overall risk approach to the organization. It is also important to link EPG to how the organization responds to business disruption, crisis, and recovery.

Portfolio Management

A single project inventory can be constructed containing all of the organization's ongoing and proposed projects. Since project portfolio management can be conducted at any level, the choice of one portfolio versus many depends on the size of the organization, its structure, and the nature and interrelationships among the projects that are being conducted. Enterprise project governance must describe the following:

- Portfolio proposals: how to select projects and programs that represent the best value to the firm and that are aligned with strategy
- Portfolio processes: how the portfolio will be managed
- Portfolio integration: integration processes (for companies with portfolios across business units or geographical areas)

American Management Association • www.amanet.org

Structure, Roles, and Responsibilities

To be effective, the individuals who direct and those who oversee governance activities must be integrated, and their contributions modeled to ensure that authority and decision making have a clear source, the work of management and oversight is efficient, and the needs for direction and decisions are addressed. The EPG plan should therefore define the following:

- Goals and expected outcomes of the EPG system: its scope, what it will achieve, and how it relates to business objectives.
- Key roles and accountabilities.
- Board roles and accountabilities: the board has oversight of the system and ultimately is the active monitor for shareholder and stakeholder benefit. The board must:
  - Address long-term issues.
  - Direct the purpose and desired outcomes of the organization.
  - Set a charter for its involvement.
  - Set business objectives and ensure they are congruent with values and risks.
  - Obtain regular assurance that the system is effective.

- Committees roles and accountabilities: most EPG work is carried out by committees, and in many organizations multiple committees work at different levels. The actual committees depend on the organization size, culture, and leadership style.
- The Role of Management:
  - Design, implement, and operate an effective EPG system.
  - Provide regular assurance about the effectiveness of the system.
  - Communicate with key stakeholders about issues arising.
  - Evaluate and optimize the performance of the system.

- The role of assurance: management should obtain and provide regular assurance about the effectiveness and performance of the EPG system. An independent expert can reveal weaknesses in design or operation, and define opportunities for integration and exchange of best practices. Internal or external independent reviews can be used. Those providing assurance, whether internal or external, should:
  - Provide assurance that risks are appropriately identified, evaluated, managed, and monitored.
  - Provide regular assurance to the board and management of the effectiveness of the EPG system in light of the organization's culture and objectives.

- Decision-making processes: a set of processes must be established as authoritative and within which portfolios, programs, and projects are initiated, planned, and executed, to ensure that goals and benefits are met:
  - Project identification: describe the processes for proposing a program or a project, including if it is a mandatory one or aligned with business objectives.

- Project selection: describe how projects and programs are selected and how to decide on go/no-go.
- Why–how framework: describe how to develop a why–how framework for each project or program.
- Project start-up: describe how to initiate a project or a program.
- Project reviews: describe the approach for programs and project reviews.
- Risk processes: describe the best practices to be applied for the program.
- Portfolio processes: describe the processes chosen to deal with handling the management of portfolios.

This roadmap provides a guideline for embarking on a program of enterprise project management. It serves as a basis for developing a customized plan for addressing the specific issues and desires of any given organization. Some of the requirements may already be in place, whereas others may require major planning and implementation effort.

Performance

Performance analysis of the EPG initiative must include a maturity analysis of how projects are contributing to the achievement of the organizational ambition, how success can be replicated, and how the organization is learning from the initiative. The result of this performance analysis must be an action program driving improvement.

Transformation

The implementation of an EPG effort and the resulting desired change affects people and as such must be planned. People need to be informed, and their actions and reactions evaluated. Organizational change management will be required.

CHALLENGES AND ROADBLOCKS IN IMPLEMENTING ENTERPRISE PROJECT GOVERNANCE

As in any other endeavor involving change in an organization, well-developed plans can pave the roadway for smooth motoring toward desired goals. Here are ways to prevent problems along the route to EPG:

- Show what the competition is doing with regard to project management.
- Demonstrate studies from professional associations, such as the Project Management Institute (PMI) and International Project Management Association (IPMA), regarding the impact of an organizational approach to project management.
- Benchmark with other companies with known expertise in high-level project management.
- Do a risk analysis of the implementation project, including factors such as probable challenges, likelihood of occurrence, and stakeholder influences.

Despite a well-planned rollout of an EPG project, unexpected challenges may appear along the way. Corrective approaches to unexpected barriers include the following:

- Put the program temporarily on pause. Sometimes time itself will sort out an issue.
- Reevaluate the situation. What has changed? What new factors have come into play?
- Replan. If a plausible plan B is on standby, then put it into play. If not, then develop a modified plan.

ERICSSON: A CASE OF ENTERPRISE PROJECT GOVERNANCE EVOLUTION

In practice, many organizations evolve over time toward a broad enterprise approach for managing projects. Such is the case of Ericsson, a global telecommunications manufacturer headquartered in Sweden, which spent decades developing project management expertise. Known as PROPS (for PROject for Project Steering), the framework's objective is to enable project managers anywhere in the world to complete their projects successfully. In the late 1980s, the company developed the first PROPS version to support the development of digital telecom switches. The introduction of mobile telecom networks sparked the need to develop a more generic model that was uncoupled from specific product lines. Later, generic versions were developed with focuses on (1) customer projects, (2) market-based R&D, and (3) internal company projects. This broadened the focus to general project management practices and encompassed the business context of projects.

Ultimately, this led to the company's *projectization*, where projects became the way of working at Ericsson, because as much as 80 percent of the company's employees work on projects. The PROPS framework has gone through multiple versions and has become a framework for enterprise project management aimed at all project-related areas, including project management, program management, portfolio management, and project offices. Focus is on the enterprise as a whole and multiple projects of sundry natures. The key points of the PROPS framework are as follows:

- Business perspective
- Human perspective
- Project life-cycle model
- Project organization model

In essence, the framework contains the basics for EPG, and is used as a basis for similar programs at Volvo, Saab, and other international companies.

The creation and evolution of PROPS was sponsored and supported by top management. A small unit responsible for project management support was given the assignment to host the framework and act as an internal consultancy team. A group of technical writers was brought in to ensure that PROPS was documented and launched in a way that would be reader friendly and attractive to potential users. Later, an internal center of excellence became responsible for development of PROPS, as well as for project management training and support. This focused group of people dedicated to PROPS cause was a key factor for its success.

Ericsson gradually developed a fully *projectized* culture from top to bottom, and did so by continuously upgrading its basic project management framework, with the full involvement and support of top managers. According to Ericsson's Inger Bergman, "Changing a company from a traditional hierarchical, functional manufacturing industry to an agile player in the IT area is not easy and takes time and effort. Project management is now seen as an important asset for the company and a competitive advantage in R&D and sales delivery." Ericsson is an example of the evolution of project governance capabilities.[4]

ACKNOWLEDGMENT

This chapter is adapted and excerpted from Paul Dinsmore and Luiz Rocha, Enterprise Project Governance *(New York: AMACOM, 2012), by permission of the publisher.*

DISCUSSION QUESTIONS

❶ Where does project and/or portfolio governance reside in your company?

❷ Thinking of a recent project or program that was challenged, how might appropriate governance made a difference?

REFERENCES

[1] Organization for Economic Co-operation and Development, *OECD Principles of Corporate Governance*, revised edition (Paris, France: OECD, 2004), http://www.oecd.org/daf/corporate/principles.

[2] World Bank, "Corporate Governance: Improving Transparency and Accountability," 2005. Quoted in "How Corporate Governance Affects the Strategy of Corporations: Lessons from Enron," in Hameed Ahmed and Ali Najam, master's thesis, Department of Management and Economics, Linköping University, Sweden, 2006, www.diva-portal.org/smash/get/diva2:21551/FULLTEXT01.pdf.

[3] Association for Project Management (APM), *Directing Change: A Guide to Governance of Project Management* (High Wycombe, UK: Association for Project Management, 2004), www.apm.org.uk.

[4] Paul C. Dinsmore and Terrance J. Cooke-Davies, *Right Projects Done Right* (San Francisco: Jossey-Bass, 2006), pp. 111–117 and 275–280.

CHAPTER 28

Performance and Value Measurement for Projects and Project Management

JAMES S. PENNYPACKER,
PENNYPACKER AND ASSOCIATES

DEBORAH BIGELOW CRAWFORD, PMP, PRESIDENT,
PM COLLEGE

Project managers excel at managing projects but have not always been very good at communicating the value of what they do. Often, the steps involved in measuring performance and value are omitted in the drive to "just get it done."

However, this is short-sighted. It is imperative that both projects and project management track and communicate performance. More than ever, investment in initiatives designed to improve organizational performance must be justified. Whether it's the implementation of a project management methodology, a project management office (PMO), project management software, or project management training, these initiatives must deliver positive and tangible results. The good news is that tangible measures of project management value and performance can be established by asking the right questions and developing an appropriate measurement system.

TWO LEVELS OF MEASUREMENT

The first measurement level is more familiar and more frequently carried out. Project managers are used to tracking budget and schedule *performance*. The missing step, however, is in relating these outcomes to the business impacts they provide. In communicating these impacts, we can demonstrate the *value* of project management processes. This key step is absent in many PMOs, which may be the reason why some PMOs have been disbanded during tough economic times.[1]

A structured measurement program enables you to identify areas for performance improvement, benchmark against the industry or competitors, set targets, identify trends for forecasting and planning, evaluate the effectiveness of changes, determine

American Management Association • www.amanet.org

the impact of project management, and tell a story about your organization's performance.

CREATING A MEASUREMENT PROGRAM

Measuring performance and value takes time and commitment. Senior management sponsorship is crucial, and there needs to be a sense of urgency about the results. Above all, make sure you have the resources to gather and analyze the data.

Common goals and objectives to measure include the following:

- Reducing costs
- Improving timing
- Improving quality
- Measuring the effectiveness of training
- Improving productivity

Choose a measurable outcome that is important to your company. For example, if improving schedule performance for all your projects over a period of a year can be translated into improvement in average project cycle time, this can be translated into improvement in time to market. Shorter time-to-market means that your organization launches more products in a given period, which can add significant value to the organization's bottom line. Value measures, therefore, provide information on the performance of the organization rather than the performance of a project. This example also demonstrates how good measures should align with organizational objectives. Figure 28-1 shows how schedule tracking metrics can lead, through careful linkage with organizational objectives, to a measurement of business value for your project management practice.

Measurement: Making the Connection

When schedule performance has been linked to increased market share, the value of training project personnel in scheduling becomes calculable. In this same way, it is possible to work backward from any strategic goal, drilling down to those measurable tasks that have an impact on goal achievement, and then developing training plans that directly impact those tasks. Using a measurement program of this type, the training function will always have a "hard" answer ready to this question: Does this training pay off? And, by how much?[2]

A Model for Performance Measurement

A model established by Project Management Solutions has been proven to work well in dozens of organizations. This model, known by the acronym PEMARI, integrates the following processes:

- **P**lanning: a process for understanding key success factors, identifying stakeholders and roles and responsibilities, identifying performance management goals, and developing a program plan
- **E**stablishing metrics: a process for identifying and selecting performance measures and developing measurement scorecards (high-level measures are

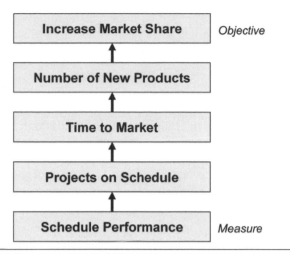

FIGURE 28-1. **FROM PERFORMANCE MEASUREMENT TO VALUE.**

defined at the governance level; specific metrics that roll up into these measures are identified at the departmental or program level)

- **M**easurement: a process for planning for data collection, including data source and information technology (IT) required; collecting data and ensuring data quality (a joint responsibility of IT and the strategic project office [SPO] as owner of the portfolio processes)
- Analysis: a process for converting data into performance information and knowledge; analyzing and validating results; performing benchmarking and comparative analysis (a joint responsibility of IT and the SPO)
- **R**eporting: a process for developing a communications plan and communicating performance results to stakeholders (a responsibility of internal communications)
- Improvement: a process for assessing performance management practices, learning from feedback and lessons learned, and implementing improvements to those practices (a joint responsibility of the SPO as portfolio owner, and executives responsible for governance)[3]

Developing Performance Measures

While there is general agreement that "you can't manage what you can't measure," the actual measurements themselves usually prove to be a source of conflict. What are we measuring, and why? What *should* we be measuring? What is the connection between the performance measures we collect regarding individuals and their tasks and the ultimate performance of the company—if any? And what, in reality, does "performance" mean, on an organization-wide scale? Is it merely making money? And if so, how much? Measures are the easy part; knowing what you want to measure, and why, is hard.

There is no single set of measures that universally applies to all companies. The appropriate set of measures depends on the organization's strategy, technology, and the particular industry and environment in which they compete. Like any aspect of any "living company," measures cannot be static: they cannot be chosen once and locked into place. Along with strategy, they evolve and are refined as the organization becomes more focused on, and skilled at, meeting strategic goals.

Measurement Planning

Planning your performance measurement program begins with identifying the measurement program team and its roles and responsibilities, and defining measurement program goals. Next, identify what, if any, current performance measurement systems are in place. What will be your implementation approach? Like any program, a measurement program needs a program plan and a clear understanding of terminology among the team members. Some suggested roles on the measurement team are as follows:

- Sponsor
- Representatives from stakeholders
- Project manager
- Data collection coordinator
- Data analyst
- Communications coordinator
- Measurement analyst

Establishing and Updating Measures

To develop a list of potential measures, start by brainstorming all the possible measures that would be meaningful to the goals you are trying to achieve. These criteria describe effective measures:

- Does this measure provide meaningful information?
- Is it supported by valid, available data?
- Is it cost-effective to capture?
- Is it acceptable to stakeholders?
- Is it repeatable? Actionable?
- Does it align with organizational objectives?

Next, prioritize and select a few critical measures, keeping the number of measures at each management level to a minimum. A few criteria for prioritization of measures might include their importance to the execution of goals, the ease of accessing the data, and the ease of acting to change the performance.

This process leads to the development of a scorecard of vital measures, with each measure clearly defined as a "measure package" that details the "what, why, when, who, and how":

- What is the measure?
- Why do we measure it?
- How will the data be captured?
- When will the data be captured?
- Where does this information reside?
- Who is the process owner for this data?

American Management Association • www.amanet.org

A sample list of prospective measures is shown in Figure 28-2. Here are detailed descriptions of what we have identified as the "top ten" measures:

1. *Return on investment:* (Net Benefits/Costs) × 100. This is the most appropriate formula for evaluating project investment (and project management investment). This calculation determines the percentage return for every dollar you have invested. The key to this metric is in placing a dollar value on each unit of data that can be collected and used to measure net benefits. Sources of benefits can come from a variety of measures, including contribution to profit, savings of costs, increase in quantity of output converted to a dollar value, and quality improvements translated into any of the first three measures.

2. *Productivity:* Output Produced/Unit of Input. Productivity measures tell you whether you are getting your money's worth from your people and other inputs to the organization. A straightforward way to normalize productivity measurement across organizations is to use revenue per employee as the key metric. Dividing revenue per employee by the average fully burdened salary per employee yields a productivity ratio for the organization as a whole. Other productivity metrics might be the number of projects completed per employee and the number of lines of code produced per employee. The key to selecting the right productivity measures is to ask whether the output being measured (the top half of the productivity ratio) is of value to your organization's customers.

3. *Cost of quality:* Cost of Quality/Actual Cost. Cost of quality is the amount of money a business loses because its product or service was not done right in the first place. It includes total labor, materials, and overhead costs attributed to imperfections in the processes that deliver products or services that do not meet specifications or expectations. These costs would include inspection, rework, duplicate work, scrapping rejects, replacements and refunds, complaints, loss of customers, and damage to reputation.

4. *Cost performance index* (CPI): Earned Value/Actual Cost. The CPI is a measure of cost efficiency. It is determined by dividing the value of the work actually performed (the earned value) by the actual costs that it took to accomplish it. The ability to accurately forecast cost performance allows organizations to confidently allocate capital, reducing financial risk, possibly reducing the cost of capital.

5. *Schedule performance*: Earned Value/Planned Value. The schedule performance index is the ratio of total original authorized duration versus total final project duration. The ability to accurately forecast the schedule helps meet time-to-market windows.

6. *Customer satisfaction:* Scale of 1 to 100. Meeting customer expectations requires a combination of conformance to requirements (the project must produce what it said it would produce) and fitness for use (the product or service produced must satisfy real needs). The customer satisfaction index comprises hard measures of customer buying/use behavior and soft measures of customer opinions or feelings, weighted based on how important each value is in determining customer overall customer satisfaction and buying/use behavior. It includes measures such as repeat and lost customers, revenue from existing customers, market share, customer satisfaction survey results, complaints/returns, and project-specific surveys.

7. *Cycle time:* There are two types of cycle time—project cycle and process cycle. The project life cycle defines the beginning and the end of a project. Cycle time is the time it takes to complete the project life cycle. Cycle times for similar types of projects can be benchmarked to determine a standard project life-cycle time. Measuring cycle times can also mean measuring the length of time to complete any of the processes that comprise the project life cycle. The shorter the cycle times, the faster the investment is returned to the organization. The shorter the combined cycle time of all projects, the more projects the organization can complete.

8. *Requirements performance:* To measure this factor, you need to develop measures of fit, which means the solution completely satisfies the requirement. A requirements performance index can measure the degree to which project results meet requirements. Types of requirements that might be measured include functional requirements (something the product must do or an action it must take) and nonfunctional requirements (a quality the product must have, such as usability or performance). Fit criteria are usually derived some time after the requirement description is first written. You derive the fit criterion by closely examining the requirement and determining what quantification best expresses the user's intention for the requirement.

9. *Employee satisfaction:* An employee satisfaction index (ESI) determines employee morale levels. The ESI comprises a mix of soft and hard measures, each assigned a weight based on its importance as a predictor of employee satisfaction levels. Examples include the following (percentages represents weight): climate survey results (rating pay, growth opportunities, job stress levels, overall climate, extent to which executives practice organizational values, benefits, workload, supervisor competence, openness of communication, physical environment/ergonomics, trust)—35%; focus groups (to gather in-depth information on the survey items)—10%; rate of complaints/grievances—10%; stress index—20%; voluntary turnover rate—15%; absenteeism rate—5%; and rate of transfer requests—5%.

10. *Alignment to strategic business goals:* Most project management metrics benchmark the efficiency of project management—doing projects right. You also need a metric to determine whether or not you are working on the right projects. Measuring the alignment of projects to strategic business goals is such a metric. Survey the appropriate mix of project management professionals, business unit managers, and executives. Use a Likert scale from 1 to 10 to rate the following statement: Projects are aligned with the business's strategic objectives.[4]

Analyzing the Data

Use a scorecard method to organize and aggregate the data, grouping measures by their relationship to key organizational areas of concern, such as financial measures, customer satisfaction measures, process measures, and employee satisfaction measures. In order to analyze and validate results, you must formulate precise questions that you are trying to answer. To validate your results, ask these questions:

COST MEASURES	QUALITY MEASURES
Project cost	Requirements performance
ROI	Customer satisfaction
Product cost variance to plan	Lessons learned implemented
Start-up costs	Project status communication
Efficiency of delivery	# scope changes/phase
Project profitability	Effectiveness
Product unit cost	AARs
Start-up cost variance to plan	Rework
Resource utilization	Internal customer satisfaction
Market share	Leadership capability
Cost of capital	Staffing conformance to plan
PRODUCTIVITY MEASURES	Project risk management
Project milestone performance	PM training satisfaction
Project success rate	**TIMING MEASURES**
Avg. sales per development FTE	Predictability of delivery
Process improvement	Time to market
Alternatives assessment	Project cycle time
Downtime	Successful phase exits
Capacity/resource planning	Project planning

FIGURE 28-2. **SAMPLE LIST OF MEASURES IN "SCORECARD" FORMAT**

- How does actual performance compare to a goal or standard?
- If there is significant variance, is corrective action necessary?
- Are new goals or measures needed?
- How have existing conditions changed?

Performance Reporting

Like any communications, performance reporting requires early identification of your target audience. Normally, with a measurement program, this will be executives, sponsors, PMO leaders, line-of-business managers, and other key stakeholders.

Relate the data to the organization's management performance goals and, where possible, to departmental and individual performance goals. Explain significant results, such as increases or decreases. The way you communicate results can be almost as important as the results themselves.

Continual Improvement

Measurement, like any organizational improvement initiative, cannot be done just once. Having baselined your measurements, you will have to iteratively measure in order to develop trends. In addition, linking the measurement program to a system of accountability for results creates a sense of urgency and relevance.

Once you start measuring performance, you can begin to start measuring value.

THE PROJECT MANAGEMENT VALUE MEASUREMENT SYSTEM:
LESSONS FROM THE FIELD

From 2000 to 2005, major companies from a variety of industries—information technology, manufacturing, pharmaceutical, new product development, government, and professional services—initiated projects to create measurement programs to measure the value that project management provides to their organizations. The goals of these project management measurement programs were as follows:

- Provide tangible metrics to senior management on the value of implementing systematic project management methods in order to reinforce the business case for project management improvement across the organization.
- Boost customer and project team members' morale by sharing statistics that show the value their work adds to the organization and the improvement they can achieve.
- Track ongoing project management performance and the business impact of project management to the organization.
- Initiate metric-based efforts to help streamline the project portfolio.[5]

Phase one focused on educating a measurement team on the Project Management Value Measurement Program to help them understand and enable them to clearly identify the program's objectives and goals. Organizational constructs that affect the program were identified, including stakeholders, organizational mission and strategies, organizational structure, key business processes, project management maturity, prior project management improvement initiatives, current measurement systems, and data availability.

Phase two focused on planning the initiative and engaging the team to identify measures, develop a project management value scorecard, and plan the implementation of the measurement program. After putting a project management value initiative plan and schedule in place, subsequent steps in this phase continue to build on the team's understanding of the project management measurement program and engage the team to develop the value scorecard and the project management value implementation plan.

Measures Development

In the measures development step, the team created and prioritized the initial list of measures for the scorecard. It is the initial pass at identifying and prioritizing measures, with the primary activity in the step being a collaborative development workshop. A comprehensive list of measures was developed, keeping in mind that they need to be logically linked to the goals described above. The measures also need to meet the criteria for good measures, which means that the measures selected must:

- Provide meaningful information.
- Be supported by valid data that are cost-effective to capture.
- Be acceptable to stakeholders.
- Be repeatable.
- Be actionable.
- Align with organizational objectives.

The measurement team then prioritized and selected measures to comprise the project management value scorecard. A simple prioritization process can be used: develop criteria for ranking the list of measures in order of importance on a scale of 1 to 5, have each of the measurement team members rank the list, and calculate average rankings.

Scorecard Development

In this step the team reviewed the prioritized measures information developed to date and developed measure packages (see below) and a cohesive project management value scorecard. The team first engaged in measures review, prioritization validation, and measure package definition. That information is then used to construct the scorecard for review and acceptance by the measurement team in preparation for implementation.

A comprehensive definition of each measure is included in a "measure package" to support the initial implementation and ongoing collection of data. Each measure package includes the following elements:

- Measure *(What)*: The data to be collected must be clearly identified.
- Objective *(Why)*: The measure's objective must be clearly defined. Why is it being collected? How will it be interpreted? What will it tell us? The measurement team must understand the objective of each measure.
- Data capture *(How)*: The mechanism for collecting the data must be identified.
- Timing *(When)*: The timing of data collection must be defined. Data collection must be properly timed to match the type of data and objective. Project management value measures are not intended to track individual project progress, so there would most likely not be a need to collect data monthly. Typically a quarterly or longer interval will support the objectives of the initiative.
- Data location *(Where)*: The location of the data must be identified.
- Data contact *(Who)*: The person responsible for maintaining the data must be identified. Who will provide the data? What is the reliability of this source?

Information from the measure packages is used to create a project management value scorecard, which is a collection and reporting tool for keeping score and reporting progress (Figure 28-3).

Measurement Program Implementation Planning

The implementation planning efforts further defined the framework around measurement processes and data collection that will be used to support ongoing measures program implementation. Key activities in this step include development of an implementation strategy and process. The Project Management Value Measurement Program process shown in Figure 28-4 describes a systematic approach to project management performance improvement through an ongoing process of establishing project management measures; collecting, analyzing, reviewing, and reporting performance data; using that data to drive performance improvement; and using lessons learned to continually improve the Project Management Value Measurement Program process.

MEASURE	OBJECTIVE	METRIC	UNITS	BASE	CURRENT	VALUE
Start-up Cost Variance to Plan	Cost Improvement	(Actual Start-up Cost ÷ Budgeted Start-up Cost) - 100%	Percent Start-up Cost Variance to Plan	64%	29%	123%
Efficiency of Delivery	Cost Improvement	(Total Man-hours Available in Dollars + Actual Labout Cost) ÷ Number of Projects	Average Labor Dollars per Project	263	260	1%
Project Status Communication	Quality Improvement	Projects Using Standard Status Reports ÷ Number of Projects	Percentage of Projects Using Standard Status Reports	20%	30%	50%
Requirements Performance	Quality Improvement	Scope Changes by Phase ÷ Number of Projects	Average Number of Scope Changes by Phase per Project	17.7	15.5	14%
Effectiveness	Cost, Quality, and Timing Improvement	Objectives Met ÷ Objectives	Percentage of Objectives Met	75%	79%	6%
Project Risk Management	Cost and Quality Timing Improvement	Projects Using Risk Management Processes ÷ Number of Projects	Percentage of Projects Using Risk Management Projects	10%	10%	0%
Project Cycle Time	Timing Improvement	Project Cycle Time ÷ Number of Projects	Average Project Cycle Time in Days	270	265	2%
Project Leader Training	Cost, Quality, and Timing Improvement	Project Leaders Trained ÷ Number of Projects Leaders	Percentage of Projects Leaders Trained	15%	20%	33%
Alternatives Assessment	Cost and Quality Timing Improvement	Project Using Formal Concept Alternative Selection Process ÷ Number of Projects	Percentage of Projects Using Formal Concept Alternative Processes	10%	30%	200%

FIGURE 28-3. **SAMPLE PM VALUE SCORECARD**

Phase three includes an initial implementation of the program and the transition to ongoing execution of the program.

The Project Management Value Measurement Program implementation is an ongoing effort to execute the program as documented in the implementation plan, using the measures packages to reinforce the data requirements, collection timing, and data contact responsibilities.

LESSONS LEARNED

- Organizational strategies and objectives set the foundation for effective measurement programs. It is essential to understand how the critical elements of the organization's strategies and objectives are linked to the measures that comprise the project management value scorecard.
- You need to have a very clear idea of the measurement program stakeholders and what their needs and expectations are regarding the program. There are

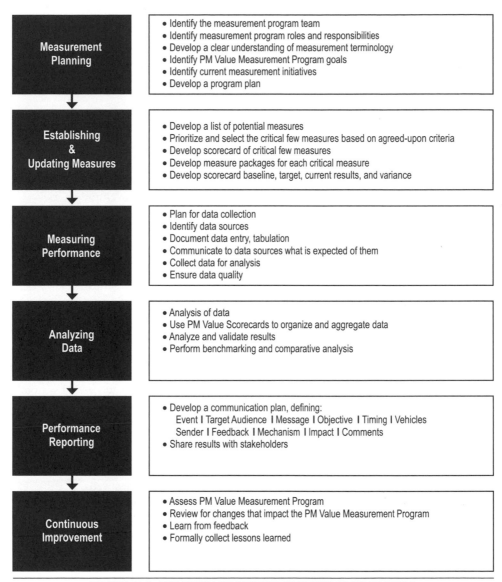

Measurement Planning	• Identify the measurement program team • Identify measurement program roles and responsibilities • Develop a clear understanding of measurement terminology • Identify PM Value Measurement Program goals • Identify current measurement initiatives • Develop a program plan
Establishing & Updating Measures	• Develop a list of potential measures • Prioritize and select the critical few measures based on agreed-upon criteria • Develop scorecard of critical few measures • Develop measure packages for each critical measure • Develop scorecard baseline, target, current results, and variance
Measuring Performance	• Plan for data collection • Identify data sources • Document data entry, tabulation • Communicate to data sources what is expected of them • Collect data for analysis • Ensure data quality
Analyzing Data	• Analysis of data • Use PM Value Scorecards to organize and aggregate data • Analyze and validate results • Perform benchmarking and comparative analysis

Performance Reporting	• Develop a communication plan, defining:
	   Event I Target Audience I Message I Objective I Timing I Vehicles
	   Sender I Feedback I Mechanism I Impact I Comments
	• Share results with stakeholders

Continuous Improvement	• Assess PM Value Measurement Program • Review for changes that impact the PM Value Measurement Program • Learn from feedback • Formally collect lessons learned

FIGURE 28-4. **THE PM VALUE MEASUREMENT PROGRAM PROCESS**

often huge differences in expectation among stakeholders; setting those expectations through clear communication of program goals is a key to success.

- Clearly identify measurement program goals and objectives. Without this clarity, selecting the right set of critical few measures will be difficult.
- In most best-in-class organizations, measurement initiatives are introduced and continually championed and promoted by top executives. When measurement initiatives are introduced from the bottom up, getting senior management buy-in is crucial and may take significant effort. Be prepared to make that effort.

- Develop a clear understanding of measurement terminology, which tends to be confusing and inconsistent, but needs to be understood and agreed upon by the measurement team and program stakeholders.
- Communication is crucial for establishing and maintaining a successful measurement program. It should be multidirectional, running top-down, bottom-up, and horizontally within and across the organization.
- The driving force to create a new or improved measurement program is usually a threat to the organization (often a crisis or strong competition). For organizations that are strategically developing measurement programs to enhance their competitive advantage, rather than reacting to their business environment, a sense of urgency must be nurtured and driven by individuals who understand the value of measurement and can evangelize the need for developing a measurement culture. Again, this takes enormous effort and communication.
- It is critical, and very difficult, to limit the number of measures in the scorecard. Selecting those critical few measures sharpens the stakeholders' understanding of the issues. Too many measures confuse and complicate (the measurement team cannot try to please everyone—selecting too many measures will ultimately kill the program).
- Pilot the measurement program before full implementation. And implementation should come in phases—implement a critical few high-value measures at first and identify more detailed measures when the organization has developed a measurement culture and is ready to collect and analyze more complex measures.
- Successful deployment of a measurement program requires a successful system of accountability—that is, all stakeholders need to buy into measurement by assuming responsibility for some part of the measurement process (sponsorship, analysis, data collection and monitoring, evangelism, etc.).
- Benchmark against industry standards if possible.
- Identify a central area of responsibility for the measurement program.
- Determine what counts as a project (what exactly will be measured).
- Reinforce the fact that project management value measurement is measuring performance change due to project management. Measures, therefore, are process focused, not project focused (you are not trying to measure the progress of a particular project).
- The measures selected are highly influenced by the project management maturity of the organization. Level-one organizations generally need to focus on process compliance and simple cost or schedule measures. As the organization matures in its project management capability, more sophisticated measures can be used.
- Analysis is one of the most important steps in project management value measurement, yet it is often one that is neglected. The insight gained from effective analysis (particularly determining root causes of the results measured) is what makes measurement a valuable business tool.
- Feedback is one of the best assets for continual improvement. Seek it and use it.

ACKNOWLEDGMENT

The material in this chapter was originally presented on behalf of PM Solutions at the 2002 PMI Global Congress in the paper J. Oswald and J.S. Pennypacker, "The value of project management: the business case for implementation of project management initiatives," Proceedings of the Project Management Institute Annual Seminars and Symposium, *2002.*

REFERENCES

[1] The Hackett Group, "Most companies with project management offices see higher it costs, no performance improvements." News release posted November 1, 2012. See also "The global state of the PMO in 2011," ESI, 2011, http://www.esi-intl.com/~/media/Files/Public-Site/US/Research-Reports/ESI-2011-PMO-global-survey-FULL-REPORT-US.

[2] PM College, *Building Project Manager Competency Improves Business Outcomes (white paper)* (Glen Mills, PA: PM Solutions Research, 2012).

[3] Deborah B. Crawford, *Mastering Performance Measurement (white paper),* PM Solutions, 2009.

[4] PM Solutions, *Measures of Project Management Performance and Value* (Glen Mills, PA: Center for Business Practices, 2005), http://www.pmsolutions.com/audio/PM_Performance_and_Value_List_of_Measures.pdf.

[5] The PM Value system is a part of the performance measurement practice of Project Management Solutions, Inc. (www.pmsolutions.com).

CHAPTER 29

Organizational Change Management

D. ALLEN YOUNG, PMP, PM SOLUTIONS

"Change management" can mean many different things to different firms and the people who work for them. To the software developer, it usually means managing version control and scheduled promotion of new or modified software components from a test, quality assurance, or the staging platform to the production environment on the "go live" date. To the project manager, it typically means managing scope, and having a solid scope change management process in place to evaluate the schedule and budget impacts of scope change requests to the project, including review, approval, and re-baselining steps, to help prevent "scope creep." While those types of change management are important, when implementing process or technology changes at the cross-functional department or enterprise level, the application of organizational change management (OCM) practices and techniques is essential for success. I would argue that, without OCM, the probability of failure lies somewhere between 50 and 75 percent, and in some cases it could be as high as 100 percent! This is based on my experience, but validated by some of the top management research firms.[1]

What exactly is OCM? In its raw form, it is a means of assessing the sponsorship, cultural resistance, maturity, and capacity of the organization to embrace and absorb the change over time, and, where weaknesses are identified, employing best practices and techniques to correct the weaknesses to an acceptable level, thereby significantly increasing the likelihood of successful adoption and utilization of the change.

That stated, OCM should not be conducted in isolation; it should be incorporated into whatever implementation methodology is used for the change initiative. To the people being affected by the change, the practices and techniques should simply appear as part of the overall implementation—tasks that naturally belong within the major phases of a project schedule. Organizational change management is not a phase unto itself. Each project phase should have OCM-related tasks within it.[2]

SPONSORSHIP

If you take away nothing else from this chapter, know that sponsorship is the first priority; without it, your change initiative will assuredly stall, and it will fail eventually. There are various levels of sponsorship that the change agent should be aware of.

Authorizing Sponsor

This is the person (or group, in some cases) who is championing the change, has the funds to pay for it or can obtain them from those who have them, has a sufficient level of line authority within the organization to lead the change, or has sufficient referent power to influence others outside of his or her direct line of authority to adopt the change. At the enterprise level, this ideally should be a C-level executive— CEO, CFO, COO. Validation of sufficient authorizing sponsorship should be one of your first tasks during the initiation phase of the project. If you do not have a true authorizing sponsor, stop the change initiative now if you can, because it will never fully get off the ground. Sponsorship of enterprise changes at the grassroots level almost never works.

Cascading Sponsorship

All of the line managers in the organization who are impacted by the change are potentially reinforcing sponsors. It is incumbent upon the authorizing sponsor to ensure that all affected managers have bought into the change. This should be confirmed before the initiation phase is completed. If an affected manager is not on board, there are various techniques that can be applied to correct the weakness, depending on the situation. Sometimes a stronger business case is needed to convince the affected managers that the change is in their best interest. Sometimes the affected managers need to be included in the decision-making process concerning the change itself (how much, how soon, to whom, etc.). Sometimes the affected managers need to be told by their superior that it is a requirement, and what the repercussions will be if they do not get on board. In some cases, the affected managers and their unit might be able to defer when they must comply with the change, or perhaps they can be "grandfathered" indefinitely.

Once all affected managers have become reinforcing sponsors, it becomes their responsibility to help communicate, promote, and enforce the change across their part of the organization. Their job becomes one of rewarding desired behaviors (adopting the new), and discouraging undesirable behaviors (continuing to adhere the old).

In some cases, the reinforcing sponsors may also be change agents, or champions, of the change, meaning that they not only have the responsibilities of a reinforcing sponsor, but are also very much an active proponent and endorser of the change.

Sustaining Sponsorship

Authorizing and reinforcing sponsors must embrace the concept that active and fully engaged sponsorship not only needs to exist throughout the change initiative, but also needs to continue after the initiative has completed. Once the change is live, the project team that implemented the change will disband, and the resulting new processes and tools will be in place from that point forward.

All sponsors are responsible for ensuring adoption by a specified cut-off date, and ongoing utilization thereafter. This should include shut-down/removal of the ability to conduct business the old way, and possibly even changes to formal job descriptions whereby people are evaluated in part on their utilization of the new way of doing things. If those steps are not taken, old habits will die hard, and the change will never be fully adopted.

SPONSORSHIP METHODS

Can the sponsors simply dictate what will be changed, and push it down through the chain of command in the organization to make it happen? Sometimes the answer is yes, but not necessarily in all cases. There are three basic methods sponsors can utilize to overcome resistance: command, compromise, and collaboration. Each one has its own merits, depending on the situation:

- Command: Sometimes a "command and control" approach works best. As the year 2000 approached, all mission critical systems needed to be tested to ensure that they would operate without any hiccups when the clock rolled past midnight on December 31, 1999. Individuals may not have enjoyed spending the extra time, but top management realized it was essential for business survival.
- Compromise: This method works best when the sponsors are willing and able to vary scope or cost based on recommendations from the targets. The goal is to find a solution that works for the majority. For example, sponsors want to bring in a project management methodology by a given date, but give the targets leeway to determine which product to purchase.
- Collaboration: The most democratic of methods, this rarely works well in its purest form for changing organizations because it is rare for everyone to agree on everything. A modified approach is for management to set boundaries, including time limits, for coming up with the best solution. When no solution is reached or stalemates occur, the issues are escalated to management to make the decisions.

CULTURAL RESISTANCE

Without OCM, when change confronts culture, culture always wins! In order to get the culture of a firm to embrace and institutionalize a significant change, several factors come into play that, depending on how they are handled, will affect the success or failure of the change effort. Generally speaking, every individual impacted by the proposed change is a member of the "target" population. That includes the sponsors, champions, change agents, and resistors. In most cases, the total number of targets represents a bell-shaped curve; a small fraction (5 to 15 percent) represents the champions who are for the change, another fraction of roughly equal size represents the resistors who are against the change, and the rest make up the targets who have not yet decided which side they will choose.

If possible, it will be advantageous to identify the resistors along with the champions. You will want to work with the champions and change agents to help sway the undecided targets to favor of the change. The last thing you want to do is intentionally agitate the resistors, because that increases the likelihood that they will recruit the undecided targets to join their ranks instead. The stronger the resistance, the more sponsorship intervention will be required to make the change happen. How do you deal with resistors?

- Leverage the sponsors and change agents to get everyone on board by target grouping. This should be done while understanding and appreciating the targets' frame of reference and highlighting what's in it for them. Target grouping might be done, for example, by department, job level, business vs. technology sides of the house, and so forth.
- Invite key resistors to join the project team, so that they are brought closer to the initiative and have a say in the final result. This often helps convert resistors to champions or change agents, or if not that, at least a nonresisting target.
- Bypass the resistors (with sponsor permission).

THE "VALLEY OF DESPAIR"

Every significant change that affects the culture of an organization goes through a life-cycle curve that looks more or less like Figure 29-1. This is normal and to be expected. The key to managing resistance is to keep the "Valley of Despair" dip—where skepticism, blame, denial, disbelief, and hopelessness thrive—as short and as shallow as possible. If it lasts too long or gets too deep, the change usually fails. To avoid this, the change initiative should be planned like a formal project. The project plan should include specific OCM tasks by phase to address the inevitable resistance that will surface throughout the life of the change—including beyond the point where the project ends, all the way through to the end of the useful life of the change. The end milestones of each phase of the curve should also be tracked in the plan. Once you get past the resistance stage, you are more than halfway there, and have a realistic chance of implementing the change.

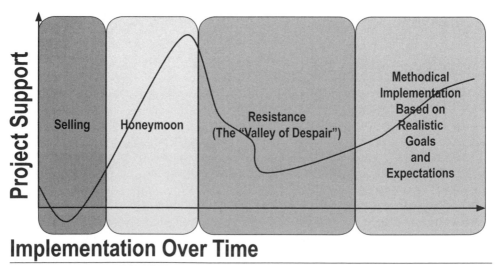

FIGURE 29-1. **THE IMPLEMENTATION SUPPORT CURVE**

THE TIPPING POINT

This is often referred to as the "burning platform"—the point at which the pain induced by the current state is perceived to exceed the level of pain that changing to the future state would invoke. The "burning platform" analogy is based on a real-life example documented by organizational change guru Daryl Connor about an oil rig in the North Sea off the coast of Scotland that exploded and caught fire one night in 1988. One of the supervisors jumped out of bed, ran to the edge of the platform, made the decision to jump, and became one of only a handful of workers who survived. He made the decision to jump because he perceived that he'd die for sure if he didn't. He jumped, believing the future state of potential hypothermia or burns from burning surface oil was less painful than remaining on the platform.

In the less death-defying world of organizational improvement, of course, the perceived intensity of pain will vary from person to person, by department, and even within the management ranks. For example, the desire to replace a desktop project management tool in favor of one with a central database might be popular with the project management practitioners, but top management might be reluctant to spend the money unless they also see value in it. The universal law is this: if the pain of the status quo is accepted by all constituents of the culture to be greater than the perceived pain of change, the change is much more easily accepted without significant sponsor intervention.

MATURITY

Determining maturity's impact on a change initiative is more art than science. Even after the scientific assessment work is done, it still takes experience and expertise to judge how much a lack of maturity will slow the change process, and thus just how much change you can introduce and how quickly it is likely to be absorbed.

CASE EXAMPLES

Here are real-life examples of how maturity impacted the speed of implementation—or in some cases stopped the project before it even got off the ground:

Major Hardware Retailer

A major hardware retailer wanted to implement earned value (EV), which it believed would help it get a better grip on its projects in terms of time and cost overruns, and give it the ability to make course corrections sooner and faster. While EV can certainly do that, I was initially concerned with whether or not the company had the foundational components in place. Earned value is a more advanced concept for most companies, especially in the private sector. I soon learned that the company's basic project scheduling practices—including a work breakdown structure (WBS), resource and cost-loaded tasks, baselining, consistent application of actuals, rescheduling, and formal scope change control—were very immature, which meant the company had no concept of schedule or cost variance, never mind more sophisticated EV measures such as schedule or cost performance indices (SPI/CPI). While the company had solid sponsorship and a "burning platform" for change, its current project management maturity level was too low for us in good conscience to recommend moving forward with an EV implementation. I suggested to the company that it would gain significant improvements from putting some of the foundational components in place, such as a project management methodology and some key metrics, run with that for a few months, and then see how the company was doing. It might still want EV, but I strongly urged the company to consider it as a release 2 or release 3 component.

"A Fool with a Tool"

In another example, many firms make the plunge into enterprise project portfolio management (PPM) tools without considering their PM maturity level or the organizational change impact such tools usually have. Tools are rolled out, only to find that:

- The majority of the project managers didn't understand project scheduling fundamentals (and had to be hastily trained after the fact).
- The organization had never done timekeeping before, but was expected to use it for capturing actuals on projects (timekeeping is also a potential cultural resistance issue, especially in high-tech outfits that hire primarily younger engineering types, who don't like "big brother watching them").
- There was no governance in place to be able to effectively take advantage of the tool's portfolio management capabilities (no project scorecard, no project list, no steering committee, no portfolio management process, etc.).

In almost every case, the sponsors who made the decision to buy the tool did so believing that their project management problems could largely be solved by a technical solution—a "silver bullet"—only to realize afterward that things got worse instead of better, so they would blame the tool, replace it with another vendor's tool, and repeat the same mistakes all over again.

Small Federal Government Agency

In contrast to the above example, a PPM tool implementation for a small federal government agency employed several tactics to help make the implementation a success, including a project management maturity assessment, an assessment of the history of the two prior failed implementations, a sponsorship assessment, an OCM chart, a communications plan with a marketing plan built in, and a training plan that included educating everyone affected by the tool at every level. At first the agency did not see the value in these activities ("This isn't project planning . . . we don't want to pay you for this!"), but it became apparent to the staff as the project moved forward the value that OCM added.

The project management maturity assessment showed that we needed to deploy the tool's functionality in four releases: (1) basic scheduling and timekeeping, (2) advanced scheduling and reporting, (3) portfolio management, and (4) EV— which was what prompted the agency to buy the tool in the first place.

CAPACITY

Like maturity, capacity does not always come up as a significant factor in OCM discussions, but it is equally as important. Capacity actually has to be considered from two perspectives: individual and organizational capacity. Neither is typically ready for change.

At the individual level, most people reach a level of proficiency that, over time, becomes a comfort zone. Preferences become habits that are hard to break. Likewise, organizations are generally not built for change. Once written and unwritten rules are established and procedures, tools, equipment, and trained personnel are in place, the organization's preference is to go into production mode and stay there. This is because changes that impact people, process, and technology simultaneously are usually disruptive and significantly reduce productivity. Publicly traded stock exchange companies, which have to report profits every quarter, are especially sensitive to this.

Individual Capacity

Measuring an individual's capacity involves assessing his/her stress level, work load, and skills. Of these three measures, stress level is the most critical. If the stress level is relatively low, the individual will be more willing to take on additional work or disruptive changes and learn new skills. When stress levels are high, getting people to commit to change becomes an arduous task. Stress levels can be gauged both by formal assessment and informal observance.

A formal assessment—the science—can be in the form of an online questionnaire, where individuals rate themselves on stress, workload and skills. You can tally the results of all staff who will be affected by an upcoming change, and quickly get an idea of how much resistance you are likely to encounter. Informal observance—the art—takes some patience and practice. I can always tell when *not* to ask my wife to do something extra for me because she wears her stress load on her face. Even if she's not really overworked, if she's had a high-stress day (usually the combination of her high-stress job plus dealing with family issues), I'll do it myself or save it for another time. Every person handles stress differently, so you have to learn how to recognize the cues. Individual or small group interviews are often a good way to gauge stress levels. Observation can also help you determine workload levels, but be aware that there are usually differences between what is considered high workloads in the private versus public sectors, and in different industries.

Organizational Capacity

Organizational capacity should also be assessed before change is implemented. This can also be done via formal surveys or questionnaires. The key questions to consider are the following:

- Does the organization have employees who can be dedicated to the change initiative? If the answer is no and it is expected that consultants alone will usher in the change, a huge red flag should go up and a critical risk added to the risk register. Changes implemented by third parties where the company itself has no skin in the game will most likely not be adopted.

- Does the organization have the right people with the right skills to support the change? If not, it may mean bringing in consultants in the short term, but sooner or later the firm will need to hire or train internal staff to carry on once the consultants leave.
- Will the change work in concert or be in conflict with the current organizational structure?
- What other changes are going on at the same time? In the workplace, too much concurrent change causes multiple projects to fail, bottlenecks to surface repeatedly, frequent escalations, a culture that becomes misaligned with corporate strategy, reduction in employee morale, and eventually burnout and resignations.
- Will the change affect the infrastructure of the organization? A Harvard Business School case study about Harley Davidson motorcycles provides an excellent example.[3] Harley Davidson had strong brand loyalty for years, but when the quality dropped to the point that approximately one third of the bikes that came off of the assembly line were defective and had to be repaired, loyalty (and thus sales) dropped significantly and internal repair costs skyrocketed, to the point that it was on the verge of filing for Chapter 11. The company knew that it had to do something drastic in order to survive, so it brought in an entirely new way of manufacturing the bikes from Japan. This not only affected the people, but the entire production operation (process and technology). Harley Davidson gradually reclaimed its strong loyalty, and is now one of the top selling motorcycles in the world.

Which OCM tactic or deliverable is the most important? The tie between the sponsor assessment and the communications/marketing plan gets my vote. Without adequate sponsorship, you have no chance of success. Without the communications/marketing plan, you can't promote the change and "win hearts and minds."

DISCUSSION QUESTIONS

❶ Thinking about a change initiative you have been involved in, which of the factors (sponsorship, culture, project management of the change, maturity, capacity) contributed to its success or failure?

❷ What would you do differently next time?

REFERENCES

[1] Claire Schooley, "Avoid the 70% failure rate of change management initiatives," Forrester.com blog posted August 31, 2011, http://blogs.forrester.com/claire_schooley/11-08-31-avoid_the_70_failure_rate_of _change_management_initiatives; see also Peter Cheese, "What's so hard about corporate change?" Fortune.cnn.com blog posted May 20, 2013, http://management.fortune.cnn.com/2013/05/20/ corporations-change-failure/.

[2] A table delineating all the OCM-related project tasks per phase can be accessed at http://www.pmsolutions .com/articles/OCM_Tasks_for_Project_Plans_by_Phase.pdf.

[3] Josef Schinwald, "Case study: Harley Davidson, Enterprise," Customer.com blog posted July 28, 2005, http://www.enterprisecustomer.com/case-study-harley-davidson-2005-07.

CHAPTER 30

Managing Multiple Projects
Balancing Time, Resources, and Objectives

LOWELL DYE, PMP, PRINCE2® REGISTERED PRACTITIONER, MANAGEMENT CONCEPTS

Downsizing, organizational restructuring, changes in technology, reduced funding, and many other factors have driven many organizations to try to do more with less. Customers, senior management, and other key stakeholders want immediate responses and are typically focused on the short term, creating a constant pressure to reduce cycle times. There is also a natural tendency for achievement-oriented project managers to want to start more projects than can logically be accomplished given the time and resource constraints found in today's business environment. Thus, project managers are often required to become multi-project managers and skilled multitaskers. On the surface, this may not seem to be too much of an issue. Hasn't everyone at some time or another handled several activities simultaneously?

The terms *program management, project portfolio management, multi-project management,* and *multitasking* are becoming more commonplace as projects are continually added, modified, and removed in response to internal and external business activity and changing economic conditions. In fact, a significant aspect of the project management software industry emphasizes the creation and integration of tools, techniques, methods, and systems for prioritizing and managing myriad projects and their associated activities.

Therefore, project managers must be familiar with several aspects of managing multiple projects:

- Understanding what multiple project management entails
- Handling the cultural, political, and organizational elements that affect the management of multiple projects
- Identifying and managing the various roles and responsibilities in a multiple project environment
- Planning, staffing, and allocating resources in a multi-project environment
- Understanding the problems of multitasking

American Management Association • www.amanet.org

- Reporting and managerial decision making
- Overcoming challenges and achieving success in a multiple project environment

WHAT IS MULTIPLE PROJECT MANAGEMENT?

The terms *program management, project portfolio management,* and *multi-project management* are often used synonymously. However, they are in fact different. In the purest sense, portfolio management has two major components: a strategic element and an operational element. The strategic element involves project selection and prioritization—making sure the right projects are selected and then prioritized according to organizational strategic goals and objectives. Table 30-1 illustrates the major differences of multiple project and portfolio management.[1]

Within the operational element, managing multiple projects is more concerned with day-to-day operational management and resource allocation of the projects within the portfolio. Add to the mix programs, strategic projects, other independent projects, and small quick-hit, short-duration projects—often referred to job assignments—and then resources become even more scarce and the project manager more stressed. Strategic projects are typically highly visible corporate undertakings that often become a high priority and pull resources from other projects and programs. An example of a strategic project is the roll-out of a corporate-wide project management-training curriculum that has been directed and sponsored by the president or CEO.

The Project Management Institute defines a program as "a group of related projects managed in a coordinated way. Programs may include elements of related work outside the scope of the discrete projects in the program."[2] Programs have a major deliverable or objective to accomplish that determines which projects are undertaken in order to meet that objective—for example, building an aircraft carrier or the overhauling an information technology (IT) infrastructure within a large global corporation. Technically, a program is a subportfolio of projects focused on a single major goal that requires several separate and unique, but integrated, projects to produce the program elements. Programs generally have an overall program manager, a common objective, and defined interfaces, so some of the issues faced when manag-

	Portfolio Management	Multiple Project Management
Purpose	Project Selection and Prioritization	Project Selection and Prioritization
Focus	Strategic	Operational
Planning Focus	Long/Medium Term (Annual/Quarterly)	Long/Medium Term (Annual/Quarterly)
Responsibility	Executive/Senior Management	Project/Resource Managers

Source: James S. Pennypacker and Lowell D. Dye, Project Portfolio Management and Managing Multiple Projects: Two Sides of the Same Coin? *Proceedings of the Annual Project Management Institute Seminars & Symposium,* 2000.

TABLE 30-1. **HIGH-LEVEL COMPARISON OF PROJECT PORTFOLIO MANAGEMENT AND MULTIPLE PROJECT MANAGEMENT**

ing several independent projects, each with its own (and sometimes competing) objectives, may not arise.

Most project managers do not manage programs or strategic portfolios; they are responsible for managing multiple short-term job assignments simultaneously. These projects are not grouped or assigned based on their contribution to a specific overall objective, but are grouped for better managerial control and tactical/operational efficiency.

Regardless of the purpose of the projects or how they are grouped, all of the programs and projects in the enterprise portfolio generally compete for the same resources. In a multi-project environment, all stakeholders need to clearly understand that resources should go to higher priority projects as determined by their urgency with respect to time, cost, customer requirements, and business objectives.

Unfortunately project priorities are not always established or maintained because of political, cultural, and other organizational factors, as well as a short-term, profit-driven motivation that almost forces a special emphasis on maximizing resources at 100 percent.

ORGANIZATIONAL ELEMENTS AFFECTING THE MANAGEMENT OF MULTIPLE PROJECTS

> That sounds fine in theory, but in real life we don't have the option of refusing or even delaying projects.

> Within our company, we don't have the luxury of dedicating any resources to a single project, let alone a project manager.

These are common laments in project management. Typically, senior managers feel that most projects are not large enough, complex enough, or economically significant enough to warrant a dedicated project manager or project team. Given the fluctuating economy and short suspense time for most projects, this perspective might not be too far off. Senior managers can contribute to multi-project success by creating a culture that facilitates effective multi-project management, however.

A study conducted in 2008 by Patanakul and Milosevic[3] and published in the *International Journal of Project Management* found three organizational-level factors that influence the effectiveness of multi-project management: project assignment (including project manager competency), resource allocation, and organizational culture. Additional research in 2013 documented the influence of team culture on multi-project success.[4]

Probably the single most significant factor in multi-project success is organizational culture—project management processes, communication, values, structure, decision making, employee and managerial attitudes, commitment, and so on. The organization's culture is demonstrated in how it assigns project managers, prioritizes projects, utilizes sound project management practices, and actively supports the project managers with respect to project assignments and workload balance. Despite the reality that resource constraints are a fact of life in any business environment, many organizations fail to admit that committing limited resources to multiple projects does not speed up delivery, but rather the reverse. Without some type of prioritization process and overall control, projects compete for limited resources, generating much shifting and coordination of resources, thereby causing throughput to decrease, resulting in negative consequences to the organization including, but not limited to, the following:

- Additional costs are incurred resulting from late deliveries because resources are working on too many projects and are not available to accomplish the scheduled work.
- Additional costs are incurred resulting from assigned resources being under-utilized because of bottlenecks created by overcommitted resources.
- Additional costs, both tangible and intangible, are incurred resulting from team member burnout, reduced quality due to overcommitment, and so on.

The senior and executive management team needs to set the culture and values, and establish systems that enable the effective management of multiple projects. In many companies there is a certain amount of "gamesmanship" in the creation of project budgets, schedules, and resource requirements. Add to this the sharing of responsibilities between functional managers and project managers—both jockeying for leadership—and things get more complicated. What saves projects in this environment are dedicated and hard-working project managers and teams that are often willing to go above and beyond the call of duty to ensure that project goals and objectives are satisfied.

Multi-project managers not only should possess the skills and experience necessary that will help them manage each individual project for which they have responsibility, but also should have the ability to coordinate work and resources among all of their projects. This is also an organizational culture issue. It is bad enough to assign unqualified managers to a project simply because they are available or have good technical skills; it is a far greater risk to assign someone who is unskilled in managing multiple projects to a situation where good administrative competencies, business skills, decision-making skills, and the ability to manage project interdependencies are crucial for project success.

Regardless of the corporate culture or the number of concurrent projects, there are a number of things that can be done to make the management of multiple projects more effective. One of the best ways to achieve this is by having clearly defined roles and responsibilities.

ROLES AND RESPONSIBILITIES IN A MULTIPLE PROJECT ENVIRONMENT

All key stakeholders, especially project managers, sponsors, and functional/resource managers, must understand their individual roles and responsibilities and be fully committed to corporate, portfolio, and project objectives. If roles and responsibilities are not aligned, each stakeholder could allow personal agendas to interfere with project decisions and negatively impact project success.

The entire leadership team has the responsibility to provide skills necessary for project success and, when possible, to put team members in positions that will encourage and enhance professional and personal development. Project managers have the responsibility to coordinate resources among their projects and provide team building for team members. Functional managers have the responsibility to ensure that resources are available when the project manager needs them. Multi-project conflict can be reduced if levels of authority with respect to resource allocation, decision making, reporting requirements, corrective actions, and baseline management are clearly defined.

Senior and executive managers need to be actively involved with the balancing of resources among active and potential projects. However, management's involvement should be at an appropriate level and not entail micromanagement. Senior management's role is primarily to ensure that projects are linked to long-term business strategy. This role includes ensuring that projects are properly prioritized, project teams are adequately staffed, obstacles to success are removed, cross-project conflicts are resolved, and so on. Senior management also has the responsibility to ensure that methods and tools are available for sharing project information among all the project managers, team members, and other key stakeholders.

Effectively managing more than one project is only possible if project managers and team members can stay focused. The challenge is in how to separate their individual responsibilities for each assigned project, as well as non-project work. In a single-project situation, the project manager is often the technical or subject matter expert. In a multiple project environment, it is unlikely that the project manager will be a technical expert in all elements of all projects. However, the project manager does need to understand the technical elements of the project and be able to manage the technical team.

Project team members, whether full-time staff members, part-time employees, or subcontractors, should be assigned because of their technical knowledge and expertise. The more specific the skills and knowledge required and the more projects involved, the more important and difficult the resource allocation process. Because the number of team members is generally limited, there is a tendency to overcommit these resources for the sake of keeping them fully engaged. Remember that team members may have assigned responsibilities that are outside their areas of expertise, creating additional pressure and stress.

Planning, Staffing, and Allocating Resources in a Multi-Project Environment

While similar to those practiced in single-project management, basic planning and control methods and techniques may not be sufficient. Managing multiple projects is a challenge because organizational practices often ignore or underestimate the significance of establishing and adhering to project priorities, defining project standards and acceptance criteria, and integrating project data. The problem increases with the complexity of inter-project links, overlapping schedule and resource requirements, and the fact that project resources cannot be concentrated on multiple projects to the extent that they can be dedicated to a single major project or program. There is also a shared misconception among executives and project managers that if someone is skilled at managing one or two projects, they can handle many projects.

Multi-project managers must have good time management and prioritization skills, and have a dashboard reporting tool in place to effectively capture and report the status of all the projects within their project portfolio. Some of the biggest challenges project managers face in a multi-project environment include the following:

- *Appropriate delegation:* Effective delegation allows the project manager time to manage the projects for which he or she has responsibility. In a multi-project environment it is even more critical that the project manager be able to step back and see the big picture. The manager needs to focus on establishing and enforcing management practices, developing resourcing strategies, and prioritizing the projects. The project manager cannot get bogged down with low-level, low-priority tasks that can be delegated to another team member. In a concurrent project situation where the project manager is the project resource, time management and self-management become even more important.

Delegating up (another way of saying no) requires tactful communication. For example, a senior manager calls a project manager into her office. She tells him that he has been assigned to manage an additional project and will be interfacing with another division. The project manager might approach it this way: "I understand. Have you already talked with the other division and made them aware that I will be contacting them?" If the manager acknowledges the need to talk to the other division's manager and takes that as an action item, the project manager has gently delegated a difficult conversation upward.

- *Effective planning and integration:* Establishing realistic project baselines and keeping individual project plans current is even more important when managing multiple projects. The more integrated the project plans, the easier it will be to manage the projects. Even if the manager is managing a portfolio of unrelated projects, a centralized approach to planning and document management is beneficial. Having an integrated master schedule of projects, including the overall life cycle, major deliverables, and resource requirements, helps the project manager maintain the necessary high-level view.

Having a common set of project management forms, templates, tools, and approved guidelines that can be reused and that are shared and communicated throughout the organization will help with the planning and integration of project resources. Shared templates help to expedite the planning process, relieve some of the administrative burdens on the project manager allowing more time for actual project management, and provide confidence on the part of management that the project management process is being consistently applied across all projects and programs.

To optimize time and resources in a multiple project environment, the use of good project management software is beneficial. During the past several years, companies have turned to a myriad of resource planning and optimization techniques with varying degrees of success. Some of the most common include resource planning, scheduling, and optimization techniques such as queuing theory, capacity requirements planning, theory of constraints, resource leveling techniques, and critical chain project management. In many situations, software may be required to properly develop a resource-loaded schedule and clearly identify time and resource conflicts. The number of projects and the size of each may determine the level of software sophistication and functionality required. If projects tend to be small, relatively simple, stand-alone projects, then something as simple as a spreadsheet or Gantt chart may be all that is necessary. For programs, large complex projects with many external dependencies, or a large number of small independent projects using a shared resource pool, then an enterprise system that integrates all projects into a master file may be necessary. A word of caution: software should never be considered a replacement for good project planning and decision making.

One of the best ways to manage resource allocation among multiple projects is to improve the quality of project effort and duration estimates. Realistic and supportable estimates can make or break project planning. Estimates, based on a well-defined work breakdown structure, provide the foundation for good time, cost, and resource planning. The importance of good estimation in a multiple project environment lies in determining resource task assignments and the creation of each project's critical path. If management clearly understands the requirements of each project and the amount of flexibility available to them, then logical decisions can be made relative to the priorities, value, and contributions of all the projects.

Some of these decisions may be difficult and may go against established norms. For example, if projects are undertaken based on their contribution to the organization's strategic goals and objectives and their benefit to the overall project portfolio, then the highest priority projects should be fully staffed first. The second priority project is fully staffed next, and so on. If sufficient resource capacity is not available, then lower priority projects should not be started. When a project is finished and capacity is again available, the next priority project can be staffed and started.

Projects started because of an external customer request or other profit potential typically get the most attention with respect to resource utilization. But many projects that compete for limited resources are not as obvious, nor do they get the attention they deserve, such as upgrades and enhancements, process improvement and cost-reduction projects, internal research and development, infrastructure systems deployment projects, facilities start-up projects, and many more. Sometimes these "non-profit" projects are started in response to a real customer or market need, but often they are initiated by management. Without defined and integrated portfolio and project management methodologies, resource requirements estimates and the subsequent resource allocation may be determined somewhat arbitrarily.

Here are four strategies for balancing the time and cost constraints of multiple projects:

1. *Increase capacity relative to demand.* Increase project team members and support staff; add new planning and management tools or enhancing existing tools; reduce non–value-added work, such as collateral assignments and meetings that take away from direct project work; provide training to team members, functional managers, and other stakeholders; and cross-train project team members in projects skills outside their area of expertise.

2. *Reduce demand relative to capacity.* Reduce the number of projects during peak demand periods, limit features, and reduce requirements if possible. Demand management is a key principle in project selection and prioritization as part of an overall portfolio management process.

3. *Implement appropriate management and control systems.* As defined in the broadest sense, systems may include a variety of tools, methods, and processes that enable management to establish realistic project/program management plans and enable project and functional manager to react quickly to changes in resource demand or project delivery times.

4. *Learn to say no.* The ability and willingness to say no is dependent on the organization and the skills of the project manager. In many organizations, saying no is not part of the culture. And unfortunately most people are not

taught how to say no tactfully, nor are they encouraged to be honest enough to address the subject of project overload. In their book, *The One Minute Manager Meets the Monkey*, Blanchard and colleagues[5] ask the basic question, "Why is it that some managers run out of time, while their staff is running out of work?" The primary answer is that too many managers are taking on too many of their employees' issues. Team members and stakeholders continually bring issues to the project manager and often the project manager is all too willing to take responsibility for addressing them. (See the earlier discussion on delegation.)

All too often, organizations and their employees, including project managers, operate under the misconception that a project manager can be given five or more projects, with each project receiving an allocation of 20 to 30 percent or less of the project manager's time. For project team members, the allocation is even worse. Assigning team members to spend 5 to 10 percent of their time on each of their many projects provides very little actual time for real work. Team members generally have non–project-related responsibilities as well, such as internal committees, company-sponsored community activities, professional development and training, and so on. The additional commitments may be important to the company, but they take energy away from assigned projects.

A well-defined and established project selection and prioritization process and a good mechanism for communicating those priorities assists in saying no to work that does not meet organizational criteria for selection.

WHAT'S WRONG WITH MULTITASKING?

Multitasking—shifting back and forth between projects or activities with the appearance of handling both simultaneously—is viewed by many project managers as a way of being more productive, facilitated by the ability to be electronically connected, and therefore busy, at all times, not just during normal working hours. Yet, if multitasking is such a timesaver, then why are so many projects late despite everyone working all the time?

For many project managers, multitasking is seen as just part of the job. However, most people are not good at multitasking, and their resulting output is generally of a lesser quality. Consider, for example, driving while talking on a cell phone—two activities that engage the same side of the brain. A 2006 study published in the *Human Factors Journal* showed that drivers talking on cell phones were involved in more rear-end collisions and accelerated slower than intoxicated drivers who has a blood alcohol content 0.08 percent above the legal limit.[6] Similarly, a study on multitasking published in 2001 in the *Journal of Experimental Psychology*, discovered that when switching from one task to another, there are "time costs" in terms of productivity, efficiency, and concentration, and that these costs increase with task complexity.[7] Logic, experience, and common sense tell us that the more projects that have to be juggled, the less efficient people are at performing any single task; and the longer it takes to return to the interrupted task, the harder it is to reengage in the previous activity. However, many project managers, even very dedicated and ethical ones, suffer from the effects of multitasking, primarily switch-tasking and continual partial attention.

Switch-tasking is shifting attention from one task to another without the first one being complete. For example, a project manager is working on a key project deliverable. A stakeholder calls, asking for information on a different project. The project manager must stop what he or she is working on, address the question, then get back to the original task. The problem is that the manager had to stop, orient to the new task, perform the new task, and reorient to the original task. All of this consumes time and energy. All too often, the manager is not able to return to the original task.

Continual partial attention means doing two or more things at once, but not being able to focus fully on any one. It is often done out of fear of missing something. For example, talking on the phone, working on the computer, and reviewing a project document feels like progress, but it only allows the project manager to skim over the tasks, picking up bits and pieces.

The following negative results of multitasking become obvious usually when it is too late to correct the problem: late projects, longer project durations, lower productivity and output, frustration, anger, chaos, and reduced communication and social interaction.

Today's business environment encourages and rewards those who *appear* to be able to juggle multiple assignments, whether they actually can or not. If someone multitasks, it is viewed as a clear sign that they are motivated and working hard. But multitasking is also an indicator of poor planning or prioritization, both for the project manager and the organization. Project managers need to realistically assess the workload and their own capabilities.

Time management can be viewed from two perspectives: urgency and importance.[8] One way to overcome the issue of multitasking is to gauge tasks from these two perspectives. Everything people experience falls into one of four categories:

- *Urgent and important:* activities such as a high-priority phone call from a critical stakeholder such as a senior manager or sponsor or a crisis that occurs and will affect an imminent deliverable.
- *Urgent, but not important:* Many interruptions, distractions, emails, and phone calls fall into this category. They say, "Deal with me now!", but will not do anything to help with project accomplishment; in fact, these items prevent goal accomplishment and are a major cause of switch-tasking and continual partial attention.
- *Not urgent, but important:* activities such as personal time, planning, project deliverables, and updating project documentation. Time needs to be provided in the project schedule and put in the project management plan. If not planned for, these items could move into the urgent-and-important category after suffering from procrastination.
- *Not urgent and not important:* These activities are simply trivial distractions and time wasters. They should be avoided to the greatest extent possible, often by ignoring them or politely saying no.

PROJECT REPORTING AND DECISION MAKING IN A MULTIPLE PROJECT ENVIRONMENT

Managers, especially when handling multiple projects, have to make difficult decisions with respect to project priorities, resources, conflicts, and so on. To make effective project decisions, project and functional managers need to have a good understanding of individual project resource commitments, how resources are shared among all the projects in the active project portfolio, and where adjustments can be made. This assumes that responsible managers have the authority and experience to shift/reallocate resources from one project to another and, if necessary, adjust activity delivery dates.

To make logical decisions, managers must be able to quickly analyze the impact of changing, adding, or removing a project, and they must be able to respond appropriately. Such analysis requires that project data be accessible, reliable, and timely. There are many reporting tools and techniques of differing levels of sophistication, such as dashboards, scorecards, and variance reports, which provide stakeholders with project status information. The information provided by these tools should be used to make timely decisions, resolve conflict, and respond proactively—not reactively—to the changing conditions.

In a multi-project environment, the value of good communication and stakeholder management plans cannot be overemphasized. A success factor in multi-project management, as in single-project management, is timely reporting and communication with applicable stakeholders. The key is to make sure the right stakeholders have the right information in a timely manner in order to make better decisions. As tough as this is in a single environment, it is compounded by the fact that in a multi-project environment there are typically a complete set of stakeholders for each project, all with different, and sometimes opposing, interests and objectives. For reporting to be effective and beneficial, project plans need to be current and up to date. A project plan that is not used or updated or is incomplete will be useless as a management and communication tool, resulting in wasting precious time trying to provide status information or justifying why more time, resources, or funding might be required.

If project managers are managing more than one project with shared resources, they need to make sure that they have current information for each individual project. Functional managers need insight into how resources are being utilized across all projects and programs, and the resource requirements projections enable them to manage their staffing plans and ensure that project managers have the resources when they are needed. Senior managers and executives require much higher level information that is more strategic, such as portfolio-level data showing how projects and programs in the aggregate are contributing to corporate goals and objectives.

In a multiple project environment, it is impossible to please all of the stakeholders all of the time, but it is possible and crucial to be honest and upfront regarding capabilities, capacity, and progress. For example, when a customer complains about late deliveries, the first reaction is to push project teams to work harder and faster—to be more productive. The problem is that they are already working on a dozen other projects. In reality, what customers and all stakeholders actually want is a realistic plan and logical delivery dates that can be met. Most stakeholders understand that unexpected events occur and are generally willing to be flexible. Stakeholders of related projects or programs often have activities of their own that must be coordinated with expected activity delivery or project completion dates in order to meet their objectives. If an integrated approach is taken to project planning and control, then managing customer and stakeholder expectations will be much easier.

Regardless of the stakeholder, it is important that the recipient have confidence in the reported data. Earned value management and variance analysis reporting for programs and major projects have been used to report progress against approved baselines since the 1960s. More recently, organizations have also added Project Dashboard reporting to their toolkit. Dashboards are simply reporting tools that present a consolidated view of the active projects or programs in a portfolio. Dashboard reports typically provide project status, baseline and revision status, project budget, and schedule information. Dashboards typically use a color-coding structure to graphically report status: green (on budget, on schedule, with no significant issues); yellow (potential budget or schedule variances, with issues that need to be addressed); and red (severe budget or schedule problems, with significant issues that could impact project success). Management may require that all projects be reported regardless of status, or reporting may be done on an exception basis—only yellow or red projects will be reported. Dashboards or some other type of consolidated reports may be managed by a program manager or a centralized project management/control office, or the responsibility may be shared by the project managers. In either case, data reporting must be consistent. As project management and enterprise software become more sophisticated with respect to features and functions, dashboard generation and data accuracy is becoming much easier.

ACHIEVING SUCCESS IN A MULTIPLE PROJECT ENVIRONMENT

There is no single right answer for how to manage multiple projects, for the best software to use, for the right organizational structure, or for how to properly engage senior managers. What is important is for management to establish a culture that encourages open and honest communication, proactive decision making, accurate documentation, and timely reporting of all project and resource information. The establishment and use of good performance metrics and measurement criteria can lead to effective management of multiple projects and can position the organization to be competitive in a dynamic environment.

DISCUSSION QUESTIONS

❶ What are the major differences and similarities among project portfolio management, program management, and managing multiple projects?

❷ What are some of the things a management team can do to balance resources, time, and cost constraints in a multiple project environment? What issues and concerns should a project manager consider when trying to balance these constraints?

❸ Reporting project performance can be difficult in a multiple project environment. What makes performance reporting so challenging, and how can the project environment support or hinder the reporting process?

REFERENCES

[1] James S. Pennypacker and Lowell D. Dye, "Project Portfolio Management and Managing Multiple Projects: Two Sides of the Same Coin?" in James S. Pennypacker and Lowell D. Dye (editors), *Managing Multiple Projects: Scheduling and Resource Allocation for Competitive Advantage* (New York, Marcel Dekker, 2001).

[2] Project Management Institute, *A Guide to the Project Management Body of Knowledge,* 5th edition (Newtown Square, PA: Project Management Institute, 2013).

[3] Peerasit Patanakul and Dragan Milosevic, "The effectiveness in managing a group of multiple projects: factors of influence and measurement criteria," in *International Journal of Project Management,* International Project Management Association, 2008, http://archive.stevens.edu/ses/documents/fileadmin/documents/pdf/MPMEffectivenessbyPeerasitPatanakulArticleinPress.pdf.

[4] Zvi Aronson and Peerasit Patanakul, "Managing a Group of Multiple Projects: Examining the Influence of Team Culture and Leader Competence," Howe School of Technology Management Research Paper Series, Number 2013-6, Stevens Institute of Technology, http/ssm/com/abstract =2205938, 2013.

[5] Kenneth Blanchard, William Oncken, and Hal Burrows, *The One Minute Manager Meets the Monkey* (New York: Quill, 1989).

[6] David Strayer, Frank A. Drews, and Dennis J. Crouch. "A comparison of the cell phone driver and the drunk driver," *Human Factors Journal* 48, No. 2 (2006), pp. 381–391, http://www.distraction.gov/download/research-pdf/Comparison-of-CellPhone-Driver-Drunk-Driver.pdf.

[7] J.S. Rubenstein, D.E. Meyer, and J.E. Evans, "Executive control of cognitive processes in task switching," *Journal of Experimental Psychology: Human Perception and Performance,* 27 (2001).

[8] Stephen R. Covey, *The 7 Habits of Effective People: Powerful Lessons in Personal Change* (New York: Franklin Covey, 1989), p. 145.

FURTHER READING

Ginger Levin, *Interpersonal Skills for Portfolio, Program, and Project Managers* (Vienna, VA: Management Concepts, 2005).

Irene Tobias and Michael Tobias, *Managing Multiple Projects* (Vienna, VA: Management Concepts, 2005).

CHAPTER 31

Program Management

**GINGER LEVIN, PHD, PMP, PGMP,
CERTIFIED *OPM3* CONSULTANT**

Increasingly, organizational leaders are using program management as a way to obtain greater benefits and opportunities and enhanced capabilities, rather than as a way to manage individual projects in a stand-alone way. Recognizing this trend, the Project Management Institute (PMI) issued a Program Management Standard in 2006, and followed it with the establishment of a Program Management Professional (PgMP®) credential in 2007. This standard is in its third edition as of 2013.

Similarly, the Office of Government Commerce (OGC) in the United Kingdom proposed a definition of a program in 2007, and described four types of programs: vision-led, emergent, compliance, and technical-led.[1] While there are slight differences in the definitions of a program and program management by both OGC and PMI, programs are strategic assets to organizations. With their typical characteristics of being long-term and complex with interdependent projects and subprograms and entailing other work, they require a different way of working and different types of competencies, rather than managing a single project for effectiveness, in realizing their intended benefits; in transitioning them to an operational unit, customer, or end user; and in sustaining them.

This chapter presents an overview of why programs are complex undertakings, describes the major themes of program management, and then discusses performance and personal competencies for program managers.

PROGRAMS ARE COMPLEX

Programs can vary from small internal initiatives to the development of large-scale products such as aircrafts or submarines or to the development and implementation of portfolio management with full support in organizations. Complexity has been researched for years and continues to be a topic of interest; thus, there are numerous definitions of it. Geraldi[2] for example, states that "mastering complexity is not a new

329

challenge but an old challenge that is being increasingly recognized and accepted." Programs and their associated projects are complex, as they represent something that is unique and uncertain. PMI explains that, while both projects and programs are uncertain, based primarily on their environment, programs have far greater uncertainty than projects.[3] Partly the increasing uncertainty and complexity of programs is due to their length and the progressive elaboration of their scope and content, with the need to consider their continual alignment with the organization's objectives. As a result, while the individual projects in a program may meet their deliverables on time, within budget, and on schedule, in the context of the program they may not contribute to the program's outcomes as initially planned, since the program's approach may be modified several times throughout its life cycle, in the face of its uncertain environment, to achieve its goals and deliver its planned benefits.

Building on the literature on complexity in the project world, program complexity further increases with politics, changing technology over the program's duration, the involvement often of several organizations working together as part of a consortium that may be competitors in other situations, the low level of maturity in program management practices, and the need to make decisions quickly, often without access to required information or experts for guidance in the process.

Complexity in programs also may arise from factors such as the interdependencies between the projects and operational work in them in that one project, if it encounters difficulties and unforeseen risks, may then jeopardize work on other projects given the interdependencies between them. The complexity of products as results of programs also is a concern given the competition and the changing requirements, as well as the desire to be the first to market, along with numerous regulations to consider. These dynamics lead to several themes that permeate program management.

PROGRAM MANAGEMENT THEMES

PMI's 2013 study, *The Pulse of the Profession,* notes that high performers in the program management field are ones with high maturity (28 percent), while low performers (3 percent) have low levels of mature processes in place.[4] A 28 percent high performance rate is unacceptable in today's environment and needs improvement. Each program requires the following for success:

First, a *common definition of success* is needed that is embraced as the organization's vision for the future or designed end state and is one that people at all levels understand and can be committed to realizing. People need to see how their work relates to this vision, requiring a formalized portfolio management system in which programs, projects, and operational work are first defined by an approved business case that sets forth its goals and shows how these goals relate to the organization's strategic goals and vision. Focusing on programs, once the business case formally is approved, and the program is then part of the organization's portfolio, its priority in the portfolio should be known by those key stakeholders responsible for success. The approved business case then leads to a program mandate to authorize resources to start the program.

However, a *focus on a governance structure* is a key theme, as it is used to oversee programs to ensure that they continue to support the organization's strategic goals and to make changes if they do not. Each program requires some type of governance board or steering committee for oversight, which should be composed of a proactive group of senior-level members who conduct periodic reviews at key stage gates of the program's life cycle, conduct performance reviews as more in-depth sessions between stage gates, approve the initiation of projects with defined business cases to be part of the program, approve the transition of these projects and other work once their deliverables are complete, and approve the overall closure of the program. As well, the governance board serves as a forum to help resolve issues and risks escalated by the program manager by discussing alternative solutions and making decisions and determining whether these issues and risks affect other programs and projects under way in the organization. The governance board's oversight ensures that programs continue to be aligned with the organization's goals and that the program *delivers its stated benefits,* which is the second key theme.

Since programs are established to attain more benefits than if the projects and other work within them were managed separately, a focus on benefits permeates programs. PMI sets forth a benefits life cycle with five phases: identification, planning, delivery, transition, and sustainment. While initial benefits are defined in the business case, they are developed further through this life cycle, especially with a benefits realization plan and continual monitoring and control to ensure that the proposed benefits can be realized as planned. The emphasis is on continually identifying opportunities to optimize program benefits, with a focus on environmental factors and the interdependencies between the program's projects. Regular reporting to the governance board on progress in benefit achievement is a best practice, along with *engagement of stakeholders,* which is the third key theme.

Stakeholders exist on projects, operational work, and on programs. The number of interested stakeholders increases exponentially on programs, meaning that the program manager and his or her team must focus on continual identification of the people or groups with an interest in, influence over, and desired involvement in the program, recognizing that everything may change based on the stage of the program. These stakeholders then need to be analyzed and classified into groups to determine not only the program's positive proponents and negative opponents but also when to engage these stakeholders at key times in the program to promote success. The program manager, in working to engage stakeholders, must prioritize his or her time in continuing to ensure the active proponents remain positive, while striving to see if by active listening and responding to the concerns of negative stakeholders, they can become positive proponents or at least neutral toward the program. One negative stakeholder has the ability to decrease overall program support and ensure that it does not meet its strategic goals, meaning the program manager's ability to work with stakeholders at all levels with different points of view is a required competence. This ability further leads to the need for the program manager to interact with and involve those stakeholders who are the ultimate recipients of the program's benefits early enough to determine their requirements when it is time to transition benefits so that they can be sustained.

Governance, benefits, and stakeholder engagement are ongoing throughout program management with a concentration on strategic alignment of the program's goals with those of the organization's to best promote not only benefit realization but also benefit transition and sustainment. Being a program manager is a rewarding profession but it has numerous challenges.

PROGRAM MANAGER COMPETENCIES

Program managers, therefore, require certain key competencies to enable them to succeed in their complex programs. PMI defines a competency as "a cluster of knowledge, attitudes, skills, and other personal characteristics that affect a major part of one's job (i.e., one or more key roles and responsibilities), correlates with performance on the job, can be measured against well-accepted standards, and can be improved by means of training and development."[5]

Building on the 2007 PMI competency model for project managers and following a similar structure, Levin and Ward[6] developed a model for program managers consisting of six performance competencies and eight personal competencies.

The performance competencies focus on the program manager's ability to apply program management knowledge to deliver the program's planned benefits. The six competencies are the following:

- *Defining the program:* determining program goals, objectives, vision, mission, and benefits; creating the business case and a high-level program roadmap; identifying stakeholders; and showing the link to the organization's strategic objectives
- *Initiating the program:* preparing the program's charter, refining the roadmap, preparing the program's financial framework, and setting up a governance structure
- *Planning the program:* preparing the program management plan, the benefits realization plan, stakeholder engagement plan, and other subsidiary plans; preparing the scope statement and the program's work breakdown structure; developing the program's master schedule and budget; establishing baselines; and setting up a program management office and a program management information system
- *Executing the program:* holding a kickoff meeting, preparing business cases for approval by the governance board for projects and other work to be part of the program, prioritizing resources, awarding contracts, focusing on quality assurance, deploying best practices across the program, implementing approved changes, and providing information to stakeholders
- *Monitoring and controlling the program:* analyzing variances, making decisions to correct deficiencies or to focus on ways to optimize benefits, managing changes, focusing on resource interdependency management and issuing change requests
- *Closing the program:* transitioning benefits, closing each project or operational work, preparing a final program report, conducting final review meetings with stakeholders and suppliers, closing all contracts, releasing resources, and obtaining governance approval to officially close the program

The eight personal competencies are as follows:

- *Communications:* also considered by PMI to be the key competency because of the large and diverse number of program stakeholders, it further includes active listening
- *Leadership:* PMI notes it is embedded in the program manager's job, and also it includes ensuring the programs vision is understood at all levels in the

program since it involves setting forth the vision and establishing the program's direction

- *Building relationships:* with different stakeholders and their different views concerning the program, the program manager works actively to note and respect the specific interests of each stakeholder or stakeholder group and work effectively to build and maintain their support for the program, engaging them throughout the life cycle
- *Negotiating:* because of the large number of stakeholders, negotiating is required to acquire resources when needed and ensure the program remains a priority in the organization's portfolio, along with enlisting support from the governance board or comparable group
- *Thinking critically:* program managers must be able to determine the right questions to ask and solve problems as issues are identified, and relevant facts and information are gathered; through critical thinking, one must think openly, not be influenced by others, and identify relevant assumptions, constraints, and the implications and consequences of decisions
- *Facilitating:* the program manager sets an atmosphere for success for his or her team by creating an environment in which people can perform tasks with limited roadblocks, and by ensuring the team's policies, procedures, and processes are ones that are conducive to realizing the program's benefits
- *Mentoring:* since most programs are long, staff turnover is expected; the program manager and others can serve as mentors to team members so they can assume additional responsibilities and advance to positions of greater responsibility as needed
- *Embracing change:* program managers recognize that the very nature of the program itself is one that involves change, and they must promote an approach to adapt by embracing changes as they occur on the program, both internal and external, and exploiting them to realize additional benefits or the optimization of those benefits in the initial business case and benefit realization plan

Each of these competencies is expanded to show performance criteria and the types of evidence required to then determine whether the criteria are met. Program managers also must decide which criteria are the most relevant to their programs, but the criteria serve as a guide to getting started. And, while models do not make decisions, competency models are effective in pointing out one's areas of strength and others where improvements may be useful. If used periodically, one can see improvements over time, which, it is hoped, can reduce the level of stress encountered when managing complex programs.

CONCLUSION

While many organizations have embraced the management-by-project environment, programs are the next level. If programs are managed as individual projects, the concern is that interdependencies may be missed, and a single change in one project then may have many repercussions in others, not to mention the reduction in benefits that may occur, and strategic alignment may not be continued. Program management is a more effective method of management, with its emphasis on a governance structure, benefit realization, and stakeholder engagement. By using a competency model, program managers can set a baseline and reevaluate their overall program management style periodically to be even more effective in their program work.

DISCUSSION QUESTIONS

❶ Thinking of a program now in progress, or one that you have recently worked on, how were each of the themes identified in this chapter handled? Where is/was there room for improvement?

❷ Comparing your own competency to the model described above, in what areas can you identify the need for further study or practice? Make a plan to include these in your professional development.

REFERENCES

[1] Office of Government Commerce, *Managing Successful Programmes* (London, England: The Stationary Office, OGC, 2007).

[2] J. Geraldi, "Patterns of complexity: the thermometer of complexity," *Project Perspectives* 29 (2008), p. 4.

[3] Project Management Institute, *The Standard for Program Management,* 3rd edition (Newtown Square, PA: PMI, 2013).

[4] Project Management Institute, *The Pulse of the Profession* (Newtown Square, PA: PMI, 2013), http://www.pmi.org/Knowledge-Center/Pulse.aspx.

[5] Project Management Institute, *Project Manager Competency Development Framework,* 2nd edition (Newtown Square, PA: PMI, 2007), p. 74.

[6] G. Levin and J.L. Ward, *Program Complexity: A Competency Model* (Boca Raton, FL: CRC Press, 2011).

CHAPTER 32

The Project Management Office
Trends and Tips

J. KENT CRAWFORD, PMP, CEO, PM SOLUTIONS

JEANNETTE CABANIS-BREWIN, PM SOLUTIONS RESEARCH

Gartner predicted in 2001 that companies that failed to establish a project management office (PMO) would experience twice as many major project delays, overruns, and cancellations as would companies with a PMO in place.[1] Since then, we have seen the percentage of companies implementing PMOs skyrocket, with research indication that they had become valued organizational fixtures,[2] followed in 2013 by a spate of negative studies questioning their value.[3] What's *really* going on with the PMO?

A decade ago, we theorized that what was then commonly termed the "project office" would become a valued player at the strategic corporate level.[4] That strategic project office has since surpassed our wildest expectations. Our experience with finalists and winners of the PMO of the Year award has shown us that PMOs—whether evolved from the grassroots or implemented from the top down—have become indispensable centers of insight and services in companies, nonprofit organizations, and government.[5]

Center of excellence, strategic project office, enterprise program management office, enterprise project services—today's PMO goes by many names and appears within our organizations in many roles. Attempts to gauge the effectiveness of this relatively new organizational entity run up against these different conceptions of the PMO, which exhibit varying spans of control, missions, functions, and process maturity.

Recently, there are been several attempts to apply process maturity modeling and language to measure the effectiveness of PMOs. The most detailed of these has been the PMO maturity cube. A full description of the cube is available at the website cited in the reference list. Its developers began from the assumption that "the better the PMO delivers its services, and only the ones related to the needed functions, the more the PMO is perceived delivering value to its organization."[6] The cube model goes on to posit twenty-one possible types of PMO and to deliver a complex scoring system to ascertain what a PMO's scope, approach, and maturity of service delivery might be.

Working with PMO leaders, corporate leadership, and consultants in the field made us concerned that a model of such complexity might not be accessible for the average organization that needs to quickly compare itself to others in the industry, receive feedback on whether its PMO was performing the types of functions that are common to high-performing PMOs, and make plans for organizational improvement. We questioned whether, in fact, the complexity of measuring PMO value was perhaps one factor that fed into negative assessments of the PMO's contributions.

In fact, we reasoned, restating the core assumption, that "a PMO delivers optimum business value to the sponsoring organization when its role—whether strategic, tactical, or operational—is guided by corporate strategy, and when its functions are selected and refined based on data about how well these functions contribute to strategy execution/goal achievement." Such value is not—or, in our view, should not be—"perceived," but rather should be measured and objective.

Was this reasoning realistic? In an effort to provide a structure for identifying and naming PMOs that is based on the business value they offer to their sponsoring organizations, PM Solutions Research then sought the input of focus groups drawn from PMO of the Year award finalists, as well as leaders of PMOs identified as "high performers" in the *State of the PMO 2012,* to develop a prototype model for PMO classification.

THE PROJECT MANAGEMENT OFFICE UNIVERSE

The first task was to develop a system of classifying PMOs, beginning with the descriptions offered in *The Strategic PMO,* 2nd edition (Figure 32-1). This system of three types works as a high-level kind of sorting mechanism to differentiate PMOs based on their span of control in the organization. Here are the descriptions of their roles:

Type 1: The Project Control Office. This is an entity that typically handles large, complex single projects (such as a Euro conversion project, or the creation of a new type of airplane). It is specifically focused on one project, but that one project is so large and so complex that it requires multiple schedules, which may need to integrate into an overall program schedule. It may have multiple project managers who are each independently responsible for an individual project schedule. As those individual schedules, and their associated resource requirements and associated costs, are all integrated into an overall program schedule, one program manager or a master project manager is responsible for integrating all of the schedules, resource requirements, and costs to ensure that the program as a whole meets its deadlines, milestones, and deliverables.

Type 2: Business Unit PMO. At the divisional or business unit level, a PMO may still be required to provide support for individual projects, but its challenge is to integrate a large number of multiple projects of varying sizes, from small short-term initiatives that require few resources to multi-month or multi-year initiatives requiring dozens of resources, large dollar amounts, and complex integration of technologies. The value of the Type 2 PMO is that it begins to integrate resources at an organizational level, and it is at the organizational level that resource control begins to play a much higher value role in the payback of a project management system. At the

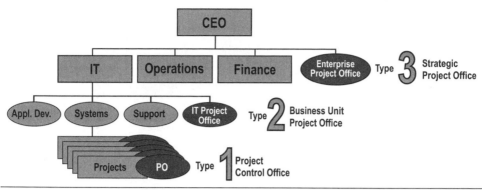

FIGURE 32-1. **THREE TYPES OF A PROJECT OFFICE**

individual project level, applying the discipline of project management creates significant value to the project because it begins to build repeatability—the project schedule and the project plan become communication tools among the team members as well as within and among the organizational leadership.

At Type 2 and higher, the PMO serves that function but also begins to provide a much higher level of efficiency in managing resources across projects. Where there are multiple projects vying for a systems designer, for example, the Type 2 PMO has project management systems established to de-conflict that competing need for a common resource and identify the relative priorities of projects. Thus, the higher priority projects receive the resources they need and lower priority projects are either delayed or canceled. A Type 2 PMO allows an organization to determine when resource shortages exist and to have enough information at their fingertips to make decisions on whether to hire or contract additional resources. Since the Type 2 PMO exists within a single department, conflicts that cannot be resolved by the PMO can easily be escalated to a department manager or organizational vice president, who has ultimate responsibility for performance within his or her organization.

Type 3: Strategic PMO. Consider an organization with multiple business units, multiple support departments at both the business unit and corporate level, and ongoing projects within each unit. A Type 2 project office would have no authority to prioritize projects from the corporate perspective, yet corporate management must select projects that will best support strategic corporate objectives. These objectives could include strategic initiatives, revenue generation opportunities, cost reduction programs, productivity enhancements, and profitability contribution, to name just a few. Only a corporate-level organization can provide the coordination and broad perspective needed to select, prioritize, and monitor projects and programs that contribute to attainment of corporate strategy—and this organization is the strategic PMO. At the corporate level, the strategic or enterprise PMO serves to de-conflict the need for competing resources by continually prioritizing the list of projects across the entire organization. Obviously, this cannot be done by the strategic PMO in isolation; thus the need for a steering committee made up of the strategic PMO director, corporate management, and representatives from each business unit and functional department.[7]

The common capabilities of these various types of PMO are shown in Table 32-1.

	Service Offering	Type 1: Project Control Office	Type 2: Business Unit PMO	Type 3: Strategic/ Enterprise PMO	Description of Services
People	Project Planning and Controls Specialists	X		X	Plans all activities for the project; manages the critical path, issues, risks, and budget. Responsible for resource management and schedule/budget status reporting.
	Project and Program Managers	X		X	Coordinates with business sponsors to manage scope of work, business issues, risks, etc. Drivers business issues and communicates to project stakeholders and team members.
	Mentoring and Coaching		X	X	Individual coaching for less experienced project managers, to reinforce training and established client methodologies.
	PM Training and Professional Development		X	X	A variety of on-site training courses including certification programs that can be customized for any organization.
	Organizational Change Management		X	X	Assessing current organization's readiness to change, including barriers to change, and developing/executing a plan to successfully implement new project management processes.
Process	PM Organizational Maturity Assessment & Improvement Planning		X	X	Uses PM Solutions' acclaimed Project Management Maturity Model (PMMM) to show how to systematically mature an organizations' project management practices.
	Project Portfolio Management		X	X	Process and software tools to select and manage the optimum set of projects that maximize business value. Provides management visibility through dashboard reporting.
	PM Methodology	X	X	X	Customized methodology—processes, procedures, templates, examples, and guides—delivered through an easy-to-use web-based tool, the PM Community of Practice (PMCOP).
	Functional Methodology		X	X	Customized methodology (SDLC, NPD, Marketing) that integrates into the overall project management methodology.
	PM Value Measurement		X	X	Tangible metrics program established to measure the benefits derived from the PMO.
Technology	PM Software	X	X	X	Proven software tools for planning, managing, and status reporting the full portfolio of project(s).

TABLE 32-1. CAPABILITIES OF VARIOUS TYPES OF PROJECT OFFICE

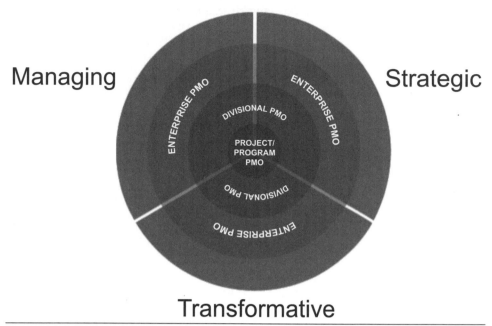

Managing

Strategic

Transformative

FIGURE 32-2. **THE PROJECT MANAGEMENT OFFICE (PMO) UNIVERSE**

Discussion with our focus group members led us to further refine these types and rename them. Figure 32-2 shows a prototype of PMO classification based on span of control plus organizational role/mission. Since several focus group members described the existence of informal or nascent (under development) PMOs in their organization, we originally added the Type 0 category—given that the goal of the model is to accurately describe the workday reality of PMOs. However, as the concept continued to evolve to focus on the *capability* of the PMO, Type 0 was dropped, recognizing that informal PMOs usually exist to initiate the development of capability but probably do not themselves display it.

PROJECT MANAGEMENT OFFICE AREA OF FOCUS: THE MISSION OR ROLE DEFINED BY THE ORGANIZATION

A primary source for information about the day-to-day world of PMOs has been our series of biennial research studies, *The State of the PMO*. Inaugurated in 2007 and repeated in 2010 and 2012, these survey-based studies are beginning to show trends in the development of the PMO as an organizational structure. For example, in 2008, a minority of PMOs functioned as enterprise-wide entities; this percentage had increased dramatically by 2012 to 41 percent.[8] In seeking to accurately depict PMOs' role in organizations, we sifted through the data compiled over 2007 to 2012, looking for key changes in the roles played by PMO. As the developers of the PMO cube also discovered, the picture is complex. Here are some findings:

- Project management offices are becoming more mature; the number moving from level 1 to level 3 in self-reported project management (PM) process maturity increased between 2007 and 2010, and the more mature PMOs represented organizations that scored higher on eight measures of organizational performance (Figure 32-3). Maturity was self-reported on a scale from level 1 to 5 (immature, established, grown up, mature, best in class). Only maturity levels 1 to 3 are shown in the figure, since too few PMOs reported at levels 4 and 5. "High performance," also self-reported, is defined as higher on a scale of 1 to 5 of how well the overall organization performs in the eight measures of performance shown in the figure, along with a measure of overall performance.

- While PMO age does correlate with maturity and capability, even new PMOs (less than one year since inception) frequently show up in the "high-performing organization" category.
- Even PMOs with a single-program focus frequently describe their role as "strategic," while information technology (IT) (divisional) PMOs frequently report managing enterprise-wide programs.[9]

Clearly, the idea of a progressive improvement in maturity tracking with increasing levels of responsibility or organizational scope was not in tune with PMO realities. In discussing this with PMO leaders in our focus group and during qualitative research interviews with respondents to the *State of the PMO 2012* study, we heard over and over again that the very idea of "levels" of PMO was flawed. Here are a few of their comments:

- "'Level' says that you start at the bottom and work your way up incrementally, starting with basic project management and adding more and more strategic roles. That isn't necessarily the case. In our company, the PMO came in as a strategic entity tasked with transforming the organization. It wasn't until several years passed that we actually hands-on managed projects."
- "Stay away from the word 'level'—it has a judgmental overtone. In fact, a 'level 1' PMO that focuses only on managing projects may be the exact PMO that is perfect for delivering the business results the company requires. There is no 'up' from there."
- "'Level' implies progression or hierarchy and that's not what that is."[10]

Taking our lead from this input, we conceptualized the "PMO universe" shown in Figure 32-2, one in which a PMO might operate:

- As a single megaproject and yet be *transformative* in nature for the organization as a whole.
- At the divisional level, and yet be involved in *strategic* initiatives.
- At the enterprise level providing project managers and project management expertise across functional boundaries, and be purely focused on *managing,* without participating in strategy formulation or other strategic or transformative roles.

These roles are described in more detail in Table 32-2. The model is circular because, in the real world, there isn't a clear, step-by-step progression in the changing PMO role and impact. An organizational structure can be implemented, for example, by experts called in to create it and jump-start it, without growing that structure from the internal grassroots. Today's organizations often grow by leaps through merger or

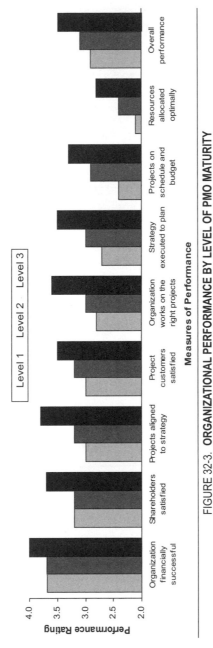

FIGURE 32-3. ORGANIZATIONAL PERFORMANCE BY LEVEL OF PMO MATURITY

Source: *The State the PMO 2010*, PM Solutions Research, 2010.

	Managing	Strategic	Transformative
Enterprise	PMO's primary focus is to manage multiple projects and/or programs across the enterprise. The PMO may manage all projects/programs or only strategic projects/programs.	PMO's primary focus is on the strategic impact of the enterprise portfolio of projects/programs enterprise. The PMO may focus on all projects/programs or only strategic projects/programs.	PMO's primary focus is on enabling projects/programs to transform the way an enterprise does business. The PMO may frocus on all projects/programs or only strategic projects/programs.
Divisional	PMO's primary focus is to manage multiple projects/programs within a division (business unit or department) of an enterprise. PMO may manage all divisional projects/programs or only strategic divisional projects/programs.	PMO's primary focus is on the strateigc impact of a portfolio of projects/programs within a division (business unit or department of an enterprise. The PMO may focus on all divisional projects/programs or only strategic divisonal projects/programs.	PMO's primary foucs is on enabling projects/programs to transform the way a division (business unit or department) of an enterprise does business. The PMO may focus on all divisional projects/programs or only strategic divisional projects/programs.
Project/ Program	PMO's primary focus is to manage a single project or program.	PMO's primary foucs is on the strategic impact of a single project or program.	PMO's primary focus is on the ability fo a single project or program to transform the way the organization does business.

TABLE 32-2. **THREE AREAS OF FOCUS FOR PMOs**

acquisition, or discontinuously, as when a new chief information officer makes radical changes to divisional structure and processes.

We called these "classes" of PMOs to make it clear that one is not better than the other, except in terms of individual organizational needs. We envisioned individual companies being able to scope a PMO that crossed all the boundaries shown, by incorporating to a greater or lesser degree the functions that might be typical of a particular class. As we discussed what made a great PMO, we heard again and again from our focus group and interviewees that the only lens through which a PMO's effectiveness should be viewed was the organization-specific lens of capability; that is, does the PMO perform those functions that add business value to their sponsoring organization?

PROJECT MANAGEMENT OFFICE CAPABILITIES

Again referring to the *State of the PMO* research, we found that high-performing organizations had PMOs that offered a wider range of functions and services (Figure 32-4). The PMOs in organizations that scored as "high performing," based

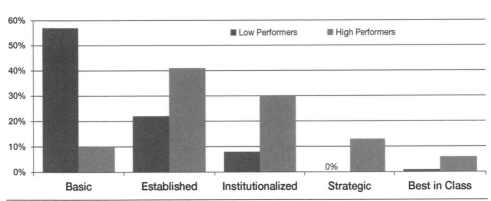

FIGURE 32-4. **PMOs IN HIGH-PERFORMING ORGANIZATIONS**

Source: *The State of the PMO 2012.*

on eight measures of organizational performance, offered more functions and services than those in low-performing organizations.

However, referring to notes from interviews and focus groups, we were struck by comments such as the following:

- "If you stretch too thin and do things poorly, then it's not true [that offering more functions adds value]. Instead the model should show that as you increase what you can do for your organization—via more functionality—more benefits accrue to your organization."
- "It's not that we are trying to roll out PPM [project portfolio management] or not roll out PPM—as a services organization, it's driven by the client and funded by the client, so PPM isn't that important to us in the classical sense. Our mission is to further integrate with the business, understand the strategic goals of the business, and develop tools and processes that serve those goals."
- "We don't see the world as 'things we need to do as a PMO' but as 'things we can do as an organization to help the company sell more products and services.'"[11]

Obviously, these PMO leaders were speaking with the voice of experience, reminding us that functional capability alone is not what matters; the PMOs should offer and refine only those functions or services that directly impact the business outcomes for their organization.

How do PMOs identify which functions and services these are? And what can they do to optimize the performance of these functions? We defined the ability to identify the correct functions, and to optimize them in concert with meeting business goals, as "capability": the ability to deliver those functions and services that are required to execute strategies, and to deliver them in ways that contribute to measurable performance improvements. To that end, we identified eight key PMO functional capabilities:

- Project management
- Program management

- Portfolio management
- Performance management
- Demand management/resource management
- Vendor management
- Change management
- Integration management

In addition, with the assistance of our focus groups, we identified four "capability enablers" that can support (or hinder) PMO capability in any of the above areas, for any type of PMO, no matter what its organizational mission:

- Governance/structure
- People/culture
- Process
- Technology

The assessment method for the degree of effectiveness of each of these continues to be under development and validation.

To recap: the PMO capability model operates as a classification system to help standardize the nomenclature of PMOs. At present, there is a wide range of organizational entities referred to as "PMOs." This model will help to clarify the terminology and assist organizations in understanding where their present or planned practices fit into the "universe" of PMOs operating in the marketplace. We felt—and our interviews confirmed—that this would be of practical assistance to PMO leaders. One interviewee remarked, "Most of us here. . .have some challenges communicating what we are trying to do. In trying to describe our PMO, we've struggled for the right language—are we hybrid? Guerilla? We need to be able to make a business case for moving the PMO out of IS [information systems]."[12] This focus on the business case has provided the lens through which we view PMOs and their many roles. The resulting model is descriptive, not prescriptive; that is, its emphasis is on defining your PMO as it stands now, and where you want it to be based on your specific business goals. It provides a "menu" of possibilities to aspire to that may be pulled from various types of PMOs.

The PMO capability model focuses on *capability* instead of maturity because, while a process improves incrementally and can be measured against a continuum, the capabilities of an organizational entity may improve via breakthroughs (hiring consultants, acquisitions, new technology). Thus the PMO model is not in levels, but by classes—with PMOs able to straddle two or more classes, depending on the business needs they serve and the services they offer.

How can this be important? An organization may attain process maturity and still not be delivering the value-adding services that the executive needs or desires. By focusing on capability we seek to keep the discussion rooted in practical business functions and outcomes. Think of it in terms of an "elevator speech": the PMO director may say to the CEO, "We achieved level 5 in PMMM (project management maturity model)!" and still get the response, "But what are you capable of doing for us today?" A transformative EPMO (enterprise project management office) leader, on the other hand, might be able to say, "We offer the following sources of business value, which we developed in response to strategic requirements."

PROJECT MANAGEMENT OFFICE IN PLACE? DON'T RELAX YET

A trend that first surfaced in 2002 at the Project Management Benchmarking Forums, and which has continued to plague PMOs despite increasing organizational clout, visibility, and proven value added, was of companies that had achieved a mature project management process under the auspices of an enterprise PMO, but which were disinvesting in project management in the name of cost-cutting exercises.

Forum participants—representatives of project management practices within some of America's top corporations—described the expressed opinions of their executive leadership as paradoxical: on the one hand they claimed to support and value project management; on the other hand they were slashing project management office budgets and cutting training for project managers. In a tight economy, management identified the entire project management exercise as an overhead expense.

Ironically, the most successful and long-standing project management offices may be the most vulnerable to cost cutting because the organization takes good project management for granted. An article in *Computing Canada* by HMS Software president Chris Vandersluis characterized the attitude as "Can't we just do all of this in Excel like we used to?" and "The projects aren't a problem; why do we spend so much money on managing them?"[13]

Once implemented, good project management becomes invisible and, paradoxically, that can be a problem. The effects of good change management, good planning, resource capacity planning, and variance management mean that projects just seem to run themselves. Management forgets that the costs associated with maintaining a project management structure are outstripped by the potential costs of having no project management structure. Vandersluis describes the PM-free environment as "projects that run late and over budget . . . a mismatch of resources to projects . . . clients [and] suppliers are unhappy . . . shareholders are unhappy . . . ," and boldly states that "losing the efficiency that comes with a corporate-wide project management environment can take a company from barely profitable to completely unprofitable in a short period of time."

PERFORMANCE MEASUREMENT: THE MISSING LINK

In reviewing the in-depth background research provided by Pinto et al,[14] one statistic stuck us as particularly meaningful. In a 2007 study, it was determined that the function of 50 percent of the PMOs studied was to "monitor and control their performance." Only 50 percent? It may seem striking that only half of PMOs put systems in place to monitor their own performance, yet this result has been borne out by the State of the PMO studies. As recently as February 2012, this number is still only 50 percent, although 54 percent report that they plan to focus on improving or implementing performance measurement within that year.[15] In terms of identifying areas for improvement in capability, or identifying where capability could be better enabled, a lack of PMO performance measurement is a serious gap. The "instability" in PMO tenure noted by Pinto et al may very well be related to the failure of PMOs to tell executive management an "elevator story" that aligns with their most pressing concerns.

Project management office directors and managers often wonder out loud why processes like accounting are accepted as costs of doing business, while the project management process constantly struggles for survival on the organizational edge. The constant effort to make visible to management costs they *didn't* incur saps energy that would be better spent on managing projects. But this vigilance is simply part of the requirements for maintaining your PMO, once established, as a visible and appreciated part of organizational life.

DISCUSSION QUESTIONS

❶ What types of PMO exist in your organization, if any? How would you classify them in terms of focus?

❷ Which of the "capability enablers" work well in your organization? Which are lacking—or even hinder PMO success?

❸ Again, for a company you are familiar with, consider ways that centralizing project management across the enterprise might streamline decision making. In particular, focus on communication and information sharing between departments and levels of management.

REFERENCES

[1] M. Light and T. Berg, *Gartner Strategic Analysis Report: The Project Office: Teams, Processes and Tools,* August 1, 2000.

[2] PM Solutions Research, *The State of the PMO 2012* (Glen Mills, PA: PM Solutions, 2012).

[3] The Hackett Group, "Most Companies with Project Management Offices See Higher IT Costs, No Performance Improvements," posted November 1, 2012, http://www.thehackettgroup.com/about/research-alerts-press-releases/2012/11012012-research-details-factors-behind-failure-pmos.jsp. Also see J. Leroy Ward, "The Life Expectancy of a PMO," posted 26 March 2012, http://www.wardwired.com/2012/03/the-life-expectancy-of-a-pmo/.

[4] J. Kent Crawford, *The Strategic Project Office* (Boca Raton, FL: Auerbach/CRC Press, 2001).

[5] PM Solutions Research, 2012 PMO of the Year Award ebook, http://www.pmsolutions.com/resources/view/pmo-of-the-year-award-2012-ebook/.

[6] A. Pinto, M. Cota, and G. Levin, *The PMO Maturity Cube, A Project Management Office Maturity Model,* Presented at the PMI Research and Education Congress 2010, Washington, DC, http://www.pmomaturitycube.org/arquivos/PMOMaturityCubeEng.pdf, p. 16.

[7] J Kent Crawford and Jeannette Cabanis-Brewin, *The Strategic Project Office,* 2nd edition (Boca Raton, FL: Auerbach/CRC Press, 2011): pp. 31–33.

[8] PM Solutions Research, *The State of the PMO 2007–2008* (Glen Mills, PA: PM Solutions, 2008); *The State of the PMO 2010* (Glen Mills, PA: PM Solutions, 2010); and PM Solutions Research, T*he State of the PMO 2012* (Glen Mills, PA: PM Solutions, 2010).

[9] PM Solutions Research, 2008, 2010, 2012.

[10] PM Solutions Research, Focus Group Proceedings, January 4, 2012. Unpublished.

[11] PM Solutions Research, Focus Group Proceedings, 2012.

[12] PM Solutions Research, Qualitative Interviews, follow-up to State of the PMO survey, March, 2012.

[13] Chris Vandersluis, "Cutting project office is detrimental to corporate health," *Computing Canada*, September 2002.

[14] Pinto et al, op cit., p. 1.

[15] PM Solutions Research, State of the PMO 2012.

Issues, Ideas, and Methods in Project Management Practice

Introduction

Project management practice is dynamic; it responds to technological, cultural, and sociological changes in the environment. In this section, authors highlight areas in project management where new trends and problems are creating new ideas and solutions.

The issues are broad and multifaceted, and the topics covered illustrate specific approaches to dealing with project management, ranging from political and cultural issues to alternative methodologies that can be applied together with project management principles.

Earned value measurement, an important method for keeping projects on track and communicating progress, is explained in detail in Chapter 33 by Lee R. Lambert.

Power and politics are always an overriding issue. Rather than simply complain about them, Randall L. Englund in Chapter 34 offers a proactive way to plan for and succeed at organizational politics.

Critical Chain and Six Sigma methodologies are proven approaches that, in certain contexts, can be applied jointly with project management. These methodologies, relatively new to the practice of project management, are described by Frank Patrick in Chapter 35 and by Rip Stauffer in Chapter 36.

Among the quality management tools and approaches that may be helpful to project managers, the Baldrige criteria, business process management, and process improvement are key; these are described by Alan Mendelssohn and Michael Howell in Chapter 37.

Interpersonal skills and teamwork go hand in hand, as Paul C. Dinsmore shows us in Chapter 38.

Dinsmore and Manuel M. Benitez Codas in Chapter 39 provide an overview of the challenges project managers face when working with the increasingly common multicultural or international project teams.

Alan Levine in Chapter 40 had perhaps the heaviest update chore of all our authors in covering new communications technologies, because so much has changed since 2009! He shows how blogs, Twitter, wikis, social networking, and the like have the potential to boost the speed and collaborative spirit of project management.

We are excited about the addition of two new topics to this section in the fourth edition. Agile Project Management's potential to revolutionize the way we work is cogently explained by Karen R.J. White in Chapter 41.

Is *sustainability* just a buzz word? Not as it is defined and promulgated by Richard Maltzman and David Shirley in Chapter 42. They challenge readers to "be the change they want to see in the world" by adopting sustainable practices in project management.

CHAPTER 33

Earned Value Management

LEE R. LAMBERT, PMP, LAMBERT AND ASSOCIATES

Earned value management (EVM), often referred to simply as earned value, is a productive technique for the management of cost and schedule that is required on many United States government contracts. In recent years, EVM has shown itself to be equally valuable when applied to other complex projects, whether in private, commercial, or government environments.

In the world of EVM, the role of the control account manager (CAM) is pivotal in the process. The project manager and all of the other traditional project management contributors are active participants and have significant responsibilities that cannot be underestimated. However, because of the critical role of the CAM, this material is suggested to help the CAM plan and manage assigned tasks.

The EVM process is essentially the same at all levels of the project or organization. Individual components of the EVM approach addresses work authorization through status reporting. Descriptions of cost accounts, authorized work packages, and planned work packages are emphasized because of their significance in the EVM approach in general and, specifically, because of the role they play in helping the CAM to be successful at the difficult job of balancing the many project management requirements and tasks.

PROCESS OVERVIEW

The first EVM concept (then known as cost schedule control system criteria [C/SCSC]) was introduced in the 1960s, when the Department of Defense Instruction 7000.2-Performance Measurement of Selected Acquisitions exploded on the management scene. The criteria included in the instruction defined standards of acceptability for defense contractor management project control systems. The original thirty-five criteria were grouped into five general categories—organization, planning and budgeting, accounting, analysis, and revisions—and were viewed by many, government and contractor personnel alike, as a very positive step toward helping to solve

• AC	–	Actual cost = ACWP	• ETC	– Estimate to complete
• ACWP	–	Actual cost of work performed = AC	• EV	– Earned value = BCWP
• AWP	–	Authorized work package*	• FM	– Functional manager*
• BAC	–	Budget at completion	• FTC	– Forecast to complete
• BCWP	–	Budgeted cost of work performed = EV	• LOE	– Level of effort
• BCWS	–	Budgeted cost of work scheduled = PV	• LRE	– Latest revised estimate
			• MPMS	– Master phasing milestone schedule
• CA	–	Cost account	• MR	– Management reserve
• CAA	–	Cost account authorization*	• PCR	– Package change record
• CAM	–	Cost account manager	• PM	– Project manager
• CAP	–	Cost account package*	• PMB	– Performance measurement baseline
• CBB	–	Contract budget base		
• CD	–	Contract directive*	• PV	– Planned value = BCWS
• CFSR	–	Contract funds status report	• PWP	– Planned work package*
• CPR	–	Cost performance report	• RAM	– Responsibility assignment matrix
• C/SCSC	–	Cost/schedule control system criteria	• SOW	– Statement of work
• C/SSR	–	Cost/schedule status report	• UB	– Undistributed budget
• CWBS	–	Contract work breakdown structure	• VAR	– Variance analysis report
			• WBS	– Work breakdown structure
• EAC	–	Estimate at completion	• WBSM	– WBS manager*
			• WPM	– Work package manager

*These abbreviations are not common. Also note that organizations may use their own terminology.

FIGURE 33-1. **ABBREVIATIONS AND TERMS**

management problems, while achieving some much needed consistency in the general project management methods used throughout the Department of Defense and, eventually, most major U.S. government agencies.

Today, many highly respected organizations around the world work within the boundaries of the criteria managing thousands of government and private projects and programs. Countless other contractors have been using the basic principles of EVM without any formal requirement to do so because they have found the concepts and techniques useful.

Numerous abbreviations and terms are employed in a description of EVM; these are explained in Figure 33-1.

CRITICAL DATA ELEMENTS OF EARNED VALUE MANAGEMENT

There are three critical data elements involved in EVM: planned value (PV), actual cost (AC), and earned value (EV).

Planned Value

The PV is the authorized budget assigned to scheduled work. The PV is more commonly known as the spend plan or cost estimate and has long been employed in the world of project management. In EVM applications, the emphasis is placed on achieving the closest possible correlation between the scope of work to be completed (work content) and the amount of resources actually required to deliver that scope.

Actual Cost

The AC is the realized cost incurred for the work performed on an activity during a specific time period. This is usually stated in terms of dollars or some monetary measure. The AC is more commonly known as the actual incurred cost or simply actuals, and it has also been employed in the world of project management since its beginning. In EVM applications, the emphasis is placed on expending and recording resource expenditures with a direct correlation to the scope of work that has been planned to be completed at the same point in time.

Earned Value

The EV is a measure of work performed expressed in terms of the budget authorized for that work. The work accomplishment status, as determined by those responsible for completion of the work, is converted to dollar amounts and becomes the focal point of all status and analysis activities that follow. The EV is the only nontraditional data element required when utilizing EVM management techniques. The EV, when compared with the PV and AC, provides the foundation for comprehensive management evaluations, projections, and (if necessary) corrective action planning and implementation.

WHAT'S IN IT FOR THE USER?

In-the-trenches experience has resulted in two separate observations on utilizing EVM: good news and bad news. Let's take the good news first. The EVM approach does the following:

- Provides information that enables managers and contributors to take a more active role in defining and justifying a "piece of the project pie."
- Alerts you to potential problems in time to be proactive instead of reactive.
- Allows you to demonstrate clearly your timely accomplishments.
- Provides the basis for significant improvement in internal and external communications.
- Provides a powerful marketing tool for future projects and programs that require high management content.
- Provides the basis for consistent, effective management system-based training and education.
- Provides a more definitive indication of the cost and schedule impact of project problems.
- Allows tremendous flexibility in its application.

On the downside, EVM also most likely does the following:

- Results in the customer asking for more detail.
- Results in greater time spent organizing and analyzing data by someone in the organization, although this is becoming less and less of an issue with today's automated project management support capabilities.
- Requires more structure and discipline than usual.
- Costs money and organizational resources to develop and implement.

Experience clearly shows the net result to be significantly in favor of utilizing the EVM approach. Figure 33-2 shows the benefits in graphic form. Without earned value, the example shows an "under-budget" situation. Using EVM, the real status of the project is revealed, showing a project behind schedule and over budget.

But even with EVM, the management user must remember at all times that using EVM will not do the following:

- Solve technical problems.
- Solve funding problems, although it might help.
- Make decisions for you, although it will help.
- In any way "manage" your program, project, or work package.

However, EVM will provide sound, timely information—the most useful commodity for today's managers faced with making extremely difficult decisions.

PROCESS DESCRIPTION

Earned value management can be successful only if the user recognizes the need for a hierarchical relationship among all the units of work to be performed on a project. This hierarchical relationship is established through the work breakdown structure (WBS). Work is done at the lowest levels of the WBS (work packages); therefore, these critical elements have particular significance when it comes to achieving the most beneficial results from using EVM.

The EVM process involves numerous specific tasks and efforts, which are described in detail below.

Control Account

The control account (CA) is the focus for defining, planning, monitoring, and controlling because it represents all the work associated with a single WBS element, and it is usually the responsibility of a single organizational unit. Earned value management converges at the control account level, which includes budgets, schedules, work assignments, cost collection, progress assessment, problem identification, and corrective actions.

Day-to-day management is accomplished at the CA level. Most management actions taken at higher levels are on an "exception" basis in reaction to significant problems identified in the CA.

The level selected for establishment of a CA must be carefully considered to ensure that work is properly defined in manageable units (work packages) with responsibilities clearly delineated.

American Management Association • www.amanet.org

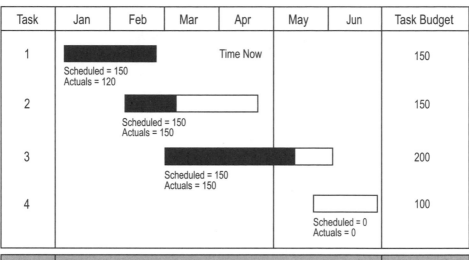

Task	Jan	Feb	Mar	Apr	May	Jun	Task Budget
1			Time Now				150
	Scheduled = 150 Actuals = 120						
2							150
		Scheduled = 150 Actuals = 150					
3							200
			Scheduled = 150 Actuals = 150				
4							100
					Scheduled = 0 Actuals = 0		

Total	Scheduled = 450 Actuals = 420 — 30 Under Budget	600

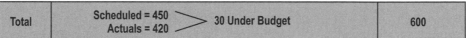

Project Control Without Earned Value

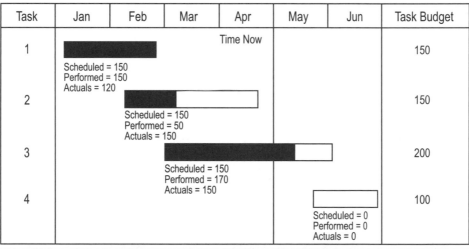

Task	Jan	Feb	Mar	Apr	May	Jun	Task Budget
1			Time Now				150
	Scheduled = 150 Performed = 150 Actuals = 120						
2							150
		Scheduled = 150 Performed = 50 Actuals = 150					
3							200
			Scheduled = 150 Performed = 170 Actuals = 150				
4							100
					Scheduled = 0 Performed = 0 Actuals = 0		

Total	Scheduled = 450 Performed = 370 — 80 Behind Schedule Actuals = 420 — 50 Over Cost	600

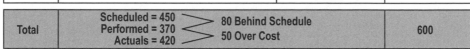

Project Control With Earned Value

FIGURE 33-2. **BENEFITS OF USING EVM**

Authorized Work Package

An authorized work package (AWP) is a detailed task that is identified by the CAM for accomplishing work within a CA. An AWP has the following characteristics:

- It represents units of work at the levels where the work is performed (lowest level of the WBS).
- It is clearly distinct from all other work packages and is usually performed by a single organizational element.
- It has scheduled start and completion dates (with interim milestones, if applicable), which represent physical accomplishment.
- It has a budget or assigned PV usually expressed in terms of dollars or labor hours.
- Its duration is relatively short unless the AWP is subdivided by discrete value milestones that permit objective measurement of work performed over long periods of time.
- Its schedule is integrated with all other schedules.

Planning Work Package

If an entire control account cannot be subdivided into detailed AWPs, long-term effort is identified in larger planned work packages (PWPs) for budgeting and scheduling purposes. The budget for a PWP is identified specifically according to the work for which it is intended. The budget is also time-phased and has controls that prevent its use in performance of other work. Eventually, all work in PWPs is planned to the appropriate level of detail for authorized work packages.

Work Authorization

All project work, regardless of origin, should be described and authorized through the work authorization process, an integral part of EVM. The EVM relates not only to work authorization, but also to planning, scheduling, budgeting, and other elements of project control, which reflect the flow of work through the functional organizations.

Although the CAM is most concerned with the work authorization process at the authorized work package and CA levels, the total process is presented to provide the CAM with a sense of specific responsibilities within the total system. The authorization flow is traced from customer authorization through contractual change authorization using the following five steps:

1. Authorization for contracted work consists of two parts: the basic contract and the contractual scope changes.
2. Work authorization for contracted work is provided as follows: The organization's general manager, in coordination with the finance director, provides authorization to the project manager to start work through a contract directive (CD). This directive approves the total project scope of work and funding.
3. Work breakdown structure planning target authorization is as follows:
    - The WBS manager prepares the WBS planning target authorization.

- The project manager approves the WBS target goal for expansion to the functional control account.
- The WBS target is later replaced by the completed WBS-package budget roll-up of CAs.

4. The procedure for CA planning target authorization is as follows: The CAM prepares a target CA goal for expansion to work packages. The CA target is later replaced by CA-package budget roll-up of all planned work packages.
5. Change control is processed as follows: The CAM submits or signs a modified work package form to the EVM information department. These modified work package forms show any internal replanning or customer contractual baseline change that alters work by addition/deletion, causing CA budget adjustments, or causes adjustment of work or budget between CAs. The processing department completes a package change record (PCR) for audit trail of baseline revisions (baseline maintenance). The project manager or delegated WBS manager approves the add/delete transactions to the management reserve/contingency account controlled by management if the budget adjustment is outside the single cost account. (*Note:* Parties to the original budget agreements must approve revisions.) The CA budget cannot be changed by such actions as cost overruns or under-runs; changes that affect program schedules or milestones because of work acceleration or work slippage; or retroactive adjustments.

Planning and Scheduling

This description of planning and scheduling from the project level down gives the CAM an overall view of specific responsibilities. Eight factors are involved:

1. Planning and scheduling must be performed in a formal, complete, and consistent way. The customer-provided project master schedule and related subordinate schedules through the control account/work package levels provide a logical sequence from summary to detailed work packages. The EVM logic network schedule works as the tool to make certain that work package schedules are compatible with contract milestones, since the networks are derived from the work package database.
2. Network logic must be established for all interfaces within the framework of the contract work breakdown structure (CWBS).
3. The responsibility assignment matrix (RAM) is an output of WBS planning. It extends to specific levels in support of internal and customer reports. The RAM merges the WBS with the organization structure to display the intersection of the WBS with the control account-responsible organizations.
4. When work plans are detailed, the lower-level work packages are interfaced and scheduled. These work packages are usually identified as either of the following:
   - *Discrete effort:* Effort that can be scheduled in relation to clearly definable start and completion dates, and which contains objective indicator milestones against which performance can be realistically measured

- *Level of effort (LOE):* Support effort that is not easily measured in terms of discrete accomplishment; it is characterized by a uniform rate of activity over a specific period of time. Where possible, work packages should be categorized in terms of discrete effort. The LOE should be minimized—typically not more than 10 percent.

5. The general characteristics of schedules are as follows:

   - Schedules should be coordinated (with all other performing organizations) by the EVM manager.
   - Commitment to lower level schedules provides the basis for the project schedule baselines.
   - All work package schedules are directly identifiable as related to CA packages and WBS elements.

   After a baseline has been established, schedule dates must remain under strict revision control, changing only with the appropriate EVM manager's approval.

6. Two categories of project schedules are used. *Project-level schedules* are master phasing/milestone schedules, program schedules, or WBS intermediate schedules. *Detailed schedules* are either control account schedules or work package schedules.

   - *Control account schedules:* (1) have milestones applicable to responsible organizations; (2) are developed by the organizations to extend interfaces to lower work package items; (3) are at the level at which status is normally determined and reported monthly to the project CA level for updating of higher level schedule status and performance measurement; (4) have planned and authorized packages that correlate to the CA, WBS, and scope of work (SOW) and which is reported to the customer; and (5) document the schedule baseline for the project.
   - *Work package schedules:* (1) provide milestones and activities required to identify specific measurable work packages; (2) supply the framework for establishing and time-phasing detailed budgets, various status reports, and summaries of cost and schedule performance; (3) are the level at which work package status is normally discussed and provide input for performance measurement; (4) are the responsibility of a single performing organization; (5) provide a schedule baseline against which each measurable work package must be identified; and (6) require formal authorization for changes after work has started and normally provide three months' detail visibility.

7. Regarding schedule change control, the control account managers can commit their organization to a revised schedule only after formal approval by at least the WBS manager.

8. Work package schedule statusing involves the following:

   - Objective indicators or milestones are used to identify measurable intermediate events.
   - Milestone schedule status and EV calculations are normally performed monthly.

BUDGETING

In accordance with the scope of work negotiated by the organization with the customer, the budgets for elements of work are allocated to the control account manager through the EVM process. These budgets are tied to the work package plans, which have been approved in the baseline. The following top-down outline, with five factors, gives the CAM an overview of the EVM budgeting process:

1. Project-to-function budgeting involves budget allocations and budget adjustments. Budget allocations involve the following:

   - The project manager releases the WBS targets to the WBS managers, who negotiate control account targets with the CAMs. The CAMs then provide work package time-phased planning.
   - When all project effort is time-phased, the EVM information is produced and output reports are provided for the project manager's review. When the performance measurement baseline (PMB) is established, the project manager authorizes WBS packages, which are summarized from the control accounts.
   - The WBS manager authorizes the control account packages, which are summed from work package planning. The time-phased work package budgets are the basis for calculating the EV each month.

   Regarding budget adjustments, the performance measurement baseline can be changed with the project manager's approval when either of the following occurs:

   - Changes in SOW (additions or deletions) cause adjustments to budgets.
   - Formal re-baselining results in a revised total allocation of budget.

2. The PMB budgets may not be replanned for changes in schedule (neither acceleration nor slips) or cost overruns or under-runs.
3. Management reserves (MRs) are budgets set aside to cover unforeseen requirements (unknown/unknowns). The package change record is used to authorize add/delete transactions to these budgets.
4. Undistributed budgets (UBs) are budgets set aside to cover identified but not yet detailed or assigned SOW. As these scopes of work are incorporated into the detail planning, a PCR is used to authorize and add to the performance measurement baseline.
5. Regarding detailed planning, the planned work package is a portion of the budget (the PV) within a CA that is identified to the CA, but is not yet defined into detailed AWPs.

COST ACCUMULATION

Cost accumulation provides the CAM with a working knowledge of the accounting methods used in EVM. There are six factors involved in cost accumulation accounting (for actual costs):

1. Timekeeping/cost collection for labor costs uses a labor distribution/accumulation system. The system shows monthly expenditure data based on labor charges against all active internal work packages.

2. Three factors are involved in non-labor costs:

   - Material cost collection accounting shows monthly expenditure data based on purchase order/subcontract expenditure.
   - The cost collection system for subcontract/integrated contractor costs uses reports received from the external source for monthly expenditures.
   - he funds control system (commitments) records the total value of purchase orders/subcontracts issued, but not totally funded. The cumulative dollar value of outstanding orders is reduced as procurements are funded.

3. The accounting charge number system typically uses two address numbers for charges to work packages: (a) the work package number, which consists of WBS-department-CA-work package; and (b) the combined account number, which consists of a single character ledger, three-digit major account, and five-digit subaccount number. Work package charge numbers are authorized by the control account manager's release of an AWP.

4. Regarding account charge number composition, an example of an internal charge number is 181-008-1-01. External charge numbers are alphabetized work package numbers. An example is 186-005-2-AB.

5. Regarding direct costs:

   - All internal labor is charged to AWP charge numbers.
   - Other direct costs are typically identified as purchase services, travel and subsistence, computer, and other allocated costs.

6. Indirect costs are elements defined by the organization:

   - Indirect costs are charged to allocation pools and distributed to internal work packages. They may also be charged as actuals to work packages.
   - Controllable labor overhead functions may be budgeted to separate work packages for monthly analysis of applied costs.

Note that actual cost categories and accounting system address numbers vary by organization. Extra care must be taken to integrate EVM requirements with other critical management information processes within the specific organization.

PERFORMANCE MEASUREMENT

Performance measurement for the control account manager consists of evaluating work package status, with EV determined at the work package level. Comparison of planned value (PV) versus earned value (EV) is made to obtain schedule variance. Comparison of EV to actual cost (AC) is made to obtain cost variance. Performance measurement provides a basis for management decisions by the organization and the customer. Six factors must be considered in performance measurement:

1. Performance measurement provides the following:

   - Work progress status
   - Relationship of planned cost and schedule to actual accomplishment
   - Valid, timely, auditable data

American Management Association • www.amanet.org

- The basis for estimate at completion (EAC), or latest revised estimates (LRE) summaries developed by the lowest practical WBS and organizational level

2. Regarding cost and schedule performance measurement:

   - The elements required to measure project progress and status: (a) work package schedule/work accomplished status; (b) the PV or planned expenditure; (c) the EV or earned value; and (d) the AC or recorded (or accrued) cost.
   - The sum of AWP and PWP budget values (PV) should equal the control account budget value.
   - Development of budgets provides these capabilities: (a) the capability to plan and control cost; (b) the capability to identify incurred costs for actual accomplishments and work in progress; and (c) the control account/work package EV measurement levels.

3. Performance measurement recognizes the importance of project budgets:

   - Measurable work and related event status form the basis for determining progress status for EV quantification.
   - The EV measurements at summary WBS levels result from accumulating EV upward through the control account from work package levels.
   - Within each control account, the inclusion of LOE is kept to a minimum to prevent distortion of the total EV.
   - There are three basic "claiming techniques" used for measuring work package performance: (a) Short work packages are less than three months long. Their earned value (EV) equals PV up to an 80 percent limit of the budget at completion until the work package is completed. (b) Long work packages exceed three months and use objective indicator milestones. The earned value (EV) equals PV up to the month-end prior to the first incomplete objective indicator. (c) Level of effort: planned value (PV) is earned through passage of time.
   - The measurement method to be used is identified by the type of work package. Note that EV must always be earned the same way the PV was planned. (See Figure 33-3 for alternate methods of establishing PV and calculating EV.)

4. To develop and prepare a forecast to complete (FTC), the control account manager must consider and analyze the following:

   - Cumulative actuals/commitments
   - The remaining CA budget
   - Labor sheets and grade/levels
   - Schedule status
   - Previous quarterly FTC
   - EV to date
   - Cost improvements
   - Historical data
   - Future actions
   - Approved changes

0/100	Take all credit for performing work when the work package is complete.
50/50	Take credit for performing one-half of the work at the start of the work package; take credit for performing the remaining one-half when the work package is complete.
Discrete Value Milestones	Divide work into separate, measurable activities and take credit for performing each activity during the time period it is completed.
Equivalent Units	If there are numerous similar items to complete, assume each is worth an equivalent portion of the total work package value; take credit for performance according to the number of items completed during the period.
Percentage Complete	Associate estimated percentages of work package to be completed with specific time periods; take credit for performance if physical inspection indicates percentages have been achieved.
Modified Milestone/ Percentage Complete	Combines the discrete value milestone and percent complete techniques by allowing some "subjective estimate" of work accomplishment and credit for the associated earned value during reporting periods where no discrete milestone is scheduled to be completed. The subjective earning of value for nonmilestone work is usually limited to one reporting period or up to 80 percent of the value of the next scheduled discrete milestone. No additional value can be earned until the scheduled discrete milestone is completed.
Level of Effort	Based on a planned amount of support effort, assign value per period; take credit for performance based on passage of time.
Apportioned Effort	Milestones are developed as a percentage of a controlling discrete work package; take credit for performance upon completion of a related discrete milestone.

FIGURE 33-3. **ALTERNATE METHODS OF ESTABLISHING PV AND CALCULATING EV**

5. The CAM reports the FTC to the EVM information processing organization each quarter.
6. The information processing organization makes the entries and summarization of the information to the reporting level appropriate for the project manager's review. [*Ed. Note:* Further information on measurement of aspects of project management performance beyond intraproject metrics can be found in Chapter 28.]

VARIANCE ANALYSIS

If performance measurement gives results in schedule or cost variances in excess of preestablished thresholds, comprehensive analyses must be made to determine the root cause of the variance. The CAM is mainly concerned with variances that exceed thresholds established for the project. Analyses of these variances provide information needed to identify and resolve problems or take advantage of opportunities. Three factors are involved in variance analysis:

1. *Preparation*
   - The cost-oriented variance analyses include a review of current, cumulative, and at-completion cost data. In-house performance reports are used

by the CAM to examine cost and schedule dollar plan vs. actual differences from the cost account plan.

- The calendar-schedule analyses include a review of any (scheduling subsystem) milestones that cause more than one-month criticality to the contract milestones.
- Variances are identified to the CA level during this stage of the review.
- Both cost variance and schedule variance are developed for the current period and cumulative as well as at-completion status.
- Determination is made whether a variance is cost-oriented, schedule-oriented, or both.
- Formal variance analysis reports are developed on significant CA variances.

2. *Presentation*

Variance analyses should be prepared when one or more of the following exceed the thresholds established by the project manager: (a) schedule variance (EV to PV); (b) cost variance (EV to AC); or (c) at-completion variance (budget at completion to latest revised estimate [LRE]).

3. *Operation*

- Internal analysis reports document variances that exceed thresholds: schedule problem analysis reports for "time-based" linear schedule, or control account variance analysis reports for dollar variances.
- Explanations are submitted to the customer when contractual thresholds are exceeded.
- Emphasis should be placed on corrective action for resolution of variant conditions.
- Corrective action should be assigned to specific individuals (CAMs) and closely tracked for effectiveness and completion.
- Internal project variance analyses and corrective action should be formally reviewed in regularly scheduled management meetings.
- Informal reviews of cost and schedule variance analysis data may occur daily, weekly, or monthly, depending on the nature and severity of the variance.

Figure 33-4 presents some sample comparisons of PV, EV, and AC.

REPORTING

The two basic report categories are customer and in-house. Customer performance reports are contractually established with fixed content and timing. In-house reports support internal projects with the data that relate to lower organizational and WBS levels. The CAM is mainly concerned with these lower level reports.

1. *Customer reporting*

- A customer requires summary-level reporting, typically on a monthly basis.
- The customer examines the detailed data for areas that may indicate a significant variance.

PV (BCWS)	EV (BCWP)	AC (ACWP)	Condition of Project
$100	$100	$100	On schedule – On budget
$200	$200	$100	On schedule – Underrun
$100	$100	$200	On schedule – Overrun
$100	$200	$200	Ahead of schedule – On budget
$100	$200	$100	Ahead of schedule – Underrun
$100	$200	$300	Ahead of schedule – Overrun
$200	$100	$100	Behind schedule – On budget
$300	$200	$100	Behind schedule – Underrun
$200	$100	$300	Behind schedule – Overrun

FIGURE 33-4. **COMPARISONS OF PLANNED VALUE, EARNED VALUE, AND ACTUAL COST**

- The cost performance report (CPR) is the vehicle used to accumulate and report cost and schedule performance data.

2. *In-house reporting*

   - Internal management practices emphasize assignment of responsibility for internal reports to an individual CAM.
   - Reporting formats reflect past and current performance and the forecast level of future performance.
   - Performance review meetings are held monthly for cost and schedule, and as needed for review of problem areas.
   - The CAM emphasizes cumulative to-date and to-go cost, schedule, and equivalent person power on the CA work packages.
   - It is primarily at the work package level that review of performance (EV), actuals (AC), and budget (PV) is coupled with objective judgment to determine the FTC.
   - The CAM is responsible for the accuracy and completeness of the estimates.

INTERNAL AUDIT/VERIFICATION AND REVIEW

The control account manager is the most significant contributor to the successful operation of an EVM process and to successful completion of any subsequent internal audits or customer reviews. Day-to-day management of the project takes place at the control account level. If each CA is not managed competently, project performance suffers regardless of the sophistication of the higher level management system. The organization and the customer should place special emphasis on CAM performance during operational demonstration reviews.

The EV approach to project management may be the most comprehensive and effective method of developing plans and providing decision-making information ever conceived. But to achieve maximum potential benefit, the extensive use of an automated support program becomes inevitable. Software especially developed to support EVM applications is currently available for nearly every computer hardware configuration.

When considering which computer hardware/software combination will best satisfy your needs, carefully evaluate your specific project application, including the size of projects, the frequency of reporting, the ease of modification, the potential for expansion, and the graphic output requirements. This computer hardware/software decision could be the difference between success and failure in an EVM application, so don't rush it! Make your selection only after a thorough investigation and evaluation. Don't let anyone sell you something you don't need or want.

DISCUSSION QUESTIONS

❶ If you are using EVM data to project the "future state" of a project, at what stage of the project would this data become useful in the decision making process?

❷ How important is the duration of a work package in successfully utilizing the earned value approach? Are there any alternatives?

❸ During the status/reporting stage (50 percent complete) you note that one of the key cost accounts on the project has an Schedule performance index (SPI) of 0.83. What does this mean and what would you propose doing about it?

ACKNOWLEDGMENT

We gratefully acknowledge Paul Lombard for updates to this chapter in the fourth edition.

FURTHER READING

Defense Contract Management Command (DCMC), *Earned Value Management Implementation Guide,* http://www.srs.gov/general/EFCOG/02GovtReferences/02D0D/EVMImplementationGuide.htm.

Industry Standard Guidelines for Earned Value Management Systems, www.ntsc.navy.mil/Resources/Library/Acqguide/evms_gde.doc.

Lee Lambert and Erin Lambert, *Project Management: The Common Sense Approach—Using Earned Value to Balance the Triple Constraint* (Dublin, OH: Lambert Consulting Group, Inc., 2000).

Project Management Institute, *Practice Standard for Earned Value Management,* 2nd edition (Newtown Square, PA: PMI, 2011).

CHAPTER 34

Dealing with Power and Politics in Project Management

RANDALL L. ENGLUND, EXECUTIVE CONSULTANT

Project management is more than techniques to complete projects on time, within scope, and within budget. Organizations by their very nature are political, so effective project managers need to become politically sensible. Astute "project politicians" assess the environment and develop an effective political plan that addresses the power structure and activities in an organization. They seek out a guiding coalition of supporters and guide them to take positive action toward desired results.

To be ignorant about political processes can be costly to the organization and the individual. Instead of lamenting a failed project, program, or initiative, it is possible to learn a proven approach to power and politics that optimizes project success. The approach discussed below can help turn potential victim scenarios into win–win political victories.

ADOPT A LEADERSHIP ROLE

Sooner or later all professionals find a leadership role thrust upon them, a team to lead, or a project to accomplish with others. Opportunity comes to those leaders who understand and meld scope, schedule, and cost management processes with skills in selling, negotiating, managing change, and politicking. This should not be viewed as a burden, but as the chance to become a *complete project manager*.[1]

A common theme for success or failure of any organizational initiative is building a guiding coalition—a bonding of sponsors and influential people who support the activity. This support, or lack thereof, represents a powerful force either toward or away from the goal. Embrace and develop negotiating skills, employing passion, patience, and persistence. Moderate success may be achieved without widespread political support, but continuing long-term business impact requires alignment of power factors within the organization. A key factor is leadership that guides organizations to be more project-friendly, which in turn leads to greater value-added, economically viable results.

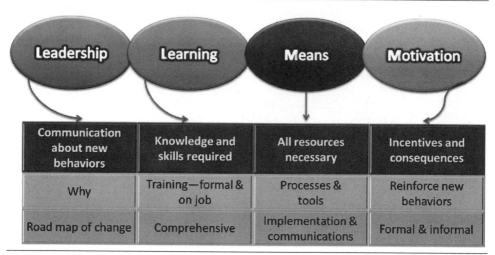

Communication about new behaviors	Knowledge and skills required	All resources necessary	Incentives and consequences
Why	Training—formal & on job	Processes & tools	Reinforce new behaviors
Road map of change	Comprehensive	Implementation & communications	Formal & informal

FIGURE 34-1. **FOUR FACTORS IN BEHAVIORAL CHANGE**

Organizations attempting projects across functions, businesses, and geographies increasingly encounter complexities that threaten their success. A common response is to set up control systems that inhibit the very results intended. This happens when we inhibit the free flow of information and impose unnecessary constraints.

By contrast, taming chaos and managing complexity are possible when leaders establish a strong sense of purpose among all stakeholders, develop shared vision and values, and adopt patterns of behavior that promote cooperation across cultural boundaries. These processes represent major change for many organizations.

An organic approach to project management acknowledges that people work best in an open environment that supports their innate talents, strengths, and desires to contribute. Many organizational environments thwart rather than support these powerful forces in their drive to complete projects on time, within budget, and according to specifications. Look for behavioral patterns and incentives that naturally guide people toward a desired result rather than implement onerous controls. Results are similar to those of a successful gardener: combining the right conditions with the right ingredients creates a bountiful harvest. By ensuring that leadership, learning, means, and motivation are all present in appropriate amounts, the right people can employ efficient processes in an effective environment (Figure 34-1).

Too late, people often learn the power of a *nonguiding* coalition. This happens when a surprise attack results in a resource getting pulled, a project manager getting reassigned, or a project getting cancelled. Getting explicit commitments up front, the more public the better, is important to implementing any activity. It also takes follow-through to maintain the commitment. But if commitment was not obtained initially, it is not possible to maintain throughout. It all starts by investigating attitudes and assessing how things get done.[2]

VIEWS OF POLITICS

Albert Einstein said, "Politics is more difficult than physics." The challenge is to create an environment for positive politics. That is, people operate with a win–win attitude. All actions are out in the open. People demonstratively work hard toward the common good. Outcomes are desirable or at least acceptable to all parties concerned. This is the view of power and politics espoused in this chapter.

One's attitude toward political behavior becomes extremely important. Options are to be naive, to be a shark that uses aggressive manipulation to reach the top, or to be politically sensible. According to Jeffrey Pinto,[3] politically sensible individuals enter organizations with few illusions about how many decisions are made. They understand, either intuitively or through their own experience and mistakes, that politics is a facet of behavior that happens in all organizations. People who are politically sensible neither shun nor embrace predatory politics. "Politically sensible individuals use politics as a way of making contacts, cutting deals, and gaining power and resources for their departments or projects to further corporate, rather than entirely personal, ends."[3]

To make politics work for you, it is important to understand the levels of power in leading a project. As depicted in Figure 34-2:

- *Control* or authority power is the one most prevalent but not one that project managers can rely on with any degree of certainty in most organizations.
- *Influence* or status depends on referent (or appealing to others) powers:
  - Be willing to challenge the status quo.
  - Create and communicate a vision.
  - Empower others.
  - Model desired behavior.
  - Encourage others.
- *Appreciation* means having awareness of areas of uncertainty outside the realm of control or influence that could nevertheless impact project success. For instance, I cannot know when an upper manager will dictate a change in the project or a system will crash, but I can appreciate that these things happen and can provide placeholders with contingencies for them in the project plan.

Power and politics are unpopular topics with many people. That ambivalent attitude hampers their ability to become skilled and effective. A negative reaction to the word *political* could be a barrier to success. Often, when people feel there is too little power available to them, they resort to a "victim mode" of feeling powerless. Yet the savvy project manager can develop sources of power by remaining alert for opportunities to lead or assist. One high-level management team almost ceased to function when the general manager could not be present at the last moment for a critical meeting. The facilitator had to help the team members realize this was their opportunity to build a power base among themselves and to take action that would present a united front when they next met with the general manager.

Lack of demonstrated power is also an opportunity to exercise personal power. Many people shine when they jump in and do something when they first see the opportunity, asking forgiveness later if necessary instead of waiting for permission.

ASSESS THE POLITICAL ENVIRONMENT

A big pitfall is not taking the time to fully assess what we are up against—that is, learning how to operate effectively in a political environment.

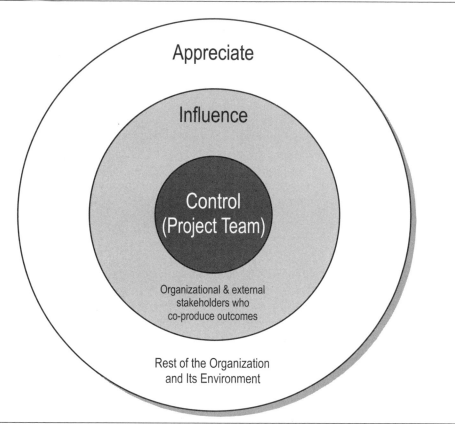

FIGURE 34-2. **TYPES OF STAKEHOLDER POWER**

What is a political environment? Being political is not a bad thing when trying to get good things done for the organization. A political environment is the power structure, formal and informal. It is how things get done within the day-to-day processes as well as in a network of relationships. Power is the capacity each individual possesses to translate intention into reality and sustain it. Organizational politics is the exercise or use of power. The world of physics revolves around power. Because project management is all about getting results, it stands to reason that power is required. Political savvy is a vital ingredient in every project manager's toolkit.

Understand the power structure in the organization. A view from outer space would not show the lines that separate countries, organizations, functional areas, or other political boundaries. The lines are figments that exist in our minds or on paper but not in reality. Clues to a power structure may come from an organizational chart, but how things get done goes far beyond that. Influence exists in people's hearts and minds, where power derives more from legitimacy than from authority. Its presence is shown by the implementation of decisions.

Table 34-1 describes the various sources of power and their effects.

Legitimacy is what people confer on their leaders. Being authentic and acting with integrity are ways a leader behaves in relations to others, but legitimacy is the

Influence Base	Organizationally Derived Components	Individually Derived Components
Authority	Position, Title Office Size Charter Budget, Resources Project Size, Importance	Respect Trust Credibility Performance Image Integrity
Reward Power	Salary, Bonuses Hire, Promote Work, Security Training, Development Resource Allocation	Recognition, Visibility Accomplishments Autonomy, Flexibility Stimulating Environment Professional Growth
Punishment	Salary, Bonuses Fire, Demote Work, Security Resource Limitations	Reprimand Team Pressure Tight Supersion Work Pressure Isolation
Expert Power	Top Management Support	Competence Knowledge Information Sound Decitions Top Management Respect Access to Experts
Referent Power		Friendship Charisma Empathy

Source: Hans J. Thamhain, "Leadership," in *The AMA Handbook of Project Management,* 3rd edition (New York: AMACOM, 2010), p. 166.

TABLE 34-1. **THE PROJECT MANAGER'S BASES OF INFLUENCE**

response from others. Position power may command respect, but ultimately how a leader behaves is what gains wholehearted commitment from followers. Legitimacy is the real prize, for it completes the circle. When people accept and legitimize the power of a leader, greater support gets directed toward the outcome; conversely, less resistance is present.

People have always used organizations to amplify human power. Art Kleiner[4] states a premise that in every organization there is a core group of key people—the "people who really matter"—and the organization continually acts to fulfill the perceived needs and priorities of this group.

Kleiner suggests numerous ways to determine who these powerful people are. People who have power are at the center of the organization's informal network. They are symbolic representatives of the organization's direction. They got this way because of their position, their rank, and their ability to hire and fire others. Maybe they control a key bottleneck or belong to a particular influential subculture. They may have personal charisma or integrity. These people take a visible stand on behalf of the organization's principles and engender a level of mutual respect. They dedicate themselves as leaders to the organization's ultimate best interests and set the organization's direction. As they think or act or convey an attitude, so does the rest of the organization. Their characteristics and principles convey what an organization stands for. These are key people who, when open to change, can influence an organization to move in new directions or, when not open to change, keep it the same.

Another way to recognize key people is to look for decision makers in the mainstream business of the organization. They may be aligned with the headquarters culture, ethnic basis, or gender, or speak the native language, or be part of the founding family. Some questions to ask about people in the organization are: Whose interests did we consider in making a decision? Who gets things done? Who could stop something from happening? Who are the "heroes"?

Power is not imposed by boundaries. Power is earned, not demanded. Power can come from position in the organization, what a person knows, a network of relationships, and possibly the situation, meaning a person could be placed in a situation that has a great deal of importance and focus in the organization.

A simple test for where power and influence reside is to observe who people talk to or go to with questions or for advice. Whose desk do people meet at? Who has a long string of voice or email messages? Whose calendar is hard to get onto?

One of the most reliable sources of power when working across organizations is the credibility a person builds through a network of relationships. It is necessary to have credibility before a person can attract team members, especially the best people, who are usually busy and have many other things competing for their time. Credibility comes from relationship building in a political environment.

In contrast, credibility gaps occur when previous experience did not fulfill expectations or when perceived abilities to perform are unknown and therefore questionable. Organizational memory has a lingering effect—people long remember what happened before and do not give up those perceptions without due cause. People more easily align with someone who has the power of knowledge credibility, and relationship credibility is something only the individual can build or lose.

Power and politics also address the priority assigned to project management's triple constraints—outcome, schedule, and cost. If the power in an organization resides in marketing, where trade shows rule new product introductions, meeting market window schedules becomes most important. A research and development (R&D)–driven organization tends to focus on features and new technology, often at the expense of schedule and cost. Low-cost market leaders obsess about cost controls.

CREATE A POLITICAL PLAN

A quest to optimize results in a convoluted organizational environment requires a political management plan. This is probably a new addition to the project manager's arsenal. Elements of a political plan may have been included in a communications plan. To conduct a systematic approach to power and politics, a key element is to prepare a stakeholder analysis. One quickly realizes that it is impossible to satisfy everyone and that the goal might become to keep everyone minimally annoyed and to use a "weighted dissatisfaction" index.[5]

Positioning

Another element of a political plan is positioning. For instance, where a project office is located in an organization affects its power base. The concept of "centrality" says to locate it in a position central and visible to other corporate members, where it is central to or important for organizational goals.[6] HP's project management initiative started in corporate engineering, a good place to be because HP was an engineering company. That put the initiative into the mainstream instead of in a peripheral organization where its effectiveness and exposure may be more limited. Likewise, a project office for the personal computer division reported through a section manager to the R&D functional manager. This again reflected centrality since R&D at that time drove product development efforts.

Most important decisions in organizations involve the allocation of scarce resources. Position and charter a project office with a key role in decision making that is bound to the prioritization and distribution of organizational resources. Be there to help, not to make decisions. Reassure managers that they are not losing decision-making power but gaining an ally to facilitate and implement decisions.

An individual contributor, project leader, or *project office of one* needs to consider where he or she is located in an organization in order to have a greater impact, make a larger contribution, get promoted, or generally gain more power and influence. Doing service projects in a field office for a manufacturing and sales-oriented company is less likely to attract attention than a product marketing person doing new product introduction projects in the factory. Seek out projects that address critical factors facing the organization. In essence, address in a political plan how important the project is to the organization, where it resides in having access to key decision makers, and what support resources are available to the project.

Driving Change

Implicit in changing a dysfunctional political environment into a successful project-based organization is the notion that change is inevitable. The use of power and politics becomes a mechanism for driving change. Politics is a natural consequence of the interaction among organizations, functional areas, teams, and individuals. View political skills as an important tool and the need for a change as an opportunity to contribute, using those skills.

A well-known political tactic that enhances status is to demonstrate expertise and earn legitimacy. Developing proficiency and constantly employing new best practices around program and project management, combined with some of the above tactics in the political plan, plus communicating and promoting the services and successes achieved, help a project gain status in the organization. This factor is a recurring theme in many case studies.

Pinto says, "Any action or change effort initiated by members of an organization that has the potential to alter the nature of current power relationships provides a tremendous impetus for political activity."[7]

A business case can be made that changes are usually necessary within organizations that set out to conquer new territory through projects and project teams, often guided by a project office. The role of upper managers may need to change in order to support these new efforts. However, it takes concerted effort, often on the part of project managers who are closest to the work, to speak the truth to upper managers who have the authority and power about what needs to happen.[8] The change may be revolutionary and require specific skills and process steps to be effective.

Here is a suggested outline or template for crafting a political plan:

- Assessment of environment
- Description of political "jungle"
- Stakeholder roles
- Potential issues
- Approach to stakeholders and issues
- Strategic response, such as positioning and steps
- Action plans

CONCLUSION

Recognize that organizations are political. A commitment to positive politics is an essential attitude that creates a healthy, functional organization. Create relationships that are win–win (all parties gain), where actual intentions are out in the open (not hidden or distorted), and trust is the basis for ethical transactions. Determining what is important to others and providing value to recipients are currencies that project leaders can exchange with other people. Increased influence capacity comes from inquiry about concerns important to others, advocacy of clear arguments and action plans, and communicating through all appropriate means. Effective project and program managers embrace the notion that they are salespersons, politicians, and negotiators. Take the time to learn the skills of these professions and apply them daily.

Embrace the role of leader and change agent. Exercise political savvy. Successfully navigate political minefields by exercising these traits:

- Act from personal strengths, such as expert, visionary, or process owner.
- Develop a clear, convincing, and compelling message and make it visible to others.
- Use your passion that comes from deep values and beliefs about the work (if these are not present, then find a different program to work on).
- Be accountable for success of the organization, and ask others to do the same.
- Get explicit commitments from people to support the goals of the program so that they are more likely to follow through.
- Take action—first to articulate the needs, then help others understand the change, achieve small wins, and get the job done.
- Tap the energy that comes from the courage of your convictions . . . and from being prepared.

Believe in and apply techniques for political coalition building. The extent that powerful organizational forces are on board (or not) enables a project to go ahead in a big way, a project to be modified or downscaled, or for people to quit and move on to something easier.

Between today's situation and a desired state lies a long road of organizational change and the required politicking. Project managers who are skilled at the political

American Management Association • www.amanet.org

arts of communication, persuasion, change management, and negotiation—and who also are authentic and trustworthy—can help their organizations make this transition.

DISCUSSION QUESTIONS

❶ What cultural context or organizational factors influence the development of a political plan? For example: open, enlightened, closed, exclusive, stimulating, supportive, productive, chaotic, messy, difficult to navigate, and so on.

❷ How will you address these factors (or forces)?

❸ Where can you find opportunities to develop your political skills?

REFERENCES

[1] Randall Englund and Alfonso Bucero, *The Complete Project Manager's Toolkit* (Vienna, VA: Management Concepts Press, 2012).

[2] Robert Graham and Randall Englund, *Creating an Environment for Successful Projects,* 2nd edition (San Francisco: Jossey-Bass Publishers, 2004); Roger Lewin and Birute Regine, *The Soul at Work: Listen, Respond, Let Go; Embracing Complexity Science for Business Success* (New York: Simon & Schuster, 2000); and Jeffrey K. Pinto, Peg Thomas, Jeffrey Trailer, Todd Palmer, and Michele Govekar, *Project Leadership* (Newtown Square, PA: Project Management Institute, 1998).

[3] Jeffrey K. Pinto, *Power and Politics in Project Management* (Upper Darby, PA: Project Management Institute, 1996).

[4] Art Kleiner, *Who Really Matters: the Core Group Theory of Power, Privilege, and Success* (New York: Currency Doubleday, 2003).

[5] Pinto, *Power and Politics.*

[6] *Ibid.*

[7] *Ibid.*

[8] Randall Englund, Robert Graham, and Paul Dinsmore, *Creating the Project Office: A Manager's Guide to Leading Organizational Change* (San Francisco: Jossey-Bass Publishers, 2003), pp. 66–73 (contains a more thorough discussion about speaking truth to power).

CHAPTER 35

Multi-Project Constraint Management
The "Critical Chain" Approach

FRANK PATRICK

Every organization also has constraints limiting what it can accomplish. With finite time and attention available from the human and other resources that make up the organizational system, it must provide an appropriate answer to the questions, "What should I/we be working on today?" and "How should I/we organize and perform the mass of work facing me/us?" These are the critical questions for which project management is meant to provide answers.

The literature on project management until recently had focused on project management related to the delivery of individual projects. While it is necessary—and nice—to be able to deliver a single project as promised, it is not sufficient to ensure the ability of an organization to address its multiple needs.

ORGANIZATIONS ARE MULTI-PROJECT SYSTEMS

Let us assume that the goal of an organization is to sustain itself so that it can profitably deliver products or services—not only today but also in the future.[1] If that's the case, then because its market environment—the demands of its customers and the responses of its competitors—cannot be reasonably expected to remain static, the organization must efficiently deliver today's business and effectively change to address its future circumstances.

Projects as the Business

There is a distinction between production-based organizations and project-based organizations, in that the former is usually dependent on delivering a lot of copies of identical (or at least very similar) units of a product or service, with minimal or easily manageable uncertainty and variation of process. In production environments, the "touch-time" associated with an individual piece of output is usually very small compared to the total duration of building that output, as components tend to spend

---

377

most of their time in queues awaiting attention or the setup of the machinery that will transform it in some way.

Project environments, on the other hand, are characterized more by uncertainty of expectations and greater variation in the performance against those expectations. Projects also involve larger chunks of "touch time" as a proportion of total project duration. If one's business is based on directly "selling" the outcome of projects developed with a shared pool of resources, as it is in industries such as custom software and information technology (IT) systems, consulting, construction, maintenance and repair, and engineer-to-build custom manufacturing, projects are "the business." In such arenas, the ability to maximize the throughput of multiple completed projects is directly related to both current and future success.

Projects Supporting the Business

The ability to effectively implement change is clearly related to what most would recognize as projects and project management. Such efforts are typically temporary efforts, with a reasonably finite span of time between launch and completion. In this context, change projects are related not only to tactical, local process improvements or highly visible strategic initiatives, but also to the ability to redefine one's offerings to meet future needs—research and new product/service development and deployment. Regardless of whether the business of the organization is production-or project-based, its future success needs to be supported by effective delivery of change.

ORGANIZATIONAL EFFECTIVENESS IS RESOURCE EFFECTIVENESS

The old saw defining efficiency largely as "doing things right" and effectiveness as "doing the right things" definitely applies to multi-project systems. Understanding the importance of getting the right things done at the task level, and behaving accordingly, are significant contributors to efficiency as well and are the basis for multi-project resource (organizational) effectiveness. Unfortunately, too many organizations overlook this and instead emphasize control of costs to the detriment of what they are trying to accomplish.

Maximizing Throughput or Controlling Costs?

Many managers look on the twin pressures of maximizing throughput and controlling costs as conflicting requirements, because pressures to keep expenses down have the potential to threaten the ability to deliver more completed projects quickly and with quality.

This sense of conflict comes from confusing organizational effectiveness with efficiency, and even worse, with resource utilization.[2] Ensuring that everyone is fully utilized all the time may seem like a reasonable strategy for getting the most out of the individual resources, and, by extrapolation, out of the organization. On the surface, this feels like it makes sense. However, if a system wants to maximize its throughput, keeping resources fully loaded across the board actually hampers that objective for several reasons.

The first reason to avoid striving for full resource utilization is that if everyone is fully loaded, there is no slack to deal with the inevitable run-ins with Murphy's Law. Given the uncertain nature of projects as unique endeavors, any negative deviation from planned expectations will require the capacity to recover. If that protective capacity is not available, problems in a project will result in either cascading problems that will threaten the promises of other projects, or burnout of resources, or both. In either case, future throughput is threatened.

Similarly, without protective capacity set aside, there is no ability to capitalize on new opportunities that arise. Potential throughput is lost.

Multitasking Multiplies Time to Complete Projects

Finally, in environments where full utilization of people's time is valued, there will usually be timesheets to fill out, or measurement-and-reward systems—formal or informal—that drive people to keep busy. In addition, in such a situation, projects are usually launched with an eye to making sure that no one is starved for work. As a result, there are usually plenty of choices of things for everyone to work on. With many active projects expecting progress, there is pressure to work on several at one time, splitting one's time and attention across them. Unless an effective multi-project management system provides clear priorities for resource attention, people will strive to make the "measurement" look good by keeping busy and keeping several balls in the air. This is multitasking—working on several significant pieces of work simultaneously, switching between them before any one piece is completed and before its output is handed off to the next task in the project.

What happens in this situation is that, as a result of trying to make sure that everyone is always fully utilized (a seemingly efficient means of controlling costs), the time it takes to convert a task input into an output that is usable by the next task is expanded because of the time it sits idle while another project gets the attention.[3] In addition, the context switching cost—the time involved in answering the question "Where was I?" when returning to a set-aside task—adds to the actual work time, adding further inefficiencies to the project. Throughput associated with these projects is lost as their completions are delayed beyond when they could have been achieved.

Resource Efficiency Is Not Organizational Effectiveness

By striving to be "efficient" through high local resource utilization—by striving for cost control through avoiding "wasted" idle resources throughout the organization—the real objective is suboptimized. Throughput of completed projects and the benefit—paid invoices, improved processes, or new products that will ring new cash registers—associated with those completions is threatened, lost, or delayed.

CONSTRAINT-SAVVY MULTI-PROJECT AND RESOURCE MANAGEMENT

In order for a multi-project system to operate effectively for an organization, it needs to ensure that the project pipeline is not overloaded. Also, when there are decisions to be made between project tasks vying for the attention of a resource, the system needs to provide a clear priority that is aligned with maximizing the benefit from the total collection of projects so that the resource in question will pick up and work the "right" task without multitasking. The first of these requirements is directly related to understanding and managing the organization through its constraints.

$$\text{Constraint} = \text{Capacity} = \text{Throughput}$$

Unless artificially forced otherwise, or unless mismanaged to the point of non-recognition by overload, systems put together for a purpose typically have one or at most very few constraints limiting their ability to deliver that purpose. Like the clichéd "weak link of a chain," a potential bottleneck resource can usually be identified as a limiting factor associated with project throughput.

The capacity of the system is the capacity of this constraining bottleneck. It doesn't pay to try to push more projects into launch mode than this constraint can handle. They'll only back up waiting for it to attend to them, and they'll distract and unnecessarily overload all the resources working upstream of the constraint. Rather than trying to tightly balance the load on all resources (and killing throughput in the process), a rational approach to managing such a system is to identify (or design in) a clearly understood constraint and manage that one piece of the system very closely.

Protective Capacity

The current constraining resource in a multi-project system could be located anywhere. By definition, other resources are nonconstraints and have more capacity than would be technically needed to support the possible throughput of the system. But to start cutting and slashing this extra capacity indiscriminately would be a mistake. At some point, that would merely shift the constraint from where it is to another, potentially unpredictable part of the system at the same or lower level of capacity, or, worse, set up a situation with hard-to-manage interactive constraints.

Instead, the means of managing the constraint for growth of throughput starts with stabilizing the system so that the extra capacity upstream of the constraint ensures that the constraint is not starved for work. The only resource that should be kept near high utilization (note "near high" is not "at full") is the constraint, since the output of the system is tied directly to its output. Project launches that are synchronized with the ability of the constraint to deal with them will, if sufficient protective capacity is available upstream, flow smoothly to the closely managed possible bottleneck. Similarly, once through the identified constraint, no downstream resource should be so tight that it delays the conversion of constraint output to a complete accrual of project benefit. Again that implies a necessary level of protective capacity downstream as well.

Once stabilized and ridded of the effects of overload and multitasking, the true capacity of the system and of its components is far more easily identified. At this point, the organization can take rational steps to grow its capacity and capabilities by systematic constraint management.

Implications for Project Portfolio Management

Once the constraint of the system is understood, it will have implications beyond just project delivery performance. It will also provide useful input to the project portfolio process. If the organization is limited to taking on projects at the rate that they can pass through the bottleneck, then those projects that have a higher relative benefit value per time required of the bottleneck will be more valuable to the organization than those that require more bottleneck time, all else being equal.[4]

One project may seem to have small face value, but if barely involving the constraint, it will be able to deliver that value while barely displacing some other project and its benefit. It is almost a "free" project, taking advantage of the slack in the nonconstraint resources. On the other hand, if a project looks very valuable when complete but requires so much constraint time that many other projects are denied or delayed, it becomes a serious strategic decision to move forward with it. If, by the nature of a bottleneck or constraint, taking on one project forces us to forgo or delay another, then this metric of benefit per constraint usage becomes an important factor in the decision to launch.

MULTI-PROJECT AND RESOURCE MANAGEMENT: MANAGING THE PRESENT AND THE FUTURE

Once an organization understands the constraints associated with its ability to deliver projects, whether for customer-driven deliverables or for internal process improvements, it has the basis not only to avoid overloading its current capacity and capability, but also to smoothly grow the capability to take on more work in the future.

"How Much Should We Take On Next Month?"—Gating Project Launches

At the border of portfolio management and project management lies pipeline management. Nothing will bog down a project delivery system faster than the premature push of projects into a system that cannot really handle them.

Once the portfolio management or sales acceptance process determines the relative ordering of projects, the process for synchronizing project launches to constraint capacity is a simple matter of staggering them at the point of use of the constraint. Once it is known when the constraint can take on a new project, it is a simple matter of placing it there in the calendar, perhaps with a bit of buffer to avoid cross-project impacts at the constraint, and examining the resulting schedule to determine where it is appropriate to start the upstream activities.

If project launches are staggered in this manner, then the constraining resource will not be overloaded. And if the constraining resource is not overloaded, then the other nonconstraining resources will also, by definition, not be overloaded, thereby reducing pressures to multitask and simplifying the question of priorities when the occasional need to choose which task to work comes up.

"What Should I Be Working On Today?"—Clarity of Priority at the Task Level

If projects are not overloading the system, the question of which task to work on is simplified by the mere reduction of active tasks in play. In-boxes are less loaded.

However, due to the vagaries of project plans, and of variation in task performance, occasionally it might occur that a resource faces the need to choose one task to pick up and finish before addressing another one that is waiting. There are several options to providing such guidance.

Assuming that the individual projects are being actively managed via critical path or Critical Chain processes, one consideration is whether any of the waiting tasks are on the critical path or critical chain of the project in question. If so, that task would most likely be the appropriate first choice over a competing "noncritical" task.[5]

If there is a choice of two or more "critical" tasks from different projects, the relative health of the projects in question can be easily assessed based on working one, then the other, and vice versa. The scenario that leaves the best combination of the resulting health of the projects' promises in best condition (or maximizes the benefits associated with both projects) would be preferred. In an environment based on Critical-Chain scheduling and buffer management, project buffers not only provide the ability of projects to absorb such decisions, but also make the assessment process straightforward. Critical path–based projects, usually relying on smaller, if any, schedule reserves, might have to add some additional recovery activities. (Note that this constraint-based approach to multi-project management comes from the same source as critical-chain scheduling and buffer management; the theory of constraints and the two processes work together by design.)

If all queued tasks are "noncritical," it is less of an issue, and while usually a first-come, first-served process will suffice, a consideration of the general health of the project promise, or in the case of a critical-chain project, buffer consumption, could also provide useful guidance.

"How Much Can We Work On Next Year?"—Current and Strategic Constraints

The previous section described the stabilization of the system around the organization's current constraint. That constraint is the result of past actions and staffing levels; it may not be an ideal leverage point for maximum strategic benefit. Once the system is stable, the organization can manage itself proactively by designing a more appropriate system based on what one might call a "strategic constraint."

An appropriate constraining resource would be one that is commonly and heavily used across a range of anticipated projects, but is also hard to augment. If it is easy to get more of it by acquiring more people or improving processes, then it is probably worth doing so to easily grow organizational capacity, assuming the protective capacity around it is also easily grown. If hard to augment, it becomes a matter of offloading or improving processes to grow capacity. A constraint that is hard to get more of while commonly and heavily required is a natural candidate for a long-term constraint against which to manage the organization.

Additionally, such hard-to-grow resources are often critical to the organization's competitiveness. For example, a system architect who knows the ins and outs of the firm's software products is far harder to replace, and is inherently more important to its capacity, than some "plain vanilla" developer skill that can be augmented with contractors. If there is some other, easily elevated constraint in place, it behooves the organization to develop plans to grow its capacity along with any others who might be limiting what can be gotten through the expert. Understanding this relationship also highlights and justifies the need to grow that expert skill as well, perhaps through shared work or by determining what it is in the work usually performed by the expert that really needs the expertise.

An interesting offshoot of effective constraint management is that if one considers a limiting factor—a constraint—to be a weakness, then the system's strength—the resource and skill that defines its core competency—should probably be that weakness. After all, you don't want any other aspect of the organizational system to limit the ability to maximize the benefit of that strength.

IT'S NOT HOW MUCH YOU START, IT'S HOW MUCH YOU FINISH

Too many organizations act as if by packing the pipeline and keeping everyone heavily loaded with work, a combination of filled queues and busy resources will result in rapid and reliable project completions. Instead, projects bump into one another, adding delays usually unanticipated in individual project promises, and resources burn out jumping between unfinished tasks that then further delay task handoffs and project completions.

Suggested exercise: Survey some of your project participants. Ask them how many different tasks they currently have open. How many different project reviews do they attend each week? Ask them how long they expect their current collection of tasks to take to complete. Then ask them if they set aside most tasks and just picked one and finished it as if it were the only thing they had to do, then another, and then another, when would the individual tasks and the total collection be complete? How much less time would it take them to complete them all if they focused on one at a time?

Constraint management suggests instead that projects only be launched at a rate that can be handled by the organizational system, and as its surrogate, by the system's constraining resource. This constraint is easily identified as a heavily used resource, skill, or facility common to most projects in the portfolio. Once the pipeline of projects quickly settles down to stability through such an approach, it becomes a matter of systematic constraint management to grow the capacity and capability of the organization to meet strategic needs.

Suggested exercise: Consider your organization. Even if it is in a chaotic state in which every resource feels overloaded, ask this question: If you could double the capacity of one and only one resource, skill, or facility, where would it be most beneficial for the organization in terms of helping more projects move to completion quicker? In most organizations, it usually quickly narrows down to a consensus on one or two candidates. Those are your initial candidates for designation as project pipeline constraint.

Every organization needs to consider how it manages the collection of projects it requires to sustain itself. Whether the business is based on delivering project work or process improvements that require attention from a limited pool of players, or if the business depends on a steady flow of new product development, maximizing throughput of completed projects is critical to organizational effectiveness.

CONCLUSION

It's not about how busy everyone is. It's not about success with one major project that would have everyone's attention anyway. It's about how many projects you finish in a period of time. It's about finishing many projects rapidly and reliably. It's about maximizing the throughput of your project pipeline, and the key to moving more through a pipeline is not forcing too much through it, creating turbulence, leaks, and spills. It's about understanding the bottlenecks and constraints, rationally loading them, and systematically growing their capacity.

DISCUSSION QUESTIONS

❶ Consider your organization: How many people are involved in project work? Is this project work revenue enhancing or primarily supporting process improvements? (Don't forget your IT department.)

❷ What would be the impact if you could finish most projects in 25 to 50 percent less time than you typically do today by eliminating multitasking?

❸ More importantly, what would be the impact if you could double or even triple the number of projects completed in a year by synchronizing project launches with your constraint?

REFERENCES

[1] Eliyahu M. Goldratt, *It's Not Luck* (Great Barrington, MA: North River Press, 1994), pp. 270–278.

[2] Eliyahu M. Goldratt, *The Goal,* 2nd revised edition (Great Barrington, MA: North River Press, 1992), pp. 26–33.

[3] Francis Patrick, "Program Management—Turning Many Projects into Few Priorities with TOC," http://www.focusedperformance.com/articles/multipm.html, October 1999.

[4] Gerald I. Kendall and Steven C. Robbins, *Advanced Project Portfolio Management and the PMO* (Plantation, FL: J. Ross Publishing, 2003), pp. 217–220.

[5] Francis Patrick, "Program Management, and Weakness as Strength," http://www.focusedperformance.com/articles/ut06weak.html, January 2001.

FURTHER READING

The "business novels" of Eliyahu Goldratt discuss the tenets of the theory of constraints in very accessible form. The author's website, FocusedPerformance.com, contains a wealth of additional resources.

CHAPTER 36

Six Sigma and Project Management

RIP STAUFFER

Six Sigma is a data driven, project-based, team driven, and customer-focused methodology for achieving breakthrough levels of performance in strategically important processes. Six Sigma is essentially a quality initiative, in the vein of total quality management (TQM), lean manufacturing, business process reengineering (BPR), statistical process control (SPC), and continuous improvement (CI). Many of these other process quality initiatives are focused largely on the ongoing management and control of processes; many of the actions taken for improvement tend to be relatively quick turnaround, "just-do-it" reactions to emergent signals from the process.

Six Sigma is the most successfully marketed quality initiative in recent years. It packages many of the tools and concepts from other approaches, including all the quality tools mentioned in the Project Management Institute's *Guide to the Project Management Body of Knowledge (PMBOK® Guide)*. The fact that it is project-based makes it of particular interest to the project management world. Six Sigma projects tend to be longer than those of other quality initiatives—four to six months is a commonly accepted standard.

The name *Six Sigma* originated as a goal for process improvement at Motorola in the late 1980s. While organizations' perceptions of Six Sigma (and so their definitions and practices) vary, most Six Sigma approaches share some common features and concepts:

- The use of data analysis and a scientific approach to problem solving
- Project teams
- Similar project life cycles—DMAIC (Define/Measure/Analyze/Improve/Control) and DMADV (Define/Measure/Analyze/Design/Verify)

This chapter explores the history of the quality movement, the evolution of Six Sigma, and the synergy between Six Sigma (along with other initiatives and their tool sets) and project management.

THE QUALITY MOVEMENT

Seeds for Six Sigma were sown in the quality movement; while Henry Ford and Frederick Taylor were developing scientific methods for reducing work to measurable components, statisticians and physicists in industry were beginning to build statistics into a coherent set of methods for providing truly scientific measurements. The physicist Walter Shewhart was hired by Western Electric to work on the carbon microphone and to develop experimental techniques for measuring its properties. Shewhart was extremely interested in statistical methods, and he began to look for more ways to incorporate them into the manufacture of telephone components.

Shewhart realized that although there is variation in everything, there are limits to the day-to-day random variation observed in most processes, limits that could be derived statistically. In 1924, he produced the first process control chart, which set the limits of chance variability according to statistical guidelines. The chart was a brilliant innovation for management, because it indicated when management action could be taken and which types of action would be effective. These charts are now used across numerous industries from health care to hospitality, from auto making to chip making, tracking everything from laser welder performance characteristics to oxygen uptake in asthma patients, from customer satisfaction scores to quarterly results.

Figure 36-1 depicts a modern control chart. It is a fairly simple tool: a time-series plot of the measure of interest, with centerlines (averages), and upper and lower control limits (UCLs and LCLs) calculated from the data. By looking both for points outside the control limits and for nonrandom patterns within the control limits,

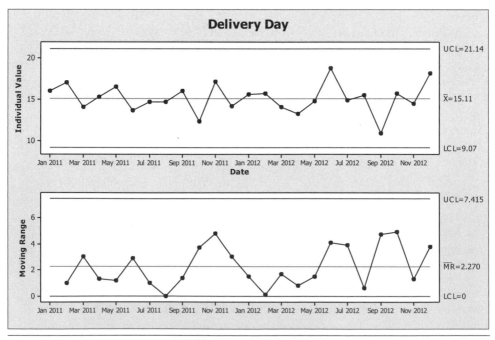

FIGURE 36-1. **CONTROL CHART**

managers can separate the common cause variation (inherent in the producing system) from assignable cause variation arising from emergent factors. In effect, the control chart articulates the "voice of the process," capturing the background noise in a way that makes it easy to discern signals when they happen.

The chart in Figure 36-1 is being used to track on-time performance, for a report that is due on the fifteenth business day of the month. On average, the process does not look too bad; the mean delivery day is "15.11," which indicates very close to on-time performance. The lower chart shows that the mean month-to-month variation is about two-and-a-quarter days. The upper and lower control limits (imagine them in red) tell us that it would not be unusual to see a month where the report was delivered on the twenty-first day; neither would it be unusual to see a month where the report was delivered on the ninth day.

The other message of the control chart is that if we do want to improve the process—if we need the average higher or lower, and want to reduce the variation—we have to make fundamental changes to the process. The process, as it is, is delivering on dates between the ninth and the twenty-first, usually closer to the fifteenth than farther away. We can predict (within limits) when we will deliver. If we want different performance, we now know that we have to make some changes to the process to get it working better. This idea, that we can set limits for predicting the behavior of processes, was the foundation of the modern quality movement.

Imagine the benefit to a project manager of having this kind of knowledge. If you were managing construction projects and knew—within very predictable limits—the amount of time it took for a given crew to complete one hundred square feet of wall framing, and how much material that crew consumed for every one hundred square feet, and its labor cost, how much better might your scheduling and resource estimates be? How much would this type of knowledge enhance your risk analysis?

Another important aspect of this knowledge is that, once you know what the real world will give you, you can compare it to what you want. Customers usually have some specified level of performance that they desire. Suppose that in our report delivery process, the customer needed the report on the fifteenth day of the month, but experience might tell them that no one can always deliver it exactly on the fifteenth, so they compromise, setting specification limits. They specify that as long as the information is delivered no sooner than six days early, it won't be obsolete by the time they include it in their report; if it's delivered any more than six days late, they won't have time to incorporate the information. Reviewing the control chart, and looking at the distribution of the control chart data compared to those specifications, we would see something like Figure 36-2. Statistically, it can be shown that an early or late delivery would be predictably rare events, considerably less than one in a hundred.

JAPANESE DEVELOPMENTS

After World War II, many of the quality initiatives of the 1930s and 1940s lost favor, as production lines were retooled for peacetime production, and civilian markets clamored for goods. In Japan, the story was different. With its industrial machinery devastated by the war, Japan was in the position of having to rebuild from the ground up. They were assisted by the United States; General Douglas MacArthur was tasked

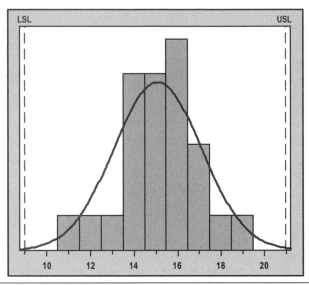

FIGURE 36-2. **PERFORMANCE "WITHIN SPECIFICATIONS"**

with helping rebuild the Japanese economy, as Secretary of State George Marshall was doing in Europe. Two of Shewhart's protégés, W. Edwards Deming and Joseph Juran, were invited to lecture and consult as part of this effort. Their influence was profound; to this day, the most prestigious quality award in Japan is the Deming Prize. Many Japanese companies began using control charts and studying customer needs. In 1960, Genichi Taguchi published a paper that "[led] unavoidably to a new definition of World Class Quality—'On Target with Minimum Variance.'"[1]

Taguchi's loss function is depicted in Figure 36-3. The vertical lines represent the upper and lower specification limits (USL, LSL) set by the customer. The two distribution curves represent predictable output from processes in statistical control. The wider one (dashed line) has its mean output on target, and most of its output will be within the specification limits, meeting customer demand. The narrower (solid line) curve is also on target, but is using about half of the specified tolerance. Much more of the output is closer to the target. Taguchi's assertion was that there is some loss (here represented as a quadratic, U-shaped function), which is very low near the target, but its magnitude accelerates as the output moves toward the specification limits.

"WHAT IS A SIGMA AND WHY DO I NEED SIX OF THEM?"[2]

The term *Six Sigma* derives from Shewhart's theories as well as from the loss function developed by Taguchi. Prior to the late 1970s, manufacturers had been striving to build "to spec," to have every part built within the specified tolerances, to have every delivery on time, to have no more than some certain number of defects in anything. Taguchi showed that it was not enough to build to spec, because variation within the specifications is costly. Take our delivery example; if one vendor could

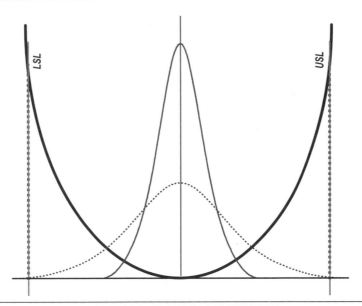

FIGURE 36-3. **TAGUCHI LOSS FUNCTION**

deliver many more of the reports exactly on the fifteenth, and was never more than three days early or late, you would have the narrower curve case on Figure 36-3.

This is where statistical terminology comes into play. In the histogram on Figure 36-2, the predictable process mean is centered between the specification limits, and there is a statistical distance of three standard deviations (three sigma) from the mean to the specification limits. Theoretically, 99.73 percent of all the reports would be delivered within the six-day limit, or about 2,700 per million. If you cut that variation in half (to create the taller curve in Figure 36-3), there would be a statistical distance of six sigma from the process center to either specification. About 70 percent would be delivered within one day of the fifteenth, 99.73 percent would be delivered within three days of the fifteenth, and only about *two reports per billion* would be delivered outside of the six-day specification.

Motorola, embarking on a long-term initiative to improve its quality, ended up using this "six sigma" capability as its goal for quality improvement. Because of the shifts in its production processes, Motorola equated six-sigma performance with what it considered to be a more realistic 3.4 parts per million defective rather than the theoretical maximum of two parts per billion. Motorola put together a phase-gated project life cycle called MAIC (measure, analyze, improve, control), and assembled a set of quality tools to use in each phase. Jack Welch of General Electric and Larry Bossidy of Allied Signal adopted the Six Sigma approach and popularized it in the business literature. As a result, the Six Sigma approach became a very marketable approach to continuous improvement. General Electric, Allied Signal and others added "D" (define) to the beginning of the life cycle acronym (becoming DMAIC), for requirements setting and chartering.

Figure 36-4 depicts some of the activities and deliverables at each phase of the DMAIC life cycle. In the define phase, the Black Belt, team and Champion (or

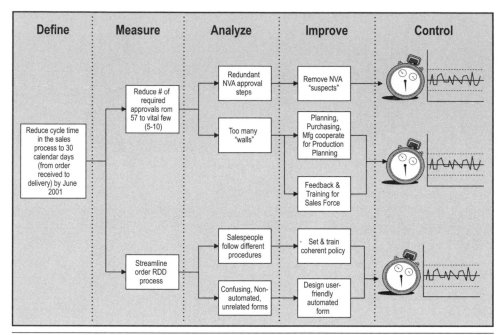

Define	Measure	Analyze	Improve	Control

FIGURE 36-4. **THE DMIAC FLOW**

Sponsor) build a business case for the project, identify the process scope and define a progress measure, and baseline the data for the progress measure. They agree on a goal and articulate an objective. These become the basis for a project charter. In the measure phase, the team develops and analyzes a detailed process map (flow chart). The Black Belt stratifies the baseline data to look for areas of interest. In the analyze phase, root cause analysis, hypothesis testing, and model building help identify the leverage points that will create the desired change in performance. In the improve phase, the team generates solutions and sets up experiments (pilots) to test them. The team studies the results of the pilot, and puts together a rollout plan to implement the total solution, full-scale. Finally, in the control phase, control plans are put in place to monitor the new process, hold the gains, measure financial or other benefits, and watch for further improvement opportunities.

SIX SIGMA AND PROJECT MANAGEMENT

What can project management bring to Six Sigma? What can Six Sigma (and other quality initiatives) bring to project management? While there are some differences in the bodies of knowledge, each discipline brings knowledge, skills, abilities, and a number of tools to the table, and elements of each discipline enhance the other.

A Quality Project Management Office

At the organizational level, any project-focused or matrix organization trying to implement a Six Sigma program would be very well served by integrating Six Sigma projects into its existing project management office (PMO). Six Sigma implementations often fail because the projects are scoped poorly, resources or data are not available, the solution is not implemented, or the projects are incorrectly assigned to Black Belts when the projects are a poor fit for DMAIC.[3] A well-run PMO, with a strategic focus and leaders experienced in scoping and resources, would avoid some of these problems. It would also be beneficial from an organizational change perspective, because Six Sigma—instead of being another add-on or "flavor of the month"— would be seen as an addition to "the "way we do business." Skilled portfolio managers in the PMO could ensure that the DMAIC and DMADV life cycles were used to best advantage on applicable projects.

At the same time, some of the process management, statistical rigor, and decision-making tools from the Six Sigma, SPC, and lean manufacturing approaches could help a PMO make more rational decisions regarding prioritization, resource allocation, logistics, and risk analysis. Understanding which aspects of certain projects are repeatable processes, and applying ongoing tracking and optimization, could greatly enhance a PMO's accuracy in scheduling and budgeting, help avoid quality problems and reduce tendencies toward "gold plating." Stochastic modeling is a very powerful tool for maximizing the potential end value of a portfolio, thus providing an excellent way to manage risks and benefits and building the optimum strategic prioritization scheme for any set of proposed projects.

As a project-based approach, it would seem intuitive that the project team leaders (Black Belts) would have—or would at least be required to learn—project management tools and skills. This is seldom the case in practice, though. Engineers, office managers, line workers, and others who get the training to become Six Sigma Black Belts usually have only Project Management Professional (PMP) certification by serendipity.

Capability Maturity Model/Project Management Maturity Model (PMMM) Improvement

For any organization trying to get beyond level 2 of the Capability Maturity Model (or any of the similar models measuring project management capability),[4] the knowledge gained through a concerted effort at quality improvement is vital. Level 3 requires standardized, managed, and defined processes; many of the tools used in the define and measure phases are very useful for studying, streamlining, standardizing, and measuring processes. What this may require is that project managers understand that some aspects of what they do are repeatable processes that can be defined using these techniques.

A level 4 process is quantitatively managed and "controlled using statistical and other quantitative techniques. Quantitative objectives for quality and process performance are established and used as criteria in managing the process. Quality and process performance is understood in statistical terms and is managed throughout the life of the process."[5] Any project manager in an organization trying to achieve level 4 in project management would need to understand and use SPC techniques (control charts, capability studies—used throughout the DMAIC model), which provide the basis for this type of quantitative management. Root cause analysis, hypothesis testing, and other statistical tools from the measure and analyze phases provide tools for managing the process, keeping it in control, and improving it. In addition, the statistical knowledge required to use these approaches would greatly enhance the project manager's understanding and skill in the area of risk analysis.

If your project management or PMO process is a key business driver and you want to take it to level 5, quality approaches become an absolute necessity. A level 5 process is:

> an optimizing process . . . a quantitatively managed capability level 4 process that is improved based on an understanding of the common causes of variation inherent in the process. The focus of an optimizing process is on continually improving the range of process performance through both incremental and innovative improvements.. . . Reaching capability level 5 for a process area assumes that you have stabilized the selected subprocesses and that you want to reduce the common causes of variation in that process.[6]

Control charts are the only set of statistical tools for understanding common and special cause; SPC, lean manufacturing, and Six Sigma provide proven approaches for both incremental and breakthrough improvements.

Project Management Training

One would think that Six Sigma Black Belts—who usually receive four to six weeks' training in team facilitation, process management and improvement tools, and statistical analysis—would also be trained as project managers. This is not always true, however. Project management skills are usually left to chance in Six Sigma. Although Black Belts are supposed to manage projects, getting project management training is considered an extra. Reasons given for this vary: reluctance to pay for more training, assumptions that project management is a skill that is easily learned on the job, assumptions that the Black Belt candidates were "already skilled project managers . . . that's why we selected them"; these top the list of the reasons given to the author.

Black Belts would gain greatly from learning formal project management skills and tools, and adopting the rigors of project management discipline. Six Sigma projects are plagued with the triple constraints of outcome, schedule, and cost, just as every other project is. Every Black Belt should be able to work up a rough overall work breakdown structure (WBS) for each phase of a DMAIC project, and a detailed WBS for each phase at the beginning of that phase, even though the final deliverables for the project itself won't be known until the improve phase. They should be able to lay out a Gantt chart and a Pert or CPM diagram, and use those tools to monitor progress toward completion. They have an excellent risk-management tool, failure mode effects analysis, which can easily be adapted for project risk management. Additionally, Black Belts need to understand that resources are not free; the ability to understand resource loading and allocation would go a long way toward managing costs associated with Six Sigma projects.

Likewise, project managers would be well served by taking some Six Sigma and lean manufacturing training. The analysis and problem-solving knowledge, skills, and abilities they would gain through a Black Belt course would greatly enhance their abilities to forecast, to plan, to deal with emergent problems quickly, and to analyze and mitigate risk.

DISCUSSION QUESTIONS

❶ For a project with which you are familiar, discuss how Six Sigma techniques might have been applied to achieve better outcomes.

❷ Comparing the Six Sigma tenets in this chapter to the *PMBOK® Guide* chapter on quality management, where are the overlaps? The disconnects?

❸ Find a Six Sigma Black Belt within your organization and compare notes. How might synergies be achieved between Six Sigma and project management?

REFERENCES

[1] D.J. Wheeler and D.S. Chambers, *Understanding Statistical Process Control*, 2nd edition (Knoxville, TN: SPC Press, 1992).

[2] B. Ragland, Presentation at Northern Trust Worldwide Operations and Technology Senior Management Meeting, 2004.

[3] L.A. Johnson, "Falling short," *Six Sigma Forum Magazine* 8, No. 3 (2009), pp. 19–22.

[4] CMMI Product Team, *CMMI for Services, Version 1.2* (Pittsburgh: Carnegie Mellon University, 2009).

[5] Ibid., p. 24.

[6] Ibid., pp. 24–25.

CHAPTER 37

Achieving Business Excellence Using Baldrige, Business Process Management, Process Improvement, and Project Management

ALAN MENDELSSOHN, PROCESS IMPROVEMENT CONSULTANT, RETIRED

MICHAEL HOWELL, ASQ, IBM CIO BUSINESS TRANSFORMATION/INFORMATION TECHNOLOGY

In the last thirty years, there have been many terms used to describe various approaches to achieving business excellence. Some of the more familiar are quality improvement, total quality control, quality management, Total Quality Management (TQM), process improvement, ISO 9000, Six Sigma, business process management (BPM), Lean, Lean Six Sigma, Baldrige, and even the more generic term *continuous improvement*. Project management, while not in the above list, becomes an enabler to help implement the different methodologies. When one takes a step back and looks at all these approaches, one finds that there are some common elements that are the keys to success, no matter what the method or methodology.

Business excellence can now be defined as a holistic, customer-focused, process-based systems approach to successfully achieving the goals of the organization. The Baldrige criteria for performance excellence provide the framework for this systems approach—what an organization must do to be successful. Embedded throughout the criteria is a proactive, integrated, process framework that uses data to make decisions. And, to continually improve all the organization's processes and keep them current with changing customer and market requirements, a process improvement approach is needed. The concepts and tools of project management are used to help implement many of the changes that are necessary to make these process improvements.

USING BALDRIGE AS A FRAMEWORK

The Malcolm Baldrige National Quality Award was established in 1987 to recognize organizations that have demonstrated excellence against a set of criteria representing best practices of role model companies. As these practices have advanced, so have the criteria.[1] The criteria provide a framework to evaluate how an organization delivers value to its customers and stakeholders and how successful it has been in doing so. Whether the criteria are used for internal self-evaluation or for assessment as part of a state or national award process, the goal should be the same—accelerate the organization forward in its journey towards business excellence. Those who focus solely on the award miss its real purpose. The most important output of an award is the feedback an organization receives identifying its strengths and its opportunities for improvement. Properly addressing the latter is what makes an organization better.

Criteria for Performance Excellence

The seven Baldrige categories that are the heart of the criteria provide the framework for an organization's approach to achieving business excellence. How they connect and integrate is shown in Figure 37-1.[2] The organizational profile at the top of figure sets the context for the way an organization operates.

The organization's leadership (category 1) uses strategic planning (category 2) processes to develop and implement strategies to support the customer focus (category 3). These categories set the organizational direction. Using the workforce addressed in the workforce focus (category 5) to accomplish the work, operations focus (category 6) approaches are implemented to achieve the desired results (category 7). The categories are linked as shown. All actions point toward results—a composite of product and process, customer-focused, workforce-focused, leadership and governance, and financial and market results. The system foundation of measurement, analysis, and knowledge management (category 4) is critical in a fact-based, knowledge-driven system for improving performance and competitiveness.

FIGURE 37-1. **THE BALDRIGE CRITERIA FOR PERFORMANCE EXCELLENCE FRAMEWORK**

The Seven Baldrige Categories

The Baldrige categories are as follows:

1. The *leadership category* examines how senior leaders' personal actions guide and sustain the organization; how senior leaders create an environment for customer engagement, innovation, and high performance; how they communicate with the workforce and key customers; and the organization's governance and how it ensures legal and ethical behavior and fulfills social responsibilities.[3]

2. The *strategic planning category* examines how the organization establishes a strategy to address its strategic challenges and leverage its strategic advantages and strategic opportunities, and deploys these throughout the organization. It also addresses how the organization makes key work system decisions and how it converts its strategic objectives into action plans.[4]

3. The *customer focus category* examines how the organization listens to the voice of the customer. It addresses how customer and market requirements and expectations are determined and how relationships are built with customers, including the key factors that lead to customer acquisition, satisfaction, loyalty, and retention.

4. The *measurement, analysis, and knowledge management category* examines how performance data and information are selected, gathered, analyzed, and improved; how the quality and availability of needed data and information are ensured; and how organizational knowledge is managed.

5. The *workforce focus category* "assesses workforce capability and capacity needs and builds a workforce environment conducive to high performance. The category also asks how the organization engages, manages, and develops its workforce to utilize its full potential in alignment with your organization's overall mission, strategy, and action plans."[5]

6. The *operational focus category* examines how the organization "designs, manages, and improves its products and work processes and improves operational effectiveness to deliver customer value and achieve organizational success and sustainability and includes effective management of operations on an ongoing basis and for the future."[6] It addresses how the organization identifies and manages its key processes and how it improves them so they are efficient and effective and stay current with changing business needs and directions.

7. The *results category* examines the organization's performance in key business areas. It measures the organization's progress toward achieving its overall strategy through implementing its approaches defined in categories 1 to 6.

Evaluation Using the Criteria

With the Baldrige criteria providing the framework for business excellence, it is important for an organization to evaluate its progress in the improvement journey. Whether doing an internal self-evaluation or as part of an external assessment, the extent to which the organization has matured in its process implementation will impact the results achieved. Figure 37-2 illustrates the steps toward mature processes.[7]

**Reacting to Problems
(0–25%)**

Operations are characterized by activities rather than by processes, and they are largely responsive to immediate needs or problems. Goals are poorly defined.

**Early Systematic
Approaches
(30–45%)**

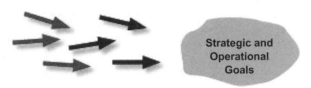

The organization is beginning to carry out operations with repeatable processes, evaluation, and improvement, and there is some early coordination among organizational units. Strategy and quantitative goals are being defined.

**Aligned
Approaches
(50–65)**

Operations are characterized by repeatable processes that are regularly evaluated for improvement. Learnings are shared, and there is coordination among organizational units. Processes address key strategies and goals.

**Integrated
Approaches
(70–100%)**

Operations are characterized by repeatable processes that are regularly evaluated for change and improvement in collaboration with other affected units. The organization seeks and achieves efficiencies across units through analysis, innovation, and the sharing of information and knowledge. Processes and measures track progress on key strategic and operational goals.

FIGURE 37-2. **STEPS TOWARD MATURE PROCESSES**

Progress is evaluated from two perspectives: process and results. The former are addressed in categories 1 to 6, and the latter in category 7.

Evaluating processes looks at the approaches used, the extent of deployment of these approaches within the entire organization, how these approaches have been improved, and how aligned and integrated the approaches are to support organizational-wide goals.

For results, the current level of performance, trends, comparisons, and integration are evaluated to assess the extent to which results address key customer, market, process, and action plan requirements.

BUSINESS PROCESS MANAGEMENT AS A FOUNDATION

Everyone engages daily in both personal and business processes. When you perform an activity repeatedly on a frequent enough basis, it is worth your attention. An example is driving to work every day. If the process is executed consistently, then the results can be predicted. Business process management is no different. It is all about managing business processes to get the desired results, to consistently and efficiently meet or exceed customer requirements, and, in so doing, enabling an organization to be successful and grow. Within the Baldrige criteria framework, BPM becomes the foundation to move an organization forward in its continuous improvement and business excellence journey.

Organizations that have not yet implemented BPM often find themselves working feverishly on everything at once. Typically, an organization has started a lot of projects, often using disciplined project management techniques and set financial expectations. The projects, however, are working in a rapidly changing environment. The more cross-functional the process, the greater the chance for miscues, and many of the projects or improvement efforts are uncoordinated, perhaps even redundant, with real savings hard to quantify. Often, work priorities shift due to the next crisis management issue or simply because of what an executive may have said. In many cases, a structured approach from which to select projects does not exist.

Business process management provides a structured approach in an environment where little structure existed before. It focuses an organization's resources on the top priority projects and on work that is aligned to the organization's vision, mission, strategies, and goals.

Overcoming the perception that BPM takes too long or that a quality system is just a theoretical exercise requires a disciplined and structured implementation. Above all else, leadership engagement and commitment is a must. Of course, marketing a few successes significantly helps to gain buy-in from those who are sitting on the fence.

Business process management provides a structured method to manage processes with data and documents, stores key work processes for easy accessibility and reuse, leverages and builds on knowledge management, captures process dependencies, uses objective process measures, and closes the gap between customer needs and actual process performance.

Implementing BPM enables an organization to control core business processes as well as the process outcome. Business process management focuses and aligns an organization on its top priorities, creates a common process language, and accelerates organizational learning. It also provides a positive return on investment by identifying and targeting process improvement and leveraging process replication across the company

Business process management implementation entails the following key steps:

- Identify top-priority, critical processes.
- Validate customer requirements.

- Model the process.
- Develop process measures.
- Monitor the process for the following:
  - Stability—consistent performance
  - Capability—meeting customer needs
  - Flexibility—for new requirements
- Manage and improve the process.

Identify Critical Processes

A process is series of repetitive and systematic actions or operations that add value and are necessary to produce and deliver a product or service. From a simplistic perspective, a process starts with an input from a supplier, work is performed, value is added, and the product or service is delivered to a customer. A business process is much more complex and is typically cross-functional in nature with multiple process levels. An activity at one level becomes a process at the next lower level. At each level, someone owns the process. Depending on the organization's process maturity, each level process owner may be accountable for the results. The concept of process ownership is important to achieving business excellence.

Top priority or critical processes are those processes that are typically operational in nature and are core to delivering a product or service to external customers. A problem with a top-priority or critical process directly results in not meeting customer requirements or expectations.

Eventually, all critical processes need to be addressed. Which one to look at first can be determined by (1) evaluating the criticality of each process to satisfying customers and achieving organizational goals, and (2) evaluating which processes are not performing as expected. The determination of the top-priority processes is extremely important. Typical corporate prioritization is done by focusing on what is "most broke" or what is receiving the most top-level scrutiny. Having a structured, disciplined approach to managing core business processes results in incremental continuous improvement, occasional radical process simplification, and a "pipeline" of projects to work on next.

Validate Customer Requirements

A customer of a process is the person who receives the product or services from the output of the process. Depending on the level of the process and where the process fits into the overall order-to-delivery of the organization, the needs of both external customers and internal customers have to be met.

In many organizations, a number of employees do not have direct interaction with the external customer. They may deal with other functional areas, management, or "next process" customer. This would be an example of an internal customer.

A requirement represents a need or a want that the customer expects to have satisfied. It is necessary to review the customer requirements frequently with customers to be sure they are specific, measurable, have not changed, and can be provided in a satisfactory format and time frame. This may involve negotiation with the customer if the above criteria cannot be met. The requirement becomes valid only

American Management Association • www.amanet.org

after agreement is reached that (1) the need can be satisfied, and (2) the party responsible for the process agrees to satisfy it. The same criteria apply in validating requirements for both internal and external customers.

In some organizations, other key stakeholder requirements may be as important as customer requirements. For example, in a healthcare environment, the needs of physicians, families, and insurance companies can play a significant role in how a hospital serves its primary customers—patients. In education, requirements of parents and other stakeholder (e.g., businesses and institutions of higher learning) could impact the way a school teaches its primary customers—students.

An organization also must carefully consider its suppliers and partners. To provide products and services that meet customer expectations and requirements consistently, employees must understand the end-to-end system and where they fit in the bigger picture.

Model the Processes

Documentation of the work processes makes them visible. All the steps necessary to achieve the final product need to be shown. A process should be described in simple terms, at a level of detail represented by four to eight activities. The process for the manager should be at a level of detail reflecting those activities that he or she will personally follow. Each activity block might represent a lower level process that must also be controlled.

In describing a process, in addition to the flow of activities and their triggering events, it is important to consider the various components that are necessary to make the different steps of the process work. These include people, systems, information and data, materials, tools and equipment, documentation, and environmental factors. Not all components apply to every process or process step. If a process is not performing properly to meet customer requirements, the activities may be correct but one or more of the components of the process could be the problem area.

When looking at any particular process, there are a number of different versions that can be considered. These versions can represent the process as defined in a procedures manual, the process as management thinks it works, the way the process is actually performed—the "as-is" process, the "ideal" process (as-is, but cleaner), or the "future state" process. The most important version to model and measure first is the "as-is" process. Since the output of a process is a direct result of what happens in the process, it is necessary to understand what is currently being done, including what is not working properly, before looking at any future state process.

In the past, processes have been documented using flowcharts. Flowcharts usually show activities, have a single symbol to represent a decision, and may identify the responsible person or function for a group of activities. This, however, is not enough. What happens to complex decisions and how are they represented? What about some of the other components of a process that are absolutely necessary if a process is to work properly?

Modeling a process has a number of benefits not available from just flowcharting. In addition to providing visual descriptions of processes, modeling addresses more complex decisions and process components; links to information technology (IT) systems, people, and other resources; uses an enterprise-wide database with a common language; permits simulation of "what if" scenarios; and can link to measures that are part of a balanced scorecard.

Develop Process Measures

Measuring process performance is important to determine if it is meeting customer requirements and to understand how the process is actually performing.

A *results indicator* measures the output of a process and determines whether a process is satisfying the customer's valid requirement, based on the customer's viewpoint as to what is most important—not what is convenient to measure or possibly an internally focused business metric. But if the process team uses a different set of indicators, its interpretation of success may be different from the customer's.

A *process indicator* is used to show whether a work process is stabilized and to provide a sense and respond capability for problems that could impact final results. This is the "voice of the process" speaking to us. It represents the process owner's view. Located upstream in the process, it alerts the team to unwanted outcomes.

If the indicators show that the targets are being met but the data show that the process is not stable, then the process owner has been favored by luck. When a process is unstable, anything can happen, and it often does. Response to this instability is usually called firefighting, and unnecessary variation is added, affecting process performance.

If the data show that a process is stable but the indicators show that the targets are not being met, then the process is not capable of achieving the desired results. It must be changed in some way. A problem-solving process is used to eliminate root causes and identify improvements to the process. Process stability is required before addressing capability issues.

Process control requires an understanding of the relationship between the process indicators and the results indicator. For example, if the forecasted date for turnover of new equipment to the customer is the result indicator being monitored, it is also important to follow the schedule for completion of each of the key activities in procuring that equipment. If the engineering activity is running late, this has a direct impact on the turnover date, unless action is taken to correct the situation. By monitoring this process indicator, the process owner can predict whether the customer's required turnover date can be met or can take appropriate action to improve the situation before it is too late. If the process is not controlled upstream of the outcome, the impact is felt downstream, but not by the people who cause the problem. Correcting the steps or activities in the engineering process that cause delays may also prevent the same factors from affecting future engineering activities.

Monitor the Process

Once the process has been defined and measures established, the process owner needs to do the following:

- Confirm the process model with all stakeholders.
- Start measuring the results and process indicators.
- Establish targets and thresholds.
- Manage and improve the process based on the data analysis from the measures.

Managing a process is an ongoing effort. The process owner has to continually confirm that the process is meeting customer requirements, especially in a changing market environment, and the process is efficiently executing so as not to waste the organization's resources. When it is not, improvements in the process are required. A process improvement approach provides the roadmap and tools to make the needed improvement.

PROCESS IMPROVEMENT

How does process improvement play a role with BPM? It all depends on how it is positioned and viewed within an organization. As part of achieving business excellence, process improvement is viewed from a problem-solving, process-by-process perspective. The benefits in integrating BPM with the problem-solving and design methodology are operational in nature: faster and cheaper. This includes root cause elimination with statistical rigor and hard dollar improvements. The integration of BPM and process improvement provides a continuous improvement loop that generates a "pipeline" for problem-solving projects (Figure 37-3) from core business process measurement and then improves the processes for continued operations and monitoring.

In using a statistical approach, however, it is necessary to weigh the depth and breadth of the use of statistics within the organization. The seven basic continuous improvement tools[8] are often more than sufficient for an organization to start with. As the organization becomes more proficient with the tools themselves, introduction of more advanced statistical methodologies is appropriate.

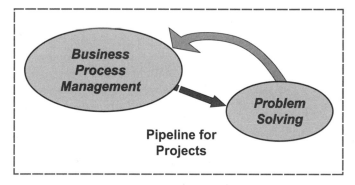

Manage core processes
Targeted implementation of a BPMS
- Core business processes defined
- Process owners given accountability
- Process metrics established
- In-depth data analysis

Continuous Process Improvement

Business Process Management

Problem Solving

Pipeline for Projects

On-going process improvement
- Process management teams
- DMAIC Teams
- Quick hits

FIGURE 37-3. **CONTINUOUS PROCESS IMPROVEMENT**

Problem solving, such as in Lean Six Sigma, is a structured, five-step approach built around the DMAIC process:

- *Define*—What is the problem?
- *Measure*—How big is the problem?
- *Analyze*—What is causing the problem?
- *Improve*—What can be done to eliminate/reduce the root cause of the problem?
- *Control*—How will the process be monitored to ensure the gains are sustained?

It does not matter which process is used: DMAIC, or a six-, seven-, or eight-step process. All good problem-solving processes have the same basic ingredients.

From a BPM system approach, process improvement is an enabler to a company's continuous improvement journey. The continuous improvement impact, if balanced correctly, can be felt in both the short and the long term. Using approaches like the design phase of the Six Sigma methods and tools in the improve phase will help achieve sustainable, long-term results. Lean tools, such as Value Stream Mapping, Standard Work, and 5S are being integrated with the original Six Sigma method, thus often referenced as Lean Six Sigma. Change management now plays a critical role in implementing solutions, and leadership must be engaged for the approach to work. Political issues and obstacles need to be addressed early. Developing, establishing, and improving processes can provide breakthrough results and increased capacity, and allow the organization to address changing customer requirements that will enable it to achieve a desired future state.

BUSINESS PROCESS MANAGEMENT, PROCESS IMPROVEMENT, AND PROJECT MANAGEMENT

Implementing the Baldrige criteria, BPM, or process improvement requires specific skill sets from quality professionals, such as "Black Belts" and Lean practitioners, involved in these efforts. Typical training for these individuals includes project management skills.

Project management skills are important because continuous improvement efforts are often project based and cross-functional in nature. The project leads are held accountable for completing projects on time and within budget (if applicable), and for delivering improvements based on customer or business requirements. This usually requires managing multiple activities at once, addressing change management issues, and meeting rigorous "tollgate" timelines. In addition, Black Belts or other quality professionals are routinely assigned multiple projects at any given time. Utilizing project management discipline, such as understanding a project's critical path and the key tasks to be completed, improves the probability of success for the projects themselves.

Business process management and process improvement are dependent on the project leads possessing the skills to successfully manage the life cycle of projects. Delivering results are absolutely critical to a program launch in order to gain credibility to the quality system initiative. Project management discipline enables project leads to successfully complete the projects and, therefore, demonstrate the much needed credibility or value to the business leaders.

American Management Association • www.amanet.org

CONCLUSION

Business excellence is a continuous improvement journey. If an organization does not keep current with changing customer and market needs, someone else will. Profitability and success are challenged, and even survival can become an issue. Only by a commitment to provide better, more responsive, innovative, and efficient products and services can an organization continually achieve business excellence.

DISCUSSION QUESTIONS

❶ Although we make the assertion that BPM is the foundation for business excellence, many organizations want to jump into other approaches and tools to reach the end state without first building the foundation. What barriers have to be overcome to be able to create a business process foundation?

❷ There appears to be a trend of the traditional boundaries of project management, quality, and other management disciplines blurring. How will this trend shape the approach to achieving business excellence in the future?

❸ With new emerging technologies, such as process modeling, workflow, and process automation, organizations are increasingly able to receive information for real-time measurement, process execution, and task management. What kind of impact will this have on achieving business excellence in the future?

REFERENCES

[1] Baldrige Performance Excellence Program, *2013–2014 Criteria for Performance Excellence* (Gaithersburg, MD: U.S. Department of Commerce, National Institute of Standards and Technology, 2013), http://www.nist.gov/baldrige.

[2] *Ibid.*, p. 1.

[3] *Ibid.*, pp. 7–8.

[4] *Ibid.*, pp. 10, 12.

[5] *Ibid.*, p. 18.

[6] *Ibid.*, pp. 22–23.

[7] *Ibid.*, p. 30.

[8] The seven basic tools are cause-and-effect diagram, flowcharts, check sheets, Pareto diagrams, histograms, control charts, and scatter diagrams. Some authors include run charts or line graphs instead of one of the other tools.

Team Building and Interpersonal Skills for Dynamic Times

PAUL C. DINSMORE, PMP, DINSMORECOMPASS

Lessons from nature abound regarding collective efforts for getting things done: bees and ants perform amazing tasks as they work in chaotic unison to achieve community goals; lions and other predators often hunt jointly to increase the poor odds against their speedy and nimble prey; and whales parade around in circles to corral schools of fish, which in turn try to elude their marine predators by flashing back and forth in darting schools. In the case of these creatures, working together is about survival. They have learned to do it through the ages, and these practices have become embedded in their DNA.[1]

For humankind, teamwork means cooperating to meet common goals; that includes all types of people doing work that calls for joint effort and exchange of information, ideas, and opinions. In teamwork, productivity is increased through synergy: the magic that appears when team members generate new ways for getting things done and that special spirit for making them happen. Teamwork is not embedded in the human DNA; therefore, in each situation that calls for it, the team needs to be built. This is where the term *team building* comes in.

The emergence of the team idea in modern times can be traced back to the late 1920s with the classic Hawthorne studies, which involved research designed to understand what happened to group workers under various conditions. The research showed that a sense of group belonging was the most significant factor that affected group performance, resulting from a sense of cohesion that came with increased worker interaction.[2]

In times past, teamwork was generally developed in settings where workers shared a common workplace and time frame. People worked at the same place, during the same hours. While that situation still exists, increasingly teams are at least partially virtual, meaning that some members may never see other important colleagues of the team. Such is the case in outsourced development of information technology (IT) projects, and in the design and construction of aircraft and ships; in both cases, the work may be scattered about the globe. This requires ways of dealing with team communications in nontraditional ways.

407

THE CASE OF VIRTUAL TEAMS

The nature of organizations is dynamic, changing faster than new editions of this book can be prepared. Some organizations are predominantly virtual settings where traditional face-to-face meetings scarcely ever take place. Virtual meetings increasingly use video, audio, and text, often with collaborative features, while meeting contents are digitally tagged so the information can be accessed promptly. Even face-to-face meetings can be recorded digitally for future reference or to share with remote members. Virtual teams face some special issues that require special attention: the project team needs to be competent in relevant communications technology; trust and rapport are a must among many stakeholders, who are spread geographically; and the project technology chosen must meet the overall project needs and be sufficiently user friendly to be appealing to team members.

The Virtual Teams Survey Report 2012 written by RW3 CultureWizard showed the profile and challenges facing professionals in the virtual environment. Here are some significant findings drawn from the survey:

- Sixty-one percent of respondents reported virtual work with individuals based both domestically and internationally.
- Respondents reported that virtual teams were most different from face-to-face teams in managing conflict (70 percent), expressing opinions (55 percent), and making decisions (55 percent).
- Time zones (78 percent) presented the greatest general hurdle to virtual teams, followed by the time required to make decisions (74 percent), different accents (69 percent), cultural differences (59 percent), and language (51 percent).
- The greatest personal challenges respondents faced were the inability to read nonverbal cues (88 percent), difficulty establishing rapport and trust (75 percent), absence of collegiality (70 percent), difficulty seeing the whole picture (65 percent), reliance on email and telephone (57 percent), and a sense of isolation (47 percent).
- The top five challenges faced during virtual team meetings were insufficient time to build relationships (79 percent), speed of decision making (73 percent), colleagues who do not participate (71 percent), different leadership styles (69 percent), and the method of decision making (55 percent).
- Only 16 percent of respondents reported that they had received training to prepare them for working on a virtual team.[3]

The challenges virtual teams face, while substantial, are not insurmountable. Here are commonsense ground rules that can help overcome the lack of in-the-room presence:

- Be aware of differing levels of language fluency.
- Speak slowly and clearly; avoid use of slang.
- Establish and communicate the agenda beforehand.
- Use visual aids during video conferencing.
- Make meetings short and objective.
- Discourage multitasking during virtual meetings.
- Develop an online directory with profiles of virtual team members.

While some of these approaches may develop intuitively or through daily practice, the effectiveness of virtual communications can be enhanced through training and coaching programs promoted by human resources departments or other facilitating parties. Selection and training of the right communication tools, along with executive support, create a promising setting for developing high-achieving virtual teams.

BENEFITS AND PITFALLS OF TEAMING—IN ALL SITUATIONS

Teamwork offers a number of concrete benefits:

- *Teamwork enhances success.* Teamwork helps your group excel at what it is doing and boosts its chances of "winning."
- *Teamwork promotes creativity.* The team approach stimulates innovation and encourages people to try new approaches to problems.
- *Teamwork builds synergy.* The mathematical absurdity "2 + 2 = 5" becomes possible.
- *Teamwork promotes trade-offs and solves problems.* Teamwork creates a problem-solving atmosphere that facilitates decisions about schedule, cost, and performance.
- *Teamwork is fun.* Working together for a common cause creates group spirit, lightens the atmosphere, and reduces tensions and conflicts.
- *Teamwork helps large organizations as well as small groups.* The team concept can be used to involve an entire company culture as well as to stimulate a small department.
- *Teamwork responds to the challenge of change.* Teams thrive on opportunities to improve performance and show how they can adapt and adjust in order to win.

There are also pitfalls to watch out for:

- *There can be negative synergy.* When the team doesn't get its act together, then synergy becomes negative and the equation becomes "2 + 2 = 3."
- *There can be excessive independence.* Poorly guided or poorly built teams wander off course and start doing their own thing as opposed to meeting overall goals.
- *Time is needed to build and maintain the team.* If company culture is not team oriented, a lot of time and effort is needed to create the team spirit.
- *Decision making may be slow.* Getting a group to make a decision on a consensus basis is a time-consuming task.

Why is teamwork increasingly important? One reason is that change—economic, societal, cultural, environmental, technological, political, and international—continues to take place at an accelerating rate. And change has a dramatic impact not only on individuals but also on organizations. Task forces, departmental teams, cross-functional teams, and project teams are replacing the cumbersome hierarchical organizational structure of the past in many organizations. Teamwork enables organizations to be nimbler, more flexible, and better able to respond swiftly and creatively to the challenge of today's competitive business environment.

Several factors have speeded this trend toward team approaches to business planning and operations:

- The success of the Japanese management style, which stresses employee involvement in all phases of the work
- The rejection by newer generations of autocratic leadership
- Rapid changes in technology that create a need for quick group responses
- Emphasis on corporate quality, which requires team effort on an organizational scale

Team building encompasses the actions necessary to create the spirit of teamwork. Oft-cited research by Tuckman and Jensen[4] indicates that the team-building process is a sequence that can be divided into five stages: forming, storming, norming, performing, and adjourning.

FIVE CLASSIC TEAM-BUILDING STAGES: STILL STANDING?

Although this view of the team-building process is not new, it appears to be standing the test of time even as social and organizational norms have evolved.

Stage 1: Forming

In this stage, the manager and the group focus more on tasks than on teamwork. They organize the team's structure, set goals, clarify values, and develop an overall vision of the team's purpose. The manager's role is to direct these efforts and to encourage group members to reach consensus and achieve a feeling of commitment.

Stage 2: Storming

This stage is less structured than the first stage. The manager broadens the focus to include both accomplishing tasks and building relationships. As the social need for belonging becomes important to group members, the emphasis is on interpersonal interactions: active listening, assertiveness, conflict management, flexibility, creativity, and kaleidoscopic thinking. The group completes tasks with a sense of understanding, clarification, and belonging, but also deals with any underlying conflicts as they begin to surface. The manager relies not only on actual authority but also on leadership skills, such as encouragement and recognition.

Stage 3: Norming

In this stage, the team-building process is more relationship-based than task-oriented. Since recognition and esteem are important for group members, the manager relies on communication, feedback, affirmation, playfulness, humor, entrepreneurship, and networking to motivate the team. Group members achieve a feeling of involvement and support.

Stage 4: Performing

At this point, the team is operating very much on its own. Management style is neither task- nor relationship-oriented, since the team members are motivated by achievement and self-actualization. The manager's role in this phase is to serve as mentor/coach and to take a long-range view of future needs. Team members focus on decision making and problem solving, relying on information and expertise to achieve their goals.

Stage 5: Adjourning

Management concern in this wrap-up stage is low-task and high-relationship. The manager focuses on evaluation, reviewing, and closure. Team members continue to be motivated by a feeling of achievement and self-actualization.

TEN RULES FOR TEAM BUILDING

The five team-building stages show how teams evolve over time. That process can be accelerated by applying the following ten principles of team building. Each principle helps create the spirit that gets people to work together cooperatively to meet goals:

1. *Identify what drives your team.* What is the driving force that makes team-work necessary? Is it an external force, such as the market? Is it internal, such as organizational demands? Is it the needs of the group itself? Is the leader the only driver? Or is it perhaps a combination of these factors?
2. *Get your own act together.* Are you a bright and shining example of team-work? Could you shine even brighter? Polish your interpersonal skills and show your teamwork talents on a daily basis.
3. *Understand the game.* All teams play games. Do you know the game and how much you can bend the rules? Each game of business is different and rules need to be rethought.
4. *Evaluate the competition.* First, know who the real market competition is. Then size it up so that your team can become competitive with a larger outside opponent.
5. *Pick your players and adjust your team.* Choose qualified players who know the basics, and teach them the skills that they don't have. Also, make sure the right team players are in the right spots.
6. *Identify and develop inner group leaders.* Team builders learn to identify inner group leadership early on. If you want to develop the full capacity of your team, then delegating, mentoring, and coaching must become part of your daily habit.
7. *Get the team in shape.* It takes practice and training to get athletic teams in shape. The same is true for other teams. Start with training in the funda-mentals of teamwork—things like active listening, communicating, and negotiating—and see that they are practiced on a daily basis.
8. *Motivate the players.* The only way to get people to do things effectively is to give them what they want. The secret is to discover what individuals really want and, as you deal with them, to relate to those desires—whether they be recognition, challenge, a chance to belong, the possibility to lead, the opportunity to learn, or other motivators.

Ten Rules		Five Phases				
		Form	Storm	Norm	Perform	Adjourn
1	Identify what drives your team	X				
2	Get your own act together	X	X	X		
3	Understand the game	X	X	X		
4	Evaluate the competition	X				
5	Pick your players and adjust your team	X	X	X	X	
6	Identify and develop inner group leaders		X	X	X	
7	Get the team in shape	X	X	X		
8	Motivate the players			X	X	
9	Develop plans	X		X		
10.	Control, evaluate, and improve			X		X

FIGURE 38-1. **TEAMBUILDING RULES THROUGH THE PHASES**

9. *Develop plans.* In teamwork, the process of planning is more important than the plan. Team members must become so involved in the planning process that they can say with conviction, "This is our plan."
10. *Control, evaluate, and improve.* Knowing the status of things at any given time is important for teams to be successful. Sometimes that's a tough task. To make sure you maintain the right spirit, involve your team members in creating your control instrument.

These ten rules apply throughout the five team-building phases. Greater emphasis, however, is appropriate during certain periods. Figure 38-1 shows the phases in which the rules tend to be most applicable.

PLAN FOR IMPLEMENTING TEAMWORK

Get People Involved

The key to successful team planning is involvement: get people involved at the outset of your team-building effort to win their personal commitment to your plan. One simple technique for involvement entails a questionnaire in which team members are asked to assess the need for team building. A sample questionnaire is shown in Table 38-1. In the test, team members rate the degree to which certain team-related problems appear. If the team is newly formed, the questionnaire should be answered from the perspective of anticipated problems. Then test results are tabulated and group discussion follows in search of a consensus on how to obtain team development. This consensus approach generates synergy when the team carries out the planned activities. In addition, potential differences are dealt with in the planning stage before resources are fully committed.

Group planning approaches are used in programs such as quality circles, total quality management, and participative management, as well as in project management. The management skills required to make these group planning efforts effective

		Low			High		Score
1.	Quality of communication among group members	1	2	3	4	5	_____
2.	Clarity of goals, or degree of "buying into" goals	1	2	3	4	5	_____
3.	Degree of conflict among group members and/or third parties	1	2	3	4	5	_____
4.	Productivity of meetings	1	2	3	4	5	_____
5.	Degree of motivation; level of morale	1	2	3	4	5	_____
6.	Level of trust among group members and/or with boss	1	2	3	4	5	_____
7.	Quality of decision-making process and follow-through on decisions made	1	2	3	4	5	_____
8.	Individuals' concern for team responsibility as opposed to own personal interests	1	2	3	4	5	_____
9.	Quality of listening abilities on part of team members	1	2	3	4	5	_____
10.	Cooperativeness among group members	1	2	3	4	5	_____
11.	Level of creativity and innovation	1	2	3	4	5	_____
12.	Group productivity	1	2	3	4	5	_____
13.	Degree that team perceptions coincide with those of upper management and vice versa	1	2	3	4	5	_____
14.	Clarity of role relationships	1	2	3	4	5	_____
15.	Tendency to be more solution- than problem-oriented	1	2	3	4	5	_____
	TOTAL						_____

Test Result: Add up your scores. If the score is over 60, then your work unit is in good shape with respect to teamwork. If you scored between 46 and 60 points, there is some concern, but only for those items with lower scores. A score of 30 to 45 indicates that the subject needs attention and that a team-building program should be under way. A score of between 15 and 30 points means that improving teamwork should be the absolute top priority for your group.

TABLE 38-1. **TEAM MEMBERS' QUESTIONNAIRE**

include interpersonal communications, meeting management, listening, negotiation, situational management, and managerial psychology.

The right planning process produces a quality plan to which the parties involved are committed. Here are some methods that enhance the planning process:

- *Creativity sessions.* Techniques for boosting creativity include brainstorming, brain-writing (a technique that has been termed "brainstorming on steroids")[5], random working, checklists, and word associations.
- *Consensus planning.* A plan reached through group discussion tends to yield a program that is well thought through, with a high probability of being implemented.
- *Decision-making models.* Formal models for making decisions can be used as a basis for planning. Some common techniques are decision trees, problem analysis, decision analysis, implementation studies, and risk analysis.

Chapter 38 • Team Building and Interpersonal Skills for Dynamic Times **413**

An effective team is built like putting together a puzzle. Individuals (like the separate puzzle pieces) match up in one-on-one contacts (like pairing up matching pieces) or find commonality to form small groups (like the subsets of the puzzle). These unite to form large groups (like the overall picture that the whole puzzle represents) and the team itself.

This means that team building, just like putting together a puzzle, requires viewing the whole range of team factors, from the characteristics and talents of individual members to the overall picture: What are the team's immediate goals and long-term objectives and how does the team fit into the larger organizational scene? Some of the concrete steps that transform groups into teams are discussed below.

Set a Good Example

Here the focus is the individual. As team leaders concern themselves with developing their own skills and knowledge bases, then the other pieces of the puzzle begin to fall into place. All team leaders communicate their management philosophies to some extent by setting both overt and subliminal examples.

The manager who trusts subordinates and delegates authority to key project members can expect others to emulate that style. Likewise, an open give-and-take approach fosters similar behavior in the team and in others associated with the project under way. Through the team leader's own actions, team members' best behavior is called to the forefront.

Coach Team Members

Coaching requires some schooling in the "different-strokes-for-different-folks" philosophy, which assumes that people with different temperaments react differently to a standardized "shotgun" approach. Thus, each individual needs to be singled out for a special shot of custom-tailored attention in order for coaching to be effective.

A coaching session can be as simple as a chat with a subordinate who made a mistake about why something happened and what can be done to keep it from recurring. It can be a formal interview by the manager, who goes into the session with a tailor-made approach. Or it can be a formal appraisal session using classic management tools, such as job descriptions and performance standards.

Train Team Members

Training may involve small groups or the overall group or may incorporate all the stakeholders involved in the team's efforts. Informal training sessions can be conducted in various forms, such as lectures, roundtable discussions, and seminars.

Lectures, though one-dimensional, can present large amounts of information in a short period of time. Lectures given by experts can bring top-quality information to the team members. When the speaker is well known, the lecture stimulates special interest.

Roundtable discussions are open-forum debates on pertinent subjects. They give participants a chance to air their views and present their opinions and ideas frankly. The goal may be to establish a consensus or to provide a basis for planning in-depth training programs.

Seminars or workshops combine the informational content of the lecture with opportunities for participation offered by the roundtable. In seminars or workshops, information is dispensed in smaller doses, interspersed with group discussions and debates. Seminars are established around a longer time frame than lectures or round-table discussions. Two- to three-day seminars are the most popular, but one-day events are acceptable, and five-day seminars are right for more in-depth coverage.

Set Up a Formal Team-Building Program

Of the approaches aimed at heightening team synergy, a formal team-building pro-gram is apt to bring the best results because the longer program duration provides greater opportunity for retention of concepts as they are reworked throughout the program, while on-the-job application of the concepts provides timely feedback. In-depth treatment can be given to subjects of interest, and enough time is available to build a consensus among participants and develop interpersonal relations.

THE KEY TO SUCCESSFUL TEAMWORK

Teamwork depends heavily on the interpersonal skills of the members. In a team setting, this personal interaction takes on a special importance because the number of relationships among members is sharply increased. Sometimes this creates a traffic problem. Just as vehicle traffic flows more smoothly when drivers have developed their abilities, observe protocol, and behave courteously, the same is true in team situations where members have learned how to work together skillfully and cooperatively.

What are some of the skills that each team "driver" needs to operate effectively in a team situation? They include listening, applying techniques to deal with inter-personal conflict, negotiating, and influencing.

Listening

Communication, no matter how clear and concise, is wasted unless someone is lis-tening actively to the communicator's message. When team members know how to listen actively, overall effectiveness is boosted. Here is the attitude that represents good listening:

> I am interested in what you are saying and I want to understand, although I may not agree with everything you say. You are important as a person, and I respect you and what you have to say. I'm sure your message is worth listening to, so I am giving you my full attention.

Here are other listening pointers:

- Maintain eye contact.
- Don't interrupt.
- Keep a relaxed posture.

Good listening also requires the listener to focus on both the communicator's content and feelings and then to extract the essential message being conveyed.

Dealing with Interpersonal Conflict the Classic Way

Interpersonal conflict can occur whenever two or more people get together. It's an inevitable part of team dynamics. There are five classic techniques for dealing with interpersonal conflict:

1. Withdrawing (pulling out, retreating, or giving up)
2. Smoothing (appeasing just to keep the peace)
3. Bargaining (negotiating to reach agreement over conflicting interests)
4. Collaborating (objective problem solving based on trust)
5. Forcing (using power to resolve the conflict)

Application of these techniques depends on the situation. Effective team members recognize that conflict is inevitable and rationally apply appropriate conflict resolution modes in each given situation. Here are some of the applications:

- Use *withdrawing* when you cannot win, when the stakes are low, to gain time, to preserve neutrality or reputation, or when you win by delay.
- Use *smoothing* to reach an overarching goal, to create an obligation for a trade-off at a later date, to maintain harmony, to create good will, or when any solution will do.
- Use *bargaining* (also called conflict negotiation) when both parties need to be winners, when others are as strong as you, to maintain your relationship with your opponent, when you are not sure you are right, or when you get nothing if you do not make a deal.
- Use *collaborating* when you both get at least what you want and maybe more, to create a common power base, when knowledge or skills are complementary, when there is enough time, or where there is trust.
- Use *forcing* only when a "do or die" situation exists, when important principles are at stake, when you are stronger (never start a battle you can't win), to gain status or demonstrate power—and when the relationship is unimportant.

Beyond Conflict Resolution

A different twist for dealing with team issues is Appreciative Inquiry (AI), which helps to shorten the "storming" period by encouraging teams to focus on possibilities instead of problems. The AI 4D process—discover, dream, design, deliver—meshes well with project management processes, and assists in building trust within teams and across the organization.[6] Excellent resources on AI are available on the Web.[7]

Negotiating

Team members are likely to find themselves dealing with both third-party and in-house situations that call for major negotiation skills. The type of negotiation that tends to be effective in team settings is called principled negotiation. This is negotiation in which it is assumed that the players are problem solvers and that the objective is to reach a wise outcome efficiently and amicably.

Principled negotiation also assumes that the people will be separated from the problem, that premature position-taking will be avoided, that alternative solutions

American Management Association • www.amanet.org

will be explored, and that the rules of the negotiation will be objective and fair. This means focusing on interests rather than on positions and implies fully exploring mutual and divergent interests before trying to converge on some bottom line. The tenet *invent options for mutual gain*—calling for a creative search for alternatives—is also fundamental to principled negotiation.

Influencing

In team situations, individual authority lags well behind the authority of the group. Therefore, effective teams depend on the ability of members to influence one another for the common good. Influence management includes the following principles:

- *Play up the benefit.* Identify the benefit of your proposal for the other party (factors such as more challenge, prestige, or visibility, or the chance for promotion or transfer). Then emphasize that benefit in conversations so that the message is communicated.
- *Steer clear of Machiavellian tactics.* Avoid manipulation. Concentrate on influencing with sincerity and integrity.
- *Go beyond "I think I can."* Successful influence managers don't waste time questioning whether things can be done. Their efforts are aimed at how the task will be performed and what needs to be done to make it happen.
- *Put an umbrella over your moves.* Effective influencing hinges on strategic planning, to give direction and consistency to all influencing efforts.
- *Tune in to what others say.* Successful influence managers learn to identify others' expectations and perceive how given actions contribute toward fulfilling those expectations.
- *Size up your plans for congruency.* Make sure there is a fit between proposed actions, testing your plans for consistency, coherence, and conformity.
- *Remember: "Different strokes for different folks."* Be sure to adapt your approach to fit each person's individual characteristics. Size up your targets and adjust your presentation to individual needs.
- *Watch your language!* Be careful with what you say and how you say it. Screen out pessimism and other forms of negativity, putting positive conviction into what you say to increase the impact of your message.

When team members are schooled in these basics, teamwork is likely to come about rapidly. Synergy is generated as people work together to meet common goals.

FAST TRACK TO TEAMING

In projects, just as in sports, teamwork is developed and honed to excellence through practice sessions and in day-to-day settings. Practice sessions for developing teamwork are built into training and are part of the formal team building program mentioned earlier in this chapter. Yet aside from the purely practice-session approach used in training, daily activities provide numerous settings for creating team climate and interaction. Kick-off meetings, review sessions, and interface meetings are examples of settings for spotlighting the team approach.

If a jump start is required to get things moving in environments where teams must ramp up rapidly (joint ventures, ad hoc teams, new projects), then experiential workshops are highly recommended. These can be of the ropes-course, adventure-course variety, or tamer versions done in indoor settings. The important factor is that is that task simulation be the focus of the training, thus requiring joint planning and execution of activities, leading to specific results.

In successful team-building undertakings, once the team concept has been kicked off through an experiential learning event, insights and lessons learned are then funneled into the formal team building program. This way, the teaming effort is not only jump-started, but further developed toward a long-lasting synergistic relationship among team members.

DISCUSSION QUESTIONS

❶ In the classic team building model (forming, storming, norming, performing, adjourning), what factors might upset the sequence outlined? How can these be overcome?

❷ Classify the ten rules of team building in two categories: "must do" and "highly desirable to do." Discuss with colleagues.

❸ Of the five conflict resolution techniques, which is most commonly used on most projects? Which in your opinion is the most effective? Are there circumstances where you have used a less desirable method with a good outcome?

REFERENCES

[1] Eric Bonabeau and Christopher Meyer, "Swarm intelligence: a whole new way to think about business," *Harvard Business Review* (May 2001), pp. 107–114.

[2] "The Hawthorne Studies," World Academy Online, http://worldacademyonline.com/article/27/383/the_hawthorne_studies.html.

[3] "2012 Virtual Teams Survey Report," RW3 Culture Wizard, http://rw-3.com/2012VirtualTeamsSurveyReport.pdf.

[4] B.W. Tuckman and M.A. Jensen, "Study of small group development revisited," *Group and Organizational Studies* 2, No. 2 (1977), pp. 419–427.

[5] "What is Brainwriting?" University of Central Oklahoma Academic Affairs, http://www.uco.edu/academic-affairs/cqi/files/docs/facilitator_tools/brainhan.pdf, 2003.

[6] Jeannette Cabanis-Brewin and Paul Dinsmore, "Appreciative inquiry: a new model for teams," presentation at Rio de Janeiro, Brazil, November 18, 2009. See also materials on AI by J. Cabanis-Brewin in Timothy Kloppenborg, *Contemporary Project Management* (Mason, OH: South-Western Cengage Learning, 2009) p. 371.

[7] Weatherhead School of Management, Case Western Reserve University, "What Is Appreciative Inquiry?" http://appreciativeinquiry.case.edu/intro/whatisai.cfm.

CHAPTER 39

Cultural Challenges in Managing International Projects

PAUL C. DINSMORE, PMP, DINSMORECOMPASS

MANUEL M. BENITEZ CODAS, CONSULTANT

The shrinking business world has presented the project management community with a hodgepodge of cultural and communication challenges. Groups from far-flung corners of the earth find themselves intimately coexisting as they implement gigantic civil works and bring complex global systems on line. The cultural challenges vary from basic ethnic differences to language and other communication barriers, including subtle unspoken forms.

A backhanded "V for victory" sign, for instance, is an uncomplimentary gesture in Australia. In Brazil, the American "A-OK" sign is also offensive. These are lessons that some presidents, diplomats, and businesspeople have learned the hard way. Awareness of such cross-cultural subtleties can spell success or failure in international dealings.

Projects conducted in international settings are subject to cultural, bureaucratic, and logistical challenges just like conventional domestic projects are. In fact, project management approaches to international ventures include the same issues common to domestic projects. Under both circumstances, successful project management calls for performing the basics of planning, organizing, and controlling. This also implies carrying out the classic functions outlined in the Project Management Institute's *Guide to the Project Management Body of Knowledge (PMBOK® Guide)* of managing scope, schedule, cost, quality, communications, human resources, contracting and supply, stakeholders, and risk, as well as the integration of these areas across the project life cycle.

Understanding culture is the starting point for planning for the challenges that face international projects. The *American Heritage Dictionary* defines culture as "the totality of socially transmitted behavior patterns, arts, beliefs, institutions, and all other products of human work and thought characteristic of a community or population." For an organization, culture may be more simplistically perceived as the guiding beliefs that determine the "way we do things around here." The challenge in international project settings revolves around the fact that projects are usually made up of multiple organizations, thus involving multiple organizational cultures in settings that place several ethnic or country-based cultures in contact with one another. An example is an Anglo-American joint venture in Saudi Arabia, working with Japanese and Indian subcontractors.

FACTORS REQUIRING SPECIAL ATTENTION IN CROSS-CULTURAL SETTINGS

Here are the primary factors that affect the management of globalized projects: functional redundancy, political factors, the expatriate way of life, language and culture, additional risk factors, supply difficulties, and local laws and legislation.

Functional redundancy means the duplication or overlap of certain functions or activities. This may be necessary because of contractual agreements involving technology transfer requiring "national counterparts." Language or the organizational complexity of the project may also be responsible for creating functional redundancy. Special attention is called for, therefore, in managing the project functions of human resources and communications.

Political factors in international projects are plagued with countless unknowns. Aside from fluctuations in international politics, project professionals are faced with the subtleties of local politics, which often place major roadblocks in the pathway of attaining project success. In terms of classic project management, this means reinforcing the communications function in order to ensure that all strategic and politically related interactions are appropriately transmitted and deciphered.

The expatriate way of life refers to the habits and expectations of those parties who are transferred to a host country. This includes the way of thinking and the physical and psychological needs of those people temporarily living in a strange land with different customs and ways of life. When the differences are substantial, this means making special provision for a group of people who would otherwise refuse to relocate to the site, or, if transferred on a temporary basis, would remain highly unmotivated during their stay. The basic project management factors related to the expatriate way of life include communications, human resources, and supply. Personal safety issues may affect the coming and going of expatriates and family members.

Language and culture include the system of spoken, written, and other social forms of communication. Included in language and culture are the systems of codification and decodification of thoughts, beliefs, and values common to a given people. Here all the subtleties of communications become of special importance. Religion must be considered, as well. For instance, in Islamic countries, Friday is equivalent to Sunday elsewhere; some Muslim-majority countries have their weekend on Thursday and Friday, others on Friday and Saturday. Ramadan means fasting from sunrise to sundown, and separation of areas for men and women is the norm. In Israel, Saturday is the day of rest and the "weekend" is a fluid period a day and a half long (although formally establishing a two-day weekend has been discussed).[1]

Additional risk factors may include personal risks such as kidnapping, local epidemics, and faulty medical care. Political turmoil, coups d'état, terrorism, and local insurgencies are also critical risk factors to be considered in some settings. Rapid swings in political and economic situations, or peculiar local weather or geology, are also potential uncertainties. The obvious basic project management tenet in this case is risk management, but often companies doing business internationally fail to include locally knowledgeable stakeholders in risk identification.

Supply difficulties encompass all the contracting, procurement, and logistical challenges that must be faced on the project. For instance, some railroad projects must use the new railway itself as the primary form of transportation for supplies. In other situations, waterways may be the only access. Customs regulations present major problems in many project settings. A new concept in logistics may need to be pioneered for a given project. Contracting and supply on international projects normally calls for an "overkill" effort, since ordinary domestic approaches are normally inadequate. This usually requires highly qualified personnel and some partially redundant management systems heavily laced with follow-up procedures. Heavy emphasis is needed in the areas of contracting and supply.

Local laws and legislation affect the way business is done on international projects. They may even affect personal habits (such as abstaining from drinking alcoholic beverages in Muslim countries). Here the key is awareness and education so that each person is familiar with whatever laws are applicable to his or her area. In this case, the project management tenets that require special attention are communications and procurement.

Issues of religion, politics, race, nationalism, and sexual orientation are specific influences that not only affect the culture of a project, but also are part of a broader trend toward multiculturalism, which calls for recognition and positive accommodation of individual and group differences through "differentiated rights." When a project developed in one cultural context receives team members of other religions, races, or sexual orientations, or when expatriate workers encounter a culture unfriendly to them, project outcomes can suffer if these issues are not appropriately planned for and managed.

COMMUNICATION AGREEMENT: A CASE IN POINT

A consulting contract carried out in September 2012 presented a peculiar communications stumbling block for members of a Paraguayan consulting firm. Hired by a Korean forestry company to carry out surveys and feasibility studies in Paraguay, the consultants were faced with virtual communication challenges between the Korean client and the Paraguayan consultants, who were receiving technical support from a Spanish specialist. The forestry project under study was estimated at $30 million, and the feasibility consulting fees were set at $100,000. Field surveys were carried out at five different sites covering an area of five hundred square kilometers.

The different time zones of Paraguay, Spain, and Korea presented an initial obstacle. Audio conferences among the parties invariably meant that at least one of these stakeholders would have to be awake very early in the morning or late at night. The quality of these verbal communications often lacked clarity, as all were speaking in English, their non-native tongue. The audio-conferencing also lacked technical fidelity, which further garbled the ability to understand one another.

An additional conflictive factor involved the tone that the Korean client representative used both in verbal and written communication. It was described by the Paraguayan lead as well as the Spanish technical specialist as "harsh, authoritative, and demanding." In an attempt to improve the quality of communications, the

PMBOK® Areas	Internationally Sensitive Factors						
	Functional Redundancy	Political Factors	Expatriate Way of Life	Language and Culture	Additional Risk Factors	Supply Difficulties	Local Laws and Legislation
Scope							
Schedule							
Cost							
Quality							
Communications	X	X	X	X			X
Human Resources	X		X				
Contracting and Supply			X			X	X
Risk					X		
Stakeholders		X	X		X		
Integration	X	X	X	X	X	X	X

TABLE 39-1. **RELATIONSHIP OF INTERNATIONALLY SENSITIVE FACTORS TO THE BASIC CONCEPTS OF THE** *PMBOK*® *GUIDE*

Paraguayan consultants proposed a "communications protocol" establishing timing for video conferencing, telephone calls, and templates for reports. In developing this protocol, it was discovered that the Korean client's English had been learned from American soldiers stationed in Korea in the 1950s. With the communications protocol in place and the understanding that the Korean's tone of voice was not meant to be offensive, the feasibility project was completed within the thirty days scheduled.

It is apparent from Table 39-1 that in terms of classic project management, special emphasis is required on international projects in the areas of communications, contracting and supply, human resources, risk, and stakeholder management. Since all of the project management areas—including the basic areas of managing scope, schedule, cost, and quality—are interconnected (a communications breakdown affects quality, for instance), extra diligence is called for in managing communications, contracting and supply, human resources, and risk. A conventional approach to managing these areas will be inadequate for international projects.

A MODEL FOR INTERCULTURAL TEAM BUILDING

The challenge in international team building boils down to creating a convergence of people's differing personal inputs toward a set of common final outputs. This means developing a process that facilitates communication and understanding between people of different national and ethnic cultures. Making this process happen signifies the difference between success and failure on international projects.

Individuals' inputs are factors like personal and cultural values, beliefs, and assumptions. They also include patterns of thinking, feeling, and behaving. Expectations, needs, and motivations are also part of people's inputs into any given system. The outputs are the results or benefits produced by a given system. They may be perceived as a combination of achievements benefiting the individuals, the team, the organization, and the outside environment. Intercultural team building thus calls for developing and conducting a program that will help transform the participants' inputs into project outputs.

SOME GLOBAL CONSIDERATIONS

The groundswell toward globalization stems from a number of factors: advances in transportation and communications technologies, international trade agreements, international standards replacing national standards that impeded the movement of goods and services, and open doors toward a more globalized economy. Increasingly, project managers will find themselves working in a global and culturally challenging context without ever leaving home.

While the trends toward globalization of project management and related technologies such as the construction industry are apparent, there still remain basic differences in the way business is performed from one country to the next. A contrast between the United States and Japan is noted, for instance, when examining the relationship between general contractor and architects. This relationship is traditionally adversarial in the United States, as is reflected by the habitual finger-pointing that goes on at the end of contracts, sometimes resulting in litigation. In contrast, in Japan these relationships are much more cooperative in nature; there is a certain congeniality between design and construction. Another contrast is that mutual risk-taking between contractors and clients is a more common practice in Japan and Europe than in the United States. Meanwhile, partnering and alliancing—a form of mutual risk-taking—is growing in the United States.

Information technology projects became increasingly globalized, largely due to massive outsourcing of services to parts of the world where the expertise exists and cost is less than in the country of origin. Some manufacturing projects are highly globalized, both in terms of development as well as fabrication. Such is the case in aircraft manufacturing, where components are developed and manufactured in sundry parts of the world and then consolidated at a central location.

The way technical information is developed and transferred also affects how business is performed and consequently how projects are managed and implemented. Various systems or models are in place for generating and transferring knowledge in different parts of the world. Here are some of the models applicable to the construction industry. In general terms, the basic models may be called the European, the North American, and the Japanese. (These terms are used only to identify trends, as all three models can be found in most countries.) The characteristics of the models are as follows:

- The European model: In Europe, highly structured, formal, and centralized national systems exist for generating and disseminating technical knowledge.

Responsibilities are clearly defined, with specific national organizations charged with generating research, while other organizations take care of transferring the result to industry. The Swedish system is a typical example, with the National Swedish Institute for Building Research responsible for knowledge generation, and the Swedish Institute for Building Documentation responsible for dissemination. National systems in Europe are often jointly financed by government and industry.

- The North American model: The system in North America is less formal than in Europe. There is, in fact, little coordination in the construction research effort in North America. In contrast with the European model, advanced construction knowledge is mainly generated at the university level. The dissemination to industry is largely performed by broad-based engineering or trade associations, such as the American Society of Civil Engineers and the Construction Industry Institute. The technical work is carried out in these associations partially by committees made up of volunteers.

- The Japanese model: In the Japanese model, research is concentrated in a handful of integrated companies that dominate Japanese construction, where technology development is considered a significant competitive tool. Therefore, as much as $100 million is invested annually by those companies, which is considered proprietary and subject to commercial confidentiality. Companies invest in research to attain competitive advantage.

In spite of these differences in philosophy and style, globalization is evident at every level of the construction industry—from material, through manufactured goods, to services. The general trend in international industrial research and development is toward strategic alliances and joint ventures to reduce the risk factor and share the spiraling costs.

Governments are now changing previous policies aimed at achieving regional goals in favor of sponsoring research and development at the multinational level. Examples are projects such as Airbus and jointly funded research and development (R&D) programs underwritten by the European community. While there is sharing going on, which points to increased globalization, the fight for the competitive edge is always under way.

Another factor that influences managing projects internationally is the increasingly active role being taken by the owner organizations in the management of their projects. In the case of developing countries, this often reflects a national policy aimed at attaining greater managerial and technical capability so as to be less dependent on the developed world. Owners in such countries have a need for contracting services in order to get their projects completed as well as for transferring experience to their own organizations.

The globalization of project management information and know-how takes place through independently published literature and through two major internationally recognized organizations that are dedicated exclusively to the field of project management—the Project Management Institute (PMI) and the International Project Management Association (IPMA)—both of which are affiliated with numerous other organizations with related interests.

INTEGRATING TWO CULTURES

While globalization is an ongoing influence on the management of international projects, success depends primarily on giving the proper emphasis to those factors that are particularly vulnerable in cross-cultural settings and on building teams capable of dealing with the challenges presented.

This discussion is drawn from the experience of coauthor Manuel M. Benitez Codas in the management of a binational project in South America that involved the merging of cultures of a project jointly owned by the governments of Brazil and Paraguay, bordering a river of staggering hydroelectric potential, the Paraná.

Binational projects are products of hard political processes that involve long and difficult negotiations. In most cases each side has a different perception about the adopted solution, and during the project phase each side may try to "win back" some of the points initially "lost" at the negotiating table. The final diplomatic agreements are lengthy texts rich in political rhetoric and poor in operational and technical considerations. This sets the stage for conflict during the implementation phase. The need for strong communications and stakeholder management becomes immediately evident in such a setting. An additional complicating factor is the fact that diplomatic documents contain writing "between the lines" and are consequently not easily decipherable by project managers and engineers.

Most binational agreements for developing projects state a philosophy of equity regarding the division of the work to be executed by each side. The unclear definition of what "equal parts" means is the prime source of inbred interest-based conflicts, which also affect the culture of the project.

THE DEVELOPMENT OF A PROJECT CULTURE

Experience in managing binational projects indicates that, for cultural convergence to take place, managers of both sides have to understand the culture of the other side by analyzing the different patterns that make up that culture. This means learning the other country's history, geography, economy, religion, traditions, and politics. Both sides, therefore, need to become aware of the differences involving educational level, professional experience, experience on this kind of project, knowledge of the language, and the country's way of life.

Aside from this information, which can be readily obtained and assimilated, other perceptions require consideration, such as beliefs, feelings, informal actions and interactions, group norms, and values. These factors strongly affect behavior patterns. A simple way of tabulating the different factors that affect cultural behavior is shown in Figure 39-1. Although the judgment criteria are basically subjective, the figure pinpoints some of the basic differences in culture that affect managerial behavior. In the binational situation used as a basis for this discussion, both sides filled out the charts and jointly evaluated the results.

Based on the analysis of the cultural differences, behavioral standards are developed. The objective is to define a desirable behavior for a "project culture" most suitable to the project objectives. In other words, cross-cultural team building must take place so that the individuals' inputs can be effectively channeled to meet the

Characteristic	Country 1 — Values					Country 2 — Values				
	Min 1	2	3	4	Max 5	Min 1	2	3	4	Max 5
Gregariousness			X					X		
Technically Oriented		X							X	
Formal Behavior		X					X			
Consensus-Oriented					X					X
Internal Project Experience	X					X				
Rational Behavior	X									X
Non-nationalistic Posture		X							X	
TOTAL			16					24		

FIGURE 39-1. **EVALUATION OF CULTURAL PATTERNS OF TWO COUNTRIES INVOLVED IN A JOINT VENTURE**

project goals. Forming a project culture is a project in itself; therefore, it requires a clear objective, a schedule, resources, and a development plan. A document such as a standard of conduct is recommended to be submitted and approved by team members. A standard of conduct committee is recommended to deal with eventual violations. Its implementation becomes the responsibility of the management team. The objective of building a project culture is to attain a cooperative spirit, to supplant the our-side-versus-your-side feeling with a strong "our project" view. The project culture is developed around the commonalities of both groups, identified in the analysis shown in Figure 39-1. As other desirable traits are identified, they are developed and refined through training programs designed to stimulate those traits.

PROJECT CULTURE THROUGH THE PROJECT LIFE CYCLE

Culture on international projects establishes itself during the early stages of the project. The participative process in the development of the work breakdown structure and the project activities network can stimulate the "our project" spirit. It is also then that the first problems arise. Problems at this stage are relatively easy to resolve, because enthusiasm on the part of the team members is generally high. The cultural model to be established at this stage is that of strong cooperation of all parties where and when necessary, in the spirit of "all for one, one for all."

If some individuals at this stage show uncooperative attitudes, project managers should seriously consider taking them off the project, because if they create problems in "blue-sky" conditions, they may be impossible to work with when "stormy weather" appears. During the maturing stages of international projects, when the organization is well defined and each unit or department is supposed to take care of its own tasks, the culture tends to become competitive as project groups try to show efficiency in relation to the other groups. Problems mainly arise at this stage because of unbalanced workloads. Some groups may claim to be overworked, while others have little work to do. Strong coordination and regular follow-up meetings are required during these intermediate project stages.

The final stage of the project is particularly difficult in terms of cultural integration. There is less work to do, and people are leaving to go on to other new international projects. At this point, project managers are hard-strapped to maintain the spirit of the remaining group. This is the moment for the managers to show their leadership capabilities to make sure that the final activities of the project are performed with the same efficiency as the previous ones.

DISCUSSION QUESTIONS

❶ From the following list of cross-cultural factors, choose the three factors that you deem most critical in an international setting: functional redundancy, political factors, the expatriate way of life, language and culture, additional risk factors, supply difficulties, and local laws and legislation. Discuss with your study group.

❷ In globalized project settings, what steps need to be taken to ensure the generation of a healthy "project culture"?

REFERENCES

[1] Ethan Bronner, "Israel debates two-day weekends, and its lifestyle," *New York Times* online, http://www.nytimes.com/2011/07/07/world/middleeast/07israel.html?_r=0, July 6, 2011.

FURTHER READING

Christine Congdon, "How culture shapes the office," *Harvard Business Review* (May 2013) http://hbr.org/2013/05/how-culture-shapes-the-office/.

Taylor H. Cox and Stacy Blake, "Managing cultural diversity: implications for organizational competitiveness," *Academy of Management Executive* 5, No. 3 (1991), pp. 45–56.

G. Hofstede, *Cultures and Organizations* (New York: McGraw Hill, 1997).

Andy Molinsky, "Common language doesn't equal common culture," *Harvard Business Review* Blog, April 3, 2013, http://blogs.hbr.org/2013/04/common-language-doesnt-equal-c/.

CHAPTER 40

Social Networking Tools
An Introduction to Their Role in Project Management

ALAN LEVINE, CHIEF INFORMATION OFFICER, JOHN F. KENNEDY CENTER FOR THE PERFORMING ARTS, AND CHAIRMAN OF THE BOARD, TESSITURA NETWORK, INC.

The trend I noticed in our workplace developed gradually, starting with one or two people and spreading. But the revelation of it came suddenly, just before the phenomenon reached critical mass.

I walked into an office at the Kennedy Center, where our software developers sat in a U-shaped arrangement facing the walls with an open space in the center, which made it easy to see what everyone was doing. I must have been unusually quiet, because nobody "alt-tabbed" to another screen when I entered the room. As I looked around, two of the developers were using instant messaging. Another was reading a blog written by one of the lead architects of the software environment he was working in. All three were hard at work. Instead of working "heads down" trying to solve the day's challenges, they were reaching out in new ways: asking questions, sharing ideas, and getting immediate help from other developers, inside and outside the organization. They were going directly to the best source of information, wherever it might be. On its own, without directives, the team had reinvented itself and its primary means of communicating and collaborating. The team had also extended its reach and the resources available to it—at virtually no cost!

This was a sea change from the traditional hierarchical, email-driven ways of the immediate past. It also represented a significant acceleration in the flow of information. Perhaps just as important was who the team was reaching. The universe of contacts they could access had grown. They were going right to the source of expertise, where before they had been limited to the people in the room, those elsewhere that they had a personal relationship with, or the support person who answered the phone at a vendor service desk. Companies that had carefully shielded their lead developers and architects from informal, regular, and direct contact learned that the fastest road to relevant innovation and market acceptance is to break down traditional barriers.

Collaborative and social networking technologies are making it possible for them to do so.

The benefit is bidirectional: customers gain access to personal knowledge and answers right from the original creators, and those creators gain a direct understanding of customer perspectives and needs. My team had quickly learned to take advantage of the availability and access to people and information. There was no question that this accelerated our project success.

Since that early revelation, the state of the art has steadily evolved. We have now reached the threshold of Social 2.0, characterized by the dominance of the "news-feed." Rather than reach out directly, we allow relevant information to find us, at the time when it is most useful and meaningful. We "follow" or "like" various people, topics, keywords, hash tags, and even business objects such as tasks, a section of source code, a physical asset, an order, an invoice, a document, or a customer. Feed engines built into project management and service management tools or enterprise applications such as CRM and ERP systems then surface information likely to be relevant to us as they are posted by other individuals, as their status changes, or as they are updated by system transactions. Rather than communicate directly or publish, we (or our systems) "post" and those posts instantly are available to anyone that might need them, and are fully searchable by anyone seeking information. In the old model, project management was designed for managers; you were a slave to your email. In the new model, we have project management designed for project workers; individuals have control, we choose who and what to follow; we choose the information to be pushed to us rather than constantly seeking it out.

McKinsey estimates that "30% of current total e-mail time could be repurposed by moving communication to a social collaboration platform, freeing up 8% of the workweek for more productive activities. Information Searching Time could be reduced by as much as 35%, freeing up 6% of the workweek."[1] What are the underlying factors that make this paradigm productive and embraceable, and what are the best ways to leverage these capabilities for project management?

SOCIAL NETWORKING AND PROJECT MANAGEMENT PRACTICE

An important, if not the most important, key to successful project management is the timely receipt and distribution of complete and accurate tidbits of information from and to all the right people in a useful format. In an ironic twist of fate, this is also one of the most challenging aspects of project management. There are many well-understood reasons for this project participants are busy and see status reporting and updates as an imposition; for many, such writing is outside of their comfort zone and thus intimidating; for others, information is power, and the withholding of information means others must pay homage, or at least attention, to you.

There may also be less obvious motivations. I'm reminded of the story of the newlywed wife who, wanting to quickly establish her place in her husband's life, decides the best route is through his stomach. She asks her mother-in-law for his favorite recipes. The mother-in-law, not wanting to refuse outright, provides her with the recipes. But no matter how much effort the young wife exerts, these dishes that mean so much to her husband never taste quite right. Years later, she learns that her mother-in-law, not wanting to be supplanted in her son's affections, had left out one or two key details from each recipe.

Project management has traditionally been a top-down means of coordination and communication, which often engendered manifestations of these very same issues. Asking for status reports or metrics, we ran smack into differing agendas, motivations, and comfort levels that limited the timeliness and value of the information we receive, as well as the utility it provides to participants at all levels.

The story of the newlywed wife and her mother-in-law is apt in another way, because cooking has always been a social activity, and the kitchen has always been the social networking hub of the family. Few of us do not have emotional memories of learning the family gossip and history as a holiday meal was being prepared; more than just gossip and stories, we were passing down the family wisdom. One of the key advantages that social project management tools offer is the effect of a collective intelligence.[2] Social networking has rapidly taken root in project management and is changing the nature of the discipline. With traditional project management the processes were designed for the managers who were managing the inputs and outputs of one project, with the goal of scheduling. Now the focus is on managing the processes and on the project participants, where the real goal is collaboration. Social networking enables this collaboration, which often starts from the bottom up. Project management is an inherently social activity, and social networking tools have evolved into useful project management tools precisely because they enable us to work more naturally.

A SOCIAL NETWORKING PRIMER

What is different about social networking tools that makes them useful project management tools? What are some of the key success factors to their incorporation and utilization?

First, and perhaps most important, is that these tools are often first adopted from the bottom up, rather than from the top down. Many of our team members, regardless of their age, have begun to use these tools in their personal and professional lives without prodding. What pressure there is to adopt these means of collaborating and sharing information is often peer pressure from friends, professional acquaintances, children, and other family members. Had I given my teams a directive to use these tools, the effort would likely have been much less successful.

Right away there is thus a trust (whether well founded or ill advised is another conversation) and level of comfort when using these tools. They feel natural. Furthermore, collaborative tools ask users to share control rather than cede control, which also helps to foster a sense of trust. This is the first lesson of success: social networking depends on a sense of community. Social networks must be trusted by the participants before they will embrace them actively. Team members often develop a higher level of trust in these social networks than in the hierarchical networks that have been imposed upon them.

This brings us to the second critical difference. The networks (communities) must be self-sustaining, self-correcting, and self-policing. The community itself fulfills these functions, not management. This involves several considerations.

To be self-sustaining, the community itself must recognize and reward the strongest contributors, providing powerful peer incentives for participation, a concept that has been studied and defined as "gamification." The tools facilitate personal recognition through community rankings and ratings of each post and participant, "counters" such as number of posts from each member or how many "friends" or "colleagues" are in their network, and the raising of successful participants higher in page displays and search results. In many organizations, this becomes a direct and very visible measure of each person's level of influence and areas of expertise, and participants are naturally incentivized to raise their visible profile to gain status and recognition. This feedback-driven recognition and reward encourages full participation and sharing of knowledge and information. Rather than gaining influence (or the perception of power) through the withholding of knowledge and making oneself the sole source of important information so that colleagues must approach and ask directly, the motivation is now to become visible and recognized by the community. This directly encourages valuable contribution to the community, which is continually reinforced by this positive feedback loop.

As a direct result, the community is self-correcting. Less knowledgeable or expert participants automatically receive less attention, and once the community reaches a critical mass there is enough active participation that an incorrect or controversial post is almost instantly questioned, rebutted, or augmented. Perhaps this is the hardest point to digest and accept, as whenever we are decentralizing control of information, as we must for social media tools to be successful, the natural fear is that bad information will creep into the system. But who better to monitor and correct this than the sources of information and the expert participants? In virtually all cases this is preferable, more rapid, and more effective than ceding such control to a centralized, sometimes overwhelmed manager with a singular viewpoint. It is a significant change for many organizations, though, and one that takes a while to digest and embrace.

Closely related is that the community is also self-policing. Communities develop social norms, and, as in any society, a member who deviates from that norm in a harmful or detracting way is quickly called out and chastised. The same recognition mechanisms that reward valuable participants are called into play to discourage disagreeable behavior.

A last critical difference embodied by social networking is the ease of information capture. More traditional forms of communication and collaboration, particularly email and formal documents, were point-to-point between sender and recipient, which resulted in duplicated and separate copies of the content in the possession of each participant. Such silos of content made the information difficult to uniformly categorize and sort and could not easily be referred back to, particularly if you were not a team member at the time. Now status updates, newsfeeds, blogs, and shared discussions replace email and Wikis supplement documents. Content is categorized immediately and tagged with useful metadata. Content can easily be searched and retrieved at any time, even by people who join the collaboration much later, providing a significant boost to onboarding new team members throughout the project life cycle. This unified body of content, metadata, and discussions provides a permanently viewable trace of the content and the thought pattern in which it was developed. This fosters the continued diffusion of knowledge across projects, a key sign of increased organizational maturity and an important project management goal.

These elements combine to make a social networking–driven project team stronger, and quite often faster, than one based solely on a formally imposed organizational structure. Tantek Celik, Technorati's chief technologist, has called social media "parallel processing for people rather than computers."[3]

The Tools

A perfect storm of new technologies arriving almost simultaneously have made this shift in paradigm feasible. We can divide these technologies into three categories: synchronous, asynchronous, and the underlying technologies that support and enhance both. Table 40-1 provides comparisons and examples of these technologies.

Synchronous technologies are often built around unified communications systems such as Microsoft Lync or Cisco UCS. They combine features such as presence, chat, desktop sharing, and audio/video conferencing, which are often integrated with newsfeeds and accessible from within many applications.

Ultimately, the "newsfeed" becomes a central platform. Everything will be feed-based. The feed is essentially asynchronous, yet feels and can indeed function synchronously. Major enterprise application vendors such as SAP, Infor, salesforce. com, and Microsoft have recognized this opportunity, and social newsfeeds with connections to business objects and people are now part of many platforms.

It is now widely recognized that social networking technologies are one of the key defining elements of modern enterprise computing along with cloud and mobile technologies. From a project management perspective, these go hand in hand. Social is extremely well suited to a mobile form. It is harder to read a Gantt chart on a small screen, yet quite easy to read a newsfeed. Mobile accelerates the flow of information and work—always available, easy to access, and in real time. Cloud services enable rapid and low-cost implementation, and enable us to unify newsfeeds and process across many projects and tasks.

To be sure, challenges remain. Saturation is a danger; newsfeeds have the potential to overwhelm with irrelevant information, potentially surpassing email as a source of spam. Context filters need to further develop a degree of autonomous learning, to ascertain what is relevant to each individual. Such filters need to be combined with intelligent alerts so important content is not overlooked. Confidentiality and privacy remain a consideration; enterprises must choose between private, "enterprise" social networks, where they can control and restrict access, or the public social networks their staff may already be gravitating to. The choice will depend on each organization's need for confidentiality, as well as e-discovery and other legal considerations; risk from competitors; and the breadth and skills of the universe of the people involved in the collaboration.

At present, social project management and enterprise social networking tools are at an early stage in their evolution, and the hype surrounding them in many cases exceeds their proven utility. It remains to be seen what will be truly necessary to achieve truly widespread adoption. (*Text continues on page 436.*)

	Technology	Features	Examples
Synchronous technologies	Instant and text messaging	Combined with presence and conversation archiving, a convenient, unintimidating, and real-time means of efficient communication.	Microsoft Lync, Cisco Jabber, Skype
	Micro-blogging	A real-time stream of communication that offers a sense of greater intimacy and awareness. As with instant and text messaging, limited number of characters per post makes it unintimidating.	Twitter; Yammer; SocialCast; ESME
	Online gaming and crowd sourcing	Offering influence and recognition rankings, or combining entertainment with communication offers enticing ways to foster community and share information. Incorporating polls, investing/ trading, or even betting features serves as a way of gathering grass-roots wisdom and perceptions, and offers a means for new ideas to rise quickly.	See http://enterprise -gamification.com/; Klout
	Web-based conferencing and unified communications	Offer easy to use, accessible and affordable multiparty voice and video conferencing, chat, desktop and application sharing, whiteboarding, bringing real-time collaboration for social networks and teams within and across organizations and distances.	WebEx, GoToMeeting; MS Lync; Adobe Connect; Cisco UCS; Avaya
Asynchronous technologies	Enterprise social networks	Social networking features integrated into enterprise applications such as CRM and ERP systems; most notably incorporate newsfeeds that allow selective following of both people and objects such as assets, orders, invoices, tasks, opportunities, and customers to receive automated related updates. Often incorporate sophisticated search capabilities.	Infor Mingle; SAP JAM; Salesforce.com Chatter; SharePoint
	Social project management applications	An emerging (at the time of this writing) class of applications merging the traditional functionality of project management systems with enterprise social networking capabilities.	Atlassian Confluence; Wrike; Spotlight; ITInvolve
	Collaborative note-taking	Allow for sharing and collaboration when creating free-form notes.	Evernote; Microsoft OneNote

TABLE 40-1. **SOCIAL MEDIA TECHNOLOGIES**

	Technology	Features	Examples
	Blogs	Websites allowing easy publication of journals, commentary, or treatments of a topic.	WordPress; Tumblr; vendor and open source community websites, internal blogs
	Wikis	Typically defined as a website containing content or documents that are collaboratively developed by a community of users. Allow for easy editing and usually provide version/revision control and history, as well as informal notes or discussions connected to but not part of the more formal content.	Wikipedia; Jive; Confluence; SocialText; SharePoint
	Discussions behind Wiki pages	Offer a means to capture the institutional memory and knowledge that underlies the more formal documentation but is not necessarily appropriate or important enough for inclusion there. The thought processes, roads not taken, further illustration, and different opinions that were otherwise lost.	On Wikipedia there are discussions behind some of the articles, which are often more fascinating than the articles themselves! See, for instance, the discussion behind the article on "Debate."
	RSS feeds	Consolidate communication from multiple sources, brings it to the reader rather than the reader going to it.	Most blogs, wikis, news sites. and collaboration portals now deliver RSS feeds built into most web browsers and collaboration tools.
	Social bookmarking	Replace top-down taxonomies with "folksonomies" that categorize content from the consumers viewpoint, surfaces useful content to the community.	Digg; del.icio.us
	Collaboration portals	Combine many social networking technologies, often with specific document management or project management features, in a single environment.	Microsoft SharePoint; BaseCamp
Key supporting technologies	Search engines	Without pervasive search capabilities, internal and external, social networking would not be possible	Coveo; Technorati.com

TABLE 40-1. CONTINUED

American Management Association • www.amanet.org

	Technology	Features	Examples
	Presence	Indicates a colleague's current availability, avoids leaving voicemail messages, creates a sense of intimacy and community for those not in close physical proximity.	AIM; GoogleTalk
	Public social networking	The ability to link to and receive information from selected colleagues or friends based on shared interests, affinities, expertise, or projects. Instantiates and links a community,	Facebook; LinkedIn; Google+; Pinterest; Plaxo
	Workflow	Allows processes to be formalized using automation, without impinging on the free-form, ad-hoc nature of social media. Allows realization of the best of both formal and informal processes.	Offered in business process management (BPM) systems such as SAP and Inforl; collaboration portals such as SharePoint and Lotus SameTime
	Mobility	To be widely embraced and feel true, social media must go with you and be easily and readily accessible on your terms. Trends such as BYOD (bring your own device) and the "consumerization of IT" have accelerated the adoption of mobile technologies as well as a growing expectation of "mobile first"— that applications will be designed from the start with an expectation that they will be used on portable devices.	Enabled by 4G broadband technolo-gies and ubiquitous access to WiFi networks and hardware such as iPad/iPhone; Blackberry, and Android devices; as well as operating systems such as iOS, Windows 8, Windows RT, and Android
	Single sign-on standards	Allows users to connect to systems with a single identity and set of access credentials, affording improved manageability and usability	SAML; OpenID; Active Directory Federation Services

TABLE 40-1. CONTINUED

THE PROJECT MANAGEMENT APPLICATIONS: TWO CASE STUDIES

The Kennedy Center

At the Kennedy Center, we've moved beyond the initial communication and research uses that first led to our revelation. We've turned project management upside down, using these tools to make everyone a project manager. Team members now use status postings throughout the day to send updates to newsfeeds to share new insights and identify challenges. They "follow" or "subscribe to" objects such as tasks, colleagues, and keywords to automatically receive the most relevant updates. These feeds are monitored by the whole team; everyone has a similar awareness in virtually real time. The social networking systems monitor their activity and suggest additional relevant keywords and people for them to follow, based on the content they view, post, and comment on, as well as the objects they choose to follow. These data flows have to a large extent replaced formal status reports; the project manager simply monitors or refers back to the stream for relevant information, and team members update objects directly as they work and post. The ease of use, lack of formality, and natural brevity enforced or encouraged by these tools combine to remove past barriers and reluctance to take the time and effort to share the information.

Our project plans are collaborative and hosted in an online portal, with key team members all having direct access to update them. Newsfeeds and automatic alerts notify everyone of any change. Everyone "owns" the plan and the project, reinforced by, and reinforcing, the sense of community.

Wikis have largely replaced formal documentation, to the same affect. They can be constantly and easily edited. When there are questions as to relevance or importance, gray or controversial areas, these can simply be added to the discussion behind the Wiki page. Everything is in one fully searchable location. This has removed the intimidation of creating formal documents, reduced the perception of the time and effort required, and made ownership shared, personal, and fun. Thus it has been widely embraced.

Project resources are accessible not only to developers and project managers, but also to business unit participants and external consultants and collaborators, further strengthening the team cohesion and sense of community, and adding even greater value and efficiency to the tools. Replacing more traditional forms of communication and collaboration with these social portals has meant project participants can access information when and where it is most needed, not just when it is sent.

Recognition based on "gamification" features encourages participation and surfaces valuable contributions and contributors. Value is self-evident and those successful are recognized by the full team. Staff members who in the past were reserved and quiet became much more vocal through the online tools. We gained new insight into who the real influencers were, who the "go-to" people were, and where the bottlenecks were.

Project management at the Kennedy Center has morphed into an integral part of everyone's existence, rather than a separate discipline imposed on the project. This has streamlined operations, and made projects more predictable and repeatable.

Tessitura Network, Inc.

Very different from the Kennedy Center is the Tessitura Network, Inc., a not-for-profit organization that develops and supports a sophisticated customer relationship management system that is highly specialized to meet the needs of performing arts organizations, handling complex functions such as ticketing and fundraising. The company is owned and governed by the over 300 arts organizations that license and use the software. Member organizations include some of the most prestigious arts organizations in the world, including the Metropolitan Opera, the Kennedy Center, the Sydney Opera House, and the Royal Opera House. The Tessitura Network was designed from the start to be highly efficient with low overhead. It is a virtual company, with no offices. The more than sixty staff members are distributed throughout the United States, Australia, and the United Kingdom. The Tessitura Network was also designed from the start to be highly collaborative and inclusive, seeking input from and involving all member organizations.

With such a distributed team and a "virtual office," social media tools have become indispensable. Missing from a highly distributed team is the sense of "being there," the kind of cohesive, personal contact a group gets from being able to look up and see who is in the office, from standing around the water cooler and gossiping, from going out to lunch together. The organization adopted a social networking platform, not just to share critical information, but also for the staff members to simply let one another know when they were going to lunch, or getting up to get a cup of coffee. At the same time, they were of course sharing critical project information. The intelligent application of social media tools facilitated the efforts of this group of isolated individuals to strengthen themselves as a cohesive, close-knit, committed team.

The Tessitura Network took on the challenge of beginning a major redevelopment effort and the re-architecting of its core application. One of the big challenges of such a project in a company of this nature was how to ensure that the customer base (in the case of Tessitura Network, the "owners") of hundreds of independent organizations was highly involved throughout the process, made even more critical by the stipulation that the new application had to be designed and built in such a way that it was forward-looking and could likely meet the business needs of its member organizations for at least the next fifteen years. This would be a big enough challenge in even a single organization, let alone across a network of independent and highly creative organizations. Social networking tools have become a critical element in the project, engendering a highly engaged community with minimal resources and expenditures.

A collaboration portal was set up very early in the project, with significant effort expended to get strong participation. The portal substantiated the community through social networking profiles and links. Project visions and charters were shared and collaborated on in document libraries and wikis. A blog from the core project team started very early. An online forum was created, with all organizations invited to actively contribute and participate. Leading questions were asked, and project members continued to seed the conversation and maintain the momentum. All of this was done before even the first in-person project summit was held. Simple polls were taken, allowing those who didn't have time, expertise, or confidence to participate in fuller conversations to still get involved, have input, and be a part of the community.

These were not just superficial marketing efforts. Tessitura Network was "crowd sourcing"—asking the community for substantial, meaningful expertise and input. The team could not have conceived of ultimate success without this, and the social media tools enabled it to be done effectively and at very low, almost no, cost.

These social collaboration efforts were so successful that a planned in-person requirements-gathering summit was reduced to only three days in a single location, versus the originally envisioned multiple weeks in multiple locations. Prior to the summit, the participants, many of whom had never met each other in person, were already using the social networking tools to plan social outings. The group of highly distributed, diverse virtual strangers quickly developed a strong self-awareness and sense of commitment and involvement in the project.

As the project continued, the portal was used to deliver prototypes, gather further input and review, and keep everyone at all levels completely informed and involved in the project every step of the way. The first version of the new software was delivered on time and under budget and achieved rapid adoption across the three hundred or so organizations, given the magnitude of its impact.

What traditionally would have been a staggering challenge—building consensus among 300 unique organizations around a highly sophisticated, integral component of their operations, in a short period of time at a reasonable cost around a highly innovative vision—became a realistic, even fun, community effort, all thanks to the fully integrated use of social media tools.

THE FOUR A'S

Lee Ramie of the Pew Internet Project described the "four A's" of communication and influence in the modern social media age:

1. Attention to information
2. Acquisition of information
3. Assessment of information
4. Action—the ability to act on information

Organizations and project teams that can effectively position social networking tools to form a community and a platform that together can address the four A's will no doubt experience a significantly higher project success rate. There has been a "perfect storm" of technologies and paradigms introduced into personal and professional lives. Social networking is one of the key tools they are turning to.

Challenges remain. Enterprises are struggling with multiple competing technologies, multiple profiles, and the difficult to distinguish boundary between personal and private. New players are constantly emerging, and it can be difficult to separate valuable trends from short-term fads.

In its study on the social economy, the McKinsey Global Institute estimates that "social technologies, when accompanied by significant management, process, and cultural transformations, could improve the productivity of 'interaction' workers by 20 to 25 percent. These productivity benefits in collaboration, coordination, and communication account for two-thirds of all the potential benefits of social technologies."[4] The potential of social networking to radically improve and change the way we approach project management is too great to ignore. Embrace what is happening, and harness it!

DISCUSSION QUESTIONS

❶ On a recent project you are familiar with, what are some examples of how poor information flow/communication hampered the work? What social networking tools might have been applied?

❷ Take an informal poll of your team(s). How many are already using social networking for personal use? How many are interested in trying it out on a project?

❸ The primary method of learning about social media is by using it. Visit Wikipedia, Wiktionary, Facebook, or Twitter. Download an instant message program. Start reading blogs and listening to podcasts. Find a way to incorporate Skype (with video) into meetings. Try replacing paper documents with an online collaborative document. Get hooked.

REFERENCES

[1] McKinsey Global Institute, "The social economy: unlocking value and productivity through social technologies," July 2012, 47, http://www.mckinsey.com/insights/high_tech_telecoms_internet/the _social_economy.

[2] http://www.wrike.com/articles/social-project-management.jsp n.d.

[3] Don Tapscott, *Wikinomics: How Mass Collaboration Changes Everything* (New York: Penguin Portfolio Books, 2006).

[4] McKinsey, p. 46.

CHAPTER 41

Agile Project Management

KAREN R.J. WHITE, CSM, PMP, PMI FELLOW, CONSULTANT

When I wrote my first book on the topic of agile project management,[1] industry was really focused on agility in software development projects. Agility in business was not yet being adopted. Now, some years later, we are starting to see agile management moving out of the information technology (IT) organization into other organizations, as corporations realize software development is not the only area that would benefit from agile management practices.

In the June 2013 issue of the *Harvard Business Review*, Rita Gunther McGrath discussed the need for agility in strategy selection and execution: "In a world where a competitive advantage often evaporates in less than a year, companies can't afford to spend months at a time crafting a single long-term strategy. To stay ahead, they need to constantly start new strategic initiatives, building and exploiting many *transient competitive advantages* at once."[2]

In other words, business needs to be agile when formulating and managing strategic initiatives. Furthermore, the Project Management Institute (PMI) recently recognized the emerging requirement for project and program managers to be adept with blending agile management methods in with the traditional project management approaches and developed its Agile Certified Practitioner designation (PMI-ACP®). Additionally, the APMG organization has developed the Agile Project Management™ (AgilePM®) Certification.

The recognition of agility by the executive suite and by certifying organizations such as PMI means that agile project management is not just a passing fad. It is indeed a much needed approach to project management with which project managers should become adept.

BUSINESS REASONS FOR AGILITY

You might ask why agile project management is becoming increasingly prevalent. Today's global economy moves at lightning speed. Millions of stock trades occur in

441

the space of time it takes me to write this paragraph. And somewhere on the globe, someone will have developed a new app that will go viral and disrupt society in a manner similar to Facebook, potentially impacting other development efforts underway around the globe. The speed at which our business and social environments change in this connected world requires all of us to be agile, to be nimble and flexible, in our plans and actions.

Uncertainty in Requirements

One result of this fast-changing environment is that business needs can change very rapidly in today's fast-paced economy. Businesses no longer have the luxury of spending months analyzing a project to develop the perfect solution. If they do take that time, chances are by the time they make a decision, the world will have lost interest. Business opportunities should be anticipated and addressed before they become "needs." Hence, agile methods are based on the principle of "rolling waves" of short sprints delivering value, coupled with continuous improvement based on lessons learned activities.

New Technology

Another driver in agility is the rapid change in technology and the ability of a business to leverage something new to a strategic advantage. Consider the role that apps play in the consumer market. Unheard of prior to the advent of the "smart phone," it would seem that every viable business now has an app available for customer interaction, be it the local news station with a weather app or an international airline with a complete booking app. If you were in the consumer business and did not immediately apply resources to developing an app for your transactions, you were losing business.

Time to Market

In today's consumer world, if you are not the first to market a product, you will be playing catch up. Think of the iPod and the number of "iPod wanna-be's" that have never achieved the sales numbers that Apple reached with the iPod. Even though some of the later models have more features, the fact that Apple had already captured the market's attention prevented those new features from becoming "got to haves."

Flexibility

As mentioned, new technology is introduced at ever-increasing speed. New markets emerge weekly. Wall Street and other exchanges around the world shift on a moment's notice. Consequently, businesses need to be flexible and nimble to respond to these rapid environmental shifts. Organizations need to be prepared to enter and leave markets and product lines within very short windows. This requires the leadership of the organization to be able to quickly review information and make decisions, sometimes with less than perfect information.

The same holds true for the project managers responsible for management of the organization's projects. They should be prepared to shift a project's direction, to respond to a significant change request, or perhaps even to shut down the project at a moment's notice. The ability to understand and communicate the reasoning behind these changes is at the core of being an agile project manager.

AGILE MANIFESTO

No discussion of agile project management would be complete without a discussion of the Agile Manifesto,[3] the document that formally started the current agile movement. Originally developed in 2001, the manifesto identifies four core principles:

- Individuals and interactions over processes and tools
- Working software over comprehensive documentation
- Customer collaboration over contract negotiation
- Responding to change over following a plan

These four principles state that although the items on the right have value, the items on the left are valued more. Agile project teams keep these principles in mind, and when there is a conflict, they will select the item on the left. That is, if a trade-off is needed between documenting a product and building the product, they will work on building the product. Of course, documentation itself could be a product unto itself, but I am referring to documentation that is not a stated desired project product.

AGILE PROJECT MANAGEMENT PRINCIPLES

A project, by definition, has a specific beginning date and a specific end date. Thus, operations and maintenance of a technology-based system or product is not a project, although there might be maintenance projects undertaken in the fulfillment of that objective. Establishing user access and answering customer services calls are also not a project, although the introduction of a new call center would be a project. Traditional project management methods might be applicable to these projects, but it is more likely that upon analysis, the call center project team would discover the current call center is exceeding its capacity, which in turn is creating a significant customer satisfaction issue. It could be very important to the organization's survival to get aspects of that new call center up and running as quickly as possible, even before the business has decided on the call center's management team. Therefore, application of agile project management would be indicated.

Agile project management has at its core certain practices[4] that have been developed to expand upon the Agile Manifesto's principles:

▶ *Rolling wave planning:* Often called "just-in-time" planning, in this approach, the team completes enough planning to understand how the project can be decomposed into iterations by applying risk analysis: how much risk are we undertaking by deferring planning this project aspect, versus how much value we will gain by deferring it until we know more? Project sponsorship and stakeholders participate in the planning activities.

▶ *Customer collaboration:* Customer collaboration is critical to the success of an agile project. The customer, that is the business representative for the project, is an integral member of the project team, making decisions on behalf of the business relative to the project's products. This representative should feel responsibility for the achievement of the project's success. He should be included in all project team meetings and status reporting, and ideally should be collocated with the team, to facilitate responding to questions and addressing issues.

▶ *Collective ownership:* In traditional project management, team members often feel the project and its products are "owned" by the project manager or the business representative, not by the team. In agile project management, there needs to be a sense of collective ownership, a feeling of mutual responsibility among all team members. The establishment of this ownership is one of the crucial undertakings that will require the project manager to be adept at leadership skills. The collective project team needs to feel empowered, not controlled.

▶ *Validation versus verification:* Agile project management puts an emphasis on delivering the "right product" as opposed to delivering a "product that is right." That is, if the call center under development is being built to the requirements, but the requirements are no longer accurate, then the project is moving in the wrong direction. It would be better to redefine the requirements and realign the project. Agile project management, with rolling wave planning and incremental delivery, would accommodate that shift more easily than would traditional project management.

▶ *Continuous improvement:* When delivering product in increments, it is much more possible for the collective project team (including business representatives) to conduct "lessons-learned" sessions, or as they are called in agile project management, "retrospectives," to understand what worked well in the prior increment and what could be improved upon, and then apply those improvements in the next increment.

▶ *Consensus building:* Agile project management relies on true consensus within the project team when decisions are made. This means there is a commitment by every team member to that decision and to its outcome. The ability to obtain consensus, and to know it is *true* consensus is another of the crucial undertakings that will require the project manager to be adept at leadership skills.

▶ *Daily standup meetings:* I have adopted this management practice in all my projects, regardless of the project management approach being used. Derived from the military, these daily meetings focus on today's priorities and issues, not what the project team accomplished yesterday. Facilitated by a different team member each day, the meetings are approximately fifteen minutes in duration and are conducted with everyone standing in front of a copy of the schedule for the current iteration. The team members are asked to identify their priority for the day and to determine if there is anything that would prevent completion of that priority. Resolving those roadblocks becomes the project manager's priority for the day.

▶ *Timeboxing:* This is another common method I have adopted in many of my projects, including a volunteer-based benefit project. Working with the business stakeholders, the project team determines the "cadence" of product delivery, that is, how often will the business receive something from the project. Once the "timebox" has been defined (often in weeks as opposed to months), the project team then determines how much functionality or product can be built in each timebox. If the timebox is not long enough, functionality will be removed, rather than the timebox extended. By using timeboxes, the project team is able to truly focus on the current tasks and not worry about the future timeboxes. It actually ends up enhancing productivity as a result.

AGILE IN ACTION: A CASE IN POINT

Here's an example of agile at work outside the usual software development space. In my volunteer-based benefit project, we established a cadence of three weeks to accomplish a nine-month project culminating in a benefit dinner. Every three weeks, we provided the beneficiary the monies raised plus other product deliverables such as marketing posters and the event program. As an extended project team, we would review our plan for the next three weeks' efforts (sponsors to be contacted, marketing efforts to be completed, etc.) and focus our energies accordingly. Using this approach kept us on track, achieving all intermediate fundraising goals and schedule deadlines, and delivering to the organization a benefit that exceeded the original project's financial goal by 100 percent.

FORMAL AGILE PROJECT MANAGEMENT MODELS

Several different approaches to agile project management have been introduced over the past decade. The techniques embedded in these approaches embrace the eight core principles of agile project management.

Scrum

The Scrum approach to agility is a team-based approach, with three specific roles: the product owner, the Scrum master, and the development team members. Note that the Scrum master is not the project manager. Rather, a Scrum master is the "servant leader" who helps the rest of the Scrum team follow the process; the Scrum master would report to the project manager.

Under Scrum, the product development increments are called "sprints" and are typically of durations of less than four weeks, culminating in an operating subset of the final product. That subset meets the defined acceptance criteria and quality (definition of "done"). The project team's plans and progress are visible to all, including the project's stakeholders, usually displayed on a wall in the team's work area. A "Scrum of Scrums" supports the management of the multiple Scrum teams typical on projects of any size.

A Scrum project would include five specific types of project management meetings—backlog refinement, sprint planning, daily scrum, sprint review, and sprint retrospective—as well as three essential management artifacts:

- *Product backlog*: the list of ideas for the product, in the order the project team expects to build them

- *Sprint backlog*: the detailed plan for development during the next sprint.
- *Product increment*: an integrated version of the product, at a level of quality that it is usable by the business

Dynamic Systems Development Method

The dynamic systems development method (DSDM) is another approach to incremental development that encourages active user participation. Most commonly used outside the United States, DSDM is considered more structured than Scrum, with eight underlying principles:

1. Focus on the business need.
2. Deliver on time.
3. Collaborate.
4. Never compromise quality.
5. Build incrementally from firm foundations.
6. Develop iteratively.
7. Communicate continuously and clearly.
8. Demonstrate control.

A DSDM project differs from a Scrum project in that it consists of three phases, the first of which is focused on project funding and commitment. This is followed by the actual project itself, and then a post-project phase including any maintenance or post-delivery repairs. During the project phase, there is a strong emphasis on upfront planning, including conducting a feasibility study and potentially the development of a functional decomposition model. A DSDM project also addresses the processes associated with product configuration management.

XP

"XP" stands for extreme programming, or pair programming. Its core premises are that "two sets of eyes are better than one" and "the earlier a defect is corrected, the less costly it is." Similar to Scrum and DSDM, XP projects are completed in increments that are timeboxed to something less than a month. However, under XP, two individuals work side by side on a product, with one doing and the other one catching errors as they are created. Think of an editor sitting next to a writer, doing real-time grammar checking and correction, or of a quality-control specialist reviewing a widget as soon as the engineer finishes it. The requirements are typically documented in the form of user stories, which are accompanied by test scenarios. These user stories and test scenarios are captured on index cards, which are assigned to an increment for completion.

A project managed under XP is customer-centric. In fact, the customer would collocate with the project team and interact with the team very closely. Thus, XP is best applied to simpler projects, as it is difficult up-front to estimate the effort required by each pair or to fully document complex requirements. It is also perhaps not the best selection for a project including the development of an underlying architecture, a development that could be dynamic in nature.

American Management Association • www.amanet.org

AGILE PROJECT MANAGEMENT MODEL

The Agile Project Management (APM) model[5] can be viewed as a blend of Scrum and traditional project management. It consists of five phases:

1. *Envision:* Determine product vision, objectives, constraints, and how the team will work together.
2. *Speculate:* Collect broad requirements, develop iterative feature-based release plan and risk mitigation plans, estimate project costs, and address project administrative requirements.
3. *Explore:* Plan and deliver product that meets user requirements.
4. *Adapt:* Review the delivered product and the team's performance, and adapt as necessary.
5. *Close:* Close the project, conduct lessons learned, and celebrate.

I used this overall model in the aforementioned volunteer-based benefit project. The outcome of our envision phase was a greatly simplified project charter, while in the speculate phase we defined the requirements associated with when marketing materials would be needed, what activities would be expected during the benefit dinner (speaker, music, auction), and what we would do in the event of inclement weather on the predetermined date. We used daily stand-up meetings (phone calls) to coordinate volunteer efforts during the explore phase, which consisted of three-week sprints. The adapt and close phases provided valuable insights for future benefit events within the organization.

ADOPTION CHALLENGES

Agile project management is an integrating approach to management. Adoption of agile project management practices requires the active support and participation of all aspects of the organization impacted by the project. These are not practices that IT or product development or marketing departments can implement in isolation. Integrated project teams empowered to make decisions within the project team, under the leadership of the project manager and the product owner are required if agility is to be achieved.

The empowerment of the project teams could be viewed as a threat by functional or line managers who have traditionally made decisions relative to work assignments and budgets. The project team members themselves could feel threatened by this new role, especially if they are used to others making crucial decisions for them. Industry spent most of the latter part of the twentieth century developing and applying formal predictive methodologies to managing projects. We became accustomed to using those approaches to remove uncertainty in the project and to prevent changes in the project's scope. With agile project management, change and uncertainty become the norm, and the project team must have the ability to adapt to ensure project success. Predicting the content of the next product release is not entirely possible, because it may contain modifications to previous product features, in addition to introducing new features.

Before embarking on the implementation of agile project management methods, the project manager overseeing such an effort should understand the organization's risk profile. Organizations that tend to be risk-averse and that have a high need for centralized control and decision making will be harder environments in which to introduce agile project management, because the concepts of agile project management do not align with the principles of the business. Management traditionally determines progress based on completion of documents and deliverables. Risk-averse organizations often place undue importance on time and status reporting, giving them a false sense of control. They have well-defined processes associated with procurement activities and acquisitions that require multiple levels of signature. Not complying with these processes is seen as subjecting the organization to undue risk and is something that is not encouraged.

One challenge that is presented frequently when implementing agile project management is the perceived lack of predictability. This challenge totally overlooks the fact that in traditional project management, the original project schedule and budget were often not representative of the final budget. Applying agile planning techniques, the organization, or the customer, would be in a position to react to these "surprises." Under the "rolling wave" planning core of agile project management, near-term activities actually have increased predictability, and there is more opportunity to consider the unknowns and to integrate them into the project plan.

INTEGRATION INTO PRACTICE

Many organizations are still based on a "chain of command" structure, where every decision, every purchase, and every action requires approval from someone higher up in the chain. These structures were developed with an eye toward minimizing organizational risk and exposure, and to ensure compliance with a predetermined way of conducting business. However, agility is not possible if the project manager needs to seek approval when a project purchase is required, or when he needs to add a resource to the project team. If you find yourself in one of these organizations, you need to communicate the value of agile project management to the executives and obtain permission to demonstrate that value to them.

For the project manager, it means recognizing the need to acquire and apply additional knowledge and skills in a more formal and disciplined manner than traditionally. Additionally, agile project managers need to consider their personal strengths when determining an agile project life cycle, and need to be leaders or facilitators rather than mere managers. When applying agile project management methods, the project manager's contributions are more focused on "roadblock removal," looking ahead in the project schedule and anticipating and addressing those actions that might impede the project team's progress. The project manager also focuses on the boundaries of the project, where integration with other organizational entities needs to happen.

For the project team members (which includes business participants), agile project methods mean understanding and appreciating their expanded responsibilities relative to decision making and communications with one another. The collective team needs to develop a sense of product ownership and not rely on the project manager to resolve all product issues. In fact, the product owner, the person responsible for defining project requirements, is an integral member of the project team, not just a bystander waiting for questions.

TRENDS IN AGILITY

Interest in agile project management is only beginning. Certainly not a temporary "silver bullet," it will become increasingly the norm for management of projects in our high-speed economy. With the advent of certification programs related to agile project management comes bodies of knowledge and educational courses. These will increase as various industries embrace agility and develop bodies of knowledge specific to their particular project needs. Eventually, these bodies and their associated models will coalesce into unified approaches, similar to the Project Management Institute's *Guide to Project Management Body of Knowledge* (PMBOK® *Guide*)[6] and Projects in a Controlled Environment (PRINCE2®), a standard approach to project management developed in the late 1980s by the British government. Today's project manager would be preparing for that future by understanding how to select and best apply the current agile methods.

DISCUSSION QUESTIONS

❶ How agile is the formal project management practiced in the organizations with which you are familiar? Consider the various roles and responsibilities and discuss how they are perceived as agile or bureaucratic.

❷ Think of a project with which you have been involved, and discuss the project's life cycle model: What activities were included? Which ones were not? Should agile methods have been considered? If so, for which aspects of the project? If not, why not?

❸ Would the corporation's adoption of agile project management assist with the challenges facing project managers in your organization in the near future? What are the barriers to that adoption and how might they be overcome?

REFERENCES

[1] Karen R.J. White, *Agile Project Management: A Mandate for the 21st Century* (Glen Mills, PA: The Center for Business Practices, 2009).

[2] Rita Gunther McGrath, "Transient advantage," *Harvard Business Review,* June 2013, http://hbr.org/2013/06/transient-advantage.

[3] Agile Manifesto, http://agilemanifesto.org.

[4] Charles G. Cobb, *Making Sense of Agile Project Management: Balancing Control and Agility* (Hoboken, NJ: John Wiley & Sons, 2011).

[5] Jim Highsmith, *Agile Project Management—Creating Innovative Products* (New York: Addison-Wesley, 2010).

[6] Project Management Institute, *A Guide to Project Management Body of Knowledge,* 5th edition (Newtown Square, PA: PMI, 2013).

CHAPTER 42

Sustainability and Project Management

RICHARD MALTZMAN, PMP, AND DAVID SHIRLEY, PMP, CO-FOUNDERS, EARTHPM, LLC

To appreciate and understand the practice of sustainable project management, the project manager should have a fundamental understanding of the drivers of what we refer to as the "green wave"—the growing awareness by individuals of the need for sustainability and the practices that support it. Project managers should have this understanding in their quivers, because knowledge of the drivers and influencers can help to better understand stakeholders' expectations. More and more organizations have sustainability goals, objectives, and intentions within their mission/vision statements, and they are very serious about achieving them. Connecting your project management efforts with those sustainability efforts of the organization is necessary for project success.

CLIMATE CHANGE

Nothing sparks more debate than the mention of global climate change (GCC). Whenever GCC is brought up, it is usually in conjunction with greenhouse gas (GHG) buildup in the atmosphere. The primary contributor to GHGs is carbon dioxide (CO_2), a by-product of fossil fuel combustion. Whether or not you believe GHG buildup is exacerbated by humankind (and there is an abundance of evidence that says it is),[1] more and more stakeholders are caring about it. Project managers have always cared about stakeholder perception, and the Project Management Institute's *Guide to the Project Management Body of Knowledge* (*PMBOK® Guide*), fifth edition, reinforces the need to consider stakeholders, as it devotes a full new knowledge area to this topic. Even when stakeholders are not conversant with the risks and impacts of GCC, it behooves the project manager to consider the risks and uncertainties exacerbated by it, as well as the economic changes it is generating. Companies that were engaged in development along the shore in New Jersey and

451

New York, for example, would perhaps have benefited from having project managers who were aware of the heightened risk when Hurricane Sandy struck in 2012.[2]

THE TRIPLE (AND MORE) BOTTOM LINE

Holistic thinking entails working as if everything is connected, because it is. To quote the memorable character Hushpuppy from *Beasts of the Southern Wild* (directed by Benh Zeitlin; Journeyman Pictures, 2012): "The whole universe depends on every-thing fitting together just right. If one piece busts, even the smallest piece . . . the entire universe will get busted" (screenplay by Lucy Alibar and Benh Zeitlin). Stated a bit more formally, we are coming to realize that the environment and the economy are connected; often an economic gain that comes at the expense of the environment proves to be a cost in the long run. Planning ahead to mitigate environmental and social impacts, instead of doing what is cheap and expedient and hoping not to be sued, is a core concept for sustainable business activities.

As a framework for thinking holistically about business activities, the triple bottom line (TBL) (Figure 42-1), which considers the social and political (people), environmental/ecological (planet), and financial (profits) aspects of a business, has been widely accepted since its introduction in 1994. It aims to measure the social, environmental, and financial performance of a company or project. The key thought behind this model is that only by figuring in all three aspects of business can an organization estimate the full cost involved in doing business. According to *The Economist*, "In some senses the TBL is a particular manifestation of the balanced scorecard. Behind it lies the same fundamental principle: what you measure is what you get, because what you measure is what you are likely to pay attention to. Only

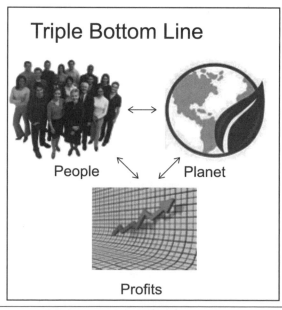

FIGURE 42-1. **THE TRIPLE BOTTOM LINE**

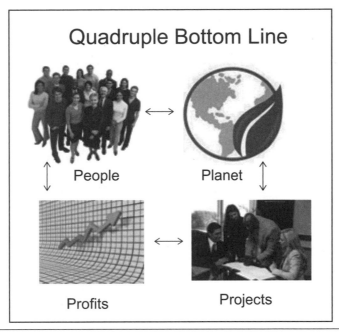

FIGURE 42-2. **THE QUADRUPLE BOTTOM LINE**

when companies measure their social and environmental impact will we have socially and environmentally responsible organizations."[3]

We have added projects to the mix to propose a quadruple bottom line (Figure 42-2). Because projects are responsible for economic activities that use resources and create change—from construction projects to new manufacturing facilities to process improvements and more—project managers have the opportunity and responsibility to be on the leading edge of incorporating sustainable practices. Almost any project can benefit in either cost reduction, morale improvement, stakeholder satisfaction, or reduction of total cost of ownership from a project manager who "thinks green."

STANDARDS AND REGULATIONS

The quadruple bottom line is not the only consideration for the project manager to be more sustainable. There is also another "P": politics. Although potentially connected to profits, there are both mandates and guidelines that can affect the organizations decision to be more sustainable. The U.S. Environmental Protection Agency (EPA) and the European Environmental Agency (EEA) both have enacted legislation to protect the environment. State and individual country regulations must also be considered. In fact, in a major speech on climate change, President Barack Obama has added significant new restrictions on new and existing power plants with respect to carbon emissions.[4] Lack of consideration of these regulatory issues can affect both the reputation of an organization as well as the bottom line. In addition, the International Organization for Standardization's ISO 14000 is a group of standards that apply to the sustainability of an organization. For example, ISO 14001 specifies requirements for an environmental management system; ISO 14010/11 provides general principle for environmental auditing reviews. To be considered ISO 14000–compliant is similar to the prestige associated with complying with ISO 9000 manufacturing standards. ISO 14000 provides another tool for the project manager to use to consider an organization's sustainability.[5]

Adherence to standards and regulations can boost an organization's reputation and keep it out of trouble with regulators, but a major influence on sustainability is the "bottom-up" demand from stakeholders. Stakeholder influence on the success of a project is becoming greater and greater. Stakeholders are becoming more and more aware of environmental issue drivers and indicators. They are bombarded by advertisements about green products and services, and they are making greener choices. In addition, major retailers like Walmart are using greener vendors to take advantage of customer (stakeholder) perceptions.[6]

GREENALITY

During the writing of our book, *Green Project Management,* we searched for a word that would capture the essence of what we and others in the field were trying to express. Authors were struggling with words like "greenness" and "environmentally friendly," but none seemed to satisfy our exact intent, which was for project management to make sustainability one of the standard factors considered in planning and risk management. The word we coined is *greenality,* which we define as the consideration of all green factors that affect a project during the project life cycle. It includes two project management processes:

1. Plan to minimize the environmental impacts of a projects.
2. Monitor and control the environmental impacts of a project and its product.

Greenality is "green" and "quality" smashed together. Taking the attributes of quality—conformance to requirements, planning (not relying on inspection for quality), not accepting "that's good enough," and following quality throughout all the processes (e.g., procurement), reducing project waste—we apply them to sustainability. Attributes for the word *green* would be applying the sustainability intent of the organization's mission/vision, planning for sustainability within the project plan, reducing project waste, checking the supply chain for sustainability, constantly improving sustainability efforts, thereby improving sustainability of the organization and considering the entire life cycle of the project's outcome.

Cost of Greenality

Further, just like quality, greenality has its cost. There is a cost to good greenality and a cost to bad greenality. Figure 42-3 is our interpretation of the cost of greenality. We've all seen a similar chart to this about quality.

Using the example of the so-called Deepwater Horizon/BP Gulf of Mexico oil spill (this was actually BP's Macondo well) in 2010, in our interpretation, the cost ofpoor greenality far outweighed the cost of good greenality. (Disclaimer: we were not in the room when these decisions were made, so we do not have all of the facts that led to the decision, and thus this is speculation based on the best information

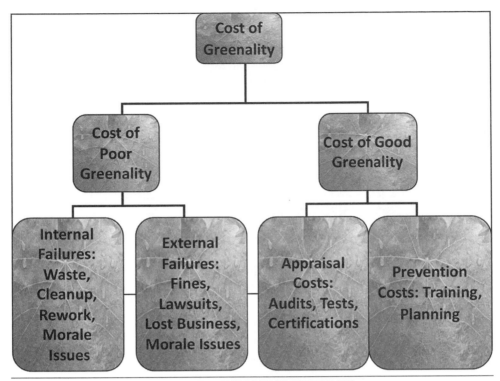

FIGURE 42-3. **THE COST OF GREENALITY**

available in the media.) While BP did conduct some testing of the well casing, we believe that a cement bond log test (a prevention cost) may have indicated some serious problems with the well casing. Whether or not that test could have prevented the disaster is unclear. But using that test as an example of the cost of greenality, a $100,000 test is always better than an estimated $50+ billion price tag for external failure, not even considering the loss of life or loss of reputation for the company. Even though the "accident" occurred three years ago, executives are still being indicted, and the long-term environmental health of the ecosystem in the Gulf remains unclear.[7]

Reducing Non-Product Output (NPO)

This element of greenality is nothing new for the project manager. Reducing non-product output (NPO) is a way to reduce resources and thereby reduce project costs. The NPOs are the "leftovers"—what is left once all the efforts for redesign and reduction have been exhausted before reuse or recycling efforts have begun. "One example of NPO is the carbon emission of the project. Once the efforts identified in the project planning process are implemented, they are monitored via performance measurements. For instance, have the efforts been implemented so that the anticipated remediation has been realized? How does the project manager measure success of that effort?"[8]

The project manager can then look at the energy (a limited resource) use of the project itself. Has the project team utilized that limited resource conservatively, exploiting energy reduction tools within their PCs, turning them and all peripherals off when not in use by using power strips? Looking at the project team environment, are the lights on motion sensors, is travel minimized by using a Skype-type virtual meeting tool?

The key to reducing NPO is to first establish a baseline. Where are we right now? Once that baseline is established, the project manager can compare that to best-in-class, organization goals, or other targets to see what improvements can and should be made to reduce NPO as well as aligning those targets with organizational sustainability strategies.

BECOMING CONVERSANT IN SUSTAINABILITY

Even if this entire handbook was dedicated to the language of sustainability, it couldn't really cover the topic. It is broad and multifaceted. However, there are a few key terms and concepts that will help the project manager be more conversant in sustainability.

The Natural Step

The Natural Step (www.naturalstep.org) is the foundational organization for sustainability. Its four system conditions and four principles of sustainability form the basis for most studies of sustainability. The four system conditions are described as follows: "In a sustainable society, nature is not subject to systematically increasing: (1) concentrations of substances in the earth's crust, (2) concentrations of substances produced by society, (3) degradation by physical means, and (4) in that society, people are not subject to conditions that systematically undermine their capacity to meet their needs."

These conditions are answered by the four principles of sustainability: "To become a sustainable society we must eliminate our contribution to: (1) the systematic increase of substances extracted from the Earth's crust (for example, heavy metals and fossil fuels), (2) the systematic increase of concentrations of substances produced by society (for example, dioxins and DDT), (3) the systematic physical degradation of nature and natural processes (for example, over harvesting forests and paving over critical wildlife habitat); and (4) conditions that systematically undermine people's capacity to meet their basic human needs (for example, unsafe working conditions and not enough pay to live on." The Natural Step conditions and principles cover the entire spectrum from the environment through corporate social responsibility. [9]

Carbon

There are descriptor words associated with carbon that should be part of the project manager's vocabulary: carbon *footprint*, carbon *trading,* and carbon *offsets.* Your carbon footprint is the measure of environmental impact that you have. For organizations it includes the impact the organization has on the environment and the environmental impact of the employees. There are various calculators for both personal and organization measures. A search of the Internet can provide the project manager with measurement tools. The results of those measurements will add to the baseline information. The more baseline information collected, the easier it will be to decide where the best efforts can be used to save valuable resources.

Carbon trading and carbon offsets are related. The Kyoto Protocol is an international agreement linked to the United Nations Framework Convention on Climate Change. The Kyoto Protocol is an agreement between nations to reduce greenhouse gas emissions. As a result of the agreement, nations are required to reduce their carbon emissions. Carbon trading assigns an economic value to carbon, and then countries can buy or sell rights. The selling country gives up its rights to burn carbon, reducing its emissions, while the buying country "buys" the right to burn carbon thus "offsetting" one country's carbon emission with another's. This is the relationship between carbon trading and carbon offsets. This works because the goal of the Kyoto Protocol is to reduce the collective carbon emissions. Carbon trading is the process and carbon offsets are the results.

Cradle to Cradle

A buzz phrase of the past was *cradle to grave*. In the traditional, project management sense, that meant that project managers' main concern was from when they took on the project to when it was turned over to operations. We assert that, by stopping at the turnover to operations, the project is not complete from a sustainability aspect. The project's holistic view includes the consideration of the final end product throughout its life cycle. For example, what happens to a bridge when the end of its useful life is reached? During the concept phase, have we considered reuse and recycling of the building materials? Has the bridge been designed with the ultimate disposal in mind? [10]

THE INTERSECTION OF SUSTAINABILITY AND PROJECT MANAGEMENT

Sustainable project management is merely an extension of traditional project management (defined above as "complete at turnover to operations"). In Figure 42-4, program and project are at the intersection of portfolio and operations, with a direct link to execution of an organization's strategy. Project management connects strategy and operations, providing the ideal facilitator for the adoption of sustainable practices. (The strategic execution framework is used as the basis of Stanford University's Center for Professional Development's Certificate in Advanced Project Management.) Strategy is part of the mission/vision of an organization. That mission/vision will increasingly include elements of sustainability. The connection between the organization's mission/vision and the project's mission/vision is critical to the success of the project. Without that connection, stakeholder expectations will not be met.

Traditionally, the project manager's role began after the business case was complete, and finished when the project (or product of the project) was turned over to ongoing operations. Sustainable project management requires that the project manager drive backward and forward. As stated above, the project manager should be involved early in the decision process to ensure that sustainability elements of the

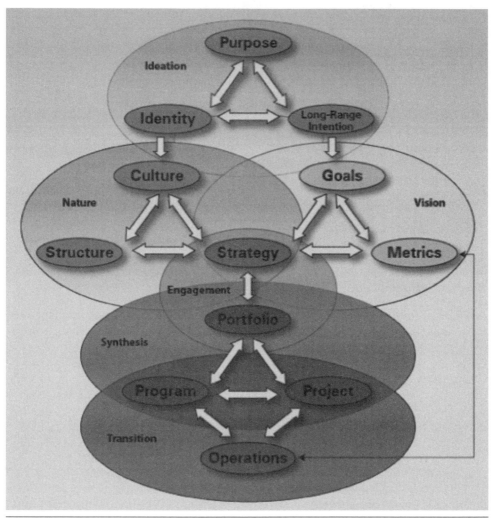

FIGURE 42-4. **STRATEGIC EXECUTION FRAMEWORK**

Source: Adapted from the Stanford Execution Framework, IPS Learning, 2013, http://ipslearning.com/content/
strategic-execution-framework. Used with permission.)

organization's mission/vision are included in the requirements, and forward into the
process to ensure that the long-term effects of the project or product of the project
are monitored and controlled.

TAP INTO THE POWER OF YOUR ORGANIZATION

There is a great deal of potential energy in your organization's purpose, identity, and
long-range intentions (Figure 42-4). These are the top leadership ideals that are often
publicly communicated to shareholders and employees. They give "ideation" to your
organization.

Now let's jump down to the bottom of Figure 42-4. Your organization's heartbeat, its flow, is its operations. This is the day-to-day *reality* of your business.

And where are we, the project, program, and portfolio managers of the world? We, dear friends, are where the rubber (the strategy) meets the road (the operations).

Project managers can gain power by aligning with the organization's strategy, but we often overlook this. In the past, we have insisted that project managers put on blinders when it comes to the "end" of their project, failing to connect with the operations of the company. Why? We're programmed to consider a project as having a definitive beginning and end, and that end occurs when we hand over the final deliverable.

But "final" is not so final, after all. When a project, such as the bridge discussed above, is "done," that only means that it can *begin* carrying vehicles over a river. Does this mean we, as project managers, have to continue monitoring each car as it goes over the bridge? Of course not. But it does mean that we should think about the long-term disposition of the bridge in the steady state. It will help us identify risk, connect with stakeholders that we might not have thought of, and in general do a better job of creating sustainable projects. In the bridge example, we assert that the project manager should consider the paving material, not just for its ability to provide improved mileage for vehicles, but also for its ability to withstand heating and cooling without breaking up and requiring repaving every year. At least ask these questions. It will help you connect to the operations below and the long-range initiatives above.

Take another look at Figure 42-4. See how important it is for an organization to plug together all of the pieces if they want to get to a sustainable steady state. And guess who is at the center of it all? You, the well-connected project, program, or portfolio manager.

The project manager can gain "sustainability power" in two ways:

1. Connect *upwards:* You don't have to be a top corporate leader or CEO to know and *live* the organizations' strategies. Read and reread your organization's mission, vision, and values statements. Check messaging from company leaders. Of course we would steer you to messages on sustainability and the environment, but you can derive power for your projects' charters from any of strategic messages communicated by the C-level.

2. Connect *downwards:* You can, and should, consider project management as distinct from operations. But that doesn't mean we have to ignore them. Get to know the people who will operate the product of your project. Understand the set of users as a stakeholder group and drink in their requirements and expectations as fodder for risk identification. Think life cycle. What happens to your final product in operations and in the long term? Can you learn anything with that mindset? We assert that you absolutely can.

Plug in! Peers in both directions are working toward sustainability, both economic and ecological. We need to pair with these colleagues and learn from both. Understand how project management processes themselves can be more sustainable.

Sustainability is not a separate process or a new knowledge area for project managers. Rather, sustainability must be integrated into the overall framework of our discipline. Having said that, there are indeed specific touch points within our discipline that warrant special attention, and we'll cover those in the next pages. But it is critical that sustainability thinking, in particular long-term, product-oriented thinking, be part of (especially) the integrating and planning processes, where it can have more of an effect on the product of the project.

Here are examples of this integrated thinking:

- Chartering the project: a broadened view of what success means for the project, in line with the organization's overall ideation.
- Identifying stakeholders: include, for example, environmental groups (and other nongovernmental organizations [NGOs]) and your company's environmental health and safety (EH&S) organization, as well as the operations group that will take the product of your project and use it in the steady state. Also consider your company's public statements and commitments in the area of sustainability and corporate social responsibility (CSR).

As far as the project itself is concerned, there are opportunities to be more efficient as a project as well. This includes reduction of waste by the project team itself (literally, turning off the lights, going paperless, etc.), but it also includes more sweeping project sustainability such as following lean management principles in the creation of your project's product.

Each time a project manager shares a best practice or lesson learned with colleagues, preventing bad decisions, poor choices of vendors or materials, and frequent rework, the project management discipline itself becomes more sustainable at your enterprise—ecologically, from a human standpoint, and from an economic perspective as well.

How else can the integration of sustainability into your project assist the project itself? Here are three examples:

1. *Support from "triple bottom line" (TBL) stakeholders:* Chances are, there are people in powerful positions—sponsors, perhaps—who already are thinking in terms of the triple bottom line. They can help you, if you get them interested in those aspects of your project. Of course, this could just as well be the case for some of your key customers. Walmart comes to mind as an influential customer of many suppliers, one that was able to assert their TBL thinking as a customer and significantly drive change back to their suppliers. And finally, project team members and project team contributors are also likely to be TBL thinkers. Assuring that sustainability is integrated will gain you buy-in from these like-minded team members.

2. *Smoother hand-off to operations:* Understanding how the product of the project will be used doesn't just help you with sustainability; it reduces the chances of surprises when the project is handed over to an operations team—which are often bad surprises, such as a product that works well in the lab but not in the field.

3. *Increased and improved risk identification, analysis, response, monitoring, and controlling:* There is nothing fundamentally different about the way in which risks related to sustainability are analyzed and responded to. What is different is that we have to remove our blinders to look for a larger set of risks, by including the longer term, and by understanding a wider set of stakeholders,

American Management Association • www.amanet.org

who, in turn, may be taking a wider view than we'd traditionally think. For example, whole new sets of risks (both threats and opportunities) may be introduced by virtue of sponsors, customers, or suppliers who are sustainability-minded. Indeed, there could be an opportunity (as Coca Cola and other large multinational companies have found) to partner with an NGO (like the World Wildlife Federation) for mutual benefit.

Examples abound in industry where sustainability risks were not properly identified at the start of the project and thus no analysis or risk response plan was created.

Take, for example, the very real case of a large multinational oil company that had zero environmental or safety risks identified in its risk register, yet had a major blowout and oil spill in an important body of water. The company had to scurry to come up with an expensive workaround plan, which did not properly treat the risk, yielding not only the (significant) workaround expenses themselves, but also billions of dollars in fines and penalties, loss of brand reputation, and still-to-be-quantified long-term damage to the ocean and shore environment.

Staying with this example for a moment, we can also consider the advantage of using sustainability thinking in identifying secondary risk. Some of the chemicals used to treat and contain an oil spill on the water have their own negative effects on the environment. Have these threats been considered when deciding to make the use of this chemical a risk response?

SUSTAINABILITY THINKING AND PROJECT QUALITY

Project managers will likely align with the concepts of quality as they pertain to sustainability for two reasons. First, much of the project quality training we receive is product related, which means it is linked to the long-term product of the project. Second, quality gurus, such as W. Edwards Deming, Joseph Juran, and Kaoru Ishikawa, were long-term, holistic thinkers. In fact, it is possible to apply each of Deming's 14 points to "green quality."[11]

LIFE-CYCLE THINKING FOR PROJECT MANAGERS

In a very interesting book, *The Discovery of Heaven* by Harry Mulisch, the table of contents looks like this:

1. The Beginning of the Beginning
2. The End of the Beginning
3. The Beginning of the End
4. The End of the End [12]

As project managers, we typically take an idea from inception to a point at which it can be handed over to operations. If you make the analogy to Mulisch's book, you could say that we manage projects from the beginning of the beginning (if we are lucky) to the end of the beginning—that point when the project's product is ready to venture into its steady-state life. We don't necessarily think of the project in its steady state, or decline, or disposal. But to address sustainability, the project manager should be thinking things through to the end of the end. Although it's beyond the scope of this chapter to provide the details, we think one way for project managers to learn how to do this is to at least gain familiarity with a tool called a life-cycle assessment (LCA), which enables the estimation of the cumulative environmental impacts—impacts from the entire life cycle of the product of your project. It takes into account those many situations in which treatment of one environmental impact causes another one instead. From a project management perspective, we can think of the LCA as a tool to aid us in better risk identification and treatment, which goes beyond the traditional boundaries of our project thinking and yields a holistic and higher quality set of risks and even advice on how to treat them. Many LCA software tools exist to aid in this highly quantitative form of life-cycle analysis. (Many resources for learning how to apply an LCA are available on the EPA's LCA resources site: http://www.epa.gov/nrmrl/std/lca/resources.html.)

CONCLUSION

If the material above seems far removed from your own job as project manager, here are five things you can do right now:

1. Accept the idea that you are a change agent. Projects are already all about change. The slogan "be the change you want to see in the world" (sometimes attributed to Mahatma Gandhi) applies here.
2. Connect your organization's environmental management plan to your project's objectives. This is one of the ways in which you can affect change. Use the statements and assertions your own enterprise is making as justification for sustainability considerations in your project and the projects' product. This can include ensuring that your project is using a sustainability-oriented procurement plan.
3. Dare to think beyond the delivery of your project's product to the sponsor. In fact, dare to think beyond that sponsor. This is part of what is already an increased discipline-wide focus on stakeholder management. Dig deeper, look further, and search more voraciously for stakeholders, and let sustainability concerns assist you in the search.
4. Understand the concept of greenality: ask yourself when planning, "How do quality and sustainability mesh on this project?"
5. Build your own credibility. As you look at job postings, you will see that sustainability is a "hot button." Building your vocabulary in the area of environment, corporate social responsibility, and the triple bottom line makes you a more valuable employee.

American Management Association • www.amanet.org

DISCUSSION QUESTIONS

❶ Does your company have sustainability policies? What are they? Look them up. How can you apply them to project planning?

❷ Who else in your department, company, or project team is interested in these issues? Connect with others to accelerate your impact. Join the PMI Community of Practice for Global Sustainability (http://sustainability.vc.pmi .org/Public/Home.aspx) or the Linked In group Green PM. See you there!

❸ Look around your office. How many aspects of the furnishings, lighting, equipment, and amenities are wasteful/toxic? Make a list. Start with the things you can control.

REFERENCES

[1] Sources for this research are too numerous to list. To get up to speed, try NASA at http://climate.nasa. gov/, or the University of New South Wales's Climate Change Research Center at http://www.ccrc.unsw .edu.au/news/newsindex.html.

[2] Doyle Rice, "*Hurricane Sandy*, drought cost U.S. $100 billion," *USA Today* online, posted January 24, 2013, *www.usatoday.com/story/weather/2013/01/24/...sandy.../1862201/*. See also *Andrew Steer,* "Listening to Hurricane Sandy: climate change is here," Bloomberg.com, posted November 2, 2012, http://www .bloomberg.com/news/2012-11-02/listening-to-hurricane-sandy-climate-change-is-here.html.

[3] "Idea: triple bottom line," *The Economist Online*, posted November 17, 2009, http://www.economist.com/ node/14301663.

[4] Juliet Eilperin, "Five takeaways from President Obama's climate speech," *The Washington Post Online*, posted June 25, 2013, http://www.washingtonpost.com/blogs/the-fix/wp/2013/06/25/5-takeaways-from -president-obamas-climate-speech/.

[5] International Standards Organization, ISO 14000—Environmental Management, http://www.iso.org/iso/ home/standards/management-standards/iso14000.htm.

[6] "Environmental Sustainability," Walmart Corporate website, http://corporate.walmart.com/global -responsibility/environment-sustainability.

[7] National Academy of Sciences, "Assessing impacts of the Deepwater Horizon oil spill in the Gulf of Mexico," ScienceDaily.com, posted July 10, 2013, http://www.sciencedaily.com/releases/2013/07/ 130710122004.htm.

[8] Richard Maltzman and David Shirley, *Green Project Management* (New York: CRC Press, 2012).

[9] Natural Step, "The Four System Conditions of a Sustainable Society," http://www.naturalstep.org/ the-system-conditions.

[10] William McDonough and Michael Braungart, *Cradle to Cradle: Remaking the Way We Make Things* (New York, NY: North Point Press, 2010).

[11] Maltzman and Shirley, p. 130.

[12] Harry Mulisch, *The Discovery of Heaven* (New York: Penguin Books, 1997).

Industry Applications of Project Management Practice

Introduction

Some professionals argue that a project is a project and, therefore, the principles of project management are generically applicable. Others proclaim that an information technology (IT) project is totally different from building a house or launching a new product. There is truth in both positions, of course. Principles of navigation are generically applicable, but putting them to proper use in the Antarctic or on the Danube requires different experiences and knowledge.

The project management principles are indeed generically applicable, yet to use them intelligently requires knowledge of the specific type of project. In this section, some of the peculiarities of project management practice across different industries are explored. In keeping with the explosion of project management into almost every type of business, this section of the book has added four new chapters in this edition.

In Chapter 43, Christopher Sauer of Oxford University explores how the mature practices of project management in the engineering and construction field may have applicability to the IT industry.

Chapter 44 features a discussion of IT project management practice and pitfalls by Karen R.J. White, PMP.

Looking to the future, the ecosystem restoration industry applies the proven practices of project management to a work environment characterized by evolving science, as discussed in Chapter 45 by Stan Veraart and Donald Ross, CEO of EarthBalance.

A veteran employee, volunteer, and board member of over a dozen nonprofits, Jeannette Cabanis-Brewin in Chapter 46 offers some insight into how project management discipline and theory can make the world a better place, when used by nonprofits and nongovernmental organizations.

Robin Markle Dumas shares insights into project management in the financial services sector in Chapter 47.

Chapter 48 covers the uses of project management in marketing initiatives; Mary Yanocha provides case studies and interviews with marketing heads, including one featuring the 2012 PMO of the Year Award winner, Verizon Wireless's Marketing PMO.

465

In Chapter 49, Janice Weaver of Norton Healthcare (short listed for a PMI Project of the Year in 2010) shares her experience with implementing project management in healthcare organizations.

Finally, Luiz Rocha and Vianna Tavares ponder ways to keep large infrastructure projects on schedule in Chapter 50.

American Management Association • www.amanet.org

CHAPTER 43

Building Organizational Project Management Capability
Learning from Engineering and Construction

CHRISTOPHER SAUER, TEMPLETON COLLEGE, OXFORD UNIVERSITY

The construction industry is widely accepted to have the most mature project management processes. Information technology (IT) project managers envy the accuracy with which their construction colleagues can estimate and predict progress on a building. They borrow their tools and techniques but struggle to emulate their results. They fall back on the conviction that "it's different in IT." Thus, they resign themselves to continuing levels of underperformance.

This is a strange response when even IT project managers would agree that there is a core of project management knowledge that is common to all projects. Who would doubt the wisdom of scope control in any project circumstance? Failure to leverage the learning of one industry into another is therefore normally explained by appeal to the need for domain knowledge. For example, the rate of change of technology, the volatility of requirements, and the invisibility of software are all supposed to make IT project management radically different. Fortunately, we do not need to resolve the debate about the importance of domain knowledge in order to improve learning.

The central point of this chapter is that industries can improve their own capabilities by adopting a model of project management capability development from the construction and engineering sector. Domain specifics may apply to projects, but they do not apply to the structures and processes by which project management itself is managed within an organization; mentoring can be effective in both construction and IT even though the learning may be different in certain respects. The domain independence of the model can be seen from its application to high-tech product development.[1] Research has shown that the construction industry has improved its performance over the last twenty years.[2] Despite embarrassing blips from time to time, it has managed down its performance variance. Many high-profile mega-projects are today successfully delivered against demanding specifications and stretch targets. These range from Hong Kong's International Airport, which met its multibillion-

467

dollar budget, to the Sydney and London Olympic facilities that were in service twelve months before the start of their respective games, to the first half of the $8 billion Channel Tunnel Rail Link project installing a high-speed rail infrastructure and service from the Channel Tunnel to London. During the 1980s and 1990s and into this century, new ways of managing projects at the enterprise level have been adopted. This has had the effect of creating enhanced capability through support for performance and learning.[3] Transfer of consruction's new ways to other industries will allow them to learn from their own experience so that any uniqueness of domain will be irrelevant. The benchmark for improvement will not be comparability with projects in other industries but improvement against your own organization's past performance and that of your industry peers.

A model of the organizational and management system by which construction and engineering companies manage project management is presented in this chapter. The model includes such practices as recruitment and development of talent, employment policies, role design, reporting processes, performance management, and organizational learning.

Engineering and construction are project-centric industries—that is, businesses that earn their revenues through projects. Transferability of the practices common to construction and engineering is an important issue covered below. There are two targets for transfer—companies in other project-centric industries, such as management consultancies and systems integrators, and companies in industries where projects are only a part of their total activity, such as new product development by an automotive manufacturer or policy development by an industry regulator.

Finally, we assess developments that indicate progress toward adoption of the capability development model, and examine new challenges for project-centric and non–project-centric organizations as the performance demands on project managers grow.

BUILDING PROJECT MANAGEMENT CAPABILITY: THE CONSTRUCTION AND ENGINEERING EXAMPLE

Project management capability operates at three levels:

1. Project level
2. Individual level
3. Organizational level

The project is both the start point and the end point. It is the focus for the application of individual and organizational capability. It is the source of experience on which learning is based.

The individual project manager is the linchpin, the essential ingredient. No project of any size or complexity can hope to be successful without an appropriately competent project manager. Equally, without project managers contributing their ideas and experience to the common pool of knowledge, organizations cannot expect to improve from project to project.

Organizational capability contributes to improving project performance by providing supports for the manager working on a project. It also assists the individual to learn, and grows the organization's communal knowledge of projects.

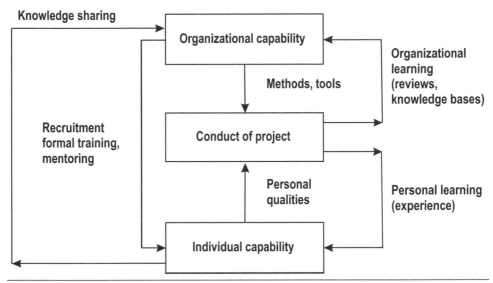

FIGURE 43-1. **MODEL OF PROJECT MANAGEMENT CAPABILITY DEVELOPMENT**

Figure 43-1 summarizes our model of project management capability development with examples of how the three levels interact.

Organizational capability consists of a number of elements. These were identified in an earlier research study in which we intensively interviewed project managers and directors of a number of top-level Australian construction companies.[1] None of the companies fully employed all the elements described, but together they amount to a coherent set of practices that support both performance improvement and the development of lasting project management capability. These capability elements have been subject to continued verification subsequently and include the following:

- Organizational structure
- Role design
- Knowledgeable superiors
- Values
- Human resource management
- Methods and procedures
- Individuals' personal characteristics
- Conduct of the project

We see these elements of capability working in a number of ways:

- Making the job easier
- Facilitating the application of knowledge
- Ensuring a supply of capable project managers
- Developing individual knowledge
- Developing organizational knowledge
- Motivating learning

Organizational Structure

Business units in construction and engineering companies typically have flat structures that serve two main purposes. They place project managers and their projects close to the locus of power and decision making in their organization, which gives them high visibility and access to resources and decisions as needed. They de-emphasize other functions, such as finance, design, and estimation, so that by contrast with non–project-centric organizations, these are clearly support functions, not internal competitors for resources and attention. By placing projects at the center of the structure, these companies eliminate a lot of possible organizational noise, and thereby make the job of project management easier.

Role Design

The crucial element of role design involves balancing responsibility with account-ability, resourcing, and authority. This equation is crucial to making the job easier and facilitating the application of knowledge. Plainly, having resources and authority are necessary to making a project doable. Without them it is hard to hold the project manager to account. To penalize a project manager who has not been given the wherewithal to succeed sends a message to others that the organization does not understand the challenge of project management and that it is not an organization in which projects represent a realistic career. Learning is likely to be retained by the individual rather than shared.

Knowledgeable Superiors

Project managers' superiors in construction have three important characteristics. First, because of the flat structure, they are likely to be people with authority and access to resources that can help solve unexpected problems. They can thus make the project easier. Second, they are typically highly knowledgeable, having graduated from many years in the project manager role themselves. This means that they understand progress reporting and have a nose for potential problems. They are thus able to prevent problems from getting out of hand and are equipped to guide their project managers through difficulties, thus enabling knowledge to be successfully applied. Third, project managers' superiors usually are involved in the client relationship from the start. They will have sold the project to the client and will have helped shape its initial stages. Because they accept responsibility for the project and will themselves be held accountable by the executives, they are highly motivated to share their knowl-edge with the project manager and do everything they can to help make the project successful.

Values

Three values underpin project capability in construction companies—a focus on performance, relationships, and knowledge. The focus on performance is evident in the reputational advantages that accrue with success—"X built the tallest high rise in Western Europe," or "Y installed the first horizontally suspended bridge." Conversely, it is also apparent in the careful weeding out of nonperforming project managers. Thus, performance management has become more sophisticated over recent years in recognizing the value of mistakes. While repetition of the same mistake will not be tolerated, the recognition that errors represent an opportunity for learning and that admission of mistakes will not necessarily be punished encourages individual and organizational learning through openness and sharing of lessons.

The focus on relationships relates to customers, partners, and subcontractors. Greater awareness that customers usually represent opportunities for future business and that retaining an existing customer is easier than winning a new one has led to contractors trying to establish contracts and relationships that encourage win–win situations. In some cases this has been extended to their supply chain. The result is that project managers see value in investing in understanding the customer, and partners and subcontractors see value in sharing their ideas and knowledge. So not only is useful knowledge shared, but the job is made easier for the project manager because of a less adversarial environment. And, as several companies have noted, because of less litigation, there is a further benefit in being able to close out projects sooner.

Focus on knowledge is apparent in the explicit recognition of project managers as an asset. In the recession of the early 1990s, a number of the companies with deep pockets kept their better managers on the payroll despite a lack of revenue-earning projects. Symbolically, this sent a strong message that the retained managers were valued, leading them to see it as worth their while to develop new and better ways of working. At the same time, these project managers had more opportunity than they had ever previously had to reflect and share their ideas. Once initiated, the practice of continual improvement has remained. So both individual and organizational learning have been encouraged.

Human Resource Management

Construction and engineering companies do not always have substantial human resources (HR) departments, but they typically do have significant HR practices designed to create and sustain a talent pool of project managers. These practices include recruitment, development, and career-appropriate talent, often at a graduate level. Development involves a managed progress through different project roles to a junior project management position. From there, subject to performance management, the project manager moves into progressively more difficult challenges. Mentoring is built into the reporting relationship because the manager's superior has a shared accountability that encourages knowledge and experience sharing. So individual capability development is strongly supported by HR practices. The availability of a career path that sees project managers in their fifties and sixties valued and rewarded for performance also encourages individuals to take the long view and to invest in building and sharing knowledge.

Few, if any, companies offer the kind of highly incentivized financial package so common among bankers and software salespeople. Project managers are paid a decent salary and may receive a bonus, although it is usually paid annually and not on the basis of performance on any single project. In fact, by selecting "project people," companies typically populate their project manager roles with individuals whose biggest motivation is to take on ever-greater challenges. Thus continual learning by the individual is built in.

Methods and Procedures

Companies typically have their own set of methods and procedures for project management. These are internalized and used with discretion rather than slavishly followed. Their principal role is to provide structure and commonality of practice so that reporting can be reliably monitored. They also provide a shared language with which to talk about projects that facilitates sharing of experience and the development of new methods.

Individuals' Characteristics

Many of the elements of organizational project management capability we have described encourage the acquisition and development of individuals with the right skills and competencies. These include the classic competencies in planning, monitoring, controlling, forming and leading teams, communicating, managing stakeholders, negotiating problem solving, and leading. These are necessary to the effective conduct of projects. But they are not sufficient. Three personal characteristics stand out as driving personal performance—a thirst for experience, personal commitment to delivering projects, and the desire to enhance one's reputation through association with a successful outcome. One project manager encapsulated the project manager mindset:

> In the construction industry, you'll find that for a lot of project managers it's a heart-and-soul type thing. It's a lifestyle. You live, sleep, and eat project. You're here six days a week. Sometimes you're working the night shift. Sometimes you're in here seven days a week. So it's a lifestyle and it's a total commitment.

All three personal characteristics are powerful motivators of individual learning.

Conduct of the Project

In describing organizational and individual capability above, we have shown how both provide essential inputs to the conduct of projects through the individual competencies of the project manager applied to the project, and through oversight, support, and intervention by knowledgeable superiors. However, projects are also the source of much learning and some companies act to capture that through encouraging informal interaction among project managers on a regular basis. Others conduct reviews and maintain more formal databases of experience that can be uniformly shared across the business and that can be used to inform future projects even when the original project manager has moved on.

The following case study shows how one leading international construction company exemplifies the model.

CASE STUDY: MULTIPLEX—THE WELL-BUILT AUSTRALIAN

Multiplex is a diversified property business, employing over 1,500 people across four divisions: construction, property development, facilities management, and investment management. Based in Australia, it has a presence in Southeast Asia and Europe. Its core construction business involves managing the design and construction of urban developments, such as office buildings, shopping centers, apartment buildings, hotels, hospitals, and sporting complexes. Landmark projects have included the $430 million Sydney Olympic Stadium and the United Kingdom's iconic sporting venue Wembley National Stadium.

Multiplex is highly regarded for its ability to compete on cost, but it does so without damage to client satisfaction and as a result seeks to secure repeat business. It operates a flat structure. The board of directors is usually fully aware of what is happening at the construction project "coalface." Head office functional managers support projects in specialist disciplines including design, contract administration, estimation, employee relations, finance, and legal affairs.

Multiplex's project managers are highly experienced in construction and project management. The company sets high performance standards, requiring its managers to deliver the building or facility to the client and continue responsibility for any subsequent modification once in service. The company gives project managers control over resources and, within broad limits, the authority to make whatever decisions are necessary to complete the project; they "can make a large number of decisions related to the project with complete autonomy."

Because performance matters, so too accountability is important. But accountability is exercised in a rounded manner. Reasonable mistakes are understood and recognized as a learning opportunity. While management does focus on project outcomes, overall performance is assessed relative to the challenge. Thus retrieving a potentially damaging situation may be valued more than the final outcome against targets. Small financial bonuses are paid against annual performance rather than specific projects. But the company recognizes that for most of its managers association with a success and the challenge of something new are the key motivators.

Control against project schedule, cost, and quality is tight. The board receives reports monthly. Formal reporting to the project director is done weekly and informal reporting daily. Senior managers actively follow progress also through site visits.

The project directors and construction managers to whom project managers report are highly knowledgeable about project management. Their involvement in business development ensures that their projects can be successfully achieved with commercial returns. The company's recognition of the challenges of projects means that project managers feel comfortable sharing difficulties with their superiors. As a result, problems are rapidly dealt with before they accumulate long-term consequences.

> Recruitment and development of aspiring project managers is based on an apprenticeship model to build long-term commitment to the company and to demonstrate its own commitment to project managers. Consequently, retention is high and turnover is low. Development includes on-the-job-training, mentoring, and formal management development courses. The company's commitment to its project managers and hence its ability to build organizational capability is reinforced by its preference for internal promotion.

Discussion

Each of the capability elements described in the Multiplex case study makes sense on its own. However, much of the power of this model to make a difference derives from the interlocking reinforcement among its elements. For example, greater tolerance of mistakes encourages openness that permits knowledgeable superiors to assist at an early stage so performance is sustained while learning is enabled. At the same time, this tolerance reflects a fairer form of performance management that in turn supports retention of individuals and retention of their knowledge.

Another way of putting this is to say that by managing the talent pool and making the job easier, the right people are given time in which to learn. By motivating learning, they are encouraged to develop individual and organizational knowledge. Through the application of knowledge, that learning is internalized. Through organizational processes, the learning is externalized and so made available throughout the company.

TRANSFER AND ADOPTION

Our model for developing project management capability has been synthesized from practice in the engineering and construction sector. For those in other sectors, the questions remain: How transferable is the model? How readily can it be adopted?

There are no in-principle barriers to transferring substantial elements of the model to other industries because it focuses on learning and support for performance within an individual company. So while a biotech company developing new drugs and an IT systems integrator implementing enterprise software systems may face radically different challenges in terms of the technologies they employ, the regulatory regime they confront, the demands of trials and testing, and so forth, each can develop its own learning, including whatever knowledge is sector- or company-specific. As we shall see in the next section, a number of IT companies have started to transfer the model to their own situation.

The one area of the model that can be problematic is transfer of those elements that are more dependent on the project-centric nature of the organization. For non–project-centric organizations, such as retail banks, supermarkets, and logistics companies, it will not be thought desirable to emulate structural characteristics that we have seen create visibility, enable executive attention, and deliver necessary resources, at the expense of the focus on day-to-day operations.

Our model was derived from the practices of large companies. This raises the concern that size may be a barrier to transfer. Obviously, large companies are to some extent better positioned—for example, for a company undertaking one hundred projects per year, the return to scale of investing in project management capability development is greater than for a company undertaking just ten each year. But the investment need not be a fixed cost regardless of size. As we noted earlier, none of the engineering and construction companies we studied exhibited all the characteristics described in the model. Learning can be seeded and performance improved even in small companies by such simple and cheap devices as organizing Friday evening drinks for project managers once a month. Celebrating their successes can be as potent a reward as financial bonuses. So, while larger companies may have the resources to dedicate to developing formal supports for project management capability, smaller companies can still gain benefit from the model.

How then should companies set about adopting the model or elements of it? Identifying an organizational lead and focal point is the first priority. For a larger company this may involve the creation of a corporate project/program office. For a smaller company, it may be the nomination of an individual, either a senior project manager or an executive responsible for project managers. In either case, an individual should be tasked with developing organizational project management capability and evaluated accordingly. The task itself should include providing processes to support existing projects, a common set of tools and knowledge bases, structures and processes to permit learning, motivation and support for the capture and sharing of learning, and support for the development of a set of performance management and HR practices to grow the talent pool of project managers.

Even with organizational commitment and resources behind the organizational lead, it takes years to design, introduce, and embed all the relevant practices. This is not a quick fix. That said, once achieved, it need not be a continuing direct cost. Some organizations we researched, such as Multiplex, had no corporate project office but had embedded the relevant practices in their everyday organizational processes.

EMERGING DEVELOPMENTS

The project environment is dynamic and it is worth reviewing a number of new developments that are now with us or just around the corner. These are extending the scope and challenge of traditional project management, extending the need for capability development to more complex organizational forms, and extending the focus of development beyond the project manager.

Though the IT sector's reputation for project performance and its track record in developing project management capability are equally poor,[4] diffusion of the capability development model is occurring. A United Kingdom government department recently asked one of its international IT suppliers what it was doing to improve its project performance. The company's inability to answer the question galvanized it into action.

In the last few years, we have seen more large IT companies, as well as hardware, software, and systems integrators, adopting some form of capability development initiative. For example, the UK arm of one major European IT company identified a project management champion as the lead for capability development. She has instituted a project management career structure, assessed its project manager pool, undertaken appraisal and mentoring, defined development paths for individuals, implemented a recruitment and selection process, and instituted a code of practice for the conduct of projects as well as for training staff in a standard methodology. And confirming that the champion role need not be an ongoing cost, she explained, "It's my aim to work myself out of a job." This kind of example suggests that much of the model is transferable.

But even while the model is diffused more widely, the environment is changing and placing new and greater demands on many project managers. Customers are increasingly demanding not merely a delivered project but the tangible benefits for which the project investment was made. In construction, BOOT (build–own–operate–transfer) contracts require the successful operation of a building or infrastructure, which implies responsibility for operational services, such as heating and elevators, and for continuing maintenance. In defense, governments require not merely the delivery of aircraft but the ability to destroy enemy targets, which implies responsibility for maintenance, spare parts logistics, and munitions. In IT, customers demand not just delivery of a system but also the achievement of cost or revenue benefits, which implies responsibility for business process change. Many companies see that, as a result, they must involve the project manager more closely in the development and selling of the business so as to ensure that the end result is deliverable. Thus, project managers are being called upon to extend their skills both at the front end and back end of projects.

Two implications are worth noting. First, as the scope of the role extends, so our model needs to reflect the new competences required. This in turn may require adjustments to performance management systems, to career structures, to tool sets, and so forth. Second, members of the current pool of project managers may no longer be suitable for the new role. Therefore, there may need to be an exit strategy for them or a reconceptualization of the role so that their skills can be exploited within the framework of the extended project.

A further dimension of added complexity for capability development is the consequence of joint venturing. Joint ventures are usually established for a quite limited duration among companies that in other circumstances may be thought of as competitors. Thus, not only may there be no long-term payoff from learning, but also sharing of knowledge may be seen as counterproductive. However, win–win contracting can counter these tendencies. In the United Kingdom, the Channel Tunnel Rail Link project has been widely seen as exemplary. A complex joint venture to deliver the railway in two sections, it created a common culture such that there were no external signs of which member company any individual works for. Identification with this enormous project was strong. Although lasting more than ten years in duration, it was necessary to have as much knowledge as possible available at the start. Learning was brought in through a policy of recruiting people with experience on two major rail projects of recent years—the Channel Tunnel itself and London Underground's Jubilee Line. Within the project, a thriving lessons-learned program generated a mass of knowledge. When the project for the second section was launched, kick-off days were organized to ensure no learning from the first section was lost. Thus where a joint venture has a long-enough life and where there are commercial advantages, capability development may still be a worthwhile investment.

Finally, two future developments are worth watching for. First, project contractors are increasingly focusing on their clients as a point of leverage for improvement. They argue that the client gets the projects it deserves. Poor contracting by clients engenders counterproductive behaviors from contractors. A better-educated client will make for better projects. The plausibility of this argument was borne out recently by an IT project manager who invested in teaching her client how to estimate a project. Subsequently, she found renegotiation of the contract much easier because she could hold a more informed conversation with the client. So it is likely that we will start to see capability development efforts extending beyond the boundaries of the contracting organization.

Second, non–project-centric businesses are becoming more dependent on projects. Recently, an insurance company conducted a work audit and discovered that its managers spent more than 50 percent of their time on projects.[5] With large-scale operational businesses of this kind finding themselves continually pressed to change and improve, they are obliged to undertake more and more projects. Over time, it is possible that the financial markets will increasingly value these companies according to their project portfolio and their capability to execute successfully. Organizing in a more project-centric way may then become common among supermarkets, banks, and insurance companies, as well as those in construction, engineering, and IT. In the meantime, there is no reason why non–project-centric businesses that nevertheless conduct projects as a continuing aspect of business improvement should not adopt and adapt elements of our model. While internal organizational structures may impede role design that balances authority and resourcing with responsibility, thereby limiting accountability, HR processes that focus on recruitment and development, mentoring, and the creation of knowledge bases can all be implemented. What is typically lacking is the organizational will to invest in project management because it is seen as noncore, but as we have just suggested, even this attitude may be about to change.

The model of project management capability development presented here, therefore, represents a solid foundation on which any organization in any industry can base its own initiative. The emerging developments we have described amplify the need for organizations to pay explicit attention to project management capability.

DISCUSSION QUESTIONS

❶ Thinking about companies that you know, how well do they manage the continuing development of their project management capabilities? What more could they do?

❷ What issues would you envisage in the acquisition and maintenance of adequate project management capability in a multiyear, multi-project joint venture? How might you tackle these issues?

❸ In what ways do extensions of the project manager's role into activities such as business case development and postimplementation benefit delivery and require capability development? What management initiatives would you take to ensure that they are adequately included in a company's capability development practices?

REFERENCES

[1] Christopher Sauer, L. Liu, and K. Johnston, "Where project managers are kings," *PM Network* 32, No. 4 (2001), pp. 39–49.

[2] Robert J. Grahamand and R.L. Englund, *Creating an Environment for Successful Projects: The Quest to Manage Project Management* (San Francisco: Jossey-Bass, 1997).

[3] A. Vlasic and P. Yetton, "Delivering Successful Projects: The Evolution of Practice at Lend Lease (Australia)," 16th International Project Management Association World Congress, Berlin, 2002, pp. 4–6; D.H.T. Walker and A. C. Sidwell, "Improved construction time performance in Australia." *Australian Institute of Quantity Surveyors Refereed Journal* (AIQS, Canberra) 2, No. 1 (1998), pp. 23–33.

[4] Sauer et al, 1999.

[5] Christopher Sauer and C. Cuthbertson, "The State of Project Management in the UK," http://www .computerweeklyms.com/pmsurveyresults/surveyresults, 2003.

Why IT Matters
Project Management for Information Technology

KAREN R.J. WHITE, CSM, PMP, PMI FELLOW, CONSULTANT

Smartphones! Facebook! Internet-enabled televisions and other appliances! Yikes! I recall a conversation I had several years ago with colleagues commiserating about not being able to escape "information technology" (IT)—the focus of our day jobs—when we left the office. In those days our car was our sanctuary, the one place where we would be sure to escape from IT. Now, with the advent of DVD displays, GPS systems, and embedded computers, we are not even free there. Information technology is playing an ever-increasing role in the delivery of the services that we rely on in our everyday lives. Information technology surrounds us, from the technology with which we manage our households, to the technology that is used in our schools and workplaces, to the technology we use to interact with one another. Information technology is no longer confined to the business community. Information technology truly does surround us, making the management of the projects that bring that technology to bear even more important.

VISIBILITY OF IT PROJECT FAILURES

An Internet search using the term *IT project failure* brings up numerous articles and blogs identifying the costs of these failures and the impact they had on the business. Failures of IT projects have been reported in cases where the failure of IT to deliver much needed capabilities or advertised services impacted a company's financial standing, market shares, or even worse. Some of the projects frequently cited include ERP implementations, "big data" projects, and large-scale modernization development efforts. One recent article referenced a $1 billion failure associated with the cancellation of an Air Force software modernization program.[1] Another publicized failure was the digital media initiative stopped after costs of nearly £100 million to the BBC.[2] While the various lessons cited in these references were certainly of interest, what is even more important a lesson is the potential impact these failures had on the

479

corporations, their markets, their customers, and their employees. Thus, IT matters in a technology-enabled world, and IT project management matters as well.

IT PROJECT MANAGEMENT MATTERS

As information technology becomes more pervasive in our lives (programmable dishwashers, cell phones, GPS systems, home networks, medical diagnostic and drug-delivery techniques, etc.), the need to treat the development of the products and software embedded in them as true engineering activities has increased. These products could have as much safety and security implications as building a bridge or constructing a house. That level of engineering requires formal project management discipline.

In addition, many corporations are feeling pressure from participation in a global economy. The need to develop products and services faster and more economically translates into a requirement for a more disciplined approach to managing their development without sacrificing time to market considerations.

What does all this mean? For companies, it means recognizing formal project management as a discipline within their IT departments and technology-based products, a discipline as crucial as database management or network security management. For the project manager, it means recognizing the need to acquire and apply additional knowledge and skills in a more formal and disciplined manner than traditionally. For the project team (which includes business participants), it means understanding—and appreciating—the contributions formal project management makes to the overall project success.

FORMAL IT PROJECT MANAGEMENT

A project, by definition, has a specific beginning date and a specific ending date. Thus, operations and maintenance of a technology-based system or product is not a project, although there might be maintenance projects undertaken in the fulfillment of that objective. Establishing user access and monitoring network security is also not a project, although introduction of a new security capability would be a project. It is important to realize that formal IT project management does not mean mounds and mounds of paper, nor does it mean lots of additional project staff. What it means is recognizing that there are some formal project management roles to be fulfilled and formal project management disciplines to be applied within an IT project.

Formal IT Project Management Roles

Formal IT project management begins with a clear understanding of the roles and responsibilities of IT project managers (including product managers of technology-based products), versus the roles and responsibilities of the project's business sponsor and of the functional manager. These roles and responsibilities are briefly summarized in Table 44-1.

Let's start with the IT functional manager role. Many IT organizations are structured around the business areas supported, which often translates into oversight of specific applications, product lines, or operational activity. Typical titles used for the

	Functional IT Manager	IT Project Manager	Business Sponsor
Responsibility	Continued operations	Completion of project objectives	Completion of project objectives
Authorization	Position in organization	Project Charter	Position in organization
Assignment	Permanent	Temporary	Temporary

TABLE 44-1. **TYPICAL ROLES AND RESPONSIBILITIES**

individuals who manage these operational activities include application manager, product line manager, and data center manager. Their responsibilities often include an operational or maintenance type of function, the "lights on" role within IT. While their daily activities are quite varied, their overall contribution to the business is the same: keep operations running, ensure the various IT capabilities are available to the business units relying on them. Information technology functional managers are often key stakeholders in IT projects, most often as providers of knowledgeable, experienced project staff, as quality control participants, and as the recipients of the project's deliverables.

Compare these responsibilities with those of the IT project manager. An IT project manager's responsibilities are established when the project is initially conceived and are concluded when the project's deliverables are completed—when the end state is achieved. The typical responsibilities associated with the project manager role include identifying the specific work to be performed, determining and obtaining the corporate resources (budget, people, and facilities) required to achieve the project's objectives, and then managing those resources as they are used to perform the project's identified work. It is the project manager's responsibility to ensure that any changes in the definition of the project's end state are reflected in the project's governing documents, and that the business sponsor agrees to the impacts on budgets or schedules. The project manager is also responsible for the communication of the project status to the business sponsor and other project stakeholders, which often include the functional IT managers.

In some organizations IT functional manager assumes the role of IT project manager on occasion, managing the enhancement of an existing application or the introduction of a new capability into the IT portfolio. It is important for the person fulfilling these two roles to be aware of the distinctions so as not to allow operational considerations, such as staff availability, to impede the success of the project. As the project manager, the IT functional manager needs to ensure that the staff time required to work on the project is made available, and that operations "hot items" do not prevent project progress.

The business sponsor role is akin to that of the homeowner in a construction project. The sponsor is the ultimate owner of the project, representing the business users for whom the IT product or service is being provided. The business sponsor is responsible for making decisions regarding scope, schedule, and budget trade-offs, after listening to the advice and recommendations from the experienced IT project manager.

Formal IT Project Management Methodology

Before discussing methodologies and application of them within IT projects, it is necessary to define some common terms often used interchangeably. A *methodology* is defined as a body of methods and rules followed in a science or discipline. Christensen and Thayer cite Institute of Electrical and Electronics Engineers (IEEE) standard 12207.0-1996 as defining a *life cycle model* as "a framework containing the processes, activities, and tasks involved in the development, operation, and maintenance of a software product, spanning the life of the system from the definition of its requirements to the termination of its use."[3] *A project life cycle* is a collection of generally sequential project phases, the names and number of which are determined by the control needs of the organization or organizations involved in the project. Finally, a *body of knowledge* can be defined as the sum of knowledge within a profession. Bodies of knowledge are often used as best-practice standards.

There are a number of bodies of knowledge with which the IT project manager should be familiar. Of particular interest is the project management body of knowledge, as described in the Project Management Institute's standards document, *A Guide to the Project Management Body of Knowledge (PMBOK® Guide)*,[4] which identifies the primary practices involved in managing any project. Now in its fifth edition, the *PMBOK® Guide* is a mature and evolving representation of the project management body of knowledge.

Project managers working within a corporation with IT projects being executed outside North America might also be practitioners of the practices called out in PRINCE2 (Projects in a Controlled Environment), a standard approach to project management developed in the late 1980s by the United Kingdom's government. PRINCE2 divides projects into stages, with reviews and go/no-go decisions specifically called out at the end of each stage. It also places an emphasis on the product via the use of a product breakdown structure.

Another guide to a body of knowledge is IEEE's *Guide to the Software Engineering Body of Knowledge* (SWEBOK).[5] At this writing, still in the early stages of industry awareness, the SWEBOK Guide provides knowledge and insight into software engineering practices such as requirements definition and management, software quality control, and software design.

One other often-cited collection of best practices with which the IT project manager should have some familiarity is the Software Engineering Institute's Capability Maturity Model (Integrated), commonly called CMMI.[6] The CMMI identifies best practices an IT organization (which could be defined as an IT project organization!) should deploy in support of successful systems development. Grouped around nine key practice areas, the CMMI associates objectives and goals with specific activities.

Most organizations have well-established systems development life cycle methodologies (SDLCs), addressing the activities required to conduct the technical work of the project. Figure 44-1 depicts a typical waterfall life cycle model, which is still the core approach to technology development. Note that the work to be performed is discussed in system development terms.

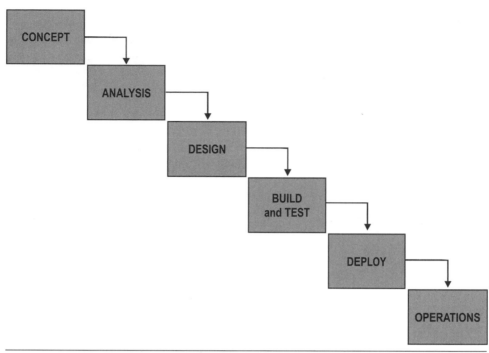

FIGURE 44-1. **TYPICAL WATERFALL LIFE CYCLE METHODOLOGY**

Much has been written recently regarding agile IT projects, including agile project management as well as agile development methods. Many software development organizations are now embracing agile approaches such as Scrum. (See Chapter 41 for descriptions of Scrum, XP, and other agile methods.) Information technology project managers should consider these approaches as another set of methods from which they can select when developing their projects' particular life cycle model. However, agile techniques are not risk-free and project managers need to carefully consider if the risks associated with agility are justified for the project being undertaken.

Whatever methodology is followed, a formal IT project management methodology would describe the activities and steps associated with each of five project phases: initiate, plan, execute, control, and close. For instance, the methodology would prescribe how to develop the project charter, the content of the project charter, and who should participate in its development, review, and signoff. The methodology would contain a sample of a project charter, as well as a template for the project manager to use.

The application of agile methods requires more leadership and less actual management. The contributions of the project manager in an agile project are those of a team leader or facilitator. With an increased emphasis on the team's (which includes the project's customers) making decisions, project managers can be focused on "roadblock removal," looking ahead in the project schedule and anticipating and addressing those actions that might impede the project team's progress. Their focus is also on the boundaries of the project, where integration with other entities such as the hardware project team needs to happen.

BEST PRACTICES

As the formal practice of project management within traditional IT organizations, as well as within technology-based product development groups, has matured over the last decade, several practices have become generally recognized as "best practices" that, when applied, can assist project teams in meeting deliverable expectations.

Establish a Formal Project Life-Cycle Model

Within formal IT project management, one of the initial activities the IT project manager undertakes is developing the project's specific life-cycle model, drawing from both a project management methodology and a systems development methodology.

It is often observed that formal methodologies impose additional work on project teams. A well-developed methodology does not impose additional work unnecessarily. Rather, the methodology provides the IT project manager and the project team with a guide by which they can conduct project activities. The project team members should use the project management methodology and a system development methodology as resources from which they can develop their project's life-cycle model, applying the concepts of "tailoring" and "just enough process" to ensure the project's life-cycle model meets their needs.

To explain further, when IT project managers survey the project management methodology and the SDLC to be applied within their project life-cycle model, they should consider the risk profile of the project. For instance, if project managers are working with a close-knit, collocated project team, they might find formal weekly team meetings and status updates with the project team are not necessary, but if the project team is working together for the first time or is geographically dispersed, it might be advantageous to have a formal time each week for the team members to interact with one another. Formal change control processes are indicated if the work is being performed under a fixed price contract with a business unit or external customer. The risk profile of the project will indicate how much formality is needed in the management of the project and which project life cycle should be followed. If the project being undertaken is deemed risky, the project manager should consider an iterative development approach, with formal scope statements and frequent schedule/budget updates, and a more rigorous approach to identifying and managing risks. A project that is viewed as being less risky, perhaps a repetitive maintenance project to an existing application, might not require as much rigor. A project with intense time-to-market considerations might warrant application of some of the agile methods associated with delivery of true sponsor value early in the project.

When the project team members have developed the project's life-cycle model, identifying the approach and processes they will use to manage the project's activities, it is recommended that the business sponsor and any internal oversight body, such as a quality assurance organization, review and approve the approach. Project managers should be able to defend the decisions made as to the degree of formal methodology compliance they will follow on the project.

Table 44-2 shows a possible partial project life-cycle model developed using a waterfall systems development methodology, in addition to a project management methodology, and expressed in terms of an activity list.

PM Methodology	Waterfall Development Methodology
INITIATING PHASE	**CONCEPT DEVELOPMENT**
Perform Project Management	**Feasibility Assessment**
Project administration	Review and document known requirements
Change control	Assess system architectures ability to support needs
Team meetings	Identify probable risk areas
Quality assurance	
Cost control	**Scope Definition**
Schedule control	Document in and out of scope conditions
Risk control	Create first level functional prioritization matrix
Status reporting	Document critical success factors
Establish System Request	**Scope Review**
Enter system request	Develop presentation
Develop project charter	Schedule review
Develop goals and objectives	Present findings
Develop business case	**Business Case Development**
Develop cost benefit	Apply ROM estimates to functional priorities
Secure sign-off	Determine risk weighting factors
Establish Project Planning Schedule	Develop probable cost model
Develop project planning schedule	
Select Project Team	
Perform skills analysis	
Select team members	
Communicate Project Charter	
Goals and objectives	
Business case	
Obtain Project Approval	
Approval	
PLANNING PHASE	**REQUIREMENTS ANALYSIS**
Establish Project Plan	**Hold Team Kickoff Session**
Develop project plan	
Develop scope statement	**Requirements Gathering**
Develop team assignments	Gather documentation
Develop communication plan	Perform necessary interviews
Develop change control plan	Establish requirements prioritization matrix
Prepare project plan document	
	Requirements Sessions
	Review critical success factors
	Review risk factors
	Validate requirements matrix
Establish Project Schedule	Prioritize requirements
Develop WBS	Validate cost estimates per functionality
Develop estimates	Develop use case scenarios
Develop critical path	Develop performance requirements
Produce project schedule	
Resource schedule by role/skill set	**Package Evaluation**
Resource schedule by name	Perform industry search
	Validate package functionality against requirements

TABLE 44-2. **SAMPLE PARTIAL PROJECT LIFE-CYCLE MODEL**

(continued)

Chapter 44 • Why IT Matters **485**

PM Methodology	Waterfall Development Methodology
Schedule and Resource Validation	Perform gap analysis and costing
Validate resources (per increment if necessary)	Develop trade-off matrix
Validate cchedule (per increment if necessary)	Vendor recommendation
Obtain Vendor Information	**Visual Specification Development**
Develop RFI	Develop story board
Issue RFI	Design screen mock-ups
Acquire Vendor(s)	Review content against requirements
Develop RFP	Develop functional flow
Develop contract and SOW	Finalize graphical presentation
Negotiation	Perform team review and validation
	Requirements Review
	Develop presentation
	Schedule review
	Present findings
	Make team recommendation

TABLE 44-2. CONTINUED

Leveraging Project Sponsors and Business Community

Most projects are not IT projects, but business projects being completed by the IT organization. Resourceful IT project managers will view their business sponsor as an equal partner in the project. Even those projects that are mostly technology in nature (for instance, an operating system upgrade) have a business sponsor, perhaps one of the IT functional managers.

Involving the business sponsor and user representatives in the planning of a project might seem risky and politically unsafe to the IT project manager. However, the more participatory and open the planning activities are, the fewer surprises there will be for the business sponsor when the project schedule or budget is presented. It has been my experience that often the business sponsor does not appreciate the details associated with developing software or implementing a new package. Involving that sponsor in the development of the project's work breakdown structure, or in the risk identification workshop, or in the development of the project's communications plan provides the IT project manager with an opportunity to educate the sponsor and to obtain the sponsor's buy-in on the project management deliverables. The sponsor will understand why these additional activities are actually to his benefit.

Representatives from the user community should also be viewed as resources to be assigned work in support of the project, to be integral members of the project team. They are the experts when it comes to defining the project's business requirements. They are also the experts as to how those business requirements should be validated as implemented. User representatives could be assigned as project team resources to participate in the definition and creation of test cases, and then in the execution of those test cases. Because they defined the requirements, they will best know when the requirement is implemented correctly.

When status reports are provided, or important project decisions are made, the business sponsor should be actively involved. In fact, one could argue that the sponsor is the *only* member of the project team empowered to make decisions regarding scope, budget, and schedule. The project manager's role is to make sure the sponsor makes an *informed* decision.

Internal Contracts

When managing internal IT projects for one of my former employers, I often negotiated contracts with my internal customers. What did this mean? It meant the project charter and associated project plan (including schedule, budget, deliverable definitions, and responsibility matrix) was a document that we both agreed to and signed. This then became a contract upon which our performances would be evaluated. I committed to delivering on schedule and within the prescribed budget; the customer agreed to actively participate in requirements management and testing activities, and to managing scope. Any change to the content of the project plan was treated as a contractual change, resulting in a new contract.

IT Project Management Office

The use of an IT project management office (PMO) was identified as an industry best practice a decade ago.[7] The PMOs proved so valuable that many of them morphed into enterprise PMOs, with mixed results. (For a survey of PMO research, see Chapter 32). The IT PMO is often implemented in one of two models: a center of excellence or shared services.

In a center of excellence model, the IT PMO serves as the keeper of the methodologies and all related activities, including methodology training and mentoring and the quality assurance mechanism, and serves as the ultimate source on all matters related to IT project management best practices. The IT PMO oversees *all* IT methodologies and standards, not just those pertaining to project management. The PMO staff oversees the systems development methodologies, the configuration management and quality control standards, and the use of any supporting tools such as scheduling and estimating tools. In this model, project managers do not report to the PMO.

An additional function often played by an IT PMO is that of project portfolio manager. Staff members within the IT PMO obtain project status data from project managers and administer periodic project reviews. They facilitate reviews of the IT project portfolio, assisting in determining which projects require additional management attention and which projects should be initiated or cancelled.

In a shared services model, the IT PMO provides the above activities in addition to being the functional provider of project managers to projects within the IT organization. This PMO is responsible for the establishment of a career path and professional training for all project managers within the organization. The PMO head would conduct performance reviews, soliciting inputs from business sponsors, team members, and others with whom the project managers had interactions.

American Management Association • www.amanet.org

Power of Technology-Based Collaboration

One of the side benefits from the emergence of technology into our everyday lives is the availability of technology as a tool for IT projects to leverage. The power of the Internet and online collaboration tools and web-based repositories means that project teams (including user representatives) no longer need to sit in the same conference room to review a presentation. They can participate in a virtual project room, where they all have access to the project documentation being reviewed. Certain technologies support real-time editing of the documents. Other products support team brainstorming and decision making. This ability to function as a team while physically dispersed means that an IT project manager potentially has a greater resource pool upon which to draw.

CHALLENGES FOR THE IT PROJECT MANAGER

The following subsections discuss the challenges that exist today and may exist in the near future for the IT project manager.

Staying Abreast with Technology

The onslaught of wireless and gaming technologies and the newer programming languages and platforms, and their integration into viable business solutions, in addition to the ongoing support of legacy mainframe and client server technologies, is changing the way we think of IT and making the role of the IT project manager more complicated. The effective use of IT is indeed a strategic market differentiator for many businesses.

The management of the projects associated with this particular endeavor can mean tremendous profits to some companies. So while the affected project managers do not need to personally be, for example, Radio Frequency Identification (RFID) experts, they do need to be sure they are comfortable with the plans and schedules they are operating under, and that any risks of schedule slippage are communicated in a timely manner to their business sponsors.

Increased Emphasis on Security and Privacy

In particular industries, notably healthcare and financial services, security and privacy are of real concern to the IT project manager. There are legal requirements that limit how one uses "live data" to create "test data" and how much data can be displayed to a particular user. Information technology project managers need to be aware of these requirements in order to ensure that the product they deliver to their user community is in compliance, just as the general contractor in a construction project needs to ensure compliance to building and safety codes.

A glance at the news reveals many instances of data privacy issues and violations resulting from overlooking these requirements. And, in some cases, hefty business fines are imposed. In a study conducted just this past year by a Harvard researcher, health data that had been "de-identified" was easily "re-identified," meaning the data in the database could violate Health Insurance Portability and Accountability Act (HIPAA) privacy rules. In 2010, the theft of a laptop containing the protected health information of over three thousand patients resulted in a $1.5 million fine for Massachusetts Eye and Ear Infirmary. The data were on a physician's laptop but were not encrypted or otherwise protected, something that could have been implemented within the application. Some might argue that the business sponsor was accountable for addressing these requirements within the project scope. However, the IT project manager, with knowledge of the domain, should ask the appropriate questions. If IT project managers are involved in a project introducing wireless technologies into an organization, they need to be sure that the activities associated with protecting the data being transmitted over that technology have been considered and are suitably addressed.[8]

Third-Party Engagements

Another trend that continues to haunt the IT project manager is the increasing pressure to expedite project delivery through leverage of third-party service providers—either in the form of software to be integrated into a solution or in the form of contract labor. This business trend can require the IT project manager to be the manager of multiple services contracts, with associated service level agreements, where the actual IT development work is performed by a third party. This means that an IT project manager needs to be up to speed on reading and interpreting contracts and enforcing their terms, as opposed to managing a project team. Many IT project managers lack the business law training required to feel totally comfortable in this role. If you are a "technology-focused" project manager, with a degree in computer sciences, enroll in a contractual law course to obtain a basic understanding of contract management.

OUTLOOK FOR THE FUTURE

The pervasiveness of information technology requires increased discipline in the management of those technology projects, while at the same time delivering the technology product ever faster. The future will indeed include some form of personal accountability for the IT project manager, especially as IT invades the healthcare industry. Just as society holds the general contractor accountable for safety and code compliance in his construction projects, so will society and specifically businesses hold the individual IT project manager accountable for safety and information privacy. There will be an increased emphasis on licensure, oversight boards, and specialized certifications in order to manage certain types of projects.

That said, the field of IT project management will indeed become more of a profession, through the efforts of organizations such as the Project Management Institute, the Association for Computing Machines, the Software Engineering Institute at Carnegie-Mellon University, and IEEE's Computer Society, to name just a few. The forward-thinking IT project manager will stay abreast of the developments within these organizations in order to be better positioned as a "professional IT project manager."

REFERENCES

[1] Kachina Shaw, "Lessons from a Billion-Dollar Project Failure, IT Business Edge," Posted December 11, 2012, http://www.itbusinessedge.com/blogs/governance-and-risk/lessons-from-a-billion-dollar-project-failure.html.

[2] Tara Conlan, "BBC Digital Media Initiative project doomed to failure, Lord Patten was told," *The Guardian* online, posted June 5, 2013, http://www.guardian.co.uk/media/2013/jun/05/bbc-digital-media-initiative-failure-patten.

[3] Mark J. Christensen and Richard H. Thayer, *The Project Manager's Guide to Software Engineering's Best Practices* (Los Alamitos, CA: IEEE Computer Society, 2001).

[4] Project Management Institute, *A Guide to the Project Management Body of Knowledge (PMBOK® Guide)*, 5th edition (Newtown Square, PA: PMI, 2013).

[5] IEEE Computer Society, *Guide to the Software Engineering Body of Knowledge* (Los Alamitos, CA: IEEE Computer Society, 2001), p. 10. Further information on the SWEBOK and the associated certification program can be found at www.swebok.org.

[6] Further information on the CMMI model can be found at www.sei.cmu.edu/cmmi/cmmi.html.

[7] Richard Pastore and Lorraine Cosgrove Ware, "The Best Best Practices," *CIO*, posted May 1, 2004, http://www.cio.com/article/32256/Findings_The_Best_Best_Practices.

[8] Pamela Lewis Dolan, "Revealed Names Expose Flaw in De-Identified Patient Data," AMEDNews.com, May 20, 2013, http://www.amednews.com/article/20130520/business/130529995/7/.

CHAPTER 45

Applying Project Management Tools and Techniques in the Ecosystem Restoration Industry

STAN VERAART, PMP, SA CERTIFIED ARBORIST, ENVIRONMENTAL CONSULTANT

DONALD ROSS, CHAIRMAN, EARTHBALANCE CORPORATION

Ecosystem restoration is a rapidly emerging industry that is firmly rooted in science. The increasing threats to our ecosystems—and their ultimate destruction—make us realize that restoring these building blocks of our planet's biological life support system has become a necessity. Introducing project management tools and techniques is essential, but before we discuss applying them in the ecosystem restoration industry, let's have a quick look at what this industry does.

THE NATURE OF THE ECOSYSTEM RESTORATION INDUSTRY

An ecosystem is the complex community of organisms and their environment functioning as an ecological unit. Restoration is defined as the return of an ecosystem to a close approximation of its condition prior to disturbance. In restoration, ecological damage to the resource is repaired. Both the structure and the functions of the ecosystem are re-created. The goal is to emulate a natural, functioning, self-regulating system that is integrated within the ecological landscape in which it occurs.

While the world's economic systems have enjoyed unprecedented expansion through the use of ecological resources, ecosystems themselves have often been degraded and diminished as a result. We live in a critical time in human history. The air, land, water, and wildlife resources of the planet are being decimated with astonishing speed. The science of restoration ecology is young and rapidly evolving. Looking ahead toward the future, we need to develop, test, and refine the science and methodology of restoration ecology further, for it to be capable of meeting the challenge of global repair. Ecosystem restoration is a growing industry because the relationship between human society and natural systems need a balance between economic growth and maintaining the integrity of healthy ecosystems. Humanity

491

must find long-term solutions to losses of biodiversity, and solutions that will support the highest levels of human fulfillment with the minimal stress on natural ecosystems. How can this be done?

SIX STEPS: THE ADAPTIVE MANAGEMENT LIFE CYCLE

Ecosystems are complex and dynamic. As a result, our understanding of them and our ability to predict how they will respond to management actions is limited. Ecosystem restoration projects are currently being implemented by making use of a formalized management process called adaptive management, which can be defined as an iterative approach in which the methods of achieving the desired objectives are unknown or uncertain—learning while doing, so to speak. Adaptive management was developed in the 1970s by C.S. Holling and coworkers at the University of British Columbia and by the International Institute for Applied Systems Analysis. Since we are dealing with a "living baseline" of a project (the ecosystem) and are facing the challenges of constant changing factors and changing understanding of the processes that take place in an ecosystem, this alternative technique is used in an attempt to increase overall project success. The typical ADAPTIVE MANAGEMENT life cycle shown in Figure 45-1 illustrates the six steps of the process:

- Step 1—*Define the challenge:* acknowledgment of the uncertainty about what policy or practice is best for the particular management issue
- Step 2—*Design a concept:* thoughtful selection of the policies or practices to be applied (the assessment and design stage of the cycle)
- Step 3—*Implement the concept:* careful implementation of a plan of action designed to reveal the critical knowledge that is currently lacking
- Step 4—*Monitor results:* monitoring of key response indicators
- Step 5—*Evaluate results:* analysis of the management outcomes in consideration of the original objectives
- Step 6—*Adjust the concept:* incorporation of the results into future decisions[1]

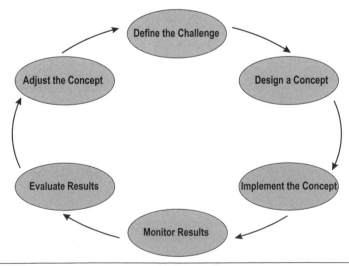

FIGURE 45-1. **STANDARD ADAPTIVE MANAGEMENT LIFE CYCLE**

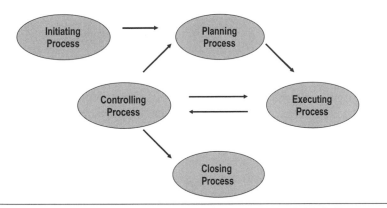

FIGURE 45-2. **STANDARD PROJECT MANAGEMENT LIFE CYCLE**

The life cycle formed by these six steps is intended to encourage a thoughtful, disciplined approach to management, without constraining the creativity that is vital to dealing effectively with uncertainty and change. How the steps are applied depends on the complexity of the problem and on the imagination of participants.

This iterative process appears to be very similar to the project management life cycle (Figure 45-2). However, whereas adaptive management provides a framework to *discover* what the best road to take is in reaching the desired project results, the project management life cycle provides a consistent, structured roadmap of *how to reach* the desired project results. In project management, we strive to meet or exceed clients' expectations by trying to describe those expectations to the finest detail as early in the project as possible. This allows us to create the scope statement, the work breakdown structure, the network diagram, critical path calculations, and the risk response plan, to name just a few. In ecosystem restoration, the final objectives and expectations are known and clear from the beginning; it is the path to get there that is unknown and uncertain. This path has to be discovered by making use of the adaptive management approach.

Ecosystem restoration is one of the last industries converting to the project management language. It is necessary that the ecosystem restoration industry be involved in new projects that deal with finding a balance between economic growth and keeping or restoring our ecosystems as early in the project process as possible. Using the tools and techniques offered by the Project Management Institute is of critical importance, enabling this industry to communicate clearly and precisely across other industries.

Fortunately, the iterative process of the project life cycle offers enough flexibility to apply the tools and techniques in this industry without too many adjustments. Project management is based on the principle of implementing controlled change. The life cycle is constructed in such a way that if deviation of the projects baseline occurs, action (replanning, followed by implementation) can be taken. After each project phase, a "phase exit" or "stage gate" provides the opportunity to reassess the project's health. It is during these phase exits that a project manager, in cooperation with the senior manager or client, can decide to kill (end) a project for measurable reasons. Some common reasons are that the deviation of the baseline is too high, that the product of the project changed, or that the original project expectations changed and are no longer in alignment with the project scope. In the ecosystem restoration industry, it is not very often that the project objectives change; however, the path to reach the project objectives often changes. Remember that the goal of ecosystem restoration is to emulate a natural, functioning, self-regulating system that is integrated with the ecological landscape in which it occurs. If the road for reaching this goal changes, it carries large consequences for the project setup. In order to compensate for this industry-specific characteristic, an easy adjustment to the project life cycle can be made during the controlling process. By adding a scope discovery process in the controlling process of the project life cycle, extra attention is given to not only the project's own baseline, by studying the project status reports, but also to the results of the adaptive management process—the reevaluation of the living baseline of the ecosystem, so to speak.

It is important that during the scope discovery process the project managers, the client, and possibly other stakeholders investigate both baselines. The scope discovery process can either be done through a meeting or through clearly written status reports. Specific attention should be given to the living baseline. Information about this baseline can be found in the adaptive management process. It is especially important that the living baseline investigation be performed during the evaluation stage of the adaptive management cycle. In case the road for reaching the project objectives needs to be changed, the project must be replanned as indicated in the project life cycle. After replanning your project, implementing the plan, and controlling your project according to your new project baseline, it again is time for implementing the scope discovery process. In this way, you allow controlled scope drift, letting your project grow and evolve, which is a necessary process in order to find the best possible solution for ecosystem restoration while maintaining good communication and management terms with other industries.

By adding this extra iterative step to the project management life cycle, it is possible to apply the project management tools and techniques to the ecosystem restoration industry. Fortunately, there are currently ecosystem restoration companies applying project management to their field of expertise, raising the industry management standards by developing a more professional and more widely recognized level of management.

An additional benefit is that the project management profession is very keen on documenting lessons learned from implemented projects. By letting our latest scientific discoveries and new technologies assist us in ecosystem restoration, and by documenting the lessons we learn from this process, it will be possible to find the lowest possible price for the maximum desired results.

If we adapt ourselves to incorporate the extra step of taking two different baselines into consideration by implementing the scope discovery process during the controlling process in the project life cycle, we can create a working symbiosis between adaptive management (currently used extensively in the ecosystem restoration field) and project management—a technique new to this industry but promising great potential. It is this symbiotic process that allows implementation of the ecosystem restoration projects, carrying, expending, and changing scope due to the living baseline, while maintaining control over the management process. This reduces risk and improves cross-industry communications by standardizing project management tools, techniques, and methodologies.

CASE STUDY: MITIGATING ENVIRONMENTAL IMPACTS THROUGH A MITIGATION BANK

The Boran Ranch Mitigation Bank in DeSoto County, Florida, provides proven, advanced wetland mitigation for public and private projects within the Peace River Basin. In general, mitigation banks are awarded "credits" as they reach milestones of improvement to wetlands they permanently protect, and these credits are later transferred to other projects as compensation for wetland losses. At Boran Ranch, land managers earn mitigation credits by restoring natural hydrology to wetlands that have been historically drained for cattle pasturing, and by establishing natural plant communities to replace the non-native pasture grasses.

This case study involves a forty-acre wetland at the Boran Ranch Mitigation Bank, informally called "the bowl" because of its obvious concavity on an otherwise flat landscape. The wetland had been drained in the 1950s and planted in pasture grasses, the most dominant of which was *Hemarthria altissima*. By studying persistent natural indicators of historic seasonal flooding, land managers had established the height and shape of the water control structure needed to reverse the drainage effects of the ditching. Before installing the structure, however, they faced decisions about the nature and intensity of measures they would take to eradicate *Hemarthria* and the other exotic pasture grasses.

Research on *Hemarthria* revealed that it was intolerant of prolonged inundation and favorably competed with other plants in a nutrient-rich environment. Since installation of the water control structures and cessation of cattle grazing would cause prolonged inundation and a gradual depletion of nutrients, land managers had to decide whether these measures alone would eradicate *Hemarthria*, or whether they need to eradicate the pasture grasses before installing the water control structure. Effective herbicides were available, but various costs were an issue. Aside from the inherent cost of herbicide application, land managers faced a regulatory requirement that success milestones (and credit release) could only be achieved after a year without herbicide treatment. Since wetland mitigation banks have highly negative cash flows in their permit approval and establishment years, land managers were reluctant to extend the establishment period by another year as a price for using herbicide. They decided to "drown" the *Hemarthria* and installed the water control structure without first eradicating the pasture grasses with herbicide.

As with many outcomes in ecosystem restoration, the bowl was both a huge success and a disappointment. Hydrology is the dominant factor in any wetland, and restoring a more natural period of inundation had immediate and profound beneficial effects. Wetland plants sprung up from the soil seed bank in response to the "just add water" prescription, but *Hemarthria* proved to be a tenacious survivor. With its roots established in the old pasture soils, it responded to inundation by sending a stem up through the water column and sprouting leaves on the water's surface. While it was less persistent in the deeper areas, it was prevalent for three years in the shallow perimeter, which was the greater land area. As its persistence became the major obstacle to reaching the success milestone, land managers decided to revisit the decision not to use herbicide.

Armed with specific experience about the use of glyphosate to eradicate *Hemarthria* and condition other sites for native vegetation, land managers were prepared to change course. Their previous experience with glyphosate provided a basis for discussions with the regulatory authorities, who not only approved of its use but also waived the one-year waiting period. The problem then became how to effectively apply the herbicide in an area with prolonged inundation.

Sometimes the vagaries of nature work in favor of the land manager. In this case, the entire state of Florida was in the second of two back-to-back years of drought, and water tables were at historic lows. Land managers waited until late in the normal annual dry cycle and were able to apply the herbicide to the shallow perimeter areas using standard land application equipment. Glyphosate is a systemic herbicide that kills roots as well as the above-ground portion of the plant. It does not, however, affect seed. Following the glyphosate treatment, the dead material was burned to complete the eradication of any plant material that may have eluded herbicide application in the heavy biomass. With the resumption of wet season rains later in the year, native wetland plants sprouted from the soil seed bank, but *Hemarthria* was absent.

The replanning of the project based on new scientific information represents an example of using adaptive management, while still applying project management tools to issues of communications, procurement, and integration.

DISCUSSION QUESTIONS

❶ How would you go about handling and simplifying the complexity of this project, while being able to stay in control of the desired outcome?

❷ For a project with which you are familiar, how might the scope discovery step be of benefit?

REFERENCE

[1] C.L. Halbert, "How adaptive is adaptive management? Implementing adaptive management in Washington State and British Columbia," reviews in *Fisheries Science* 1 (1993), pp. 261–283. See also the explanation of the adaptive management model archived on the British Columbia Ministry of Forests and Range website at http://www.for.gov.bc.ca/hfp/amhome/Amdefs.htm.

CHAPTER 46

Rescue Mission
Project Management in the Helping Professions

**JEANNETTE CABANIS-BREWIN,
PM SOLUTIONS RESEARCH**

A new commercial jet. A skyscraper. A software product. These are the kinds of deliverables that project management cut its teeth on, and with which project managers can readily identify. But increasingly, project management is being applied to enterprises where the ultimate deliverable might be expressed as something like "lessened human suffering," "improved understanding of a social problem," "a safer society for children," or "an increased awareness of the arts." Is the discipline of project management, as currently understood, applicable to projects where outcomes concern individual and social welfare, education, and development?

Every year, all across the globe, billions of dollars are invested in projects to alleviate poverty, improve public health, bolster infrastructure, and address other quality-of-life issues. Yet, until recently, project management has remained a foreign language to most staff members in the nongovernmental organizations (NGOs) and nonprofit organizations who perform the majority of this important work. This chapter examines two branches of the helping professions—community development NGOs and not-for-profit organizations—to discover what barriers exist to employing project management discipline and tools to making the world a better place for all.

COMMUNITY DEVELOPMENT: "THE PROJECT HAS FAILED US"

Early in my study of project management, one of the most moving experiences involved a project to measure participant satisfaction with a program that sought to improve maternal and child health in five African countries by improving household garden yields. In Africa, women farmers produce the bulk of crops for household consumption. Sorting through the questionnaires I had developed, and which had been administered in the field by a colleague, I came across one that was smudged with dirt and splashed by droplets of sweat. In neat, laboriously penciled script, an African woman had written, "The project has failed us because we have not learnt

497

new ways to market our cassava crop. Also, we need access to credit for farm machinery, which we did not get."[1]

This unnamed woman, sitting perhaps in the shade of an acacia tree somewhere in the Kenyan uplands on a blazing June day in 1997, was the end-user of a multi-million-dollar, multiyear project that had some considerable successes: new, blight-resistant strains of crops introduced, and new farm technologies that conserved natural resources adopted. But like many projects aimed at improving quality of life in developing nations, this one was designed around the requirements of a granting agency, not those of the population it served. In project management terms, this would be like asking the bank to draw up the blueprints for a bridge, or the accounting department to create a requirements document for the ATM software.

The Language Barrier

Why this gulf between two disciplines with so much to gain from each other? Partly, it's an artifact of a siloed educational system. Community development folks come to their work from the social sciences, economics, agriculture, or public health programs. Project managers, traditionally, have been in a building on another part of campus. Schooled to separate professional dialects, they can find it hard to communicate with each other. Write "end user" in a proposal and the community development expert will likely cross it out and write "beneficiary." Critical path? No, LogFrame.[2]

Then, too, in the heady atmosphere of big government grants that once reigned, there was little emphasis on getting a project done right the first time, on time, and within budget. A culture developed of sinking money into five-year projects that looked good on paper and later sending someone out to evaluate whether or not the project had succeeded when the money was gone and the dust had settled.

In the 1960s, development agencies were briefly excited about project management scheduling technologies; however, in the absence of automated tools like MS Project, and given the degree of uncertainty in the environment, the existing tools did not allow enough flexibility to be truly useful. Frustrated and disappointed that project management had not lived up to their expectations, development agencies turned away from standard tools that came to be summarized in the Project Management Institute's *Guide to the Project Management Body of Knowledge* (*PMBOK®* *Guide*), and developed their own tools, such as the logical framework approach. Now with so many user-friendly project planning, scheduling, and tracking tools on the market, there has been a resurgence of interest. Beginning in the 1990s, and led by initiatives from the World Bank (in partnership with Microsoft), project management became a regular feature of World Bank funded initiatives, and Humber University in Canada, among others, offers a master's program in project management for international development.[3]

But much more than technology has changed in the environment. When institutions like the World Bank start contracting for project management training, you can bet that other, more powerful drivers for change are also on the scene.

Global Village

Global commerce requires global markets. But if recent indicators can be believed, we are gearing up to sell products to people who will be unable to buy them. While it is true that incomes have increased somewhat in developing nations, the United Nations Development Program maintains that poverty cannot be measured in terms of income alone, but should be looked at as an accumulation of illiteracy, malnutrition, early deaths, poor health care, and poor access to water and urban services.[4]

Although global expansion of trade and investment is proceeding at breakneck speed, the benefits have mostly gone to the more dynamic and powerful countries in the north and south. By 2000, annual losses to developing countries from unequal access to trade, labor, and finance were estimated at well over $500 billion—ten times what they receive in foreign aid. In 1963, the poorest 20 percent of the world's population held 2.3 percent of world income. Today, their share is less than 1 percent. The increasing income inequality is a cause for concern everywhere, because of the threat of political instability it brings, as well as because expanding markets require customers who are able to participate in them.[5] Nevertheless, the United Nations holds that poverty can be erased in the twenty-first century if governments manage things better. Some of the strategies they recommend—investing in human capital (especially in women as farmers, artisans, and small-business owners) through education and training programs, and stimulating exports by fostering small enterprises—are things that development agencies have had some success with in the 1990s. But to keep up, development agencies are going to have to do more with less, and do it faster and more effectively.

Convergence

In some ways, community development provides an acid-test environment for the efficacy of project management. The external environment of the projects is very complex; social realities like drought and civil war, as well as subtle balances of cultural factors, must be understood and appreciated. It is a necessity to involve the beneficiaries, because they will be responsible for sustaining the outcomes of the project over time. It is fundamental to improve the design of the deliverables in order to achieve sustainability, yet the relationship between deliverables and their impacts is often extremely difficult to understand. Resources are limited, and the impacts can sometimes mean the difference between life and death. A social development project involves large numbers of stakeholders, and the impacts are of great interest to many parties, so project scheduling by necessity becomes a social process. This necessitates large-scale collaborative implementation of project technologies—a challenge for practitioners in both fields.

At the same time, there is synchronicity in the way that project management and community development have grown as disciplines over the last thirty years. While project management has begun to focus more and more intensively on the integrative and human aspects, community development has learned to design projects from the bottom up, beginning with the beneficiary. Yet somehow, in both disciplines, these human-centered ideas have to be much talked about before they are consistently implemented. Information systems projects still falter because of poor teamwork, and development agencies still fund public health projects that talk about participation without being truly participatory. Nevertheless, the two disciplines are converging; it took time for development agencies to see beneficiaries as customers or stakeholders with a role to play in project design, but now they can turn to scheduling technology.

In project management it was the other way around: the tools worked fine as far as that went, but when they were applied to projects of more complexity, the discipline had to expand into the human dimension. Today, agile methods hold promise for both traditional project management applications and the nonprofit/NGO world. In particular, the use of adaptive models of management and leadership can improve evaluation processes that have been overly cumbersome, allowing planners to proceed even under conditions of uncertainty, using project management principles to create a flexible and iterative plan that is responsive to conditions on the ground and to stakeholder input.[6]

This increasing convergence is highlighted by the growth and activities of the Project Management Institute's international development Community of Practice. Since a key part of building a profession is a mission of service to society as a whole, the institute and its associated membership groups take a keen interest in development projects these days, and offers an avenue to involvement for practitioners. A new, project-related mindset carries the potential to make good on the promise of community development in countries where, so far, project failure has been the rule rather than the exception. And it helps the project management profession become just that: truly professional.

NONPROFITS: THE BIG BUSINESS OF HELPING PEOPLE

Most people—including nonprofit managers and board members themselves—do not realize the potential power of nonprofit business. Statistics show that the "third sector" is necessary to our survival as a civil society:

- If the nonprofit sector were a country, it would have the seventh largest economy in the world, according to gross domestic product (GDP) data compiled by the World Bank.[7]
- With 9.4 million employees and 4.7 million volunteers, the nonprofit workforce consists of more than 14 million people and 10.5 percent of America's workforce, and contributes almost $322 billion in wages to the American economy. In fact, the nonprofit workforce outnumbers the combined workforces of the utility, wholesale trade, and construction industries. Nationally, the nonprofit arts and culture industry generates $166.2 billion in economic activity every year—$63.1 billion in spending by organizations and an additional $103.1 billion in event-related spending by their audiences.
- United States nonprofits possessed over $2.6 trillion in total assets in 2007—up from $500 million in just a little over a decade.[8]
- The sector has been growing at twice the rate at which the private and public sectors are growing.[9]

Demands on the nonprofit sector continue to grow as government strives to slim down by shedding social program responsibilities. For many communities, welfare reform has meant that the safety net once provided by government programs must now be stitched together from a patchwork of underfunded, volunteer-dependent private charities, many of which concurrently face the loss of government grants. At the same time, individual contributors, an important source of revenue, have grown more cynical about nonprofit leadership in the wake of several widely publicized scandals involving mismanagement at major nonprofit corporations. Also, recent economic upheavals began to impact charitable giving in the first quarter of 2009. Clearly, an infusion of creative management solutions is required if the nonprofit sector is to meet the challenges of this combined market expansion and resource crunch.

From Charity to Business Enterprise

One way that many nonprofits are striving to close the gap is by developing and launching nonprofit business initiatives. From the mail-order gift catalog that supports public radio programming to the thrift shop that helps underwrite a local soup kitchen, nonprofit business initiatives are multiplying rapidly. But while these endeavors offer a bright future for those organizations that successfully launch and manage them, they also pose a great risk. Frequently such enterprises are hampered by the fact that most nonprofit sector managers and staff have little experience or skill in ordinary business management—and none in the project management areas that are so critical to kicking off a successful new endeavor.

In addition, the kind of annual event-based fundraising that has always been the bread and butter of small nonprofit entities can benefit from the application of project management tools and techniques.

But project management is not a language that is spoken in most nonprofit organizations. A glance at the bible of nonprofit management, the *Jossey Bass Handbook for Nonprofit Leadership and Management* (1994), yields no references to project management and only a few pages concerning risk management and management control systems. While some organizations—notably healthcare institutions and larger nonprofits such as the March of Dimes and the Nature Conservancy—have signed on to the project management bandwagon, the small organizations that form the backbone of charitable and educational work in the United States still, from a project manager's point of view, operate in the dark. What are the barriers?

Special Management Challenges

Those versed in project management who seek to put the value of their expertise to work in nonprofit organizations will encounter numerous special conditions. For example, in grant-funded organizations, project startup can be complicated because no design and planning work can be charged to the budget until the funds to support it exist; yet design and planning must take place in advance of even applying for a grant that may eventually fund the project. In essence, many projects must accomplish the entire startup phase before any resources—either monetary or human—can be allocated.

This Catch-22 situation is compounded by the fact that, especially in small nonprofits, staff resources are limited and frequently seriously underpaid. Employees in the nonprofit sector often grumble that their love of the work is expected to reimburse them for the long hours, in lieu of money—a deal that few architects, engineers, or financial planners would accept no matter how much they loved their professions. Thus many nonprofit managers are reluctant to ask for unreimbursed extra efforts from an already overburdened staff to get new projects off the ground.

Volunteer labor is usually the resource that is relied on to solve this problem. However, anyone who has ever steered the board of a nonprofit or has managed volunteers knows that this resource base is high-maintenance and extremely variable as to time commitment, knowledge, and accountability.

When a project is mission-critical it frequently becomes the purview of a volunteer board of directors—a volatile animal at best, as any nonprofit manager can tell you. "Effective governance by the board of a nonprofit organization is a rare and unnatural act," the writers of a 1996 *Harvard Business Review* article stated flatly.[10]

Tension between the governing board and the managers of nonprofits is ubiquitous; board members may have personal agendas that conflict with the mission of the agency and that can lead to scope definition problems that, being emotionally charged, are difficult if not impossible to resolve.

While boards of directors are often skilled businesspeople, they usually do not have any of the special knowledge or experience necessary to effectively manage nonprofit organizations; this lack is exacerbated by the fact that most nonprofit managers themselves have little or no business management experience. Instead they tend to be subject matter experts in whatever the mission of the agency happens to be, whether it is domestic violence prevention, arts education, or environmental protection. So comparatively basic skills such as cost-benefit analysis, business communications, and strategic prioritizing can be missing. Business-savvy board members may be speaking Greek when they talk of risk management or change control with the program's managers.

In addition, it can be hard for a nonprofit to steer a straight strategic course when it is primarily funded by grants and contributions. Most grants and many large contributions are earmarked for very specific purposes, so the program manager has little flexibility in how to expend the organization's resources. Often an organization's progress toward its goals resembles the track of a sailboat beating against the wind: it must zig and zag according to how the latest grant or contribution forces it to frame its objectives.

Introducing Project Management to the Nonprofit

Despite the differing environments, when nonprofits convert to project management principles the payoffs can be rewarding for the organization and all its stakeholders. Project management is such a needed set of ideas in nonprofit management that the *Harvard Business Review* article cited earlier actually proposes projectizing the work of the board (without, of course, ever referring to project management as such!). The article recommends that nonprofit boards abolish committees and "organize around what matters," forming temporary task forces (read: project teams) to accomplish time-limited, goal-driven projects.

Project management experts who have worked in the nonprofit sector are very enthusiastic about the discipline's untapped potential to make these organizations more effective. While it is a bit of a stretch for people who work in nonprofits to take their long-term strategic vision and projectize it, shifting gears to project management can happen fairly quickly, precisely because foundations tend to fund organizations for specific projects. Within the familiar context of a grant application nonprofits can learn to do scope definition, define the specific problem, and define the period of time. Grant applications force an organization, in most cases, to develop measurable goals—in terms of numbers of people served, for example. Most foundation grants are actually couched in project management terms: steps, sequence, time limit, budget, and performance measures. The problem is principally one of perception. There tends to be a lot of project work going on in nonprofits that is never called a project. There is never clear scope containment; the plan is never thought through in project terms. Nonprofits need to learn to look at their programs in terms of a series of projects that have some strategic direction, and then seek funding for specific projects to serve a specific purpose, as opposed to asking the community to "fund us to do our ongoing good work," which can be a challenge to measure. Additionally, funds for "ongoing good work" can be raised by operating nonprofit businesses—and this is also an area where project management skills will be of tremendous benefit.[11]

Table 46-1, drawn from the experiences of a project management practitioner, tallies the differences between the for-profit project management environment and the nonprofit environment.

While many nonprofits strive to operate on business principles similar to those in the corporate world, the realities are quite different for a nonprofit manager. Project management techniques require some customizing to fit the volunteer and donation-driven organization.[12]

Project management techniques are most easily applied to such endeavors as annual fundraising events or a capital campaign (a major fundraising drive devoted to raising capital, usually for a major investment such as a building). Practitioners

Driver	For-Profit	Nonprofit
Responsible to:	Shareholders/Top management	Volunteers, donors, community/client base, and the governmental agencies, and foundations who supply funding
Labor base	Professional paid staff	Volunteers, professional staff (frequently underpaid)
Income	Profit-based	Contributions, grants, government funding, nonprofit business proceeds
Time/Commitment base	Consistent	Variable with volunteers; paid staff activities often circumscribed by grant stipulations
Knowledge base	Focused	Variable with volunteers and board members; finance and management knowledge tend to be limited in paid staff.

TABLE 46-1. **DIFFERENCES IN FOR-PROFIT AND NONPROFIT PROJECT MANAGEMENT ENVIRONMENTS**

who hope to "proselytize" in the nonprofit world must remember to keep it basic: basic risk management, developing a schedule, and scope definition. Over time, when the staff members of a nonprofit see that they can pull out the timeline and work breakdown structure from last year and reuse them to pull off the annual fundraiser, they begin to see the usefulness of it. Even something as simple as establishing meeting agendas with action items can be something of a revelation.

CONCLUSION

The burgeoning nonprofit section is one in which project management and the organizations it helps to improve can grow together, providing opportunities for the profession while bringing much needed skills to nonprofit management. All that, plus you get to feed the hungry, build a museum, combat AIDS, or save the rainforest.

REFERENCES

[1] Jeannette Cabanis, "'The project has failed us': the case for more and better project management in community development," *PM Network* (February 1998).

[2] More information about the Logical Framework process can be found on the MindTools website: http://www.mindtools.com/pages/article/newPPM_86.htm.

[3] Robert Youker, "The Nature of International Development Projects," Proceedings of the 2003 PMI Global Congress, PMI, 2003, http://www.pmi-idsig.org/content/PMI%2003%20ID%20ProjfromBobY.pdf.

[4] *United Nations Human Development Report*, posted annually at http://hdr.undp.org/en/, offers statistics related to the impacts of globalization, trade liberalization, and development aid projects.

[5] "For richer, for poorer," *The Economist Online*, posted October 13, 2012.

[6] Karen R.J. White, *Practical Project Management for Agile Nonprofits: Approaches and Templates to Help You Manage with Limited Resources* (West Chester, PA: Maven House, 2013).

[7] *World Development Indicators Database*, World Bank, updated July 2, 2013, http://data.worldbank.org/data-catalog/world-development-indicators.

[8] These and other statistics on the nonprofit sector can be found in *The Nonprofit Sector in Brief: Facts and Figures from the Nonprofit Almanac 2011: Public Charities, Giving, and Volunteering*, published annually by The Urban Institute, and posted at http://nccsdataweb.urban.org/kbfiles/797/Almanac 2008publicCharities.pdf, or at the National Center for Charitable Statistics page: http://nccs.urban.org/statistics/quickfacts.cfm.

[9] Economic impact statistics for the nonprofit sector are continually updated on the Council of Nonprofits website, http://www.councilofnonprofits.org/?q=economy/npstatistics.

[10] B. Taylor, R. Chait, and T. Holland, "The new work of the nonprofit board," *Harvard Business Review* (September–October 1995), p. 36.

[11] Jeannette Cabanis, "Reinventing the Business of Doing Good: Project Management in the Nonprofit Sector," *PM Network*, April 1998.

[12] The exhibit was adapted from one shared with us by Pat Barber, PMP, who first published about working with nonprofits in *Project Management Consulting News*, an Electronic Data System (EDS) internal newsletter, in October 1997.

CHAPTER 47

Focus on Financial Services
Mitigating Risk with Transparency in a Regulated Environment

ROBIN MARKLE DUMAS, MBA, SIX SIGMA BLACK BELT, EPMO CONSULTANT

Governance and risk mitigation are critical factors in the project life cycle, and are known drivers of project success.[1] Finding a balance between effective oversight and bureaucracy can be challenging for any project leader. But what happens when external stakeholders take a more active role in project oversight? Such is the case in heavily regulated industries. In the financial services sector, for example, regulatory requirements shift continually as a result of the aftermath of the worst market correction since the Great Depression. In order to remain compliant, firms must stay ahead of changing legislation while ensuring that projected spend is contained within paper-thin margins. As a result, project practices are adapted to better serve the unique challenge of driving change under robust governance.

This chapter focuses on how to implement three strategic practices designed to build trust and transparency in a regulated environment:

1. Develop financial modeling and forecasting core competencies in project leaders.
2. Communicate in terms of results rather than statistics in project reporting.
3. Manage significant change through structured dialogue and highly accessible reports.

MODEL FINANCIALS AT THE PROJECT TEAM LEVEL

Preparing the business case is historically a task for the executive sponsor. In many organizations, the project team is assembled only after the project is presented and funding approved. This approach is changing as thought leaders move project practices to more flexible methodologies.[2] No project is launched for the sole purpose of spending time and money. Project leaders must fully understand the financial goals of the project and the economic drivers of those goals in order to effectively manage project costs and drive committed results. In order to do so, project leaders must

505

develop financial modeling core competencies and accept responsibility for accurately forecasting the impact of activity on financial outcomes. Project leaders who communicate in terms of results are far more valuable than those who simply track due dates and spend.

One best practice approach to integrating the vision with the plan is to migrate responsibility for compiling financial data and pro-forma modeling to the project leader. This approach broadens the scope of the project leader to include preparing accurate and manageable budgets through partnership with the executive sponsor and subject-matter experts (SMEs). While the ultimate accountability for the benefit commitment remains with the executive sponsor, the project leader's understanding of the expected outcomes helps align reality with the vision. The project leader is not expected to approve the direction or validate the input, but must thoroughly understand each item and feel free to challenge or discuss any practical concerns on the front end. Adoption of a simple but thorough pro-forma spreadsheet template is all that is needed to master the input.

CASE EXAMPLE

To keep up with competitors' offerings, a bank approves an online banking project to spend $1.2 million in a capitalized expense to deliver an online loan application and a new set of report functionality for customers. The project will take one year to complete. The benefit is added revenue from sales of the new product and a small fee increase for existing customers. The new product will require newer hardware and software, and full-time employees will replace the contract labor supporting the current product. The new product will launch near the end of the first year and the budget will account for increasing sales momentum over the course of the second year for a steady state by Year 3.

The project lead meets with the executive sponsor to gather the revenue commitments and details regarding staffing changes. The SMEs in technology provide the cost estimates from the vendor along with any internal requirements. Guidelines for amortization are obtained from organizational process assets.

The model depicted in Table 47-1 is a very simplistic view of a pro-forma template for project budgeting. There are many different versions that can serve as well, and project leaders should ensure that organizational process assets are used where they exist.[3]

If the cost and revenue estimates require an investment to complete, an initial pro-forma can serve as a gate to cap the incremental outlay for the initiation cycle until estimates can be obtained for knowledgeable decision making. The timing can also be adjusted to accommodate the organization's unique needs and project life cycle. As long as the project lead facilitates the information gathering through funding approval the project will realize enhanced tracking and understanding from the entire project team.

		Year 1	Year 2	Year 3	Year 4
Benefit Commitment					
Added Revenue					
Increased retail sales		100,000	700,000	800,000	800,000
Price increase for product X		25,000	100,000	100,000	100,000
Total Added Revenue		–	125,000	800,000	900,000	900,000
Cost Saves					
Current maintenance		35,000	35,000	35,000	35,000
Depreciation old hardware[a]		5,000	5,000		
Eliminate contract labor		21,000	350,000	350,000	350,000
Total Cost Saves		61,000	390,000	385,000	385,000
Total Benefit Commitment		186,000	1,190,000	1,285,000	1,285,000

Budgeted Outlay	Capital	Expense			
Hardware	900,000				
Software	300,000				
Maintenance		(10,000)	(10,000)	(10,000)	(10,000)
Added salaries		(200,000)	(200,000)	(200,000)	(200,000)
Total Budgeted Outlay	1,200,000	(210,000)	(210,000)	(210,000)	(210,000)
Amortization[b]					
Hardware		(75,000)	(300,000)	(300,000)	(225,000)
Software		(25,000)	(100,000)	(100,000)	(75,000)
Total Depreciation		–	(100,000)	(400,000)	(400,000)	(300,000)
Impact to Run Rate (Revenue)		125,000	800,000	900,000	900,000
Impact to Run Rate (Expense)		(310,000)	(610,000)	(610,000)	(510,000)
Net Impact to Run Rate		**(124,000)**	**580,000**	**675,000**	**775,000**

[a]Assumes write off of corporate asset rather than redeployment. Organizational process assets should be followed.

[b]Assumes 3 year straight-line depreciation schedule for simplicity of illustration only. Organizational process assets should be followed.

TABLE 47-1. **EXAMPLE OF A PRO-FORMA TEMPLATE FOR PROJECT BUDGETING**

When deployed as an enterprise strategy, this process also provides for the following:

- Standard formatting, which enables integration and aggregation at the portfolio level
- An enterprise view of resource requirements, vendor liability, and SME scheduling

- A stronger partnership between the project leader and the executive sponsor
- Transparency
- A view of project status for third parties without involving SMEs

COMMUNICATE RESULTS RATHER THAN STATISTICS

Building trust in a heavily regulated environment, or any environment, for that matter, is a function of transparency and predictability. When communicating the status of any project or effort, it is important to clearly relay the impact of the current activities, issues, and risks to the benefit commitment. The complexity comes into play for the project manager when there are too much data and not enough story. This is especially true when there is no agreement in place as to what constitutes success.

In the example scenario used in Table 47-1, an unexpected date slippage should be communicated as a delay in bringing the new functionality to market, with a forecast of any run rate impact. Avoid presenting progress in terms of tasks unless specifically requested to do so.

Where external stakeholders are actively involved in oversight, the project leader is expected to balance the requirements of regulatory/compliance processes while meeting the needs of the executive sponsor. Although in most cases the expected results are the same for both stakeholders, the stakeholder responsible for oversight is likely to be far more interested in mitigating risk through effective project processes, whereas the executive sponsor is interested in results. To balance the two, status reports can be presented in terms of both risk and outcome with a few simple adjustments to the work breakdown structure.

Using the case example cited earlier, Table 47-2 depicts a typical project status report of technical milestones, such as requirements definition, development, testing, and deployment.

The project leader takes the role of translator and uses the report to address schedule, cost, and risk mitigation statuses.

Table 47-3 illustrates that, with simple adjustments in the milestone labels to describe the deliverable rather than the task, the message becomes much clearer.

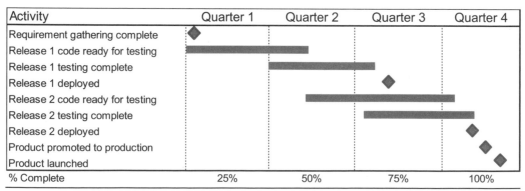

Activity	Quarter 1	Quarter 2	Quarter 3	Quarter 4
Requirement gathering complete				
Release 1 code ready for testing				
Release 1 testing complete				
Release 1 deployed				
Release 2 code ready for testing				
Release 2 testing complete				
Release 2 deployed				
Product promoted to production				
Product launched				
% Complete	25%	50%	75%	100%

TABLE 47-2. **EXAMPLE OF A PROJECT STATUS REPORT WITH TECHNICAL MILESTONES**

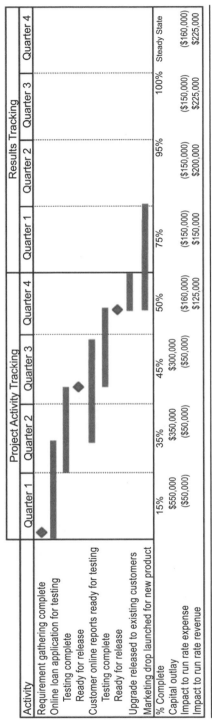

Activity	Project Activity Tracking				Results Tracking			
	Quarter 1	Quarter 2	Quarter 3	Quarter 4	Quarter 1	Quarter 2	Quarter 3	Quarter 4
Requirement gathering complete								
Online loan application for testing								
Testing complete								
Ready for release								
Customer online reports ready for testing								
Testing complete								
Ready for release								
Upgrade released to existing customers								
Marketing drop launched for new product								
% Complete	15%	35%	45%	50%	75%	95%	100%	Steady State
Capital outlay	$550,000	$350,000	$300,000					
Impact to run rate expense	($50,000)	($50,000)	($50,000)	($160,000)	($150,000)	($150,000)	($150,000)	($160,000)
Impact to run rate revenue				$125,000	$150,000	$200,000	$225,000	$225,000

TABLE 47-3. **EXAMPLE OF A PROJECT STATUS REPORT**

Additionally, the "% Complete" data field is expanded to include results tracking through steady state. Lastly, a high-level view of the planned impact on the run rate has been added as well as the planned capital outlay.

Although the steps within the work effort have not changed, the understanding of the work effort is increased. Examiners and other key stakeholders can determine if cost and schedule are on track, as well as the financial implications of date slippage. Similarly, internal stakeholders can understand and plan for resource needs and manage any potential impact on the customer.

Lastly, key executives can better guide the volume of organizational change as schedules shift or budgetary issues arise if status reports are results oriented. A CEO is more likely to understand the full impact of a delayed product launch than that of a failed code test.

MANAGE ENVIRONMENTAL CHANGE WITH STRUCTURED DIALOGUE

Highly regulated industries are constantly shifting and changing to address risk. As a result, business models must be flexible to allow for quick adoption of new compulsory requirements. Some changes can directly impact the ability of the project team to deliver committed results. And some are significant enough to warrant closing the project altogether.

Changes in legislation, changes in regulatory or compliance requirements, and abrupt shifts in the capital markets are all examples of environmental change. These changes often require adjustments to the scope of enterprise-level projects to ensure compliance and mitigate risk. Project leaders must be quick and transparent regarding the cause and impact of environmental shifts to minimize disruption. Here are some examples of actions that should be taken:

- Assess the impact of proposed change including downstream effects on affiliated projects, resources, and deliverables.
- Seek input from executive sponsors and decision makers to determine the best course of action.
- Review planned adjustments with regulators and third-party stakeholders for feedback.
- Communicate final changes in the plan to all constituents.
- Follow established change request processes to update plan documents and budgets on all projects affected.
- Ensure all resource management models are adjusted where needed on all projects affected.
- Add any additional risks to the risk matrix with applicable mitigation plans.

Disruption as a result of change, whether environmental or otherwise, is only detrimental to a project when the effect is an unpredictable outcome. If the organization knows what to expect when change occurs, the risk of change is minimized. Many projects have been delayed at the last minute as a result of an uninformed and surprised key stakeholder. There are two strategies to use for managing time-sensitive project communications:

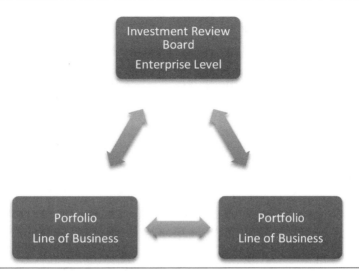

FIGURE 47-1. **COMMUNICATION FLOW BETWEEN AND AMONG LINES OF BUSINESS AND EXECUTIVES**

1. *Implement structured dialogue through a predictable forum where updates are given and issues are escalated.* The framework should include the following:

   - Consistent, recurring meetings scheduled in advance at predictable dates/times
   - A planned agenda with reports distributed in advance of the meetings
   - Participants who are at a senior level of the organization are responsible for enterprise-level project results
   - Project leaders presenting template-based reports for discussion
   - Formal minutes accessible to key stakeholders (internal and external)

   Figure 47-1 illustrates a structured dialogue within portfolios as well as oversight from an enterprise-level investment review for senior executives.

2. *Create a single repository of highly accessible reports.* Open access to certain project information creates a nimble environment able to adapt more quickly to changing needs and requirements. It also builds trust with key stakeholders charged with oversight of project processes and enables more efficient monitoring for internal and external auditors and examiners. The repository need not include sensitive data, but should allow read-only access to plans, reports, and forecasts, noting the dates of all approved changes with commentary notes.

CONCLUSION

Project leaders must understand fully the goals and expected results of any project. Adding a simple pro-forma template to project initiation documents as an exercise performed by project leaders enhances their command of the financial detail. Project leaders are better positioned to engage as partners with executive sponsors if they demonstrate financial modeling and forecasting skill sets and can put together the cost/benefit analysis.

It is important when presenting project status updates to use language that the audience can understand. Two key stakeholders in a highly regulated environment are the examiners and the executive sponsor. The project manager must balance information presented to accommodate risk mitigation through effective processes and governance as well as expected results and financial commitments. Project status reports should address potential impacts to the expected results. Simple adjustments can be made to the work breakdown structure to focus on results rather than on tasks. Adding run-rate impact to presentations helps the audience to understand the full impact of the progress made and issues at hand.

Highly regulated industries are constantly shifting and changing requirements to address risk. Shifts can be significant enough to delay a project or stop it altogether. Communication and transparency are critical to adapting to new compulsory rules or requirements. Strong partnerships with internal and external stakeholders responsible for governance are important to the success of work efforts. Two strategies for managing time sensitive communications are (1) implement structured dialogue through a predictable forum where updates are given and issues are escalated, and (2) create a single repository of highly accessible reports.

All of the strategies and practices outlined in this chapter are given within the context of highly regulated industries, with a focus on financial services. Open dialogue, inclusion, and transparency are always the best ways to mitigate risk in any project endeavor.

DISCUSSION QUESTIONS

❶ Revise the pro-forma template and remove the revenue. Discuss the implications of a project that negatively impacts run rate. When would such a project be approved?

❷ Create a structured dialogue model for your current organization. Discuss the reasons for your choices.

❸ Why should everyone have access to project information? What sensitive data elements should not be accessible in the repository?

REFERENCES

[1] "Federal Financial Institutions Examination Council (FFIEC) Information Technology Examination Handbook, Development and Acquisition Booklet", last modified April 2004, http://ithandbook.ffiec.gov/it-booklets/development-and-acquisition.aspx.

[2] Team Technologies, Inc. of Middleburg, VA, in cooperation with Operations Core Services, "The Logframe Handbook, A Logical Framework Approach to Project Cycle Management," public disclosure authorized, The World Bank, 1997.

[3] Project Management Institute, *A Guide to the Project Management Body of Knowledge (PMBOK® Guide)*, 5th edition (Newtown Square, PA: PMI, 2013), p, 27.

CHAPTER 48

Project Management for Marketing
Keep It Lean, Don't Slow Us Down

MARY YANOCHA, PM SOLUTIONS AND PM COLLEGE

Marketing by its very nature is a creative endeavor. The people that tend to work in marketing (be it a functional area within an organization or on the agency side) tend have big ideas. They are artistic, expressive, free form. In other words, marketing and communications professionals shun too much process for fear it will stifle or slow down the flow of these creative juices. But having some form of organization in this creative work is essential in order to meet a stated business objective. That's where project management comes in.

The American Marketing Association officially defines marketing as the activity, set of institutions, and processes for creating, communicating, delivering, and exchanging offerings that have value for customers, clients, partners, and society at large.[1] A much simpler definition of marketing is offered in the popular college textbook, *Marketing Management,* which describes it as "meeting needs profitably."[2] Those "needs" are ever changing. Therefore, the more rapidly that an organization's marketing efforts can capitalize on conveying that its products and services are the solution, the more profitable the organization stands to become. Marketing can accomplish this consistently by incorporating fundamental project management practices into marketing operations.

THE PROCESS GROUPS IN A MARKETING CONTEXT

Regardless of size, all projects have the same essential components, namely, a beginning, a middle, and an end. All marketing projects should also be aligned in some way with the organization's business needs. To consider how project management can save time and money with a repeatable approach to meeting objectives, let's begin by looking at a synopsis of the five process groups of managing a project, as defined in the industry-standard, the Project Management Institute's *Guide to the Project Management Body of Knowledge (PMBOK® Guide),* and the typical activities within each step.[3]

① Initiate	② Plan	③ Execute	④ Monitor/Control	⑤ Close
Create a project charter	Create a project plan	Get and develop the project team	Monitor and control project work	Collect lessons learned
Write a preliminary scope statement	Plan the scope	Run the project	Control quality	Recognize the team
	Develop the work breakdown structure	Ensure quality	Manage the work of the project team	Complete the project
		Distribute information		
	Plan for risks		Manage stakeholders	
		Work with vendors		
	Plan purchase and acquisitions		Report on performance	
	Plan contracting		Mitigate risks	

FIGURE 48-1. **PROCESS GROUPS AND TYPICAL ACTIVITIES WITHIN EACH STEP OF A PROJECT'S LIFE CYCLE**

As the figure demonstrates, the beginning of the project is initiate and plan, the middle is execute and monitor/control, and the end is close. The important thing is to understand the general elements of each process group (also considered steps or phases in managing a project), select the appropriate processes, and scale the tasks for each group to suit the specific project.

When leading a marketing project, each step of the process requires some diligence in ensuring that the questions shown in Figure 48-2 are answered. Note the larger volume of questions under "Plan." It's no coincidence. Planning is one of the most critical and often hastily overlooked elements of delivering any project successfully.

THE PEOPLE SIDE: BASIC PROJECT MANAGER COMPETENCY IS ESSENTIAL TO MARKETERS

Marketers may not hold the formal title of project manager, but they certainly are involved in delivering projects. Learning some basic project management principles will help anyone working on marketing projects maintain momentum and support for the initiative and help enhance the chance of project success.

One of the quickest ways to do this is to provide your marketing team a foundational level project management training course that covers the core technical components of project management (defining scope, scheduling, estimating, etc.). This gives the team a common understanding of how work should be performed. Customizing the training with your own marketing terminology and existing processes makes the content even more meaningful to the team members (and increases the likelihood that they will put the concepts into practice). Technical skills should be balanced with leadership skills. Marketing is an area that supports other segments of the business such as sales, customer service, and executive management. Therefore, sharpening the team's ability to manage expectations, navigate through difficult

① Initiate	② Plan	③ Execute	④ Monitor/Control	⑤ Close
Do we have an accurate description of the project? What objective do we want to achieve? Who is the sponsor? Who are the key stakeholders? Do we have formal authorization to begin the project? Is there funding? When is the project due?	What are the requirements? Which resources do we need to assign? Are they available? Will we need to contract out all/part of the work? Are there subject-matter experts we need to involve? What is the list of activities we need to accomplish? What is the timeline to complete the activities? What marketing channels will we use to meet our objective? How will we be communicating the plan and status updates to key stakeholders?	What approvals do we need along the way? Are we following the plan as it was defined?	Are deadlines being met? Are we within budget? If a change is needed, how will it be addressed? Are we communicating effectively with key stakeholders? Are we taking the proper corrective actions to potential problems before they escalate? How are we measuring success?	Did we meet our stated objective? Did the project complete on time and within budget? Do we need to document lessons learned for similar projects in the future? How do we recognize the team's efforts?

FIGURE 48-2. **SAMPLE QUESTIONS TO ASK WHEN LEADING A MARKETING PROJECT**

conversations, and resolve conflicts will garner further respect from both peer groups and the C-suite, and foster positive working relationships, making it that much easier to get the job done!

Here is an example of where building project management competency has paid off: The innovation function of one of the largest consumer products manufacturers in the world owns the commercial, marketing, and technical aspects of the company's initiatives. Innovation team members were expected to be able to communicate issues and status directly with business unit general managers. With this increased visibility came the added need for stronger leadership and communication skills. In addition, the innovation function needed to standardize processes in order to be more successful in launching initiatives and improving the percentage of projects and programs meeting milestone targets. The company brought in customized versions of both leadership and project management essentials training. Over the last five years, nearly 1,500 participants have taken one or more of the over 150 course offerings at nine different sites around the world. Most significant is that since that time, the percentage of milestones achieved on schedule has improved steadily. To date, the rate of milestone achievement is ten times higher than it was five years ago. A measurement of the value of the program showed that raising the competency level of a program manager made it twice as likely that an initiative will meet all targets once it is launched. These data make a powerful argument for continuing to raise the competency level of program managers who lead high visibility, multibillion-dollar initiatives for the company.

THE OTHER PEOPLE SIDE: STAKEHOLDER MANAGEMENT

Any interested party associated with your marketing endeavor is considered a stakeholder. Customers (internal or external), team members, project sponsors, executives, and vendor partners such as creative agencies can all be among your key stakeholders. How you identify, understand the motivations of, engage with, and manage the expectations of your stakeholders can make or break your project.

Likewise, "the bigger the organization, the more diverse the stakeholders are likely to be, and the more controversial the change, the more difficult it can become to sell the change," notes Nigel Lucas, a United Kingdom–based public relations and communications consultant whose client roster has included Network Rail, Jaguar Land Rover, HP, and Royal Bank of Scotland. He points out that one of the earliest lessons learned in marketing is that you need to sell the benefits before selling the features. He advises other marketers to "slice and dice" the benefits messages when a change is complex, in order to affirm the positive perceptions of certain stakeholders and help realign the negative perceptions of other stakeholders. "And, of course, you can't do any of this until you know exactly what your various stakeholders think, feel, believe and worry about," states Lucas. "We can all inform and make people aware of what's happening. That's the easy part. But true success can only be measured by the number of stakeholders you engage with and listen to, and, more importantly, actually persuade to get involved."[4]

COMMUNICATION: IT'S OUR JOB, AFTER ALL

Communication is inherent to marketing. But how well we convey our messages to our identified stakeholders (see above) depends on how well we plan them. Hence the communications plan is an essential component of a marketing initiative. In preparing to write this chapter, I did some communicating of my own by reaching out to other marketing and communications professionals via discussion threads on shared industry Linked-In groups. I simply asked, "What project management practices are most valuable to your marketing and communications initiatives?" Two of the many responses I received emphasize key actions you should consider when developing your own communications plan.[5]

Rob Simms, director of Life Science Solutions at UL in Princeton, New Jersey, shared what he feels to be key questions to ask when developing the communications plan that also help circumvent delays with the internal message-approval process when executing a marketing campaign:

- Are the messages relevant to the business objectives?
- How will the message be conveyed (via social media, collateral, web content, etc.)?
- Has the messaging been vetted against existing content, including that of competitors?

These questions cover the areas of strategic alignment, channels for delivery of the message, and due diligence around message creation. Also valuable to include within a marketing/communications plan are sections for target audience identification (stakeholders), goals for what you want the plan to accomplish, a defined way to measure if the goals were met, and timelines for implementing your plan (including resource requirements and budget). Central to all of this is gathering the right inputs upfront.[6]

"Requirements gathering is, for me, one of the most important components of project managing a marketing or communications initiative. Service line/business stakeholders always jump to tactics without taking the time to really define the objective and the strategy for achieving it," noted Allison Whitney, director of marketing for MedAmerica in San Francisco. She went on to say,

My requirements-gathering process starts with an initial pre-kickoff meeting where everyone can get their ideas off their chest about what poster, mailer, email, website, etc. needs to be created. I use that conversation as background information for a second more strategic discussion with the business decision makers (official project kick-off) to define and get agreement on the objectives. This process helps clearly delineate needs and wants and allows the marketing communications staff to develop strategies that speak to the true requirements of the client. This is one of the first things I train new junior (and not so junior) staff on when they join my team.[7]

TECHNOLOGY: THE GREAT ENABLER

Without question, technology is, and will remain, the backbone of marketing execution. Social media, CRM systems, websites, apps, mobile, marketing automation tools, and collaboration applications are among the many platforms and outlets being actively used by marketers in organizations of all sizes. Countless articles and data have been published about each and every aspect of these technologies that have broken down so many barriers to connectivity. While we can't cover them all here, one aspect particularly relevant to marketers is the increasing use of online collaboration tools to facilitate and accelerate project delivery.

Keeping everything and everyone organized as a project progresses through its life cycle can be no easy task. Having a home base for project team conversations, documentation, schedules, and deliverable checklists facilitates keeping all aspects moving along as planned. There are many tools available to serve this purpose, many of which are also cost-effective for even smaller organizations to afford. Here is an example of how online collaboration tools can be useful at the project level:

MARKETING OPERATIONS AT THE ENTERPRISE LEVEL: THE PROJECT MANAGEMENT OFFICE AS CHANGE AGENT

The larger the organization, the more complex and challenging it becomes to break down cultural resistance and shift the way work gets performed. Marketing is no different. Silo mentalities are very much still in existence in organizations and often inhibit getting to market quickly. Establishing a marketing project management office (PMO) as a means to centralize the delivery of the organization's strategies is an approach being taken by some forward-thinking organizations looking for ways to cut out the nonsense of a fractured operating environment. Instead, the PMO becomes the "mission control" for marketing, determining standards for delivery, for governance of the portfolio of projects that are prioritized in order of value to the business, and for enhanced capabilities of those delivering projects.

One such organization is Verizon. It has an enterprise PMO (EPMO) at the corporate level, and various PMOs at the functional levels within each line of business that operate independently. The EPMO facilitates a "PMO community" made up of representatives from each of the various business unit PMOs with the goal of collectively improving project performance to meet customer expectations.

Among these PMOs is the Verizon Wireless Marketing PMO, winner of the 2012 PMO of the Year Award (see case study below). "The marketing PMO is the business transformation function," noted Sara Nunez, director of the EPMO for Verizon and part of the team that originated the Verizon Wireless marketing PMO nearly a decade ago. "Everything the marketing PMO does becomes part of the DNA of Verizon Wireless, and that's key for success. By focusing on the business results and measuring them, we are ensuring that we are delivering what the business expects of the marketing function."

Nunez offers her advice for those looking to create a similar marketing PMO structure:

> Quantify why your PMO should exist. Remove the perception that everything can't be quantified. It can. To gain and retain executive support, provide real data, such as what a day late to market costs your business, and define what the expected return will be on improvements to project delivery as a result. Establish a common language around project work and benchmarks in how the PMO will measure its value to the business. Define the capabilities required to gain process excellence and build a project delivery framework that has enough flexibilities built in to be used and scaled as needed. These actions will set the tone for adoption and agility, with just the right amount of structure to drive the right business changes.[8]

CASE STUDY: THE VERIZON WIRELESS MARKETING PMO SURPASSES AMBITIOUS GOALS

verizonwireless operates the nation's largest 4G LTE and 3G networks and offers global voice and data services in more than 200 destinations around the world. With more than 94 million customers in the U.S., Verizon Wireless can truly be said to have "a household name," and its Marketing department plays a large part in its success. Yet, less than a decade ago, it operated in a much more siloed fashion. Departmental leaders within the marketing organization resisted sharing project resources with one another for fear of jeopardizing achievement of their respective P&L objectives. At that point, the vast majority of the work completed by key functional areas was focused on the consumer market, while the minority of all project work was being directed to business and governmental clients, which was a key piece of the Verizon Wireless strategy.

The Chief Marketing Officer at the time recognized the need to create a more efficient, integrated approach to delivering against his organization's strategies, and commissioned the creation of the Marketing PMO as a way to meet ambitious goals including:

- 50% cycle time reduction
- 90% on-time delivery for top projects

- 70% on-time delivery for all other projects
- 100% alignment of organizational resources to top prioritized projects

The PMO's mission was and continues to be "the financial advisor and delivery arm for the strategies of the organization." To that end, it is accountable for the portfolio and the delivery of top tier projects for the entire Verizon Wireless enterprise. Verizon Wireless has shown its executive commitment to a project management culture by funding and growing the PMO every year since 2006.

To deliver on its mission, the PMO consists of an array of skilled project management leaders with a strong grip on the business rationale and impacts of the portfolio. There is also a focus on individual performance appraisals and making sure that each team member is clear that their performance expectations are tied to project success. To refine its delivery approaches, the PMO has utilized the standards of the Project Management Institute and other key methodologies as the basis for its methodology and processes. It began by implementing a governance process, called VZLaunch, to refine its product development process. The model established stage gates that defined the cross-functional work required in each gate. A team of cross-functional gatekeepers decide if the project is ready to move to the next gate and the next stage of development. This process guaranteed that cross-functional teams built products correctly and reduced re-work. It resulted in project management functions applied consistently across the enterprise.

In 2008, the first iteration of portfolio management was established at Verizon Wireless. Over the next year, the organization began the facilitation and allocation of the enterprise's resources to the top-priority projects. It also drove cross-functional organizations to commit resources and timelines resulting in the effective use of the enterprise's resources. By the end of 2008, these collective efforts improved the cycle-time of product delivery by 25 percent. Another two years showed that the initial goals for the PMO set out at its inception had been achieved or surpassed:

- Cycle time had been reduced by 58% despite the increasing complexity of projects.
- Top projects were being delivered on-time 100% of the time.
- All other projects were delivered on-time 80% of the time.
- A manual process provided 100% alignment of organizational resources to top-prioritized projects.
- Prioritization of the entire enterprise's work (over a US$1 billion portfolio investment) is completed every month.

Verizon Wireless now knows which projects will advance its strategy. It has predictability; when a product is scheduled for launch, the launch will be accomplished on-time. In 2012, the Verizon Marketing PMO was the winner of the PMO of the Year Award. Administered by the Project Management Institute

(PMI®), the award salutes a Project Management Office that has demonstrated excellence and innovation in developing and maturing an organizational structure to support the effective management of projects.

DISCUSSION QUESTIONS

❶ Identify the standard process that is used by your marketing group to deliver its projects (refer to Figure 48-1). If a documented process does not exist, can you map out a basic approach that would serve as a framework for how work gets delivered?

❷ Does your marketing team have any formal training in project management approaches (both technical and leadership aspects)? If not, what type of professional development would be most beneficial to the group in order to boost their delivery competency most quickly?

❸ Think about a project you recently completed. How could you have improved upon your project communications?

❹ Would a marketing PMO structure work within your organization? What are the cultural change implications that would need to be considered? Is there appropriate executive support for a structure like this?

REFERENCES

[1] American Marketing Association, "Definition of Marketing," 2007, http://www.marketingpower.com/aboutama/pages/definitionofmarketing.aspx.

[2] Philip Kotler and Kevin Lane Keller, *Marketing Management,* 14th edition (Upper Saddle River, NJ: Prentice Hall, 2012).

[3] Project Management Institute, *A Guide to the Project Management Body of Knowledge* (*PMBOK® Guide*), 5th edition (Newtown Square, PA: PMI, 2013).

[4] Personal interview with Nigel Lucas. Conducted via emails July 20–22, 2013.

[5] Research survey. Conducted via LinkedIn on the IABC (International Association of Business Communicators) Group discussion board, July 13–25, 2013, www.linkedin.com.

[6] Personal interview with Rob Simms. Conducted via emails July 20–22, 2013.

[7] Personal interview with Allison Whitney. Conducted via emails July 20–22, 2013.

[8] Personal interview with Sara Nunez. Conducted via telephone and email July 25, 2013.

[9] PM Solutions Research, 2012 PMO of the Year Award, ebook posted at http://www.pmsolutions.com/resources/view/pmo-of-the-year-award-2012-ebook/.

CHAPTER 49

Project Management in Healthcare
Making a Difference Through Compassion, Caring, and Respect

JANICE WEAVER, PMP, NORTON HEALTHCARE

Among the unique challenges faced by project managers in healthcare, primary importance must be placed on this: *Healthcare cannot afford project failures. The risks are too great.* Aside from the monetary impact and negative press, a failed project in healthcare can mean the difference between life and death.

Project management success in healthcare is thus too critical to be left up to software programs or even skilled technical controls. Seasoned healthcare project managers know success depends on their soft skills, and perhaps most crucially on cultural sensitivity and communications.

Healthcare has been slow to adopt formal project management. In the past, healthcare consisted primarily of single hospitals usually formed by charitable organizations. Projects were simple and project teams were small. Project deliverables were manageable when coordinated by someone with good organization and planning skills. These projects were frequently implemented successfully. Project management was not critical for success.

Over time, healthcare and healthcare projects have become more complex. Most projects now encompass people, process, technology, and, frequently, construction.

The benefit of project management was not evident until large healthcare systems or integrated delivery systems (IDSs) evolved. An IDS is a collaborative network that links various healthcare providers to offer a coordinated continuum of care. They are accountable both clinically and fiscally for the outcomes and health status of the population and community they serve.

Consisting of multiple hospitals, an IDS provides a wide array of services such as acute patient care, multiple medical specialties (e.g., cancer, heart disease, neurology, orthopedics, pediatrics, women's services), physician practices, outpatient medical facilities, and affiliations with medical schools. These multihospital health systems are the most common organizational structure in the hospital industry today. Small community hospitals still exist and are often affiliated with these systems where they share services, programs, and medical staff.

In IDS organizations, large projects (and programs) are the norm. Projects are highly visible, high risk, with huge capital investments and long durations. These projects are not limited to information technology or construction. There are many interrelationships among various deliverables. Some projects extend beyond the hospital system itself and encompass affiliated organizations, increasing the complexity even more. Formal project management is critical for success.

Healthcare organizations have limited funding, schedule constraints, strict quality requirements, and competitive pressures. There are more projects to be done than resources to do them. Some projects are discretionary, but most are nondiscretionary.

TYPES OF PROJECTS

There are various types of projects in healthcare. Some projects are specific to a particular area, while others cross multiple disciplines. The need for, and the degree of, project management depends on the project.

Construction Projects

These projects are managed by a project manager knowledgeable in the construction industry. If the hospital does not have a construction department, then this position is usually outsourced. Examples:

- Building a new physician office
- Building or renovating a medical office building
- Making renovations to a department within the hospital

These project managers interact with architects, construction crews, and regulatory agencies. They plan and oversee the work to ensure healthcare codes are followed. Deliverables consist of the design, construction, interior finishes, furniture, and equipment.

Information Technology Projects

Information technology (IT) projects are usually managed by a project manager familiar with various aspects of IT. Examples:

- Major network upgrade
- New virus scanning software
- Web development

The project manager works with technical staff in IT as well as hardware and software vendors. Together, they plan and oversee completion of the work.

Process Improvement Projects

Process improvement projects are very common in healthcare. These are more complex due to the increased number of stakeholders and higher risk involved. Process improvement projects are managed by a clinical quality process improvement expert who specializes in Six Sigma and Lean techniques. Clinical processes needed to be reviewed on a regular basis to do the following:

- Improve the quality of care.
- Improve patient satisfaction.
- Comply with new regulations.
- Improve throughput and increase revenue.

Hospitals typically have several active process improvement projects at any point in time. This creates a dynamic environment for caregivers to adapt to a steady flow of process changes. Education of staff is a critical deliverable in all of these projects.

CASE EXAMPLE: DOOR-TO-BALLOON PROJECT

A process improvement project was launched to reduce the time from "door-to-balloon" for heart attack patients to less than ninety minutes.

This time interval starts when the patient arrives at the emergency department (ED) with heart attack symptoms. It ends in the cardiac catheterization lab (CCL) when a catheter guidewire crosses the suspected lesion and a balloon is inflated, relieving the blockage. "Time equals muscle" in these situations: any delay in treating the patient increases the likelihood and amount of cardiac muscle damaged.

This is an important core quality measure for the Joint Commission on Accreditation of Healthcare Organizations. The ability of hospitals to reduce the duration of this process saves lives and improves the quality of life for those patients post-discharge.

This project team consisted of nurses and physicians from the ED and CCL as well as quality management, educators, and emergency management services (EMS) personnel.

Medical Equipment Projects

Medical equipment includes any device used in patient care. Most medical equipment replacement projects do not require project management. For example, an effort to replace all patient beds is a straightforward process. As long as there is a coordinator with organization skills, these projects are successful. However, often medical equipment projects require project management because the device is more sophisticated and requires network connectivity, interfaces, facility renovations, marketing/communication, training, and education. There are internal and external stakeholders. These projects could impact hundreds or thousands of employees in a large healthcare system—as well as large numbers of current and potential patients. Examples:

- Computer-aided tomography (CAT scan)
- Magnetic resonance imaging (MRI)
- Glucometer (glucose or sugar meter measuring device) replacement

Clinical staff must be involved in the decision-making process. Testing is needed and signoff must be received before the equipment can be installed in the hospital and used for actual patient care. Installation of the equipment needs to be coordinated so it does not interfere with normal operations. Formal project management is critical for these projects. Failure to do so increases risk and can jeopardize patient care if not implemented properly.

CASE EXAMPLE: SMART INFUSION PUMP IMPLEMENTATION

Fluids and medications are frequently administered to patients directly into a vein via intravenous (IV) methods. An IV pump infuses fluids, medication, or nutrients into a patient's circulatory system. The pump regulates the rate at which the fluid is infused into the body. This is a very convenient method for medication delivery; however, harmful reactions can occur more rapidly and be more severe when given in this manner.

Hospitals can reduce/eliminate adverse drug reactions by converting to smart pumps. Safe, effective, and easy to use, this technology blocks attempts to run medication exceeding established limits, thereby preventing administration errors and harm to patients.

Implementation of this technology is not as simple as a patient bed replacement. Once the desired vendor is selected, smart pumps need to be configured and programmed with criteria such as the appropriate drug and infusion rate, and when and how warnings or full alarms should sound.

Smart pumps also track and record usage data that can be downloaded and reviewed by clinical quality effectiveness staff. Corrective action needs to be taken when "near misses" occur that could have led to patient harm. Infusion practices are assessed and new opportunities are identified for process improvements.

In this project, bedside clinicians were involved as well as pharmacists, physicians, clinical engineering staff, educators, clinical quality staff, and IT. Formal project management and a dedicated project manager were essential to ensure this project was implemented successfully.

Integrated Projects

Many projects in healthcare cross all of these lines: construction, technology, process improvements, and medical equipment. There are many internal and external stakeholders. Some work is done by the hospital system itself, while other work is contracted out to vendors. These are mission-critical projects that are required to achieve the strategic plan of the organization.

Due to their size and complexity, these initiatives are normally managed as a program under the direction of a program manager and multiple project managers overseeing their area of expertise. Examples:

- Building a new hospital
- Building a new ambulatory center
- Implementing a new service line
- Implementing clinical information system
- Making major renovations to an existing hospital

These are all multimillion-dollar capital investments impacting several aspects of the organization, involving hundreds or thousands of employees, that are visible to the entire community, and that are under the scrutiny of local and state regulatory agencies. Formal project and program management are absolutely necessary.

CASE EXAMPLE: PEDIATRIC HOSPITAL RENOVATIONS PROGRAM

Renovations were needed to a children's hospital to meet the expectations of clinicians, patients, and families. The program was approved with a not-to-exceed budget of $90 million. The estimated duration of the program was three to five years, depending on the implementation approach selected for each renovation project.

One project consisted of changing to single-family patient rooms in the neonatal intensive care unit (NICU). Deliverables included the following:

1. Architectural design
2. Construction
3. Relocations
4. Medical equipment
6. Process improvements
7. Staff education
8. Communication
9. Information technology

One of the greatest challenges in this project was developing a phasing plan for the work. Renovations needed to be done in a way that would create the least amount of disruption to patient care.

Creation of the phasing plan required meetings with NICU leadership to evaluate options and develop an acceptable plan that would still meet the minimum capacity requirements for the hospital. A four-phase approach was selected. Work was broken down into sections consisting of twelve to fifteen patient rooms. Each section required six to nine months to complete.

It would have been much easier and faster to close down the entire unit, make the renovations, and reopen, but this is not possible in healthcare. The hospital had to maintain the ability to care for the normal volume of patients throughout the renovations.

CRITICAL SUCCESS FACTORS

Project managers are responsible for delivering projects within budget, on time, and with a high degree of quality. This requires a combination of hard skills and soft skills, but in healthcare, project managers need to be most adept with the soft skills. Project managers who are unable or unwilling to focus on the soft skills will not be successful in healthcare project management.

American Management Association • www.amanet.org

This does not mean healthcare project managers can disregard the hard skills. Project managers still need to create a project schedule, evaluate the critical path, address variances, and take corrective actions. The project manager needs to be willing to make tough and frequently unpopular decisions. Finding the right balance between soft skills and hard skills can be challenging. The successful healthcare project manager focuses on two primary areas: attitude and relationships.

Attitude

Attitude is a culmination of what we believe and feel about ourselves and the situation. Project managers' attitudes impact the way they manage the project, the way the project team members approach the project, and ultimately the success or failure of the project.

Successful healthcare project managers always display a positive attitude. This does not mean that every day is perfect. There will be times when things go awry. How the project manager responds to those events sets the tone for the project.

The project team needs the project manager to stay positive, maintain his or her professionalism, and be willing to take the necessary actions at all times, even in the face of adversity. A negative attitude causes doubt in the ability of the project manager and fear of failure for the project as a whole.

Successful healthcare project managers also display an attitude of service. The project manager does not own the project. The project manager is responsible for completing project management tasks and bringing project management expertise. Other project team members bring different skills sets to the project such as clinical, technology, construction, education, and so on. The project manager must ensure that the team operates in a cohesive fashion to achieve the goal and objectives of the project.

Most of the project team members are responsible for patient care and do not have any time to waste. The project manager must make the project work as easy as possible for the clinicians assigned to the project. The project manager can do this in a number of ways:

- Remove roadblocks that can keep the clinical project team members from completing their project tasks in the most efficient and timely manner.
- Lift the project burden by taking on tasks that do not require clinical decisions. There is rarely enough administrative staff to do these tasks. Project management is considered overhead and a non–revenue-generating function. Project managers need to show value in other ways by making it easier for the clinicians to take care of patients and work on the project.
- Make the project work as easy and pleasant as possible. This includes keeping the project team organized, which can frequently add more work to the project manager.
- Adopt a rule of "no surprises." Send information out ahead of time so project team members know what is expected. This allows them to come to all meetings prepared.
- Display a "can do" and "will do" attitude whenever the project sponsor or project team member needs assistance. The words "not my job" are not in the healthcare project manager's vocabulary.

American Management Association • www.amanet.org

Role	Responsibilities
Ancillary services	Provide supplemental services such as lab, pharmacy, imaging, respiratory therapy, dialysis, and end-of-life care
Care management	Assists patients in understanding their health status, coordinates the discharge process and any postdischarge care needs
Clinical engineering	Maintains all medical equipment and coordinates repairs with vendors
Clinical quality	Ensures compliance with accreditation standards of the Joint Commission
Construction	Manages renovations to existing facilities and new construction
Education	Ensures proper education and training of staff on processes, equipment, and technology
Hospital administration	Provides leadership including nurse managers, chief nursing officer, and hospital presidents
Information technology	Supports all aspects of technology including applications, network, cabling, end-user devices, help desk, web, etc.
Medical staff	Responsible for patient care and developing appropriate plans of care
Nursing	Provides direct patient care and carries out the plan of care provided by the physician

TABLE 49-1. **KEY STAKEHOLDERS IN HEALTHCARE PROJECTS AND PROGRAMS**

Relationships

Project management in healthcare is all about relationships. Depending on the project, stakeholders can come from a variety of sources. Some are clinical and others are administrative. While not a comprehensive list, examples of stakeholders include those shown in Table 49-1.

The most frequent stakeholders in any healthcare project are nurses and physicians. Establishing solid working relationships with these groups is critical.

Nurses

In most healthcare systems, the number of nurses typically outnumbers any other job group. People enter the nursing profession for a number of reasons, some for all the reasons described below. Project managers in healthcare will encounter nurses from all these perspectives:

Altruism

Altruistic nurses are concerned about the welfare of others. Many feel nursing is a "calling." They want to make a difference in the world by helping people. Unassuming and unselfish, these nurses freely give of their time and talents. They find satisfaction knowing they touched someone's life. These nurses may worry about their patients when they are called away for a project meeting. Their minds may not be fully engaged in the agenda topics. At times they may appear to be preoccupied or uninterested in the meeting. This should not be misconstrued.

Project managers need to recognize and embrace the strong people skills of these nurses and the value they can provide to the project. Some project managers will need to get out of their hard skills comfort zone to make this happen. Engage in casual conversation with these nurses and show that you are interested in them as people and not just as project team resources.

Interest in Science

Some nurses enjoy the science side of nursing. These nurses are more task-oriented. They like to do things in a certain order every time. They take pride in the quality of their work. The project manager needs to show how the project will benefit them and make their work life better. When they enter a project meeting they want to get down to business.

These nurses are very interested in the nursing profession as a whole. They keep abreast of changes by reading journals, being involved in committees, and being members of professional organizations. Project managers need to include these nurses in the evaluation phases of a project. These nurses will be able to translate the nursing practice into the technology or equipment and vice versa.

Nurses interested in this aspect of nursing are motivated by knowing that their expertise is appreciated on the project. The project manager needs to recognize their technical skills.

Flexibility

There are many opportunities and different areas in which a nurse can work. Nursing is one of the few careers that offer such an abundance of choices. Nurses are able to move from one specialty to another to gain valuable experience across the nursing spectrum (e.g., surgery, pediatrics, emergency department, labor and delivery, oncology, etc.). Nurses with a broad range of experience provide a wider perspective. Project managers are very fortunate to have these nurses on the project due to their breadth of experience. They bring lessons learned from many areas of medicine to the project table.

Job Security

There continues to be a shortage of nurses due to the changes in healthcare and the aging population. People are living longer and will need healthcare. Some nurses enter the nursing profession because of the job security it offers, especially if this is a second career. The perception is that you do not have to worry about job security in nursing. Some of these project team members may view their position more as a job than a profession. While still valuable project team resources, these nurses may not display the same passion for the profession. The project manager needs to establish clear roles, responsibilities, and expectations.

Nurses from all of the above perspectives want to be a valued member of the project team. They believe they can make an impact on changes in healthcare by participating in projects. At the same time, the project manager must be aware that nursing can be a high-stress, fast-paced job. Nurses may be working twelve-hour shifts. The project manager needs to be sensitive to the pressure nurses are under when scheduling project team meetings. Meetings must always be scheduled at the nurses' convenience—not the project manager's.

The project manager must be respectful of time constraints and not add to the stress. All project activities must be organized with clear roles, responsibilities, and due dates.

Physicians

People enter the medical profession for a number of reasons and these reasons have changed over time. The project manager's relationship-building techniques differ depending on the physicians' viewpoint.

Altruism

We are seeing more and more doctors who are choosing medicine for this reason. They are passionate about their field and willing to fight for the interests of their patients. Similar to nurses, these physicians have the best interest of mankind at heart and want to heal people of illnesses; they see medicine as a "calling." Altruistic physicians cultivate relationships with patients and their families. Physicians treasure the gratitude they receive for helping someone through a difficult illness. Approach these physicians from the point of view of a shared goal in helping patients.

Prestige

Being a physician is honorable and held in high esteem in our society (the "white coat"). A doctor is not simply someone with special skills; doctors preserve life, bring life into the world, and diagnose problems in the lives of people. They are healers, revered and powerful. They deserve our respect and at the same time can be difficult to work with if they are not convinced of the importance of the project goals.

Compensation

The medical profession can be a financially rewarding career, especially in the specialty fields. But this doesn't come without personal sacrifice. Many physicians work grueling hours and are on call through nights and weekends.

Regardless of the reason why doctors and nurses decided on a career in healthcare, they make many personal sacrifices. They frequently work long shifts. Some physicians are not only practicing medicine in the hospital but they also have a private practice, do research, and teach. The pace is fast and tiring. The project manager must be accommodating and willing to bend the rules to meet the needs of the project and stakeholders.

American Management Association • www.amanet.org

Physicians are usually honored to be asked for their advice and want recognition for the tangible results they obtain. When preparing a progress report, the project manager should cite the physician who is responsible for that achievement.

As with nurses, physicians expect organization and structure. They do not want their time wasted in unproductive project team meetings. If this occurs, the project manager will find that the physicians refuse to attend the meetings or appear to be disgruntled when they do attend.

Project managers must be flexible and willing to work around the physicians' availability when scheduling or rescheduling project meetings. Even though some physicians may be perceived as being difficult to work with, the project manager still needs to display the same degree of respect for them as with all other project team members. The success or failure of a healthcare project hinges on your ability to gain the confidence of the physicians on the team. Physicians who are resistant to organizational changes will have great influence on their peers, so work early and proactively to get them on board.

CONCLUSION

Healthcare is one of the most complex and challenging industries for project managers today. The industry is changing dramatically, as is the science that generates the need for new equipment, clinical approaches, and facilities. Project managers need to be fully committed to the project twenty-four hours a day, seven days a week, and willing to do whatever it takes to ensure the project is successful. And rarely does the healthcare project manager have the luxury of managing only one or two projects.

Managing projects in healthcare is a very humbling experience. Even with all the challenges, pressures and stress, there is nothing more rewarding than knowing that, at the end of the project, lives may be changed or saved.

DISCUSSION QUESTIONS

❶ Discuss the cultural divide between clinical stakeholders and project management practitioners. What are some project communications strategies to help overcome these?

❷ Given the impact on human lives, what ethical issues would you expect project managers in healthcare organizations to face (whether working on information technology or clinical projects)? How would you handle these?

RECOMMENDED RESOURCES

François Chiocchio, et al, *Stress and Performance in Health Care Project Teams* (Newtown Square, PA: PMI, 2012).

Randy Englund and Alfonso Bucero, *The Complete Project Manager* (Vienna, VA: Management Concepts, 2012).

David Shirley, *Project Management for Healthcare* (Boca Raton, FL: CRC Press, 2011).

CHAPTER 50

Global Infrastructure Projects
A Better Way

LUIZ ROCHA, PMP, RIO DE JANEIRO FEDERAL
UNIVERSITY, BRAZIL

VIANNA TAVARES, MSC, MBA, SCPM, PMP, ICCPM,
ASSOCIATE PARTNER, BRAZIL

The United Nations estimates that the world's population reached seven billion by the end of 2011. In the last fifty years, humanity more than doubled, surging from three billion in 1959, to four billion in 1974, to five billion in 1987, and to six billion in October 1999.

The United Nations Population Division anticipates eight billion people by 2025; the urban population of developing countries is expected to grow by a million people every five days until 2030. The world economy has almost doubled in size over the past twenty years. This scenario suggests that we should all be very concerned because human demands are huge, although planet earth remains the same size.[1]

As a consequence of population growth and urbanization, demand for infrastructure and public utilities is increasing, putting pressure on governments, infrastructure assets, and resources. Infrastructure can generally be defined as the set of interconnected structural elements that provide framework supporting the development of a country or region. When problems exist with the performance of infrastructure, the effects can be widespread.

The European Sustainable Investment Forum, Eurosif, a not-for-profit association of institutional investors, financial service providers, academic institutes, research associations, and nongovernmental organizations (NGOs) that represents assets totaling over €1 trillion through its member affiliates, produced an infrastructure report stating that "the major issues affecting the infrastructure sector include a growing population, underfinancing, security, and climate change. As governments struggle to make ends meet, private investors are filling in the gaps for these projects, and the implications for environmental, social, and governance factors on the sector are intensifying."[2] Certainly, private investors will play a key role in the absence of sufficient government financing for these projects if their investments can be allocated in a context with clarity of rules, regulations, and returns.

According to McKinsey's report "*Infrastructure Productivity: How to Save $1 Trillion a Year,*" just keeping pace with projected global gross domestic product (GDP) growth will require an estimated $57 trillion in infrastructure investment between now and 2030.[2] That's nearly 60 percent more than the $36 trillion spent over the past eighteen years. The $57 trillion investment required is more than the estimated value of today's infrastructure.

The report has identified that eliminating waste, improving the selection of projects, streamlining their delivery, and using best practices from around the world would make a decisive difference if scaled up globally to optimize the use of capital. This means that practical steps can boost productivity to achieve critical cost savings. Although not sufficient, this can be a first step to a sector where productivity has been a long-time laggard.

COMMON FEATURES OF INFRASTRUCTURE PROJECTS

Infrastructure projects are important because they transform the physical landscape and contribute to the improvement of social and economic systems where they are located. These investments tend to be long-term and their benefits are felt over many years. These projects are generally characterized by some common features:

Large Capital Requirements

Normally, infrastructure projects require large investments over long gestation periods. An example is the Brazilian Logistics Investment Program, designed on the basis of a strategic partnership with the private sector and focused on the renewal and integration of the Brazilian transportation network. The goal is to meet the growth demands of a country with continental dimensions. In order to facilitate investment projects in infrastructure, which will add around $235 billion in the coming years, the government has enacted a number of tax and bureaucratic benefits.

Sensitive to Political Environment and Policy Changes

Because of their long life cycles, these projects experience many uncertainties and changes including transformations in the regulatory environment and institutional framework. Henisz performed a two-century analysis on the determinants of infrastructure investments in over one hundred countries and concluded that policy makers seeking to attract investment should pay attention to how they structure political institutions, and investors should look carefully at all the governmental pledges that may have an impact on the return of potential investments.

Multiple Stakeholders

It is common for projects to have a great number of stakeholders in multiple sectors related to regulatory and financing agencies, funding institutions, constructors, suppliers, and communities impacted, among others. Part of the conundrum public authorities face is the balancing of multiple interests and objectives and the need to

American Management Association • www.amanet.org

respond to the growing expectations of citizens to have their views heard while ensuring that consultation processes are conducted in an effective fashion.

Complexity in the Planning-to-Implementation Process

Infrastructures are complex collections of interacting components in which change often occurs as a result of learning on the go, making them adaptive systems. What happens to one infrastructure can directly and indirectly impact large geographic regions, and send ripples throughout social economic layers. On top of that, the necessary steps to protect the public interest and tendering procedures add more complexity. Shaping the opportunity and thinking about the regulatory permits and the organizational arrangement may take years. Then there is the planning process that requires more time. The way the planning process is conducted is a great determinant of success or failure. The problem is that governments are enforced for four or five years and normally take a short-term vision inconsistent with the long, long, long-term view required by these investments to get to the authorization stage. The reality produced is that the planning is accelerated and costs escalate during execution.

High Rates of Failures

The uncertainties, complexities, and relationships involved do not contribute to a great number of success stories. Infrastructure projects have presented poor results from their management perspective. Cost and time overruns are very common, and disputes with stakeholders are business as usual. Contributing to this reality are the forgotten lessons. A lot is commented about the importance of determining the lessons learned. The problem is that governments change, contractors move from one opportunity to another, and the lessons that should be learned for future investments are forgotten in the minds of many.

DELUSIONS OF SUCCESS

Many authors point out that the industry's capacity to deliver infrastructure projects is not at the right pace. As a result, significant overruns in budgets and schedules are rising in frequency. Flyvbjerg et al, Kain, Pickrell, and Skamris and Flyvbjerg, among others, have come out with such findings.[4]

Morris and Hough, Gaspar and Leite, and Ganuza attribute cost overruns to technical constraints.[5] According to these studies, delays and cost overruns are a result of imperfect estimation techniques on the part of government officials. The list of infrastructure projects funded on overly optimistic forecasts of initial usage is huge. One of the explanations for these flawed forecasts can be that the investment bankers and consultants who put together the deals get most of their fees irrespective of whether or not the forecast patronage materializes after construction. If their clients don't get the project, they don't get their hefty bonuses.

Other researchers such as Wachs, Kain, Pickrell, and Flyvbjerg attribute cost overruns to political factors. In order to make projects sellable, politicians understate costs and exaggerate benefits. As shown by Flyvbjerg, artificially low costs, exaggerated benefits, and underestimated risks are common strategies employed by the proposing institution to have a large infrastructure project approved.[6]

Pricewaterhousecoopers (PWC) stated,

> Large construction projects can suffer from many problems, ranging from optimism bias in the original estimate to poor communication to slow decision making. Many owners fail to establish the proper project management structure, monitoring procedures, and risk management processes. As a result, they don't anticipate unforeseen events and don't build in the necessary contingency plans. Because of shortcomings in project controls, they often don't realize the severity of delays and cost overruns until well after a project has foundered.[7]

Despite the fact that governments, investors, and financial sources use well-known consultants to make projections and estimations, it is very common to have gaps between the the projected future and the emerging reality. Miller and Lessard[8] comment on the risks involved related to market forecast, potential difficulties attracting investors, technical risks involving engineering difficulties and their novelty, construction, regulation, operation, and social-acceptability. Risks emerge along the project life cycle in conditions of strong uncertainty, and turbulence makes them very susceptible to crisis. For this reason, risk and crisis management processes must be well thought out.

CHALLENGES AND OPPORTUNITIES

The World Economic Forum (WEF) has analyzed the future of long-term investments and has shown that "in 2009 long-term institutional asset owners owned slightly under half of the world's professionally managed assets—approximately US$27 trillion out of US$65 trillion. However, constraints on these investors allow roughly 25% of their assets (US$6.5 trillion) to be used for long-term investment."[9] Interestingly enough, this $6.5 trillion is available for direct private equity and venture capital, strategic stakes in public companies, and major infrastructure investments, which means that infrastructure can only attract a fraction of that amount, indicating a huge gap between infrastructure investment demand and the total amount of capital available worldwide.

Governments will need to complement the search for sources of capital with a wide array of other measures. The great challenge is how to increase investors' interest in infrastructure projects. Traditionally, companies take varied but conventional approaches to infrastructure project organization design based on previous experiences, partnership philosophy, and risk appetite. Most organizations are set up adequately at the outset. However, over time, many of them fail to adapt to how a project's needs change at different phases, thereby leading to poor governance, control, and management.

The WEF strategic infrastructure report also states that "in such an environment, Public-Private Partnerships (PPPs) can accelerate infrastructure development by tapping the private sector's financial resources as well as its skills in delivering infrastructure effectively and efficiently on a whole life-cycle cost basis."[10] Despite this need for private sector participation, projects are lacking well-planned commercial and technical feasibility studies, risk allocation, and clarity on the institutional and legal framework.

American Management Association • www.amanet.org

RELIEVING THE DEADLOCK

A number of international organizations have been studying how to tackle infrastructure issues. Organization for Economic Cooperation and Development (OECD) published the *Infrastructure to 2030* report, which recommended finding innovative approaches to finance including public–private partnerships and the investment of pension funds, improving regulatory and institutional framework conditions, reducing the vulnerability of long-term infrastructure planning and implementation to short-term thinking and priority setting, and strengthening governance and strategic planning by ensuring the involvement of a broader range of stakeholders in the process of needs assessment and prioritization.[11]

A report from the World Energy Forum comments on a "project preparation gap" that includes poor demand forecasts, delayed land acquisition and approvals, and inadequate risk allocation.[12] Additionally, if the tender documents are deficient or unclear, the bidders have to generate the required information via due diligence. This process can be costly and wasteful unless the bidder is prepared to tender low amounts, expecting to make high returns through effective claim management.

The report proposes four areas to be addressed: (1) managing a rigorous project preparation process by effectively setting up the project team and leadership, designing the project governance structure and project management, and securing the required preparation funding; (2) conducting a robust and high-quality technical, commercial, legal, and environmental feasibility study with proactive stakeholder management; (3) structuring a balanced risk allocation and regulation with the adoption of a life-cycle–oriented model aligned with policy objectives to ensure a successful long-term partnership between the public and the private sectors; and (4) creating a conducive enabling environment by establishing a solid legal framework with independent regulators and dispute resolution forums and enforcing transparency to enhance public, private, and societal readiness.

Considering the views from these two global institutions, we suggest starting with some critical issues to solve the deadlock.

Opportunity Framing

Opportunity framing is the process by which the essential attributes of a potential infrastructure project are evaluated. Information needs to be collected, forecasts produced, and the value created allocated to the various stakeholders in order to make it sustainable.

Javernick-Will and Scott[13] identified three pillars that must be understood in the shaping of a project: regulative knowledge that includes the rules of formal governance structures and legal processes within a given society; normative knowledge that specifies how things should be done, including adopting socially accepted practices and processes and fulfilling expectations for roles; and cultural-cognitive knowledge that includes common beliefs, shared conceptions, and meanings. Whereas normative knowledge is morally governed and regulative knowledge is legally sanctioned, cultural cognitive behavior occurs because of cultural beliefs and perceptions.

Merrow[14] states that the one requirement for a successful megaproject is the need to assess and then shape the opportunity into a framework that will allow the project to be managed. Five steps are considered in the shaping process. The first one is the context, including the physical location, the history of prior projects in the area, the political and institutional environment, the regulatory climate, the local content requirements, cultural considerations, the labor availability, and quality. The second step is assessing the potential value of the project. If the value to be created cannot be understood, the risk of losing control is high. This value needs to be linked to the project ambition, the benefits to be delivered, and the future state resulting from the transformation. The third step is assessing the comparative advantage and the purpose of the project. Answering why the project is fundamentally better than alternatives gives convincing reasons to execute it. The fourth step is identifying and understanding the stakeholders. Identifying stakeholders early can guide the opportunity framing. The final step is thinking about partners, investors, and sources of financing.

Stakeholder Engagement

The effect of infrastructure projects on economies is influenced by the involvement of governments, communities, and regulators. A sustainable development mindset for people, the environment, and communities, and a positive attitude to keep teams motivated and to deal with setbacks over extended periods are particularly important. The combination of all these factors takes the stakeholder challenge to an entirely new level.

As early as possible, the stakeholders must know what the planned project entails. The decision makers must clearly explain the project ambition, and the possibilities and limitations they face in a realistic and understandable way. Stakeholders must be actively prepared for changes. It is vital to avoid surprises. Negative impacts communicated openly can cause short-term annoyance but generate trust in the long-term. A continual constructive dialogue may not avoid opposition but offers the opportunity to share knowledge and exchange perspectives that may result in fewer barriers to the achievement of the expected benefits.

A sensitive issue on stakeholder management is the suppliers' network. There is a need to carefully select suppliers and consider their compliance with issues such as human rights, work conditions, environment, and corruption fighting. A good starting point on these issues is the United Nations global compact.

Effective stakeholder engagement is an increasingly critical factor in ensuring successful delivery of infrastructure projects. Disputes, poor stakeholder relations, and disgruntled community groups can cause significant delays and impact the project.

Risk Management

Infrastructure projects are inherently rife with risks, suggesting that they must be viewed from a full life-cycle perspective. The complex multilayered dimensions involved associated with the existing interdependencies make it difficult to determine the possible risks. Identifying, understanding, and analyzing such interdependencies are significant challenges. Affecting all areas of daily life such as electric power, natural gas and petroleum production and distribution, telecommunications, transportation, and water supply, the degree to which the infrastructures are coupled, or linked, strongly influences their operational characteristics

American Management Association • www.amanet.org

The risks involved include the technical, economic, business, social/political, legal/regulatory, public policy, health and safety, and security concerns that affect infrastructure operations. It is therefore essential to have a robust risk-based governance approach so that the leadership team can sense risks and take decisive action in a timely manner.

Governance and Assurance

Governance can be understood as the art of deciding how to decide. It is a process of understanding project decisions across multiple organizational layers, organizations, and institutions. In contrast, the assurance process guarantees throughout the entire life cycle all the required compliances and adherence to the adopted methodological approaches. There are three assurance mechanisms that have proven particularly effective. The first is stage gate reviews. Stage gate reviews are points at which a project is reviewed and a decision is made on whether to move forward, to recycle, or to stop a project.

The second assurance mechanism is independent reviews, which involve external parties. It is always important to bring different perspectives to a project as a form of enhancing value creation and bringing new ideas and experiences to the project team.

The third assurance mechanism is front-end planning. This is the process of developing a detailed project definition so that the owner can evaluate the risks involved, and allocate resources in such a way that the chances of success are enhanced. The Construction Industry Institute indicates that projects that effectively implement front-end planning can improve their performance 10 percent with respect to costs, 7 percent with respect to schedule, and 5 percent with respect to change orders. One common issue is that owners can argue that they are spending a lot of money during the planning phase, forgetting that if they don't do so they may be cultivating the seeds of failure and have higher costs at the end.

Governance and assurance processes must be in place in order to support infrastructure shaping, planning, execution, and operations. Although governance and assurance approaches do not guarantee success, they can significantly increase the probability of success.

CONCLUSION

Clearly there is a need to find better ways for planning, financing, governing, and executing infrastructure projects, taking into account their various impacts and the interests of the multiple stakeholders involved.

Good infrastructure project planning requires upfront investment in opportunity framing, early stakeholder management, formalized risk management, and governance and assurance to ensure that the project can progress without facing major hurdles. Since infrastructure projects are engines of value creation and transformation, changes are normal and expected. However, poor application of these processes will increase the chances of failure in project delivery. Companies and institutions involved in infrastructure should invest in ensuring that the issues cited in this chapter are considered.

REFERENCES

[1] Joel Cohen, Seven Billion, *New York Times*, October 23, 2011, www.nytimes.com/2011/10/24/opinion/seven-billion.html?_r=0; and Robert Engelman, "What a population of seven billion means for the planet," *The Guardian*, July 18, 2011, www.guardian.co.uk/environment/2011/jul/18/population-7-billion-planet.

[2] Eurosif, Infrastructure Sector Report, http://www.eurosif.org/research/sector-reports/infrastructure.

[3] McKinsey, "Infrastructure productivity: how to save US$ 1 trillion a year," *McKinsey Insights and Publications,* January 2013, www.mckinsey.com/insights/engineering_construction/infrastructure_productivity.

[4] B. Flyvbjerg, M.K.S. Holm, and S.L. Buhl, "What causes cost overrun in transport infrastructure projects?" *Transport Reviews* 24, No. 1 (2004), pp. 3–18; J.F. Kain, "Deception in Dallas: strategic misrepresentation in rail transit promotion and evaluation," *Journal of the American Planning Association* 56, No. 2 (1990), pp. 184–196; D.H. Pickrell, *Urban Rail Transit Projects: Forecast Versus Actual Ridership and Cost* (Washington, DC: U.S. Department of Transportation, 1990); M.K. Skamris and B. Flyvbjerg, "Inaccuracy of traffic forecasts and cost estimates on large transport projects," *Transport Policy* 4, No. 3 (1997), pp. 141–146.

[5] J.-J. Ganuza, "Competition and cost overruns in procurement," *International Journal of Industrial Organization* 55, No. 4 (2007), pp. 633–660; V. Gaspar and A. Leite, "Selection bias induced cost overruns," *International Journal of Industrial Organization* 8, No. 3 (1989), pp. 443–467; P.W.G. Morris and G.H. Hough, *The Anatomy of Major Projects: A Study of the Reality of Project Management* (New York: John Wiley and Sons, 1987).

[6] M. Wachs, "When planners lie with numbers," *Journal of the American Planning Association* 55, No. 4 (1989), pp. 476–479; Kain, 1990: Pickrell, 1990; Flyvbjerg et al, 2004.

[7] pricewaterhousecoopers, *Correcting the Course of Capital Projects.* (London: PWC, 2013), p. 2, www.pwc.com/en_GX/gx/scapital-projects-infrastructure/assets/pwc-correcting-the-course-of-capital-projects-v3-pdf.pdf.

[8] R. Miller & D. Lessard, *The Strategic Management of Large Engineering Projects* (Cambridge, MA: MIT Press, 2000), pp. 75–92.

[9] World Economic Forum, *Strategic Infrastructure: Steps to Prepare and Accelerate Public-Private Partnerships* (Geneva: World Economic Forum, 2013).

[10] Ibid.

[11] OECD, *Infrastructure to 2030: Main Findings and Policy Recommendations* (Paris: OECD, 2007), www.iva.se/upload/Verksamhet/Projekt/Forskning%20Innovation/Bibliotek/OECD_long.pdf.

[12] World Energy Forum, *The Future of Term-Investing.* 2011, http://www3.weforum.org/docs/WEF_FutureLongTermInvesting_Report_2011.pdf.

[13] Amy Javernick-Will and W.R. Scott, "Who Needs to Know What? Institutional Knowledge and International Projects," Working Paper, Collaborative for Research on Global Projects, Stanford University, 2009.

[14] Edward Merrow, *Industrial Megaprojects* (Hoboken, NJ: John Wiley, 2012).

▶ **William P. Athayde, JD, PMP,** Senior Instructor, PM College. Bill's project management experience includes construction, environmental remediation projects, IT rollouts, training, and as the program manager of a 120-member multiagency team. He has extensive experience in Latin America and is a member of the State Bar of Texas.

▶ **Manuel M. Benitez Codas** is a consultant in project management and strategic planning in Brazil. Prior to starting his own consulting company in 1990, he worked for more than twenty years in large Brazilian and Paraguayan engineering organizations, involved with large hydroelectric and mass transport projects. He has published articles in the *International Journal of Project Management* and *RAE-Business Administration Magazine.* A member of the Project Management Institute since 1979, he is the founder of the São Paulo Project Management Association and of PMI Asunción Paraguay Chapter.

▶ **Theodore R. Boccuzzi, PMP,** has over 30 years of capital, manufacturing, IT and product development project experience serving as Portfolio Manager, Program Manager, Project Manager, Engineering Manager, Construction Manager, and Mechanical Design Leader supporting worldwide programs. He is the holder of three patents for work associated with web conveyance. He is a graduate of the Rochester Institute of Technology and a contributor to *A Guide to the Project Management Body of Knowledge, Third Edition,* and *Organizational Project Management Maturity Model (OPM3®), Second Edition.*

▶ **Deborah Bigelow Crawford, PMP**, is well-known within the project management industry as a former Executive Director of the Project Management Institute, where she served through 1996. Since leaving PMI, she has served as the Executive Vice-President of PM Solutions and since 2002, as President of PM College, its training division (www.pmcollege.com). She has authored numerous articles in *PM Network*-and *Optimize* magazines and is the editor of the third edition of *Project Management Essentials* (Maven House, 2013). She has presented many papers at international symposia and conferences, and is a member of the National Association of Female Executives and PMI.

▶ **J. Kent Crawford, PMP,** is founder and CEO of Project Management Solutions, Inc. (www.pmsolutions.com). His experience spans over thirty years, during which he has been responsible for the design of integrated project management systems for many Fortune 500 organizations. He is the Former President and Chair of PMI, and a recipient of the PMI Fellow Award, the Institute's highest individual honor. A prolific speaker, he is the award-winning author of *The Strategic Project Office: A Guide to Improving Organizational Performance* (for which he won a David I. Cleland Project Management Literature Award from PMI), and many other related titles.

▶ **Lynn H. Crawford,** through Human Systems International (www.humansystems.com.au), helps organizations assess and improve corporate project management capability. Ongoing research includes competence, business change, and contextual variation. She is Co-Vice-Chair of PMI's GAC Board, Life Fellow of AIPM, Honorary Member of IPMA, and was recipient of the 2011 IPMA Research Achievement Award.

▶ **Robin Markle Dumas, MBA** (robinmarkle@yahoo.com) is an award-winning PMO leader and consultant with over 20 years experience delivering transformational change. Robin's former organization was a finalist in the PMO of the Year Award (2012) for innovation and results. She holds a MBA and a B.S. in Finance/Economics from Christian Brothers University and is a 6 Sigma Black Belt.

▶ **Lowell Dye, PMP,** is a senior consultant and trainer with Management Concepts, Inc. (ldye@ ManagementConcepts.com). He has also been on the adjunct faculty of several colleges and universities and is co-editor of *Project Portfolio Management: Selecting and Prioritizing Projects for Competitive*

541

Advantage and *Managing Multiple Projects: Scheduling and Resource Allocation for Competitive Advantage*. Mr. Dye holds a BS from Excelsior College, an MS in Operations Management from the University of Arkansas.

▶ **Andrew Edkins** is the Director of the Bartlett School of Construction and Project Management which is a part of UCL's faculty of the Built Environment. His academic background spans both economics and project management and his career has been spent in both academe and in industry where he has worked in both major construction project management and complex public private procurement.

▶ **Judith A. Edwards, PHD, PMP, IEEE (SM),** counsels small businesses on technical organization as a member of SCORE®. Prior to retirement, she worked at Diebold on process improvement initiatives involving SEI CMMI® and ISO 9000, at Loral Defense Systems, and at General Dynamics. She continues to teach mathematics and computer science at the university level. Ms. Edwards has a BS in mathematics education, MA in mathematics, and PhD in Computer Science. She served as reviewer for *A Guide to the Project Management Body of Knowledge, Third Edition* and several IEEE computer standards efforts. Her professional memberships include PMI, the Association for Computer Machinery, and IEEE.

▶ **Ruth H. Elswick, PMP** (relswick@pmcollege.com) is a senior faculty member for PM College. Her experience involves practical project management ranging from small to multi-million dollar projects. Ms. Elswick holds a BA from the University of South Carolina and an MA from East Carolina University. She has been a contributing author to all three editions of *Project Management Essentials* (Maven House, 2013).

▶ **Randall L. Englund** is an executive consultant, author, and speaker. Formerly a senior project manager with Hewlett-Packard's Project Management Initiative, he has coauthored *Creating an Environment for Successful Projects*; *Creating the Project Office: A Manager's Guide to Leading Organizational Change; Project Sponsorship: Achieving Management Commitment for Project Success; The Complete Project Manager: Integrating People, Organizational, and Technical Skills,* and *The Complete Project Manager's Toolkit*. View references and stakholder templates at www.englundpmc.com.

▶ **David Hillson, PHD, PMP, PMI Fellow, HONFAPM, FIRM, FRSA** (david@risk-doctor.com) is known globally as The Risk Doctor. An award-winning thought-leader and expert practitioner, he consults and writes widely on risk management. His ground-breaking work in the field was recognized by honorary fellowships from both the Association for Project Management (APM) and PMI and he was "Risk Personality of the Year" in 2010–2011 by the Institute of Risk Management.

▶ **Valis Houston, PMP** (valis@acacia-software.com) possesses a broad range of international experience with specific know-how in Agile Project Management and Software Process Improvement. A graduate of Prairie View A&M University, he also holds a Master's Certificate in IT Project Management from George Washington University, an MS in Management Information Systems from Bowie State University, and a MS in Software Engineering from Southern Methodist University. He is also a 6 Sigma Green Belt. A former Adjunct Professor for the Keller Graduate School of Management, he currently sits on the Industry Advisory Board for Southern Methodist University's Computer Science Department.

▶ **Michael Howell, ASQ,** is a Business Process Excellence Manager and Master Black Belt (MBB) with the IBM CIO Business Transformation / Information Technology (BT/IT) team. Prior to his current role he served as a Lean Six Sigma MBB with BearingPoint. He also served in the role of Director of Six Sigma, Six Sigma MBB, Black Belt, and quality manager with Sears Roebuck & Co. Mike has experience with multiple continuous improvement methodologies such as TQM, ISO9000, Malcolm Baldrige, Lean, Lean Six Sigma, Business Process Management (BPM) systems. Mike has a bachelor's degree in Electrical Engineering, is a Senior Member of the American Society for Quality (ASQ) and is a certified Master Black Belt.

▶ **Kam Jugdev, PHD, PMP** (kamj@athabascau.ca), is a Professor, Project Management & Strategy, in the Faculty of Business at Athabasca University, Alberta, Canada. Prior to becoming an academic, Kam worked in both the public and private sector industry as a project manager. She develops and teaches project management courses at both the undergraduate and graduate levels. Her research has been funded at the university and federal levels. Kam's research program spans: project management lessons learned and communities of practice; project management tools and techniques; project success/failure; and project management as a source of competitive advantage. Kam enjoys being able to relate theory to practice with students and through her research. She has published in a variety of project management and management journals. Kam actively contributes to the advancement of academic and professional communities of management practice across Canada and internationally.

▶ **Gerald I. Kendall, PMP,** Principal, TOC International (gerryikendall@cs.com), is an expert in strategic planning and project management, management consultant, public speaker, and facilitator. He has worked with many multi-national firms, government agencies, and not-for-profit organizations, to better manage large-scale organizational change issues. Clients include Telstra, British American Tobacco, Raytheon, Babcock & Wilcox, Alcan Aluminum, Covad Communications, Lockheed Martin, and many others. Certified by the TOC International Certification Organization (www.tocico.org) in all six disciplines of Theory of Constraints, he is a graduate of McGill University. Gerald is the author of *Advanced Multi-Project Management, Viable Vision, Advanced Project Portfolio Management and the PMO,* and *Securing the Future: Strategies for Exponential Growth Using the Theory of Constraints* and of a chapter on Critical Chain in Harold Kerzner's *Project Management, A System's Approach, Eighth Edition.*

▶ **Joan Knutson, PMP,** president of PM Guru Unlimited, enjoys an international reputation as a project management thought-leader. Founder and for 25 years director of Project Mentors, a multimillion dollar project management training and consulting firm, in 1999 Joan led the through a merger/acquisition by a prestigious training conglomerate, staying on for three more years as President. She then established PM Guru Unlimited. Joan was recognized by PMI as one of the "25 Most influential Women in Project Management." Ms. Knutson was a Contributing Editor to *PM Network* magazine for over a decade and is the author of several books on project management; including *Succeeding in Project-Driven Organizations* (John Wiley & Sons).

▶ **Lee R. Lambert, PMP,** principal of Lambert Consulting, has shared his knowledge with over 40,000 students in 22 countries. Mr. Lambert has a Masters Certificate in Project Management from George Washington University. He is a Founder of the Project Management Institute's PMP Certification program and was named a Distinguished Contributor to the profession by PMI in 1995. Author of three books and dozens of articles, as well as a popular speaker at project management events, he was PMI's 2007 Professional Development Provider of the Year.

▶ **Ginger Levin, PhD, PMP, PGMP,** is a Senior Consultant with 47 years of experience in portfolio management, program management, the PMO, metrics, and maturity assessments. She is the editor, author, or coauthor of 18 books. She is an Adjunct Professor at UW-Platteville, SKEMA, and RMIT. See linkedin.com/in/gingerlevin.

▶ **Alan Levine** is the Chief Information Officer of the Kennedy Center for the Performing Arts in Washington, DC. Under his direction, the Kennedy Center developed a unified information architecture and a personalized, interactive website for its patrons, which includes a nightly Internet broadcast of a live performance daily. Through the Kennedy Center DeVos Institute of Arts Management, he teaches the application of technology in arts organizations and provides consulting services to organizations worldwide.

▶ **Paul Lombard, PMP, CQM,** a senior faculty member of the PM College (plombard@pmcollege.com), is an internationally recognized Project and Program consultant and educator. He has authored numerous articles and papers on project and quality management and coauthored foundational book, *Project Management Essentials.* A certified master trainer and curriculum developer, he has developed numerous on-site and distance learning training courses in Project Management, Leadership, Team Skills, Core Facilitation, Quality Management, Program Management, Complex Project Management, and Strategic Management.

▶ **Rich Maltzman, PMP** (rich@earthpm.com) is leader, learning, and professional advancement, at a major telecom's PMO. He is the cofounder of EarthPM, LLC, and in that role is coauthor of the book *Green Project Management* (CRC Press, 2011). Rich was VP of Professional Development for PMI's MassBay Chapter and has presented on PM/Sustainability in the US, South Africa, Costa Rica, and Malaysia.

▶ **Alan Mendelssohn** (asmquality@aol.com) is a retired Process Improvement Consultant. He has extensive experience in the design, implementation and management of process management, continuous improvement, Lean and Six Sigma initiatives. He served as a Master Black Belt and a Business Process Consultant at Sears, Roebuck and Company and a Senior Manager Organizational Performance at

American Management Association • www.amanet.org

OfficeMax, among other professional experiences. Alan has a Master's Degree in Nuclear Engineering, is a Fellow of the American Society for Quality and is an ASQ-Certified 6 Sigma Black Belt and has served as an Examiner for the Baldrige Award.

▶ **Thomas Mengel, PHD, PMP** (tmengel@unb.ca), is Professor of Leadership Studies and the chair of the faculty Research Ethics Board at Renaissance College, University of New Brunswick. He developed the model of Values-Oriented-Leadership and helped many leaders to implement business and project ethics processes. Previously he served as a faculty member at Athabasca University's Center for Innovative Management, MBA in Project Management Program. In addition to graduate studies and degrees in computer science, business administration, and adult education, Thomas has a PhD in theology and an MA in history.

▶ **Peter W. G. Morris** is Professor of Construction and Project Management at University College London (UCL) and the author of many books, including *The Wiley Guide to Managing Project* (Wiley, 2005) edited with Jeffrey Pinto; *The Management of Projects* (Thomas Telford, 1994), and *The Anatomy of Major Projects* (John Wiley & Sons, 1987), with George Hough. He has also worked on the linkage between corporate and project strategy (*Translating Corporate Strategy into Project Strategy* [PMI, 2004] with Ashley Jamieson). He is the joint editor, with Jeffrey Pinto and Jonas Söderlund, of *The Oxford Handbook on Project Management* (Oxford University Press, 2011) and the author of over 120 papers on project management. His latest book is *Reconstructing Project Management* (Wiley-Blackwell, 2013). His many awards include PMI's Research Achievement Award (2005) and the International Project Management Association's Research Award (2009). He was previously Chairman of the APM and Deputy Chairman of the IPMA.

▶ **Francis "Frank" Patrick** was founder and principal consultant of Focused Performance, a management consultancy focusing on the application of the Theory of Constraints (TOC) to help organizations achieve more of their goals. Prior to Focused Performance, Mr. Patrick had over 25 years of industrial experience with Revlon, Johnson & Johnson, Nabisco, and AT&T/Bell Labs. More of his thoughts on organizational effectiveness can be found at www.focusedperformance.com, and at his new website, http://frankpatrick.tumbir.com/.

▶ **David L. Pells** (editor@pmworldjournal.net) is Managing Editor of the *PM World Journal,* Executive Director of the PM World Library, and president and CEO of PM World Services, a consulting firm providing advisory services for major government programs. David has over 35 years of experience on a wide variety of programs and projects, including engineering, construction, defense, transit, high technology and nuclear security. He served on the board of directors of PMI® twice, and founded the Global Project Management Forum during the 1990s. David was awarded PMI's Person of the Year award in 1998 and Fellow Award in 1999.

▶ **James S. Pennypacker** (jim@thinkpennypacker.com) is President and CEO of Pennypacker & Associates. Formerly he was Director of the Center for Business Practices, where he led the development of an active thought leadership marketing and research program. He previously served as Publisher and Editor-in-Chief of the Project Management Institute. Jim is the author and editor of more than twenty books and research reports on a variety of business issues. He holds an M.B.A./Technology and Electronic Commerce from West Chester University and a B.A. in philosophy from Temple University. His new venture, Maven House Press, is the publisher of leading-edge books for business transformation.

▶ **Luiz Rocha, PMP** (Luiz.Rocha@Dinsmore.com.br) has more than 35 years of experience, having worked with Andersen Consulting and Deloitte in in Latin America, North America and Europe. He then served for five years as Project Director with Dinsmore Associates in Brazil. An engineer by education (MSc. in industrial engineering from UFRJ – Brazil), Luis is also the author/co-author of several books including *Enterprise Project Governance* (AMACOM, 2012) and *Business Metamorphosis in Brazil.* He is presently IPMA-Brasil vice president and professor at UFRJ and FGV.

▶ **Donald Ross,** Certified Professional Wetland Scientist and Senior Ecologist, is the founder of Earth-Balance Corporation, one of the nation's largest privately-owned ecosystem restoration and mitigation banking firms. He has applied his wetland expertise from Alaska to Florida, and is an acknowledged leader in the wetland mitigation banking industry. He holds a BS in Forestry and an MS in Ecology from the University of Tennessee. He can be reached at ross@earthbalance.com.

▶ **Christopher Sauer** is Fellow in Information Management at Oxford University's Said Business School and Green Templeton College. In his early career he designed, built and managed IT systems projects. As an academic, his research has focused on the challenges of IT projects. In addition to four books, his work has been published in the *Project Management Journal*, the *International Journal of Project Management*, and MIT's *Sloan Management Review*, among others. Short summaries of his recent research can be found at www.PMPerspectives.org. He is an active member of the Major Projects Association, and Joint-Editor-in-Chief of the *Journal of Information Technology*.

▶ **David Shirley, PMP** (dave@earthpm.com) is a consultant, educator, course developer and trainer in project management, sustainability and corporate social responsibility. He is presently teaching at Boston University and Southern New Hampshire University-Online. He co-authored *Green Project Management* (CRC Press 2010) and authored *Project Management for Healthcare* (CRC Press, 2011).

▶ **Rip Stauffer** (rip@woodsidequality.com) is currently Manager, Quantitative Analysis and Improvement at WBB, Inc., in Northern Virginia. He has developed and presented comprehensive and dynamic courses in Six Sigma, SPC, QFD and lean. A Senior Member of ASQ, a Certified Quality Engineer, Manager of Quality and Organizational Excellence, Six Sigma Black Belt and Master Black Belt, and a contributing member of the W. Edwards Deming Institute, Rip has an MS in applied statistics from Cal State and a BS from Regents College. He is an adjunct professor at Walden University, and a Ph.D. candidate in Leadership and Organizational Change.

▶ **Alan M. Stretton** was Chairman of the Standards Committee of PMI from 1989 to 1992 and is on the faculty of the University of Management and Technology, Arlington, VA. In 2006 he retired from a position as Adjunct Professor of Project Management at the University of Technology, Sydney (UTS), Australia. Prior to joining UTS, Mr Stretton worked in the building and construction industries in Australia, New Zealand and the USA for some 38 years. He has degrees in Civil Engineering, Mathematics, and an honorary PhD in strategy, program, and project management.

▶ **Geree Streun, PMP, CSQE, PMI-ACP, CSSGB, CSM,** is Principal of GVSoftware and has also served as a Principal Quality Engineer in the Program Management Office of Boston Scientific. She received her Master's degree in Computer Science from Southern Methodist University and her Bachelor's in Computer Science from Kansas State. She is a Senior Member of IEEE, a PMI-certified Project Management Professional, and an ASQ Certified Software Quality Engineer. She has a wide range of experience in Project Management. Ms. Streun was a Team Leader for developing two chapters for the *PMBOK® Guide, Third Edition* and also a key volunteer leader in the Fourth Edition update. She has presented papers at the Project Management Institute's Software Special Interest Group and at International Test Conferences. She has published several papers on transitioning an organization from structured techniques to Object Oriented (OO) Techniques, while evolving project management maturity within the organization.

▶ **Vianna Tavares, MSC, MBA, SCPM, PMP** (javtavares@globo.com) has been involved in the management of Large Engineering and R&D Projects for more than 18 years. ICCPM Associate Partner and NETLIPSE representative in Brazil. Prior to that, the ARES Operations Director. He has also been the Manager of the Digital Systems Division at the Brazilian Navy Research Institute, where he supported a team of more than 100 engineers working on a broad range of Defense and Aerospace projects. He was the recipient of the Brazilian Navy Engineering Merit of Honor, among other awards.

▶ **Hans J. Thamhain, PHD, PMP** (hthamhain@bentley.edu) is a Professor of Management and Director of MOT and Project Management Programs at Bentley College, Boston. His industrial experience includes 20 years of management positions with high-technology companies, like GTE/Verizon, General Electric, and ITT. Dr. Thamhain has written over 70 research papers and five professional reference books in project and technology management. He is the recipient of the Distinguished Contribution Award from the Project Management Institute in 1998 and the IEEE Engineering Manager of the Year 2000 Award.

▶ **Janice Thomas, PHD,** has 30 years of experience in the project management field as a practitioner, researcher and educator. She is the author of four books and over 100 conference, practitioner or academic articles. From 2004 to 2008 she co-led PMI's largest ever, ground-breaking research into the Value of Project Management. In 2006, she was recognized as one of the 25 most influential women in project management by *PMNetwork* and in 2010 was awarded the Research Achievement Award by PMI.

▶ **Chris Vandersluis** (chrisv@hmssoftware.ca) is the president and founder of HMS Software based in Montreal, Canada. He has an economics degree from Montreal's McGill University and over 25 years experience in the automation of project control systems. He is a long standing member of both PMI and the American Association of Cost Engineers (AACE), served for five years on Microsoft's Enterprise Project Management Partner Advisory Council. Mr. Vandersluis has been published in numerous publications including *Fortune Magazine, Heavy Construction News, PMI's PM Network,* and *Computing Canada* magazine. He teaches Advanced Project Management at McGill University's Executive Institute. HMS Software is the publisher of TimeControl. Visit his blog at www.epmguidance.com.

▶ **Stan Veraart, PMP, ISA Certified Arborist,** is an independent international consultant who assists in applying project management tools and techniques to various environmental companies. He holds an MS degree in Project Management and a BS in International Agriculture. He has worked for the Dutch Government, private companies, institutions, and NGOs in nine countries on six continents. Mr. Veraart believes that the project management profession can greatly contribute solutions to the challenges of environmental protection and building a sustainable economy. He can be reached at stan_global@yahoo .com.

▶ **Janice Weaver, PMP**, is Associate Vice President of the Enterprise Program Management Office (2007 PMO of the Year) at Norton Healthcare in Louisville, Kentucky. Janice is a senior program manager with over 25 years experience and a 2010 PMI Project of the Year finalist for the Norton Brownsboro Hospital project.

▶ **Francis M. Webster, Jr., PHD,** is a retired professor emeritus of management at the School of Business, Western Carolina University, in Cullowhee, NC, where he specialized in teaching project management courses and concepts. For many years, he served as editor-in-chief for the Project Management Institute. He was manager of Operations Research at Chrysler Corporation and served on the DOD/NASA PERT/ COST Coordinating Council during the early days of the development of modern project management concepts and practices.

▶ **Karen R.J. White, CSM, PMP** (krwhite@appliedagility.com) has over 25 years of experience in the software development and project management fields. The founder of Applied Agility, Karen provides consulting services to Fortune 500 companies as well as non-profit organizations. Karen has chaired PMI's Ethics Review Committee, served on its Ethics Standards Development Committee, and chaired its Education Foundation Board of Directors. She is the author of *Agile Project Management: A Mandate for the 21st Century* (Center for Business Practices, 2009) and *Practical Project Management for Agile Nonprofits* (Maven House Press, 2013). A recipient of the US Army Commendation Medal for demonstrated leadership within the U.S. Army Reserves, Karen holds an MS in Information Systems from Northeastern University's Graduate School of Engineering.

▶ **Mary Yanocha** (myanocha@pmsolutions.com) leads the marketing and new business growth initiatives for both PM Solutions and PM College, where she has managed the development of innovative thought leadership pieces such as primary research reports, books, white papers, and case studies; she also led the creative team responsible for launching the company's app, PMP® Flashcards for Project Management. Previously, Mary held positions at the Project Management Institute and Systems and Computer Technology Corporation (now part of Ellucian). She holds an MBA from St. Joseph's University, and a BA in Communication Studies from West Chester University. She is an Accredited Business Communicator (ABC) by the International Association of Business Communicators (IABC), and a member of the American Marketing Association and PMI.

▶ **D. Allen Young, PMP,** is an Account Executive/Engagement Director at PM Solutions, headquartered in Glen Mills PA USA. He has over 35 years of combined project, program, portfolio and Project Management Office (PMO) experience across multiple industries, integrated with organizational change management best practices. He has successfully established, enhanced and managed PMOs; implemented enterprise project portfolio management tools for multiple companies; run mission-critical projects and programs for Fortune 500 firms; taught project management classes; and has written several trade magazine articles. Allen has a Bachelor's degree in Business Administration from the Wharton School of the University of Pennsylvania.

Consensus building/planning, 413, 444
Constraints, 47
  competing, 3
  current, 382–383
  definition of, 90
  effect on project throughput, 379–380
  financial, 47
  in multiple project management, 323–324
  in project portfolio management, 270, 381
  resource-related, 95, 96, 382–383
  on schedules, 47
  strategic, 382–383
  theory of, 66
  time-related, 95, 96, 98
Construction industry, 423. *See also* Infrastructure project management
  BOOT (build-own-operate-transfer) contracts in, 476
  capability in, 467–474
  healthcare projects of, 524
  project monitoring and control in, 63–64
  technical information models in, 423–424
Construction Industry Institute, 539
Contingency allowances, 41
Contingency costs, 109
Contingency plans, 55
Continual partial attention, 324, 325
Continuous improvement (CI), 385, 395, 403–404, 444
Contract directives (CDs), 356
Contracting, 41, 477
Contracts
  administration of, 58
  bidding for, 37
  BOOT (build-own-operate-transfer), 476
  in construction industry, 423, 476
  for information technology projects, 487, 489
  in international projects, 421
  in procurement management, 158, 159, 162
Contractual closure, 72
Contract work breakdown structure (CWBS), 357

Control. *See also* Cost control; Monitoring and control
  over bodies of knowledge, 217–218
  as power, 369
  during project execution phase, 41
  of risk, 149–150
Control account managers (CAMs), 351, 357, 359, 364
Control accounts (CAs), 354, 356–357
Control account schedules, 358
Control charts, 118, 119, 386–387, 388, 391, 392
Controllers, 198
Control plans, 57
Coordinators, of projects, 200
Corporate governance. *See* Governance
Corporate project management office (CPMO), 285
Corporate social responsibility, 460
Cost(s)
  contingency, 109
  direct, 360
  of failure, 108
  of greenality, 454–455
  indirect, 360
  overruns, 40, 64, 535
  of professionalization, 223–224
  of quality, 108, 117, 297
  trade-offs with schedules, 98
Cost accumulation accounting, 359–360
Cost baseline, 106, 109
Cost budgeting, 8
Cost control, 110–111, 378–379
Cost efficiency, 297
Cost estimates, 52, 53, 106–112
  activity, 108
  basis of (BOE), 108, 109
  definition of, 8
  development methods for, 106, 107–108
  objective of, 106
  performance measurement of, 57
  risk analysis combined with, 55
  sensitivity analysis of, 55
  verification methods for, 106, 108

Cost management, 8, 15, 16, 105–113
Cost performance index (CPI), 297
Cost performance report (CPR), 364
Cost reduction, 228
Cost variance, 360
CPM (critical path method), 5, 98
Cradle-to-cradle concept, 457
Crashing, 98
Crawford-Ishikura Factor Table for Evaluating Roles (CIFTER), 24
Credentials, as basis for career development, 201
Credibility gaps, 372
Critical chain method, 66, 273, 377–384
Critical path method, 5, 98
CRM (customer relations management) systems, 430
Cross-cultural settings. *See* International projects
Crowd sourcing, 434, 438
Culture. *See also* International projects; Organizational culture
  components of, 420
  definition of, 419
  role in communication, 136–137
Customer(a)
  collaboration with, 444
  expectations of, 80, 116
  feedback from, 71
  performance reports for, 363–364
  validation of requirements of, 400–401
Customer focus, as Baldrige criterion, 396, 397
Customer relations management (CRM) systems, 430
Customer satisfaction index, 297–298
Cycle time, 298

Dashboards, 6, 67, 110, 321, 327
Data
  coding of, 259–260
  storage of, 258–259, 263
Decision making
  in enterprise project governance, 289–290

in cost control, 110
in modeling, 62
in process groups, 30–34
in product life cycles, 4
in project control process, 62
in risk management, 149–150

Japan
  construction industry in, 423
  management style in, 410
  Quality Movement in, 387–388
  technical knowledge models
    in, 423, 424
Japan Project Management
  Forum, 21, 220
Joint Commission on Accred-
    itation of Healthcare
    Organizations, 525
Joint ventures, 476–477
*Journal of Experimental
  Psychology,* 324
Juran, Joseph, 388, 461
"Just-in-time" (rolling wave)
    planning, 443, 448

Kanban boards, 100–101
Kennedy Center case study, 429,
    436–437
Kleiner, Art, 371–372
Knowledge
  as basis for certification, 175
  as competency, 192
  explicit *vs.* tacit, 250–251
  value of, 470, 471
Knowledge areas, 29-30. *See also*
    Body(ies) of knowledge
  ethics in, 207
Knowledge management, as
    Baldrige criterion, 396, 397
Kyoto Protocol, 457

Leadership
  authentic, 171–173, 370–371
  autocratic, 410
  Baldrige Criteria for, 396, 397
  business-focused, 228–234
  characteristics of, 194–195
  as competency, 191, 194–195,
    332–333
  in enterprise project
    governance, 282
  guidelines for, 126–128
  of high-performing teams,
    124–126
  inspirational, 123
  legitimacy of, 370–371

managerial, 121–130
political aspect of, 367–375
power of, 124–126
in project initiation, 42
servant-oriented, 210
situational factors in, 128
of Six Sigma process, 389–390,
  391, 392–393
of teams, 198, 411
values-oriented, 210
Leadership-oriented project
    managers, 191–192
Lean manufacturing, 385, 391,
    392–393, 395, 404, 524
Lectures, 414
Lessons-learned sessions,
    101–102, 444
Level of effort (LOE) work
    packages, 358
Licensing, 220, 222–223
Life-cycle assessment (LCA),
    461–462
Life cycle cost, of products, 3
Life cycle models. *See also*
    Project life cycle
  definition of, 482
LinkedIn, 516
Listening skills, 415
Logic plans, 53
Logistics plans, 52
Loss function, 388–389

MAIC (measure, analyze, im-
    prove, control) process, 389
Malcolm Baldrige National
    Quality Award, 395. *See
    also* Baldrige Criteria
Management of projects (MoP)
    model, 36–37
Management reserves, 359
Mandatory project
    interactivities, 2
Marketing management, 513–521
  at enterprise level, 518–519
  online collaboration tools in,
    517–518
  project management offices
    (PMOs) in, 518–521
Material cost collection
    accounting, 360
Matrix organizations, 49, 51,
    390–391
Maturity cube model, 335–336
Maturity levels, 311, 312
  in process implementation,
    397–399

in program management, 330
of project management offices,
    339–340, 341
Maturity models, 253–254, 258,
    335–336, 391
Maturity tracking, 6
McKinsey Global Institute, 430,
    439, 534
Measurement. *See also*
    Performance measurement
  Baldrige Criteria for, 396, 397
Medical equipment projects,
    525–526
Meetings, 100–101, 149, 444,
    445–446
Mega-projects, 467–468, 537–538
Memorandum of understanding,
    157–158
Mentors and mentoring, 6, 197,
    199, 333
Metadata, 432
Methodologies, in project
    management, 252–253
  definition of, 482
Metrics, 6, 67
Milestones
  in marketing management, 516
  in scheduling, 81, 98, 358
  technical, 506, 508–510
Mirror probability-impact
    matrix, for risk, 146, 147
Mission statements, 46, 457–458
Mobility, technologies sup-
    porting, 436
Models
  in agile project management,
    445–447
  of competency, 193–196
  financial, 505–506, 511–512
  maturity models, 253–254,
    258, 391
  of processes, 401–402
  in quality improvement,
    391–392
  in risk analysis, 147–148
Monitoring and control, 61–68
  of activities, 99
  components of, 82
  ethics in, 207
  factors affecting, 65–68
  in multiple project
    management, 274–275, 323
  of processes, 402–403
  in program management, 332
  of project execution phase,
    33–34